personal finance and money management

personal finance and money management

robert s. rosefsky

john wiley & sons

new york / santa barbara / chichester / brisbane / toronto

Library of Congress Cataloging in Publication Data:
Rosefsky, Robert S

  Personal finance and money management.

  1. Finance, Personal
    I.   Title.
HG179.R67   332!.024   77-20283
ISBN 0-471-01740-X

Printed in the United States of America

10 9 8 7 6 5 4 3 2 1

preface

The past ten to fifteen years have been revolutionary ones in the field of personal finance, affecting individuals of all ages and income levels. Those just launching their careers and financial futures, especially women, are experiencing the effects of recent changes in our credit laws. Most of us have felt the impact of the 1976 Tax Reform Law; individuals planning for security in retirement by now have heard of the 1974 Pension Reform Law.

Reports on new laws, new regulations, proposed consumer legislation, new debt instruments, and innovative investment opportunities crowd the pages of newspapers and magazines. Television news and advertisements devote considerable time to the same topics. The options for individuals and families interested in prudent management of their personal finances have multiplied. As the options have increased, so have possible pitfalls.

In part, this book is a review of the recent revolution in personal finance. It is also an introduction to many of your options and an examination of some of the hazards you may encounter as you follow your financial course. It *is not* a book that prescribes or offers absolute formulas. It is, I hope, a resource tool that you will call upon as you establish your financial goals and make your financial decisions.

The contents of the book are not accidental. They reflect the surveyed opinions of teachers of personal finance and consumer economics in colleges, community colleges, and adult education programs around the country. An attempt has been made to address the students of those teachers—a student audience who in recent years is more diverse in age and income level and includes a higher percentage of women planning their financial futures.

The effort to communicate with such a diverse audience has resulted in the inclusion of such features as:

☐ Chapter 1, Work and Income, which focuses on a primary ingredient of our financial lives—income—and the means by which we acquire it. Special attention is paid to recently raised questions about the value of higher education and the subject of mid-life career change.

v

☐ Two chapters on housing, reflecting the high interest in the subject and the myriad of questions raised by potential home buyers and home owners.

☐ Extensive discussion of the 1976 Tax Reform Law.

☐ A review of the new laws affecting credit and borrowing, especially the Truth in Lending Law, the Fair Credit Reporting Act, the Equal Credit Opportunity Act. Note too the explanation of APR and the lenders' responsibilities to quote it.

☐ Discussion of relatively new phenomena on the personal finance scene: REIT's (Real Estate Investment Trusts), IRA's (Individual Retirement Accounts), MUNIfunds and trading in stock options—topics not often discussed in more descriptive, traditional textbooks.

☐ A review of the 1974 Pension Reform Law and its implications for retirees as well as for those just beginning to plan their financial futures.

The Issues and Incidents following each chapter were written specifically for this textbook, and were included for these reasons: (1) to simulate the kinds of narratives found in popular periodicals and to encourage the pursuit of information in such sources, (2) to extend the textual material by offering examples and applications of principles, (3) to reveal the human side of personal finance, and (4) to provide points of departure for class discussion and interpersonal communication.

The effort in creating this book has been challenging and I have received invaluable assistance and advice from many. I particularly want to thank Robert Y. Allen (Northwestern Connecticut Community College), Thomas A. Bankston (Angelo State University), Lawrence Dukes (Waubonsee Community College), Martin Ivener (Los Angeles Harbor College), H. Lynn Miller (Central Florida Community College), and W. S. Phillips (Memphis State University) for their careful and competent review of my manuscript. I owe a special debt of gratitude to my editor, Gary DeWalt for his assistance and encouragement in all stages of this work.

Robert S. Rosefsky
Phoenix, Arizona
London, England

contents

contents

chapter 1 **work and income: attitudes, issues, goals**

People are always blaming their circumstances for what they are. I don't believe in circumstances. The people who get on in this world are the people who get up and look for the circumstances they want, and, if they can't find them, make them.

GEORGE BERNARD SHAW

Hell begins on the day when God grants us a clear vision of all that we might have achieved, of all the gifts that we have wasted, of all that we might have done that we did not do.

GIAN-CARLO MENOTTI

And unto Adam He said: Because thou hast...eaten of the tree...curst is the ground for thy sake; in toil shalt thou eat of it all the days of thy life. Thorns also and thistles shall bring it forth to thee...in the sweat of thy face shalt thou eat bread, til thou return unto the ground...

GENESIS CHAPT. 3, VERSES 17–19

the role of work in our lives

Work is perhaps the single most powerful force involved in shaping our lives.

It is our work that creates the vast bulk of all our income. And it is that income, put to proper use, that allows us to be self-sufficient. It provides us with the necessities of life as well as whatever luxuries may be within our reach. Income that isn't needed for current uses can be put away for our future welfare.

Work is a form of training ground. Whatever job we may be doing today gives us experience. That experience should enable us to accept future work tasks that will be more challenging, more rewarding, and more promising of greater benefits.

And work can—for better or for worse—play an important role in many of the nonfinancial aspects of our lives. The type of work we do can clearly shape a great deal of our social life, leading us into friendships and activities that generate from the working environment.

Our work can also influence the uses we make of leisure time—not only weekends and vacations during our working years, but also that commonly vast expanse of leisure time that befalls us when we retire. Some of us may engage in leisure-time activities and involvements directly related to our work activity. Others may charge off in the opposite direction seeking activities as remote from our work as possible. And still others, because of their psychological involvement with their work, may be unable to find any leisure activities that offer an ongoing sense of pleasure or reward. For this group, leisure time can be frustrating and retirement bleak: "It takes me the first half of my vacation to unwind from work, and during the second half I'm gearing myself up to go back to work. I really didn't relax at all." Or, "I worked so hard all my life I never generated any outside activities. Now here I am with all the time in the world and nothing to do with it."

As a well-planned working career progresses, it should create increasing leisure time along with increasing dollars to spend in that leisure time. If we fail to take advantage of this very important by-product of work, we are the losers.

attitudes and aspirations

If we are to cope with, and make the most of, this powerful force that shapes so much of our lives, we must look at work in a broader perspective. Not just what we might be doing today, tomorrow, or next week, but where our aspirations and abilities may lead us; how we might improve ourselves so that we can maximize the pleasures and rewards available to us through work; and how we can most efficiently use the fruits of our labor—our income—to satisfy current and future needs and desires.

To an extent, each of us shapes our own ideas about the style of life we would like to live. But to another extent—perhaps an even larger one—we tend to shape our future in the direction of how we see others living. A combination of our own personal desires and the achievements we perceive in others can very strongly influence the work and career goals we set for ourselves.

To aid in achieving a better perspective on our own attitudes and aspirations, let's take a closer look at the attitudes and aspirations of others, as expressed in a survey conducted biannually by the American Council of Life Insurance. The results of the most recent survey were published in 1977, reflecting the views of over 2000 Americans up to the age of 25.

Whether your career is just beginning, well established, or nearing its end, these survey results should provoke some thinking and planning helpful in shaping your financial future. They may well inspire questions that you've never asked yourself, and your answers may make you focus on directions you want to take or re-examine paths you are now embarked on.

the traditional american way

In a broad sense, much of our attitude toward work will be shaped by our overall feeling toward the traditional American system. If we tend to be in accord and comfortable with "the way things are," it's much easier to be a part of the system. If we feel rebellious, it will be that much more difficult to reconcile our own working situation with that of everyone around us.

The majority of responses to the survey indicate that people are indeed receptive to traditional patterns. Fifty-seven percent stated that they "would most like to adopt the type of life that society has typically offered: a good job, a nice family, living in a pleasant neighborhood, and becoming part of the community." Some found the traditional way acceptable, but with reservations: 17% responded "Although I have some reservations, I will probably have no choice but to accept the typical job-marriage-children-home way of life."

But slightly more than one out of four respondents found difficulty in accepting traditional patterns. Sixteen percent replied "I have serious problems in accepting the typical way of life, so I don't know what I'm going to do." And 10% stated "I find the prospect of a typical way of life in the society as it now exists intolerable, so I shall probably not adopt it."

life style   Respondents were asked which of the following life styles was most appealing to them, least appealing, and which they thought best described them fifteen years hence:

☐ A. A successful executive or professional, living with spouse and children in a good residential neighborhood.

☐ B. A single person with a good job, living well in an expensive apartment in a major city.

☐ C. Someone free of social responsibility and obligations, living where and with whom you please and not worrying much about money or work.

☐ D. A dedicated person working to solve serious social problems, but not too concerned with the material comforts of life.

☐ E. (For men) A family man, working at a nine-to-five job—one that doesn't involve a great deal of pressure and leaves time to spend with your family and on outside interests.

☐ E. (For women) A housewife, raising children and enjoying a fairly pressure-free life attending to family and personal interests.

Table 1-1 illustrates the responses to the survey, from 1970 through the most recent survey in 1976. It's particularly interesting to note the substantial shift among women from 1970 to 1976 in the number that find the "successful executive" style most appealing. The percentage increased from 26% in 1970 to 34% in 1976. During the same span, there was an even greater shift in the number of women who found the housewife life style most appealing, dropping from 42% in 1970 to 25% in 1976. These responses are indicative of the very definite trend of a higher percentage of women in the American work force, a trend we discuss later in the chapter. Note also that many preferred life styles aren't expected to be actual life styles fifteen years hence.

The issue of most appealing life style varied considerably depending on marital status and financial background of the individual respondents; this is illustrated in Table 1-2.

life goals   The survey reveals some interesting trends regarding specific goals that individuals set for themselves. Respondents were

table 1-1 **survey results: life style**

	Life Style Most appealing (%)				Life Style Least Appealing (%)				Life Style expected in 15 years (%)			
	1970	1972	1974	1976	1970	1972	1974	1976	1970	1972	1974	1976
a. "Successful executive"												
Men	30%	32%	35%	32%	11%	9%	8%	10%	34%	36%	43%	35%
Women	26%	31%	30%	34%	7%	7%	7%	8%	27%	28%	30%	29%
b. "Single person"												
Men	26%	24%	24%	25%	16%	16%	16%	14%	10%	9%	9%	13%
Women	14%	15%	17%	19%	19%	16%	19%	15%	6%	6%	5%	8%
c. "Free of obligations"												
Men	15%	13%	12%	16%	28%	29%	32%	30%	10%	9%	7%	9%
Women	10%	8%	9%	10%	42%	43%	42%	38%	5%	5%	5%	5%
d. "Working on social problems"												
Men	9%	11%	8%	6%	21%	19%	18%	23%	9%	9%	9%	7%
Women	7%	11%	8%	8%	19%	18%	17%	17%	7%	7%	8%	6%
e. "Average man/housewife"												
Men	20%	20%	21%	20%	24%	27%	25%	20%	35%	37%	32%	34%
Women	42%	35%	36%	25%	12%	16%	15%	18%	52%	53%	51%	49%

asked to choose which of the following was the most important goal to them:

☐ The opportunity to develop as an individual
☐ A happy family life
☐ A fulfilling career
☐ Making a lot of money

In 1974, 45% picked the "opportunity to develop as an individual" as the most important goal of the respondents. By 1976, that percentage had jumped to 51%. During the same period, the "happy family life" goal had dropped from 42% to 32%. "A fulfilling career" was picked by 9% in 1974 and by 10% in 1976. "Making a lot of money" was chosen by 5% in 1974 and by 7% in 1976.

Does this mean a decrease in the importance of the family as an institution? Does it suggest that people feel they can grow better as individuals on their own instead of within a family unit?

table 1-2 **life styles based on marital status and financial background**

| | Most Appealing Life Style—1976 | | | | |
| | Marital Status | | Financial Background | | |
	Married	Single	Above average	Average	Below average
a. Successful executive					
Men	41%	30%	36%	30%	21%
Women	27%	37%	40%	32%	22%
b. Single person					
Men	9%	27%	24%	25%	28%
Women	7%	23%	17%	19%	25%
c. Free of obligations					
Men	9%	17%	14%	16%	23%
Women	9%	10%	12%	8%	11%
d. Working on social problems					
Men	2%	6%	6%	4%	11%
Women	13%	7%	8%	8%	13%
e. Average man/housewife					
Men	37%	17%	18%	22%	17%
Women	41%	20%	19%	30%	25%

the value of a college education

Respondents were asked whether they agreed with the statement "A college education today is a necessity for anyone who wants to get ahead."

As Table 1-3 indicates, only a slight majority (53%) agreed with that statement. And of that, more than half only agreed somewhat. Less than a majority of college graduates responding to the survey agreed. Perhaps experience has shown them that their education did not provide them with the tools of getting ahead they had hoped for. Or perhaps they have not waited long enough to determine exactly how to put those educational tools to the fullest and best use.

responsibility for financial well-being

Much of our attitude toward work and our career will be shaped by our underlying feeling as to who is ultimately responsible for our own well-being. In other words, how highly do we value self-sufficiency?

table 1-3　**survey result: value of a college education**

"A college education today is a necessity for anyone who wants to get ahead."	Total 1976	By Education					
		Not in school/ Not high school graduate	In high school	Not in school/ high school graduate	In college	Not in school/ some college	College graduate
Agree strongly	25%	21%	34%	16%	27%	20%	19%
Agree somewhat	28%	18%	33%	25%	35%	19%	29%
Disagree somewhat	28%	38%	21%	33%	25%	29%	27%
Disagree strongly	18%	18%	10%	25%	13%	31%	25%

Respondents to the survey were asked which of the following two statements comes closer to expressing their individual point of view:

☐ A. Each individual should be responsible for his or her own financial well-being.

☐ B. It is perfectly all right to rely on others (such as government, family) for financial assistance.

Table 1-4 indicates that from 1970 to 1976 there has been a considerable shift from the self-sufficiency attitudes. Why? Very

table 1-4　**survey results: responsibility for financial well-being**

	1970				1976			
	Total	Age 22–25	College graduates	Married people	Total	Age 22–25	College graduates	Married people
Each individual should be responsible for his or her own financial well-being.	81%	89%	86%	92%	75%	75%	66%	78%
It is perfectly all right to rely on others (e.g. family, government) for financial assistance.	18%	11%	14%	8%	23%	25%	34%	22%

table 1-5   **survey results: woman's role (A)**

"If a woman has children, she shouldn't go to work until they are grown, unless it's an economic necessity."	Total 1976	Male	Female	Not in school/ not high school graduate	In high school	Not in school/ high school graduate	In college	Not in school/ some college	College graduate
a. Agree strongly	35%	39%	31%	42%	38%	31%	31%	33%	30%
b. Agree somewhat	30%	33%	26%	26%	33%	30%	31%	29%	11%
c. Disagree somewhat	21%	17%	25%	18%	17%	22%	25%	19%	33%
d. Disagree strongly	13%	8%	17%	12%	8%	15%	13%	19%	25%

likely, the economic turmoil during those years, particularly the recession of 1974–1975, accompanied by high inflation and unemployment, contributed to an understandable feeling that there were forces in the world too great for any individual to control, and a turn to others for help would consequently not be at all improper.

woman's role   Respondents were asked whether they agreed or disagreed with the following statements:

☐ A. "If a woman has children, she shouldn't go to work until they are grown unless it's an economic necessity."
☐ B. "While there are some exceptions, the statement that 'woman's place is in the home' still makes sense."

Tables 1-5 and 1-6 contain the responses to these questions.

emerging trends regarding work and careers

Patterns of work life in America are changing. Over the next two decades, many now-emerging phenomena will have modified much of what we take for granted in the field of work and careers and very few individuals will be left untouched by some of these forces. Even people in the middle or later stages of their careers will experience effects, though perhaps not as drastically as the younger people at their early career stages. To be aware of the emerging trends that can affect your career is to be prepared to cope and to adjust. Let's briefly examine some of these trends.

attitudes

As the survey pointed out, a large number of younger Americans accept the traditional values of our nation and intend to live in conventional ways. However, the survey notes, "many other young people continue to be forerunners in the emergence and expansion of a new focus on self fulfillment, and in a changing work ethic that emphasizes job satisfaction and the psychological benefits of work. This considerable minority, remaining critical of our society's institutions, politics and life styles, comprises a major force for change."

This conclusion suggests the likelihood of an ongoing struggle between a dissatisfied younger segment of the population and a satisfied older element, grown content with status quo. It's difficult to predict what specific results might be expected from such a struggle. But if the dissatisfied minority is vocal and persuasive enough, one institution that might suffer is seniority. Traditions in seniority tend to favor older workers, particularly in rehirings after lay-offs and job advancement opportunities. This may be so even though younger workers may be more productive and efficient. Although seniority traditions are an obvious advantage to older workers, they may be disadvantageous not only to younger workers, but to the company and its shareholders. Seniority can inhibit profitability, which in turn can restrict the ability of a company to create new jobs and pay higher wages to existing workers.

table 1-6   **survey results: woman's role (B)**

"While there are some exceptions, the statement that 'Woman's place is in the home' still makes sense."	Total 1970	Total 1976	Male	Female	Not in school/ not high school graduate	In high school	Not in school/ high school graduate	In college	Not in school/ some college	College graduate
a. Agree strongly	28%	15%	16%	14%	27%	12%	13%	15%	17%	12%
b. Agree somewhat	31%	33%	37%	30%	25%	35%	41%	34%	26%	18%
c. Disagree somewhat	21%	26%	28%	25%	21%	30%	19%	25%	29%	33%
d. Disagree strongly	19%	25%	18%	31%	24%	21%	25%	26%	29%	37%

(*Note:* All columns except "Total 1970" refer to 1976 responses)

Further, unions sometimes tend to limit the number of new young apprentices they will welcome into their ranks in order to protect jobs of older workers. By thus limiting access to training, the tradition makes it that much more difficult for younger workers to enter the job market in the first place.

the changing composition of the work force

The percentage of qualified males participating in the work force is actually diminishing, while the percentage of qualified women is sharply increasing. As Table 1-7 indicates, the participation rates for men of all ages has declined from 82.4% in 1960 to 77.2% in 1975 and a further decrease is projected through 1990 to 76.7%. For females of all ages, the participation rate has climbed from 37.1% in 1960 to 45.8% in 1975, with a further projected increase to 51.4% in 1990.

Men are actually entering the work force later in life than in past years due to longer schooling, and are leaving the work force sooner because of earlier retirement programs. Improvements in disability and health care benefits in recent years have also enabled men to leave the labor market when health problems have arisen; in past years the limited availability of such benefits tended to keep the men tied to their jobs longer.

Further, a drastic drop in the birth rate—from 23.7 births per 1000 population per year in 1960 to 14.9 births per 1000 in 1974—has resulted in more women being able to work uninterrupted by childbearing. Expanded day care facilities have also provided alternatives.

These factors, plus rapid gains by women in achieving equal educational and job opportunities, will result in dramatic shifts in the roles assigned to men and women. Role separation will become replaced by role sharing within the marriage structure for vast numbers. Earnings will equalize between men and women, thus providing some protection to a married couple in the event of a lay-off—compared to the current situation with the family unit predominantly dependent on the male's income.

changing careers

A 1977 study by the U.S. Department of Labor based on census surveys indicates that nearly one-third of all American workers may be changing their careers over a given five-year period. Changing careers; not just jobs. A job change implies going from one employer to another, but doing the same work. A career change is much more drastic: altering virtually the total mode of one's work, whether with the same employer or with a new one, or on one's own.

table 1-7   **labor force participation rates 1960–1990**

Sex	Age	Participation rates (percent)*				Projected	
		1960	1965	1970	1975	1980	1990
Male	16–19	58.6	55.7	57.5	60.2	62.0	62.6
	20–24	88.9	86.2	85.1	84.5	84.5	82.7
	25–34	96.4	96.0	95.0	94.1	93.4	93.7
	35–44	96.4	96.2	95.7	94.9	94.7	94.0
	45–54	94.3	94.3	92.9	91.9	90.5	89.3
	55–64	85.2	83.2	81.5	74.7	73.8	69.2
	65+	32.2	26.9	25.8	20.8	19.4	16.2
	TOTAL	82.4	80.1	79.2	77.2	77.4	76.7
Female	16–19	39.1	37.7	43.7	49.0	51.3	54.9
	20–24	46.1	49.7	57.5	64.0	67.5	74.7
	25–34	35.8	38.5	44.8	54.4	58.4	66.0
	35–44	43.1	45.9	50.9	55.7	58.1	63.4
	45–54	49.3	50.5	54.0	54.3	56.3	59.9
	55–64	36.7	40.6	42.5	40.7	41.6	42.2
	65+	10.5	9.5	9.2	7.8	7.7	7.2
	TOTAL	37.1	38.8	42.8	45.8	47.9	51.4

* Proportion of each age in labor force.
Source: U.S. Bureau of Labor Statistics, Special Labor Force Reports, 1977.

Although there are no valid statistics concerning the success quotient in career changes (did the change bring the money, the happiness, the challenge, the contentment you were seeking?), it would seem to be an infectious phenomenon that will attract increasily larger numbers of people.

Children have been reared from their earliest days to think in terms of "what do you want to be when you grow up?" They are seldom asked, "How many different things would you like to be when you grow up?" Many individuals choose a career at an early age with the assumption that it will be their one and only career—that they will learn, grow, and flourish in that endeavor. Little if any thought is ever given to the possibility that the chosen career may be limited in its overall satisfactions. Many people are poorly prepared for the day that often arrives when they find their careers have reached a dead end. They acquired neither the skills nor the outside interests or the sense of flexibility that could assist them in a career change. Many may recognize the need or value of making such a change, but may be reluctant to do so for fear of giving up the security of what they have already accomplished. They may thus resign themselves to continuing an unsatisfying career without ever knowing the consequences of a change.

Many others, though, will have acquired other skills, other interests, and a sense of flexibility that could broaden their perspective and allow them to easily adopt to a new career situation.

You may never have the slightest notion about changing your career—until you encounter one of the various factors that can motivate you to begin to seek a change. Figure 1-1 illustrates the typical flow patterns of a career change experience. Notice the arrow flowing *back* from "employment in new occupation" to the beginning. Obviously, not all new careers work out as hoped for, and many career changers will find themselves starting the process all over again.

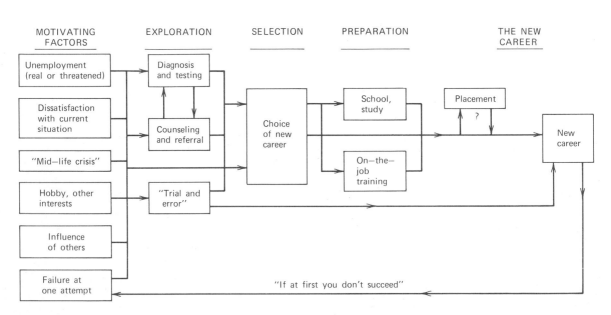

Source: Adapted from a study by the Rand Corporation,
          "Mid—life Career Redirections", 1975.

Figure 1-1   Typical flow patterns in a career change.

There's a great deal to be risked as well as gained in a career change. The prudent individual will take the fullest advantage of diagnostic and testing procedures available, plus all the counselling and referral sources within reach. The "trial and error" process can be costly, time consuming, and frustrating.

the role of education

Old assumption: "A college education is the way to get ahead."

Newer assumption: "The old assumption isn't necessarily valid any longer."

Question regarding both assumptions: "Just what is meant by a 'college education' and by 'getting ahead'?"

What is a college education worth today in terms of what might be called "getting ahead"—achieving career satisfaction and a level of income capable of satisfying basic needs and reasonable desires? The issue has been subject to growing debate in recent years, particularly as the cost of obtaining such an education skyrockets and young people seem to question traditional values. The survey discussed earlier noted that 67% of those young Americans still in high school agreed that a college education is a necessity for anyone who wants to get ahead. But only 62% of those actually in college agreed with the statement, and only 48% of those who had already graduated college agreed.

There is no doubt that the cost of a college education is increasing dramatically. Table 1-8 indicates the recent trend and there's no reason to suspect a reversal in the near future.

Nonetheless, if statistics can be relied on, there is a definite correlation between the level of education one achieves and the amount of income one is able to generate over a lifetime. (See Table 1-9.)

But there are those who say that the correlation between education and earnings doesn't tell the whole story. It has been suggested that if one took the money spent on a college education and invested it conservatively over an expected working span of 45 years, the nest egg that builds up, added to the earnings from the years otherwise spent in college, would give the high school graduate considerably more than the earnings the college graduate would have achieved.

For example, if an excellent college education cost a total of $40,000 (including everything—tuition, books, rooms, board, travel expenses, fees, spending money, clothing and accessories), and that $40,000 was invested very conservatively (say, in a savings account yielding 5½% interest per year, compounded quarterly), the total nest egg would grow to almost half a million dollars at the end of a normal 45 year working span. That sum, added to what the high school graduate might otherwise expect to earn, as set forth in Table 1-9, would considerably exceed the total earnings of the college graduate. If a college career costs even half of that amount, or roughly $20,000, the mathematics indicate that the high school graduate who banked his or her college expense money would be about on a par at the end of 45 years with the college graduate.

A premise such as this may superficially justify avoiding college, at least in terms of total income earned over a lifetime working career. But this can be grossly misleading. Even assuming the truth in the mathematics, the college graduate still will be enjoying a higher annual income during his or her lifetime career, which would obviously translate into a more affluent style of living. The high school graduate who banked this money might have to wait until retirement age before taking advantage of the accumulated funds. In the interim, the college graduate could have been accumulating a nest egg out of earnings that could provide as abundantly for retirement as the high school graduate's savings.

table 1-8 rising college costs*

Public Institutions	1965	1970	1975	1976
Tuition and fees	$298	$427	$653	$731
Board charges	462	540	685	746
Room charges	291	395	565	627
TOTAL	1051	1362	1903	2104
Nonpublic institutions				
Tuition and fees	1297	1809	2701	3013
Board charges	515	607	790	860
Room charges	390	503	702	771
TOTAL	2202	2919	4193	4644

* Estimated cost, in dollars, for average charges to full time resident credit-degree students in four year universities, for entire academic year.
Source: U.S. National Center for Education Studies, *Digest of Education Statistics*, 1976.

table 1-9 **income and education***

	Elementary		High school		College	
	Less than 8 years	8 years	1–3 years	4 years	1–3 years	4 or more years
From age:						
18 to 64	$251,000	$305,000	$343,000	$421,000	$480,000	$655,000
25 to 64	231,000	284,000	324,000	393,000	461,000	627,000
18 to death	280,000	344,000	389,000	479,000	543,000	758,000
25 to death	260,000	323,000	371,000	452,000	525,000	731,000

*Lifetime income by years of school completed calculated using 1972 constant dollars as base; data for males only.
Source: Statistical Abstract of the U.S., 1977.

Earnings aside, the value of a college education becomes a very relative and very personal matter to judge.

College—and junior college—offers more than simply career training opportunities. Available to students are educational opportunities beyond those strictly required for career matters, and the broader the background, the better equipped the student may be in the future to take advantage of changing career potentials. Also available are the opportunities to interact with people from different backgrounds, different cultures, different attitudes—a life experience otherwise difficult to duplicate in an on-the-job situation.

The debate over the value of college may never be resolved, but there can be very little argument as to the point that *education*—college, on-the-job-training, or self-education—can play an integral role in career advancement. Learning job skills, in whatever fashion, can provide entrée to the job market where further skills can be learned and further advancement attained. Sharpening existing skills can help provide more rapid advancement. And acquiring outside skills not necessarily related to the specific employment can broaden one's entire career horizon and income potential.

In short: educational facilties *alone* do not necessarily equip a person for a bigger or better or more rewarding career. It's *what one does* with the educational facilities available that will make all the difference.

elements in choosing a career

The world of work is a marketplace, an arena of buying and selling. Our careers, with very few exceptions, involve selling our services, not necessarily to the highest bidder, but to the one who offers good value in return for our work, plus working conditions that will be satisfactory to us, advancement opportunities that will be challenging and rewarding, and a measure of security that is satisfactory. At the start of a career, most of us will find these various elements most readily by working for someone else. A few may prefer to start off on their own; and later in life many others may prefer the course of self-employment.

The highest bidder for our services may seem to be the most attractive alternative in the short run. But in the long run it may not turn out that way. A high starting salary with little apparent chance for advancement may be to the detriment of our ultimate human potential. Or a high starting salary where working conditions are uncomfortable or where the demands on our time and/or energy are unreasonable may be similarly counterproductive.

If one is thinking strictly in terms of "a job," the lure of the higher pay may be too tempting to resist. But when one is thinking more of a career, the long-range potential must be evaluated at the very outset and be constantly reviewed as the months and years go by.

knowing your own aptitudes

Aptitude, in the career sense, generally means what you're best suited for. But what one is best suited for may not necessarily be the thing one enjoys most or from which one can generate the level of income commensurate with the desired life style. For example, a young man worked in his father's clothing store after school hours and during vacations. During those years, his father innocently, but persuasively, convinced the young man that he should take over the clothing store when he graduated from college. Because of the extensive on-the-job training, the young man had an aptitude for retailing; security and income seemed assured by following that course. But the young man never really liked retailing; and he always resented—though never questioned overtly—his father's persuasions; and while the income and security were comfortable enough, he swiftly felt stifled, unproductive, discontent. By common methods of measurement, his aptitude was for retailing. But for him it was the wrong career.

What, then, is aptitude? It's a very precarious balance of a number of personal elements, some of which can be measured, some of which defy measurement. Few and fortunate are those who have a good grasp of all the various elements, for they might enjoy fulfilling careers in every sense of the word. Most of us have to compromise on one or more points, but that doesn't mean a rich and active career can't be attained. Guidance counselling can be of some help in aiding us to sort out these various elements, and it would be recommended if a clear focus isn't available at any point. The elements, in brief, are these:

☐ What do you enjoy doing?
☐ What do you do well? (This is not the same as the above element. Many of us do things well but don't necessarily enjoy doing them. And many of us enjoy doing certain things that regretably we don't do that well. The difference should be noted.)
☐ What can we do that will generate a desirable level of income, security, and future potential income and security?
☐ To what extent, if any, are we seeking to satisfy, or must we satisfy, the expectations of others? Many people, such as the young retailer noted earlier, embark on careers not necessarily because that's what they would have chosen on their own, but because others—parents, spouses, in-laws—expected it of them.

financial rewards and life style

Which comes first in choosing a career: do we envision a life style that we'd like to attain and then strive to meet it? Or do we generate as much income as we can and then establish a life style commensurate with the income? Or do we succumb—as many do—to the constant bombardment of advertising urging us to acquire without regard to the income to pay for our modern American consumption tendencies?

As with aptitudes, balance is the key. Prudence dictates that a very careful balance be struck between the life style you would reasonably be comfortable with and the income you can reasonably expect to generate. As time goes on, of course, a revision of both can be expected, and modifications made accordingly. An excessive life style with relation to income can cause severe financial difficulties that can, in turn, interfere with one's performance at work, thus compounding the problem. An excessively modest life style may mean doing without certain comforts, which could dull the overall quality of one's day-to-day life, which could in turn also interfere with job performance. There is no precise formula suitable to even a small group of individuals, but later chapters in this book offer guidance as to how that balance can be achieved to suit your individual needs.

career opportunities

The more your chosen field of work is expanding, the more, theoretically, your own opportunities should expand.

The Bureau of Labor Statistics of the U.S. Department of Labor has projected future trends in a broad number of occupational areas. The study, published in late 1976, highlights those occupations that are expected to grow the fastest by 1985. See Table 1-10.

The "latest employment" is based on the employment figures in 1974, the latest date at which such calculations were taken. The projection assumes that there will have been a sustained recovery from the 1974–1975 recession, and that an unemployment rate of 4% will have been reached by 1985. It's important to note that these figures are only projections, subject to considerable possible change from unforeseen economic shifts and other trends that could reshape various occupational groupings. The figures are also based on a total national count—there is no attempt to break down job figures on a localized basis. Although these are the latest and best occupational projections available, they should only be used as a very broad and general guideline.

how much money?

Earnings surveys are, at best, only a very rough indication of the *relative* earning levels available in various occupations. The following table should not be construed as anything more than a starting point for your own further research into the kinds of monetary opportunities available in different fields.

Table 1-11 indicates the monthly salary offers to candidates for degrees in various professions and careers in 1975. The figures represent average beginning salaries based on offers (not acceptances) made by business, industrial, and governmental employers to graduating students in selected curricula and graduate programs during the year. The data is from representative colleges throughout the United States.

table 1-10 **where the jobs will be**

Job Description	Latest Employment	Estimated by 1985	% Change
Administration			
Accountant	810,000	995,000	23%
Bank, finance managers	478,000	705,000	47
Building managers	123,000	177,000	44
Health administrators	150,000	250,000	67
Office managers	337,000	473,000	40
Postmasters	31,000	26,000	−16
Public administrators	285,000	362,000	27
Restaurant managers	530,000	572,000	8
School administrators	260,000	371,000	43
Computer Specialists			
Programmers	195,000	290,000	49
Systems analysts	97,000	160,000	65
Key-punch operators	249,000	200,000	−20
Data-machine repairers	50,000	93,000	86
Peripheral-equipment operators	246,000	335,000	36
Engineers			
Aerospace	51,000	57,000	12
Chemical	50,000	62,000	24
Civil	167,000	225,000	35
Electrical	287,000	374,000	30
Industrial	193,000	224,000	16
Mechanical	183,000	234,000	28
Teachers			
College	518,000	507,000	−2
Elementary school	1,300,000	1,463,000	12
Secondary school	1,190,000	1,090,000	−8
Preschool, kindergarten	191,000	215,000	12
Adult education	69,000	100,000	45
School monitors	34,000	55,000	62
Teachers' aides	270,000	507,000	88
Mathematics			
Mathematicians, actuaries	20,000	29,000	45
Statisticians	23,000	30,000	30
Scientists			
Biologists	32,000	41,000	28
Geologists	27,000	37,000	37
Chemists	121,000	145,000	20
Physicists, astronomers	22,000	29,000	32

table 1-10 **continued**

Job Description	Latest Employment	Estimated by 1985	% Change
Merchant Marine			
Officers, pilots, pursers	34,000	33,000	−3
Sailors, deck hands	33,000	29,000	−12
Longshoremen	55,000	50,000	−9
Health Service			
Physicians, osteopaths	315,000	468,000	48
Dentists	100,000	138,000	38
Dental hygienists	23,000	58,000	152
Dental assistants	118,000	155,000	31
Registered nurses	790,000	1,190,000	51
Pharmacists	120,000	152,000	26
Medical-lab workers	155,000	236,000	52
X-ray technologists	82,000	112,000	36
Dietitians	33,000	43,000	30
Veterinarians	24,000	34,000	42
Nurses' aides, orderlies	916,000	1,506,000	64
Practical nurses	490,000	965,000	97
Social Sciences			
Economists	95,000	132,000	39
Psychologists	53,000	77,000	45
Technicians			
Draftspersons	298,000	423,000	42
Agricultural	42,000	49,000	17
Chemical	83,000	104,000	25
Surveyors	73,000	116,000	59
Other Professions			
Airline pilots	69,000	86,000	25
Air-traffic controllers	25,000	31,000	24
Architects	78,000	812,000	41
Authors	28,000	32,000	14
Clergy	245,000	275,000	12
Designers	135,000	174,000	29
Foresters, conservationists	48,000	61,000	27
Funeral directors	43,000	40,000	−3
Radio operators, teletypists	34,000	50,000	47
Lawyers	345,000	490,000	42
Librarians	172,000	206,000	20
Radio, TV announcers	22,000	25,000	14
Recreation workers	102,000	150,000	47
Social workers	305,000	436,000	43
Musicians, composers	140,000	175,000	96

table 1-10 **continued**

Job Description	Latest Employment	Estimated by 1985	% Change
Personnel, labor relations	325,000	450,000	38
Photographers	80,000	95,000	19
Painters, sculptors	149,000	186,000	25
Clerical			
Banktellers	337,000	449,000	33
Bill, account collectors	63,000	85,000	35
Billing clerks	146,000	214,000	46
Billing-machine operators	58,000	63,000	9
Bookkeepers	1,690,000	1,875,000	11
Cashiers	1,111,000	1,340,000	21
Clerical supervisors	216,000	297,000	26
Counter clerks	335,000	428,000	28
Expeditors, production controllers	214,000	270,000	26
File clerks	276,000	320,000	16
Insurance adjusters	125,000	152,000	22
Mail carriers	267,000	275,000	3
Messengers, office helpers	56,000	60,000	7
Postal clerks	293,000	302,000	3
Real-estate appraisers	28,000	39,000	39
Receptionists	459,000	635,000	38
Shipping clerks	465,000	560,000	20
Secretaries	3,189,000	4,786,000	50
Statistical clerks	324,000	375,000	16
Stenographers	103,000	78,000	−24
Payroll clerks	192,000	239,000	24
Stock clerks	488,000	610,000	25
Ticket, station, express agents	98,000	114,000	16
Typists	1,038,000	1,400,000	35
Utility meter readers	38,000	41,000	8
Vehicle dispatchers	71,000	92,000	29
Weighers	46,000	48,000	4
Sales			
Insurance agents, brokers	466,,000	536,000	15
Real-estate sales agents, brokers	394,000	480,000	22
Retail-trade salesworkers	2,696,000	3,116,000	15
Wholesale-trade salesworkers	768,000	880,000	14
Peddlers	214,000	203,000	−5
Manufacturers' sales agents	409,000	451,000	10

table 1-10 **continued**

Job Description	Latest Employment	Estimated by 1985	% Change
Services			
Airline flight attendants	41,000	56,000	36
Barbers	131,000	138,000	5
Bartenders	233,000	300,000	29
Child-care workers (except private households)	401,000	627,000	56
Crossing guards	48,000	58,000	20
Hotel baggage porters	20,000	18,000	−1
Cleaning-service workers	2,104,000	2,775,000	32
Cooks, chefs	955,000	1,250,000	31
Cosmetologists	495,000	622,000	26
Dishwashers	210,000	250,000	19
Firefighters	219,000	270,000	23
Food workers	447,000	530,000	18
Garbage collectors	102,000	175,000	71
Gardeners, grounds keepers	590,000	645,000	9
Guards, watchmen	473,000	508,000	7
Police officers	457,000	665,000	45
Private-household workers	1,228,000	900,000	−27
Sheriffs, constables, bailiffs	57,000	78,000	37
Waiters, waitresses	1,182,000	1,440,000	22
Waiters' assistants	160,000	180,000	12
Welfare-service aides	55,000	95,000	73
Building Trades			
Bricklayers	165,000	205,000	24
Carpenters	1,073,000	1,300,000	21
Cement masons	90,000	120,000	33
Dry-wall installers and lathers	85,000	100,000	18
Electricians	531,000	690,000	30
Painters	466,000	500,000	7
Excavating-machine operators	277,000	420,000	52
Plasterers	26,000	25,000	−4
Plumbers and pipe fitters	385,000	535,000	39
Roofers	90,000	130,000	44
Structural-metal workers	85,000	112,000	32
Tile setters	42,000	47,000	12
Bulldozer operators	126,000	190,000	51
Paper hangers	20,000	25,000	25
Machine Occupations			
Die setters	104,000	136,000	31
Drill-press operators	76,000	74,000	−3
Freight handlers	800,000	815,000	2

table 1-10 **continued**

Job Description	Latest Employment	Estimated by 1985	% Change
Machinists	440,000	475,000	8
Metal molders	58,000	62,000	7
Metal rollers, finishers	23,000	24,000	4
Patternmakers	41,000	38,000	−7
Tool-and-die makers	170,000	200,000	18
Sheet-metal workers	155,000	180,000	16
Mechanics and repair personnel			
Air conditioning, heating mechanics	208,000	285,000	37
Aircraft mechanics	130,000	160,000	23
Appliance service workers	137,000	170,000	24
Auto, auto-body mechanics	1,053,000	1,276,000	21
Farm equipment mechanics	61,000	75,000	23
Millwrights	95,000	115,000	21
TV, radio-service technicians	134,000	180,000	34
Heavy-equipment mechanics	776,000	913,000	18
Office-machine repairers	65,000	97,000	49
Printers			
Bookbinders	33,000	35,000	6
Composing-room occupations	166,000	157,000	−5
Photoengravers, lithographers	36,000	43,000	19
Printing pressmen	139,000	161,000	16
Telephone Industry			
Line operators, cable splicers	55,000	52,000	−5
Installers, repairmen	349,000	402,000	15
Operators	390,000	385,000	−1
Other Crafts			
Bakers	122,000	120,000	2
Boilermakers	40,000	62,000	55
Carpet installers	65,000	78,000	20
Dispensing opticians, optical mechanics	39,000	62,000	59
Food-counter, fountain workers	351,000	425,000	21
Foremen	1,457,000	1,770,000	21
Upholsterers	76,000	77,000	1
Hoist, crane operators	185,000	199,000	7
Locomotive engineers	53,000	48,000	−9
Shoe repairers	30,000	27,000	−10
Power-line installers	114,000	144,000	26
Railroad conductors	40,000	41,000	2
Stationary engineers	193,000	193,000	—
Window dressers	85,000	95,000	12

work and income

table 1-10 **continued**

Job Description	Latest Employment	Estimated by 1985	% Change
Driving Occupations			
Bus drivers	265,000	325,000	23
Routemen	594,000	645,000	8
Taxi drivers, chauffeurs	173,000	142,000	−18
Truck drivers	1,750,000	1,900,000	8
Parking attendants	42,000	45,000	7
Fork-lift operators	347,000	400,000	15
Other Operatives			
Asbestos, insulation workers	30,000	50,000	67
Assemblers	1,139,999	1,350,000	18
Bottling, canning operatives	59,000	57,000	3
Checkers, inspectors	757,000	972,000	28
Clothing pressers	162,000	129,000	−20
Dressmakers, except factory	110,000	108,000	−2
Earth drillers	63,000	73,000	16
Grinding-machine operators	149,000	152,000	2
Knitters, loopers, toppers	34,000	25,000	−26
Lathe operators	156,000	155,000	−.6
Meat cutters	282,000	286,000	1
Meat wrappers (retail stores)	52,000	66,000	27
Oilers and greasers (except autos)	50,000	46,000	−8
Packers, wrappers	676,000	720,000	6
Photo-lab occupations	77,000	110,000	43
Production painters	182,000	187,000	3
Riveters, fasteners	29,000	31,000	7
Sewers, stitchers	902,000	965,000	7
Shoemaking-machine operators	54,000	40,000	−26
Stamping-press operators	170,000	182,000	7
Stationary firemen (boiler)	90,000	85,000	5
Textile spinners	146,000	136,000	−7
Timber cutters, loggers	86,000	63,000	−27
Stock handlers	789,000	933,000	18
Vehicle washers	178,000	195,000	9
Warehouse laborers	151,000	145,000	−4
Weavers	42,000	32,000	−24
Welders, arc cutters	646,000	815,000	26
Farmers, farm managers	1,644,000	1,012,000	−38
Farm laborers, supervisors	1,404,000	848,000	−40

table 1-11   **monthly salary offers to candidates for various degrees—1975**

Field of study	Bachelor's	Master's	Doctor's
Accounting	$ 981	(NA)	(NA)
Business, general	843	1,250	(NA)
Engineering:			
Chemical	1,196	1,310	1,645
Civil	1,064	1,183	1,382
Electrical	1,081	1,228	1,550
Mechanical	1,122	1,274	1,624
Chemistry	956	1,118	1,503
Mathematics	915	1,138	1,523
Physics	(NA)	1,216	1,473
Humanities	723	931	(NA)
Social Sciences	770	953	(NA)
Marketing	801	(NA)	(NA)

NA: not available.
Source: Statistical Abstract of the U.S.

the job quest

Seeking a job—that will lead to a career—is a matter of selling. If a prospective employer is to buy your services on terms you are seeking, he or she must be convinced that your services will be able to generate a profit once you have acquired the necessary training, if any specialized instruction is called for.

Any successful sales person knows that advance preparation is essential if a sale is to be concluded on favorable terms. In the selling process that we call seeking employment, advance preparation is most critical. Your "sales kit" consists of a number of different elements.

☐ Your resume is the history of your past experience in school and at work. It should accurately and succinctly inform your prospective employer of all the various forms of training you've had that would be appropriate to the employment, as well as personal and social activities that would establish your broader profile as an individual. The value of an employee lies not just in getting a specific task accomplished. The employer wants the tasks accomplished by individuals who will get along well with their fellow workers, who will exhibit a constructive and productive attitude, and who will be, in general, well-rounded members of the community.

☐ Your references. Written references from anyone you've been involved with in terms of work or responsibility are important. This would include not just full-time work situations, but part-time and charitable work, and involvement with civic, religious, or social organizations. The thicker your file of references, the more easily you'll be able to establish your reputation for trustworthiness, integrity, and industriousness. Lack of references may not necessarily mean that you won't get a job. But an accumulation of honest references from responsible individuals can enhance your opportunities for current employment and future advancement.

☐ Your presentation. Resumes and references may depict the experience you've had. But they don't necessarily tell a prospective employer what you can do with this experience. This is perhaps the most critical aspect of your "sales pitch": what can you do for the employer that other applicants for the job might not? Applicants normally have an opportunity to make their presentation during the job interview.

Prior to that inverview, the aggressive job seeker will have taken the time to learn as much as possible about the prospective employer—products, services, strengths, weaknesses. There are a number of sources that you can investigate to build your information. Check the local newspaper for stories about and advertising by the firm. The local Chamber of Commerce and Better Business Bureau might have more detailed information. The firm might publish information about itself that can be helpful, and if you can speak with current employees of the firm you might be able to generate even greater insight.

If the firm is publicly held—that is, its stock is traded on one of the exchanges—stockbrokers will be able to acquire more specific financial information, particularly any recent prospectus that the company has issued in conjunction with an issuance of stock, as well as annual earnings reports that the company is expected to make available to its stockholders. Stock brokerage firms can also put you in touch with reports by financial analysts that may go into even greater depth regarding the company, its past, present, and projected future. Much of this information you'd probably want anyway just to determine if the company is one with whom you want to make a lasting involvement; and much of it will enhance your presentation when you go to your job interview. It involves a reasonable amount of homework that could pay off handsomely.

experience: an invaluable teacher

Job seekers are often disappointed that they can't find exactly what they're looking for. You may be distressed in thinking that you have to settle for second best, or third or fourth best. But in reality, such a decision need not be detrimental to your long-term career goals. In fact, choosing other occupational activities could enhance your ultimate career.

Experience is an invaluable teacher. Even though a given work activity may not directly coincide with your chosen career goals, you can learn from it. You can learn added skills that may be of value in the future. You can learn about people, about corporate intrigue and the workings of the hierarchy; you can learn about the kind of energy it takes to improve yourself and how its lack can set a person back. The experiences of learning, observing, and always doing your best at whatever task is assigned will be to your ultimate credit.

For many people, career goals may not come into clear focus until they have gone through a variety of work experiences. Over a period of perhaps many years, certain work activities that seem pleasurable and profitable may evolve from the varied background one has gone through. Job hopping in search of instant gratification is certainly not recommended. But reasonable job experimentation with an eye toward choosing a permanent (or even semi-permanent) career could be effective.

When Work Goes Bad

It may be long in coming, or it may come like a bolt out of the blue. Whether it arrives gradually or suddenly, the feeling is intense: "I'm sick of my work. I feel bored . . . frustrated . . . unchallenged . . . underpaid. I'm heading up a blind alley, and there's no way out. HELP!"

Nobody is immune. Young and old, salaried executives and hourly wage earners, those who rely on their muscles and those who rely on their brains—all can become victims of this common plight.

For many, the complaint may indeed be legitimate. Working conditions may be intolerable. Internal competition for advancement may be excessive and unrewarding. The pay scale for the work done may be unrealistically low compared to what other employers are offering. Career opportunities may be in jeopardy because of poor management of the company. Working skills are being wasted on unproductive matters. Personality differences may be impossible to resolve.

For others, however, the complaint may be founded in some other aspect of life—problems outside of work that are brought to work. More about such matters shortly.

The solution

The solutions to the dilemma range from the "grin-and-bear it" attitude to taking another job. Between those two extremes lie a number of other possible compromises that could, in the long run, be more sensible.

The wrong reaction to an uncomfortable work situation can be more dangerous than the situation itself. The grin-and-bear-it attitude, if taken home at the end of each workday, can have a decidedly adverse effect on one's family and social life. A change in jobs, if not carefully and correctly planned, can be detrimental to one's long-range career. An improper job change could mean sacrificing valuable pension or profit-sharing benefits, or giving up such fringe benefits as life and health insurance that might not be replaced. Other would-be employers may be skeptical of your reasons for having left a job—"personal reasons" may be difficult to explain, particularly if they are founded on your inability to adjust to disciplined working conditions. Although some job changes do advance one's career, many can also hold back advancement. In order to maintain a desired level of income, the job changer may have to move to a position with no greater fulfillment than the previous job held.

In short: job changing for a clearly improved opportunity can be advantageous. But job changing as a result of desiring to escape an uncomfortable situation can result in a change for the worse—if you've switched jobs for the wrong reasons. Consequently, the risk of making the wrong move in reaction to a bad work situation must be taken into account.

Let us examine some of the common situations that must be analyzed. If your dissatisfaction is based not on actual working factors, but on other influences, it might well be better to concern yourself with changing those other factors rather than sacrifice what might otherwise be an acceptable work situation.

Personal factors

Your work, it seems has turned sour. But in reality it may be something outside your working environment that's bothering you. Marital and family difficulties, financial problems, medical worries, and other personal anxieties of known or unknown origin can cloud our common sense, and we may fail to recognize the true nature of our problems.

Just as distressing personal

28

factors can cause dissatisfaction in the working environment, so can pleasant personal factors make an unpleasant work routine more tolerable. The amount of tedium or restlessness one is able to endure can be vastly increased by the promise of various joys and pleasures once the work hours have ended. Good personal relationships, intriguing hobbies, an active social routine, and invigorating community involvement can enhance the whole of life, even if the work routine is not as rewarding as we might like.

If one is burdened with a personal problem that affects other aspects of life, particularly work, the danger is all too obvious to change jobs as a means of escaping the unscratchable itch. In all likelihood, the personal problem will follow the individual from job to job, causing a frustration that can build to a crescendo.

It's necessary to evaluate carefully all the personal factors that may affect your work routine—and it's equally important to evaluate the work factors that can affect your personal life. Something of a minimally unsettling nature in your work routine could be creating friction outside of work that can compound itself back into a heightened dissatisfaction with work—which in turn reflects back on your personal life. And round and round it goes.

Many of us tend to keep our personal problems locked inside. This increases the danger all the more. Open and honest communications with family members, spouse, clergy, doctor, lawyer, banker, friends, the personnel officer at work, guidance counsellors, and with yourself are helpful ways of putting the problem into perspective so that it can be understood and coped with accordingly.

Working conditions

Working conditions can include many factors: the personal comforts and conveniences available to you at work; your attitude and the attitude of your co-workers; your relationship with your co-workers; and the ease with which undesirable conditions can be altered.

Among the comforts and conveniences might be the availability and quality—or lack thereof—of employee parking, public transportation, cafeteria, restrooms, infirmary, employee's lounges, recreational facilities, library and other learning facilities, temperature levels, lighting intensity, and even the comfort of the furniture for employees. Certain pluses and minuses exist in any working environment within this overall category, and anyone can adjust to a few of the minuses while enjoying the pluses. But an accumulation of negatives within the overall working environment can certainly provoke one into thinking that the entire job itself is not satisfactory. The importance that any worker gives these items is strictly individual. There may be those who prefer to work for less money and less chance of advancement, but in a country club surrounding. Oth-

ers would choose an opposite situation.

Avoid the problem

It certainly might be better to try to analyze the negative working conditions and attempt to change them rather than to change a job because of a handful of annoyances. Often, however, we don't stop to analyze and discern what is bothering us, preferring to react to the overall feeling of discontent rather than trying to change those items causing the discontent. Human nature can often set a chain reaction in motion: one petty annoyance can cause us upset in other petty areas, and a silly grievance can easily evolve into an overall feeling of malcontent. This does not suggest that anyone put up with unsatisfactory working conditions, if in fact they are honestly unsatisfactory, uncomfortable, or detrimental to your health or welfare in any way. But it also does not suggest that you should go seeking a new job because of certain conditions that, when viewed in the overall perspective of the work and personal environments, can easily be adjusted to without any sacrifice.

Company policy

If you had known what to expect, your reaction might have been totally different.

☐ You're doing volunteer fund-raising work for a local char-

ity, and you approach your employer for a contribution. To your shock and dismay you are told that "company policy" requires all charitable requests to be approved by the Board of Directors. Try again next year.

☐ A co-worker is in line for an important promotion. He's a good friend and you're rooting for him. Your disappointment is intense when you learn that someone from outside the company has been brought in to assume the cherished post. Your disappointment isn't lessened any when you learn that "company policy" encourages promotion from within, but in certain job categories the company may prefer to look outside for the talent capable of filling those certain posts.

☐ The head of the division you work in has been a capable, friendly, and encouraging leader. He is suddenly shifted to another division of the company so that the president's son—whom you feel is an incompetent—can take over the position. "Company policy" pretty much permits the president to do as he pleases.

Company policy is one of the more basic elements of job satisfaction or dissatisfaction. Even when all other factors regarding your work environment are favorable, negative feelings

about basic company policy, even though it may not affect you directly, can cause minor disappointments to turn into bitterness.

The better you understand your company's basic underlying policies in certain areas, the more easily you'll be able to adjust to them so that they will not interfere with your otherwise satisfactory job situation. These policies may include such matters as unionization; promotion from within; stockholder, employee, and community relations; incentive programs for management and employees; profitability targets; fringe benefits; and nepotism. Further, by making proper inquiry as to what these policies are, you'll be showing your employer that you're an employee who cares, and his esteem for you could well increase as a result.

The individual who has a good grasp on his or her career goals and working capacities can avoid false alarms in the work-goes-bad syndrome by carefully analyzing all the factors seemingly causing malcontent. An employee who expects calm seas throughout is bound to be in for some rude shocks. The more canny employee will know that there are ups and downs in every kind of endeavor, and he or she will be prepared to ride them out with gaze firmly focused on long-term achievements rather than short-term satisfactions.

1. Discuss the statement, "A college education is a necessity for anyone who wants to get ahead."
2. Another statement from the survey discussed in this chapter is, "It's perfectly all right to rely on others for financial assistance." Do you agree or disagree?
3. What are some reasons why women are entering the work force in increasing numbers?
4. Explain the difference between a job change and a career change.
5. What is wrong with the question, "What do you want to be when you grow up?"
6. Give suggestions for solving the problem of increasing college costs.
7. Besides long-term income advantages, why do you think it is advisable to go to college?
8. List three jobs of possible interest to you the openings for which are expected to show at least a 30% increase by 1985.

**cases
for
study**

1. Rita and Joan are high school seniors who have been discussing the value of a college education. After looking at Table 1-9, what can you tell them about the differences in lifetime incomes? Is this the result of a college education? What other factors are there to account for the difference?
2. Research a prospective career and summarize the following items about it: educational requirements, other qualifications, possible openings, entry pay, status, and chances for advancement.
3. Prepare a resume for yourself. Even though you may not be searching for a job, the resume gives you a chance to look at yourself as a prospective employer would. Remember, a resume is not a letter—it is a summary of your background and qualifications for a job.
4. Examine your resume. List your strongest points and your weakest. Set up a schedule for improving your weakest points so that when you must use a resume, yours will be better than it is today.

chapter 2 **creating a workable financial plan— budgeting and spending**

setting goals

To cope with your personal finances efficiently and to manage your money most productively, there must be a plan. This plan should set forth as clearly as possible your goals, current and future, and the steps you'll take to meet those goals. Further, for the plan to be truly functional, it must be re-examined periodically and revised when necessary. Personal circumstances change over the years, and as they do, so will many of our needs, desires, and long-range aspirations.

The essential element of any personal financial plan is how to distribute income to best accomplish current and future needs and desires? How much will I spend today and how much will I put away for the future?

To answer the above questions, let's look at the matter in terms of goals or objectives—specific uses to which your dollars will be put. Let's further break down our spendable money into two broad categories: Today Dollars and Tomorrow Dollars. Today Dollars are those applied toward meeting our current and continuing needs and goals. Tomorrow Dollars are those that, while available today, aren't spent for current needs but are put away in one form or another for future use.

Tomorrow Dollars can be accumulated directly; we put aside a portion of our spendable Today Dollars into savings plans and other forms of investment. Or, Tomorrow Dollars may be accumulated indirectly; deductions are made from our paychecks for pension plans, profit-sharing plans, and Social Security. Also, some of our spent Today Dollars may come back to us in the future; a portion of our mortgage payments on our homes will theoretically come back to us when we later sell or refinance the home; and a portion of our ordinary life insurance premiums may be available to us in the future should we wish to cash in or convert our policies.

sorting out goals

An efficient financial plan demands that we maintain a focus as clear as possible on our specific goals. Obviously, it will be much easier to focus on the more immediate goals than it will on the longer term ones. Many long-term goals may not really have taken complete shape yet and some will arise that we may not have fully anticipated. Not only do we have to attach numbers to our goals (how much will we need for what purpose, and when will we need it), but we also must assign *priorities* to our goals: which are more important, and which must we strive more deliberately to accomplish?

There are two main sorting processes. The first is to determine current and continuing goals on the one hand and the future goals (near term and far term) on the other. The other sorting process concerns the priorities of our goals. Some goals will naturally demand a higher priority than others, although it's up to each individual and family to make such determinations.

Let's look at an example of the difference between "must" and "maybe" goals with regard to one family's future aspirations. Howard and Hedda have an eight-year-old child and it is their fervent desire that the child receive a college education on graduation from high school some ten years hence. When that day arrives, Howard and Hedda don't want to say, "We're sorry but you can't go to college just now. We don't have enough money."

They know that they must have either the money, or the ability to borrow or generate the money, for their child's college education at a specific future point. For them this is a Must goal. If they have not reached their goal at the appointed time, the results would be most unsatisfactory.

On the other hand, Howard and Hedda have also dreamed of taking a trip to Europe. They'd like to do it within about five years if they could, but it's not that critical. If circumstances dictate that they're never able to take the trip, they'll be disappointed but it wouldn't be all that devastating. This aspiration falls into the Maybe goal category: if they don't ever achieve it, not that much has been lost in the trying.

Although each individual and family sets its own goals based on desires and needs, there is one particular goal that has a Must quality for most everybody: having enough money to live on when work ceases—that is, on retirement.

If, on reaching that time, we find we don't have adequate funds, we can't go back ten, twenty, or thirty years and accumulate the necessary nest egg that will provide us with the retirement life style we were hoping for. We must have the needed funds at that appointed time. It's all too easy at the age of twenty or thirty or even forty to ignore the importance of this must goal—it's too far off to warrant thinking about. But sound financial planning, even at a very young age, requires that this must goal be kept in mind, and planned for at the earliest possible time.

Common sense suggests that the prudent person create a well-disciplined plan that will allow one to reach the Must destination at the appointed time. This generally entails putting away future dollars in such a form as to give the highest degree of assurance that we'll have the needed money at the right time. The techniques that offer the highest level of assurance for this program are "fixed income investing" techniques.

Once a well-disciplined program is underway to meet the Must goals, the prudent individual might begin planning for the Maybe goals, using more speculative techniques, such as the stock market, to achieve them. These various investment techniques are discussed in later chapters, along with other matters relating to our spending programs.

changes and trade-offs

It would indeed be attractive if, at any age, we could program all our financial needs and desires into a computer, and let the machine create and maintain a plan that would help us achieve our various goals. But alas, technology can not yet take into account the shifting patterns of human activity. As we grow and mature, old goals are accomplished or abandoned, and new ones arise, perhaps unexpectedly. These shifts, whether drastic or imperceptible, will require a revision of our financial plan.

Further, as we pass old goals and strive toward new ones, we may have to make certain trade-offs—adjustments in priority to allow us to accomplish something that may not have been there yesterday.

In short, a workable financial plan is only as valid as its revisions. In addition to developing the disciplines of saving wisely and spending prudently, one must also develop the habit of periodically reviewing and, where needed, revising the overall plan that will most clearly satisfy the sought-after life style. For the family, it may be a yearly meeting at which everyone sits down to discuss, analyze, evaluate and make plans for the future regarding family finances. For the individual it may be an annual meeting with a banker, accountant, lawyer, or other adviser to do the same. An important part of such a review is to go step by step through each expense and each item of future needs and ask yourself: "Am I doing it right; am I getting bogged down in unproductive spending habits; will I arrive at my appointed destination on time with the right amount of dollars in my pocket?"

a goal worksheet— current needs

We all have a number of current and ongoing expenses that must be maintained to provide us with the life style we are living. Table 2-1 is designed as a worksheet. It lists all the common immediate and continuing goals that we must be constantly achieving and contains spaces for inserting the amounts you are currently spending (or setting aside) to meet these goals, as well as projected amounts that you will be spending one and two years from now. The exercise of filling out the worksheet serves several purposes: it can help to provide a clearer picture of your actual current financial situation; it will aid you in anticipating future goals as your needs may change; and it can help you determine what expenses might be modified to supply more spendable dollars in another area.

Each of the items contained in the worksheet is discussed in more detail. For your own purposes, you might want to break down any of these items into its more specific components.

It may take a bit of subdividing and figuring to finally achieve the correct detailed picture. As you calculate each monthly expense, whether current and actual or anticipated, include within the expense any debt repayment that may be a part of the total expense. In other words, any principal payments on an automobile loan would apply toward your overall transportation expense. Try also, to the best of your ability, to separate from

table 2-1   **goal worksheet—current and ongoing expenses**

	Current estimated monthly expenses	Estimated monthly expenses one year from now	Estimated monthly expenses two years from now
1. Food and beverage	_____	_____	_____
2. Shelter	_____	_____	_____
3. Clothing and other textile needs	_____	_____	_____
4. Protection against risk (insurance)	_____	_____	_____
5. Entertainment	_____	_____	_____
6. Education	_____	_____	_____
7. Medical and health care costs	_____	_____	_____
8. Transportation	_____	_____	_____
9. Little "rainy day" fund	_____	_____	_____
10. Cost of credit	_____	_____	_____
11. Travel and recreation	_____	_____	_____
12. Personal business matters	_____	_____	_____
13. Children's allowances	_____	_____	_____
14. Miscellaneous personal expenses	_____	_____	_____
15. "Luxuries"	_____	_____	_____
16. Charity and religious expenses	_____	_____	_____
17. Income taxes	_____	_____	_____

debt payments that portion attributable toward interest, and include those interest items under the category "cost of credit." It's important to get a clear cut picture of what all of your credit is actually costing you, and it may come as quite a surprise.

1. Food and beverage. This would include food and beverages consumed at home and at restaurants. Don't overlook alcoholic beverages, lunch money, snack money, and the tips you might leave when dining or drinking out.

2. Shelter. Your overall shelter costs should be broken down into various components, which include the following.

Basic expense: rent or mortgage payment. If you are an owner, remember that a portion of your mortgage payment applies to the reduction of your debt. This portion, referred to as principal, will theoretically be recovered at some future time when you sell or refinance the property. But because that future time is probably unknown at present, the total mortgage payment should be considered as a current expense.

Property taxes. In most communities, property owners are billed twice each year for property taxes. The tax bill may include separate allocations to the city, the county, the school district, and any other jurisdictions with the right to tax local properties. In addition to this overall property tax cost, home owners must include separate taxes for any special assessments. Special assessments are levied when, for example, a sewer line is installed, sidewalks are put in, streets are widened, and so on.

Property insurance. Commonly, property insurance includes forms of protection in addition to the basic coverage of your dwelling and its contents, such as public liability coverage and medical payments coverage for costs incurred by people who may be injured on your premises, plus specially scheduled protection for loss or theft of valuable property. It would be appropriate to include the total cost of your property insurance in this category, but do continue to be aware of the different coverages included within this overall cost.

Utilities. In an ever-increasing energy conscious world, the cost of utilities (electricity, heat, water) is no longer taken for granted. Indeed, those costs have mounted considerably, and have imposed a particularly harsh burden on many people. In evaluating current and future utility costs, it would be wise to also evaluate how those costs can be reduced by various energy-saving techniques. Ample literature on this is generally available from utility company offices, home improvement supply dealers, and at your local library or bookstore. It might be worth investing in a periodic inspection of the various mechanical elements in your home—heating system, air conditioning, plumbing, wiring—to determine if there is any energy waste involved, and correcting it. Any machine can lose its efficiency as it grows older, and an inefficient heating plant or air conditioning unit could be costing you needlessly.

Telephones are another form of utility. A simple evaluation of your telephone service could result in substantial cost savings— if you're paying for more telephones than you realistically need or for "fancy" equipment, you might be able to eliminate those extras and realize extra dollars in your pocket instead. If your local calls are measured on a time basis, how much a month could you save by reducing each conversation by simply a minute or two? If you make frequent long distance calls, are you taking full advantage of the night time and weekend discounts available?

Maintenance and repairs. Typically, this will be an accumulation of small amounts, but in the annual aggregate can become a substantial sum. Further, there is always the possibility of inevitable minor disasters, some of which are preventable through an alert maintenance system; others are totally unpredictable. A program of preventive maintenance can be decidedly less costly than one of after-the-fact maintenance.

Renovation and improvements. We may renovate and improve our dwellings cosmetically or functionally. Cosmetic improvements would include redecorating, painting, landscaping. Functional improvements might entail new kitchen equipment, adding or expanding rooms, installing a pool, converting a storage area into usable living space and so on. Much of this renovation and improvement activity is appropriate and worth the expense and much of the expense can be recaptured on a later sale of the property. But caution must be noted with regard to certain improvements that can be excessive. Because modernization costs can be extensive, the home owner embarking upon such projects must bear in mind the ability to recapture those expenses on subsequent resale and might best consult a local real estate firm first to determine the potential value of the improvements.

Appliances, and Reserves for Replacements. Under the general category of shelter, there are a number of expensive items many of us take for granted: television sets, kitchen appliances, water heaters, and the like. All of these items have a limited lifetime and will have to be replaced. Many people choose to wait until the end is at hand, and then there often ensues a scramble to find money in the budget for this. A more prudent course might be to establish a "Reserve for Replacements," a fund that would build a little month by month and alleviate much of the pain accompanying replacement costs.

3. Clothing and other textile needs. Clothing expenses tend to be based on two predominant factors: need (function) and style (frivolity). No guidelines are suggested other than prudence, and the caution that all too many budgets are thrown into disarray because of excessive purchases of clothing and accessories.

Other textile needs include sheets, towels, blankets. Although these may be relatively minor budget items, shopping with an eye toward durability and washability can keep replacements at a minimum.

4. Protection against personal risk. This category includes your program, for individual or family, of protecting your cash flow against the risks of illness, accident, and the unexpected premature death of the breadwinners. Health insurance, disability income insurance, and life insurance are discussed in more detail in later chapters. But as current and continuing expenses, actual out-of-pocket costs must be carefully discerned and allocated in your overall budget/goal program. Much of this protection may be available to you in the form of fringe benefits at work, and you may not actually incur out-of-pocket expenses. To the extent that you do, however, you must include them in your expense listings. Regarding ordinary life insurance that you have purchased privately, a portion of what you pay in will be available at some later time should you cash in the policy. Insofar as the premium payments now represent an out-of-pocket expense, you should consider them as such, and utilize the conversion values in your future planning.

5. Entertainment. Much of the money we spend on entertainment tends to be spent impulsively. This is natural; when we get the urge to escape, we don't always stop to examine how the expenses might affect our normal budgetary program. The frequent result: a severe budget "leak."

Take the time to make a detailed listing of all entertainment expenses so that you can determine where excesses might lie.

Among your overall entertainment costs you might include the following: admissions to movies, theaters, musical events; cable television subscription costs; admissions to sporting events; costs of sporting equipment and fees or memberships at sports facilities; books and periodicals (for other than educational purposes); dining and drinking out, if you haven't already included them in "food and beverages"; at home parties and get-togethers; special events, including not just the cost of tickets, food, and drink, but also special clothing and accessories purchased for that event and that might seldom be used again.

6. Educational expenses. This should include any expenses for private school tuition, religious education tuition, adult education expenses, and all reading materials related to such schooling or used apart from normal schooling activities. Include also the expenses of tutors, as well as fees and expenses for school clubs, uniforms, equipment, and printed materials.

7. Medical and health care costs. Over and above any premiums you may pay for health insurance, include here any costs you incur that are not reimbursable by any insurance program. In addition to doctor visits, include prescriptions, dental expenses, eye glasses, ambulatory devices (e.g., crutches), hearing aids, therapeutic equipment, and the costs of any other special treatments or devices needed.

8. Transportation. This should include the cost of both privately owned vehicles and public transit—and don't overlook the cost of motorcycles and bicycles, their maintenance, repairs, and parts.

Transportation can be one of the most critical factors in your overall expense program. If you live within easy access to public transit, you might be able to do without an automobile, or with one instead of two in a family situation. Further, the type of car you choose can make a notable difference in your overall life style. The cost difference between driving a compact car as opposed to a standard is roughly $50 per month. The difference in monthly cost between a standard and a subcompact can be in excess of $100 per month.

The above figures include two main factors: operating costs and purchase costs. Operating costs, based on 1976 Federal Highway Administration figures, indicate a total cost per mile of 15.9¢ for standards, 12.9¢ for compacts, and 11.2¢ for subcompacts. Based on 10,000 miles driven per year, that comes to totals of $1590 per year, and $132.50 per month for the standard; $1290 per year or $107.50 per month for the compact; and $1120 per year or $93 per month for the subcompact. These operating costs include depreciation, maintenance, accessories, tires, gas, oil, garages, parking, tolls, insurance, and taxes. Figures are calculated on a ten-year life of the car, which is not commonplace; in reality, where cars are traded more frequently, the depreciation factor would be much higher, thus boosting operating costs considerably.

Assuming a difference in original price of $1000 between standard and compact, and $2000 between standard and subcompact, and assuming the average going rate of interest on a 36-month car loan, the standard car will have monthly payments about $35 higher than the compact, and about $70 higher than the subcompact. Adding those purchase costs to the operating costs, we arrive at the total differential: the standard costs roughly $100 more than the subcompact and roughly $50 more than the compact.

If you were to drive a compact instead of a standard, or subcompact instead of a compact, thereby saving $50 per month in transportation costs, what else might you do with those dollars? If you were buying a house on a 30-year mortgage at 9% interest, that extra $50 per month would buy you approximately $6000 more house. If you decided to save the money, that extra $50 per month, invested in a conservative savings account paying 5% interest, would leave you with a total nest egg of about $7800 after ten years, $13,400 after fifteen years, and $20,600 after twenty years. The potential trade-off—less car in exchange for more spendable or saveable dollars—has some obvious advantages.

The Federal Highway Administration figures presumably are comparing cars that are equally equipped. They don't disclose the added cost factors of the "optional extras" that we tend to load into our automobiles, for purposes not always particularly clear. Some of these items increase the cost by many hundreds of dollars. Further, we pay extra interest when we finance these added costs, and we buy additional gasoline to carry it all around. If you're paying more than you need for the simple basics of adequate transportation, you must ask yourself if that money can't be put to better use in some other category of your overall expense program.

9. Little Rainy Day funds. We should distinguish between "little rainy day" funds to be used in your immediate and continuing budget program as opposed to "big rainy day" funds for your long-range budget program. The little rainy day fund is a handy source of money—perhaps kept in a savings account— that can be used to equalize some of the inevitable fluctuations that occur in a month-to-month spending program. It should be added to regularly and tapped as little as possible. The more it can grow, the better off your big rainy day fund will be, should major future needs arise.

10. Cost of credit. Apart from interest that you may be paying on your home mortgage, which is included in the shelter category, you should distinguish what costs you are incurring for all your other credit uses. This would include revolving charge accounts at department stores, interest on loans at banks and credit unions and consumer finance companies; interest on credit card lines, interest on overdraft checking lines, interest on personal loans payable to other individuals, interest on second mortgages you may have taken out on your home, interest on insurance premiums (which may be charged to you if you are paying monthly or quarterly instead of annually). The cost of credit is too easily buried in your overall payments, and not enough attention is paid to this cost, which can add from 10% to 30% of the goods and services you're purchasing, depending on the sources of credit. Only by determining a clear picture of the actual dollar cost of your credit will you be able to decide if you are using credit excessively. The use of credit is discussed in more detail in later chapters.

11. Travel and recreation expenses. This should be considered as a category separate from your normal transportation and entertainment expenses. Primarily it refers to vacations, travel to visit family, attend out-of-town weddings, and other functions. The cost of children's activities, such as summer camp, should also be included. Expenses in this category include transportation, lodging, meals, entertainment, tips, shopping (souvenirs, etc.), car rental fees, babysitting fees, special clothing and equipment, and any costs involved in maintaining your dwelling while you are away.

12. Personal business. Into this category fall all those expenses you incur in keeping your personal and family matters under control: legal fees, accounting fees, income tax preparation charges, investment advisory expenses, safety deposit box rentals, checking account costs, and the purchase of necessary equipment and supplies related to these matters (a calculator, stationery, filing equipment, etc.).

13. Children's allowances. A minor item perhaps, but important in setting the tone of a family's financial status. Factors to be considered in establishing allowances are: the degree of control over spending habits that parents wish to exert, the amount of allowance received by your children's peers (peer group pressure can be stronger than you might think), the amount that the children themselves contribute to family needs (housework, odd jobs). Although allowances themselves may be of low to medium priority, the establishment of discipline and control regarding the children's own financial status is of the highest priority. The size and conditions under which an allowance is given can have a considerable effect on a child's ability to establish a sense of self-sufficiency and self-worth. The matter should not be regarded lightly, even when children are at an early age.

14. Miscellaneous personal expenses. This is somewhat of a catch-all, but it can't be ignored. Experience has shown that individuals and families with financial problems will have an excessively large and unspecified "miscellaneous" category in their expense program. If all the miscellaneous expenses are carefully noted, it's much easier to bring a runaway budget under control.

Among myriad other common miscellaneous expenses you should include: money for snacks; cosmetic expenses (haircuts, beauty parlor costs, and all related accessories, salves, etc.); gifts purchased for others or for yourself; pet supplies and veterinarian fees; tobacco costs; various toys and trinkets purchased for your children or yourself; equipment and supplies for hobbies. Another miscellaneous expense is gambling, whether for state lottery tickets or other forms of betting. If you have any doubts about whether or not you are including every one of your personal miscellaneous expenses, follow a simple program that will help capture them all: for a period of two or three months carry a notepad and pencil and jot a quick note each time any expense is registered. If you can discipline yourself to make these notes, you'll stop and think twice before you make each expense; you'll also have a much better idea of how the dollar drain has eroded your budget.

15. "Luxuries." This is an optional category designed for those who genuinely have a goal of acquiring certain luxuries as a part of their immediate and continuing expense program. What are such luxuries? It all depends on the individual—obviously, what one might consider a luxury, another might view as an ordinary acquisition. Luxuries must be designated in terms of priority with regard to all your other expenses. What else might you be willing to give up in order to acquire them?

16. Charity and religious expenses. This would include membership in religious organizations, contributions to them, as well as other ongoing charitable contributions made during the year, such as the local United Fund, Red Cross, medical-oriented charities (heart fund, cancer association, muscular dystrophy fund), and so on.

17. Income taxes. Most of us never see the money we pay to the government (federal, state, and local where applicable)—it's simply deducted from our paychecks. If we have instructed our employers to withhold the proper amount, the annual withholding sum will cover our total tax obligation. If we have under-withheld, we will have a tax bill to pay each April. If we have overwithheld, we have a refund coming. Your employer will ask you to complete a W-4 form in which you list your exemptions and dependents. That form controls how much will be withheld from your regular salary. Some people may prefer to overwithhold, looking forward to a "bonus" when their tax refund comes each year. In a sense, this is a form of enforced saving, except that you don't get any interest on your money.

If you are self-employed, you will have to make quarterly payments of your estimated income tax due, as well as of your self-employment tax (the parallel to Social Security for the employed). Because those estimated tax payments are due only four times each year, it might be overly tempting not to worry about them until they fall due. But coming up with one-fourth of your annual income tax bill at those appointed times might be difficult if you have not embarked on a well-disciplined program to set aside the money for meeting those payments. One method would involve setting aside the necessary amount each week in a separate "untouchable" fund so that you don't have to throw your budget out of joint each quarter in order.

coordinating current goals with future goals

Once you've established what the spending patterns are in meeting immediate and continuing goals, you'll next have to assign priority to those goals. But first you must get the broad picture of your future goals, both near and long term. If, after making all the appropriate adjustments in your immediate goal program you can find excess dollars available, you must then choose whether to apply those dollars to other immediate goals or to perhaps more important longer term goals.

"Discretionary income"—the excess dollars available once your basic needs are met—now enters the picture. How will you spend those excess dollars? They could be spent on frivolities that might be quickly forgotten. Or they could be allocated to future needs, to provide pleasures whose values may be much more treasured.

The ability to meet your long-term goals will be largely shaped by the demands of your immediate goals. Only you can determine what each of those sets of goals will be. You are unique. A budgetary program should serve as a discipline in meeting the goals that you individually have set. Often, individuals and families will adopt "rule of thumb" budget programs to keep their spending habits in line. Such programs may work to an extent, but if they haven't been created with the individual's own particular needs in mind, the ultimate result can be a high level of dissatisfaction.

shaping future goals

Table 2-2 lists some of the more common major goals that most individuals and families anticipate. These goals are not listed in any order of priority; this is for you to determine. If you can complete the columns accompanying the goals, even in rough fashion (since many may be several years away for you), you'll begin to get a better idea about what priorities you want to attach to them.

How can one anticipate these major future needs without knowing the effects of inflation? Not only are these effects uncertain, but those of a continuing increase in personal income are also not known. Historically, with a few exceptions, the rate of personal income in the United States has exceeded the rate of inflation. It would not be totally safe to say that this trend would continue, though studies indicate it should. Thus, for purposes of completing this worksheet, it might be best to assume your future needs based on current dollar values, and then adjust the worksheet each year or two to reflect changes that have occurred. If expenses and income continue to increase at approximately the same rate, then the portion of your budget set aside for future goals should show a similar increase. In other words, if you're earning $12,000 a year and are able to put aside 5% of that after all expenses have been met ($600), and some years from now your earnings are $15,000 and you're still able to put aside 5% after all expenses have been met ($900), your annual savings/investments will be growing at a rate to help you meet the higher priced goal when it arrives at that future time.

Let's now take a closer look at each of the suggested items in the future goal list.

Education. This refers to higher education for children, and, in the light of current trends, it can be a most foreboding goal. Educational costs are increasing rapidly in both public and private school sectors. College education is a goal that traditionally must be met at a fairly fixed point. Though it is possible, most young individuals would not want to delay their college training by more than a year or two because of a shortcoming in the financial area.

Preparations to meet this goal must begin at the earliest possible time. These preparations can include a savings/investment program; acquiring an awareness of loan, grant, and scholarship programs; and communications between parents and child regarding the child's own contribution to the financial needs, such as through work.

table 2-2 **major future goals**

	How much will be needed	When will it be needed	Amount per year
Education	_____	_____	_____
Housing (new shelter)	_____	_____	_____
Retirement	_____	_____	_____
"Stake" for your children	_____	_____	_____
"Stake" for yourself	_____	_____	_____
Care of elderly or disabled	_____	_____	_____
"One shot" expenses	_____	_____	_____
"Big rainy day"	_____	_____	_____

Housing *(new shelter).* The individual or family currently owning a home and anticipating buying a bigger and better one in the future have an advantage over those currently renting: they will be building some equity in their existing home that can be applied toward the purchase of a new one. Current renters must accumulate a large enough down payment to enable them to obtain their first home. That home, once acquired, can become a growing asset that will assist them in meeting other goals later in life. Throughout the 1970s, many people played a "waiting game," hoping that interest rates or housing costs would eventually come down to enable them to make their purchase. For the most part, this proved fruitless and it's difficult to speculate what trends in the 1980s might bring. Later chapters on housing provide assistance in working out the arithmetic of buying versus renting and focus on this particular priority and how it can be accomplished.

Retirement. With rare exceptions, this is the most predominant "Must" goal for everyone. You don't have a chance to do it over if you reach a point when work ceases and there's not enough to live on. Whatever your aims, it's not too early to begin focusing on this important goal. The chapter on financial planning for retirement contains more guidelines to help you achieve that focus.

Stake for your children. Many families have a goal of acquiring enough money to provide their children with a stake to help them get started in life. The stake might be used to help them buy a home, get started in business or professional practice, or just to provide a cushion to assist them in coping with the world's vagaries. If this is one of your goals, you must give it priority in line with other goals.

A stake for yourself. As discussed in Chapter 1, career changing is becoming a more prevalent phenomenon in our society. Many of these changes involve going into business for oneself, and very often a substantial stake is needed. Unfortunately, the concept of going to work for oneself does not always loom clearly on the horizon and so it's difficult to put a priority on such a goal. Consider it accordingly, and keep it in mind each time you renew and revise this list of goals and priorities.

Care of elderly or disabled. This should perhaps be called a need rather than a goal, since we all hope that those near and dear to us will be able to maintain themselves throughout their lifetime. But it doesn't always work out that way. Parents and other close relatives may, through circumstances beyond anyone's control, become dependent on us for a measure of support. If this likelihood can be anticipated, it can be planned for and better coped with.

"One shot" expenses. These might be "must" goals, or they could be "maybe" goals. They can include such items as a "once in a lifetime" trip, a large wedding for one's child, a major purchase of jewelry or luxury items, or a generous gift to a charity or other institution. These are voluntary goals, and their priority may be high or low, depending on you. The higher the priority, the earlier the planning must be done.

Big rainy day. In the discussion of current and continuing goals and needs we mentioned the "little rainy day" fund. The big rainy day fund is directed more to major unanticipated expenses that any individual or family might confront—uninsured medical expenses and recuperative costs; extended periods of lay-off from work; emergency needs of other family members for various purposes; uninsured losses, and so on. Generally, this is an item of fairly high priority. Proper insurance programs can minimize much of the risk and there's always the possibility that the fund will never be needed and that it can, at some point, be allocated into other goal requirements.

the sources from which future goals can be accomplished

In addition to keeping a careful watch on your goals and their shifting priorities, it's also important to maintain a careful vigil on the sources of money that will allow you to accomplish these goals. They, too, might be subject to change over the years, and it's obviously important to be able to adjust goals and priorities in line with adjustments in the sources of money.

income from work

This, obviously, is the primary source from which your current and continuing goals will be met. To the extent that you don't use all your current income in meeting your current goals, the remainder will be put aside to meet future goals.

savings/investments

This is actually a double source, consisting of the income you earn in your savings and investment plans and the principal that you ultimately might use to meet various goals. Depending on the manner of placement of these funds, you may have a reliable or an unreliable source of dollars. Prudence can assure your future; speculation can demolish it. Be well aware of possible consequences before you make any decisions in this extremely important area.

equities

Home owners are building a source of future funds as they reduce their mortgage debt. Owners of ordinary life insurance policies likewise are building a source of future funds. Both forms of equity—your share of ownership—can amount to substantial sums. If they are tapped too early, by refinancing your home or prematurely cashing in your life insurance policies, the ability to meet future goals may be seriously impaired. Know what these values are and what they can amount to in the future. Later chapters on housing and life insurance will assist you in determining those future values.

borrowing

Borrowing can provide a most convenient way of meeting goals. Certainly with regard to housing, transportation, and such other major items as college tuition, borrowing allows you to accomplish what otherwise may take many years of accumulating. But borrowing is little more than a means of accelerating the use of future income, with an added cost factor of 10% to 30%, depending on the credit source used. It should also be well noted that funds that are borrowed and have to be repaid in the future will probably affect the budget flow when the funds are being repaid. Prudent borrowing can enhance your current, continuing life style; imprudent borrowing can devastate your future life style.

enforced savings—
pensions,
social security,
profit-sharing plans

These represent a form of what would otherwise be current income, shifted to future accessibility. To many people, these forms of enforced savings represent all, or a substantial part, of the sources for meeting long-range goals, particularly retirement. But a danger exists in overestimating the total of these sources. Many people may find their reliance on these sources has been in error—there simply isn't as much as expected. Even though access to these sources may be many years off, it's vital that a reasonably close estimate of what will be available is maintained on a continuing basis.

inheritances, gifts,
and other windfalls

For most of us this category may be a complete imponderable. But if you have any reasonable assurance that inheritances or gifts will be coming your way, it would be wise to try to determine the amount involved; this can have a considerable effect on your other ongoing financial plans. Whenever an inheritance can be anticipated, be sure you understand the impact of the tax laws on it. Federal taxes can take a substantial bite out of inherited property if it is sold at a gain. It's the net amount, not the gross amount, that you should assimilate into your budget.

**the financial
statement—
a planning tool**

Can you imagine buying an automobile with no dashboard indicators on it? No speedometer, no gas gauge, no mileage indicator, no oil, brake, or battery warning lights? And to top it off, the hood is sealed shut, requiring two days in the shop every time you want to check your oil, battery, and other innards.

It might be okay for an occasional spin down to the supermarket, but to take it out on the highway would be risky, to say the least.

In much the same sense, any individual, family, or business needs a proper set of financial indicators plus easy access to the inner workings, so that periodic tune-ups can be done quickly and simply.

A thoughtfully prepared and *regularly updated* financial statement is a neat and invaluable package of gauges, meters, and warning lights. It can tell you how fast you're going, how your fuel is holding out, how much fuel you'll need in the future, how smooth your ride is.

Financial statements provide a picture, at any given time, of the exact financial condition of the person or business involved. But it's important to remember that these financial statements reflect the condition only on the given day. The value of a single statement is limited. The true value comes in comparing it with past statements, so that changes in growth and strong and weak points can be spotted and evaluated.

The financial statement consists of three major elements: assets, liabilities, and net worth.

assets   Assets are the sum total of everything you own, plus everything owed to you. The value of assets is figured as of the date of the statement. Because the value of many assets can and does change, it's essential to evaluate them anew each time a statement is prepared, if it's to be accurate.

Included among your assets are your house, cars, personal property, bank accounts, cash value of life insurance, stocks, and other securities. Also included are money or property due you as a result of a pending inheritance, personal debts owed to you, property settlements, and so on.

liabilities   Liabilities are debts—everything you owe. As with assets, these are figured as of the date of the statement, and values must be updated accordingly to insure the accuracy of your statement.

Included among liabilities will be the mortgage on your home, amounts owed on personal loans, amounts owed on contracts, and other personal debts. A detailed financial statement will break down financial liabilities into long term and short term. This can aid an analysis of your condition by distinguishing which debts will fall due within, say, one year and which will fall due at some more distant point.

net worth   Your net worth is the difference between assets and liabilities. It should be on the plus side. You arrive at net worth by subtracting liabilities from assets. The business executive regards it this way: if he wanted to close up shop altogether, he would sell off all assets and use the money to pay off all liabilities. What's left would be his net worth.

other components   Simple personal financial statements will also include a brief summary of your annual earnings and living expenses, as well as schedules of your life insurance holdings, your investments, and your property, both real and personal.

From time to time you might be required to provide personal financial information to obtain credit or other services. In such instances, you'll probably have to sign a statement that says, in essence, that the information you have given is accurate; that you have given the information with the intent that the other party can act in reliance on it; that you have not withheld any pertinent information; and that you agree to notify the other party of any adverse changes in your circumstances. In providing this information and then signing the statement, you are legally binding yourself to the accuracy of the information given. If you give false or incomplete information, and the other party acts on it, you may be putting yourself in jeopardy. An insurance policy can conceivably be voided, a loan can be declared in default, a debt can be refused discharge in bankruptcy proceedings. Although such happenings may be rare, they can occur and the proper way to avoid them is to be certain that the information on any kind of financial statement is accurate. Figure 2-1 illustrates a typical financial statement provided by financial institutions (usually at no cost). After you have filled it out, consider the uses to which it can be put.

the uses of the financial statement program

as a safety valve

An ongoing program of updated financial statements can help you spot troubles before they get out of hand. A financial mess can be lurking beneath the surface for years before it begins to hurt. For example, you may be involved in a gradual buildup toward becoming overly extended with debts. By tracing your indebtedness over the years via your financial statement, the signals might become evident early enough to warn you to correct the situation. Or, your nest egg may not be growing as rapidly as it should be, and this can be spotted by comparing a series of annual financial statements. It's all a matter of "keeping track" and the financial statement program can be a most important tool for this.

for keeping the reins on your credit

Good credit, wisely used, can be of immense value. Knowing well in advance your borrowing needs and your borrowing capabilities helps assure the wise use of credit. Through your financial statements, you can maintain a close vigil on your current debts, your depreciating assets (items that need replacement in the future, such as a car), and your anticipated future income (your ability to afford tomorrow's obligations). Of course, you realize without looking at some figures that you'll need a

FINANCIAL STATEMENT
Personal Form

TO:				
		OFFICE	NO.	TELEPHONE NO.
NAME	ADDRESS		SOCIAL SECURITY NO.	
SPOUSE	OCCUPATION		FINANCIAL CONDITION AS OF ,19	

ASSETS			LIABILITIES		
CASH IN THIS BANK — (Checking) DEMAND			NOTES PAYABLE TO THIS BANK (Sch. 4)		
(Savings) TIME			NOTES PAYABLE TO OTHER BANKS AND OTHER FINANCIAL INSTITUTIONS (Sch. 4)		
CASH IN OTHER FINANCIAL INSTITUTIONS (Checking) DEMAND			CURRENT BILLS PAYABLE (Other than Instalment Loans)		
(Savings) TIME					
ACCOUNTS RECEIVABLE			INCOME AND OTHER TAXES PAYABLE		
NOTES OR MORTGAGES RECEIVABLE (Due within one year) (Sch. 1)			DUE TO BROKERS		
STOCKS AND BONDS — LISTED ON MAJOR EXCHANGES (Sch. 2)					
CURRENT ASSETS			CURRENT LIABILITIES		
REAL ESTATE AND BUILDINGS (Sch. 3)			LOANS ON LIFE INSURANCE (Sch. 5)		
AUTOMOBILE AND OTHER VEHICLES — MARKET VALUE (Describe)			OTHER LONG TERM OBLIGATIONS (Due after one year) (Sch. 4)		
HOUSEHOLD GOODS AND OTHER PERSONAL PROPERTY (Describe)					
OTHER SECURITIES (Sch. 2)					
CASH VALUE LIFE INSURANCE (Sch. 5)					
LONG TERM RECEIVABLES (Due after one year) (Sch. 1)					
OTHER			TOTAL LIABILITIES		
			NET WORTH		
TOTAL ASSETS			TOTAL LIABILITIES AND NET WORTH		

GROSS INCOME	Monthly	Annual	FIXED EXPENSE	Monthly	Annual
Alimony, child support, or separate maintenance income need not be revealed if you do not wish to have it considered as a basis for repaying this obligation.					
SALARY			INSURANCE PREMIUMS		
SPOUSE'S SALARY			RENTAL		
INCOME FROM SECURITIES (Sch. 2)			R.E. MTGE. & INSTALMENT PAYMENTS (Sch. 4)		
RENTAL OR LEASE INCOME (Sch. 3)			INCOME AND OTHER TAXES		
MORTGAGES OR CONTRACT INCOME (Sch. 3)			OTHER		
OTHER					
TOTAL GROSS INCOME			TOTAL FIXED EXPENSE		

SCHEDULE 1. Notes, Contracts, and Mortgages Receivable

DUE FROM	AMOUNT DUE Within One Year	AMOUNT DUE After One Year	DATE OF MATURITY	AMOUNT OF PAYMENT RECEIVED Monthly	AMOUNT OF PAYMENT RECEIVED Annually	TYPE OF OBLIGATION AND COLLATERAL IF SECURED
TOTALS						

CR–1 Rev 4.77

new car two years from now. But considering what other things you might have to borrow for between now and then, how will that car loan fit into your overall plans at that time? The financial statement gives you the current data that can help you cope with the future.

to help protect you against loss

If you keep your financial statements up to date—at least yearly—you'll be forcing yourself to keep accurate current valuations on all your property. The value of any property is subject to change, and only by knowing true current values can you be sure of obtaining the necessary insurance to protect you against loss.

in maintaining a sensible life insurance program

Sound planning dictates that provision be made to maintain comforts in the event of the premature death of a breadwinner. Life insurance is the most common means of providing for this. A life insurance program should be planned in conjunction with the availability of other assets that can be cashed in to provide for needs. The financial statement provides a reliable current indicator of available assets that can be converted readily into cash without undue sacrifice should the necessity arise. This can help you tailor your life insurance program to your specific needs rather than guessing what that program should consist of.

to help establish a worry-free estate plan

Your progressive financial statements provide the best possible at-a-glance gauge of how much and what type of estate planning you need. Prudent estate planning requires a regular checkup of your net worth: which assets and liabilities are increasing and decreasing? At what rate? Until what time? Which assets and liabilities can be shifted out of the estate to obtain maximum tax benefits and assure a proper distribution to survivors? Which assets have actual earnings or income potential and to what extent? A concise inventory and evaluation of these factors can be gained from your financial statements.

in helping to plan your long-range budget

The financial statement, regularly updated, is a simple device to keep your current and future goals in clear focus, and to provide an ongoing measurement of the sources from which those goals will be met.

as an aid in borrowing

On those occasions when a financial statement is required as a condition to getting a loan, you'll expedite matters considerably if you are prepared with a current statement as well as those of recent years. It will speed up application processing and will serve as evidence of your financial good housekeeping.

some thoughts on spending habits

It's the object of this chapter, this book, and this course of instruction to help guide you in establishing financial habits that will allow you to accomplish your individual goals. But all too often we are waylaid from those ultimate goals by strange and often inexplicable outside circumstances. We live in an age of instant gratification, constantly bombarded by commercial messages urging us to acquire products that will provide happiness and satisfaction in almost every phase of our day-to-day life.

Spending habits born out of impulse, gullibility, or low sales resistance can be extremely counterproductive to one's financial welfare. To some degree, we are all subject to impulsive spending but the more aware we can become of this susceptibility, the more readily we'll be able to control it.

Spending habits may have been unconsciously dictated to us by our observations of our parents and we should evaluate what spending habits are inherited and determine their good and bad points. Peer group pressure—"keeping up with the Joneses"—can also influence our spending habits, and succumbing to it can be costly and unsatisfying.

Spending habits can be a powerful force in shaping your overall financial well-being, which in turn can have a considerable effect on your social, psychological, and personal well-being. To the extent that spending habits control you, you'll have a much more difficult time achieving your own personal potential; when *you* control these habits, you will indeed be the master of your fate.

A Reporter's Notebook: Supermarket Savvy

Curiosity quickly became a challenge: how much money can you save by taking a little extra time and care in supermarket shopping?

Some of the basic tactics of supermarket survival are fairly simple. For example, don't go to the market when you're hungry because you're too likely to load up on nonessentials and luxuries that will boost your cost unnecessarily. Also, be aware that the highest profit margin items (and thus the ones providing less value for your dollars) tend to be on eye level shelves. If you're willing to reach up or bend down, you can probably do better in trimming costs.

But some techniques may require a little calculating and so you might take along your pocket calculator. These techniques include: 1) avoiding convenience foods; 2) using your own water; 3) buying store brands instead of name brands; 4) shopping for size.

Armed with these techniques, I proceeded to a nearby supermarket to test my thesis that the careful shopper can save at least 10% to 20% and in many cases much more than that on a substantial number of common staple items. I compared only items that were not on special sale so as to get a valid apples-versus-apples comparison.

There were scores of situations where ample money could be saved.

Avoiding convenience foods

Time is money, so they say, which is probably why business executives fly from one city to another rather than taking a train or car. But when it comes to the preparation of food, there's a serious question as to whether the time saved is worth the considerable added expense of convenience foods. *Examples*: A box of frozen French toast (6 slices) costs $.67. Making six slices of French toast from scratch, using your own milk, eggs, and bread, would cost about $.35—roughly half the cost of the convenience food. Does it really take that much longer to do it from scratch?

Next to the frozen French toast was frozen pancake batter. For $.69 you could buy a container stating that it would make 10 to 12 four-inch pancakes. Over in the pancake mix department you could buy a box of complete mix (only add water) for $1.39, and that would make 48 four-inch pancakes. To make that many pancakes using the frozen batter you'd have to buy four containers at a total cost of $2.76—again, the convenience product costs roughly double what the do-it-yourself product costs.

The produce department offered many additional opportunities for similar savings: fresh carrots were $.19 a pound that day; frozen cut carrots were $.53 for 20 ounces. Fresh onions were $.20 a pound, while frozen chopped onions were $.35 for 12 ounces. Fresh ears of corn were $.17 each while frozen ears were $.22 each. A ten pound bag of potatoes was fetching $1.08 while frozen hash browns were $.59 for a two pound pack.

Using your own water

These examples provided the comic relief for the day. A popular brand of fruit punch was selling for $.61 in a 46-ounce can. A concentrate of the same product was available for $1.69. With the concentrate you could make your own punch—6 quarts of it or 192 ounces—by adding your own water. Let's do a little math here. In order to get 192 ounces of the prepared punch you'd have to buy 4.17 cans which, at $.61 per can, would cost a total of about $2.55. That's $.86 more than the concentrate would cost. In other words, you're paying $.86 for six quarts of water when you buy the readymade punch. That comes out to about $.57 per gallon, which was the same price that a quart of milk was selling for that day.

We then come to the canned ice tea department. Canned ice tea was selling for $1.33 for a six-pack of 12-ounce cans. That's 72 ounces, no more, no less. Instant powdered iced tea, in a name brand bottle was $1.79 and according to the label it was capable of making 120 8-ounce glasses of iced tea. That's 960 ounces, maybe a little more, maybe a little less. To obtain the same amount of iced tea from the canned product as you could from the powdered product you'd have to buy approximately thirteen 6-packs, at a total cost of $17.29. That would give you about 7½ gallons of iced tea—perhaps a month or two supply for thirsty individuals. The bulk of iced tea, no matter how you buy it, is water. And if you go the canned route, you're paying essentially $2.30 per gallon of water. You can either give it to the supermarket or you can save it for something worthwhile.

Brand name products versus store name products

Most major supermarkets offer a wide variety of products packaged in their own labels. In such cases, the supermarkets have generally bought those products from the same manufacturers who make the brand name products. In fact, the goods may actually come out of the same vat. For the most part, you're getting a virtually identical product with these various local label purchases that you get in the advertised brand. Try it. If you don't like it, you can always go back to the more expensive product. In the meantime, here are some examples of the savings you can realize by shopping for the store label.

Mayonnaise: a 32-ounce jar of the store's brand was $.95, the name brand was $1.15.

Ketchup: 32-ounce bottle of the store's label was $.77, the name brand was $.89.

Vegetable oil: 38-ounce jar of the store's brand was $1.49 compared with $1.65 for the brand name product.

Yellow popping corn: a 16-ounce jar of the store's brand was $.25, the name brand was $.35 for the same size. A "gourmet label" was $.93 for a 15-ounce jar. These products were taste tested, and a large family couldn't tell the difference between any of the products.

Vodka: which by federal law must be all alike, was selling for $3.49 per fifth in the store's label, and $4.99 in a popular, nationally advertised brand.

Laundry bleach: $.84 per gallon for the nationally known product and $.63 per gallon for the store's label.

Brand name products may be perfectly fine and may satisfy you more than comparable products. It's your money, and if you'd just as soon spend part of it on advertising (which is why brand names generally cost more), go right ahead.

Buying by size

It's no secret that many products are cheaper if you buy a larger quantity. Hundreds of common supermarket items are available in varying quantities and substantial savings can be realized by buying larger packages. Properly stored, there should be no loss if the product isn't consumed as rapidly as one in a smaller container.

Some supermarkets offer a shopper's aid known as "unit pricing." In the unit pricing stores, there will generally be a sign on the shelf indicating the cost per ounce of each product on the shelf. (The information may also be contained on the label itself.) Unit pricing can be

Tomato juice consumers had a wide choice: 46-ounce cans ranged in price from $.57 for a store label to $.59, $.67, and $.69 for various advertised brands. For the extravagant, there was a 6-pack of one of the national brands: 33 ounces for $.75.

Among various nonfood products: a common deodorant sold for $.99 in a 4-ounce container, and $1.39 in a 7-ounce container. That's a difference of a nickle an ounce. A popular men's hair grooming substance was $1.49 for 7 ounces and $1.89 for 13 ounces—almost twice the product for an extra 40¢. An 8-ounce bottle of a popular conditioning shampoo was $1.59 while a 16-ounce bottle was $2.69.

a valuable tool for the shopper by providing quick and easy reference to the relative cost of various sized containers of the same product. Obviously, by combining the unit pricing technique—whether the store does it for you or you do it yourself—with the brand name versus store label technique, you can amplify your savings considerably. Here are a few examples of savings available in the size category:

The cereal department offered much more than food for thought with those little "6-packs" containing a variety of cereals; they priced out at $.59 for 5.34 total ounces, or 10.3¢ per ounce. (Sirloin tip steaks were selling for the same price per ounce that day.) A name brand of corn flakes was selling for $.39 for an 8-ounce box (4.88¢ per ounce), and for $.75 in an 18-ounce box (4.16¢ per ounce).

Candies that don't melt in your hand could be purchased for $1.43 in a one-pound pack, or in two half-pound packs that totalled $1.58.

Perhaps the most difficult problem to overcome in getting the most for your supermarket dollar is the inbred impulse to which we are all subject. It arises, no doubt, from a combination of susceptibility to advertising and habit. It's easier to follow our impulse and buy the product we've always been buying or the one we've been programmed to buy, even if it costs more, than it is to stop and do some simple calculating. But the difference is clear when we get to the checkout counter. Impulse costs money; it's as simple as that.

review
questions

review questions

1. What is the one *must* goal for everyone?
2. Name the investment techniques suitable for *must* goals.
3. What investment techniques are suitable for *maybe* goals?
4. Make an estimate of the savings possible by driving a smaller car. If you are now driving a subcompact, compare its costs with those of driving an intermediate to determine how much you are actually saving. Use the cost figures provided in the chapter.
5. Indicate some expenditures that might involve using the *little* rainy day fund.
6. What are some expenditures the *big* rainy day fund might be used for?
7. List any forms of enforced savings for you or your family.
8. Explain what unit pricing is and how it can help you.

cases for study

1. Complete a goal worksheet. Write a short paragraph describing some possible future events that would require a revision of your plan.
2. Complete a similar worksheet for your major future goals. You should realize that some of the items will be zero.
3. Barry Cohen completed a financial statement for his lender when he bought a new car. To be sure of obtaining his loan, he conveniently forgot some of his bills. Discuss the possible consequences of this oversight.
4. Rita and Bob Mateo have carefully analyzed their food purchases for one week. They determined that the items they buy most frequently are bread (one loaf), milk (two gallons), fruit punch (two 42-oz. cans), orange juice (five 12 oz. cans), corn flakes (one 16 oz. box), round steak (4 lbs.), hamburger (4 lbs.), green beans (3 lbs.), potatoes (5 lbs.), and American cheese (8 oz.). Check on the possible savings they might obtain by careful shopping.

chapter 3 **income taxes**

the importance of understanding the basic income tax laws

Income taxes are more than just an annual form filling event. Virtually every major facet of our financial concerns—housing, insurance, investing, pensions and retirement, estate planning, and so on—are affected in one way or another by federal income tax laws. An awareness of how the tax laws operate can aid us in many ways besides the filing of our annual return. A good grasp of the tax structure will help us plan much of our annual spending so as to take maximum advantage of what the law allows. It can motivate us to be better record keepers in conjunction with tax law requirements. It can improve our investment expertise. And it can, overall, help us to be better managers of our financial affairs. (For those who must be concerned with state or city income taxes, a knowledge of the federal system can also prove beneficial.)

The federal income tax system is complex and in a constant state of change. Tax laws are initially passed by Congress. Once a law is passed, the Internal Revenue Service issues rules and regulations that dictate how the laws apply to individual taxpayers. If a dispute arises—as it often does—between taxpayers and the Internal Revenue Service, the courts may then further interpret precisely how a specific law is to be applied.

The average individual would find it an enormous challenge to keep up with the constant flow of new laws, rules, regulations, and court decisions. To an average taxpayer, the whole spectrum of income taxes is focused on the 1040 form (or the short form, 1040A) that must be filed each year by most of us. This chapter concentrates on the 1040 form as the "manual" for grasping the basic elements of the tax laws and how they affect us. Although the 1040 form itself undergoes a degree of change each year, its essential elements remain generally constant.

The basic income tax laws, in their simplest and most understandable form, are as follows.

☐ You *must* report all income that is subject to taxation. But you need *not* report income that is *not* subject to taxation. If you do report income that is not subject to taxation, you're liable to end up paying more taxes than you should.

☐ You *may*, if you so choose, reduce your taxes by taking advantage of a number of provisions in the law. You don't have to do this. You won't be violating the law if you don't; but if you don't do it, nobody else will do it for you. In other words, it's up to you to take the steps available to reduce your taxes. If you do so, you might reduce your obligation to the government, perhaps considerably. If you don't take these steps, you may end up paying more than you have to.

The items that can allow you to reduce your taxes are: exclusions, exemptions, adjustments, deductions, and credits. Each is explained in more detail shortly.

a 10-step formula

The steps taken in computing your taxes are the following:

1. You total all of your *income* that is subject to tax.
2. You then subtract from the above figure any *exclusions* to which you may be entitled.
3. You then subtract any *adjustments* that you may be entitled to.

4. The result (income less exclusions and adjustments) is a figure called your *adjusted gross income*. This figure is important because a number of other later calculations are based on it.

5. From the adjusted gross income you subtract whatever *deductions* you're entitled to.

6. Then you subtract whatever *exemptions* you're entitled to.

7. The result (adjusted gross income less deductions and exemptions) is your *taxable income*.

8. Using the tables in the tax instructions, you compute the tax due on your taxable income.

9. From the tax due, you subtract any *credits* to which you may be entitled.

10. The result (the tax less the credits) is the amount you actually owe the government, or the amount that may be refunded to you, if more than you actually owe has been withheld from your earnings, or if you have paid in more than was needed in your estimated tax payments.

Let's now put some people, facts, and numbers into those oversimplified statements and see how it all really works in practice.

jerry and joan smith—a case study

We'll consider the case of Jerry and Joan Smith. Their income situation is well above the national average, but we had to create a situation that would enable us to demonstrate the wide variety of problems encountered in filling out an income tax return.

Jerry's income as a sales agent was $16,000. Joan earned $6000 as a substitute teacher (but she had to incur babysitter expenses of $2500 while she was at work). In addition, the Smiths took in $3000 in rents from a property they bought many years ago. They have some money invested in the stock market, and they earned dividends of $570. Their various savings accounts earned $450 in interest. Their income thus totalled $26,020.

Over and above their normal living costs, the Smiths had the following deductible expenses: $1327 for medical fees, including premiums on a private health insurance policy; $1566 in taxes, including property taxes on their house and state and local sales taxes; $2342 in interest expenses, including the interest on their mortgage and on their charge accounts; $350 worth of charitable contributions; $15 for a safety deposit box rental in which stock

certificates are kept; $40 for subscriptions to professional maga-
zines that Jerry uses in his business; and $20 for dues to a
professional association that Joan belongs to.

A number of other items affect the Smiths' income tax situation:
during the year, Jerry's CB radio was stolen from his car. He had
just recently bought it, and had not yet notified his insurance
agent to cover it for theft. The radio was worth $180. The Smiths
bought a new car late in the year with a $5000 price tag. They
contributed $1500 to their Individual Retirement Account. And
Jerry's mother moved in with them, totally dependent on Jerry for
her care and well-being (Figure 3-1).

Let's refer again to the ten steps used in figuring taxes, filling
in the blanks with Joan and Jerry's situation.

1. Total income for the year was $26,020.

2. The law permits the Smiths to exclude up to $200 of dividend
   income. (This is explained more fully in a later section.)
   Thus, $200 is subtracted from the figure in item one.

3. The law states that contributions to an Individual Retirement
   plan are considered as an adjustment to income. Thus,
   another $1500 is subtracted from the Smiths' total income.

4. The total income of $26,020 has been reduced by the two
   items, $200 worth of exclusions and $1500 worth of adjustments, giving the Smiths an adjusted gross income of
   $24,320.

5. Their allowable deductions total $5740.

6. There are a total of five exemptions available in the Smith
   family: Jerry, Joan, the two children, and Jerry's mother.

Income		Expenses	
Jerry's income	$16,000	Child care	$2,500
Joan's income	6,000	Medical	1,327
Rental income	3,000	Taxes	1,566
Dividends	570	Interest	2,342
Interest	450	Charity	350
		Safe deposit box	15
Also note:		Subscriptions	40
C.B. radio loss	$ 180	Dues	20
New car purchased	5000		
I.R.A. contribution	1500		
Mother-in-law moved in			

Figure 3-1   Jerry and Joan Smith's Situation.

Each of these five exemptions is entitled to a $750 reduction, or a total of $3750.

7. Subtracting the deductions ($5740) and the exemptions ($3750) from the adjusted gross income ($24,320) leaves us with a taxable income of $14,830.

8. The tax due on the above taxable income, according to the tax tables, would be $2966.

9. However, the Smiths are entitled to certain credits against their taxes. The amount spent on child care expenses entitles them to a credit against their taxes of $500, and the general credit available on 1976 returns entitles them to another $180 in credits. Their credits thus total $680.

10. Subtracting the credits ($680) from the tax due ($2966), the Smiths end up with an actual tax obligation of $2286. However, since the Smiths had a total of $2500 withheld from their earnings throughout the year, they actually end up being entitled to a refund of $214.

Regretfully, the tax forms aren't quite that simple. To look at them in their entirety is like trying to identify the individual strands in a bowl of spaghetti. But if we take the forms apart and examine them piece by piece, bearing in mind the ten-step formula noted earlier, we can make sense out of the chore of computing taxes and learn to handle it efficiently. Some of the lines and numbers on these forms change from year to year, as do some of the specific laws and regulations. But once a grasp of the basic pattern is gained, the year to year variations can be handled with relative ease. We will consider the major points applicable to most taxpayers. Because state and city income taxes, where applicable, vary from locality to locality, there is no discussion of those tax returns. However, they generally follow the same patterns of the federal return, and a grasp of the federal return will thereby assist you in handling any state or city income taxes you may be obliged to pay.

The following is not intended to be a comprehensive course in income taxes. It's intended as a *general guideline* to alert you to the highlights of the tax laws and to increase your awareness of how to take maximum advantage of what the law allows. We're examining the generalities as they apply to most people. Space does not permit discussion of many specific situations that may apply to individual taxpayers. Although this chapter should help you to determine and resolve any of these specific matters, professional assistance still might be advisable in order to obtain the proper legal position regarding such points. For example purposes we'll use 1976 forms and laws. Check for changes that have occurred since then.

Before we examine Jerry and Joan's return more closely, we must first answer two preliminary questions: who must file a return, and what forms should be used in filing the return?

who must file a federal income tax return

Whether or not you are required to file a federal income tax return depends on three things: your age, your status (married,* single, widowed, child), and your gross income. Gross income refers to income subject to taxation. Certain types of income are not subject to taxation and need not be reported. Such income is not included when you calculate the gross income to determine whether or not a form must be filed. These forms of nontaxable income are discussed in a later section.

single persons

- ☐ If you were single and under 65, you have to file a return if you had a gross income of $2450 or more for the year.
- ☐ If you're single and 65 or over, you have to file a return if you had gross income for the year of $3200 or more.
- ☐ If you can be claimed as the dependent of another taxpayer, such as a parent, and you had *unearned* income (dividends, interest, and other investment income) of $750 or more you must file a return.

married persons and certain widowed persons

- ☐ A married couple may file a single tax return together, or a joint return, or they may prefer to file separate returns for each of them. See the later section on filing status for more detail.
- ☐ If you and your spouse were both under 65 *and* living together at the end of the taxable year, *and* if you file a joint return, you must file if your gross income was $3600 or more for the year. This was the case for Joan and Jerry Smith.

* Your marital status is determined as of the last day of the tax year, which is December 31 for most taxpayers.

☐ If one of the spouses was 65 or over, the gross income requirement is $4350, and if both spouses are 65 or over, the income requirement is $5100.

☐ If you're married, but filing separate returns, of if you're married but not living together at the end of the year, you must file a return if your gross income is $750 or more.

☐ Certain widowed persons may be eligible for benefits when filing a tax return. If a widowed person meets the following requirements, he or she is considered a *qualified* widow or widower; (1) the spouse must have died within the two tax years preceding the year for which the return is being filed; (2) you must have been entitled to file a joint return with your spouse for the year of death whether you actually did so or not; (3) you have not remarried before the close of the current tax year; (4) you have a child or stepchild who qualifies as your dependent; (5) you furnish over half the cost of maintaining your home, which is the principal residence of your dependent child or stepchild during the year.

A qualifying widow or widower whose age is under 65, and who has a dependent child, must file a return if gross income was $2850 or more (compared with a single person or nonqualifying widow or widower who must file if income exceeds $2450). If a qualifying widow or widower is 65 or over, a return must be filed if gross income exceeds $3600 (as compared with the nonqualifying widow or widower or single person who must file if income exceeds $3200).

In addition, and probably more important, the qualifying widow or widower is entitled to use the *joint return* tax rate category rather than the *single* tax rate category. For example, with a taxable income of $14,000, a single tax rate category indicates a tax of $3203, whereas the joint tax rate category indicates a tax of $2754, a difference of $449. At higher income levels, the advantage to the qualifying widow or widower increases accordingly.

self-employed persons

If you are self-employed, you must file a return if you had net earnings from self-employment of $400 or more, regardless of your age, even if you're over 65 and receiving Social Security benefits. As a self-employed person, you also have to pay a self-employment tax on your self-employment income. This tax is comparable to the Social Security tax that's withheld from an employee's wages.

exceptions

If you did not earn enough to require you to file a return, but income taxes were withheld on whatever you did earn, then you are required to file a return so that you can get any refund due. Also, you may be entitled to what is known as the "earned income credit" that offers certain benefits to low income taxpayers. If you want to take advantage of this credit, you will also have to file a return, even though your income may not have been enough to otherwise require you to file. Briefly, you may be eligible for the earned income credit if your earned income, or your adjusted gross income, whichever is larger, is less than $8000, and if for the entire year you have maintained a residence that is the principal residence for you and your children. The credit may also be extended to workers who have disabled dependent adult children living with them. If the amount of the earned income credit to which you're entitled is greater than the taxes you owe, the difference will be refunded to you. The maximum amount of credit available is $400.

which form should you file?

Individual taxpayers have a choice between the "short form" 1040A and the regular form 1040. The short form 1040A may be used if all income was from wages, salaries, tips, and not more than $400 in dividends or $400 in interest was received.

But the regular form 1040 must be used: if you don't qualify as stated above; if you wish to itemize your deductions; if you can reduce your gross income by adjustments resulting from a contribution to an Individual Retirement Account or from moving expenses, or other eligible adjustments; or if you choose to take advantage of the income averaging provisions. (Income averaging is generally advantageous to a taxpayer whose income has fluctuated considerably from one year to the next. The law permits you to average your income over a period of years, and may thus allow you to pay a lower tax on a particularly high income year.)

Check your tax form instructions for further specific regulations requiring use of the 1040 instead of the short form 1040A.

Each year the Internal Revenue Service will send taxpayers instructions with forms based on the type of return they had filed in the previous year. If you wish to use a form different from the one used in the previous year you can obtain the appropriate instructions and forms directly from the Internal Revenue Service, from local financial institutions, or you may find them contained in tax guide books available at most newsstands.

a walk through the 1040, one step at a time

Let's now break the regular form 1040 down into easily digestible bites, using Joan and Jerry Smith's situation as an example. Within each segment, you will be required to make evaluations and decisions—will you qualify for certain benefits that the law allows you? Remember that if you don't take advantage of provisions enabling you to reduce your ultimate tax bill, no one else will do it for you.

The five major segments of the tax return are the following.

☐ Identifying the parties, including choosing the proper status under which you're filing, and listing all available and eligible dependents who can qualify for valuable exemptions.

☐ Tallying the total income subject to taxation, and reducing that income by taking advantage of eligible exclusions and adjustments.

☐ Calculating deductions: standard versus itemized, and who should do what about which ones.

☐ Computing the tax.

☐ Taking advantage of all eligible credits that can reduce your tax bill.

who's who—the identity label, your status, your exemptions

This segment consists of three parts, as illustrated below.

identity label

The first part is the identity label. If you've received your forms and instructions from the government, the mailing label will be a peel-off one that you should remove from the instructions booklet and place in the square at the top of the form. This will help to assure that your return is properly processed. If you don't have the mailing label, write in your name and address as instructed. If the mailing label is incorrect, change it as appropriate. To the right of the label are spaces for your Social Security number and your spouse's Social Security number, as well as statements regarding your occupation. These should be filled in.

filing status

Below the identity label is the segment called "Filing Status." Status #2 (married and filing a joint return) and status #5 (qualifying widow or widower) pay at the same tax rate. The other three each have their own separate tax rates. The highest tax rate of the five is the #3 status (married, filing separate). The

---

IDENTITY

Form 1040 Department of the Treasury—Internal Revenue Service
U.S. Individual Income Tax Return 19__   This space for IRS use only

For the year January 1–December 31, 1976, or other taxable year beginning ___, 1976 ending ___, 19 ___

Name (If joint return, give first names and initials of both)	Last name	Your social security number
JERRY & JOAN	SMITH	111 22 3333

Present home address (Number and street, including apartment number, or rural route)
999 FAIRVIEW LANE

For Privacy Act Notification, see page 5 of Instructions.   Spouse's social security no. 444 55 6666

City, town or post office, State and ZIP code
ANYTOWN

Occupation: Yours ▶ SALES   Spouse's ▶ TEACHER

FILING

1 ☐ Single   **(Check only ONE box)**
2 ☒ Married filing joint return (even if only one had income)
3 ☐ Married filing separately. If spouse is also filing give spouse's social security number in designated space above and enter full name here ▶ _____
4 ☐ Unmarried Head of Household. See page 7 of instructions to see if you qualify ▶
5 ☐ Qualifying widow(er) with dependent child (Year spouse died ▶ 19). See page 7 of Instructions.

EXEMPTIONS

6a Regular ☒ Yourself ☒ Spouse   Enter number of boxes checked ▶ 2
b First names of your dependent children who lived with you TOM MARY   Enter number ▶ 2
c Number of other dependents (from line 7) . ▶ 1
d Total (add lines 6a, b, and c) . . . . . . ▶ 5
e Age 65 or older . ☐ Yourself ☐ Spouse   Enter number of boxes checked   Blind . . . . ☐ Yourself ☐ Spouse
f TOTAL (add lines 6d and e) . . . . . . ▶ 5

7 Other dependents:

(a) Name	(b) Relationship	(c) Months lived in your home. If born or died during year, write B or D.	(d) Did dependent have income of $750 or more?	(e) Amount furnished for dependent's support — By YOU. If 100% write ALL.	By OTHERS including dependent.
ETHEL SMITH	MOTHER	12	NO	$ ALL	$ ____

next highest is status #1 (single) followed by status #4 (unmarried head of household). The lowest tax rate is enjoyed by married couples filing jointly and by the qualifying widows and widowers. This is the status that Joan and Jerry Smith are entitled to.

Naturally, you should choose the proper status that will give you the lowest tax rate. In other words, a qualifying widow who erroneously chooses to file as a single person will pay a much higher tax than necessary. Similarly, if you qualify as a head of a household but you choose to file as a single person, you will also be paying more tax than you should.

Married couples may choose between filing separate returns and filing jointly. A husband and wife should calculate the taxes due both ways—if they filed separately and if they filed jointly—to determine which would be the lower rate. Generally, if both spouses have income that is equal or close to equal, there may be a slight advantage in filing separately. However, the added time and possible cost of filling out two separate returns may offset this slight advantage. If one spouse has income that is substantially more than that of the other spouse, it will probably be advantageous to file a joint return.

Table 3-1 illustrates the advantages in filing jointly or separately. It gives examples of the *total* tax obligation of married couples filing separate returns compared with those filing joint returns. For example, with total combined income of $22,000, a joint return will result in a tax obligation of $5020, regardless of which spouse earns what portion of the total. If the spouses are filing separately, and they've each had a taxable income of $11,000, their total tax due will be $5004, which is $16 less than if they filed a joint return. However, if one spouse earns $16,000 and the other earns $6000, their total tax would be $5445, substantially more than they have to pay if they had filed a joint return.

Exemptions For each legitimate exemption you can reduce you income by $750. (Further, for the taxable year 1976, certain exemptions

table 3-1 **filing separately or jointly**

Total taxable income	Spouse #1	Spouse #2	Total Tax Separate Returns #1	#2		Joint Returns
$16,000	$ 8,000 +	$8,000	$ 1,624 +	$1,624	= $3,248	$3,254
	10,000 +	6,000	2,183 +	1,125	= 3,308	3,254
	12,000 +	4,000	2,822 +	685	= 3,507	3,254
$22,000	11,000 +	11,000	2,502 +	2,502	= 5,004	5,020
	14,000 +	8,000	3,541 +	1,624	= 5,165	5,020
	16,000 +	6,000	4,320 +	1,125	= 5,445	5,020
$28,000	14,000 +	14,000	3,541 +	3,541	= 7,082	7,100
	18,000 +	10,000	5,160 +	2,183	= 7,343	7,100
	20,000 +	8,000	6,059 +	1,624	= 7,683	7,100
	22,000 +	6,000	7,030 +	1,125	= 8,155	7,100
$34,000	17,000 +	17,000	4,740 +	4,740	= 9,480	9,500
	20,000 +	14,000	6,059 +	3,541	= 9,600	9,500
	24,000 +	10,000	8,030 +	2,183	= 10,213	9,500
	28,000 +	6,000	10,090 +	1,125	= 11,215	9,500

entitled the taxpayer to an additional credit against taxes other-wise due. This specific credit may or may not be continued beyond the taxable year of 1976.) If taxpayers do not claim all of the legitimate exemptions available, they will pay more tax than necessary.

Each taxpayer may claim an exemption of $750 for himself, plus another $750 for his spouse. Additional exemptions are allowed the taxpayer if he, or his wife, is 65 or over, or is legally blind within the definitions set forth by the IRS. For example, if both taxpayer and spouse are over 65, they may claim a total of four exemptions.

dependents   In addition to the personal exemptions, a taxpayer may also claim exemptions for dependents. For a person to qualify as a dependent, and thus entitle the taxpayer to an exemption, the dependent must meet five tests. These five tests, briefly, are:

1. *The Support Test.* The taxpayer must furnish over one-half of the dependent's total support during the calendar year.

2. *Gross Income Test.* In order to claim a person as a dependent, that person must not have earned more than $750 of gross income during the year. If, though, a child is under 19 years of age at the end of the year, this gross income test does not apply. Further, if the child is a student, the gross income test does not apply regardless of the child's age. Even though a child or child/student is exempted from meeting the gross income test, he or she must meet all of the other four tests in order to qualify as a legitimate dependent.

3. *Member of Household or Relationship Test.* A person claimed as a dependent must be either a relative or a member of your household. However, a qualifying relative need not actually live in your house in order to be a dependent. And a member of your household need not necessarily be a relative to qualify as a dependent.

4. *Citizenship Test.* To qualify as a dependent, a person must be a citizen or resident of the United States or a resident of Canada, Mexico, the Republic of Panama, or the Canal Zone.

5. *Joint Return Test.* To qualify as a dependent, a person must not have filed a joint return. For example, if you have a child who otherwise meets the above tests, but is married and files a joint return with his or her spouse, you may not claim that child as a dependent. There is an exception to this: if a

married dependent is not otherwise required to file a tax return for the year, but does so in order to claim a refund on taxes withheld from their earnings, you may still claim an exemption for that person.

As you can see from the sample return duplicated above, Jerry and Joan Smith claim a total of five exemptions: one each for Jerry and Joan, one each for their two dependent children, and one for Jerry's mother who lives with them and meets all the dependency tests.

totalling the income and reducing it by exclusions and adjustments

The income segments of the 1040 form are where the hopscotch starts. The main section for reporting income is on the *front* of the 1040. This is what it looks like:

INCOME

9	Wages, salaries, tips, and other employee compensation (Attach Forms W-2. If unavailable, see page 6 of Instructions.)	9	22,000
10a	Dividends (See pages 9 and 16 of Instructions) 570 , 10b less exclusion 200 , Balance ▶	10c	370
	(If gross dividends and other distributions are over $400, list in Part I of Schedule B.)		
11	Interest income. {If $400 or less, enter total without listing in Schedule B} {If over $400, enter total and list in Part II of Schedule B}	11	450
12	Income other than wages, dividends, and interest (from line 37)	12	3000
13	Total (add lines 9, 10c, 11 and 12)	13	25,820
14	Adjustments to income (such as moving expense, etc. from line 42)	14	1,500
15a	Subtract line 14 from line 13	15a	24,320
b	Disability income exclusion (sick pay) (attach Form 2440)	15b	
c	**Adjusted gross income.** Subtract line 15b from line 15a, then complete Part III on back. (If less than $8,000, see page 2 of Instructions on "Earned Income Credit.")	15c	24,320

On the *back* of the 1040 are two additional segments relating to income. The first is referred to as Part 1, which looks like this:

Form 1040 (1976)   Page **2**

Part I   **Income other than Wages, Dividends and Interest**

29	Business income or (loss) (attach Schedule C)	29	
30a	Net gain or (loss) from sale or exchange of capital assets (attach Schedule D)	30a	
b	50% of capital gain distributions (not reported on Schedule D—see page 10 of Instructions).	30b	
31	Net gain or (loss) from Supplemental Schedule of Gains and Losses (attach Form 4797)	31	
32a	Pensions, annuities, (rents,) royalties, partnerships, estates or trusts, etc. (attach Schedule E)	32a	3,000
b	Fully taxable pensions and annuities (not reported on Schedule E—see page 10 of Instructions)	32b	
33	Farm income or (loss) (attach Schedule F)	33	
34	State income tax refunds (does not apply if refund is for year in which you took the standard deduction—others see page 10 of Instructions)	34	
35	Alimony received	35	
36	Other (state nature and source—see page 11 of Instructions) ▶	36	
37	**Total** (add lines 29 through 36). **Enter here and on line 12** ▶	37	3,000

Part 1 includes income other than wages, dividends, and interest, and, as you can see, it may require filling out a separate schedule. If you have had income or loss from a business activity, you will have to complete and attach Schedule C. If you've had income or loss from the sale or exchange of capital assets, you will complete and attach Schedule D. If you have had income from rents—as did Jerry Smith—or from pensions, annuities, royalties, partnerships, estates, or trusts, you will have to complete and attach Schedule E. If you have had income or loss from farming, you will complete and attach Schedule F. These separate schedules are on separate forms, and they are not duplicated here.

Next is Part 2, *adjustments to income*, which is also on the back of the 1040. As you can see, this may also call for completion of additional forms if you have qualified for these particular adjustments. This is what Part 2 looks like:

Part II	Adjustments to Income		
38	Moving expense (attach Form 3903)	38	
39	Employee business expense (attach Form 2106)	39	
40a	Payments to an individual retirement arrangement from attached Form 5329, Part III	40a	*1500*
b	Payments to a Keogh (H.R. 10) retirement plan	40b	
41	Forfeited interest penalty for premature withdrawal (see page 12 of Instructions)	41	
42	**Total** (add lines 38 through 41). **Enter here and on line 14** . . . . ▶	42	*1500*

Further, if you have reported income from interest or dividends of more than $400 each, you will have to complete a separate form called Schedule B, Parts 1 and 2, which looks like the form on p. 75.

These segments of the 1040 form are filled in with the appropriate entries from Jerry and Joan Smith's return, outlined earlier. You can see where each entry from Part 1, Part 2, and Schedule B was inserted, as per instructions, into the income segment on the front of the 1040 form. The ultimate calculation is for "adjusted gross income," which is a figure used to determine the allowable deductions.

If the various income segments of the Smith's 1040 form were unscrambled and restructured in logical sequence, this is what it would look like (in abbreviated form).

Income

1. Income from wages, salaries, tips, and other employee compensation $22,000

Schedules A&B (Form 1040) 1976   **Schedule B—Dividend and Interest Income**   Page **2**

Name(s) as shown on Form 1040 (Do not enter name and social security number if shown on other side)   Your social security number

Part I — Dividend Income

Note: If gross dividends (including capital gain distributions) and other distributions on stock are $400 or less, do not complete this part. But enter gross dividends less the sum of capital gain distributions and non-taxable distributions, if any, on Form 1040, line 10a (see note below).

1 Gross dividends (including capital gain distributions) and other distributions on stock. (List payers and amounts—write (H), (W), (J), for stock held by husband, wife, or jointly)

XYZ CO	200
SUPER MUTUAL FUND	250
ZYX CO	120

2 Total of line 1 570

3 Capital gain distributions (see page 16 of Instructions. Enter here and on Schedule D, line 7). See note below

4 Nontaxable distributions (see page 16 of Instructions) . . . .

5 Total (add lines 3 and 4) . . . . .

6 Dividends before exclusion (subtract line 5 from line 2). Enter here and on Form 1040, line 10a **570**

Part II — Interest Income

Note: If interest is $400 or less, do not complete this part. But enter amount of interest received on Form 1040, line 11.

7 Interest includes earnings from savings and loan associations, mutual savings banks, cooperative banks, and credit unions as well as interest on bank deposits, bonds, tax refunds, etc. Interest also includes original issue discount on bonds and other evidences of indebtedness (see page 16 of Instructions). (List payers and amounts)

NATIONAL BANK	250
CREDIT UNION	150
H BONDS	50

8 Total interest income. Enter here and on Form 1040, line 11 . . . . **450**

2. Income from dividends   570
3. Income from interest   450
4. Income (or loss) from business—attach Schedule C
5. Income (or loss) from sale or exchange of capital assets—attach Schedule D
6. 50% of capital gain distributions not reported on Schedule D
7. Income (or loss) from supplemental schedule of gains and losses—attach form 4797
8. Income from pensions, annuities, rents, royalties, partnerships, estates, or trusts, and so on—attach Schedule E   3,000
9. Income from fully taxable pensions and annuities not reported on Schedule E
10. Income or loss from farm operations—attach Schedule F
11. State income tax refunds
12. Alimony received
13. Other income not included above
    TOTAL INCOME   26,020

Exclusions from Income

14. Dividend exclusion	200
15. Disability income exclusion (attach form 2440)	
TOTAL EXCLUSIONS	200

Adjustments to Income

16. Moving expenses (attach form 3903)	
17. Employee business expenses (attach form 2106)	
18. Payments to an Individual Retirement Account (attach form 5329, Part 3)	1,500
19. Payments to a Keogh (HR 10) retirement plan	
20. Forfeited interest penalty for premature withdrawal from savings account	
TOTAL ADJUSTMENTS TO INCOME	1,500
21. Subtract Total Adjustments and Exclusions from Total Income. The result is adjusted Gross Income.	24,320

This list has also been filled in with the results of Jerry and Joan Smith's income for the year. As you can see, the results are the same as those on the 1040 form.

In completing the income segments, each taxpayer must determine what income was taxable and what income is not subject to taxation. The law requires that you must report all income subject to taxation. But you need not report income that is not subject to taxation. Obviously, if you include nontaxable income, you will be paying more taxes than the law says you must.

income that is taxable

The following are the major types of income that are taxable and that you must report as such.

□ *Wages, salaries, and tips.* You should attach the W-2 form that your employer will have given you shortly after the first of the year. If you report an amount different from what the W-2 form indicates, the Internal Revenue Service will want to know why.

□ *Interest.* All interest that you receive on savings accounts, certificates of deposit, corporate bonds, and mutual funds is subject to taxation. The firms that paid you this interest may be required to file a form 1099, indicating the amount of interest paid during the year. IRS computers may compare the amounts reported on the 1099 forms with the amount of interest income you actually report. If these figures don't match, the Internal Revenue Service will expect you to make the proper adjustments. If you receive interest payments from someone who owes you money, such as on a personal IOU or on a mortgage, that interest is also subject to taxation and must be reported. If you own E-Bonds, you have an option as to whether or not to report the interest. Interest earned on E Bonds may be reported in the year in which it is earned, or you may defer the reporting of the earnings until such time as you cash the bonds in.

☐ *Dividends.* Dividends that you receive from stock ownership or through mutual funds are taxable. However, you are permitted to exclude up to $100 worth of dividends earned. (If a married couple owns stock jointly and is filing a joint return, up to $200 worth of dividend income may be excluded.) As with interest income, dividend income is reported on 1099 forms by the payers of the dividends, and those figures should match the amounts that you actually report.

☐ *Capital gains.* If you realize gains on the sale of property or securities, those gains are to be reported. Some of them may be subject to taxation at a lower rate than the ordinary types of income noted above.

☐ *Business income, including sales commissions.* This income, properly reduced by allowable expenses incurred in generating the income, is reported on Schedule C.

☐ *Certain income from pensions and annuities.* This may be reportable, depending on whether the contribution to the respective fund was made by the taxpayer or an employer.

☐ If you are a *beneficiary of an estate or a trust fund*, and that estate or trust fund has earned income during the year, the earnings will be taxable to either the trust or you as the beneficiary, but not to both. Note the difference between the tax status of the original *bequest* and the *income earned* by the bequest. An inheritance itself is *not* subject to taxation. If you inherit $10,000 from good old Uncle Charlie, you don't pay a tax on that $10,000. But if, before the money is paid out to the beneficiaries, it is invested in a savings account where it earns $500 during the course of a year, that $500 worth of income *is* subject to taxation. Also, once you've received your bequest, if *you* invest it or sell it at a profit, the income and/or gain will be taxable to you.

☐ *Other business endeavors* such as rental income investments and partnerships are subject to taxation on their earnings, after appropriate expenses have been deducted from the earnings.

☐ *Alimony* that is received by a divorced spouse is subject to taxation. Child support payments received by a spouse on behalf of dependent children are not subject to taxation.

☐ *Gambling winnings* are subject to taxation. If, though, you itemize your deductions, you may deduct your gambling losses during the year, but only up to the amount of your winnings. Lotteries and raffles are included in the gambling category. If you win something other than cash—say, a car or a TV set—the fair market value of that price must be included in the taxable income.

☐ *Certain prizes* are considered taxable income, including contest winnings, awards and bonuses given for employee performance or suggestions, and even door prizes.

This is by no means a complete list of all forms of taxable income. Refer to the IRS regulations for a more complete detailing of taxable income items.

nontaxable income

The following items are among those not subject to income taxation. As with the taxable items, you should refer to the law for a more thorough list of nontaxable income items.

☐ Insurance proceeds are not subject to taxation. This would include benefits paid on health and accident policies, reimbursement from casualty losses, and life insurance proceeds payable to beneficiaries.

☐ Gifts and inheritances are not taxable, but, as noted above, if those funds have been invested, the earnings themselves are taxable.

☐ Tax-exempt interest is not subject to federal taxation, although it would be subject to state and local income taxation. These forms of interest arise from IOU's issued by municipalities when they borrow money, and they are known as "tax-exempt municipal bonds." An investor may purchase these securities directly through a bank or stockbroker, or may invest in mutual funds that specialize in such securities.

☐ E Bonds: as noted above, the taxpayer has a choice of reporting the interest earned during the current year on E

Bonds, or of delaying reporting all the income until the bonds are cashed. (Interest earned on federal government bonds, including E bonds, is not subject to state income taxes.)

☐ Unemployment compensation benefits are not subject to taxation.

☐ Certain scholarships and grants may be excluded from taxation, particularly if they've been made to the taxpayer primarily for the purpose of furthering his or her education and training. If, however, scholarships or grants are awarded in exchange for services rendered, the amounts may be subject to taxation.

☐ Social Security, Railroad retirement, and welfare benefits are not subject to taxation.

☐ In recent years, cash rebates have been popular in the automotive industry. If you've purchased an automobile and received such a rebate offered to the general public, the amount of that rebate is not taxable income.

☐ Certain awards, made in recognition of past accomplishments in religious, charitable, scientific, artistic, educational, literary, or civic fields are not included in your taxable income.

exclusions from income

The 1040 form refers to two types of exclusions—that is, income received that need not be reported. In other words, it is excluded from the total income that you will report.

Dividend exclusions. You need not report the first $100 of dividends you receive from qualifying corporations. Spouses may also exclude up to $100 each, but they may not "borrow" from the other to reach the maximum allowable exclusion. For example, if a husband earns $120 in dividends in his own name, and the wife earns $80 in dividends in her own name, he may only exclude $100 of the $120 from his income, and she may exclude the entire $80. Thus, they will take a total exclusion of $180, whether they file jointly or separately. If they own stocks jointly, they may exclude up to $200 worth of dividends received in stocks thus held.

The disability income exclusion. Prior to 1976 the law was relatively liberal concerning the exclusion of certain kinds of sick pay received by an employee. But in 1976 the law was changed drastically. Now, in order to claim any exclusion for disability income, the taxpayer: (1) must not have reached 65 at the end of the taxable year; (2) has not reached mandatory retirement age at the beginning of the taxable year; and (3) was permanently and totally disabled at the time of the forced retirement. If a taxpayer meets all qualifications, he or she can exclude up to $5200 per year of disability pay from total income. Very few taxpayers will qualify for this exclusion, but those who do certainly should examine the regulations and take full advantage of them.

Sale of residence at age 65 or over. This item is not included in the form 1040, but many taxpayers may be eligible for it. Generally, if a taxpayer sells a house and realizes a profit, that profit can be taxable unless the taxpayer takes certain steps to delay the tax, such as investing the proceeds in another residence of equal or greater value. However, for taxpayers 65 or over, it is possible to *exclude* such gain from your income altogether.

adjustments to income

Your total income can be reduced by taking advantage of the so-called "adjustments." If you qualify for any of these five adjustments, you report the appropriate amount in Part 2 on the back side of form 1040. These adjustments may occasionally be referred to in conversation as "deductions." Technically, they are not. They do have the same effect as deductions—that is, they reduce your overall income on which the tax is ultimately paid. But the adjustments are subtracted from *total income* in order to arrive at the *adjusted gross income*. Deductions, on the other hand, are subtracted from the *adjusted gross income*. In many cases, the actual amount of deduction that one can take is dependent on the adjusted gross income.

The primary reason why the adjustments are figured prior to the adjusted gross income calculation is that they are available to taxpayers who do not otherwise itemize their deductions. For example, you are permitted to reduce your income by an amount contributed to an Individual Retirement Account, whether you itemize your deductions or not. For taxpayers who do not itemize their deductions, but who do make contributions to an individual retirement account, this is the place and manner in which it is done.

The allowable adjustments are as follows.

Moving expenses. If you have moved during the taxable year, and you satisfy certain minimum distance and work tests, all or a portion of your moving expenses may be included in the adjustment. Moving expenses for which you've been reimbursed are not includable. See the discussion on moving expenses in Chapter 7 for further detail.

Employee business expense. If you, as an employee, incur expenses for travel, entertainment, and gifts in connection with your employment, you may be entitled to reduce your income by these expenses—to the extent that you are not reimbursed for them—either in the adjustment section of the 1040, or in some cases in the deductions section of the 1040 form, if you itemize your deductions. The regulations differ for those who are outside sales people and for those who are not.

Payments to an Individual Retirement Account, or payments to a Keogh (HR-10) retirement plan. The IRA and Keogh plans, more fully described in Chapter 11, permit considerable tax benefits to taxpayers taking advantage of them. The Keogh plan is designed for self-employed individuals; the IRA plan is for individuals—whether self-employed or employed by others—who are not otherwise covered by a qualified pension plan. In a nutshell: if you put $1000 into your savings account during a year, with the intention of letting it ride there until retirement time, you get no tax advantage. However, if you place that $1000 into a savings account with an IRA or Keogh designation, which you can establish at your local bank, that $1000 reduces your otherwise taxable income by that amount. If, for example, you're in the 25 percent tax bracket (tax brackets are explained later), a $1000 contribution to an IRA plan will reduce your taxable income by $1000, and your tax obligation by $250. The contribution to a normal savings account has no such effect. Jerry and Joan Smith made a $1500 contribution to an IRA plan, and have entered it in the "adjustments" segment.

Forfeited interest penalty for premature withdrawal from a savings certificate. Say you have a savings certificate for $1000, paying $60 per year. The institution may credit the $60 of interest earned to your account, even though it has not entered that credit in your passbook or on your certificate. The $60 worth of income is reportable in full as taxable income. However, you withdraw the $1000 before the certificate matured, and in accordance with the deal you made with the institution, you must suffer a penalty. Instead of the full $60 interest, you're entitled only to $45, for example. Your withdrawal then totals $1045. The other $15 is forfeited. Although you report the $60 in income in the appropriate interest segment of the 1040, you deduct the $15 penalty in the adjustment section, thus showing the true picture of your actual earnings.

Total exclusions and total adjustments are subtracted from total income, and the result is adjusted gross income.

deductions: standard or itemized, and who should do what

Deductions are certain expenses you've incurred during the year that, according to the law, can be subtracted from your adjusted gross income. If you take full advantage of what the law allows you regarding deductions, you can cut down your adjusted gross income and thus minimize your taxable income and the actual tax due. The law does not require you to take full advantage of the deductions provisions. If you do not, you may well pay more tax than necessary.

Taxpayers have the choice as to how they will take their deductions: the standard deduction or the itemized deductions. The choice is made by checking off a box on line 44A if you choose the itemized deductions, and on line 44B if you choose the standard deduction. These lines are contained in Part 3, Tax Computation, which is on the *back* side of the 1040 form. This is what that section looks like:

Part III   **Tax Computation**

43 Adjusted gross income (from line 15c). If you have unearned income and can be claimed as a dependent on your parent's return, check here ▶ ☐ and see page 9 of Instructions	43	24,320
44a If you itemize deductions, check here ▶ ☒, and enter total from Schedule A, line 40, and attach Schedule A		
b Standard deduction—If you do not itemize deductions, check here ▶ ☐, and:		
If you checked the box on line . . . { 2 or 5, enter the greater of $2,100 OR 16% of line 43—but not more than $2,800; 1 or 4, enter the greater of $1,700 OR 16% of line 43—but not more than $2,400; 3, enter the greater of $1,050 OR 16% of line 43—but not more than $1,400 . . }	44	5,740
45 Subtract line 44 from line 43 and enter difference (but not less than zero)	45	18,580
46 Multiply total number of exemptions claimed on line 6f by $750	46	3,750
47 Taxable income. Subtract line 46 from line 45 and enter difference (but not less than zero) . .	47	14,830

● If line 47 is $20,000 or less and you did not average your income on Schedule G, or figure your tax on Form 2555, Exemption of Income Earned Abroad, find your tax in Tax Table. Enter tax on line 16 and check appropriate box.

● If line 47 is more than $20,000, figure your tax on the amount on line 47 by using Tax Rate Schedule X, Y, Z, or if applicable, the alternative tax from Schedule D, income averaging from Schedule G, tax from Form 2555 or maximum tax from Form 4726. Enter tax on line 16 and check appropriate box.

the standard deduction

The amount of the standard deduction is fixed by law. You may take the standard deduction regardless of your actual deductible expenses. For the taxable year 1976 the standard deduction was equal to 16 percent of your adjusted gross income, with certain maximums and minimums. As the segment of the form indicates on line 44B, if you have chosen the status of married and filing a joint return (box 2 in the Filing Status segment), or the status of a qualified widow or widower (box 5), you are entitled to a standard deduction of at least $2100 or 16 percent of your adjusted gross income, whichever is greater. But your standard deduction may not exceed $2800.

If you are filing as a single person or as an unmarried head of household, you're entitled to a minimum standard deduction of $1700 or 16 percent of your adjusted gross income, whichever is greater, but not more than $2400. A married person filing a separate return is entitled to a minimum deduction of $1050 or 16 percent of the adjusted gross income, whichever is greater, and not more than $1400.

Table 3-2 illustrates how the selection was made.

For example, if your adjusted gross income was $10,000, and your actual deductions totalled $1500, you should take the standard deduction, for the standard amount allowed—$2100— is greater than the amount of your actual deductions. On the other hand, with an adjusted gross income of $10,000, if your actual deductions totalled $2500, you should take the itemized deduction, because the actual deductions exceed the minimum allowed of $2100, and they also exceed the 16 percent limitation; which would be $1600.

If your adjusted gross income was $15,000, the 16 percent allowable deductions would total $2400. If, in such a case, your actual deductions totalled $2000, you should take the standard deduction, which would be $2400 or 16 percent of your adjusted gross income. However, if your actual deductions totalled $3000,

table 3-2   **standard or itemized deductions? (joint return)**

Adjusted gross income	Actual deductions total	Standard allowed	Which to take
$10,000	$1,500	$2,100 (min.)	standard
10,000	2,500	2,100 (min.)	itemized
15,000	2,000	2,400 (= 16%)	standard
15,000	3,000	2,400 (= 16%)	itemized
20,000	2,500	2,800 (max.)	standard
20,000	3,500	2,800 (max.)	itemized

you should itemize your deductions, since that sum exceeds the amount allowed in the standard deduction, which would be $2400.

itemized deductions

Itemized deductions consist of the sum total of all allowable deductible expenses for which you have adequate proof. You're entitled to deduct whatever this allowable total might be.

In order to make an accurate determination of whether to take the standard or the itemized deduction, you should prepare a list of all eligible deductions and see whether or not the total exceeds the amount you could otherwise take under the standard deduction.

As a general rule, you will probably be better off taking the itemized deductions if you own your own home and have a mortgage on it. The interest you pay on your mortgage is deductible, as are the property taxes. For example, if you own your home and you have a mortgage with a balance of, say, $25,000, which has an interest rate of 9 percent, you will, during the year, have accumulated interest expenses of approximately $2250. In addition, your property taxes will probably have been in the neighborhood of $600. The total of these two items is $2850, which exceeds the maximum allowed under the standard deduction. These two items alone, then, would dictate that you take the itemized deduction, for there are a number of other available deductions that will boost the total even higher.

In addition to owning your own home, there are some other guidelines that might dictate itemizing your deductions. If you have had large uninsured dental or medical expenses during the year, or if you have paid a substantial amount of qualifying alimony, or if you have made large charitable contributions, or if you have had a large uninsured casualty loss, it will probably pay you to itemize your deductions.

Once you have totalled all of your allowable deductions, Table 3-3 indicates whether or not you should in fact take the itemized deductions instead of the standard.

table 3-3
when should you itemize? (based on 1976 returns)

Single Returns Should Itemize *if*:		
Adjusted Gross Income Is	and	Deductions Exceed
Less than $10,625		$1,700
$10,625 to $15,000		16% of A.G.I.
Over $15,000		$2,400

Joint Returns Should Itemize *if*:		
Adjusted Gross Income Is	and	Deductions Exceed
Less than $13,125		$2,100
$13,125 to $17,500		16% of A.G.I.
Over $17,500		$2,800

schedule a: listing your itemized deductions

If you itemize your deductions, you will have to fill in Schedule A of form 1040, which is a separate sheet of paper from the 1040. It's on the back of Schedule B, where interest and dividend income are reported. The following is a copy of the Schedule A that the Smiths filled in for their 1976 return.

Schedules A&B—Itemized Deductions AND
(Form 1040) Dividend and Interest Income

Department of the Treasury Internal Revenue Service

▶ Attach to Form 1040. ▶ See Instructions for Schedules A and B (Form 1040).

19

Name(s) as shown on Form 1040

JERRY & JOAN SMITH

Your social security number

111 22 3333

Schedule A—Itemized Deductions (Schedule B on back)

Medical and Dental Expenses (not compensated by insurance or otherwise) (See page 13 of Instructions.)

1 One half (but not more than $150) of insurance premiums for medical care. (Be sure to include in line 10 below) . . .	*100*
2 Medicine and drugs	*320*
3 Enter 1% of line 15c, Form 1040 . . .	*243*
4 Subtract line 3 from line 2. Enter difference (if less than zero, enter zero) . .	*77*
5 Enter balance of insurance premiums for medical care not entered on line 1 . .	*100*
6 Enter other medical and dental expenses:	
a Doctors, dentists, nurses, etc.	*680*
b Hospitals	*750*
c Other (itemize—include hearing aids, dentures, eyeglasses, transportation, etc.) ▶	*350*
7 Total (add lines 4 through 6c) . . .	*1957*
8 Enter 3% of line 15c, Form 1040 . . .	*730*
9 Subtract line 8 from line 7 (if less than zero, enter zero)	*1227*
10 Total (add lines 1 and 9). Enter here and on line 34 . . . . ▶	*1327*

Taxes (See page 13 of Instructions.)

11 State and local income	*220*
12 Real estate	*660*
13 State and local gasoline (see gas tax tables)	*115*
14 General sales (see sales tax tables) . .	*571*
15 Personal property	
16 Other (itemize) ▶	
17 Total (add lines 11 through 16). Enter here and on line 35 . . . . . . ▶	*1566*

Interest Expense (See page 14 of Instructions.)

18 Home mortgage	*2250*
19 Other (itemize) ▶	
DEPT STORE	*27*
BANK CREDIT CARD	*19*
CAR LOAN	*46*
20 Total (add lines 18 and 19). Enter here and on line 36 . . . . ▶	*2342*

Contributions (See page 15 of Instructions for examples.)

21 a Cash contributions for which you have receipts, cancelled checks or other written evidence	*350*
b Other cash contributions. List donees and amounts. ▶	
22 Other than cash (see page 15 of instructions for required statement)	
23 Carryover from prior years	
24 Total contributions (add lines 21a through 23). Enter here and on line 37 . . ▶	*350*

Casualty or Theft Loss(es) (See page 15 of Instructions.)
Note: *If you had more than one loss, omit lines 25 through 28 and see page 15 of Instructions for guidance.*

25 Loss before insurance reimbursement .	*180*
26 Insurance reimbursement	*-0-*
27 Subtract line 26 from line 25. Enter difference (if less than zero, enter zero) .	*180*
28 Enter $100 or amount on line 27, whichever is smaller	*100*
29 Casualty or theft loss (subtract line 28 from line 27). Enter here and on line 38 . ▶	*80*

Miscellaneous Deductions (See page 15 of Instructions.)

30 Alimony paid	
31 Union dues	
32 Other (itemize) ▶	
SAFE DEPOSIT BOX	*15*
SUBSCRIPTIONS	*40*
DUES	*20*
33 Total (add lines 30 through 32). Enter here and on line 39 . . . . . . ▶	*75*

Summary of Itemized Deductions **A**

34 Total medical and dental—line 10 . .	*1327*
35 Total taxes—line 17	*1566*
36 Total interest—line 20	*2342*
37 Total contributions—line 24	*350*
38 Casualty or theft loss(es)—line 29 . .	*80*
39 Total miscellaneous—line 33	*75*
40 Total deductions (add lines 34 through 39). Enter here and on Form 1040, line 44 . . . . ▶	*5740*

medical and dental deductions

You are allowed to deduct certain medical and dental expenses for which you have not been reimbursed by insurance or otherwise. Jerry and Joan had the following nonreimbursed medical and dental expenses: health insurance premiums, $200; medicines and drugs, $320; doctors, $680; hospitals, $750; other miscellaneous, $350. The total is $2300. However, not all of that amount is deductible.

These are the limitations on the deductibility of medical and dental expenses.

Medical insurance premiums. Up to one-half of your medical insurance premiums, but not in excess of $150, is directly deductible. The balance of your medical insurance premiums are treated as a medical expense, subject to those limitations.

Medicines and drugs. Expenses for these items for which you are not reimbursed may be deducted, but only to the extent that they exceed 1 percent of your adjusted gross income. *Example*: if your adjusted gross income was $10,000 and you had valid expenses for medicines and drugs of $90, you would not be able to deduct anything. One percent of your adjusted gross income would be $100, and your expenses for medicines and drugs do not exceed that figure. If, though, your expenses for medicines and drugs were $120, you would be allowed a deduction of $20—the amount by which the expenses exceed the 1 percent limitation. The allowable deductions for medicines and drugs is further limited to the 3 percent limitation on the overall medical and dental expenses that are as follows.

Medical and dental expenses. These are deductible only to the extent that they exceed 3 percent of your adjusted gross income. *Example*: if you had an adjusted gross income of $10,000 and allowable medical expenses of $200, you would not be able to take any deduction, for the actual expenses did not exceed the 3 percent level, which would be $300. If, though, your actual medical and dental expenses totalled $400, thereby exceeding the 3 percent limitation by $100, you'd be entitled to a $100 deduction.

The Schedule A reproduced indicates how Jerry and Joan Smith's medical deductions were figured. Line 1 indicates one-half of their total insurance premium, or $100. Line 4 indicates the allowable deduction for medicine and drugs—their actual expenses of $320 exceeded the 1 percent limitation of $243 by $77. (Ten percent of their adjusted gross income is $243). Thus,

$77 is an allowable deduction for medicine and drugs. Line 7 is the total of all allowable expenses. Line 9, $1227, is the amount by which their actual expenses exceeded the 3 percent limitation. (Expenses total $1957; 3 percent of their adjusted gross income, rounded off, was $730. Thus, the amount on line 9: $1227.) The total allowable deduction for medical and dental expenses is the $1227 on line 9 plus the $100 on line 1, representing one-half of their insurance premium, for a total of $1327.

deductions for taxes

The Smiths had a total of $1566 in expenses on various kinds of taxes, all of which were deductible. The state and local income taxes are based on what they actually paid during the year to their state and city for income taxes owed. The real estate taxes are those paid on their property.

The instruction booklet that each taxpayer receives with the tax forms contains tables that allow you to determine the gasoline and sales taxes you've paid during the year. The gasoline tax tables list the amount of tax on gasoline for each state, and illustrates the appropriate deductible amount depending on miles driven during the year. The state sales tax tables indicate the appropriate state sales tax for each state, as well as the allowable deduction for families of various sizes. In many cases, local sales tax will have to be added to the state sales taxes to give you the proper amount deductible. If you can prove that you paid more in either gasoline taxes or sales taxes than the tables allow, then you can take the larger deduction. For example, the Smiths found from the sales tax table that they were eligible for $321 worth of deductions; in addition, they had purchased a new car for $5000, and paid a 5 percent sales tax on it, or $250. Thus, their total deduction for the sales taxes was $571.

interest expenses

Generally, mortgage lenders will notify their accounts yearly as to the total amount of interest paid on the mortgage. But with other types of interest expenses—such as charge accounts and credit cards—you may not receive notification from the creditor concerning the annual interest expense. It would be up to the taxpayer, therefore, to inquire of each and every account that may have had interest expenses as to the total amount paid during the year, in order to record the accurate deductible amount.

contributions

In addition to actual gifts made to qualified charitable organizations, you can also deduct amounts you paid for gasoline and other expenses required for you to carry out volunteer work for charitable organizations and civil defense programs. In 1976, the standard allowance for mileage was 7¢.

casualty or theft loss

Losses of personal property, for which you are not reimbursed by insurance or otherwise, are subject to a $100 "deductible." In the case of Jerry and Joan Smith, Jerry's CB radio was stolen from his car before he had a chance to report the purchase to his auto insurance agent. After subtracting the $100 limitation, he's entitled to an actual deduction of only $80. Casualty or theft losses of business or income producing property are not subject to the $100 limitation.

miscellaneous deductions

As you can see from the reproduction of Schedule A, only two miscellaneous deductions are listed, with space for "other" possible deductions. Further, the official instructions issued by the Internal Revenue Service are very sketchy regarding other deductions.

There are many dozen other possible deductible expenses that taxpayers should be aware of. But taxpayers are on their own to search through available guide books and consult with professionals in order to determine what these deductions are. If you're eligible to take deductions that you're not aware of, and you fail to do so, you might end up paying more tax than you have to. Further, you may have incurred deductible expenses and not realized that they were deductible, and thus neglected to keep the proper records that would verify those expenses. If you do claim any kind of deduction, you must be prepared to verify it. If you have not kept the necessary receipts or other documentation to verify a deduction, you should attempt to obtain copies from the person to whom you paid the deductible dollars.

The following is a partial listing of various miscellaneous deductions. More complete listings are available in the IRS publication 17, "Your Federal Income Tax," as well as many privately published tax guides.

☐ Alimony can be deducted if you make periodic payments or separate maintenance payments based on a court decree or a written separation agreement entered into after August 16, 1954, or a decree for support entered into after March 1, 1954.

You may not deduct lump sum cash or property settlements, or voluntary payments not made under a court order. The person who receives alimony payments must report them as income. Payments made for child support are not deductible.

☐ Union dues are deductible as are dues paid to professional societies. In Jerry and Joan Smith's return, they deducted $20 for dues payments to a professional sales society to which his wife belonged.

☐ Subscriptions to periodicals relating to your trade or business are deductible. Jerry Smith had a $40 deductible subscription.

☐ If your employer requires you to wear special apparel or equipment, and if that special apparel or equipment is not generally adaptable to normal street usage, you may deduct its cost and its maintenance, to the extent that your employer does not reimburse you for that apparel or equipment. Examples of such deductible special work clothes include those worn by professional athletes, fire and police officers, letter carriers, nurses, theatrical clothing used by musicians and entertainers if used solely in the course of their employment, uniforms used by transportation employees (air, rail, bus, etc.) unless such uniforms are easily converted to general use, and protective clothing used in the course of business.

☐ The expenses of maintaining an office in your home may be deductible, but only under very stringent conditions. Generally, if you're required for the convenience of your employer to provide your own space and facilities for performing your duties, and you use a portion of your home regularly and exclusively for that purpose, you may deduct a pro rata portion of the maintenance and depreciation expense on your home. If you're not an employee, but you use your home, or a portion of it, for business purposes, deductible expenses are allowed only if you do use that portion of your home regularly and exclusively as your principal place of business, and it's used by you for meeting and dealing with your clients, patients, or customers in the normal course of your trade or business.

☐ Certain expenses connected with your employment may be deductible. These can include (in addition to expenses noted earlier under the section on adjustments) expenses relating to travel, transportation, gifts, and entertainment on behalf of your employer; certain expenses in connection with education relating to your job; employment agency fees incurred in seeking new employment in the same trade or business; and travel and transportation expenses incurred in seeking employment in your present trade or business. Also, if you have to acquire small tools and supplies for use in your trade or business, the cost of those may be deductible. Any expenses incurred relating to your employment are deductible only to the extent that you have not been reimbursed.

☐ Income-producing expenses can be deductible. Generally, if you incur expenses relating to the production, collection, management, or taxation of income, those expenses can be deductible. These would include collection fees incurred in the collection of debts owed to you; investment counselling; clerical help that you hire to assist with your income-producing activities; office rent; interest on a stock margin account; custodial fees to a bank or a trust institution or brokerage firm for holding cash or other securities; safety deposit box when used for the storage of materials relating to income-producing activities; and legal expenses incurred with relation to income-producing activity. Note that personal legal expenses incurred for nonincome-producing expenses are not deductible. Jerry Smith had an expense of $15 for a safety deposit box in which he kept stock certificates. That was a deductible expense. If he had stored only jewelry in that box, it would not be a deductible expense.

nondeductible expenses

Taxpayers often make the error of claiming deductions for expenses that are not technically deductible. The following is a partial list of common expenses claimed as deductions but which in fact are nondeductible.

Burial and funeral expenses.

Licenses and fees, including auto licenses, marriage licenses, pet licenses.

Fines and penalties.

Repairs to your home.

Insurance premiums for life insurance and property insurance. (Remember that a certain portion of medical and health insurance premiums can be deductible; see the section on medical deductions.)

Losses on the sale of noninvestment property.

Personal legal expenses.

Commutation to and from work.

Child or dependent care expenses. Prior to 1976 dependent and child care expenses were deductible. However, in 1976 this deduction was changed to a *credit*. Thus, a family making payments for child or dependent care, such as Joan and Jerry Smith did, can still get tax benefits from it, but it must be claimed as a credit, not as a deduction.

All of your eligible deductions should be totaled at the bottom of Schedule A, and the total should be then subtracted from the adjusted gross income. You're now about ready to compute your tax.

computing the tax: adjusted gross income less deductions and exemptions equals taxable income.

Part 3, on the back side of the form 1040, is the tax computation segment. It was reproduced on page 82.

We previously arrived at the adjusted gross income and the amount of deductions available to Jerry and Joan Smith. The next step is to calculate the value of their exemptions. Based on 1976 laws, each exemption claimed in the exemption segment on the front portion of the 1040 form is worth $750. The Smiths, with five exemptions, are thus entitled to deduct $3750 for exemptions in addition to the $5740 for deductions. Subtracting these two items from their adjusted gross income of $24,320, we arrive at a taxable income of $14,830. Once the taxable income is calculated, the taxpayer must then turn to the appropriate table to determine what the tax *before credits* will be. If the taxable income is $20,000 or less, the so-called "tax tables" are used. If the taxable income exceeds $20,000, the taxpayer will refer to tax rate schedule X, Y, or Z.

Some taxpayers may be eligible for the "income averaging provisions" that may result in a lower tax due than the tables indicate. Income averaging is generally beneficial if a taxpayer has had a year of very high income in relation to previous years. The calculations are somewhat complex, and professional assistance may be advisable. If a taxpayer chooses the income averaging method, he or she should complete Schedule G and attach it to the 1040 form.

The Smiths had a taxable income of $14,830. The instructions indicate that they would use the tax tables to compute their tax. The following is a sample segment of the tax tables in the bracket that would apply to the Smiths.

income taxes

If line 47 (taxable income) is—		And you are—			
Over	but not over	Single	Married filing sepa- rately	Head of a house- hold	Married filing jointly *
			Your tax is—		
14,750	14,800	3,450	3,852	3,197	2,954
14,800	14,850	3,466	3,872	3,211	2,966
14,850	14,900	3,481	3,891	3,225	2,979
14,900	14,950	3,497	3,911	3,239	2,991

As you can see from the table, their income is over $14,800, but less than $14,850. Filing a joint return, as they are, means that they would have a tax due, *before credits*, of $2966. A single taxpayer with the same taxable income would have a tax due of $2466. Note a curious quirk with these tax tables: If the Smiths' income had been exactly $14,850, their tax still would have been $2966. But if their taxable income had been $14,851, dropping them down to the next line, their tax would have been $2979—a $13 increase in taxes because of a $1 increase in taxable income. That's an illustration of why it pays to take advantage of every possible deduction, exemption, adjustment, and exclusion available. Even $1 or $2 worth of such reductions can save much more than that in the final tax due.

What if a taxpayer had a taxable income of $25,000, and was filing a joint return? He or she would refer to the appropriate segment of Schedule Y, a small portion of which is reproduced below.

schedule Y—married, filing joint return, and qualifying widow(er)s

If the amount on Form 1040, line 47, is:		Enter on Form 1040, line 16:	of the amount over—
Over—	But not over—		
$20,000	$24,000	$4,380+32%	20,000
$24,000	$28,000	$5,660+36%	$24,000
$28,000	$32,000	$7,100+39%	$28,000
$32,000	$36,000	$8,650+42%	$32,000
$36,000	$40,000	$10,340+45%	$36,000

In accordance with the table, the taxpayer with a $25,000

taxable income would pay $5660 plus 36 percent of the amount over $24,000. Since the amount over $24,000 is $1000, the added tax is $360. Thus, the taxpayer pays $5660 plus $360, or a total of $6020. The 36 percent figure is referred to as the "tax bracket" that the taxpayer is in. Note, however, that the taxpayer is not actually paying 36 percent of taxable income in taxes. $6020 is only 24.08 percent of $25,000.

credits: they reduce your taxes directly

When the taxable income is known, the tax *before credits* is computed from the tax tables or tax schedules. In the case of the Smiths, their taxable income resulted in a tax from the tables of $2966 before credits.

What are credits and how do they affect your tax obligation? There is often a lot of confusion over the difference between deductions and credits. Let's examine that difference. A deduction reduces the income on which your tax is figured. A credit reduces the tax directly. Here's an example. If a family had a joint taxable income of $15,100, their tax would be $3041. Assume that before they completed their return, they came up with another deduction for $100 that they had overlooked. Their new calculation would be to subtract the $100 from the income of $15,100, giving them a new taxable income of $15,000. The tax on that amount of taxable income would be $3016. In other words, the $100 deduction reduced their tax due by $25.

Taking the same family, instead of coming up with an extra $100 deduction, they came up with an extra $100 credit. The effect of the credit would be to reduce their *taxes* from the previous level of $3041 to $2941. It would have taken a deduction of $400 to do the same thing that a credit of $100 did. Credits indeed can be valuable and should not be overlooked by any taxpayer.

Once again, the designers of the 1040 form require a bit of hopscotching for the taxpayer seeking all available credits. Most of the common credits are contained in Part 4, Credits, on the back side of the form 1040. This is what it looks like:

Part IV	Credits		
48	Credit for the elderly (attach Schedules R & RP)	48	
49	Credit for child care expenses (attach Form 2441)	49	*500*
50	Investment credit (attach Form 3468)	50	
51	Foreign tax credit (attach Form 1116)	51	
52	Contributions to candidates for public office credit (see page 12 of Instructions)	52	
53	Work Incentive (WIN) Credit (attach Form 4874)	53	
54	Total (add lines 48 through 53). **Enter here and on line 19** . . . . ▶	54	*500*

As you can see, Jerry and Joan Smith took a credit of $500 for their child care expenses. In order to do so they had to fill out and attach form 2441 to their 1040 return. Briefly: if, in order to work, you have had to hire household help to take care of children, disabled dependents, or a disabled spouse, you may be entitled to a tax credit of up to 20 percent of those expenses.

Other credits available under Part 4 include the following.

☐ Credit for the elderly. If you are 65 or older, or if you are under 65 and are receiving pension benefits from a public retirement system, you may be entitled to a credit against your tax of up to 15 percent of your retirement and earned income. Those over 65 will complete Schedule R and attach it to their 1040 form; those under 65 will complete Schedule RP and attach it to their 1040 form. The amount of retirement income against which you can take a credit is fixed by law. For example, if you're filing Schedule R, for persons over 65, the maximum amounts against which the credits can be taken are: $2500 if you're single; $2500 if you are married and filing a joint return and only one spouse is 65 or older; $3750 if you are married and filing a joint return and both spouses are 65 or older; or $1875 if you are married and filing a separate return and have not lived with your spouse at any time during the year.

These amounts must be further reduced if you have received certain kinds of pension and annuity income under the Social Security Act or the Railroad Retirement Act; then they are further reduced by portions of actual earned income during the year. After reducing the initial amount eligible for credit by the retirement and earned income factors, the final credit allowable is 15 percent of the remaining sum. The following facsimile of Schedule R illustrates how one taxpayer would compute the credit.

The initial amount for this taxpayer, who is single and over 65, is $2500 (line 1). He had received, as indicated, $1450 in pertinent pensions or annuities; his adjusted gross income was $8000; thus, as line 2B indicates, he must deduct an additional $250. The total deductions are $1700, and the credit is thus figured on 15 percent of the remaining $800. The credit would be $120.

Note well that no credits may be larger than the actual tax you owe. In the above case, the actual tax owed was $747, so the full credit applies. If, however, the actual tax owed by this taxpayer had been only $100, then only $100 worth of the credit could

Schedules R & RP—Credit for the Elderly

(Form 1040)
Department of the Treasury
Internal Revenue Service

(Public Retirees Under 65 See Schedule RP on Back)

▶ Attach to Form 1040. ▶ See Instructions for Schedules R and RP (Form 1040).

1976

Name(s) as shown on Form 1040

Your social security number

Schedule R—Credit for the Elderly—Individual(s) 65 or Over Having Any Type of Income

Important: You may elect to use Schedule RP if you are married filing a joint return and one spouse is 65 or over and the other spouse is under 65 and has public retirement system income. However, unless both spouses elect to use Schedule RP, you must use Schedule R.

R

Filing Status and Age (check only one)

- A ☐ Single, 65 or over
- B ☐ Married filing joint return, only one spouse 65 or over
- C ☐ Married filing joint return, both spouses 65 or over
- D ☐ Married filing separate return, 65 or over, and have not lived with your spouse at any time during the taxable year

1 Initial amount of income for credit computation. Enter $2,500 if block A or B checked, $3,750 if block C checked, or $1,875 if block D checked	1	2,500 00
2 **Deduct:**		
a Amounts received as pensions or annuities under the Social Security Act, the Railroad Retirement Acts (but not supplemental annuities), and certain other exclusions from gross income (see instructions)	1,450 00	
b Enter one-half the excess of your adjusted gross income (Form 1040, line 15c) over: $7,500 if block A checked, $10,000 if block B or C checked, or $5,000 if block D checked	250 00	
3 Total of lines 2a and 2b	3	1,700 00
4 Balance (subtract line 3 from line 1). If zero or less do not file this schedule	4	800 00
5 Tentative credit. Enter 15% of line 4	5	120 00
6 Amount of tax shown on Form 1040, line 18	6	747 00
7 **Credit for the Elderly.** Enter here and on Form 1040, line 48, the amount on line 5 or 6 whichever is smaller . . . . ▶	7	120 00

have been taken. A credit cannot reduce your tax bill below zero. It will not entitle you to a rebate from the government. A credit can only reduce your tax to zero, but no further.

Many taxpayers may find the computations for Schedule R and RP to be somewhat complex. The Internal Revenue Service can compute it for you if you desire.

☐ Investment credit. If you bought property for use in your trade or business and that property has a useful life of at least three years, you may be able to take a credit equal to 10 percent of the cost of such property.

☐ Foreign tax credit. If you paid income taxes to a foreign government, the amount that you paid may be claimed as a credit against your United States income taxes.

☐ Political contributions may be claimed as a credit, or as an itemized deduction, but not both. If you take political contributions as a credit, you can claim one-half of the amount contributed, but not more than $25 ($50 if married and filing a joint return).

Two additional types of credits are *not* calculated in Part 4 but *are* calculated in the "Tax, Payments and Credits" segment on the *front* side of the 1040 form. Those two credits are the general credit, which was available in the taxable year 1976, and the earned income credit.

Two additional types of credits may be available to a small number of taxpayers. They include the credit against federal taxes paid on special fuels, and credit from a regulated investment company. These items are recorded, with the proper forms attached, in Part 6 of the form 1040. Part 6 also includes a claim for rebate if you have paid an excess of withholding taxes on your Social Security obligation.

Part 5 of the 1040 form lists any other tax obligations that you may have in addition to the basic income tax.

who owes whom: the final calculation

The ultimate arithmetic on your 1040 form takes place in the segment that looks like this:

16	Tax, check if from: [X] Tax Table / Schedule G / Tax Rate Schedule X, Y or Z / Form 2555 OR / Schedule D / Form 4726	16	2966
17a	Multiply $35.00 by the number of exemptions on line 6d	17a	175
b	Enter 2% of line 47 but not more than $180 ($90 if box 3 is checked)	17b	180
	Enter larger of a or b	17c	180
18	Balance. Subtract line 17c from line 16 and enter difference (but not less than zero)	18	2,786
19	Credits (from line 54)	19	500
20	Balance. Subtract line 19 from line 18 and enter difference (but not less than zero)	20	2,286
21	Other taxes (from line 62)	21	
22	Total (add lines 20 and 21)	22	2,286
23a	Total Federal income tax withheld. (attach Forms W-2, or W-2P to front)	23a	2500
b	1976 estimated tax payments (include amount allowed as credit from 1975 return)	23b	
c	Earned income credit. (from page 2 of Instructions)	23c	
d	Amount paid with Form 4868	23d	
e	Other payments (from line 66)	23e	
24	TOTAL (add lines 23a through e)	24	2500
25	If line 22 is larger than line 24, enter BALANCE DUE IRS (Check here [ ], if Form 2210 or Form 2210F is attached. See page 10 of instructions.)	25	
26	If line 24 is larger than line 22, enter amount OVERPAID	26	214
27	Amount of line 26 to be REFUNDED TO YOU	27	214
28	Amount of line 26 to be credited on 1977 estimated tax ▶ 28		

Pay amount on line 25 in full with this return. Write social security number on check or money order and make payable to Internal Revenue Service.

You will have determined the tax due, based on your taxable income that was computed in Part 3 on the reverse side of the 1040 form. Taxpayers in 1976 were entitled to an additional credit of $35 per exemption, or 2 percent of their taxable income (but not more than $180), whichever was greater. The facsimile illustrates this calculation on lines 17A and 17B. The Smiths were entitled to a credit of $180, which was subtracted from their tax of $2966, leaving them with a balance of $2786. Further, the Smiths were entitled to a $500 credit for child and dependent care expenses, which gives them a balance showing on line 20 of $2286. They had no other taxes to pay, so the balance carries down to line 22. Line 23A illustrates that during the year they had a total of $2500 withheld from their pay. They had made no estimated tax payments, and are not eligible for the earned income credit.

(The earned income credit, available for the taxable year 1976, was generally available to a taxpayer with an income under $8000 who maintained a principal residence for himself and his children. Special forms in the tax instructions illustrate how this credit is to be claimed.)

The Smiths are filing their return on time. They could have requested an extension of time to file, which would have automatically extended the filing deadline by two months. Had they done so, they would have had to file a form 4868, and would have had to have included with that form an amount of money tentatively equal to the amount that they would ultimately declare on their 1040 when filed.

Thus, the $2500 withheld is the only item to offset their obligation. But the $2500 withheld exceeds their tax of $2286; thus, on line 26 they indicate that they've overpaid by $214, and on line 27 they indicate that the $214 is to be refunded to them. Their signatures follow, as well as the signatures of anyone who has prepared their return for them.

getting help with your taxes

A taxpayer opinion survey conducted by the Internal Revenue Service indicates that less than half (actually 47%) of all taxpayers prepare their own returns. The remaining percentage can be broken down: 20.1% use a lawyer or an accountant, 17.2% use commercial tax services, 7.9% use a family member or relative, 3.5% use a neighbor or friend, 1.3% use the Internal Revenue Service office, and 3.0% use other sources. In other words, out of the more than 80 million individual returns filed each year, more than 40 million of them are seeking help from other sources.

In addition to turning to outside help for preparation, millions of taxpayers buy the various tax guides that abound on newsstands from the first of every year until the April 15 filing date. For the few dollars, many of these tax guides prove to be a good investment. Some are more complex and comprehensive than others. Some are nothing more than exact duplicates of the Internal Revenue Service publication 17, "Your Federal Income Tax," which is available at no charge at local IRS offices.

The Internal Revenue Service itself maintains a taxpayer information service, either by telephone or by person. You can determine the telephone number and address of the nearest office in the white pages of your telephone book under "U.S. Government—Internal Revenue Service."

Help should be sought when needed, but the best prepared taxpayers are the ones who have taken the time to study and learn the basic tax laws on their own. Awareness of what constitutes taxable income and nontaxable income, and awareness of the means by which income can be reduced (exemptions, deductions, adjustments, credits, and exclusions) will make taxpayers more alert to how they can take advantage of what the law permits. With the proper discipline, they'll find their bookkeeping and record-keeping techniques adjusting to the tax laws, thus giving them the most complete and accurate records to enable completion of their returns each year with maximum efficiency and maximum savings.

The world of investments demands a reliable knowledge of tax laws. The value of any investment portfolio is directly related to how income taxes affect the earnings on that portfolio. There are taxable investments, tax-free investments, tax-deferred investments, and tax-sheltered investments. To distinguish among these, and to make use of those investment techniques that will best help you meet your goals, it's necessary to understand the precise effect of the tax laws on these various forms of investment. The chapters on investments discuss this relationship between taxes and investments in greater detail.

Computer Picks Tax Returns for Audit

If your tax return doesn't measure up to a closely guarded secret formula residing in an Internal Revenue Service computer, your return may be selected for audit. Contrary to popular belief, only a very small percentage of all returns chosen for audit are picked on a random sampling basis. Actually, more than two-thirds (68.8 percent in 1975) of all returns audited are chosen by the sophisticated program known as the Discriminate Income Function, or DIF for short. The IRS has been using the DIF program since 1969.

Historical studies by the IRS revealed that certain tax returns were more likely than others to result in added taxes being recovered as the result of an audit. Elements of these returns followed certain patterns—such as the relationship of income to deductions. The various patterns were reduced to the computer formula, which weighs all the various elements of your individual return, and scores them based on the historical figures. Returns with the highest scores are chosen for audit. The weighting of the specific items is a closely held secret by the IRS, even exempt from the Freedom of Information Act, according to an IRS official.

Most audits require nothing more of the taxpayer than to produce verification of statements he or she has made on the return. If, though, a taxpayer has violated the law willfully or excessively (though innocently), an audit can probe more deeply and can cause

more distress for the taxpayer.

Before returns are actually selected for audit (and roughly one out of every fifty individual returns filed are actually audited), they go through preliminary screening procedures.

After a return is filed at the appropriate IRS service center, it is screened by hand to determine that everything is in order: that it's properly signed, that the W-2 forms are attached, and so on. It is then processed through a computer that verifies the arithmetic, and seeks "unallowable items," particularly those involving incorrect calculations.

If the computer spots mathematical errors or unallowable items, the taxpayer will normally be notified by mail of the error, and the problem can usually be handled through simple correspondence. In 1975, out of more than 81 million returns that were screened, mathematical errors were found in almost 4 million. Nearly half of these resulted in refunds to taxpayers, averaging about $93 each. The balance resulted in increased taxes, averaging about $134 each. Correcting unallowable items can also be handled by correspondence, and is not considered an audit as such. If the computer catches an unallowable item, it doesn't necessarily mean that the whole return will be examined. But it could spark curiosity or suspicion on the part of an examiner, which could lead to an actual audit.

Many unallowable items occur where an error in arithmetic has been made. For example, deductions for medical expenses have certain specific limits. An error in arithmetic might result in an excessive deduction being claimed for these expenses. This would be considered an unallowable item, and would be caught by the computer. Other unallowable items can include excessive dividend exclusions, improper deductions for casualty or theft losses, claiming fractional exemptions, improper moving expense deductions, and exces-

sive deductions for Individual Retirement Accounts.

After the screening for mathematical verification and unallowable items, the actual selection for audit occurs. As noted, in 1975, 68.8 percent of all the returns selected for audit were chosen by the DIF method. The balance of returns selected for audit were chosen on the following basis:

3.5 percent of the returns audited were selected out of the total batch of taxpayers who claimed refunds.

4.8 percent of those returns selected for audit were selected as a part of a multi-year audit: for example, if your 1973 return had been chosen for audit, the IRS might also call up your 1974 and 1975 returns for audit as well.

5 percent of the returns chosen for audit were selected because of "related pickups." If, for instance, your business partner was chosen for audit, you might also be chosen. The questionable deductions claimed by the one might be suspect with regard to the other. Further, if the statements on your return do not match statements submitted about your status, you might be tabbed for an audit. In this regard, if your W-2 form (your employer's report of the income paid you) does not match the income that you, yourself, report, you may be a candidate for an audit.

Roughly 8 percent of the returns audited are chosen as part of the Taxpayer Compliance Measurement Program. These are selected purely at random, and generally are subjected to a more intense audit than average. The purposes of the TCMP program are to police the voluntary compliance aspects of the law, and to unearth more statistical data to support the DIF program.

The balance are chosen for miscellaneous reasons.

Under the DIF audits, which represent the majority, 23 percent resulted in no change in the taxpayer's liability in 1975. Then 6.6 percent of the returns audited resulted in refunds to taxpayers totalling $302.8 million. The balance resulted in $5.3 billion worth of additional taxes and penalties recommended.

What are the odds of being audited? Based on returns filed in 1976 for the taxable year 1975, if a taxpayer had an adjusted gross income of under $10,000 and took the standard deduction, there was a .7 percent chance of being audited, or 7 out of every 1000 returns. For taxpayers with an adjusted gross income of under $10,000 taking itemized deductions, the odds jumped to 4.3 percent or 43 out of every 1000. Taxpayers with an adjusted gross income between $10,000 and $50,000 ran a risk of 2.5 percent, or 25 out of every 1000; and taxpayers with an adjusted gross income of over $50,000 ran a risk of 12.6 percent, or 126 out of every 1000.

Individuals filing business returns (Schedule C returns) ran the following risks of audit: adjusted gross income of under $10,000—2.9 percent; adjusted gross income between $10,000 and $30,000—2.3 percent; an adjusted gross income over $30,000—9.3 percent.

Of a total of 81,271,762 individual returns filed in 1975, 1.8 million were audited, or 2.3 percent.

Accuracy of your return and the ability to authenticate all of your claims will minimize your chances of being subjected to a rigorous audit.

If, though, you are selected, the IRS suggests (and accountants agree) that ready cooperation is the best advice for simplifying the procedures. You'll be notified by mail of the IRS intention, and you have extensive opportunities to defend your claim if you believe that the IRS is wrong.

If the amount claimed by the IRS is considerable, you may want professional assistance at the earliest possible time. If the amount is nominal, you may prefer to handle the matter on your own, particularly if the cost of the professional outweighs the amount in question.

The IRS publication 17, "Your Federal Income Tax," contains more detailed information on what to do if your return is audited, what your rights of appeal are, and how you may claim a refund.

1. Explain why it is important to understand our tax laws.
2. What is the term for adjusted gross income minus deductions and exemptions?
3. Explain when a person should file an income tax return even though it is not required.
4. Joe and Nancy Schmidt had dividends of $432 from common stock that they jointly own. How much of this is taxable?
5. Sue Scott has adjusted gross income of $10,000 and medical expenses of $285. How much medical cost is deductible?
6. Mark Palmer had a television set stolen from his home but his insurance did not pay for it. The value of the set was $329. His adjusted gross income is $10,000. How much can he deduct for the loss?
7. What is the penalty for failing to take all available deductions?
8. Maria Gomez has a part time business of preparing income tax returns. Last year she earned (net income) $740. Maria lives with her parents and is attending college. Is she required to file an income tax return?

**cases
for
study**

1. Sue and Bruce Helm have the following medical expenses:

Health insurance	$360
Medicine	210
Other medical costs	300

Their adjusted gross income is $12,000. Calculate their medical deduction.
2. Mark and Michele Krekorian have an adjusted gross income of $15,000, with actual deductions of $2000. In filing their joint return, should they itemize or take the standard deduction?
3. Look through the financial data of the Smiths in this chapter. Try to suggest some tax planning for the next year that would reduce their tax bill.
4. Millie and Jim Madden own a vacation condominium in Kona, Hawaii. While they were away they suffered a theft loss of $575. Explain the amount that can be deducted. If the condominium is an investment and not used for vacation, how much could the Maddens deduct as a business expense?

chapter 4 **financial institutions**

the middlemen

Financial institutions play an important "middleman" role in our nation's economy and in our own personal financial situation.

At any given point, there are countless individuals (and businesses and governments) who have more money on hand than they need for their immediate purposes. Simultaneously, there are countless others who do not have the money they need for specific purposes.

Financial institutions act as intermediaries by providing a safe place for those with excess money to keep it until they need it, and at the same time supplying access to needed funds to those who seek to borrow at a fair and reasonable cost.

The middleman views this activity as a business. He must acquire his raw material (other people's money) at the lowest possible price consistent with competitors, and he must lend it out on the most prudent basis, taking into account the ability of the borrower to repay the money and the agreed on interest at the agreed on time. In order for a middleman to survive as a business executive, he must make a profit. Thus, he must charge the borrower more for the use of the money than he has to pay to the investors entrusting him with their money.

Certain middlemen may not be operating as a business enterprise, but as a service to members of an association. The members may have banded together to pool their excess money and provide for the needs of borrowers. Although it is not important for the association to generate a profit, members must still generate enough income within their operation to pay for personnel and overhead needed to run the operation efficiently and comfortably.

Financial institutions that seek to generate a profit and thus fulfill the needs of the community are commonly referred to as commercial banks and savings institutions (mutual savings banks and savings and loan associations). Those institutions operating for the benefit of the membership of a group are known as credit unions. In this chapter we will examine financial institutions, how they operate, how they can serve you, and how you can best utilize them.

commercial banks

There are roughly 15,000 commercial banks in the United States. These banks have a total of approximately 32,000 branch offices, for a grand total of 47,000 banking offices. Total assets of these commercial banks nears $1 trillion. Commercial banks run the gamut from small country institutions to giant banks in such major cities as New York, Chicago, Los Angeles. Of all the commercial banks in the United States, the fifty largest control roughly one-third of all the deposits. The remaining 14,950 commercial banks control the other two-thirds.

Commercial banks are commonly referred to as "full service" banks. They offer a broad range of services, including savings accounts, checking accounts, trust facilities, and virtually all types of loans.

Commercial banks may be chartered by the state in which they're located or by the federal government. Deposits in commercial banks are insured by the Federal Deposit Insurance Corporation (FDIC) for up to $40,000 per account in the event of the bank's failure. The FDIC is a federal agency that constantly scrutinizes the operations of all banks it insures for the protection of the depositors and the community. All federally insured banks pay an annual premium to the FDIC, and the total is set aside as a reserve to be used should a bank be liquidated and the depositors paid off. In addition to its own funds, the FDIC can call upon the U.S. Treasury for additional money to back up its guarantee to depositors. But the strength of the FDIC lies not just with its funds, but also with its constant surveillance and expertise in determining when banks are in trouble and in intervening as swiftly as possible to prevent financial loss.

examination of banks by state and federal authorities

In addition to FDIC examination, banks may also be examined by state or federal authorities, depending on their charter. They are also examined by their own internal auditors, and commonly by outside independent auditors on orders from the bank's own Board of Directors. Examinations are generally by surprise and very rigorous. All cash is counted. All loans are scrutinized in detail, including original credit information, current payment status, and prospects for ultimate full payment. Where loans seem to be in jeopardy, the examiners will notify the bank officials. If an excess of loans seem to be in jeopardy, the examiners will instruct the bank to take whatever steps appropriate to correct the situation. The results of examinations are kept confidential between the examiners and the bank's officials. But examiners will follow up to determine whether or not the bank has taken whatever corrective steps the examiners have requested to keep the operation in healthy condition.

mutual savings banks

Mutual savings banks are few in number (476 of them located in roughly one dozen states, generally throughout New England and the Northeast, plus Ohio, Minnesota, Oregon, and Washington). But they are substantial in size, controlling a total of over $120 billion in assets. Mutual savings banks are state chartered and insured by the Federal Deposit Insurance Corporation, which also examines them as it does commercial banks. Mutual savings banks generally are limited in the scope of their business to accepting only time deposits and making loans on real property—mortgages and home improvement loans. Some New England mutual savings banks have been granted permission to offer a breed of checking account, called NOW accounts (Negotiable Order of Withdrawal). The banking industry has expressed concern that this new step (created in the mid-1970s) could lead to a gradual changeover whereby all financial institutions offer the same services. In short, the commercial bankers seem concerned that savings institutions will infringe on their territory regarding checking accounts.

savings and loan associations

Savings and loan associations, like mutual savings banks, are generally limited to savings deposits, and their lending activity predominantly involves mortgages and property improvement loans. There are over 5000 savings and loan associations throughout the nation. Like commercial banks, they may be either federally chartered or state chartered. Assets of all of America's savings and loan associations exceed $340 billion, and they are the largest type of mortgage lender, with approximately $280 billion outstanding in mortgage loans (compared with approximately $140 billion in mortgage loans at commercial banks, and $78 billion in mortgages at mutual savings banks). Savings and loan associations (as well as mutual savings banks) tend to pay a slightly higher rate of interest on savings accounts and certificates than commercial banks. Savings and loan associations are insured by the Federal Savings and Loan Insurance Corporation (FSLIC), which acts in a manner similar to the Federal Deposit Insurance Corporation.

credit unions

Because credit unions don't advertise the way commercial banks and savings and loan associations do, they're not as familiar to the public as those other institutions. But credit unions are playing an increasingly important role in the American financial system. They are associations of individuals who have a common bond—they work for the same employer, they belong to the same religious order, or they are members of the same union or trade association. Credit unions are not operated for profit; further, they are tax exempt. They are operated solely for the benefit of their membership, which is open generally to all individuals who meet their requirements.

Credit unions accept savings accounts and may pay a slightly higher interest than other institutions. This is possible because they do not have the profit motive, generally are located in very modest quarters, and do not have to pay any federal income taxes. Credit unions in some areas may make loans to their members at a rate slightly more favorable than that charged elsewhere. Loans usually are of the installment variety.

There are currently about 23,000 credit unions throughout the United States, supported by over 30 million members. Their assets total roughly $40 billion. In recent years, credit unions have been gaining the authority to offer a form of checking account, which would add another measure of competition to the overall banking industry.

Slightly more than one-half of all the credit unions are federally chartered and the balance are state chartered. Insurance on credit union accounts is available through the National Credit Union Administration (NCUA).

consumer finance or "small loan" companies

These are private businesses, operating generally under state licensing, that make small loans available to credit-worthy seekers. Consumer finance companies do not accept public deposits. They obtain their money by borrowing from larger institutions such as banks and insurance companies. A small number of these companies have branches throughout the entire country, but most are limited to individual states or cities in their sphere of operation.

merchant lenders and credit card companies

Technically, these are not financial institutions in the same sense as banks and savings and loan associations are. But they do provide a financial service to many millions of Americans: making credit available virtually at the request of the customer. A merchant lender, generally, is a retail or service establishment that will accept a customer's IOU as payment for goods sold or services rendered. In other words, rather than pay cash, the customer can "charge it."

Commonly, the customer will sign an agreement in which he or she agrees to make payments over a specified period of time with an agreed on rate of interest. In effect, the merchant lender is lending the money to the customer to enable the customer to buy the product. Many merchants do this strictly as a convenience for their customers, and to be in line with services that their competitors might offer. Often the merchant lender will sell the customer's loan agreement to another financial institution, such as a bank or a consumer finance company, so that it can get its money right away. In some cases the merchant lender will retain the loan agreement, and the customer will make payments directly to the merchant instead of to the third party institution.

Some companies—such as gasoline companies, hotels and motels, airlines—operate nationally. To induce the public to use their services and products, they will issue credit cards to credit-worthy applicants. These credit cards allow the users to charge their purchases, thus creating a loan to the issuing company. The loan will be repayable based on the terms contained in the original credit card agreement.

Another form of quasi-financial institution is the credit card company: American Express, Diner's Club, and Carte Blanche are the prime examples. They have made arrangements with many thousands of businesses across the nation and around the world to accept their credit cards in lieu of cash. When a purchase is made by a customer on a credit card charge, the credit card company makes payment to the specific merchant, and then seeks repayment of the amount borrowed from the customer. The credit card company is thus acting strictly as a middleman between the merchant and the customer. Most commercial banks also issue various forms of credit cards— BankAmericard (VISA) and Master Charge. Where a purchase is made with a bank credit card, the bank pays the merchant and seeks repayment directly from the customer.

services available at financial institutions

Commercial banks frequently refer to themselves as "full service banks." The following financial services are those commonly found at commercial banks, although smaller banks might not offer some of the more sophisticated services such as trust departments, international departments, and electronic banking facilities.

1. Checking accounts
2. Savings accounts
3. Safety deposit boxes
4. Trust departments
5. Installment loans
6. Credit cards
7. Business loans
8. Mortgage loans
9. Travellers checks and money orders
10. Notarial services
11. Electronic banking
12. Collection services
13. International banking facilities
14. Investment Departments

As noted earlier, savings and loan institutions, mutual savings banks, and credit unions are generally limited to savings accounts, although they are beginning to make inroads in the offering of various forms of checking accounts. Savings and loan institutions and mutual savings banks are generally limited to residential and commercial mortgage loans, and home improvement installment loans. Credit unions offer personal installment loans, and are beginning to establish mortgage lending departments. Some of the lesser services, such as notarial, travellers checks and money orders, and collection might also be found at savings and loan institutions, mutual savings banks, and credit unions.

Let's now take a closer look at what these services consist of. *Note:* savings accounts (passbooks and certificates of deposit) are briefly noted here and are discussed in greater length in the chapter on fixed income investments. Installment, credit card, and business loans are dealt with in the chapter, Credit and Borrowing, and mortgages are discussed fully in the chapters on housing.

checking accounts

It would be both inconvenient and risky if we had to conduct all our financial transactions with cash. Inconvenient if for no other reason than the sheer massive volume of cash that would have to be available in all segments of the economy at all times; risky because a loss of cash is irreplaceable.

Checks, simply stated, act as a substitute for cash. Checks are more convenient and the risk of loss is virtually eliminated.

The efficiency of our checking system is founded on a combination of mutual trust and law. We have grown accustomed to accepting these money substitutes as having the value represented; and in those rare cases when the document proves invalid, there are laws that can punish those who have violated the law and the trust between the parties.

how checking accounts work

Bob lives in Phoenix, Arizona, and works for the Ajax Supermarket. Each day the supermarket gathers up all the money it has collected from its customers and deposits the money in its checking account at the Arizona National Bank. The essential agreement between the bank and the store is as follows: the bank agrees to hold the money safely for the store and to pay out the money to any persons that the store directs them to make payments to. The store will then issue checks to its employees for their wages, checks to the landlord for the rent on the building, checks to suppliers for the food that it obtains from them, and so on.

The checks order the bank to make payment to the holder of the check. That's the essence of the words "pay to the order of" that appear on all checks. The check—the order to pay—must be signed by a properly authorized representative of the store. The bank will have obtained copies of all the authorized signatures permitted on the checks, and can compare those signatures with the signatures on the checks if they wish to determine the validity of the order to pay.

Bob's weekly paycheck, after all deductions have been taken out for income taxes, Social Security, and fringe benefits, looks like this (Figure 4-1):

The check document, duly authorized by the treasurer or Ajax Supermarkets, orders the Arizona National Bank to pay the sum of $250 to Bob Rosefsky when he presents that check to them.

"negotiating" a check
Bob might then do a number of things with that check:

1. He might take it directly to the bank and request that they pay him in cash. The teller at the bank will see to it that Bob signs his name on the back of the check so as to show that he has received the money promised him by the maker of the check, the supermarket. This signature on the back of the check is called an "endorsement." The teller will then give Bob the cash and the check will be processed. In the processing procedure, the bank will deduct the $250 from the store's account and will return the check to the store to show that the amount has actually been paid. During the processing, the bank will also take a microfilm picture of both sides of the check so that they will have a permanent record of the item, which can also be available to the customer (the store) should they ever need it.

2. Bob can deposit the check to his own checking account at the Citizens Bank of Phoenix. If he does, the Citizens Bank technically does not know whether or not the check will be honored by the Arizona National Bank. They simply have no way of knowing whether or not the Ajax Supermarket has money in its account at that time to honor the check. They could thus say to Bob, "Technically, we can't permit you to draw against this check until we're sure that it is honored by the bank on which it's drawn." Bob's bank will actually send the check to the store's bank where it will be processed as in the above example. The Arizona National Bank does not notify Bob's bank

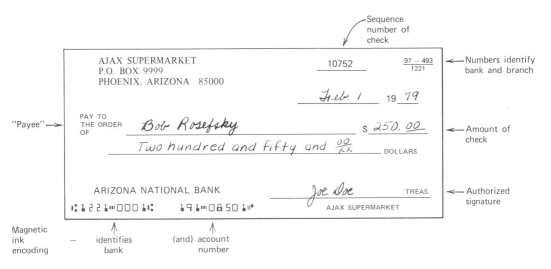

Figure 4-1   Sample Check.

that the check was good. Bob's bank will know that the check was good and was honored only if they do not get it back from the Arizona National Bank. If, in fact, the supermarket did not have enough money in its account to honor the check, the Arizona National Bank will return it to Bob's bank with a note that it was dishonored, in this case for lack of sufficient funds, or insufficient funds.

Because both banks are in the same city, it customarily will only take one or two days for the check to go from one bank to another. Thus, Bob's bank can be reasonably sure that the check has been honored if it hasn't heard otherwise within two or three days—the time it would take for the check to go round trip, if in fact that was its fate.

In common practice, Bob's bank knows that he has been depositing these checks on the Ajax Supermarket for many years and there's never been a problem. Thus, they would probably allow him to draw against those funds without waiting for the check to be cleared by the originating bank.

3. Rather than cash the check or deposit it to his own account, Bob decides to send it to his friend Gary Hartman in Connecticut, for he owes Gary $250 and wants to settle the debt. Bob realizes, though, that if Gary takes the check to his Connecticut bank, the bank will most likely refuse to process it: "That check doesn't belong to you, Gary, it belongs to Bob. We really can't process it to your account."

Bob thus endorses the check, writing his name across the back, to show that the money has passed through his hands. He further adds an endorsement: "Pay to the order of Gary Hartman in full settlement of debt." By so doing, Gary will have to acknowledge that the debt has been paid in full because he'll have to endorse the check still further in order to process it through his bank.

Gary will then deposit the check in his bank, which will have to send it back to the originating bank, the Arizona National, where it will have to clear through the store's account. Gary's bank tells him, "We won't know if this check is going to be honored or not for perhaps six to ten days, because it has to go clear across the country, and if it's not honored, it has to come all the way back to us again. Until the money is actually collected, or until we know that it won't be refused, we can't allow you to draw on it. Technically, it's what we call 'uncollected funds'."

This disturbs Gary, because he's anxious to have the use of the money right away. He asks his bank why they can't simply call the bank in Arizona to determine if there are adequate funds. His bank explains that that won't do any good: there might be funds in the bank when we call, but that's no assurance that there will be money in the account when the check actually gets there.

Though Bob technically could have paid off his debt to Gary in this fashion, it would have been unwise for him to do so. He should have deposited the store's check to his own account and then drawn his own check payable directly to Gary. He would subsequently receive the cancelled check back and would have adequate proof that Gary had received the payment and that the debt was paid. As it is, the store will get the check back, and Bob would have to seek the store's help in verifying that Gary had received the money.

Gary also could have taken steps to alleviate his anxiety. If he had asked Bob to send a "certified check" instead of a regular check, his Connecticut bank could have been assured that the money was in the account. A certified check means that the money is in the account and that the bank will hold at least that much money to honor the payment of the check that they have certified. Bob could also have sent Gary a "treasurers" or "cashiers" check that would have been a check drawn on the bank itself and not on Bob's account. It's more than likely that the Connecticut bank would immediately honor a check drawn against the funds of another bank, as opposed to a check against the funds of an individual.

stopping payment

The treasurer of the Ajax Supermarket learns that the computer has erroneously issued a check to one of the store's meat suppliers. The check is for $500 more than it should be, and the treasurer is concerned that the meat supplier will cash the check and will refuse to refund the excess $500 because there had been an ongoing dispute between them over a previous bill. The treasurer wants to stop the check before the meat supplier can cash it at his bank.

It's literally a race against time. The proper course for the treasurer is to go to his bank, Arizona National, and issue a "stop payment" order. He must inform the bank in writing as to the amount of the check, the date it was issued, and to whom it was paid, and then sign the order. This done, the bank will then refuse to allow payment on the check when it is presented. But if the meat supplier gets to the bank first and is able to cash the check, he will have the money in hand and it will then be a hassle between the supplier and the store as to who is entitled to the money.

Once a proper stop payment order has been filed with the bank, the bank might be responsible to the store if they make payment on the check in error. Thus, once a stop payment order has been signed, the bank alerts all of its tellers and the appropriate bookkeeper on the Ajax account to refuse payment should the check be presented. If a stop payment order is conducted verbally, and the proper documents haven't been signed, the bank might not be responsible if it does pay the check. Banks customarily charge a few dollars for the processing of a stop payment order.

overdrafts

What if a checking account customer doesn't have enough money in the account to cover all the checks written against the account? In other words, what if he or she doesn't have sufficient funds to pay these checks? He is, in such a case, "overdrawn" and the checks may be returned to the individuals or firms to whom they were made payable. This is not only embarrassing, but it can also be costly because the bank will levy a charge of a few dollars for each item overdrawn. If a customer overdraws an account too frequently, he or she could jeopardize their credit standing with the bank.

In some instances, a bank may pay a check even though it would overdraw the account. This may occur because the customer is in good standing, rarely has overdrawn, and the overdraft is for a relatively slight amount. The bank isn't worried about getting its money, and rather than inconvenience the customer, they'll allow the check to be paid.

In other cases, banks offer overdraft privileges to their customers. If a check overdraws an account, the bank will automatically loan the customer at least enough money to cover the overdraft, and will deposit that loaned money in the customer's checking account. The loan must then be repaid at a specified rate of interest. This program can be convenient and eliminate embarrassment, but it can be as costly, if not more so, than basic overdraft charges; and it might also act as too easy a temptation for a customer who lacks the discipline to keep a checking account in the proper balance.

making deposits

The check is the means for taking money out of a checking account. How does the money get into the account? The document commonly used is a deposit slip, and this is a sample of one (Figure 4-2):

The bank code numbers written in at the indicated place represent the bank's identifying number, which is taken from the check seen in Figure 4-1. This particular deposit slip represents a combination of transactions. Bob is depositing a part of his check and taking a part of it in cash. After depositing $250 and taking $50 in cash, the net deposit is $200. This is simpler than depositing the whole check and then writing out another check against the account for $50.

Deposit slips are enclosed in the customer's checkbooks, and they can also be obtained for bank-by-mail use, in which the bank customarily pays the postage and then returns another bank-by-mail envelope to the customer.

the register

The register, or stub, is where the checking account customer keeps a record of all deposits and checks. The register should be updated immediately with each transaction. One of the most frequent causes of overdrawn accounts and other errors is customer failure to enter deposits and checks. If you neglect to enter a check transaction in your register, you run the risk of forgetting that transaction and subsequently overdrawing. Reg-

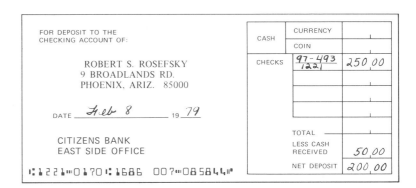

Figure 4-2   Sample Deposit Slip.

isters come in several forms. Figure 4.3 shows some sample registers, indicating how transactions are noted in them.

the statement and reconciliation

Periodically—usually monthly—the bank returns a statement to each of its checking account customers. This statement contains an itemized listing of all transactions made on the account, and includes all checks written and cleared during the previous month as well as all deposit slips. In that way, the customer has written verification of every transaction. As noted earlier, the bank also makes a microfilm record of all items, which the customer can refer to if necessary.

The statement also contains instructions for determining that the balance shown by the bank matches the balance shown in the customer's account. This is known as "reconciling" the account. Figure 4-4 illustrates an example of a monthly account reconciliation.

checking account costs

Banks customarily charge customers for the services rendered in a checking account. The two most common types of charge structures are the Minimum Balance Account and the Per Item Account.

minimum balance account

In this type of account the bank will not levy any service charges, provided the customer keeps a specified minimum balance in the account at all times. If the minimum monthly balance drops below the specified level, charges will be levied according to a fixed schedule. For example, the bank will not

CHECK #	DATE	CHECK ISSUED TO (or description of deposit)	AMOUNT OF CHECK	AMOUNT OF DEPOSIT	BALANCE 139.90	
143	2/21	To Joes Gas Sta. / For Gas	7.75		CHECK OR DEP. 7.75	BAL. 132.15
Dep.	2/27	To (net Paycheck) / For		200.00	CHECK OR DEP. 200.00	BAL. 432.15
144	3/5	To Electric Co. / For Feb. bill	28.10		CHECK OR DEP. 28.10	BAL. 404.05
145	3/5	To Savings & Loan / For march pmt.	242.00		CHECK OR DEP. 242.00	BAL. 162.05

(a)

CHECK # 144	DATE 3/5
TO Electric Co Feb. bill	
BALANCE	432.15
CHECK	28.10
DEPOSIT	
NEW BAL.	404.05

CHECK # 145	DATE 3/5
TO Savings & Loan march pmt.	
BALANCE	404.05
CHECK	242.00
DEPOSIT	
NEW BAL.	162.05

(b)

Figure 4-3   a) Sample Checkbook Register b) Sample Checkbook Stubs.

require any service charges if the customer always keeps at least $500 in the checking account. If the balance drops below $500, there will be a monthly charge of 50¢ and a charge for each item (checks, and possibly also deposits) of 15¢. This can be an economical form of checking account, provided one does maintain the required minimum balance. However, that minimum balance is not drawing interest as it might if it were deposited in a savings account. This must be taken into account in comparing the costs of checking accounts so that the customer can get the best possible deal, all factors considered.

per item accounts

In a per item account, the customer generally pays a fixed monthly fee, plus a set fee for each item. The monthly fee might be 50¢, plus a charge of 10¢ per item. In this account, the customer does not have to maintain any minimum balance.

1. Arrange cancelled checks and deposit slips by number or date.
2. Check them off in your checkbook, verifying each amount as you proceed.
3. *Add* to your checkbook any deposits or other credits recorded on this statement that you have not already added.
4. *Subtract* from your checkbook any checks or other charges recorded on this statement that you have not already subtracted.
5. List at right each check you gave written that is not yet paid by bank (does not show on statement). Total them, and enter total on line 10.

CHECKS NOT YET PAID		
DATE	#	AMOUNT
3/8	149	52.50
3/9	150	7.50
3/10	151	10.00
TOTAL		70.00

6. List any deposits you have made that do not show on statement, and enter total on line 8.

DEPOSITS NOT YET CREDITED	
DATE	AMOUNT
3/10	100.00
TOTAL	100.00

7. Ending balance as shown on statement $ 182.00
8. Add total from line six   + 100.00
9. Subtotal   282.00
10. Subtract total from line 5   − 70.00
11. This total should be the same as the balance in your checkbook $ 212.00

Figure 4-4   Sample Reconciliation of Checking Account.

other arrangements

In some situations, commercial checking account customers who carry large balances and have a high number of transactions might negotiate a separate arrangement for their checking account charges. Also, many banks across the country have, in recent years, offered "special package deals." These consist of a bundle of various services included at one fixed monthly cost. For example, a package deal might consist of all the checking services used by the customer, free travellers checks and money orders (usually up to a set limit), a safety deposit box, a bank credit card, overdraft privileges, and notarial services—all for a fixed monthly charge of perhaps $3 to $5, depending on the bank and the competition.

shopping for checking accounts

Unless you prefer one specific bank for convenience or other personal factors, it can be wise to shop around for the best available deal on a checking account. In order to determine that, one must consider the structure of the service charges, the average amount of checks and deposits transacted each month, the minimum balance one wants to remain in the account without drawing interest, the banking hours, the convenience of getting to and from the bank (or of using bank-by-mail facilities), and any other personal or financial arrangements.

Once you have estimated the probable number of checks and deposits you'll be transacting in a month, the following chart (Figure 4-5) can help you work out the best overall program in terms of out-of-pocket costs.

savings accounts

Savings accounts are available at commercial banks, mutual savings banks, savings and loan associations, and credit unions. Generally, they take one of two forms: passbook account and savings certificates of deposit (CD).

Unlike checking accounts, where money flows in and out constantly, savings accounts are relatively inactive. They're used as a device to accumulate money over a long period of time.

Financial institutions are willing to pay savings accounts customers for the use of their money. The payment is referred to as "interest." In effect, customers are lending their money to the institution and the institution is paying interest for the loan.

passbook accounts

The most common type of savings account is the passbook account. A passbook account may be opened with any amount of money, and the customer may make deposits to or withdrawals from the account as desired. (Some institutions might limit the number of withdrawals permitted in a month or in a quarter, and if that number is exceeded, the institution might levy a modest service charge.) Passbook savings account customers will usually receive a small booklet, or passbook, in which each deposit and withdrawal is entered, and in which the interest earned on the account is added to the customer's balance.

certificates of deposit   Increasing in popularity in recent years has been the savings certificate or CD. This is a contractural agreement between customer and institution whereby the customer agrees to leave a certain sum of money with the bank for a fixed period of time—perhaps as short as ninety days or as long as ten years. Certificates generally pay a higher rate of interest to the customer than passbook accounts because the institution is assured that it will have the fixed sum of money available for lending for a known period of time. If a certificate customer wishes to withdraw funds before the agreed on time has elapsed, he or she will suffer a penalty in the interest due and may end up receiving slightly less than if the money had been kept in a normal passbook account.

1. Average number of checks you'll write each month: _____
2. Average number of deposits you'll make each month: _____
3. Amount you can make available to satisfy minimum balance requirements: _____

	Min. balance required for no service charge	Service charge if min. balance not kept	Cost per check written (and deposits made, if any)	Estimated total monthly cost
PLAN A	_____	_____	_____	_____
PLAN B	_____	_____	_____	_____
PLAN C	_____	_____	_____	_____
PLAN D	_____	_____	_____	_____
PLAN E	_____	_____	_____	_____

Note: The minimum balance could be earning interest if placed in a savings account. However, that interest will be subject to income taxes. If a minimum balance of, say $300, was kept in a checking account, and as a result you avoided having to pay, say, $30 per year in checking account costs, that minimum balance will have "earned," in effect, 10% for you, without your paying income taxes on the "earnings."

Figure 4-5 Worksheet For Calculating Checking Account Costs

Competition is keen among institutions for savings accounts of all types. Generally, mutual savings banks, savings and loan associations, and credit unions pay a slightly higher rate of interest to savers than commercial banks. To offset that possible disadvantage, commercial banks offer a broader range of services.

Because many consider savings accounts as a form of investment, they are treated more fully in the chapter on fixed income investments.

safe deposit facilities

Safe deposit boxes provide the ultimate security for valuable items and documents that cannot be replaced or duplicated. Financial institutions that rent safe deposit facilities will make boxes of varying sizes available, generally on a yearly rental basis. The amount of the rent depends on the size of the box. The person or persons renting safe deposit facilities must sign a signature card at the time the box is rented and then only those persons who have signed the cards are permitted entree to the box. A key is given to safe deposit customers and it must be presented in addition to signing the entry form. It takes a combination of two keys—the one held by the customer and the one held by the institution—to allow entry into a box. If the customer loses a key, the likelihood is that the institution will have to drill the door open, probably at the customer's expense. Naturally, access to the box is available only during normal banking hours.

Some institutions may offer safe deposit box facilities at a reduced charge for customers who utilize other services.

trust services

Trust departments are usually found in larger commercial banks. The basic function of a trust department is to act as a trusted custodian of money or property for customers who require such services.

One very frequent use of trust services arises when an individual dies and directs that property go to his survivors "in trust." He will have established an agreement with the bank to act as trustee of the stated money and property. The trust department will then be responsible for investing the money prudently, for managing property (such as real estate), for selling any securities or properties that it deems proper to sell, for assisting with the necessary tax returns and other accounting matters on behalf of the trust, and for distributing the proceeds in accordance with the wishes of the individual who established the trust. Charges are levied for trust services depending on the total value of assets in the trust, and the complexity of instructions that the trust department must follow. See the chapter on estate planning for further discussion of trusts.

loans

See Chapter 5, Credit and Borrowing, for a full discussion.

mortgages

See Chapter 7, Housing: Actions and Transactions, for complete information.

travellers checks and money orders

Travellers checks provide a safe and convenient means of having funds available when one is travelling—whether in the United States, where personal checks may not be acceptable outside your own home community, and particularly in foreign countries where neither personal checks nor American dollars may be acceptable as exchange. Travellers checks can be purchased at most financial institutions in denominations of $10, $20, $50, and $100. The common charge is $1 per $100 worth of travellers checks. The most popular brands of travelers checks are issued by the American Express Company, Citicorp, Thomas Cook and Sons, and Bank of America, and are readily accepted by most hotels, restaurants, and merchants throughout the world; they also can be changed into local currancy at banks in foreign nations. If lost, they can be replaced at offices of the issuing agencies, or by mail, as directed in the instructions included with each packet of travellers checks. Some institutions may offer the travellers checks at less than the normal cost to customers who make use of other services.

Money orders are a form of check that one purchases at financial institutions (and at the United States Post Offices) usually for payment of bills, or for any other personal needs. Money orders can be purchased in any denomination. They generally cost more than checks, and one must go to the institution in order to purchase one; thus, they aren't nearly as convenient as a checking account. They might be suitable for someone who issues very few checks each month, but if more than a handful of checks are issued, it might be cheaper to use a checking account instead of purchasing money orders.

notarial services

We often have to sign documents requiring that our signature be "notarized." This service is performed by a notary public, and most financial institutions have a notary public on their staff available to serve their customers. The purpose of notarization is to verify that the signature is indeed that of the person indicated. When a signature is to be notarized, the document must be signed in the presence of the notary, and the notary must know that the signer is who he represents himself to be. Many institutions do not charge for notarial services, particularly for their own customers. Where a charge is levied, it's usually under $1. Notarial services can also be obtained through law firms, governmental offices, insurance agencies, and other businesses.

electronic banking

Many commercial banks throughout the nation have begun installing electronic tellers—machines that offer twenty-four-hour service on a variety of transactions: withdrawals, deposits, loan payments, and transfers from one account to another. Customers wishing to utilize these services are generally issued a plastic card with a secret code number assigned to it, thus preventing anyone except the authorized user from making use of the card. Currently, banks do not charge for this electronic banking service, because most consider it a competitive tool to attract accounts. It does offer considerable convenience, particularly to individuals who might find it difficult to do their banking during normal banking hours. Industry observers have speculated that someday electronic tellers may replace human tellers for most simple transactions. Although the technology certainly exists to accomplish this, it's far from certain whether the American public is willing to accept machines in place of the human element in their common financial transactions.

collection services

Business and commercial accounts are more likely to make use of this little known service. For example, a landlord who lives in a distant city may find it more convenient for tenants to make their rent payments to the local bank, which will in turn deposit the payments into the landlord's account in that bank. He may feel that there's a psychological advantage in getting the rent paid more promptly if the payments are made to a local bank rather than to some distant address. Charges are made in accordance with the volume of service rendered.

international banking

This is predominantly a service for the business executive, found in larger commercial banks. As American business spreads throughout the world, the need has arisen for banking services to exchange foreign currency for American currency, to establish business contacts in foreign countries, and to assist with the various business negotiations and transactions taking place between American and foreign firms.

investment department

As noted earlier, what banks don't lend out to the public or keep in reserve, they invest, usually in high quality government and corporate bond issues. Many individual investors who seek those types of securities find it more convenient and less costly to acquire them through their bank investment department rather than through stock brokerage firms. Anyone contemplating investing in government or corporate securities would do well to inquire at their local bank to see if their investment department can provide comparable or better service than local brokerage firms.

laws that govern financial institutions and their transactions

Financial institutions, and the transactions that emanate from them, are governed by a complex system of state and federal laws. As noted earlier, each institution is given its original license to operate, either by the state in which it is located or by the federal government. The respective government then generally oversees and regulates the operation of the institution including periodic audits and examinations to ascertain if the institution is complying with governmental guidelines. Additional state regulations that institutions must comply with include laws of negotiable instruments (an important aspect of which is the concept of the "holder in due course"), laws of usury, and laws regarding secured transactions. Federal laws with which institutions must comply include the Truth in Lending Law, the Fair Credit Reporting Law, the Fair Credit Billing Law, and the Equal Credit Opportunity Law. Let's examine each of these.

the negotiable instruments laws

The negotiable instruments laws refer to instruments—such as checks, promissory notes (IOUs)—that are negotiated—sold, exchanged, and otherwise passed from hand to hand. Each state has its own laws of negotiable instruments, but they all tend to be quite similar. In essence, negotiable instruments laws determine what constitutes a valid negotiable instrument and what does not. They also may set forth the penalties involved when one attempts to transact an instrument that is not negotiable. A check is a good example of a negotiable instrument. It carries an unconditional order to pay a fixed sum of money to the holder; it's dated; and the person who has drawn the check has signed it. If a check does not contain any of these elements—such as the signature of the drawer—it could be construed as being nonne-gotiable, and need not be processed in the manner that valid checks are processed. In short, it could be returned to the person who drew the check and the intended transaction would thus not occur.

Another example would be a promissory note: you buy a TV set from a local appliance dealer, and instead of paying cash for it, you sign a promissory note in which you agree to make payments over a specific period of time. The promissory note is payable directly to the dealer. The dealer in turn sells your promissory note to a local bank or finance company so that he can get his money out. You then end up making your payments to the bank. The bank has become a *holder* of your negotiable instrument *in the due course of business*, assuming that the instrument has been properly created and executed. If you had neglected to sign it, the TV dealer would not have been able to sell it to the bank. If the TV dealer had not properly endorsed it, the bank would not have bought it from him.

We noted in the above example that the bank had become a holder of your promissory note (or negotiable instrument) in the due course of business. The bank, in such a case, is referred to as the "holder in due course" and this brings up one of the more important aspects of the law of negotiable instruments. Let's follow the example a little further. After you've taken possession of the television set, you find it doesn't work properly. The store refuses to make adjustments, claiming, perhaps, that you have somehow damaged or abused the set. You disagree, of course, and claim that you shouldn't have to pay for something that doesn't perform as you expected it would. You inform the store that you intend to refuse making payments until they have honored the warranty and put the set in proper working order. The store owner smiles and shrugs and tells you that that's out of his hands: they have sold your promissory note to the bank, and it's the bank that you owe money to, not the store. "Settle it up with them," the store owner tells you.

You inform the bank of this situation, and that you don't intend to make any payments. But they tell you you're out of luck: you owe them the money regardless of any claim you have against the store. They are, as they say, a holder in due course of your legitimate promissory note, and they bought that promissory note regardless of any claims or disputes that might have existed between you and the store.

The disadvantage to the buyer is obvious: the strongest defense—witholding payment for an unsatisfactory product—is effectively cut off by the operation of the holder in due course doctrine.

On the other hand, the lender's viewpoint is not without some merit, in effect: "if we had to make certain that every buyer was totally satisfied with his or her purchase before we got involved with the financing, the wheels of commerce could grind to a halt. We simply don't have the time, nor does the consumer want to absorb the expense, of having the lender make certain that everyone is happy before the money changes hands. Granted there are abuses, but they are extremely rare in relation to the volume of transactions that occur in which there is no complaint of any kind."

Throughout the 1960s and 1970s, the abuses began to come to the attention of consumer protection agencies. A few states passed regulations that put limits on the holder in due course doctrine, and eventually in May 1976, the Federal Trade Commission acted to impose limits to the doctrine on a nationwide basis.

Under the new regulations, most consumer credit contracts must contain a notice stating that the holder of the contract or promissory note will be subject to the same claims and defenses that the buyer could have asserted against the seller.

It may take many years before the full impact of the law and the size of its loopholes are clear to the public. Insofar as the new regulations directly contradict established law and custom, it's difficult to know whether or not they will survive the court challenges likely to arise.

In the meantime, the wary buyer of goods should become aware of the protections that the law now allows, and should rapidly assert his or her rights if in the least suspect that they may be violated.

usury laws

Each state has its own laws of usury. The usury laws dictate the maximum rate of interest that can be charged for various types of loans.

Each separate state has a number of specific loan categories, and different interest rates limitations may apply in each. New York State, for example, has ten different loan categories, including auto finance, small loans, insurance premium finance, revolving credit, educational loans, mobile home loans,

and others. Each has a separate maximum interest rate structure. (The only exception among the fifty states is Arkansas,
whose constitution has a flat 10% maximum interest rate.)

You should determine what the maximum interest rates allowable for various categories of loans are in your own state.

If a lender charges an excessive, or usurious, rate of interest
on a loan or on any kind of financing, he may be subject to
penalties. The borrower, or debtor, in a usurious transaction
should determine what his or her rights are in such a case and
take appropriate action.

In most states the laws of usury apply to individuals only.
Corporations do not have the same measure of protection when
they borrow.

secured transactions laws

You purchase an automobile and arrange for financing through
your local bank. In the common transaction, you will sign
documents that give the bank the right to take back your car if
you fail to make the payments as promised. As a result of your
signing these documents, the bank has what is known as a
"security interest" in your new automobile.

Suppose you then decide to be devious and dishonest. You go
to the bank across the street and tell them that you have just
purchased a brand new car for cash and you would like to
borrow against it. Before making such a loan, the second bank
would (or should) check to determine whether or not your
automobile has any other claims against it. Their check would
reveal that indeed the first bank has filed a "financing statement" that reveals their security interest in the car.

Three years later: you still own the car, but now you've paid
off the loan. The car is still worth a few thousand dollars and
you need money. You go to a different bank and request a loan
and offer to pledge your car as collateral in order to obtain the
loan. The bank checks and determines that the original bank
that financed the car in the first place still has a security interest
in the car. But they shouldn't. They should have released that
security interest when your loan was paid off.

These are instances of how the laws can affect the parties in a
secured transaction—that is, when the borrower pledges property as collateral, or as security, for a loan. The law allows the
seller to protect himself, and offers protection to the buyer/
borrower as well. Secured transaction laws are slightly different
in each state, but they all derive from one uniform recommended law called the Uniform Commercial Code. The state

laws describe how a lender goes about protecting his security interest in a property, and how he must release that security interest when the loan is ultimately paid off. The law does not dictate when or if a borrower must put up security for a given loan, nor how much security should be put up. That's between the borrower and the lender. The law does, though, describe the means by which each party is protected in such a transaction.

The Federal Laws: Truth in Lending

Congress passed the Truth in Lending Law in July 1969. The main purpose of the Truth in Lending Law (also referred to as Regulation Z) is to inform borrowers and consumers of the exact cost of credit so that they can compare costs offered by various credit sources.

The Truth in Lending Law is very broad in scope. It applies to virtually all issuers of credit, including commercial banks, savings and loan associations, credit unions, consumer finance companies, residential mortgage brokers, department stores, automobile dealers, furniture and appliance dealers, artisans (such as electricians and plumbers), and professionals (such as doctors, dentists, and lawyers). If these parties, or any others issuing credit to the public, extend credit for personal, family, household, or agricultural uses, or for real estate transactions, they must comply with the regulations of the Truth in Lending Law. (Credit transactions in excess of $25,000, except for real estate transactions, may be excluded from coverage of the law.)

The main objective of the Truth in Lending Law is to establish a uniform means of quoting credit costs. Prior to the passage of this law, grantors of credit frequently quoted interest costs in a variety of different forms—add-on, discount, simple, per month, per year, and so on. This variety of quoting costs made it quite difficult for the typical consumer to compare the true cost between one lender or credit grantor and another. It was, in a sense, like trying to compare apples with oranges.

The Truth in Lending Law dictates that any grantor of credit must clearly set forth the *total finance charges* that the customer must pay, directly or indirectly, in order to obtain the desired credit. The finance charges can include any of the following costs: interest, loan fees, finders fees, service charges, "points" (commonly, the added fees charged in a residential mortgage transaction), appraisal fees, premiums for credit life or health insurance, the cost of any investigation or credit reports.

(It should be noted that certain costs involved in some loan transactions need not be counted in the finance charge. These include taxes, license fees, registration fees, title fees, and some real estate closing fees.)

In addition to stating the total dollar amount of finance charges, the credit grantor must also express the cost in terms of a percentage. This is known as the *Annual Percentage Rate* or *APR*. A formula was devised whereby all finance charges could be translated into APR, and it is the APR that must be quoted by all credit grantors. Technically, the APR formula now requires all lenders and credit grantors to quote credit costs using the same mathematics. APR, then, is the pure way of comparing credit costs between different lenders.

The Truth in Lending Law does not fix the interest rates that may be charged on credit. That's between the lender and the borrower within the limitations of state usury laws. But where interest or other finance charges are involved, the law states that the cost must be expressed in terms of APR.

The provisions of the Truth in Lending Law apply not only to installment loans granted by lenders or to credit contracts, but also to what is known as "open end credit." Open end credit is generally that form of credit granted with credit cards and revolving charge accounts in retail stores, and check overdraft plans in banks. Detailed information about the finance charges and the APR must also be given to users of this form of credit.

The following example of a typical retail installment contract shows the various aspects of the credit transaction as referred to in the Truth in Lending Law (Figure 4-6).

Although the Truth in Lending Law sets forth a means of comparing credit wisely and prudently, it does not necessarily instruct the consumer how to make a decision as to which lender to do business with. The cost of credit is not the only factor that must be considered in making a borrowing decision. Thus, while two credit grantors may offer varying APRs on a specific loan application—such as automobile financing—the lowest rate may not ultimately prove to be the best arrangement for the borrower. For example, if a local bank offers an APR slightly higher than an out-of-town credit firm, the borrower might still be better off doing business with the local bank where other services and considerations may be provided that wouldn't otherwise be found at the out-of-town institution. The Truth in Lending Law goes a long way toward helping the consumer,

Dear Customer,

We welcome the opportunity to be of service to you and would appreciate your acknowledging your agreement to these charge account terms by signing below and returning this item either in the enclosed envelope or with your regular payment. Please tear off the lower portion for your records.

Important Information

I will be billed monthly for all purchases made on the Account. Within **25** days of the billing date stated on each monthly statement, I have the option of paying the New Balance shown on the monthly statement, in which case I will incur no **FINANCE CHARGE**, or I may make a minimum payment of the greater of **$10.00** or 10 % of the New Balance, in which case a **FINANCE CHARGE** will be added to the Account on the next monthly statement computed by a periodic rate of **1½%** for that part of the previous balance which is less than **$500.01** and **1%** of that part of the previous balance which is in excess of **$500.00** (or a minimum charge of **$.50** for balances under **$33.33**), which correspond to **ANNUAL PERCENTAGE RATES** of **18%** and **12%** respectively. Payments and/or credits within **25** days after the billing date will not be deducted from the previous balance before computation of the **FINANCE CHARGE.**

THE STYLE SHOP
SANTA ROSA   CA 95401

CURRENT THANK YOU
ACCOUNT NUMBER   4108-03226-5

198852

PERIODIC RATE %	BETWEEN	AND	ANNUAL PERCENTAGE RATE
1.50	.01	500.00	18.00
1.00	500.01	OVER	12.00

BILLING DATE 11/05/ — PURCHASES 40.94 — MIN PAYMENT 10.00 — NEW BALANCE 40.94

MRS. MARY DOE
SEBASTOPOL   CA   95472

Thank You

PLEASE RETAIN THIS PORTION FOR YOUR RECORDS

Figure 4-6 Typical Retail Installment Contract

but the consumer must ultimately weigh other factors in making his or her decision.

The Truth in Lending Law also sets forth regulations regarding the use of credit cards, the liability for their unauthorized use, and the means by which credit may be advertised.

the fair credit billing law

The Fair Credit Billing Law was passed in October 1974 as an amendment to the Truth in Lending Law. It was designed to put an end to the frustration that certain credit customers have when they receive a bill that contains an error and then cannot get the error properly corrected. It pertains to open-end credit—credit arising out of revolving charge accounts, checking overdraft plans, and credit card obligations. It does *not* apply to normal installment loans or purchases that are paid in accordance with a set schedule of installments.

The Fair Credit Billing Law covers only billing errors on your periodic statement. Billing errors are those that might arise as a result of the following: charges that you did not make or charges made by a person not allowed to use your account; charges billed with the wrong descriptions, amount, or date; charges for property or services that you did not accept or that were not delivered as agreed; failures to credit your accounts for payments or for goods you have returned; accounting errors, such as arithmetic mistakes in computing finance charges; billings for which you request an explanation or written proof of purchase; and failures to mail or deliver a billing statement to your current address provided you gave at least ten days notice of any change of address.

The law does not cover disputes over the quality of goods that you have received. In certain cases, however, you might be able to withhold payment under the Fair Credit Billing Law if you have purchased merchandise or services on a credit card and the goods or services prove to be unsatisfactory. In effect, if you would have had the right to withhold payment from the seller of the merchandise, you might also be able to withhold payment for that merchandise from your credit card account. The law won't help you settle the dispute, but it could give you the right to withhold payment while the dispute is being settled.

The Fair Credit Billing Law requires that open-end creditors give a notice summarizing the dispute settlement procedures to all customers who have active accounts or who open new accounts after October 28, 1975. After the first notice, additional copies must be provided to customers every six months.

The dispute settlement procedures regarding a billing error, as outlined by the Federal Trade Commission, are as follows.

1. *How you notify the creditor of a billing error.* If you think your bill is wrong, or if you need more information about an item on your bill, here's what you must do to preserve your rights under the law. On a sheet of paper separate from the bill, write the following: your name and account number; a description of the error and an explanation as to why you think it's an error; a request for whatever added information you may think you need, including a copy of the charge slip; the dollar amount of the suspected error, and any other information you think will help the creditor to identify you or the reason for your complaint or inquiry. This would include your address, and photocopies of the bill itself and the charge in question.

   Send your billing error notice to the address on the bill listed after the words: "Send inquiries to," or similar wording indicating the proper address.

   Mail it as soon as you can, but in any case early enough to reach the creditor within sixty days after the bill was mailed to you.

   Do not attempt to notify the creditor by telephone. You may do so, but this will not necessarily protect your rights under the law. The proper way to protect your rights is to notify the creditor in writing.

2. *What the creditor must do.* The creditor must acknowledge all letters pointing out possible errors within thirty days of receipt of such letters, unless the creditor is able to correct your bill during that thirty days. Within ninety days after receiving your letter, the creditor must either correct the error or explain why he, the creditor, believes the bill is correct. Once the creditor has explained the bill, the creditor has no further obligation to you even though you still believe there is an error, except as provided in 5 below.

3. *How you are protected from collection and bad credit reports.* After the creditor has been notified, neither the creditor nor an attorney nor a collection agency may send you collection letters or take other collection action regarding the amount in dispute. But periodic *statements* may be sent to you, and the disputed amount can be applied against your credit limit. You cannot be threatened with

damage to your credit rating or sued for the amount in question, nor can the disputed amount be reported to a credit bureau or other creditors as being delinquent until the creditor has answered your inquiry. However, you remain obligated to pay whatever portion of your bill is not in dispute.

4. *What happens if the dispute is settled?* If it is determined that the creditor has made a mistake on your bill, you will not have to pay any finance charges on any disputed amount. If it turns out that the creditor has not made an error, you may have to pay finance charges on the amount in dispute, and you will have to make up any missed minimum or required payments on the disputed amount. Unless you have agreed that your bill was correct, the creditor must send you a written notification of what you owe. If it is determined that the creditor did make a mistake in billing the disputed amount, you must be given the same amount of time to pay as you are normally given for undisputed amounts before any more finance charges or late payment charges on the disputed amount can be charged to you.

5. *What happens if the dispute is not settled?* If the creditor's explanation does not satisfy you, and you notify the creditor in writing within ten days after you receive his explanation that you still refuse to pay the disputed amount, the creditor may report you to credit bureaus and other creditors and may pursue regular collection procedures. But the creditor must also report that you do not think you owe any money, and the creditor must let you know to whom such reports were made. Once the matter has been settled between you and the creditor, the creditor must notify those to whom he had reported you as being delinquent.

6. *How the creditor can be penalized for not following the procedure.* If the creditor does not follow these rules, the creditor is not allowed to collect the first $50 of the disputed amount and finance charges, even if the bill turns out to be correct.

7. *When can you withhold payment for faulty goods or services purchased with a credit card?* If you have a problem with property or services purchased with a credit card, you may have the right not to pay the remaining amount due on them if you first try, in good faith, to return the item or give the merchant a chance to correct the problem. There are

two limitations on this right: (a) you must have bought the item or services in your home state, or if not within your home state, within 100 miles of your current mailing address; and (b) the purchase price must have been more than $50. However, the above two limitations do not apply if the merchant is owned or operated by the creditor, or if the creditor mailed you the advertisement for the property or services.

In brief, the Fair Credit Billing Law gives you the right of extensive protection against alleged errors in billing. But you must exercise your rights as they are stated in the law. If you fail to do so, you may have waived those rights. Further, if the creditor is in error or does not follow the instructions regarding the law, it's up to you to take the steps to protect yourself accordingly.

The most important aspect of the Fair Credit Billing Law is the dispute procedure. There are some additional protections offered the public by the Fair Credit Billing Law. They include:

☐ If an open-end credit customer is given a time period within which to pay a bill without a finance charge, the creditor must mail or deliver the bill to the customer at least fourteen days before the end of that time period.

☐ An open-end creditor must credit a customer's account with payments as of the date that they are received, unless not doing so would not cause extra charges.

☐ Open-end creditors must promptly credit any customer overpayment to the account, and, if requested by the customer, must promptly refund the overpayment.

☐ Open-end creditors must, where the merchant accepts returns, credit a customer's account promptly for any refunds on returns.

☐ Under the Fair Credit Billing Law, merchants may, if they wish, grant discounts to customers for paying by cash instead of by credit card.

the fair credit reporting act

The Fair Credit Reporting Act, which went into effect in April 1971, is designed to give access to any information that may be on file at local credit bureaus regarding your own individual credit history. It also enables you to take steps to correct erroneous or outdated material that may be in your file.

It should be noted, contrary to what many people think, that credit reporting agencies are *not* governmental agencies. They are generally private firms, either operating on their own, or as a cooperative of various merchants and lenders within the community. It is their job to accumulate appropriate credit information on individuals and make it available to their respective participating members. Most individuals aren't aware of it, but when we make application for credit of various kinds and sign our name to the application, we are giving permission to the lender to seek any information about us at the local credit bureau and to relay any information obtained on us to the bureau. This clause will normally be contained in the loan application statement. Easy access to credit information on the citizens of a community makes it easier and more convenient for credit to be granted to credit-worthy seekers. To this extent, the local credit bureau, as a clearinghouse of information, serves a most valuable purpose. But there have been abuses within that industry, as in any industry, and the Fair Credit Reporting Act was designed to correct those abuses.

Under the Fair Credit Reporting Act, you can, on presenting proper identification, learn the contents of your file at your local credit bureau. The identification requirements are for the borrower's own protection. This aspect of the law would eliminate the chance of a stranger walking into a credit bureau claiming to be you and viewing your credit file.

Regarding erroneous information, you can request the bureau to reinvestigate any items you question. If the information is found to be inaccurate or cannot be verified, it will be deleted. If the reinvestigation doesn't resolve the problem, you can write a brief statement explaining your position and the statement will be included in all future credit reports. If an item is deleted, or a statement added, you can request that the bureau so notify anyone who has received regular credit reports on you during the last six months.

If you've been denied credit during the past thirty days because of a report from the credit bureau, or if you've received a collection notice from a department affiliated with the credit bureau, the law states that you're not to be charged for viewing your file. If the above doesn't apply, a reasonable charge can be imposed for the privilege of viewing your file.

Information in your credit file that is adverse may not be disclosed to creditors after seven years have elapsed—except if you have had a bankruptcy in your past. That information may remain in your file and be available to inquirers for up to fourteen years.

As with the other laws, the Fair Credit Reporting Act gives the rights to the individual, but it's up to the individual to see that those rights are obtained when deserved. The credit bureau will not call you to tell you what's in your file. It's wise to examine your credit file every few years to make sure it does not contain any adverse information. Through nobody's fault, adverse or incorrect information can find its way into an individual credit file. Mix-ups in names and addresses can occur—whether via computer or human error—and erroneous information can be released without your knowledge. Viewing your credit file for potential errors or inaccuracies is a simple and inexpensive way to facilitate all your credit and borrowing needs.

the equal credit opportunity law

The Equal Credit Opportunity Law went into effect in October 1975. Essentially, it's designed to prevent any discrimination in the granting of credit regarding sex or marital status of any person applying for credit.

In the most general sense, this law was designed to correct an apparent abuse that often prevented women from receiving credit to which they might otherwise be entitled. Highlights of the law include the following.

☐ Creditors must not discriminate against any applicant on the basis of sex or marital status in any phase of a credit transaction.

☐ Creditors must not make any statement to any applicant that would discourage a reasonable person from applying for credit because of sex or marital status.

☐ Creditors must not demand information about an applicant's childbearing intentions or capability, and may not ask about birth control practices.

☐ Creditors must open separate accounts for husbands and wives if requested and if both are credit-worthy.

☐ Creditors must consider alimony and child support payments as they would any other source of income in assessing credit-worthiness if the applicant wishes to rely on those means of income.

☐ Creditors must not consider sex or marital status in any system of evaluating credit worthiness.

table 4-1 **federal enforcement agencies of truth in lending law, fair credit reporting law, equal credit opportunity law, and fair credit billing law**

NATIONAL BANKS	Comptroller of the Currency Washington, D.C. 20219
STATE MEMBER BANKS	Federal Reserve Bank serving the area in which the State member bank is located.
NON-MEMBER INSURED BANKS	Federal Deposit Insurance Corporation Supervising Examiner for the District in which the nonmember insured bank is located.
SAVINGS INSTITUTIONS INSURED BY THE FSLIC AND MEMBERS OF THE FHLB SYSTEM (EXCEPT FOR SAVINGS BANKS INSURED BY FDIC)	The FHLBB's Supervisory Agent in the Federal Home Loan Bank District in which the institution is located.
FEDERAL CREDIT UNIONS	Regional Office of the National Credit Union Administration, serving the area in which the Federal Credit Union is located.
CREDITORS SUBJECT TO CIVIL AERONAUTICS BOARD	Director, Bureau of Enforcement Civil Aeronautics Board 1825 Connecticut Avenue, N.W. Washington, D.C. 20428
CREDITORS SUBJECT TO INTERSTATE COMMERCE COMMISSION	Office of Proceedings Interstate Commerce Commission Washington, D.C. 20523
CREDITORS SUBJECT TO PACKERS AND STOCKYARDS ACT	Nearest Packers and Stockyards Administration area supervisor.
RETAIL, DEPARTMENT STORES, CONSUMER FINANCE COMPANIES, ALL OTHER CREDITORS, AND ALL NONBANK CREDIT CARD ISSUERS	Federal Trade Commission Washington, D. C. 20580
SMALL BUSINESS INVESTMENT COMPANIES	U.S. Small Business Administration 1441 L Street, N.W. Washington, D.C. 20416
BROKERS AND DEALERS	Securities and Exchange Commission Washington, D.C. 20549
FEDERAL LAND BANKS, FEDERAL LAND BANK ASSOCIATIONS, FEDERAL INTERMEDIATE CREDIT BANKS, AND PRODUCTION CREDIT ASSOCIATIONS	Farm Credit Administration 490 L'Enfant Plaza S.W. Washington, D.C. 20578

☐ Creditors must allow applicants to open or maintain accounts in their birth-given name if they so desire.

☐ Creditors must require a co-signature of both spouses on loans only if the same requirement is imposed on all similarly qualified applicants without regard to sex or marital status.

☐ Creditors must give the reason why credit has been denied or terminated when asked by the applicant.

☐ Creditors must not terminate or change the conditions of any credit solely on the basis of a change in marital status while a person is using or is liable for an account.

☐ However, a creditor may require reapplication on a change in marital status where the credit has been granted to an applicant based on income that was solely earned by the applicant's spouse.

☐ Creditors must include a notice of the right to equal credit opportunity on written application forms, together with the name of the federal agency that supervises compliance.

☐ Creditors must report all information on joint credit accounts opened after November 1, 1976, in the name of both spouses and both spouses use the account or are liable for it.

enforcement of the federal laws

Generally, the Federal Trade Commission administers all the foregoing federal laws regarding retail firms, department stores, consumer finance companies, all other creditors, and all non-bank credit card issuers. Table 4.1 indicates which federal agency enforces the various federal laws regarding credit and borrowing.

Rashomon—at Your Friendly Neighborhood Bank

Rashomon is the title of a classic Japanese tale that raises the ever perplexing question: "What is the truth?" In the tale, an incident occurs between a man and a woman that is witnessed by some passers-by. The incident is described differently by each of the individuals involved. The reader of the tale is free to draw whatever conclusions he or she wishes regarding what actually might have happened. But the only conclusion that can be drawn with validity is that the truth, indeed, is difficult to perceive.

The following composite of incidents presents a "banking rashomon": each character in the tale will tell it as he or she perceived it, and readers are left to draw their own conclusions.

Mr. Breck's story

"It's unbelievable, but I'm likely to lose my job and my car because of some dumb mistake by one of the clerks at that bank!

We'd gotten into a financial bind because of some illness and other personal matters, and had fallen behind in a lot of our payments, including one to a loan company where we had financed a car. We were expecting a $3000 inheritance from my wife's aunt, and I knew that would bail us out of our trouble.

The check finally came in, drawn on a bank 1000 miles away. I immediately deposited it to my account, then wrote all the checks to cover our debts and personally delivered them to each place of business.

When I finally got to work that day I was astounded. My boss called me into his office and told me that he had received a call from the loan company. Our check had bounced, and the loan company had called to tell him they were starting legal proceedings to have my paycheck sent directly to the loan company. Then I called the loan company, and the manager told me they were following their legal rights, which also included the start of repossession proceedings to take back the car.

By the time I called the bank I was in a rage. The clerk in the bookkeeping department was as rude as she could possibly be. She told me the check to the loan company had bounced because it was drawn on uncollected funds. We had deposited a check from one of the biggest law firms in the Midwest and she wouldn't honor it! That check was as good as gold! I was so angry at that point that I really didn't understand the technicalities she was talking about and demanded to talk to the branch manager.

He wasn't very helpful. He explained that they couldn't honor the check until at least five business days had elapsed, because the check would have to go back to the bank on which it was drawn, and we wouldn't know if that check was good or not until the originating bank had agreed to pay on it.

I tried to then explain this to the manager of the loan company, and asked him to wait just a few days until the check had cleared. But he would have none of it, and stated that he was going ahead with all of the legal paperwork to repossess our car and have my paycheck mailed to him.

As far as my job is concerned, I don't know what to think. My boss is looking over my shoulder at everything I do, and the slightest wrong step on top of this incident could mean the end.

My lawyer explained to me that the bank technically was correct. They could have handled it more decently, but you can't sue anybody for rudeness.

I hope to salvage everything, but it won't be without a lot of cost and aggravation.

The bank clerk's story

"I was just doing my job. And believe me, I often wonder whether it's worth it, what with the little they pay and the guff I have to take from customers such as the Brecks.

That day was a bad one. I had a splitting headache. I was in no mood to put up with problems I otherwise might have handled a little better.

As for the Brecks—I don't know if all banks do this, and I'm sure our customers aren't aware of it, but we actually rate our checking account customers. Most everybody overdraws their checking account once in a while. I've done it myself. If the overdraft is not large, and if we know the customer, very often we'll pay the check even though it's overdrawn. We know the customer will make good on it without any hesitation. Of course, we have to charge a few dollars for the paperwork involved even if we do pay the check.

If the overdraft is sizeable enough, or if we're not sure about the customer, we simply return the check, as well as impose the service charge. We have no choice. Unless a customer has an overdraft privilege, which they can arrange through our loan department, we have to return their checks. If a customer overdraws an account too frequently, we'll flag the account.

Anyway, the Brecks' account had been flagged because they had had a serious number of overdrafts in the past year or two. Every time we charged them for an overdraft, either Mr. or Mrs. Breck would come into the bank stating that the mistake had been the bank's and not theirs. They really weren't very pleasant to deal with. Every time they came in, one of the clerks—usually myself—had to sit down with them and go through their statement to point out the error. I'm not saying we never make mistakes, but with the Brecks it was always their error. Either they had forgotten to enter a check when they drew one or they had made errors in arithmetic.

Then along comes this $3000 check from 1000 miles away. Technically, we could assume that the check would be good, but we don't know for sure until it gets back to the original bank on which it was drawn. In a case where we have a flagged account, such as this one, we withhold honoring the check until the funds are, in fact, collected. Why isn't the customer told this? I don't know. It's not my department. If they didn't know to ask, that's not my problem either. I'm just doing my job as they told me to do it.

The bank manager's story

I wasn't aware of the Brecks' problem until Mr. Breck called me. He had already talked to his boss, the loan company manager, and our clerk before he got to me. By the time he

and I spoke, he was in a terrible fury. I wasn't meaning to be rude, but I was just talking to him in a way that would allow me to penetrate his own anger.

Yes, our clerk was right in refusing to honor the check. And yes, I have the discretion to overrule her. But under the circumstances, I don't think I would have overruled her, even if I had known of the facts in advance.

As for all the problems—I'm not so sure that he didn't blow it all out of proportion. That happens a lot you know. A boss looks at an employee cross-eyed, and the employee is sure he's going to be fired. I've seen too many cases where customers use that kind of overblown tactic to intimidate us into changing our minds about a particular matter.

Why wasn't he aware of drawing checks against uncollected funds? I'm not sure. Our customers are notified of this matter at the time they open their account. He's probably forgotten, or didn't stop to think about it. But that's not really our fault, is it? Problems rarely arise in this area, and it's a shame that one family has to get into such a hassle because of it. I'm sorry it happened, but who knows, I might do the same thing all over again next week. Then again, there's the human factor. Everybody seemed extra edgy that day, and I'm sure that contributed to all of the misunderstanding. Could the same thing happen to one of our better customers? Probably not. Somebody else makes the rules and I just follow them. Rule making isn't my department."

The loan company manager's story

"I've been getting the run-around from the Brecks for months. Their payments kept getting later and later, and they were running a full two months late. The extra interest charges and late charges had also started to mount up heavily. Every time I'd call and ask about their payment, I'd get phony promises that they would have the money in next week. And I never saw them.

When he finally came into my office with that $400 check to bring everything up to date, he was far from a gentleman. Matter of fact, he was downright abusive. Naturally, I was angry at his attitude, but I was just as happy to have his check so that his account would be up to date. Just to play it safe, though, as I do in many cases, I

took this check directly to the bank. When it bounced, I was furious!

I called him immediately at home, but got some kind of recorded message on his phone. I thought it was one of those messages that the phone had been disconnected. That made me all the angrier, and I tried to reach him at work. He wasn't there.

Then I started the paperwork to repossess his car. I wasn't going to wait any longer. If I don't do my job like I'm supposed to, I'm in just as much trouble as the Brecks are.

If he had only come in to see me earlier, we might have been able to work the whole matter out. But he didn't. That's his problem, not mine."

The boss's story

"Fire Breck? Let me put it this way. He's been a good employee. Not the best we've ever had. I wouldn't fire a person because of an incident like this, but it's certainly going to stick in the back of my mind. I knew that he was having some problems, and I was trying to cooperate with him. I'm sure he didn't mean anything wrong. But the thing that particularly irks me is when an employee lets his personal financial matters get to a point that I have to start getting telephone calls from some loan company. And I didn't even talk to the loan company manager. I just happened to pick up the phone in the middle of the conversation

between the loan company manager and my secretary, and that was all I had to hear."

The bank vice-president's story

"Well, we finally got everything nicely resolved. I didn't hear about the whole matter until some days after it happened. But when I did, I called Mr. Breck and asked him and his wife to pay me a visit. We sat and talked quietly and calmly, and I was able to explain the whole thing to him.

Of course, I pointed out to the Brecks that all would have gone much better for them from the beginning of their problems if they had come in personally to discuss the matter with us. Funny, but people rarely do that. They try to resolve problems over the telephone or through the mail; it's simply just a lot easier if they come in in person so that we can sit down and discuss it at length.

We certainly don't like things like this to happen. But I can appreciate how complicated the financial world can be to people, and how they can overlook some things that we on the inside take for granted. I wish we could do more to educate them about how banking works and how they can best take advantage of the services we offer. But the head of our marketing department says we don't have enough dollars to spend on projects like that. I find that hard to believe, but then again, that's not my department."

1. Who insures the deposits of commercial banks?
2. Explain the advantages of having your bank insured.
3. What is a NOW account and what is its main advantage?
4. In credit terms, what is a store that extends credit to its customers?
5. Explain what usury laws do.
6. What is the main objective of the Truth in Lending law?
7. Name the two items available to the borrower under the Truth in Lending law.
8. What is the one general area covered by the Fair Credit Billing law?

**cases
for
study**

1. Complete a worksheet similar to Figure 4-5 for at least three banks. If you or your parents have a checking account, be sure to include that bank.
2. Connie and Pete Mandic are interested in financing a car. They have been quoted APRs that are very close. Discuss other comparison points when deciding on a lender.
3. You have decided to apply for credit at a large department store. To your surprise, you are turned down. Carefully outline the steps you should follow to determine if there has been an error in the evaluation of your credit application.
4. Joan Richards is single. She has a savings account at Big Savings and Loan and because of the size of her account, Big will give her free money orders. She uses these to pay her bills each month. Joan does not have a checking account. What are some reasons why she should consider opening a checking account?

chapter 5 **credit and borrowing**

buy now, pay later

Most of us take the "buy now, pay later" aspect of our economy for granted. But it was not always so.

It wasn't until about 1916, with the development of a phenomenon called the Morris Plan, that the individual working person could borrow from banks and other financial institutions. Prior to that, businesses, governments, and wealthy individuals were the predominant borrowers. Their loans were generally on a "demand" or "time" basis. A demand loan would be repayable in its entirety upon the demand of the lender. A time loan would be repayable after the passage of the stated amount of time. If the borrower wished, and the lender were willing, such loans could be renewed for an additional period of time, once the borrower had paid the interest due. It was generally felt that if the working man borrowed on such a basis, he would spend the borrowed funds on goods and services, and would not be able to repay the lump sum at the agreed on time.

Then, in 1916, a man named Arthur Morris devised a plan that would enable the individual working man to borrow money that he needed for his immediate purposes. Today, Mr. Morris' plan seems commonplace, but it was a revolutionary concept when originally devised.

The key to his idea—which came to be known as the "Morris Plan"—was that a loan could be repaid in monthly installments over a fixed period of time. The Morris Plan was the origin, and grandfather, of the installment loan, the time payment plan, the revolving charge account, the credit card loan, and all other forms of borrowing that we are accustomed to.

Morris' reasoning was simple enough: although it might be difficult for the typical worker to repay one large lump sum, if the individual was prudent and well employed, he or she should be able to set aside a fixed amount each month to apply to the debt. This type of debt would command a higher rate of interest from the borrower, and the lender would have a constant inflow of money as payments were made each month on the loans, thus enabling the lender to keep putting the available money back to work on a constant basis.

The Morris Plan was scoffed at by the established institutions, but Morris had faith that his plan represented a reasonable and prudent way to lend money to the working class and to make a profit in the process.

From an initial institution in Virginia, the Morris Plan proved itself. Within a few years there were scores of Morris Plan institutions in operation around the country. In many states they became known as "industrial banks" because they were designed to fill the needs of industrial workers—factory employees and the like.

Commercial banks soon saw the advantages and profits in making such loans, and merchants began to accept the installment IOUs of customers for many products. The buy now, pay later years were on their way.

The Morris Plan, and all that developed from it, proved successful on more than one level. By putting borrowing power into the hands of millions of American workers, more goods could be manufactured and sold. This, in turn, helped to create more jobs, which in turn created more income for more people. This then enabled a much larger segment of the population to borrow and buy.

The assembly line concept might never have been successful if there weren't people waiting with cash at the end to buy the products coming off the line. The Morris Plan and the installment loan created the availability of that cash to keep the lines moving and growing.

Today, there are very few adults in America who do not carry one of the descendants of the Morris Plan with them in their wallets or purses: the credit card. The credit card, in effect, allows a holder to write a personal installment loan—within limits—whenever and wherever he or she chooses. Just as Mr. Morris and his plan were originally scoffed at as being imprudent, the credit cards are often damned as being an evil temptation to squander money.

Understanding the workings of credit and borrowing is essential to any individual or family who wishes to manage their personal and financial affairs wisely. Let's now take a closer look at these workings and how they can be put to proper and sensible use.

how interest rates are calculated

simple interest

The fee you pay for the use of someone else's money is called interest. Interest rates are expressed as a percentage of the amount borrowed, and for a given period of time. For example: if you were borrowing $1000 for one year, and the interest rate was 10% per year, you would pay a fee of $100 (10% of $1000) for the use of the money for a period of one year. If you were borrowing $1000 and the interest rate was expressed as 1% per month, you would pay a fee of $10 per month (1% of $1000 equals $10), or a total over the year of $120 in interest. In these examples, you would have the use of the entire $1000 for the full period, be it one year or one month. This calculation is what is commonly known as "simple interest."

Loans calculated on a simple interest basis are loans that are generally repayable in one lump sum at a specific time. That time might be a fixed future date, such as thirty, sixty, ninety, or one-hundred twenty days hence. Or the loan may be repayable on the demand of the lender. Businesses generally borrow on a simple interest basis, and some individuals may also be able to borrow on that basis. (The expression "prime rate" refers to the simple interest rate that banks charge their most creditworthy borrowers. Prime rate loans in theory are the safest and lowest risk loans that lenders make. Thus, the prime rate is the lowest interest rate that a lender will offer. Borrowers who do not have the financial strength and credit-worthiness of prime rate borrowers will pay a higher rate of interest. As the prime rate moves up and down, as it tends to do regularly, other interest rates usually follow accordingly.)

Of more concern to the average individual is the mode of calculating interest on installment and open-end credit. Installment loans are those that are repayable in equal monthly installments; open-end credit refers to debts generated through charge accounts, credit card accounts, and checking account overdraft accounts. In an open-end account, you will be billed for a minimum monthly payment (commonly one twenty-fourth of the total balance outstanding) but the loan is not necessarily repaid in equal monthly installments.

add-on interest

Probably the most common way of calculating interest in an installment loan is the "add-on" method. Here's how it works. Say you want to borrow $1000 for twelve months, and the rate is 6% add-on per year. Your rental fee for the use of the bank's money will be 6% of $1000, or $60. The lender will then add the $60 on to the $1000 worth of principal, making a total of $1060.

That sum, $1060, is divided by twelve, giving you twelve equal monthly payments of $88.33 each. Thus, with the add-on loan, you receive the $1000 in cash and, over the course of one year, you will repay $1060. It sounds like simple interest, but it is really quite different. In the simple interest loan, you have the use of the full $1000 for the full one year. Under the installment method, such as add-on, you have the use of the full $1000 only during the first month of the loan, at the end of which you make your first payment. During the second month, therefore, you have the use of only 11/12 of the money, and proportionately less each month until the final month, when you have the use of only 1/12 of the money. In effect, then, you are paying $60 rental but you don't have the use of all the money all the time as you would in the simple interest loan. However, you do have the use of whatever it is you obtained with the money you borrowed— be it a car, an appliance, whatever.

discount interest

Another way of figuring interest on installment loans is the "discount" method. A loan of $1000 for twelve months at a 6% discount per year rate works like this: working from a prefigured chart, the lender notes that 6% of $1064 equals $63.84. Let's round that off to $64 for ease in figuring. The sum of $1064 minus $64 equals $1000 which is the cash you get. A promissory note is signed for $1064, and the lender "discounts" the interest from that leaving you with $1000 in cash. The $1064 is divided by twelve, giving you twelve equal monthly payments of $88.66. You receive $1000. You repay $1064. Comparing the discount with the add-on method, you can see that the discount results in a slightly higher cost to the borrower and a slightly higher return to the lender. In other words, in the above examples, the 6% discount method will cost the borrower $4 more per year than will the 6% add-on method.

What if the loan is for more than one year? In the add-on method, the interest rate would be multiplied by the number of years. For example: if you are borrowing $1000 for two years at a 6% per year add-on rate, your total interest obligation would be $120 over the full two year period. (6% per year, or $60 per year, times two years equals $120.)

Sometimes interest rates might be calculated on a per month basis rather than on a per year basis. A simple interest rate of 1% per month would equate to a simple interest rate of 12% per year. And an add-on rate of 1% per month would equate to an add-on rate of 12% per year.

how interest costs are expressed: APR

Prior to the passage of the Truth in Lending Law in 1969, a borrower could be very easily confused or misled by the manner in which interest rates were quoted. A borrower shopping around for credit might be quoted from different sources rates of 4% on a specific loan request. But is it 4% add-on? 4% discount? 4% simple? 4% per year? 4% per month? Lenders would not always divulge the full facts and borrowers often didn't inquire about the full facts. The Truth in Lending Law was designed to put an end to this confusion. Under the Truth in Lending Law, lenders and grantors of credit may *calculate* their interest rate and other finance charges in any way they want (within the limitations of the state's usury laws). But no matter how those rates are calculated, they must be *expressed* in terms of Annual Percentage Rate (APR). The Federal Trade Commission has prepared extensive tables by which any lender can convert add-on or discount rates to APR terms. Table 5-1 shows the conversion of add-on rates for common installment loans to APR.

For example, a 6% per year add-on rate for a twenty-four-month loan is equal to an APR of 11.13. A 6% per year add-on rate for a thirty-six-month loan is equal to an APR of 11.08.

Under the Truth in Lending Law all lenders are required to quote their rates only in terms of APR, even though many of them may still calculate their rates on an add-on or discount basis.

table 5-1 **converting ADD-ON to APR**

Term (months)	ADD-ON rates (in percentages)			
	5½	6	6½	7
12	10.00% APR	10.90% APR	11.79% APR	12.68% APR
18	10.18	11.08	11.98	12.87
24	10.23	11.13	12.12	12.91
30	10.23	11.12	12.00	12.88
36	10.20	11.08	11.96	12.83
48	10.11	10.97	11.83	12.68
60	10.01	10.85	11.68	12.50

open-end credit

In the typical installment loan, the borrower receives a lump sum of money and pays it back in equal installments. In open-end credit, that's not necessarily the case. If, for example, you have a credit card account and you have not paid all of your charges, you will be carrying an "open-end loan." Open-end means, in effect, that you can, at will, add to that debt by making additional charges, or diminish it by making payments. Because the total balance you owe at any given time can fluctuate almost daily, the APR is normally calculated on the average balance owed throughout the monthly billing period. The APR rate will be expressed on the billing statement each month.

The Truth in Lending Law requires finance charges to be quoted as APR for installment loans and open-end credit. The Truth in Lending Law does not apply to simple interest loans or to loans repayable in four installments or less.

figuring your installment loan costs

The APR gives us the means of comparing the *rate* and costs of various loan quotations. To determine how the actual *dollar cost* of any given loan is arrived at, it may be necessary to convert the APR back into the original calculating method, most frequently the add-on method.

The following formulas and tables will enable you to figure the actual dollar cost of an installment loan. If you have been quoted an APR rate, use the conversion table (Table 5-1) to find the equivalent add-on rate. (Space does not permit the inclusion of the entire add-on to APR conversions, but the figures contained in Table 5-1 contain the more common loan rates. Your banker can assist you in finding other conversion figures.)

Note: where "monthly payments" are referred to, they include principal and interest only. Extra amounts that might be paid for insurance, recording fees, and other charges should be determined from the lender and added in accordingly. Also, many of the figures used in the charts are rounded off for purposes of simplicity; consequently, figures you might obtain from other sources could differ slightly.

Table 5-2, the Interest Cost Finder for installment loans, is the basic tool we'll use to find the dollar costs of typical installment loans. Here's how it works:

1. Determine how much money you want to borrow. Let's say it's $1000. We'll call that M.
2. Assume that you want the money (M) for a twenty-four-month period, and that the going rate is 11.13 APR. The conversion table (Table 5-1) indicates that an 11.13 APR is equal to a 6% add-on rate for a twenty-four-month term. Now turn to the

table 5-2 **interest cost finder for installment loans**

No. of Months in Loan	"Add-on" Rate—Per Annum (In Percentages)								
	4	4½	5	5½	6	6½	7	7½	8
12	.04	.045	.05	.055	.06	.065	.07	.075	.08
15	.05	.056	.062	.069	.075	.081	.088	.094	.10
18	.06	.068	.075	.083	.09	.098	.105	.113	.12
21	.07	.079	.088	.097	.105	.114	.122	.132	.14
24	.08	.09	.10	.11	.12	.13	.14	.15	.16
27	.09	.101	.112	.124	.135	.146	.157	.169	.18
30	.10	.112	.125	.137	.15	.162	.175	.187	.20
33	.11	.124	.137	.151	.165	.179	.192	.206	.22
36	.12	.135	.15	.165	.18	.195	.21	.225	.24
39	.13	.146	.162	.179	.195	.211	.227	.244	.26
42	.14	.157	.175	.192	.21	.227	.245	.262	.28
45	.15	.169	.187	.206	.225	.244	.262	.281	.30
48	.16	.18	.20	.22	.24	.26	.28	.30	.32
54	.18	.202	.225	.247	.27	.292	.315	.337	.36
60	.20	.225	.25	.275	.30	.325	.35	.375	.40

Interest Cost Finder chart (Table 5-2) and find the factor on the chart where the 6% add-on column meets the twenty-four month column. The number there is .12, and we'll call that the factor (F).

3. Multiply the factor (.12) by the money ($1000). The answer is $120. That's your interest cost and we'll call that I.

4. Now add the money (M) and the interest (I). The total is $1120, which is the total debt you'll have to repay. We'll call that D.

5. Divide the debt (D) by the number of months (24) and your answer is $46.67. That is your monthly payment, which we'll call P.

Thus we have three formulas that can be used to determine the interest cost in dollars, the total debt, and the monthly payment for any loan within the limits of the chart:

Formula One: Interest (I) = Money (M) × Factor from chart (F).
Formula Two: Total debt (D) = Money (M) + Interest (I).
Formula Three: Monthly payment (P) = Debt (D) ÷ Number of months.

Here's another example using these formulas. How much will the monthly payments be on a loan of $2000 for thirty months at an APR of 12.88?

Using the add-on to APR conversion table, we find that on a thirty-month loan a 12.88 APR is equal to a 7% add-on rate. Using the Interest Cost Finder table we find that a 7% add-on rate on a thirty month loan gives us a factor (F) of .175.

Now we turn to Formula One: I = M × F
I = 2000 × 1.75
I = $350. That's your interest cost.
Formula Two: D = M + I
D = $2000 + $350
D = $2350. That's your total debt that you must repay.
Formula Three: P = D ÷ Number of months
P = $2350 ÷ 30
P = $78.33. That's your monthly payment for interest and principal.

credit insurance

Many lenders may offer or suggest that you obtain credit insurance as a part of your installment loan transaction. There are two common types of credit insurance: life and health. If you obtain credit life insurance as a part of the transaction, the insurance will pay off any remaining balance on the loan should the borrower die before the loan is paid off. The borrower's survivors need not, therefore, pay the remaining balance on the loan.

If you obtain health insurance as a part of your loan transaction, the insurance company will make your payments for you in the event you become disabled for an extended period of time due to poor health or an accident. Credit health policies may differ from lender to lender regarding the initial waiting period involved before the insurance takes effect. In other words, if the waiting period is fifteen days, then you must be disabled for more than fifteen days before the insurance will take effect. In this case, if you are disabled for, say, twenty-five days altogether, the insurance will protect you for ten days out of that month. They will, in effect, make roughly one-third of your monthly payment for you.

If your loan does include charges for life or health insurance, the lender, in effect, is lending you the amount of the premium for that insurance in advance. The amount of such premiums should, therefore, be added to the "M" before you start using the above formulas. In other words, if in the earlier example, the life insurance premium is $30, that amount should be added to the money you need, bringing the total of M to $2030. Your interest costs would then increase accordingly, which would change the results in the other formulas slightly.

paying off an
installment loan ahead
of schedule

Loan officers frequently have to resolve a perplexing dispute that arises when customers wish to pay off their installment loans ahead of schedule. Here's a typical situation. Charlie had borrowed $5000 for a thirty-six-month term. The interest cost for the three years was $900, which, when added to the $5000, gave Charlie a total debt of $5900, and monthly payments of $164. Eighteen months have elapsed, and Charlie has accumulated some unexpected funds and wishes to use them to pay off his installment loan. Against the original debt of $5900, Charlie has, during these first eighteen months, made payments totalling $2592. That would reduce his debt to $3308.

Charlie then figures that since he's half way through the loan he should only pay half of the interest that he originally committed to, or $450. Subtracting the $450 from the $3308, Charlie calculates that he owes the bank $2858 to wipe the loan off the books. But the bank figures differently. They figure that Charlie is entitled to get back only 25.7% of the original $900 worth of interest, which would make his payoff figure $3077.

Charlie is enraged to learn that he owes the bank $219 more than he had expected to. What happened to that $219? The Rule of 78s happened.

the rule of 78s

It was noted earlier that in the typical installment loan the borrower has the use of the full original amount borrowed only during the first month of the loan. Then, as the borrower makes periodic payments, he or she has the use of progressively less and less of the original amount of the loan. That's the basis for the so-called Rule of 78s, which is used to determine how each month's payment is broken down into interest and principal.

In an installment loan, the borrower commits himself to pay a certain amount of interest over the term of the loan. If he pays off the full balance of the loan before the full term elapses, the borrower is entitled to get back a portion of his interest cost, plus a portion of any other rebatable charges such as insurance. But the borrower does not get back an amount directly proportional to the amount of time the loan has run. As in Charlie's case, if you have a thirty-six-month loan, and you pay it off at the end of eighteen months, your interest rebate does not equal one-half of the original amount of interest, even though one-half of the loan has elapsed.

Here's an example of the rule of 78s in action.

On a twelve-month loan, the borrower has the use of all the money during the first month. She then makes her first payment. During the second month she has the use of only 11/12 of the money. For the third month it becomes 10/12. And so on until the last month when she has the use of only 1/12 of the money.

Because the borrower has the use of more money in the earlier months, she has to pay proportionately more for it. Actually, the borrower has the use of twelve times more money in the first month than in the last month.

In the Rule of 78s, the sum of the number of months in a twelve-month loan equals 78. (1 + 2 + 3 + 4 . . . to 12 = 78) During the first month of a twelve-month loan, you're charged with 12/78 of the total interest. During the second month of a twelve-month loan you're charged with an additional 11/78 of the total interest. During the third month of a twelve-month loan, you're charged with an additional 10/78 of the total interest. The last month you'd be charged with 1/78. The total of the twelve fractions is 78/78, or 100% of the total interest.

If, therefore, you paid off a twelve-month loan at the end of six months, you'd be charged for 57/78 of the total interest owed. (12 + 11 + 10 + 9 + 8 + 7 = 57) Your rebate would be the remaining 21/78, or about 27% of the original interest charged to you. If the original interest had been $60, you'd thus get back about $16. For loans of other than twelve months, the key number becomes the sum total of the number of months.

Table 5-3 converts the fractions into percentages to enable you to figure the rebate on loans ranging from twelve to sixty months at six month intervals. For loans set to run for other terms than those shown in the table, your banker can give you a precise rebate breakdown. A good working knowledge of installment loans and how rebates are figured can be most important in determining when, how, and why you should consolidate loans, refinance them, or pay them off. Here's how you can figure the rebates on any loans included in the table.

1. Determine the total interest you have been charged for the loan.
2. Decide at what point you want to figure the rebate—say, after nine months of a twenty-four-month loan. Locate the factor on the rebate chart where the column "loan has run— 9 months" meets the row "original term of loan—24 months." That factor is 40%, which is the percentage of your interest charge you will get back or that will be credited to you if you pay off a twenty-four-month loan after nine months have run.

3. Multiply your original interest cost by the rebate percentage to get the actual dollars to be rebated.
4. From your original total debt, subtract the amount of payments made so far. Then subtract the dollar amount of your rebate. The final total is your payoff figure.

Here's an example using this formula. You had originally borrowed $2000 repayable in thirty months. The interest cost was $250, making your total debt $2250. Monty payments are $75. You want to pay off the balance due after nine months.

table 5-3   **rebate schedule from the rule of 78s (showing percentage of finance charge to be rebated)**

No. of months loan has run	Original Term of Loan							
	12 Mos.	18 Mos.	24 Mos.	30 Mos.	36 Mos.	42 Mos.	48 Mos.	60 Mos.
1	84.6	89.5	92.0	93.5	94.6	95.3	95.9	96.7
2	70.5	79.5	84.3	87.3	89.3	90.8	91.9	93.5
3	57.7	70.2	77.0	81.3	84.2	86.4	88.0	90.3
4	46.1	61.4	70.0	75.5	79.3	82.1	84.2	87.2
5	35.9	53.2	63.3	69.9	74.5	77.8	80.4	84.1
6	26.9	45.6	57.0	64.5	69.8	73.7	76.8	81.1
7	19.2	38.6	51.0	59.3	65.3	69.8	73.2	78.2
8	12.8	32.2	45.3	54.4	61.0	65.9	69.7	75.3
9	7.7	26.3	40.0	49.7	56.8	62.1	66.3	72.5
10	3.8	21.0	35.0	45.2	52.7	58.5	63.0	69.7
11	1.3	16.4	30.3	40.9	48.8	54.9	59.8	66.9
12	-0-	12.3	26.0	36.8	45.0	51.5	56.6	64.3
13		8.8	22.0	32.9	41.4	48.2	53.6	61.6
14		5.8	18.3	29.2	38.0	45.0	50.6	59.1
15		3.5	15.0	25.8	34.7	41.9	47.7	56.6
16		1.7	12.0	22.6	31.5	38.9	44.9	54.1
17		.58	9.3	19.6	28.5	36.0	42.2	51.7
18		-0-	7.0	16.8	25.7	33.2	39.5	49.3
19			5.0	14.2	23.0	30.6	37.0	47.0
20			3.3	11.8	20.4	28.0	34.5	44.8
21			2.0	9.7	18.0	25.6	32.1	42.6
22			1.0	7.7	15.8	23.3	29.8	40.5
23			.33	6.0	13.7	21.0	27.6	38.4
24			-0-	4.5	11.7	18.9	25.5	36.4
25				3.2	9.9	16.9	23.5	34.4
26				2.1	8.3	15.1	21.5	32.5
27				1.3	6.8	13.3	19.6	30.7
28				.65	5.4	11.6	17.9	28.8
29				.22	4.2	10.1	16.2	27.1
30				-0-	3.1	8.6	14.5	25.4
31					2.2	7.3	13.0	23.8
32					1.5	6.1	11.6	22.2
33					.90	5.0	10.2	20.7
34					.45	4.0	8.9	19.2

table 5-3   **rebate schedule from the rule of 78s (showing percentage of finance charge to be rebated)**

No. of months loan has run	Original Term of Loan							
	12 Mos.	18 Mos.	24 Mos.	30 Mos.	36 Mos.	42 Mos.	48 Mos.	60 Mos.
35					.15	3.1	7.7	17.8
36					-0-	2.3	6.6	16.4
37						1.7	5.6	15.1
38						1.1	4.7	13.8
39						.66	3.8	12.6
40						.33	3.1	11.5
41						.11	2.4	10.4
42						-0-	1.8	9.3
43							1.3	8.4
44							.85	7.4
45							.51	6.6
46							.26	5.7
47							.09	5.0
48							-0-	4.3
49								3.6
50								3.0
51								2.5
52								2.0
53								1.5
54								1.1
55								.82
56								.55
57								.33
58								.16
59								.05
60								-0-

What will your rebate and your payoff amount be? (*Note:* the rebate schedule is the same for all interest rates.)

1. The percent of your total original interest that will be rebated to you is 49.7%. That's where the thirty-month column (original term of loan) meets the nine-month row (number of months loan has run).

2. Your rebate is $12.25 (49.7% of $250).

3. Your payoff figure is $1450.75. From the original total debt of $2250 you subtract $675, representing the nine payments you made at $75 each. From that sum you further subtract the $125.25 that is your rebate. In other words, your payoff figure is your *original debt* less *payments made to date* less *rebate due you.*

   Other rebatable charges, such as insurance premiums, are figured on the same basis. Thus, if you had a life insurance premium charge on the above loan of $30, you would receive a rebate of that charge of $14.91 (49.7% of $30).

   Does it make sense to pay off an installment loan early? In the above example, the borrower presumably found himself with a windfall of $1450. Even though his loan was only 30% paid off (nine months out of thirty), more than half the total interest he was committed to pay has been used up. If he uses the $1450 to pay off the loan, he'll save about $125, representing the remaining interest he's obliged to pay. If, though, he puts that $1450 into a savings account, it will earn roughly $150 over the next twenty-one months.

   On the other hand, if he pays off the loan early and puts the $75 per month into a savings account—instead of paying it on the loan—he'll build up a comparable-sized nest egg at the end of twenty-one months. Much of the decision depends on individual human nature. It might be easier to put away the lump sum in a savings account and thus realize a sizable nest egg at the end of the period than to deposit $75 each month into the savings account.

refinancing an installment loan

Having the money to pay off an installment loan is a pleasant dilemma rarely faced. Much more frequent is the desire to refinance the loan, perhaps to reduce the monthly payments. The Rule of 78s applies in this situation just as it would in an early pay-off. Following the above example, an individual might wish to refinance the original $2000 loan after nine of the thirty months had elapsed. As the formula indicates, he would have a balance owing of $1450. Assuming that he wished to refinance that balance for a new thirty-six-month term at an 11.08 APR (6% add-on), the earlier tables indicate that he would have to oblige himself for an additional $261 in interest. The $261, added to the $1450 remaining payoff figure would give a new debt of $1711 and monthly payments (interest and principal) of $47.51. He thus reduces his monthly payments by almost $30 but in so doing incurs added interest expense and an ongoing debt for fifteen months longer than previously obliged. Whether or not it's wise to do this would depend on personal circumstances, and refinancing of a debt in such a manner should only be done after counseling with a loan officer. To extend the debt could create a bottleneck years down the road when other credit needs arise.

increasing an installment loan

As with refinancing, frequently individuals will want to add a new sum of money to their credit line. For example, in the above situation assume that the borrower wished to acquire another $1000. He did not wish to take out a separate new loan, but wanted to add the $1000 to his existing installment loan to run for a period of thirty-six months. His payoff balance on the original loan is $1450. To that the lender adds the $1000 new money and then must add the interest onto that. Assuming an 11.08 APR (6% add-on), the additional interest would be $441. This would give him a total debt of $2891 with monthly payments of $80.30. For roughly $5 more than he is now paying each month, he has another $1000 cash in hand. But, as with the refinancing, he has stretched his payment schedule out for an additional thirty-six months—fifteen months longer than he was otherwise obliged to make payments for. And, as with refinancing, adding on to debt in this manner should be done only after adequate consultation.

comparing interest costs

A slight difference in the interest rate on an installment loan can have a considerable impact on the overall cost for the term of the loan. Table 5-4 illustrates the effect of varying interest rates on a sampling of different loans. You can work out similar charts for loans of different amounts and terms by using the Interest Cost Finder formula referred to earlier.

the effect of down payment size

To the extent that you borrow to buy anything, the cost of borrowing can add as much as 10% to 30% to the cost of the item. The less you can borrow, the less interest you'll be paying, and the lower your monthly payment and overall obligation.

The question may arise as to whether or not one is better off financing the whole amount of a purchase, and putting the available down payment dollars into a savings account where it can earn interest. Generally, when you're starting from scratch with an installment loan, before the Rule of 78s comes into play,

credit and borrowing

table 5-4 **comparing interest costs**

on a loan of $1000 for 12 months		Total interest	Total to be repaid	Monthly payments
APR	(Add-on)			
10.00%	5½%	$55	$1055	$87.92
10.90	6	60	1060	88.33
11.79	6½	65	1065	88.75
12.68	7	70	1070	89.33

on a loan of $2000 for 24 months

on a loan of $2000 for 24 months				
10.23	5½%	$220	$2220	$92.50
11.13	6	240	2240	93.33
12.12	6½	260	2260	94.16
12.91	7	280	2280	95.00

on a loan of $3000 for 36 months

on a loan of $3000 for 36 months				
10.20%	5½%	$495	$3495	$97.08
11.08	6	540	3540	98.33
11.96	6½·	585	3585	99.58
12.83	7	630	3630	100.83

you probably wouldn't do as well in going for the larger financing. Because a savings account pays less than what you must pay a lender for a loan, you'd probably be better off applying your available cash toward the purchase price and reducing the amount of the loan accordingly.

Table 5-5 illustrates the dollar effect of varying down payments on a specific loan. You can work out similar charts for loans of different amounts by using the Interest Cost Finder formula.

how long should your loan run?

The amount of time, or term, of an installment loan can effect overall costs considerably. The longer the term, the lower the monthly payments and the higher the interest costs. Do the lower payments make up for the higher interest costs? Table 5-6 illustrates the effect of different terms on loans of varying sizes.

table 5-5 **effect of down payment on loan costs on a $3000 *purchase*, at 11.08% APR (6% Add-on), for a 36-month loan**

Down payment	Amount of loan	Total interest cost	Total to be repaid	Monthly payment
0	$3000	$540	$3540	$98.33
$300	2700	484	3184	88.44
500	2500	450	2950	81.94
800	2200	396	2596	72.11
1000	2000	360	2360	65.55
1200	1800	326	2126	59.05
1500	1500	270	1770	49.16

table 5-6 **the effect of different terms on loan costs***

Amount borrowed	Term of loan (months)	Total interest cost	Total to be repaid	Monthly payment
$1000	12	$ 60	$1060	$ 88.33
1000	18	90	1090	60.55
1000	24	120	1120	46.67
1000	30	150	1150	38.33
1000	36	180	1180	32.77
2000	12	240	2240	93.33
2000	18	300	2300	76.67
2000	24	360	2360	65.55
2000	30	420	2420	57.62
2000	36	480	2480	51.67
3000	12	360	3360	140.00
3000	18	540	3540	98.33
3000	24	630	3630	86.42
3000	30	720	3720	77.50
3000	36	900	3900	65.00

* All loans are calculated at 6% add-on per year; APR will vary according to length of loan.

The best plan to adopt is one best suited to your own credit needs and credit capacity, current and future.

There are other basic guidelines helpful in determining how long an installment loan should run. Generally speaking, the life of the loan should not exceed the expected life use of the product or service you're borrowing for. Also, when one borrows for a recurring need, the loan should be paid off before the need occurs again. Examples of recurring loans include those for the payment of taxes, vacations, winter expenses, automobiles.

For example, say you borrow $600 on June 1 for a summer vacation. With a twelve-month loan, you'll be all paid up by the next summer. But with an eighteen-month loan, you'll be paying for this year's vacation well into next fall. If you were to borrow again in June of next year for that year's vacation, you'd have a few hundred dollars of this year's loan still unpaid if you had taken the eighteen-month plan. If you then combined the remaining old balance and the new loan for yet another eighteen-month loan, you could still be paying for part of this year's vacation three years from now. This is an example of "pyramiding," and it can be a dangerous practice.

Car loans should be geared to the time you expect to retain the car. If you trade every two years, for example, your loan should be paid off within that period. Running the loan longer than the life of the car makes the borrower prone to the risk of pyramiding. In recent years, four-year car loans (and in isolated cases, five-year car loans) have begun to appear, partly because of the desire to keep payments lower while the cost of buying and operating a car goes higher. Unless certain that the car will be retained for at least the life of that loan, one should be very aware of the pyramiding problem that can arise by obtaining a new car before paying off the old one.

Major household items, such as large appliances, might not need replacing for a decade or more. But they should not be financed for as long as they will last. These debts should be eliminated as quickly as your budget will allow in order to make room for other borrowing needs and to keep your interest expenses down. Most lenders won't exceed a few years for such loans anyway, but avoid the temptation of becoming involved in longer plans that might allow for lower monthly payments. The interest cost will be that much higher, and you could still be paying off a loan when you'd rather have that credit capacity available for some other purpose.

One-shot loans, such as those for special events (weddings, etc.), special trips, and other nonrecurring personal needs should also be paid up as quickly as your budget will allow. The needs won't recur, but taking such a loan for too long a term can clutter up your future borrowing capacity and have you paying more interest than may be wise.

Home improvements, particularly major additions such as patios, pool, extra rooms, and so on, can get a bit tricky. These items can easily run into many thousands of dollars, and common installment financing plans run to five years, occasionally longer. For the most part, these improvements become a part of the house—you won't take them with you when you move. You should recapture all or a better part of the cost when you sell the house.

When these improvements are integral to the house, you might find it better to add the cost on to your mortgage if you can. Check with your mortgage lender to evaluate cost and feasibility. For example, a $4000 home improvement loan for five years could entail monthly payments of roughly $83. If you added that same amount to a mortgage that had twenty years left to run, the monthly payments would be about $35. If you expect to be selling the house within about ten years or less, it could be better to add the home improvement costs to your mortgage.

uses and abuses of credit

Credit—the ability to borrow—is not a right. It's a privilege earned through careful planning and faithful performance. Good credit, properly used, can be a most valuable asset. Wise borrowers will have studied their own financial situation with great care. They will know the difference between needs and luxuries. They will know within pennies their ability to repay. They will know how to approach the lender, what to ask for, what not, and what to expect. They will resist the temptations that scream out "Buy me now!" and "Easy credit!."

They will have carefully defined their access to credit, credit needs, and credit capacity. And they will keep each in proper perspective and balance. Let's take a closer look at these three important elements of credit.

access to credit

Access to credit refers to the amount of credit readily available to you, through such means as charge accounts, credit cards, and installment loans. Access to credit is, of course, directly related to lender and merchant willingness to grant credit. That in turn depends on your past performance, income, other debts, work, and the purposes for which you may wish to borrow.

credit needs

Credit needs refer to the various needs you may have that can or should be fulfilled through borrowing. Common needs for borrowing include purchasing an automobile; revolving charge accounts at your department stores so that a large clothing purchase, for example, can be paid for over an extended period of time, thus making it easier on the monthly budget; home improvements; personal emergencies. *Note*: we are referring to *needs*, not luxuries. Most of us would like to obtain certain luxury items and indeed may be able to through the use of credit. But using credit to acquire luxuries, as opposed to using credit to fulfill needs, can be dangerous. If your available credit is used excessively to obtain luxuries, you can cut off your access to credit for the more important needs.

credit capacity

Capacity for credit refers to the amount of borrowing you can realistically handle within your current situation of income and other expenses, as well as your future situation regarding anticipated income and other expenses.

Many people find themselves having access to more credit than they realistically need, and they also often have needs for credit that are in excess of their credit capacity. For example, Charlie and Charlotte estimate that they have access to roughly $15,000 worth of credit. Based on past experience, they're confident that their bank would lend them up to $5000 without collateral if necessary. The sum total of all of their credit cards and charge accounts would allow them to go into additional debt of about $5000. And a representative of a lending firm has told them that the equity in their house would allow them to borrow another $5000—if, naturally, they were willing to give a second mortgage on the house. Their current credit needs are much more modest. Their automobile is all paid off and next year they'll need a new one. They estimate that they might need between $4000 and $5000 for this purpose. Over and above that, their credit needs don't exceed $1000—to be used in their charge accounts to even out the monthly cost of clothing and home necessities.

Currently, then, their capacity for credit exceeds their credit needs. They can easily carry the projected needed debts within their current income and expense structure. However, Charlie and Charlotte are well aware that in three years their oldest child will be starting college. They haven't saved for his tuition and other expenses, and they expect to borrow quite heavily to meet those expenses. Thus, in three years, their credit capacity for debts other than the college expenses will be sharply limited. But their normal credit needs will continue. Their needs, then, will probably exceed their capacity. If they plan properly in advance, they can keep everything in a sensible balance and get through the squeeze. But, if they abuse the access to credit that they have, and use it for luxuries rather than needs, or even obtain more than is necessary for their needs, they can be in trouble in a few years.

We often have access to more credit than we need because credit is sometimes granted too indiscriminately. When we apply for a loan at a bank, they scrutinize our overall financial situation and generally will not permit us to borrow more than we are capable of handling. But when we acquire credit cards and charge accounts, the scrutiny is not as severe. If we succumb to the easy temptation to let the credit card or charge account debts mount up, we can find ourselves in a severe financial crisis.

Each individual and family should, at least every two or three years, visit a lending officer at a financial institution and review their access to credit, needs for credit, and credit capacity for the present and the next three to five years. Only by such a periodic review can credit be put to the most satisfying and economical use. Everyone's situation changes at least slightly over the years, and so too will their credit situation.

abuses—pyramiding

As noted earlier, pyramiding occurs when a loan for a recurring purpose has not been paid off by the time the purpose recurs. Let's look at a specific example.

Otto has been in the habit of trading his cars every three years. He's always taken three-year car loans, so that the loan has been paid off each time he buys a new car. This year a fancy new model catches his eye and he's determined to buy it. He'll need $5000 over and above his trade-in on his old car, but he can only afford payments of roughly $130 per month. His banker tells him that the interest on a three-year loan for $5000 would be $900, making the total debt $5900, and the monthly payments $164. The dealer tells Otto that they can arrange financing for a four-year term and that the payments would only be $129 per month. (The interest would be $1200, making the total debt $6200.)

Otto prudently realizes that if he's financing the car for four years he should keep the car for that time. Even though that's contrary to his habit, he vows he will do this.

Three years later: Otto has dutifully made thirty-six monthly payments of $129 each, reducing his original balance from $6200 to $1556. An advertisement lures him into the automobile dealer's showroom, where he promptly falls in love with a brand new model. He realizes he shouldn't trade for at least another year, until the loan is paid off, but habit and desire get the best of him.

After allowing for the rebate due on his existing loan, his payoff figure is $1477. (A rebate would be $79: 6.6% of the original $1200 interest obligation—see the rebate tables.) Naturally, inflation has boosted the price of the cars, and in order to acquire the new model, Otto will need $6000 over and above his trade-in. The $6000, added to the payoff figure on the previous loan, means that Otto will have to borrow $7477. In order to afford the car, he'll have to obligate himself for another four-year loan, which means added interest of $1795, bringing the total debt to $9272—forty-eight monthly payments of $193 each.

Three years later: Otto has made his payments of $193 for thirty-six months, reducing his original balance of $9272 to $2324. Another advertisement almost lures him into the auto dealer's showroom again, but first Otto does some arithmetic.

Over the previous six years, he has paid $2916 in interest for his loans ($1200 for the first loan plus $1795 for the second one, less $79 rebate on the first loan when he refinanced.) In addition to having paid $2916 in interest, he still has a debt of $2324.

Otto calculates the arithmetic if he had stayed with his three-year financing plans. His interest cost for the first three-year loan would have been $900, and the loan would have been paid up at the end of three years. If he had bought the next new car at the end of three years, he would have needed a loan of $6000, which would have meant an interest cost of $1080, giving him a total debt of $7080, with monthly payments of $197 (compared with the $193 he was paying for the second four year car loan). After the second thirty-six months he would have been all paid off. By using the two three-year plans, Otto's total interest expense would have been $1980, and he'd have no debt remaining. As it is, his interest expense has been almost $1000 greater and he still has a debt remaining of $2324.

Table 5-7 illustrates the effect of Otto's pyramiding.

Where does Otto now stand after six years of unwitting

table 5-7 **effects of installment loan pyramiding**

	Amount borrowed	Interest cost	Total debt	Monthly payments	No. of months	"Payoff" after 36 months
Otto's first loan	$5,000	$1,200	$ 6,200	$129	48	$1,477
Second loan, 36 mo. later	7,477	1,795	9,272	193	48	2,206
Status after six years, if Otto borrowed $7000 for a 36-month term	9,206	1,657	10,863	302	36	0

pyramiding? If he wants to buy a new model car (whose price has gone up to $7000 over and above the trade-in), and wishes to revert to the more prudent three-year financing, he'll have a total debt to finance of $10,863. This would be made up of the $7000 needed for the new car plus $2206 to pay off the old debt (the $2,324 debt remaining less a rebate of $118), plus an added interest cost of $1657. The payments for a three year loan at this point will be $302!

If Otto had not been pyramiding and wanted to buy the $7000 car at the end of six years, his interest cost would be $1260 for a thirty-six-month loan and the monthly payments would be $229.

As Otto's case illustrates, pyramiding can be a costly mistake, whether it originates innocently or as a result of lack of financial discipline. Otto took undue advantage of his access to credit, and exceeded both needs and capacity to borrow.

The pyramiding trap is equally as dangerous, if not more so, regarding credit cards and charge accounts. For example, an individual runs up $50 in gasoline bills for her car during a month. She charges them on a credit card. At the end of the month the bill comes in and rather than pay the full $50, which isn't necessary if she chooses to let the credit line run, she decides to send in only the minimum payment, say $10.

The same thing happens the next month: $50 worth of gas bills and a $10 payment. And so on throughout the year. Unless the individual comes to her senses, she could be paying for her January gas in December and even well into the following year.

The interest costs continue to mount, adding between 15% and 25% per year to the cost of the goods so purchased.

The simple way to avoid pyramiding is to remember that an installment loan or an open-end credit account should be eliminated before the need to borrow for the same purpose occurs again.

abuses: ballooning

Which is more appealing: a twelve-month loan for $1000 with monthly payments of $88.33, or the same loan with monthly payments of only $60? The temptation is to take the loan with the smaller monthly payments, but obviously there's a catch—with the smaller monthly payments there will be one very large payment at the end of the loan, for the loan is to run for only twelve months. In this particular case, after making payments for eleven months at $60 each, the borrower will still owe roughly $400 in the twelfth month. This is what's known as a "balloon" payment, and it can be dangerous. If the borrower isn't equipped to meet the large payment, it may be necessary to refinance that payment and incur additional interest costs. Although the Truth in Lending Law requires lenders to disclose the Annual Percentage Rate and the total costs involved in making the loan, there may not be adequate disclosure regarding the size of the monthly payments. Any borrower should make certain that he or she knows whether or not there are balloon payments at the end of the loan. Unless there are compelling circumstances for a balloon payment program, prudence generally dictates that equal monthly payments are more acceptable to the typical repayment budget.

abuses: oversecuring

If you were borrowing $1000 to pay for your summer vacation, it would not seem wise to have to put up your car, your house, your bank account, and all of your other assets for security for that loan. Reputable lenders would certainly not require such collateral. But it can happen that some lenders may seek more security than reasonable for certain loan situations. This security may include a general assignment of your wages and your personal property. If a borrower does pledge those assets to obtain a loan, the legal aspect is that the lender can take action to recover those assets should the loan become delinquent. The individual borrower must determine when collateral is required for a loan and that that collateral is reasonable, proper, and not excessive. If it is excessive, the borrower is putting assets in jeopardy, which could create severe future problems. The borrower should determine exactly what collateral is being given to the lender and if more is being required than seems necessary, the borrower would do well to shop around at other institutions.

abuses: loan sharks

Despite all the consumer protection laws and publicized warnings, there will always be loan sharks as long as there are people willing to pay exorbitant fees for borrowed funds. Loan sharks operate outside the limits of the law. Their interest rates are generally far above what the state usury laws allow and their collection techniques have been well publicized. If anyone becomes involved with a loan shark, they can expect to bear what could be severe consequences. Before entering such a situation, an individual should consult a banker or attorney to determine the legal methods that may alleviate his or her debt problems.

abuses: loan consolidation

The appeal is almost irresistible: "Why suffer along with all those big monthly payments when you can consolidate all your debts into one loan with a much smaller monthly payment?"

If a family or an individual has accumulated too much debt, loan consolidation seems a logical and convenient way out of the crisis. It's a line of least resistance too often taken by borrowers not aware of the potential pitfalls. Poorly planned, or impulsively embarked on, a consolidation loan can cause more ultimate troubles than the original loans did. Sound, prudent planning might provide other, more suitable, alternatives. Using the following example of a loan consolidation program, and consulting the interest finders and rebate formulas, you can plan any consolidation and judge its value.

Charlie and Charlotte have the following loans:

1. A car loan, whose original total amount was $3540, including interest of $540. The loan has run for twenty-four months, and has twelve months to go. Monthly payments are $98.33.
2. A home improvement loan that originally totalled $2480, of which interest was $480. The loan has already run for thirty months and has eighteen months to run. The monthly payments are $51.67.
3. A personal loan, originally totalling $1090 of which interest was $90. Twelve months of the loan have already expired with six months still to run. Monthly payments are $60.55.

Table 5-8 illustrates Charlie and Charlotte's debts and how much they would need to pay them all off.

Charlie and Charlotte need roughly $2330 to pay off their existing debts. At an interest rate of 11.08 APR (6% add-on), they can obtain a loan of that amount for three years, which would entail an added $419 in interest, giving them a total new debt of $2749. Their thirty-six monthly payments would be $76.30 each, compared with the $210.55 they're now paying.

It seems like an easy way out of what to them has become a serious jam. But is it wise? Is it worth it? If they wait just six more months, the personal loan will be all paid off, reducing their monthly payments to $150. In twelve months the car loan will be paid off, reducing their payments to $51.67. And in eighteen months the home improvement loan will be paid, eliminating their monthly payments altogether.

The consolidation loan will have cost them an additional $419 in interest and will require payments of $76.36 for thirty-six more months. During the next thirty-six months Charlie and Charlotte will in all likelihood have new reasons to acquire debt. Rather than consolidating their loans, they might be far better off in the long run if they could simply tighten their belts and continue with their current debt load. It will be lightened considerably in just six months.

If proper loan planning is done in the beginning, the need for a consolidation loan might never occur. If this need does occur, careful communications with a lending officer are necessary if a sensible consolidation plan is to be arrived at.

table 5-8   **loan consolidation: charlie and charlotte's debts**

Loan	Current balance	Monthly payment	Months to run	"Payoff" figure now
Car	$1180	$ 98.33	12	$1117
Home improvement	930	51.67	18	860
Personal	363	60.55	6	352
Total		$210.55		$2330

cures for overindebtedness

As the above example indicates, Charlie and Charlotte might be candidates for a severe case of overindebtedness. The problem, if not promptly treated, can lead to serious impairment of one's credit history, and can complicate—if not prevent—the ability to obtain credit for many months or possibly years, or, it might force the borrower into obtaining credit through sources that specialize in higher risk situations, and charge higher interest rates accordingly.

The first symptom of overindebtedness is late payments. Not only will late payment entail late charges, which can be as much as 5% of the amount of the payment (the law varies from state to state), but it can also result in a bad rating on your credit history.

Borrowers who *anticipate* that they might be running into a delinquency problem should act *before* the actual delinquency occurs. Borrowers in such straits should visit *in person*, not by phone or by mail, with the creditors in question and explain the overall circumstances. It might be possible to arrange a different payment date that would be more convenient; or to remake the loan on favorable terms; or get a temporary reduction in payments; and it might even be possible to have late charges waived if your reason for delinquency is acceptable to the creditor.

It's up to the borrower to keep the lender informed of the circumstances. If the lender doesn't know what the borrower's problems are, he could rightfully assume that the borrower is being willfully delinquent. The borrower is subject to the terms of a legal contract—the promissory note—and it's the borrower's job to persuade the lender to amend the terms to alleviate the problem.

Frequently, lenders will attempt to communicate with the delinquent borrowers to determine the causes for the problem and when and how it might be resolved. It's always better for the borrower to take the initiative and contact the lender before the lender has to resort to his steps, for by that time the lender may consider that the account is in a "collection" status, which will appear, in all likelihood, on the borrower's credit history.

If the borrower has not complied with the terms of the loan agreement, the lender may deem that the borrower is in default. In that case the lender can commence whatever legal rights have been reserved to him in the loan agreement. If collateral has been pledged for the loan, the lender can take steps to recover the collateral and sell it to pay off the loan. If a co-signer is involved in the loan, the lender can look to the co-signer for payment. In some instances the lender may be able to attach, or garnish, the borrower's wages.

Even if a debt situation has decayed to the point of default, it is still valuable for a borrower to make every effort to work out a satisfactory arrangement with the lender. If such an arrangement can be worked out, and the borrower can perform accordingly, the situation might be alleviated. But often, by the time a loan account falls into the default category, there is such ill will between the parties that a borrower makes no attempt to solve the problem.

debt counseling services
In many communities, lending institutions cooperate to create a debt counseling service to assist people in financial trouble. The agency usually contacts your creditors and gets them to hold off on their collection procedures while you make an effort to reorganize your financial matters. You'll have to make a show of good faith by making some regular periodic payments. If the counsellors have been successful, those payments will be smaller than what your normal payments might otherwise have been.

(Be on guard against some commercial firms who offer debt reduction services. Federal and state consumer protection agencies have reported numerous cases of such firms charging excessively for those services rendered; in many cases the firms simply disappear with the customers' money and no debt reduction is accomplished.)

If a debt counseling service of good repute is not available to you or not capable of helping you, the next step might be to visit with an attorney who can arrange for an Assignment for the Benefit of Creditors. This is similar to the services offered by the debt counseling firms in that it tries to convince creditors to accept a smaller monthly payment until the full debt is paid off.

bankruptcy
The ultimate way out of overindebtedness is bankruptcy. Federal bankruptcy laws offer several ways to obtain shelter from creditors. If you come to this ultimate move, you should seek the aid of an attorney. Bankruptcy is a last resort for solving overindebtedness problems and, whatever the reasons for declaring it, bankruptcy can remain on your credit history for as much as fourteen years. Many lenders will honestly attempt to rehabilitate a bankrupt family or individual, particularly if the reasons were beyond their control, but an ex-bankrupt can still

find it very difficult to obtain the kind of credit otherwise needed for a desired lifestyle. Indeed, bankruptcy often requires individuals to seriously reduce their lifestyle for an extended time.

shopping for credit

Two very important aspects of an individual financial program are gaining access to the *credit* you'll need for the various purposes you have in mind; and obtaining the *guidance* to help you use your credit wisely. Both of these important assets can be acquired through lending officers at your local financial institutions. It's worth the time involved to interview a number of these individuals to find one with whom you seem to be able to communicate openly and constructively. A loan officer can be an important ally in helping you achieve your financial goals, short term and long term. But a word of warning: loan officers are often transferred to other departments and one day you may find your friendly favorite helper no longer at the desk. It's always wise, therefore, to make an effort to know more than one loan officer so that there can be some continuity on a personal level between yourself and the institution.

The following list of basic suggestions can help you communicate better with your lender and make the best use of the credit available.

1. Do all of your shopping and homework beforehand. Whenever possible, know exactly what you're going to borrow for, how the money will be used, and what the total needs will be.

   Borrowers often ask a loan officer, "How much can I borrow to buy a new car?" or "How much can I borrow to buy a new house?" Unless the loan officer has a detailed familiarity with your individual credit history, it can be difficult to answer such questions.

   When you finally make your application, remember that the loan officer can serve you best when your specific needs are clearly stated. A loan application with question marks on it simply can not be processed as readily as a completed one.

2. Make sure all your other credit accounts are up to date before you apply for credit. If necessary, check with each creditor and with your local credit bureau. The Federal Fair Credit Reporting Act permits you to see your credit file (there may be a modest fee involved) and it's wise to review your file every few years to make certain it contains no erroneous

items. If there are errors, the law stipulates how they can be corrected. If you have credit accounts that are not up to date, it would be wise to update them before you make your application. A credit history showing late accounts may not kill your chances of getting a loan, but it could well cause delays and aggravation.

3. Get an idea of the rates charged by various lenders. This can be done quickly, discreetly, and, if you wish, anonymously. Be certain that any quotes you receive are expressed in terms of APR (Annual Percentage Rate) and determine what the total dollar charges are for interest and any other fees the lender may impose.

In comparing interest rates, remember that the interest rate isn't the only item you're shopping for. You might be able to obtain a more attractive interest rate if you make a larger down payment on the purchase in question, and you may have to inquire whether or not this is possible. You also might get a more attractive interest rate if you are a customer of the institution in other departments. Service and convenience must also be considered.

Should you finance directly through an institution or through a dealer that offers access to financing? Financing through the dealer can often be a time-saving convenience and rates may be comparable to those of local institutions. But it may be more important to have the personal contact directly with a local institution. The institution may be able to help you in a number of other ways, whereas the dealer-financed situation could place you in the hands of an out-of-town institution or a local institution where you're nothing more than a number on a computer. The personal relationship is important, and you may lose that with dealer financing.

4. Before you make your loan application, prepare a list of all your other debts, including the name of each creditor, purpose of the loan, original amount borrowed, current amount owed, and the monthly payment. This will make the loan officer's job much easier, and your application simpler to process. Divulge all pertinent credit information, even if you think it may not look good. The lender will probably discover it anyway, and if you haven't mentioned difficult accounts, they're liable to wonder why. Also, when you've compiled the list of all your debts and payments, double check that this new debt you're seeking can be properly taken care of within your current and future budget.

5. Inquire in advance if the lender has any specific requirements or taboos. Some lenders have strict requirements regarding the borrower's years on the job, period of residence in the community, and minimum down payment for specific purchases.

6. Be sure to tell the loan officer clearly and specifically just what the money is for. The more concise you are, the more the officer will be able to advise you if it appears you might be going overboard on a certain debt since loan officers listen to dozens of requests each day.

7. Make sure your requested time for loan repayment does not exceed the use period of whatever you're borrowing for. If you let the lender know you've considered this, it will demonstrate your prudence and could enhance your application and relationship with the lender.

8. Be prepared to discuss your budget in detail. The loan officer wants assurance that there will be money available to pay off the loan, and if he or she doesn't see room in your current budget for the repayment, your request might be declined—and perhaps wisely so. If you plan to trim other expenses to make room for this debt, or if you are anticipating a higher income in the future, discuss these factors with the loan officer.

9. Bring your spouse, if you have one, to complete the application and sign all the necessary papers. Granted, under the Federal Equal Credit Opportunity Laws it may no longer be necessary for both spouses to sign credit agreements. That may satisfy many people, but traditional prudence still dictates that debt is a family obligation—morally if not legally—and both partners should have a full and complete understanding of their involvements.

10. Don't be embarrassed to seek the loan officer's specific advice on related financial matters. It's part of the job and he or she might be able to discover and solve other money problems you aren't aware of.

11. Don't try to get a better interest rate by telling a loan officer that you can do better elsewhere. Chances are you'll be told to go ahead and do so. And, if you can do better elsewhere, you might as well. It doesn't hurt to ask if rates are flexible,

but petty bickering will very likely gain nothing and may well lose a potential ally—the loan officer.

12. Don't caution the loan officer not to check a certain credit reference. If there is a problem or a dispute with one of your other creditors, clear it up in advance. If you raise suspicions in the loan officer's mind, he or she will undoubtedly take steps to find out what it's all about.

13. Don't act as if you're doing the lender a favor by coming to him. And don't make it appear as if the lender is doing you one by making you a loan. This is a business deal and should be treated as such by both sides.

14. Don't be disturbed if the loan officer asks you to do your other business such as your savings or checking account, with his or her institution. This is part of the job. Very often, a loan applicant may be upset by such questions and this can destroy an otherwise good relationship. A simple "I'll be happy to consider it" should suffice if you don't want to change at the moment.

15. Don't fret if the loan officer starts "selling" life or health insurance for your loan. It's very common, and the cost is not unreasonable. If, after you understand their program, you still don't want it, merely decline politely. The loan officer should know that a "hard sell" is not becoming, nor is it liable to win friends or influence people.

16. Don't expect the loan officer to tell you if your intentions regarding your borrowing are wise. If you aren't sure of the wisdom of your loan, maybe you shouldn't be asking for it.

17. Don't be surprised, however, if the loan officer does volunteer to question your wisdom. You may be absolutely certain in your own mind, but you may have overlooked something. The loan officer is in the business of evaluating personal financial decisions, and his professional knowledge might enable him to correct or amplify your thinking. The officer might be able to suggest other alternatives, some of which might provide a better solution than the one you're seeking.

18. Don't wait until the last minute to apply for a loan. Anticipate your needs far enough in advance to take care of all the details. If other matters hinge on whether or not you get the loan, keep the other parties informed of your progress. Careful and thoughtful planning in this regard can avoid serious problems.

19. Don't demand an answer to your application within a certain time. You have a right to have your papers processed promptly, assuming that everything is in order. The lender will make every effort to do so. But delays, such as receiving an incomplete report from the credit bureau, can happen.

Often, too, an application may have to be considered by the loan committee. The loan officer isn't "passing the buck" when he or she refers an application to the loan committee. Your request may be for more than he has authority to approve, or he may just want to get other opinions on a puzzling point in the application. The committee can often be very helpful simply by giving the borrower the benefit of all its best collective thinking.

When you make your application, the officer should be able to give you a fairly good idea of how long it will take to process. Perhaps he can speed it up a bit for you if circumstances warrant. But if you give him a deadline—an "or else"—you might antagonize him.

20. Don't balk if the loan officer asks you for a co-maker or collateral to support a given loan request. He's trying to help you get your loan, but lending policies may require security. You may disagree, but rather than argue about it (which won't help matters), ask for an explanation.

There is often room for compromise. A request for collateral or a co-maker doesn't necessarily mean your credit isn't good. There just might not be enough of it—due to your age, job tenure, and so on. Remember—the loan officer doesn't have to ask you for the extra security. He or she can turn you down flat, but may not want to. It doesn't hurt to inquire if the request for collateral or a co-signer can be altered, so that the co-signer is only obliged for a part of the loan, or the loan is only partly collateralized.

The loan officer is there to help and advise you, but as part of the job must stick to certain patterns. Know those patterns. Be prepared. Make a good friend and build your credit and your personal financial structure on a firm foundation.

Minutes of a Loan Committee Meeting at the Citizens Bank of Anytown

CHAIRMAN OF THE LOAN COMMITTEE: "What's first on the agenda?"

LOAN OFFICER #1: "I've got a real stickler here. It's the Holloways. They've been excellent customers for over ten years; I've been taking care of them myself for the last five. They want to buy a $15,000 motor home and finance it for five years. They can only put $2000 down, and the loan, with the interest and other charges, is going to be hitting close to the $20,000 range."

CHAIRMAN: "That's a good loan for us. What's the problem?"

OFFICER #1: "I thing they're going over their heads and could be in some serious trouble. They've always had reasonable loan requests, and we've always met their requests without hesitation. They've been trading cars every two years and have been financing them with us on two year loans. Their payment record is perfect. Never late a day. They have their checking account with us and a substantial savings account. And I know for a fact that they've sent a lot of customers our way. We've had a

most satisfying relationship with them all along.

But about a year ago, Mr. Holloway got a nice promotion and a good raise, and I think it may have gone to his head. He came to see me about a new car loan. He had decided to buy a much more expensive car than he ever had in the past, and in order to keep the payments down, he financed it over a four year term. I was a little leery at the time, knowing of his regular two year trade cycle, but he assured me that he'd be keeping this car for at least four years and wouldn't have any problem. I made the loan hoping that he was right, but I'm still a little concerned about his first departure from that two year trade cycle he's been on so long.

"Now they come in wanting to finance this motor home. It's purely a luxury, and they know it. But he's sure that he can rent it out to friends and co-workers and take in enough to cover a large portion of the payments. I'm not so sure. We've seen in the past how those good plans go astray, particularly in fall and winter months

when nobody wants to be taking trips in the bad weather.

"They were rather upset when I told them that I would have to submit their request to the loan committee. As good as they've been with us, I'm really concerned that this loan could put them in financial jeopardy and us with it."

CHAIRMAN: "Their credit history is certainly excellent, his job seems secure, and he has otherwise been a valuable customer to us. There seem to be as many reasons to make the loan as to deny it."

OFFICER #1: "When I see trouble signs on the horizon, I feel it's only fair to analyze them thoroughly for the customer's benefit as well as for our own."

CHAIRMAN: "Can't you get him to make a bigger down payment or pledge his savings account as additional security?"

OFFICER #1: "I tried. The savings account is set aside for his kids' college tuition and he doesn't want to dip into it or tie it up in any way."

CHAIRMAN: "What about a cosigner?"

OFFICER #1: "I raised it with him and he was offended to think that we'd even ask him to come up with extra security for us."

CHAIRMAN. "I don't care. Un-

178

der the circumstances he's got to understand that it's a difficult request. What about the dealer? We could ask him to sign for all or a portion of the loan."

OFFICER #1: "The dealer's been calling me three times a day to see if the loan's been approved yet. He's as anxious as can be because he smells a nice profit in the deal. The dealer is sound, and he might well go along with it. But that's not really the question. The question, as I see it, is whether or not the loan should be made at all, even with a co-signer. You know what happens a lot of times with these luxury pur-

chases—after a year or so of playing with their new toy, the people get tired of it and end up selling it at a considerable loss. Then they remain saddled with a big chunk of debt for years to come."

CHAIRMAN: "Why don't you try to convince them to rent one of the blasted things for the summer, and if they really do like it and think they want to own one, then we can discuss the terms of financing with them. Maybe we can avoid the problem altogether."

OFFICER #1: "Good idea. Worth a try. But what if they refuse?"

CHAIRMAN: "If they refuse, tell them that we either have to

have a larger down payment or a co-signer before we can approve their request. If they want the thing badly enough, they'll just have to take some more of the risk on their own shoulders. We're not going to take the chance of his being able to rent it out to his friends, or of his deciding he doesn't like it after a year or so. I'd like to make the loan, but I think you're right in anticipating the troubles that may lie ahead. So that's how we'll do it. Is everybody in accord? Fine. What's next on the agenda?"

LOAN OFFICER #2: "I have a young couple that was caught in one of those 'easy credit' traps, and I'd like to help them if we possibly can. After I first interviewed them, I thought we had some flim-flam going on, but I did some further digging into the matter and came up with the horrible truth. I could make approval of the loan on my own, but I thought I should run it by you just so we all know what's happening.

"Here's their story: They were married about two years ago and made plans to move into a one bedroom apartment. They needed furniture, but they were strapped for cash and had no credit experience whatsoever. As the young wife puts it, they were too embarrassed to seek credit at a bank, because they had no track record. They ended

up at one of those furniture stores that has a big 'easy credit' sign over the front door. You know the kind—no down payment, easy terms, past history no problem! They bought about $1000 worth of furniture and appliances, and the dealer financed it directly for them. They claimed that they made all of their payments right on time, and paid off the loan just a few months ago on schedule.

"They're expecting a baby and they want to move into a better apartment and they need another $2000 to buy additional furniture and furnishings. Now they weren't embarrassed to come to a bank because they felt that they had a good credit history as a result of their loan with the furniture dealer. Aside from paying their rent and utilities, that furniture loan was their only credit history. They both work and have good salaries, and on the face of the application I'd have been willing to make the loan, taking the furniture as collateral, of course.

But then I checked their credit history and found absolutely no record of the loan with the furniture store. I even called the store directly, and was told that there had been no loan. My first reaction, of course, was that the young couple had lied to me

in order to finagle the $2000 loan from us. They came right in to see me about the problem, and were absolutely confused at what had happened. They brought with them their cancelled checks to show payments to the furniture dealer, every one of which was on the first of the month as promised. They also brought along a copy of the original loan agreement."

CHAIRMAN: "Don't tell me. I've heard this one before. You found out this store was trying to create captive customers. They know that this young couple won't be able to get credit anywhere else without an existing credit history, and they'll have to come back to that store to buy the goods they need and finance them. And I wouldn't be surprised if the financing terms are as exorbitant as the law will allow. Right?"

OFFICER #2: "That's right. They're not required to report such performance to the credit bureau, but as you say, in not doing so, they are depriving the borrowers of a credit history. If we turn down this young couple, I have no doubt that they'll go back to that same store, mad as they may be at them, in order to get the financing they're seeking."

CHAIRMAN: "Well, then, if everything else checks out all right, as it seems to, I see no

reason why we shouldn't make the loan."

OFFICER #2: "Just off the record for a moment, isn't there some way that we can generally educate the public—particularly these young people—about the availability of credit through banks so that they don't fall into these easy credit traps that can be so costly? The credit may be easy, but they always find out that the repaying is tough indeed. The interest rates are high and the collection procedures, if they become delinquent, can be harsh. It's a regular catch-22—you can't get credit until you've had some credit history, and you can't get a credit history until you've had some credit."

CHAIRMAN: "That's true to an extent, but not necessarily. If a young couple has a good work record—as you know, our bank requires at least one year's steady employment—and they're living within their means, we certainly can consider them as credit-worthy. Often it may take a co-signer to help a young couple get started. A lot of them are embarrassed to ask family or friends to co-sign, but they should remember that that's probably how their families and friends originally got started.

CHAIRMAN: "Now what else is on the agenda? If there's nothing else on the agenda, I'll call the meeting closed."

1. What company started the concept of the installment loan?

2. Explain who can borrow money at the prime rate.

3. A loan is set up as follows:

$1000 at 8% for 1 year
$1000 × .08 = $80 interest
$1000 borrowed + $80 interest
= $1080 ÷ 12 months = $90/month

   What interest calculation method is this?

4. What loans are not covered by the Truth in Lending law?

5. How much will the monthly payment be on a loan of $3000 for 3 years at an APR of 11.08%?

6. In borrowing money to buy a car, what factors should be considered in determining how long the loan should run?

7. Explain the difference between access to credit and the need for credit.

8. What is the last resort in getting out of debt?

1. Comparison shop the cost of credit to buy a new car. The amount of the loan is $4000. From each lender get the number of months, the monthly payment, and the APR. Try to compare an automobile dealer, a commercial bank, and a credit union or some other lender.

2. Go to two stores and compare the cost of credit for an appliance or furniture with a total cost of at least $300. You could also check the cost of borrowing that much money from your bank or credit union. Obtain the same information as in Case 1.

3. Joan and Tim Robertson have been saving money for a down payment on a house. They have accumulated $7000. They now want to borrow $3000 to buy a car. Joan says they are earning $5\frac{1}{4}$% on their savings, so it makes sense to withdraw the money rather than pay 12% on an auto loan, which would cut the interest cost in half. Tim says the money should stay in the savings account for the down payment. Discuss their options.

4. Two of your friends have been having financial difficulty. Their bills have been running up and they seem to have lost control of their budget. What suggestions could you make before they consider consolidating their debts?

chapter 6 **housing: an overview**

the dilemma

Where to live? House, apartment, condominium? Central city, suburban, or somewhere in between? How much of the available budget should be devoted to housing, at the possible expense of other needs or desires? Scrimp now for the sake of something better in the future, or spend now and not worry about the future?

There is no easy answer. Each individual or family must decide what will best suit their own specific needs and desires, based on careful consideration of a number of important factors. Broadly speaking, these factors are: financial, geographical, architectural, and personal.

financial factors

A house (or condominium) is the single largest purchase that most individuals will ever make and they have to generally live with it longer than most other purchases. A mortgage loan is the biggest debt most people will ever incur, and monthly payments (including utility costs and maintenance obligations) will represent a major portion of most budgets.

183

Home ownership, if desirable, will largely depend on the amount of down payment one has available. If the amount currently available is not adequate, it may be necessary to wait until a larger amount is accumulated. Or a compromise on the location or the type of housing may have to be made.

geographical factors

One cannot afford to overlook the expenses involved in getting to and from work, shopping, schools, and other places. The costs of owning and operating an automobile must definitely be taken into account in choosing a location for housing. A more costly dwelling that's more readily accessible to mass transit lines may prove in the long run to be less costly than the lower priced dwelling that necessitates the need for an automobile.

One must consider the convenience elements of a given housing location. How much time is one willing to spend in an automobile shopping, visiting, seeking entertainment, and, above all, commuting to work?

The condition of the general neighborhood must also be considered. Is it in a state of decline or likely to be so? Is it stable? Is it showing signs of improvement? These matters not only can affect your comfort and state of mind, but, particularly where ownership is concerned, they can have an important bearing on the future value of your house when you decide to sell. Two otherwise equal dwellings could have considerably different price tags because of the condition of the neighborhood. It might seem tempting to save money by choosing the dwelling that's in the declining neighborhood, but in the long run that might prove to have been an imprudent decision.

architectural factors

When making a housing decision you should consider the architectural aspects: design, layout, size, and physical condition of the premises. Design is largely a matter of taste, but communities generally dictate that certain designs command a higher price. All other elements of a given choice of dwellings being equal (layout, size, and physical condition), a choice of the more costly design can be a ticklish matter. Do the esthetics of the design offer a level of satisfaction that will be rewarding and that will continue into the foreseeable future? Does the more costly design add a measure of prestige to your status, which may be desirable? Or, on the other hand, is the design merely cosmetic, offering nothing more tangible than a diminished checking account?

Layout and size are very practical considerations that the individual or family must weigh in regard to specific needs, both current and future. Will the layout be comfortable and functional? Will the size be correct for the future as well as the present? If you have a family, will the dwelling accommodate added members should they occur; will the size be more than is needed in the future when children move out on their own?

The physical condition of the premises is one of the most important aspects to be considered in choosing a dwelling. Most of us can tell if walls need painting, or if doors and windows close properly, or if roof shingles are falling off. But the prudent dwelling shopper could find it valuable to invest in a professional service that can evaluate all of the physical aspects of the premises. In larger cities, there are firms that specialize in home inspection; in smaller cities, one might hire a building contractor who can render the service. The service should include a close examination of the structural elements of the building, the mechanical elements (plumbing, electrical wiring, built-in appliances), and the likely need for repair or replacement of any of the building's components. If one is renting, such extensive inspection may not be necessary. But a thorough check of the premises is still called for if one is to avoid aggravations and hassles with a landlord.

personal factors

Personal considerations must be balanced with all of the other above factors. Often, we can be subtly motivated into making a housing decision based not on what we ourselves prefer, but on what we think others might prefer for us—friends and family urging us to live in a particular area because that's the "in" area, and so on. We must suit our own life style rather than the whims of others.

Some people may be just plain apartment dwellers and nothing may ever change that. Others may abhor apartment living and would never be satisfied with one regardless of how much money they may save in the process. Some people may hate the thought of commuting long distances or of travelling on public transit. Others may find it to their liking.

Some people may have a green thumb and an urge to own their own "turf," and a house is the only thing that will satisfy them. Growing potted plants in an apartment just isn't the same for them.

Some people may prefer the privacy that a house offers, while an apartment or condominium may be desirable to those who feel more comfortable with other families close at hand.

If an individual or family hasn't yet settled into a fixed living pattern, an apartment may be more appropriate because of the flexibility it offers. When a lease is up, you can simply move on.

Some people enjoy the pleasures of their own dwelling— whether house, condominium, apartment—while others are constantly on the go, enjoying the other pleasures—skiing, hunting, fishing, travelling. The former might prefer to invest more of their funds in their housing because they'll make greater use of it. The latter might prefer more modest housing since a larger portion of their spendable dollars goes to outside pleasures.

The person with a knack for patching, painting, fixing up, and taking care of things might feel more comfortable in his or her own home, whereas the person with ten thumbs is likely to feel put upon if faced with taking care of the myriad items that need attention in a home. To such a person, the apartment or condominium might be preferable, particularly if the landlord or condominium developer is responsible for most of the maintenance on the premises.

Future personal plans must also be considered. Some may desire to live more modestly than they can otherwise afford, looking forward to bigger and better things in the future. Others, perhaps feeling that their future is secure, may prefer to spend to their upward limits for their current housing needs.

If one is to arrive at a decision best suited to current and future needs, as well as current and future budgets, all these factors must be taken into account.

Table 6-1 provides a checklist of the various factors that must be considered in making a decision on a dwelling.

types of housing

houses

Inflation—particularly rising labor costs and rising material costs—has pushed the price of the average new single family home skyward. Along with the sharply escalating costs of building a home come comparable expenses for financing it. Interest rates on mortgages, which had been in the 5 to 6% range through the 1950s and well into the 1960s, shot to upwards of 9% by the late 1970s. Higher prices and higher interest rates

187   **types of housing**

mean larger down payments and larger monthly payments, and a great many people found the house of their dreams priced out of their reach.

Although it is possible to rent a house, outright ownership is the more common means of acquiring this type of dwelling. The usual mode of purchasing involves a cash down payment that might represent as little as 5% of the purchase price, up to a more common range of 20 to 30%. The balance of the purchase price is paid over an extended period of time, frequently running as long as twenty to thirty years. The buyer's promise to repay the remaining balance is secured by signing an IOU commonly referred to as a mortgage. (In some states this is referred to as a "trust deed.")

The expenses of home ownership just begin with the mortgage payment; there are property taxes, property insurance, utilities, and maintenance.

property taxes   *Property taxes* (also called real estate taxes) provide the money that allows the municipality to operate. Owners of all kinds of property are required to pay these taxes, in return for which the municipality provides services. A portion of the property taxes may also be allocated to the county and state jurisdictions within which the city is located to enable them to provide their respective services.

How are property taxes calculated? The residents of each city, at least in theory, determine the amount and type of services they wish. In order to meet the expenses of these services, the city must generate income from taxation. The city officials determine what types of property will carry what share of the overall tax burden. The city, through its assessor's office, undergoes a program by which each property in the city is evaluated. Representatives of the assessor's office visit each property in the city periodically to determine the actual value of each parcel. When the current value of every property is known, the *assessment rate* is applied. For example, a given city may determine that residential property will be assessed at 20% of market value, while commercial property will be assessed at 25%, and industrial property at 30%. (Business and industrial areas frequently contribute a heavier share of tax dollars because they are using the property for income-producing purposes.) Thus, a house with a market value of $30,000 may be assessed at $6000. In theory, all properties of the same type with equal market values are assessed equally.

table 6-1 **checklist for evaluating a housing purchase**

	House	A	B	C

A. Location

   1. Condition of neighborhood:
      a. Declining
      b. Could decline
      c. Stable
      d. Could improve
      e. Improving

   2. Proximity, in miles, to:
      a. Work
      b. Schools
      c. Local convenience shopping
      d. Major shopping
      e. Public transit stops
      f. Church or synagogue
      g. Entertainment facilities
      h. Other (Close friends, family, etc.)

   3. Approximate miles driven per month to each of the above:
      a. Work
      b. Schools
      c. Local convenience shopping
      d. Major shopping
      e. Public transit stops
      f. Church or synagogue
      g. Entertainment facilities
      h. Other

   4. Transportation costs, per month:
      a. Automobile
      b. Car-pooling
      c. Public transit

B. Building Characteristics

   1. General Physical Condition:
      a. Foundation
      b. Exterior walls
      c. Interior walls
      d. Roof
      e. Plumbing
      f. Wiring
      g. Heating equipment
      h. Air conditioning equipment
      i. Landscaping

table 6-1 **continued**

	House	A	B	C
j.	Water heater	___	___	___
k.	Kitchen appliances (dishwasher, disposal, range, oven)	___	___	___
l.	Doors and windows (fitting and operation)	___	___	___
m.	Gutters and downspouts	___	___	___
n.	Driveway and walkways	___	___	___
o.	Porches, patios	___	___	___
p.	Cabinetry	___	___	___
q.	Furnishings included (carpeting, draperies, blinds, appliances)	___	___	___
r.	Insulation (attic, exterior walls)	___	___	___
s.	Storm windows and doors	___	___	___
t.	Basements	___	___	___
u.	Attic	___	___	___
v.	Garage or carport	___	___	___

2. Estimated expenses to refurbish to suit your needs:
   a. Painting (Exterior and interior)   ___ ___ ___
   b. Plastering   ___ ___ ___
   c. Wallpapering   ___ ___ ___
   d. Repair or replace appliances   ___ ___ ___
   e. Lawn and landscaping   ___ ___ ___
   f. Carpet, drapes, blinds   ___ ___ ___
   g. Insulation; other weather protection   ___ ___ ___
   h. Kitchen modernization (fixtures, cabinets)   ___ ___ ___
   i. Bathroom modernization (fixtures, cabinets)   ___ ___ ___
   j. Paving driveways, walkways   ___ ___ ___
   k. Repair or replace mechanicals (heating plant, water heater, air conditioning, etc.)   ___ ___ ___
   l. Structural (foundation, walls, roof)   ___ ___ ___

3. Size and Layout:
   a. Is it adequate for current needs?   ___ ___ ___
   b. Will it be adequate three years hence? Five years? Ten years?   ___ ___ ___
   c. Is room layout suitable?   ___ ___ ___
   d. If not, can layout be altered? At what cost?   ___ ___ ___

4. Design
   a. Compared with other houses of comparable size, condition, location and layout, are you paying extra for design?   ___ ___ ___
   b. How much?   ___ ___ ___
   c. Is it worth it?   ___ ___ ___

table 6-1 **continued**

	House	A	B	C

C. Terms of Purchase

1. Asking Price   ___ ___ ___

2. Price of comparable sales (houses or condominiums similar in size, location, condition and layout) in recent months. Real estate agent can help obtain this information.   ___ ___ ___

3. Price that you think it can realistically be purchased for.   ___ ___ ___

4. Down payment required by seller   ___ ___ ___

5. Down payment you have available   ___ ___ ___

6. Mortgage terms currently available in your community:
   a. Lender #1
     i. Down payment required   ___ ___ ___
     ii. Interest rate   ___ ___ ___
     iii. Number of years to run   ___ ___ ___
     iv. Other costs   ___ ___ ___
     v. Prepayment Penalty   ___ ___ ___
     vi. Other clauses (See section on financing)   ___ ___ ___
   b. Lender #2
     i. Down payment required   ___ ___ ___
     ii. Interest rate   ___ ___ ___
     iii. Number of years to run   ___ ___ ___
     iv. Other costs   ___ ___ ___
     v. Prepayment penalty   ___ ___ ___
     vi. Other clauses   ___ ___ ___
   c. Lender #3
     i. Down payment required   ___ ___ ___
     ii. Interest rate   ___ ___ ___
     iii. Number of years to run   ___ ___ ___
     iv. Other costs   ___ ___ ___
     v. Prepayment penalty   ___ ___ ___
     vi. Other clauses   ___ ___ ___

7. "Apples vs. Oranges": What extra features are included that aren't found in others?   ___ ___ ___

8. Date available for occupancy   ___ ___ ___

table 6-1 **continued**

	House	A	B	C

9. Can existing mortgage be assumed? If so, what are its terms (Interest rate, payments, years left to go) ___ ___ ___

D. Costs

  1. Acquisition expenses—cash at the time of closing
    a. Down payment ___ ___ ___
    b. Moving expenses ___ ___ ___
    c. Closing costs (legal, survey, appraisals, etc.) ___ ___ ___
    d. Mortgage expenses (legal, "points," recording fees and taxes, etc.) ___ ___ ___
    e. Repair and renovation ___ ___ ___
    f. New furnishings, appliances ___ ___ ___

  2. *Monthly* operating costs, including items in D 1 above not paid in cash at time of closing, but included in total mortgage, or otherwise financed over a period of time.
    a. Moving expenses (related to moving in) ___ ___ ___
    b. Mortgage expenses   " " " " ___ ___ ___
    c. Repair and renovation   " " " " ___ ___ ___
    d. New furnishings, appliance   " " " ___ ___ ___
    e. Mortgage payment (interest and principal) ___ ___ ___
    f. Property taxes ___ ___ ___
    g. Property insurance ___ ___ ___
    h. Estimated utility bills ___ ___ ___
    i. Lawn and yard care ___ ___ ___
    j. Common area usage fees (such as in condominiums) ___ ___ ___
    k. Maintenance fees, re: Condos, co-ops ___ ___ ___
    l. General building maintenance ___ ___ ___
    m. Ongoing renovation costs (beyond any such costs incurred at time of move-in). ___ ___ ___
    n. Reserve for replacement of appliances, furnishings, mechanical elements (heater, water heater, etc.) ___ ___ ___
    o. Reserve against major future repairs (roof, etc.) ___ ___ ___
    p. Transportation costs (From A 4, above) ___ ___ ___

Once the assessment rates are established, the city officials look at the outgo side of their budget and determine how much money is needed on the income side. They then determine the *tax rate*. Based on their budgetary needs, they may determine that the tax rate for a given year will be $100 for each $1000 of assessed valuation. Thus, the house with the $30,000 current value, which has an assessment of $6000 (20% of the current market value according to the formula) will pay taxes of $600 for the year.

The tax *rate* is adjusted annually to keep the city's income and expenses as close to equal as possible. Periodically, depending on local law and custom, all properties in the city, or a selection of properties in the city, may be reassessed to make sure that they are in line with the prevailing assessment program.

Commonly, home owners are billed for their property taxes in two installments six months apart. If the home owner has a mortgage escrow account, the tax bills will be sent to the mortgage lender who will then pay the taxes. They will be paid out of this account to which the owner has made added payments each month in addition to interest and principal.

property insurance   A necessary expense for every home owner is property insurance, usually referred to as a "homeowners policy." The basic coverage protects the owner in the event the property is damaged by fire or other stated causes. In addition, personal property within the premises can be covered for damage and certain kinds of loss or theft. The cost of this insurance—the premiums—may be paid directly by the owner to the insurance company, or, as with property taxes, may be added to the monthly mortgage payment, where it is held by the lender who pays the bill directly to the insurance company when it falls due.

utilities   The owner of a house will make arrangements with the local utility companies for them to provide gas, electricity, and telephone service. The individual owner will be responsible for paying for the utilities used. Utility bills, particularly for heating, can vary considerably throughout the seasons. Some utility companies offer budget payment programs in which the estimated annual total cost is broken down into relatively even payments, allowing the home owner to maintain a program less disruptive to other budget elements.

maintenance and repairs   Human nature being what it is, we often don't get around to doing preventive maintenance for a house—such as seasonal lubrication and servicing of a heating plant—until we hear the creaks and rattles, and one thing or another is about to self-destruct. Unexpected maintenance costs can be a severe jolt to any budget.

To the home owner, a periodic inspection is an inexpensive insurance policy, alerting you to potential dangers and expenses. In addition to paying for current ongoing maintenance costs, the wise homeowner will set aside a reserve for replacements—a fund that will allow him or her to take care of these costs without having to interfere with borrowing lines, savings account, or ongoing regular budget.

apartments   Apartments are individual dwelling units within a larger building complex—either high-rise or garden-type—that are rented by the occupants for a stated period of time. Typically, the owner of the building (the landlord) and the occupant (the tenant) will enter into an agreement called a lease that will set forth the rights and obligations of both parties. The lease will normally specify the amount of rent payable by the tenant, the length of time the tenant has the right to occupy the apartment, and any renewal rights that the tenant may have. The lease will also stipulate who pays for utility costs, and what the landlord's rights are if the tenant fails to pay what is legally obligated.

The landlord, as the owner of property, will be responsible for paying property taxes, property insurance premiums, utility costs, and maintenance expenses on the building. Indirectly, therefore, the tenant is paying a share of property taxes and insurance; part of the rent goes to meet those expenses, which the landlord is obliged to pay directly.

The tenant has no ownership rights in the dwelling, and is responsible to the landlord in accordance with the terms of the lease.

Not all tenants have a written lease. Many people occupy dwellings on a "month-to-month" basis, without the benefit of any written documents. This, in effect, is a one month lease, which allows the landlord to alter the terms by giving one month's notice, and allows the tenant to vacate by giving one month's notice. Laws may differ from state to state on precisely what the rights of the parties are on a month-to-month lease. Generally, a landlord wishing to raise rents or a tenant wishing to move out must give at least 30 days notice from the start of any month of their respective intentions to do so. For example, if a tenant wishes to vacate on March 1, he or she should give proper notice to the landlord not later than the preceding February 1. If this is done, the rental obligation will cease after February, as will the right to occupy the apartment. If, though, notice isn't given until, say, February 10, the landlord might technically be able to hold the person on as a tenant, and expect the rental due for the month of March.

In an apartment dwelling, the tenant is customarily responsible for care and upkeep of the individual unit, and the landlord is responsible for the care and upkeep of common areas.

In leasing apartments, a landlord may require one or two months rent payment in advance before the tenant takes occupancy. The purpose is to assure the landlord that at least some monies will be available should the tenant vacate the lease before the elapsed time, and to provide some cash in hand should the landlord have to undertake repairs caused by the tenant's negligence. If a tenant does vacate prior to the end of the lease, or if a tenant does cause damage to the property, the amount of the rental deposit will not be the total limit of his or her liability. The tenant may still be liable for additional amounts owed over and above the rental deposit, and the landlord can take legal action to collect those amounts.

condominiums and cooperatives

Condominiums and cooperatives are a relatively new form of dwelling ownership. They are somewhat similar, and are often confused, but their differences should be well understood. Both refer to multiple housing complexes, and in each case an individual resident has a form of ownership. In a *cooperative*, each resident owns what's called an undivided percentage of the total building. In a condominium, the resident owns only his or her own specific dwelling unit.

Here's how they both work. Picture what you would call an apartment house, five stories high, with four apartments on each floor. All of the apartments are of equal size and value. On a cooperative basis, each of the twenty residents would own an undivided one-twentieth of the total building. In effect, it's like twenty partners owning the whole project, each having an equal vote. The cooperative owners enter into an agreement that sets forth what type of vote is necessary to take various actions. For example, it may require a simple majority vote—

eleven out of the twenty—to commit the group to improvements or repairs of a certain value. It might take a three-quarters vote, or 15 out of the 20, to commit all of the members to major expenses. And it may take a unanimous vote to reach an agreement to sell the project. Each cooperative group determines its own rules and regulations.

Each member, or family, that belongs to the cooperative will have an individual lease agreement with the cooperative for the premises they occupy. If not an actual lease, there will be some form of agreement in the cooperative documents permiting a particular member of the cooperative to occupy a particular apartment within the building. This master agreement among all the cooperative members will also spell out such matters as the right to sublease one's apartment to nonmembers of the cooperative; the right to sell one's interest in the cooperative to outsiders; the rights of members to sell, gift, or bequeath interest in the cooperative to members or nonmembers of their family. Not unlikely, any members of the cooperative who wish to dispose of their interest in one way or another may first be required to offer it back to the other members of the cooperative, perhaps at a pre-agreed-on price, or based on a pre-agreed-on formula for setting a price.

The business affairs of the cooperative may be run by a volunteer member of the group, or by a hired professional, depending on the size and complexity of the building management. The cooperative as principal owner, and its members indirectly, will be responsible for all of the building occupancy costs, including property taxes, property insurance, utilities, and maintenance. In all likelihood, the cooperative will have borrowed money—a mortgage—to make the property purchase (or construction) in the first place. Each of the individual members will have signed on the mortgage to individually insure payment.

In a *condominium* each of the twenty occupants, individuals or families, will own their own separate and distinct unit. As in a cooperative, all of the individual owners will enter into agreement with all of the others regarding basic management of the property, maintenance of the common areas, and rights of the individual owners to sublease and sell to parties of their own choosing. Each owner will be responsible for individual property taxes and property insurance, and, as with a cooperative, will be additionally responsible for taxes and insurance as they apply to the common areas of the building.

Condominiums and cooperatives can come into being in one of two ways: An existing building can be converted into condominium or cooperative ownership, or a new structure may be developed and sold to occupants on a condominium or cooperative basis. In the former case, the owner of an existing apartment house will negotiate with the tenants for them to "buy" their apartments either jointly (cooperatively) or individually (as condominium owners).

In the latter case, a developer will begin construction of a building and instead of renting each individual unit to tenants, will sell each individual unit to the owners. This is particularly common with condominiums, and is not without problems. As a new condominium project is being developed, there is a dual form of ownership. The developer owns all of the unsold units, and each buyer owns his or her separate unit. As each occupant buys into a new condominium development, he or she will sign a contract with the developer that sets forth the rights of the developer and of the individual owners until such time as an agreed on percentage of all units are sold, at which time the condominium owners association will take over the developer's position to determine management and occupancy policies. But the developer, to protect his own interests, will likely reserve many rights to himself that would otherwise not be reserved to the association.

For example, the owner may reserve the right to rent units that have not yet been sold, at whatever price the owner deems fit. He would do so, obviously, to create income while waiting for the units to be sold. This could create a serious conflict, for part of the building consists of owner-occupied units and part of the building consists of rental units, which tend to be more transient. The owners may resent the tenants, particularly if the tenants are paying a considerably lower sum for the privilege of occupancy than the owners. But if the developer's lawyer has drawn a tight contract, the individual unit owners will have very little they can say or do about the situation.

A number of other serious problems can occur in new condominium developments. Many of these problems have occurred in such abundance in various parts of the country that state laws have been created to control the advertising and sales of condominiums.

• The developer may reserve ownership of the recreational facilities, for which he charges a use fee to the occupants.

Unless the contract states otherwise, the developer may reserve the right to increase those fees to whatever level he sees fit. Thus, what may have been represented in the sales brochure as a fixed monthly expense can increase considerably shortly after an individual owner takes occupancy.

- The developer may scrimp on construction, knowing that once each individual unit is sold it will be up to the individual owner to take care of individual maintenance of the unit. If he was to remain a landlord, and therefore responsible for ongoing maintenance, he more likely would use better quality materials and labor in the construction process. But since he is going to walk away from it as soon as the condominium contract is signed, he may try to save money on construction and let the owners worry about taking care of the problems that will inevitably arise.

- An owner may complete and sell a portion of a project and then run into financial difficulty. If things get bad enough, and the developer defaults, the construction lenders might find themselves with the project in their hands, and the individual owners who have already bought units may find themselves having to pay off such loans, as well as taxes and insurance for the entire project, including those units that have yet to be sold.

In a house, owners are free to do as they please as long as they don't break any laws or create any nuisances. They can sell when they like, to whom they like, at the price the market will bear. But in condominiums and cooperatives many of the rights of the owners are subject to their contract with the condominium or cooperative association, and also possibly with the original developer who has retained certain rights in the complex. Owners may be required to offer their units back to the association before they can sell them on the open market, and their rights to sublease may be severely limited. Although many have regarded condominiums as the best of both worlds—the convenience of apartment living with the advantages of home ownership—these contractual agreements often prove that this is not the case.

mobile homes

A generation ago, mobile homes had a poor image. The parks were often sloppily kept by the managers, banks were reluctant to lend money on mobile home purchases, and the units themselves were often subject to severe depreciation over the years. Today, however, mobile homes have a vastly new and better image. Many parks are well located, efficiently laid out, handsomely landscaped, and comparable in many respects to permanent home subdivisions. Lenders have opened the door to mobile home financing, and builders are constantly improving their construction techniques.

Mass production construction methods allow manufacturers to offer a mobile home buyer a better value in terms of square footage than a buyer of a permanent home of equal size may be able to obtain. Further, mass purchasing of furniture and appliances allows dealers to offer fully furnished units at very attractive prices.

A mobile home dwelling customarily involves a combination of ownership and rental. The unit itself is purchased from a dealer, and is often financed on a long-term installment loan basis. Such financing can be more costly than conventional mortgage financing, but the conventional long-term mortgages aren't that frequently available for mobile home purchases. The unit is then shipped to the owner's destination, usually at the owner's expense, where it is moored on its pad and hooked up to the available water, gas, and electricity. The owner pays a rental for the pad to the park management and is responsible for individual insurance and utility costs. In some instances, of course, a mobile home purchaser may have the unit installed on property which he or she already owns, and thus avoid the rental fee.

Though mobile homes may really not be as mobile as they were a generation ago, an owner does have some limited degree of flexibility in moving the dwelling from one site to another. The farther the distance, the higher the cost, so long-range moves may not be feasible. If there's a slight possibility that a mobile home may be moved to a different location, the would-be buyer must understand explicitly what costs he or she may be confronting. Such costs may offset the initial lower price of the mobile home when compared with a permanent home.

Because mobile homes are not of the same permanent construction as regular houses, an owner must be alert to the possibility of a depreciation in value, compared with the more customary increase in value that permanent homes enjoy. In shopping for a new mobile home, one should compare the prices of similar *used* mobile homes to get an idea about the likely future value of the current purchase. In making a final decision, this depreciation should be carefully evaluated.

**multiple units,
townhouses, and
rowhouses**

Other forms of dwellings are represented by multiple-unit build-ings and townhouses (or, as they're called in some parts of the country, rowhouses). The multiple-unit housing is most com-monly the *duplex*, where two dwelling units occupy the same building, either side by side, or one above the other. Some structures may even house three units (a *triplex*) or four dwelling units (a *fourplex*). Beyond four, the buildings would more normally be referred to as apartment houses, although there is no precise legal definition of an apartment house. One may buy a duplex, or a triplex, or a fourplex with the intention of living in one of the units and renting out the others. This can prove to be an attractive situation if the style of living is suitable to you, for the rental income can offset your own dwelling costs, and even provide some attractive tax shelter. (A more detailed discussion of the tax-shelter benefits of rental real estate is provided in Chapter 13.) It's also possible for the occupants of a multiple housing complex to own their units on a condominium basis, or as a cooperative.

Townhouses, or *rowhouses*, are a series of connected dwell-ing units sharing common walls. These walls allow economy in construction, and the higher density of units on a given piece of property can also result in cost efficiencies. Townhouses, which may be owned individually, as a condominium or a coopera-tive, or which may be rented, offer a combination of house and apartment living that is attractive to many. They can provide more space than an apartment, at a lower price than a compar-ably sized single family home. If the walls between the adjoin-ing units are well insulated, a homelike privacy can be main-tained.

**certain laws
regarding housing**

There are a number of laws that can affect the rights and obligations of both property owners and tenants. These laws will differ from state to state and from city to city, and you should make inquiry in your own locality as to any laws that might affect you.

zoning

Cities commonly reserve the right to specify that certain areas may only have certain kinds of uses permitted on them. The city map will be divided into zones according to the uses allowed in those zones. The broad categories in zoning regulations are residential, commercial, industrial, and agricultural. Within each category there may be subcategories. For example, within a residential category there may be zones for single family housing only and zones in which multiple housing is permitted. Each specific zone may carry within it certain regulations applicable to that zone. In a commercial zone, for example, there may be a requirement that so many off-street parking places are available for each thousand square feet of building space.

Generally, zoning regulations are like a pyramid: higher uses are permitted in any of the lower use zones, but lower use zones may not be permitted in the zones above them (Figure 6-1). For example, the highest zone is usually single family housing. Single family housing can often be erected in any of the lower zones, down through commercial and into industrial, if an owner chooses to do so. But a lower use, such as industrial, is usually not permitted in any but its own specific zone.

Zoning ordinances may be changed from time to time as the city officials deem proper. You may be living in a single family zone that is adjoined by an agricultural zone. Farmer Jones, who occupies a large section of the agricultural zone, is approached by a residential home builder to sell the land to him. At the same time, he's approached by a commercial shopping center developer who also wishes to buy the land. The homebuilder and the shopping center developer would both have to seek a change in the zoning from agricultural use to either residential or commercial use. You, as a resident in the adjoining single family zone, could have a considerable stake in the outcome of this struggle. Conceivably, the development of an

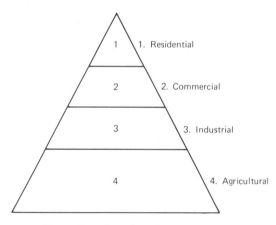

Figure 6-1 Pyramidal Zoning Structure.

attractive housing subdivision could enhance the value of your property while a shabby development could cause a decrease in value. Similarly, a high quality shopping center development could be to your advantage, whereas a low quality shopping center could be unattractive to you and your property value.

Residents of any municipality should make themselves aware of current zoning regulations and be on the alert for the possibility of any change in the immediate vicinity that could affect the value of their residence. Zoning hearings are usually open to the public, and customarily there are appeals that can be taken from unfavorable zoning rulings. If many people are affected by the possibility of a zoning ordinance change, they can group together and hire an attorney to represent all of their joint interests.

nuisances

Your next-door neighbor keeps a rooster that crows at dawn each morning, or plays a stereo at high volume each night into the wee hours, or starts running a massage parlor on the premises, or burns strange or noxious chemicals at odd hours, or permits dangerous conditions to exist. These items, and scores of others like them, fall into the general category known as nuisances. If you're located in a multi-unit building, such as an apartment house or a condominium, you may be able to get some assistance from a sympathetic landlord or from the condominium owner's association. If you're a home owner, you may have to resort to the local police, or to your own attorney, to get some satisfaction. Nuisance laws exist in most every city, but enforcing them can involve feats of diplomacy that the local magistrates may be incapable of carrying out to your satisfaction. Some nuisances will fall under the jurisdiction of other laws. For example, opening a business in premises where businesses are not permitted could be in violation of zoning laws. Matters relating to health and safety could fall under the multiple housing unit laws or health and safety codes of the city. If a nuisance exists within your immediate vicinity, it might be better for you to explore the possibility that laws other than nuisance laws control the situation.

eminent domain

The law of Eminent Domain permits a local government—perhaps city, county, or state—to acquire private property where they can prove that the need exists for the public welfare. The process is generally known as "condemnation," and it occurs where new highways and bridges are to be constructed, where urban renewal programs take place, and where other public uses are called for. Owners of property threatened by condemnation are entitled to fair payment for their property. Procedures vary as to how property owners are compensated. Often there will be a hearing at which property owners present their claims for fair compensation. If an owner isn't satisfied with the offer, he or she may appeal, and if the appeal does not satisfy, the person may take the matter into the courts. The aid of a lawyer and competent real estate appraiser is necessary in any condemnation situation.

The law of Eminent Domain can also affect your property indirectly, without actually taking any portion of it. For example, a new highway nearby may create noise and pollution problems for your house. None of your property has actually been taken, but the value of the property may suffer as a result. You may be entitled to some claim for damages as a result.

Anyone who is either buying or already owns property, whether residential, commercial, or industrial, should be aware of any possible eminent domain that could take place within proximity of your property. Knowledge of an impending condemnation might discourage you from buying certain property, and that knowledge can also permit you to take early action to best protect your interests if a condemnation threatens currently owned property.

liability

As an owner or tenant of property, you can be responsible to others if they are harmed as a result of your negligence in maintaining the property. To protect yourself against claims for injuries by such persons, you obtain a public liability insurance policy. The law does not require you to maintain such insurance, as it does in most states regarding automobiles. But the law will require you to pay damages should a court find that you in fact were responsible. The matter is a bit more complicated for apartment tenants and condominium owners than it is for single family house owners or tenants because a person may be injured in the common premises, not simply in your own unit. That will not necessarily prevent the injured party from suing both the landlord (or condominium owners' association) as well as yourself, assuming that the injured party was your guest on the premises. In such situations the resident of a multiple unit dwelling should see to it that either the landlord or the condominium owners' association has adequate public liability insurance to protect all interested parties in the event of a claim for damage.

As noted earlier, each property owner is required to pay property taxes based on the city's evaluation of the property, and in conjunction with the tax rates set forth by the city, which can change from time to time. Tenants are also indirectly paying a share of the tax because a portion of their rent is applied by the landlord to his tax bill on the property. If a property owner defaults in the payment of taxes, the property can eventually be sold at auction to satisfy the unpaid taxes due.

Local laws also provide measures by which property owners can protest the assessment on their property and, if successful, reduce the assessment and thereby the taxes.

Tenants, who have an indirect stake in the taxation on the property they occupy, can also take steps to have the assessment reduced. They can act as a group, in conjunction with the landlord, in the same way that individual property owners can.

Although it is the express object of each local assessor's office to value equal properties equally, errors and inequities occur. (Equal properties are those comparable in size, date and quality of construction, and location.) If an inequity exists concerning property that you own or occupy, nobody will take steps to correct that inequity other than you. Because an improper assessment can mean hundreds of dollars lost each year, year in and year out, it behooves any property owner or tenant to examine the assessment roles every few years to determine that the property is in fact being properly assessed.

The steps are relatively simple, and in many communities do not require the assistance of an attorney unless and until you have proceeded through the normal appeal systems and find it necessary to go to the courts. Visit your local assessor's office and with their assistance locate your property on the assessment roles. Usually it's listed by a code number, and also may be listed by the name of the owner and the street address. Compare as best you can the assessment on your property with comparable properties in the immediate adjoining area. If the assessment on your property seems to be higher than that of your neighbors, you might well have a chance of getting your assessment reduced.

You might want to confer with a real estate agency in your area. They can assist you in determining the value of actual sales in the immediate neighborhood during the past year or two. Actual sales of property are usually a good indication of the true market value of the property, but often sales will be made on a forced basis, or other circumstances might dictate that the sale does not in fact reflect the true market value. If you can determine these factors, you'll be in a better position to evaluate what your true assessment should be.

renting versus owning—pros and cons

In addition to choosing the type of dwelling one wishes to live in, one must also consider the manner of occupancy: as owner or tenant. Indeed, houses can be rented as well as owned, and apartments—condominiums and cooperatives—can be owned as well as rented. Let's examine the pros and cons of renting versus owning.

flexibility

One of the primary advantages of renting—whether it's a house or an apartment—is the flexibility available. When a lease expires, the tenant is free to move on (or renew, assuming he or she and the landlord agree on renewal terms). There's no need to worry about selling, and no danger getting caught with making payments on two dwellings, such as where sale is not completed by a home owner prior to the time of moving out. The flexibility is even greater where furnished units are rented, for the chores of physically moving are considerably minimized. Largely for this reason, renting is often preferable for younger persons who have not yet settled into their chosen lifestyle or career, and who may not yet know what ultimate size their family will be. The same is true for older persons at or near retirement who may wish to be able to come and go as they please without the concerns of ownership.

money tied up

With very rare exceptions, ownership requires a substantial sum of money to be tied up in the property. When one buys a house or condominium, it's necessary to make a substantial down payment. Further, as you make your monthly mortgage payments, a portion of which goes to reduce your mortgage debt, those additional sums are effectively tied up in the property. Money that's tied up in property ownership is money you do not have direct access to, and it's money that could otherwise be earning income for you if it were invested. Until you sell or refinance the property—either of which could be time consuming and costly—you cannot get at your money. In a rental situation, there's no need to tie up any large sums of money. A rental deposit, usually not in excess of two months rent, will frequently be called for, but this is not a large enough sum so as to create any noticeable disadvantage.

income tax implications

Ownership conveys certain income tax advantages that are not duplicated in a rental situation. Tax laws state that interest paid on your mortgage and property taxes paid on your property are deductible items on your income tax return. This can mean a substantial savings of income tax dollars. For example, if a family is in the 25% tax bracket (taxable income of roughly $15,000 per year and filing a joint return), every dollar's worth of interest and property taxes that they pay will result in a savings of 25¢ in their income tax obligation. If, say, their total interest and real estate taxes for the year run to $2000, that $2000 worth of deductions will diminish their tax bill to the federal government by $500. (In order to take advantage of these deductions the taxpayer must file form 1040, not the short form 1040A.)

These tax advantages have often been the deciding factor for many families to purchase a home rather than to rent. But a closer look at this situation reveals that in many cases the advantages may not necessarily be as attractive as they seem. Let's look at one case.

A couple contemplates buying a house that will have a mortgage of $20,000 with an interest rate of 9% per year. During the first year of their mortgage, their total interest cost will be roughly $1800, diminishing slightly in subsequent years. Their real estate taxes are estimated at $400, probably increasing slightly in subsequent years. Their alternative is to rent an apartment that will, all costs considered, be $50 per month cheaper than the house purchase. However, because of the deductibility of the interest and real estate taxes, totalling $2200, they feel that arithmetic favors the house purchase.

Does it? Not really. If money alone is their only concern, some sharp pencilling will reveal that they may be making a mistake. Let's assume that their adjusted gross income is approximately $15,000 and that in addition to the interest and property taxes they have another $400 worth of eligible deductions. In their income bracket the standard deduction would be 16% of their adjusted gross income, or $2400. They can take this standard deduction *without* itemizing. If they were to itemize, their deductions would total $2600. Thus, by itemizing, they are gaining only $200 more in deductions than they would have if they took the standard deduction. This extra $200 worth of deductions will reduce their taxes by $50 per year. That would hardly offset the extra $50 per *month* that they're obliging themselves to pay by purchasing the house instead of renting the apartment.

When analyzing the specific financial advantages in renting versus owning, this income tax factor should be carefully calculated regarding any individual or family income tax situation. Obviously, the more costly the house and the higher the other eligible deductions, the more favorable these tax advantages will be to the owner. But it's not an automatic bonanza. Many years ago, when the standard deduction was much smaller than it is today, the advantage was much more obvious. But in recent years, the standard deduction has grown to such a relatively high percentage of income that careful arithmetic is necessary before final decisions are made.

In a rental situation, the tenant does not get any of these income tax advantages. Even though a portion of the tenant's rent may go to pay the landlord's property taxes and mortgage interest, the tenant gets no direct benefit. The landlord does get those advantages, and presumably may pass them along to the tenants in the form of slightly lower rentals. But that's too thin a presumption to bank on, and the tenant would be better off simply assuming that he or she has no tangible tax advantages as a result of renting.

chance of profit

One of the attractions in ownership is the chance that one may profit on a later resale. The tenant, of course, has no such chance for profit, but he or she also faces no risk of loss.

Indeed, the lure of profit often bears fruit. But profit is often the direct result of inflation, and although you may profit on the sale of your existing home, you'll soon realize that you have to live somewhere else, and the cost of acquiring new housing will have likely risen in step with the price of your old housing. Thus, your profit can be easily absorbed by the simple change from one dwelling to another.

Profit can also be reduced by two other factors: real estate commissions and income taxes. In all likelihood you will have used a real estate agent to help you sell your house, and a commission of 6 or 7% of the selling price goes to the agent. Further, if you sell your house at a profit, that profit is subject to federal income taxes. (If you sell your house at a loss, that loss is not deductible on your income tax return.)

You can delay the payment of the income taxes on the profitable sale of your house if you reinvest the proceeds in another principal residence of equal or greater value within the eighteen-month time limit set by the Internal Revenue Service. This delay can be virtually indefinite until you sell the subsequent house or houses and do not reinvest in another principal residence. If that time is delayed until after you've turned 65, it's possible that all or a portion of the taxes due can be avoided altogether. But, if you sell your house and move into an apartment, you will not be able to delay the payment of the taxes on the profit.

fixed overhead

Neither owning nor renting can assure you of a fixed overhead, unless there's a complete reversal of the inflationary trend that we've been living with for the past decade. During the term of a lease, a renter will be able to enjoy a period of fixed overhead, particularly if the landlord is responsible for the payment of utilities and repairs. But it should be assumed that on renewal of a given lease, the rental will be increased to compensate for the increased overhead that the landlord has had to absorb with respect to higher property taxes, insurance, maintenance, utility costs, and so on.

In ownership, the major expense—monthly mortgage payments—will remain fixed throughout the life of the mortgage. But other expenses can be assumed to be on the rise: property taxes, property insurance, maintenance, repairs, utilities, and so on. If a trend that began in the late 1970s continues, even the mortgage payments for forthcoming new homes may not be fixed. That trend is toward the "variable rate mortgage," which dictates that the interest rate on the mortgage can fluctuate up and down within a fixed range depending on overall interest rates throughout the nation.

hedging against inflation

The renter has virtually no protection against inflation. On each lease renewal rents will increase as the overall cost of living increases. The owner can enjoy more protection against inflation because interest and principal payments remain fixed. Owners also may enjoy an appreciation on the value of their houses over the long term, but the substantial profit envisioned could be somewhat eroded by the necessity of paying real estate commission costs and an income tax on any profit realized if the proceeds of a sale are not reinvested in another principal residence within the required time. Some protection, no doubt, is better than none at all.

building equity

"Why rent and collect worthless rent receipts when we can own and be building a hefty equity in our home?" Fact or myth? Although it's true that rent receipts have no tangible value, the other side of the question can be misleading. The average stay in a dwelling by a typical American family is from seven to ten years, and during those early years of the common 30 year mortgage, the amount of actual equity actually built up is very small indeed.

Equity is that portion of your mortgage payment that goes to reduce your debt. The rest of the payment is interest. Theoretically, when you later sell your property, you recapture the equity that you paid in.

The later chapter on financing discusses in more detail how interest is figured on mortgages. For the moment, note that during the first seven years of a 9% 30 year mortgage, the amount of equity that is accumulated is only about 6.4% of the total original mortgage.

For example, during the first seven years of a $30,000 mortgage that is set to run for 30 years at a 9% interest rate, that portion of your mortgage payments allocated to reducing the debt totals 6.4% of the total original mortgage, or $1920. In other words, after seven years of making payments on such a mortgage, you will have reduced your mortgage indebtedness from $30,000 to $28,080. The amount of equity you've built up during that seven year period probably is about the same as the real estate commission you'd pay if you sold the house at that time. In reality, it's not until the later years of a long-term mortgage that the equity really builds in any substantial degree.

repairs and alterations

If you're a tenant, the cost of certain repairs may be borne by the landlord, depending on the terms of the lease. If you're an owner, you'll usually have to bear most of these costs yourself, except in certain condominium or cooperative situations. As a tenant, you're probably limited in the amount of alterations and modifications you can make to the premises. Again, the lease will control. Unless you're willing, on terminating your lease, to correct any personal modifications that you might have installed, you will be very limited in what you can do in a rental unit. As an owner, you're free to do as you please—paint the walls purple and pink if you like—as long as you're aware of the implications of such modifications when it comes time to sell the house or condominium. You run the risk of overpersonalizing your premises and scaring away would-be buyers. You can also run the risk of overimproving the premises and thus pricing the dwelling out of the market for comparable units within that neighborhood. But bearing those factors in mind, the freedom of modifying your dwelling is vastly greater in an ownership situation than in a rental one.

to buy or
not to buy—
a case history

Let's now examine a situation in which a family is debating between buying and renting. We won't take into account personal preferences, because that's an individual item with each individual. Nor will we consider the potential for profit on the resale of a house, for that also is an imponderable. The example does not presume to answer the dilemma. It's merely intended to serve as a guide, a framework, to help you arrive at a clear view of the alternatives that you may be confronted with.

The Browns are a family of four. They have an adjusted gross income of $16,000. Each year, on average, they accumulate $2000 worth of tax-deductible expenses not related to housing. (All references to income taxes are for the federal taxes, and do not include state or local income taxes.)

They are comparing a property that they can buy for $30,000 with another one that they can rent for $350 per month.

They have $10,000 in cash that they can use as a down payment if they purchase. The property they have in mind has an existing $20,000 mortgage, with an annual interest rate of 7½%. Monthly payments on interest and principal total $140. Property taxes are $100 per month, property insurance is $25 per month, and utilities and maintenance total $85 per month. Thus, their total monthly cash outlay would be $350.

The monthly rental in the rental unit would be $350, which would include all utilities and maintenance.

During the first year of occupancy in the owned dwelling, the Browns will pay a total of roughly $1500 in interest on their mortgage. (This amount will decrease slightly during successive years.) That $1500 worth of interest payment is tax deductible. In addition, they'll pay $1200 in real estate taxes, also deductible. For ease in figuring, let's assume that as the annual interest cost decreases, the real estate taxes will go up by an equal amount, keeping their annual total deduction at around $2700.

Now we subtract their housing related deductions of $2700 and their nonhousing related deductions of $2000 (totalling

$4700) from their adjusted gross income of $16,000. We also subtract their $3000 worth of personal exemptions (four persons times $750 each). We thus come up with a taxable income of $8300, which results in a tax of $1452. (Social Security taxes and any applicable credits are not included in these computations because they would be approximately equal for both the ownership and rental situation.)

If they were to rent instead of own property, their deductions would total $2000. However, the standard deduction would allow them to deduct $2560. Taking the obvious advantage that the standard deduction offers in these circumstances, and again subtracting the same $3000 worth of personal exemptions, the Browns as tenants come up with a taxable income of $10,440. This results in a tax of $1914.

Thus, by owning instead of renting they are saving $462 in income taxes (the difference between the $1914 income tax as renters and the $1452 income tax as owners). That's an average of about $39 per month. Subtracting the saved $39 per month from their outlay of $350 per month as owners they end up with a net out-of-pocket cost of $311.

As renters they don't get this tax advantage, but they still do have their $10,000 nest egg that can go to work for them. By investing that sum very conservatively in a federally insured savings account at 5% per year interest, they will earn about $500 during the first year, or an average of about $42 per month.

As owners		As renters	
Mortgage	$140	Base rental	
Property tax	100	(including utilities)	$350
Property insurance	25		
Utilities & maintenance	85	Less: Earnings on	
	——	invested $10,000	−42
	$350		——
		Net cost	$308
Less: Saved via tax			
deductions	−39		
	——		
Net cost	$311		

Figure 6-2 Renting and Owning: A Monthly Comparison.

By deducting this $42 per month income from their $350 per month outlay as tenants, they end up with a net out-of-pocket cost of $308.

We've struck pretty much an equivalent situation. For about $310 out-of-pocket each month, the Browns can choose between a $350 rental unit with utilities and maintenance provided, or a $30,000 purchase (house, co-op, or condominium) assuming the expenses as noted above.

This does not mean that all $350 per month rental units are equal to all $30,000 purchase units, be they houses, apartments, or whatever. In some areas they may be very similar regarding location, size, and quality. In other areas the rental units may have a lot more to offer for the money than the house, and vice versa.

Figure 6-2 illustrates the arithmetic of the above example. You can work out examples to suit your own individual situation by following the same general formula.

Swindlers Bilk Homeowners of $1 Billion Per Year

"It was a nightmare! Just horrible!" said Mrs. Roger Purvis. "That couple was so nice when they first came around to see us. We believed everything they said. We fell for it hook, line, and sinker. Now, two years after, we just can't believe what has happened to us."

A tale of woe

Mr. and Mrs. Purvis were victims of a home improvement swindle. The Council of Better Business Bureaus estimates that home improvement swindles are one of the major forms of public bilking in the United States. Over $1 billion per year is taken from unsuspecting people.

Mr. and Mrs. Purvis were first approached two years ago by an alleged husband and wife team who were travelling from city to city selling what they referred to as an "advertising program." As Mrs. Purvis relates it, "They knocked on our door one evening and told us that they could arrange for us to get a complete aluminum siding job on our entire house at absolutely no cost to us if we would cooperate with them in an advertising program. They claimed that they were representing a major national brand name manufacturer of alumi-

num. They showed us advertisements with the name of this manufacturer included, and that kind of lulled us into believing it was a square deal. If a well-known national firm such as that put their name behind it, how bad could it be? Very bad, we soon found out."

The couple asked the Purvises to sign what they referred to as a "good faith" agreement. "My husband and I read quickly through the agreement," Mrs. Purvis went on, "and noticed that it referred to us having to make payments of $3500. They explained to us that the $3500 was there to indicate the value of the work we'd be receiving. They told us the advertising program required us to recommend this firm to our friends and neighbors for similar siding jobs. For each person we recommended who actually signed up for a job, we would get a credit of $700. All we had to do was get five home owners to sign up, and our job would be totally free. It sounded so easy. They gave us advertising materials to help us, and told us that they would be on call for the next two months to help us convince our friends. Ours would be a 'model' home, and anyone

taking a look at it would see its worth. They even convinced us that a $3500 siding job would increase the value of our property by twice that, or $7000. In other words, when we sold the house, we'd get double our money back from this siding job, if in fact we had had to pay for it, which they assured us we wouldn't. So we signed the agreement. We didn't really read it carefully, and they convinced us we didn't need a lawyer to review it. I've regretted that moment ever since."

The work begins

Workers showed up two days later and actually did install siding on the Purvis home. "But it was terrible," Mrs. Purvis complained. "It was out of line, and there were loose ends sticking out all over, and we weren't even sure that it was really aluminum. The colors were uneven, they punched a lot of holes in the walls, and they left a mess all around. When we tried to get the workers to correct the situation, they told us that another crew would be back in a few days to do the final touch up and clean up work. We never saw the workers again. We waited two weeks and tried to call the couple that had originally sold us the deal. Their phone was disconnected. We sent them a letter, and it was returned marked 'no such

212

addressee.' We felt like fools trying to convince any of our friends that they should get a siding job from this company. We did try it with one couple, and they all but laughed at us."

The trouble begins

"Another week or two later we received a coupon book from a finance company in another state. With it was a letter telling us that we had to make payments to them for our home improvement job. We compared the amount of payments with the $3500 that was set forth in the agreement and realized that we were paying an exhorbitant interest rate. We called the finance company immediately to complain that since the job was so poorly done we didn't feel we should have to pay for it. A very gruff man told us that it was none of his business if we didn't like the work. They had bought our contract and the interest rate that they were charging was what we had agreed to pay in the contract. He told us that the payments would be due on the first of every month thereafter, or, as he put it, 'you'll be sorry'."

"He also told us that it wouldn't do us any good to see an attorney because we had a perfectly legally binding contract, and their own attorneys had already gone over the papers and there was nothing we could do about it except to make the payments. If we were unsatisfied with the work, he

said, we'd have to locate the company that sold us the job and get them to correct it."

Intimidated, the Purvises began making the payments. Four months after the job had been completed, the siding began to warp and pull off the walls. "Not only was the work totally worthless," Mrs. Purvis complained, "but we realized during those winter months how much actual damage they had done to the house in installing the siding. We decided to stop making the payments, come what may. Three weeks after the next payment was due, we received a knock at our door and there was a bill collector. He all but threatened us with physical violence if we didn't give him a check for the payment right there on the spot. Rather than get involved in a fracas, we made the payment. At about that time we thought we should seek some legal help. We visited a lawyer, and he wrote a letter to the finance company asking them for copies of the various documents. Little did we know that now our troubles were just beginning."

Shortly after the attorney's letter was received by the finance company, the Purvises were visited by an alleged representative from the finance company. "He was as slick and smooth as you can imagine," Mrs. Purvis said. "In a very pleasant way, he offered us a chance to settle up the whole agreement. If we would pay

them $2000 within the next ten days, they would cancel the whole obligation. We told him that we wanted to discuss it with our attorney, but he said that he had to have an immediate answer and we would have to sign the appropriate papers right then and there. He got talking very fast and had us sign a lot of papers that we really didn't read. But he kept reassuring us that the matter would be all settled as soon as we sent him the check for $2000. The next day we went to our bank and withdrew that amount from our savings account. We sent him the check, and we didn't hear from them again for a few months."

"What happened next you may not believe," Mrs. Purvis almost laughed. "After a few months we received a phone call from the finance company. They told us they were now the owners of our house, and that the balance of the original $3500 was still due. If we didn't make the payment in whole within thirty days, they would commence to have us evicted from the house. That was beyond our comprehension. We immediately went to our lawyer and urged him to investigate the matter fully."

The investigation

The lawyer quickly learned that among the papers the Purvises had signed for the slick smooth visitor was a deed to their house. They had, in fact, trans-

ferred the ownership of the house to the finance company. However, gross fraud was involved in the transaction. Realizing this, the attorney contacted the State Attorney General, and civil and criminal actions were commenced against the finance company and the bogus home improvement company to have the amount of the debt set aside, the money returned, and compensation made to the Purvises for the damage done to their home.

The swindlers weren't finished. By legal maneuvers, they delayed the Purvises still more, and it wasn't until the Attorney General was ready to bring them into court that they consented to reimbursement, cancellation of the debt, and signing a deed back over to the Purvises. They also agreed to restore the house to its original condition, but, before a penny was ever paid, the firm disappeared into the night. Subsequent investigation by the Attorney General's office disclosed that the finance company was not a properly licensed finance company operating within the state but a phony corporation set up to act as a front for the equally phony home improvement company. In communicating with neighboring states, the Attorney General's office learned that there had been dozens of prosecutions against firms using virtually the same method of operation. The Purvises ended up out of pocket almost $3000—the money that they had paid into the firm was never recovered, nor was the repair work ever done on the house. They had to do it themselves at their own expense.

Roger Adams, executive director of the State Home Improvement Contractors Association observes: "There are dozens of legitimate and reliable home improvement contractors in every city. They are as disgusted as the public is with the tactics of these fraudulent operators. These operators offer a deal that sounds too good to be true. It just doesn't work out that way. Home improvement jobs can be very complex and need competent skilled technicians to deliver true value for your money. You should obtain proper plans and specifications for the work you want done, and then ask reliable local contractors to submit bids for the work. Based on reputation, the bid price, and your feeling of 'good vibes' with the contractor, make your decision accordingly. A carefully detailed contract should be agreed upon by both parties, and it certainly doesn't hurt to have your attorney look over the contract before you sign it. But as long as people are willing to fall for these con men's pitches and these 'something for nothing' deals, there will always be victims and there will always be losses suffered."

review questions

1. What is the largest purchase most individuals and families will ever make?
2. What other budget expenses are closely related to housing cost?
3. List some personal factors that affect choice of housing.
4. Why does a landlord usually require two months' rent in advance?
5. What type of dwelling unit is most likely to increase in value?
6. Describe the dwelling unit most likely to decrease in value.
7. Why are zoning changes important to a home owner?
8. How should you determine if your home is properly assessed?

cases for study

1. Lisa Rodriguez has a mortgage escrow account with her lender so that her property taxes and insurance are collected by the lender. She gets one bill each month for the whole thing. Discuss her other housing costs.
2. Discuss the problems a condominium owner will have in selling in addition to those experienced by a home owner.
3. Joe Smith is considering the purchase of an older house with the idea of refurbishing it. Carefully outline the factors he should examine before deciding if this is a wise choice.
4. Carolyn and Lee Chang have the following financial resources:

Savings	$4800
Investments	7300
Combined monthly income	1300

Discuss their housing options by considering the financial factors. Use your local newspaper for information on houses for sale plus the tables in this chapter for the monthly payments on various loans.

chapter 7 **housing: actions and transactions**

a matter of complications

You agree to buy a house with an occupancy date set for 90 days hence. One week before you are to take occupancy, the seller informs you that there will be an indefinite delay because he has had some personal problems. Meanwhile, you've already made arrangements to give up your apartment, and the new tenants are set to move in on the promised date. If you can't convince the new tenants to cooperate, you may end up living in a motel for weeks, until your seller can get his problems cleared away.

Once you finally move in, you run into the following: a water main bursts and floods the premises, and because there was no warranty between you and the seller, you have no recourse to him, and you find that your homeowner's insurance doesn't cover such damages.

A neighbor claims that the fence you're erecting on what you thought was the true property line is actually two feet inside her property.

A stranger knocks at the door stating that he's the heir of a gentleman who owned the property twenty years ago, and claims he has a legal right to the property.

217

A lawyer for the Ajax Painting Company sends you a nasty letter stating that his clients had performed certain work on the house for the prior owner for which they were not paid. The lawyer claims that his clients have a legitimate claim against the property and they want you to pay up or suffer the consequences.

The mortgage lender informs you that the mortgage you have assumed when you bought the house states that you have 90 days from that date to come up with the entire balance due on the mortgage. If you can't, they're willing to continue the mortgage as is, but at an interest rate two percentage points higher than what you had thought you would be paying.

These incidents illustrate some of the problems that can arise with the basic transactions of acquiring real estate: the execution of and compliance with the sales contract; the condition of the property and the presence or absence of any warranty; the legal title to the property; the legal description of the property; and the financing documents. The knowledgeable buyer will make proper use of professional help—lawyer, realtor, appraiser, insurance agent, and so on—and will avoid such incidents. With correct professional help, you can anticipate and understand the possible complications that may arise, and avoid the usually costly and time-consuming headaches that can befall the victim of a fouled-up real estate transaction. Before we discuss each of these aspects, let's first consider one critical question that every buyer must answer: How do you determine a fair price?

striking the best bargain

How much should you pay for a house? An old rule of thumb floating around for decades stated that an individual should have monthly house payments roughly equal to one week's take home pay. That may have been a reliable guideline back in the days when mortgage interest rates were in the 5 to 6% range, as compared with the current range, and when electricity and heating fuel were relatively cheap and in ample supply. But today's home buyers must look beyond such simple rules in order to determine that they are getting the best value for their money, and as much house as they need and can adequately afford. In determining a reasonable and fair price, a buyer must consider the following: personal needs, comparable values, warranty, financing terms, utility costs, furnishing costs, and resale potential.

Before we discuss each of these items, let's consider one very common aspect of arranging a purchase: bargaining over the price. It's virtually a tradition that the seller will ask one price, the buyer will offer a lower price, and they will ultimately settle for something in between. One might say that this kind of hassling is almost expected, unless, as in rare instances, the demand for houses vastly exceeds the supply—in which case an anxious buyer may be more than ready to pay whatever the asking price is. There's no rule of thumb to guide a would-be buyer in this delicate area other than the old saying "Nothing ventured, nothing gained."

personal needs

A good price on a too-small house today may prove to be a regretable decision if, in a few years, you have to either enlarge the house or tolerate the inconvenience of inadequate space. Similarly, if a house later proves to be too large for your needs, you may look back at the original purchase as having been more costly than necessary. Although changes in household size aren't always predictable, the possibilities must be considered, particularly when you're putting out many thousands of dollars for down payment, and signing an IOU for many more thousands.

comparable values

Assuming you've located an area in which you want to live, and taking into full account the costs of commuting to work, shopping, schools, and other facilities, you should try to determine if a specific house you're interested in is priced in a range comparable to others in the vicinity. Your real estate agent can help you by examining the records of recent sales in the area. All other things (size, quality, location) being equal, comparable houses should sell for comparable prices. You may be fortunate in finding a seller who is disposing of property on a distressed basis. That is, personal circumstances are requiring him or her to sell at less than what otherwise might be obtained. Such circumstances could be a job transfer, a drastic change in family situation, or the need for cash. Likewise, you may find someone who is asking the maximum they think the traffic will bear and unless you, the buyer, do some checking, you may succumb to their asking price, when in fact you could have perhaps obtained a better buy if you were armed with knowledge of comparable sales in the neighborhood.

Be careful not to compare apples with oranges. This is particularly true concerning houses that otherwise are equal in size and quality, but differ in age. The age of a house can have a distinct bearing on the value you may or may not be getting for your money. Aside from elements of decor, you have to evaluate the physical deterioration that may have occurred regarding either the old or the new house. In certain neighborhoods the old saying "They don't build them like they used to" may be perfectly true. Certain older homes may have been built with better quality materials and greater craftsmanship than more recent homes. However, the reverse can be true. It will take a detailed inspection by a qualified contractor to reveal to you the current condition and need for maintenance and replacement of such things as foundation, sidewalls, roof, heating system, plumbing, wiring, and specific appliances.

One advantage that may often be found in older homes is an older mortgage that carries a lower rate of interest. There can be an obvious benefit in assuming an older mortgage: not only may the interest rate be lower than the current going rate in your community, but the older mortgage will build up your equity at a faster rate. The older a mortgage gets, the greater portion of each monthly payment goes to principal and the less to interest.

For example, on a 30 year mortgage with 9% interest, you'll reduce the principal amount owing by 10.6% during the first 10 years, and by an additional 25.9% during the second 10 years. Assume that you had a $30,000 mortgage at 9% interest, set to run for 30 years. During the first 20 years, you will have reduced your debt from $30,000 to $19,050. You will have paid off, in other words, $10,950 of the total amount due. But that $10,950 reduction in your debt is not spread evenly over those first 20 years. During the first 10 years, the debt is reduced by $3,180; during the second 10 years, the debt is reduced by $7,770. Thus, if you step into a seasoned mortgage as opposed to a brand new mortgage, and you stayed for 10 years before moving on, a substantially larger portion of the payments you've made will come back to you when you sell.

Possibly offsetting this advantage will be the fact that with the older mortgage you may have to make a larger down payment, and thus tie up that much more of your money. A large down payment may also require a proportionately larger down payment from a buyer on a subsequent sale of the house. This could possibly prove to be a detriment. Careful analysis is called for.

warranties   Unless warranties are specifically spelled out in a contract and agreed to by the parties, they might not be enforceable. Customarily, brand new homes are sold with a one year warranty by the builder. (It is not customary for used homes to have warranties, but in recent years many real estate brokerage firms have been offering limited warranties to buyers of used homes.) New home warranties will generally cover the premises with respect to cracks, leaks, and breakdowns of mechanical equipment. In addition to such warranties, the buyer and seller might agree to specific clauses that should be included in the contract of sale. A seller may warrant, for example, that the roof is in excellent condition, and that if it leaks within the first 12 months, it will be repaired at his own expense. This is an agreement between these two parties, and if properly drawn and executed would bind the seller to perform his promise if, in fact, the roof does leak. A seller may offer such warranties as an inducement to a buyer; or a buyer may request such warranties from the seller as part of the overall bargain. It's strictly a matter to be negotiated between the parties. There is no legal requirement that a seller offer such warranties, and lacking anything in writing, the buyer has little protection.

Another form of warranty that may accrue to the buyer's benefit is the warranty on specific mechanical equipment. For example, a water heater may be installed with a seven year guarantee. During the seven year period, the house changes hands. The remaining guarantee on the water heater could accrue to the benefit of the new buyer. The same might be true of any other mechanical equipment.

In the purchase of a new house, the buyer should take care to determine whether or not mechanical equipment warranties are included in the builder's overall warranty and, if they are not, exactly what one's protection may be. For example, the warranty on a water heater may begin as of the date of installation. The unit may actually have been installed one year prior to the sale of the house to the ultimate buyer. Thus, one full year of the warranty may have already elapsed before the buyer even begins to use the appliance.

Any warranty—be it on a house, an appliance, or any other product or service—is only as good as its specific legal statements, and it's only as good as the ability of the warrantor to perform.

A salesperson may state that a warranty covers every conceivable thing that goes wrong with the house (or other product or service), but if the specific wording of the warranty itself does not so state, you might not be protected if a variety of things actually do go wrong. The salesperson's statements may not be enforceable and the actual wording of the agreement would control.

Or, the warranty may actually state in full legal terminology that everything conceivable is covered. But such a warranty may be valueless if the person or firm who stands behind it cannot be expected to fulfill the terms of the agreement. If, say, a homebuilder is in severe financial distress, he may offer an unlimited warranty to attract customers, hoping to improve his business. If the unlimited warranty is in fact a successful sales tool, he may honor the terms of the warranty. But if the warranty doesn't sell enough homes, he may not be around to honor the warranties on those homes he has sold. The ultimate precaution, therefore, is to take steps to determine the financial solvency of the firm making the promise to perform on the warranty. If it's a well-known national manufacturer, you may not care to go to that trouble. But if it's a local firm or individual, it may be worth a few dollars to run a credit investigation through your local credit bureau. This can avoid the problem of having to come up with a lot of cash out of pocket to make your own repairs or replacements should a warranty not be honored by the person who made it.

financing terms   "How much down and how much a month?" Those are the predominant questions asked when considering any kind of financing—an appliance, a car, a house. It's not always as simple as that, though. To get the best value for your money in a housing buy, the amount of the down payment has to be compatible with the amount you actually have available, or have access to, without interfering with your other predictable financial needs. It's essential to bear in mind that once money has been used for a down payment on a house, that money cannot be retrieved unless you either refinance the house or sell the house, and both transactions can be costly and time consuming, if in fact they're feasible at all. If you have other possible needs projected for the amount of money you've saved up and are contemplating using as a down payment, you must carefully evaluate the effect of placing that money in the house. Other such needs could include emergency medical purposes, future tuition for your children's education, and plain old rainy day funds.

The monthly payments must similarly be compatible with your current and projected ability to meet them. In this respect, it's essential that you or your attorney closely examine the terms of a proposed mortgage. You must determine whether or not the payments will be constant, and for how long. In the last decade or two many mortgage lenders, caught off guard by sharply increasing interest rates since the early 1960s, have built in clauses that can allow them to increase interest rates on mortgages at pre-established points. For example, mortgage payments may be set based on a 30 year payout, but the lender may have reserved the right to increase the rate of interest after the first 10 years of the mortgage have elapsed. These escalation privileges are discussed in more detail under the section on financing. In making your initial buying decision, these factors must be taken into account.

utility costs

Heating and electrical costs have risen drastically in most parts of the country in recent years. A generation ago, a home buyer may have paid little attention to utility costs, for they were a relatively small portion of the total out-of-pocket expenses involved in home ownership. Not so any longer. Energy conservation is not just a patriotic slogan; it's an economic necessity, and must be considered carefully during the home buying decision-making process. If you're buying a used home, it's necessary to determine the utility costs that the former owners incurred. Obviously, not all families will utilize the available energy in the same way, but that's at least a beginning guideline to help you determine the costs you'll be facing. If you're buying a new home, this task is more difficult. But if the same builder has erected comparable homes in the immediate vicinity, you might attempt to visit the owners of those homes and inquire as to their utility expenditures. A visit to the local utility companies might also be helpful in getting these preliminary estimates. Also, a physical examination of the insulation in the house can be important. If there's adequate insulation, you'll be realizing a better bargain. If insulation is inadequate, you should evaluate the cost of bringing it up to standard compared with the cost of additional fuel you'll use because of its lack. Your local utility company and local building contractors can assist you in these considerations.

furnishing costs

Beyond the cost of the house itself, the cost of the money with which to finance the house, and the cost of utilities, you must also consider the cost of furnishing the house to suit your desires. If the decor is not satisfactory, how much will it cost to repaint, repaper, and otherwise change it? Other items that can run into considerable expense include carpeting, draperies, and cabinetry. You'll also want to determine how much of your existing furniture can be used in the new dwelling, and how much additional furniture you may need to complete the interior satisfactorily. Two houses, with all other things being equal, can differ considerably with regard to the furnishings that may be included or may have to be added. Evaluating these elements is part of your initial buying decision. Where will the money come from to provide the necessary furnishings and changes in decor? Do you have the cash available? Will you finance these purchases over the customary three to five year term of a home improvement installment loan? Can you add the cost of these purchases to your overall cost of the home and include them in the mortgage? Whichever step you take, or whichever combination of steps, how will it affect the balance of your regular budget?

The bulk of the money you spend on furnishings cannot be recaptured. Used furniture has very little resale value. Changes in decor, including carpeting and draperies, may enhance the value of the property on a subsequent resale, but if they are too deteriorated or out of style, they could detract from the price. In other words, before you commit dollars to furnishing expenses on the new home, you must carefully evaluate the effect of such expenses on your overall budget.

resale potential

When buying a house, it may seem foolish to exercise your brain in guesstimating what you might be able to sell it for five or ten or fifteen years in the future. Granted, there's no way to assuredly predict what any property in any community might bring even a year or two after purchase. But it may be foolish to ignore the question altogether. Some neighborhoods will evidence signs of slow and gradual deterioration, while others will seem to have a fairly assured future of increase in property values. There may be subtle changes underway in the neighborhood characteristics. This can have a decreasing effect on the value of property. If you envision the possibility of reselling the home within a relatively short period of time—say, four to seven years—your real estate agent should be able to help you estimate the possibility of increase or decrease in value. If you'll be in the home for longer than that, you'd probably do best to put your thoughts into the hunch category and hope for the best.

Once you've made all the necessary evaluations, you're ready to visit your attorney and discuss the terms of the sale.

making the purchase

All of the elements of a real estate transaction are of concern to both the buyer and the seller. But since the buyer may be said to have more at stake in the transaction, the following material is slanted more toward the buyer's concerns and considerations. Separate matters that are of concern to the seller are discussed subsequently.

the memo

Often, when a buyer and seller have agreed on the basic terms of the transaction, they will enter into a brief agreement pending the execution of the actual sales contract. This agreement may be referred to as a memorandum or memo, and it will commit the parties to negotiate the terms of, and sign, the final purchase agreement. Commonly, the buyer may deliver a check for a token amount—perhaps a few hundred dollars—to bind the deal. This cash payment is referred to as "earnest money" or good faith money (also called a binder in some areas). It should be understood that this money will be returned to the buyer if the parties, acting in good faith, fail to agree on the final contractual terms. A memo may not be necessary, particularly in a case where a real estate agent is handling the transaction for the seller, and will be able to prepare the actual contract swiftly upon the agreement between the parties. But both buyer and seller may prefer to enter into a memo agreement, if for no other reason than the peace of mind in knowing that the deal is moving forward.

the purchase contract

The purchase contract is a very important aspect of a real estate transaction. It sets forth the names of the parties involved, describes the property, dictates the terms and conditions of the sale, stipulates the kind of deed that the seller will deliver to the buyer, and states where and when the closing is to take place. Generally, a purchase contract will be prepared by the seller's representative, either a real estate agent or an attorney. One of the primary rules in the world of financial and legal transactions is that if the other party's representative has prepared a contract for your signature, you can and should assume that the contract will be structured to favor the other party. Only by having your own representative review the document can you be assured of the fullest protection of your own interests.

the parties to the contract

The names and addresses of the buyers and the sellers are set forth in the contract. Customarily, a married couple will acquire a house in joint names, or what is referred to as "tenants by the entirety." Although complications concerning the names of the parties may be rare, they nevertheless can occur. For example, the house may originally have been in the name of Mr. and Mrs. Jones. Since they bought the house, though, they have become divorced. By the terms of the divorce settlement, Mrs. Jones still retained a one-half interest in the house, even though she is no longer Mrs. Jones. In order for Mr. Jones to properly and legally sell the house, he would have to get his ex-wife's signature on the contract and deed. Lacking her signature, the contract may not be valid. If the buyers sign a contract unaware that all proper parties in interest have not signed it, and if Mrs. Jones is unwilling to go along with the deal, the buyers could end up in a muddle. They'd probably be able to get back any money they had paid in, but they could have sacrificed considerable time in the process.

Similar situations could result if one of the spouses had died. If the property had been held jointly by husband and wife, the surviving spouse would likely have full ownership, and would be able to sign a valid contract conveying full rights in the property. But the husband may have owned the house solely in his own name, and on his death, his will stipulated that the house would go into a trust for the use of his widow and children, and on the widow's death, would pass to the children. In such a case, the trustee of the trust would be the proper party to sign the contract.

What if the buyers sign a contract and before the actual closing decide that they don't want to actually buy the house? Perhaps a job transfer has been cancelled. Perhaps they've found another couple who wish to buy the house at a price higher than what they are paying for it? If the contract permits a "right of assignment," then the buyers can transfer their interest in the contract to another party.

For example, the Smiths, having been told of a job transfer, contract to buy the Jones' house for $30,000. Shortly thereafter the job transfer is cancelled, and the Smiths no longer have any need or desire to buy the Jones' house. But in the meantime they have met the Whites, who would be willing to pay $31,000 for the Jones' house. The Smiths, under the right of assignment clause, can assign their rights in the contract to the Whites and the Smiths could profit by $1000 as a result. In effect, then, the names of the buying parties would be changed in the contract. The Smiths would have to notify the Joneses that they were assigning their rights to the Whites. Unless the Joneses had reserved the right to approve of any such assignments, the

Whites would then legally stand in the shoes of the Smiths as contractual buyers of the property.

description of the property

In most purchase contracts, the description of the property will be simply the street address of the property in question. That indeed may be the legal address as far as the post office and the Social Security Administration is concerned, it is not the technical legal description of your property. Such a description will more normally be contained in the deed to the property.

To be certain that you as a buyer are buying everything that you have bargained for, it is necessary that the property description in the deed you receive matches the property description in the deed that the seller himself holds.

Modern descriptions tend to be of two varieties. One is the individual description, which indicates the exact boundaries and the distance between them, as described in technical surveying terms. The other is the subdivision description. Local laws, which differ slightly from place to place, require land developers to file maps of their subdivisions with the appropriate local offices, usually county. These maps become the legal description for the overall subdivision itself, and for individual lots within the subdivision. Thus, a property description of a parcel within a subdivision may refer to it as "lot #17 of the XYZ subdivision." This may be an adequate legal description, but the cautious buyer would still want an attorney to double check that the numerical description of the property does indeed fit the physical piece of land that is being purchased.

The street address normally referred to in the purchase contract is not the ultimate description of the property that you may be buying. The seller may innocently misunderstand exactly where the boundary lines are, and you could easily inherit this misunderstanding. You could live in a house for decades—and many people probably do—without every really knowing or caring where the precise property boundaries are. But when you eventually sell your property, the buyer may be a fussy sort who wants to know precisely what's what, and you may then learn that what you thought was really yours isn't. For such reasons, it's best to have the property description clarified before a contract is signed.

title

Your title to a piece of property represents the rights you have regarding that property. There may be certain restrictions as to how you can use any given piece of property; and your use of the property may be subject to the rights of other people. The purchase contract will commonly state that you are receiving "title free and clear of all liens and encumbrances, except as otherwise noted." What does this mean? It means that you are receiving the property without any restrictions and subject to no other rights of other people, unless such other restrictions or rights are specifically spelled out. If your contract says that you are receiving the right to use the property "free and clear," when in fact you are not, you may have the right to get out of the contract. Your lawyer or your title insurance company will search the appropriate records to determine if, in fact, any other such rights or restrictions do exist. If you take title to property without being aware of other person's rights or restrictions on you, you could find yourself in a difficult position when it comes to financing the property or later selling the property. It could also mean lawsuits to resolve whether or not the rights and restrictions are in fact valid. Restrictions on your use of the property, and rights that others may have to use your property are referred to as "blots" on the title. The most common forms of blots are easements, liens, and restrictive covenants.

easements

Many years ago the owner of a piece of property may have given a neighbor the right to lead cattle across the property to a watering hole. The neighbor may have paid for this right, and in return received a document setting forth that right. Later, when the owner of the property sold to another buyer, the neighbor's right to cross the property was included as a part of the deal. Thus, the new buyer acquired the property subject to the neighbor's right to use it. Unless and until the owners of the respective adjoining properties agree to terminate this right, making whatever payments and exchanging whatever documents are necessary, that right would continue down through all subsequent owners of the property.

This is a form of easement, and it exists today in many forms. It's not uncommon for a utility company or the telephone company to have easements across residential property for the purpose of installing utility lines and underground piping. These rights may have been reserved, but not yet exercised by the utility company. The fact that they have not yet exercised their rights does not mean that their easement has expired. Easements may have been created many years or many decades ago, yet they will continue to run with the property until they are terminated by mutual agreement.

liens

Laws on the subject of liens differ from state to state. A lien on the property comes into being when the owner of the property has a debt that has not been paid, and the creditor takes legal action to collect the debt. If the legal action is successful, the creditor may wind up with the right to force the owner to sell his or her property (real estate and personal) in order to satisfy the debt.

For example, John had borrowed $10,000 from Mary, and could not repay it when the debt became due. Mary began legal action, but John still refused to pay. Mary won a judgment against John that technically gave her the right to force a sale of John's house to satisfy the debt. Mary, in effect, had a lien on John's house. The lien was properly recorded according to state law. Anyone then buying John's house would own it subject to Mary's right to force a sale in order to satisfy John's debt to her.

Other liens can arise out of a property owner's failure to pay taxes, in which case the government will have a lien. Or if a property owner has failed to pay contractors or workers who have performed work on the property, what's known as a "mechanics lien" can arise.

Note that a debt alone does not give rise to a lien. The creditor must pursue the legal requirements set forth in the state in order to "perfect" the lien. Not until the lien is legally perfected does the creditor have any claim on the property. However, if a creditor is in the midst of a lawsuit that ultimately might lead to a lien on a property you're contemplating buying, the existence of that lawsuit can be determined by a title search, and caution should be exercised. Because there are often many months between the signing of a purchase contract and the final closing of a real estate transaction, a pending lawsuit could be resolved in the meantime and result in a lien coming into being prior to the actual date of closing. Thus, it's common for a title search to occur both on the signing of the purchase contract and again just before the closing to make certain that no liens have arisen in the interim. A proper purchase contract should disclose the existence of any actual liens. If the contract does not disclose actual liens, the seller is promising to sell something that he can not in fact deliver: a "free and clear" title. In such a case the buyer should have the right to bow out of the contract and recoup any monies he had paid in. He might possibly also be entitled to damages suffered as a result of entering into the contract.

restrictive covenants

Restrictive covenants may prevent you from doing certain things on your property. For example, a restrictive covenant may state that you may not build a house of less than a certain value. Such a covenant, or promise, may have originated with the subdivider of the property who wanted to insure that the subdivision was developed with homes of at least a minimum quality. He would do so to protect the financial interests of all those persons buying his lots, for they would want to know that their investment in a house would not be tarnished by the construction of buildings of lesser values. Not long ago it was common to see restrictive covenants that would prevent an owner of property from selling to persons of certain races or religions. Such restrictive covenants are now illegal, but they still appear in various property documents, simply because lawyers have not bothered to delete them from the documents.

In condominium situations there may be restrictive covenants concerning the sale of the property. The owner of the condominium may be restricted from selling on the open market until he or she has first offered the property to other members of the condominium owners' association, or to the association as a whole.

Zoning regulations discussed in Chapter 6 are a form of restrictive covenant, although they don't actually appear on your title.

title insurance

Both the buyer of the property and the mortgage lender should be duly concerned with the nature of the title. Although the seller of the property may make promises that the title is as stated, he or she may not be able to adequately live up to the promise to make good on any claims against the title. Therefore, a form of insurance is needed to protect the buyer's interest in case of some future claim. If, for example, the seller was not aware that Charlie Junior had a valid claim on the property, and you bought the property unaware of the existence of Charlie Junior's potential claim, the insurance that you would obtain would protect you against such claim. This is known as title insurance. It's an insurance policy, for which you the buyer pay, that protects you in the event of any such claim. A title insurance policy does not establish the *value* of your property. It sets forth the maximum amount of monetary damages that you can expect to recover in the event a claim is successfully made against your title, and where the insurance company has not exempted such a claim from its coverage. In some areas of the country, lawyers' certification is the practice preferred over title insurance. In such cases, your lawyer will certify as to the accuracy of the title, and if claims arise, you will seek reimbursement from the attorney.

A title search is a procedure whereby your attorney or a representative of the title insurance company examines all of the existing legal records that could possibly pertain to the ownership of the property. These records are normally contained in an office of the county government.

Clear title is as important to a mortgage lender as it is to the buyer, for a lender will not advance you money for a mortgage unless certain that the title is clear, subject to known exceptions. A mortgage itself becomes a lien on the property—if you default on your payments, the lenders have the right to foreclose, which involves selling the property to satisfy the unpaid debt. In most cases, liens take precedence in the order in which they are recorded. First in line is first satisfied. The mortgage lender wants to know that there will be no liens prior to his, so that in the event of a forced sale he will have first grab on the proceeds.

The purchase contract should accurately describe exactly what blots, if any, there are on the title, or it should describe other documents, such as the deed, which would in fact fully describe the clarity of title. If your purchase contract states that you will be receiving anything less than a completely free and clear title, you should know before you sign exactly what those blots are and what their possible consequences might be. Once you have agreed to accept the title as offered by the seller, you will have to live with the known blots, even though you may be protected by title insurance for the unknown or unstipulated blots.

the deed   The deed is the legal document by which the title to the property passes from the seller to the buyer. It's the actual symbol of ownership. The purchase contract should spell out when you will get it.

The contract should also stipulate that the deed will be

transferred at the time of closing. If the contract does not call for the deed to be delivered at the closing, you should receive an explanation before consenting to sign the contract. There is one type of transaction wherein the deed is not delivered at the closing but at a later date. This is referred to as a "land contract" transaction. In such a transaction, the buyer and the seller agree in writing that the deed will not be delivered until some future point, by which time the buyer will have made an agreed on amount of payments to the seller. There can be a number of reasons for the parties to enter into a land contract arrangement. One may be that the seller does not yet have the deed to the property. He may have purchased on a land contract himself, and will not have his own deed until some future time. Or, the buyer may not be able to obtain conventional financing, and the land contract is a convenient way for the buyer to have access to the property, with the seller taking the payments directly. Or, the seller may have doubts about the buyer's ability to make payments, and the land contract generally allows him to reclaim the property more efficiently than he would through foreclosing proceedings, if a default did occur to the seller.

There are different kinds of deeds, and they convey different interests in a piece of property. The highest and most complete form of deed is called a "full warranty deed." In such a deed, the seller warrants that he has clear title to the property (subject to any stated exceptions), that he is conveying the title to you, and that he will protect you against any outside claims made against the property.

The lowest form of deed is called a "quit claim deed." By this document the seller conveys to you whatever interest he or she may have in the property, with no further assurance as to title. By virtue of a quit claim deed the seller is saying, in effect, "I hereby quit, or give over to you, the buyer, any claim I may have to this property." If in fact the seller has full and complete title to the property, this is what is conveyed to the buyer. If in fact he has no claim whatever to the property, that too is what he is conveying to the buyer. In other words, a seller could convey to a buyer via a quit claim deed "all of my right, title, and interest in the Grand Canyon." The seller has no interest whatsoever in the Grand Canyon, but it's still a valid deed. He is simply giving over any rights that he may have, and it's up to the buyer to determine that those rights are worthless.

Once a buyer takes title to a property, he can only convey the title that he has received. You can't convey more than you actually own. If you receive a quit claim deed to a piece of property, and later want to sell it, you can't give anything more than a quit claim deed—unless it's been otherwise legally established that you do, in fact, have free and clear title.

The buyer should demand the highest form of deed that the seller is capable of delivering. If your purchase contract calls for you to receive a certain type of deed, and at the closing the seller does not deliver the type of deed he has committed himself to deliver, you technically might be able to void the deal or bargain for better terms.

manner of payment   The purchase contract will set forth the manner in which the buyer is to pay the seller for the property. The manner of payment will usually take one of three forms: all cash at the time of closing, part cash at the time of closing and the balance over a stipulated period of time, or a cash down payment with the buyer assuming the mortgage debt of the seller.

Where a buyer agrees to pay all cash, usually arrangements for mortgage financing for a major portion of the total price are made. A mortgage lender will have advanced the agreed on sum to the buyer, who, in addition to his own down payment check, turns over the entire amount to the seller. The seller then must pay off any debts that he may have with respect to the property.

If the seller himself is going to finance the purchase, the buyer will pay him the cash down payment and will sign an IOU to the seller—a mortgage—for the remaining amount due.

Very commonly, the seller will still be obliged on his own mortgage and the buyer then will pay him the cash difference between the purchase price and the amount remaining on the existing mortgage. The buyer, with the consent of the lender obtained in advance, will then assume the seller's debt for the remaining amount due on the mortgage. If this latter mode is the agreed on manner of payment, the buyer should take care to determine that the purchase contract spells out the terms explicitly.

For example: the buyer and seller *verbally* agree to a purchase price of $30,000. The seller has told the buyer that the remaining balance on the mortgage is $25,000. The contract is prepared by the seller and it states "that the buyer agrees to pay the sum of $5000 in cash, and also agrees to assume the remaining debt on the existing mortgage." The buyer later learns to his dismay that the actual amount remaining on the debt is not $25,000 but $28,000. Technically he has contracted to assume a debt $3000 larger than what he had believed. Although such matters can be ironed out, it's always better practice to take advance precautions to see that they don't happen. In a case such as this, the actual purchase price should, of course, be spelled out in the purchase contract. As a further precaution, the buyer may require the seller to deliver what's known as an "estoppel certificate," which is a statement assuring the true amount of the debt remaining that the buyer will be assuming.

Many purchase contracts will have an important "but if" clause, usually for the protection of the buyer. That clause will make the final closing contingent on the buyer's ability to obtain the necessary financing. If the buyer is not able to obtain the necessary financing by the agreed on date, and the parties cannot negotiate an agreeable amendment to the deal, then the deal should be off and the contract should state that the buyer would be entitled to his or her money back.

In some cases, something other than cash or IOU's will be used in the transaction. The parties may be exchanging pieces of real estate, for example, or the buyer may be delivering personal property, securities, or other items of value as his part of the deal. In any such event, the specific nature of the payment should be spelled out clearly in the purchase contract.

closing date

For the fullest possible protection of both parties, the purchase contract should set forth the date and the place of the closing. The closing is the official event at which the transfer of deeds, checks, and IOUs takes place. When a closing date is fixed, both parties must perform by that date or risk forfeiture. Of course, the parties can subsequently agree to amend the date of closing. This is often done, particularly in cases where financing arrangements have been delayed, or where personal circumstances unavoidably alter the plans of either or both of the parties. If the closing date arrives and one party is ready to perform and the other is not, the party standing in potential default will have to satisfy the other party or risk losing his position. A purchase contract that does not stipulate a closing date can be disadvantageous to both parties.

seller's obligations

As part of the negotiations, the seller may agree to perform certain services or work regarding the property. For example, the buyer and the seller reach an agreement in September with the closing and occupancy to take place in December. The buyer would like to have the house painted, but can't do so until he becomes the owner, which will be in the dead of winter. He'd thus have to wait until spring for the work to be properly performed. The seller agrees to have the house painted between September and December for the buyer's benefit. Presumably the purchase price would be adjusted accordingly. December, and the closing date, and the occupancy date arrive and the seller has failed to perform as agreed. What recourse does the buyer have? It all depends on how carefully the seller's obligation was worded in the original purchase contract. The buyer may have no recourse beyond an adjustment in the purchase price. But if the buyer was careful enough and fussy enough to protect himself to the fullest, the seller's obligations would have been spelled out in detail, including the nature of the paint to be used, the number of coats to be put on, and specific damages should the seller not perform in accordance with the contract.

default and recourse   What if either of the parties fails to perform in accordance with the agreement? What are the rights of the other party? Much depends on the nature of the default, and how serious it is concerning the overall transaction. As noted above, if the seller has indeed performed as substantially agreed on, but has neglected to complete some minor touch-up work, such a default would not likely destroy the entire transaction. But a more serious default, such as the seller's failure to pay off a substantial tax lien on the property prior to the date of closing, could conceivably destroy the whole transaction. But bowing out of the deal might not satisfy the buyer, who, in anticipation of closing as agreed, has already moved out of his prior dwelling and has the moving van standing ready in the driveway to go into action as soon as the final papers are signed. Nor, on the other hand, will the seller be satisfied to keep the $500 earnest money that the buyer has paid him, only to later learn that the buyer is running away from the deal. The seller has relied on the promises of the buyer, he has taken his house off the market for an extended period of time, and has made other personal arrangements.

If the respective remedies of the parties are not clearly spelled out in the contract, lawsuits will surely result, and those can involve expenses of time and money not satisfactory to either party.

Thus, it could be advantageous for the parties to agree on

specific remedies within the purchase contract itself. They might agree, for example, that either party failing to perform the terms of the contract and complete the conveyance as agreed, will be responsible to the other party for a fixed sum of money as damages. A more gentle form of agreement might be to submit any disputes to arbitration. Even with an agreement as to damages, each party has to satisfy himself that the other will, in fact, make good on any such claim. But at least having an agreement at the outset is preferable to leaving the matter up in the air where it may never be resolved to the satisfaction of either party.

In some states the signed contracts and other documents are held by a third party pending completion of all of the buyer's and seller's obligations. This is known as "escrow" and it is commonly performed by a title insurance company or by an attorney. The party holding the papers in escrow (the escrow agent) will have been instructed by both buyer and seller not to release the papers for the ultimate closing until all of the various obligations of buyer and seller have been performed as agreed.

getting the money— financing

If you don't have all of the cash on hand needed to buy a house, you'll have to borrow it, or assume the existing debt that the seller already has. A mortgage is a form of debt whereby the borrower pledges the property as security for the loan. If the borrower should default, the lender has the right to take legal steps to acquire the property. This is known as a foreclosure proceeding. In a foreclosure proceeding the lender will acquire title to the property, and will sell it, usually at public auction, to satisfy the remaining debt. In many cases, the actual cost of the foreclosure proceeding will be added to the amount owed. If the sale of the property does not bring enough money to satisfy the debt completely, the lender may be able to take additional steps to acquire a "deficiency judgment" against the borrower. This deficiency judgment would permit the lender to pursue additional courses to gain complete satisfaction.

There are two aspects of a mortgage: the IOU and the security agreement. In some states there will actually be separate documents, with the IOU referred to as the "bond" and the security agreement referred to as the mortgage. In other instances, the two aspects of the mortgage are combined into a single document. The IOU portion, or the bond, sets forth the terms of repayment of the debt. The security portion sets forth the lender's rights in the event the borrower does not meet the payments when due.

A mortgage agreement, including both the bond and security aspects, is a binding legal contract that can contain a variety of different clauses that can affect the financial status of the borrower. Many of these clauses can be negotiated between the lender and the borrower at the time a new mortgage is initiated. If you assume an existing mortgage, you will be subject to the existing clauses, although there still may be room to negotiate and change existing clauses, assuming that both parties are in accord.

Whether you're obtaining a new mortgage or assuming an existing one, it's important to be aware of the existence of these clauses and the effect they can have on you. Of primary importance are those aspects of the mortgage that will determine how much the debt will cost you. To help you understand how these clauses might work, let's first examine how interest on a mortgage is figured.

paying for your mortgage

There are three elements of cost in the standard mortgage: the interest, which is the "rent" that you pay for the use of the lender's money; the acquisition fees; and the insurance costs.

interest

In the standard mortgage, your interest cost is calculated on the unpaid principal balance at each given monthly point. Here's an example of how mortgage interest is figured. In a $25,000, 25 year, 7½% mortgage, the monthly payments for interest and principal would total $184.75. During the first month of the mortgage, the principal balance that the borrower owes the lender is $25,000. By computing 7½% of $25,000 you get $1875, which would be the total interest for the year if the principal balance did not change. One twelfth of $1875 is $156.25. That represents the amount of interest due for the first full month of the mortgage. Thus, in the first month of the mortgage, the total payment of $184.75 is broken down as follows: $156.25 for interest and the remaining $28.50 for principal.

Now the full balance due has been reduced by $28.50, from the original $25,000 to $24,971.50. During the second month of the mortgage, then, the interest is based on this new principal balance of $24,971.50. One-twelfth of 7½% of that amount equals $156.07. That's the amount of interest due during the second month. In the second month, therefore, your total payment of

$184.75 is broken down into $156.07 for interest and $28.68 for principal.

The principal has now been reduced by an additional $28.68, leaving it at $24,942.82 during the third month. In the third month, then, the interest due is one-twelfth of 7½% of $24,942.82 or $155.89. The payment for the third month is then broken down into $155.89 for interest and $29.86 for principal.

That's the basic formula on which mortgage interest is figured. In each succeeding month the interest will be based on the current balance remaining after the previous month's principal portion has been applied to reduce the balance. As each month goes by and the amount of the debt shrinks, the interest factor for each subsequent month gets smaller and smaller, albeit by very slight degrees. As the interest portion of your total monthly payment decreases, the principal portion obviously then increases. As you can see from this example, and from Table 7-1, the payments during the early years of a mortgage are mostly interest. It's not until many years into the mortgage that the principal and interest portions of each monthly payment equal each other. In the last few years of a mortgage, the principal portion is substantially greater than the interest portion.

acquisition costs   Although the interest that you pay on your mortgage is, as noted, the rent you're paying for the use of the lender's money, you will also likely have to pay certain fees to reimburse the lender for his costs in putting the mortgage on his books. Practices vary in this regard from place to place and from time to time, but it's not uncommon for the lender to expect you to reimburse him for the legal expenses involved in preparing the papers, for the credit bureau costs involved in checking your credit history to determine your credit worthiness to take on the loan, for out-of-pocket expenses for appraisals on the property, and for the cost of the title search that the lender conducts for his own benefit.

In addition to the above fees you might be asked to pay "points" to the lender. The "points" are an added fee that the lender is imposing on you to improve the yield on his investment. Generally, a point equals one percent of the amount of the mortgage. Thus, two points on a $30,000 mortgage would total $60. All of these added costs—the fees and the points— should be explained to you at the time you make application for the mortgage. The manner of payment of these expenses may be dictated by the lender, or they may be negotiated between

table 7-1 **typical mortgage reduction schedule (annual interest rate: 9%; term: 30 years)**

Years elapsed	% of original balance remaining	On a mortgage of $30,000, monthly pmts. = $241.39 annual pmts. = $2,896		
		Balance due	Approx. portion of annual pmts. applying to Principal	Interest
1	99.3	$29,790	$210	$2,686
2	98.6	29,580	210	2,686
3	97.8	29,340	240	2,656
4	96.9	29,070	270	2,626
5	95.9	28,770	300	2,596
6	94.8	28,440	330	2,566
7	93.6	28,080	360	2,536
8	92.4	27,720	360	2,536
9	91.0	27,300	420	2.476
10	89.4	26,820	480	2,416
11	87.8	26,340	480	2,416
12	85.9	25,770	570	2,326
13	83.9	25,170	600	2,296
14	81.7	24,510	660	2,236
15	79.3	23,790	720	2,176
16	76.7	23,010	780	2,116
17	73.8	22,140	870	2,026
18	70.7	21,210	930	1,966
19	67.3	20,190	1,020	1,876
20	63.5	19,050	1,140	1,756
21	59.4	17,820	1,230	1,666
22	54.9	16,470	1,350	1,546
23	50.0	15,000	1,470	1,426
24	44.6	13,380	1,620	1,276
25	38.8	11,640	1,740	1,156
26	32.3	9,690	1,950	946
27	25.3	7,590	2,100	796
28	17.6	5,280	2,310	586
29	9.2	2,760	2,520	376
30	-0-	-0-	2,760	136

Note: The apparent discrepancies in some years are due to rounding.

the lender and the borrower. They may be expected to be paid in one lump sum at the time the loan is made, or they may be spread over all or a portion of the life of the loan. The effect of the former will be to reduce your available cash on hand; that of the latter will be to increase your monthly payments slightly for a period of years.

One other type of expense that you might encounter is a mortgage brokerage fee. If, for example, you were unable to obtain normal mortgage financing on your own, perhaps because of an inadequate down payment or some problems with your credit history, you may turn to a mortgage broker to find a loan for you through sources other than your local banks and savings and loan associations. He might arrange for the loan through private sources or through out-of-town institutions. He'll receive a fee for this service, which should have been negotiated in advance of retaining him. You may have the choice of paying his fee in cash at the time he obtains a firm commitment for you, or you may be able to add the fee to the amount of the mortgage and pay for it over the life of the loan. Although private mortgage brokering is an upstanding and legitimate business, abuses have been known to occur. Alleged mortgage brokers may demand a fee in advance in order to work on your case. They may deliver a mortgage whose terms are unacceptable to you (the interest rate may be too high) or, if worse comes to worst, they have been known to disappear into the night with your advance fee in their pocket. Prudence would dictate that no fees would be paid until a firm commitment is obtained, and even at that point you should check personally with the lender to determine that the mortgage commitment is in fact firm and reliable.

insurance costs The lender may require you to obtain certain insurance to protect the lender's interest primarily, and to protect your own interest secondarily. Title insurance, as discussed earlier in this chapter, is almost universally expected by the lender, the cost of which will be born by the borrower. The lender will also expect the borrower to carry adequate fire insurance on the premises so that the lender will be protected in the event of such catastrophe. The lender may also urge the borrower to obtain life insurance, so that the mortgage debt can be paid off by the insurance proceeds in the event the borrower dies. And default insurance may be involved: this kind of insurance guarantees that payments will be made for a set period of time in the event the borrower defaults. FHA and VA insurance include this kind of protection for the lender. In addition, many private firms in recent years have begun offering mortgage default insurance, which, if carried by the borrower, will usually be at the borrower's own expense.

escrow, or reserve, accounts

Escrow accounts don't actually represent an added expense to the borrower, for the money ultimately goes to pay obligations of the borrower. But they do represent an added out-of-pocket amount the borrower must be aware of. In the typical escrow account, the borrower pays in an added monthly sum to cover property insurance premiums and property taxes as they fall due. Some lenders may require an escrow account; some may offer it as an option; some may not offer it at all. Typically the lender will not pay interest on the funds he holds for your benefit, but neither will he charge you for the service in seeing to it that the payments are made as they fall due. The escrow account can be an excellent way of levelling out one's total annual budget program, for the property insurance premiums and property tax bills can be very large and very disruptive to the normal budget.

An escrow account can cause some minor fluctuations in your monthly payments from year to year. Escrow accounts are normally analyzed once a year to determine how much will be needed in the account for the following year. This estimate is based on the expected amount of property insurance premiums and property taxes that will be due in the following year. Because these amounts generally are on the increase, a borrower can expect a slight increase in total monthly payments from year to year to cover the rising costs of insurance and taxes.

important clauses in your mortgage

There are a number of possible clauses that can be contained in a mortgage that would have the effect of changing your interest rate and thus your monthly payments. If you consent to such clauses on the signing of a new mortgage, or by assuming an existing mortgage that contains such clauses, you have given the lender the right to exercise those privileges and you should assume that he will take advantage of those rights.

rate increase clauses

Prior to the 1970s, interest rates throughout the economy fluctuated only mildly. Mortgage lending institutions (primarily banks and savings and loan associations) would acquire their raw materials (depositors' savings accounts) and would be fairly well assured that the cost of those raw materials (the interest rate that they paid on deposits) would remain fairly stable over an extended period of time. Thus, say, in 1965 a lender who was at the time paying 4% interest on savings accounts, granted a mortgage loan for a 30 year term at a 6% interest rate. The difference between what he was paying his depositors (4%) and what he was receiving from his borrower (6%) was his margin on which he would operate and hopefully realize a profit. He was committed to receive the 6% over a 30 year period, and he assumed at that time, based on prevailing conditions and anticipated conditions, that he would continue to pay out the 4% over an indefinite period of time.

But by the 1970s, economic conditions in the nation and in the world caused interest rates to start fluctuating wildly. In 1975 that same lender looked at his 6% mortgage loan, now 10 years old, and realized that he was now paying not 4% but upwards of 7% on many of his savings accounts and certificates. In other words, he was paying out as much, if not more, than he was taking in. Naturally, he had adjusted the interest rate of subsequent brand new mortgages to a figure higher than what he was paying out on savings accounts, but that didn't help him with regard to the older mortgages that had already been on the books. He would have to live with them for their expected life.

Thus, many lenders began to build into their mortgage agreements clauses that would allow them to vary the interest rate as conditions warranted. These clauses normally will take one of three forms: the escalator clause, the variable rate clause, and the balloon or call privilege.

the escalator clause

This clause will specifically amend the interest rate at stated points in time. For example, the clause may state that the mortgage will run for a total of 30 years, and that the interest rate for the first three years will be 7%, for the next three years, 8%, and from the seventh year onward, 9%. In the late 1970s, a number of lending institutions began to experiment with this program, hoping that slightly lower than standard rates in the first few years of a mortgage would make it easier for home buyers to afford the payments, with the lender making up the difference by a slightly higher rate some years after the inception of the mortgage.

the variable rate clause

This clause will allow the lender to vary your interest rate from time to time depending on prevailing interest rates throughout the country. Variable rate clauses are usually pegged to the prevailing prime rate, which is the interest rate large banks charge their major borrowers on short-term loans. For example; if the current prevailing prime rate is 7%, a lender might write a new mortgage loan at a 9% rate, with the right to vary that rate up or down as the prime rate fluctuates. If the prime rate were then to rise by one-half of one percent, so would the interest rate on the mortgage. Likewise, if the prime rate were to drop one-half of one percent, so would the interest rate on the mortgage. Variable rate clauses are usually activated only at pre-stated points in time, such as each six months or each twelve months. There should be a ceiling and a floor on any variable rate clause, such as a 1% change. In other words, the rate may vary upwards or downwards, but will not exceed 1% from the original rate. In the above example, therefore, the rate could not ever exceed 10% nor could it ever go below 8%.

the balloon clause, or call privilege

Such a clause would permit the lender to demand that the entire loan be paid off at a set point in time. For example, a loan for $30,000 may be set to run for 30 years at an 8% interest rate. This would require monthly payments of $220. The balloon clause, or call privilege, would state that at the end of 10 years the lender had the right to demand that the entire remaining balance be paid off. Ten years into the above mortgage would leave a remaining principal balance of $26,310. The borrower would, at that time, have to pay off or refinance the existing balance. The lender might be willing to refinance the remaining balance, but at a higher interest rate. With 20 years yet to go on the mortgage, the lender might rewrite the loan at a 9% interest rate for 20 years, which would mean monthly payments of roughly $237 per month, a $17 per month increase. Or, the lender might be willing to rewrite the remaining balance of the loan for a new 30 year term at a 9% interest rate, which would mean monthly payments of about $212 per month, an $8 reduction, but considerably more interest expense over the remaining years.

These escalation clauses will vary from lender to lender and from time to time, but all are subject to the laws of usury—the interest rate may not exceed the legal limit established by the state. Anyone shopping for a new mortgage or considering assuming an existing mortgage must determine whether any of these escalation clauses exist, and what their effect might be over the anticipated period you'll be occupying the dwelling.

assumption clauses

Most mortgages contain clauses that permit assumption of the debt. That means that the owner of a house can sell the house to another party and the new buyer can assume the existing debt. The new buyer, in other words, steps into the shoes of the former owner and becomes liable for the remaining balance on the debt, and all other terms and conditions of the mortgage. Assumption privileges are subject to the right of approval of the lender. The lender might, for example, refuse to allow a person with a known bad credit history to assume an existing mortgage. The reasons are obvious. Even if a mortgage does not contain an assumption privilege clause, the lender might still permit a subsequent buyer to assume the debt, but conceivably could require such an assumption to be at a higher rate of interest. If you are contemplating buying a house and assuming an existing mortgage, you should determine in advance whether or not you will be permitted to assume the mortgage, and at what interest rate. If you are entering into a new mortgage, the existence of or absence of an assumption clause can have an effect on your ability to later sell the house.

prepayment clauses

You might come into a sum of money and wish to make advance payments on your mortgage, either wholly or partially. Do you have the right to do so, and if so, will it cost you anything? Some mortgages will contain prepayment privilege clauses, which will allow you to make such advance payments on your debt without suffering any penalty. On the other hand, some mortgages will have prepayment penalty clauses that will state that you must pay a penalty if you do prepay early. The prepayment penalty clauses are obviously an attempt by the lender to discourage prepayment during the early years of the mortgage. Why would they want to do this? At the time they make the loan, they feel they have a good long-term situation. During the early years of the mortgage they may think that they will not have recovered all of their costs of putting the loan on the books, and will not have gotten the return they were seeking over the long pull. This, in spite of the fact that they may have charged advance fees and may have been reimbursed for many of their initial expenses. The lender simply wants to keep costly turnovers at a minimum and the prepayment penalty clause is one way of doing so.

open end clauses These are rare, but might be negotiated if requested. A typical open end clause permits the borrower to borrow back up to the original amount of the mortgage at the same interest rate, perhaps without paying any costs or fees in the process.

shopping for the best mortgage If you're buying a house with an existing mortgage that you plan to assume, you're more or less locked into the terms of that mortgage. That doesn't mean that you can't discuss revision of any of the terms with the lender. It might be worth your while to do so to help tailor a payment program that would be best suited to your own financial circumstances.

If you're buying a house and seeking your own original financing, the following shopping list and tables can help you work out the deal that's best suited to your own circumstances.

acquisition costs What "points" and other fees will you have to pay? These should be clearly explained to you at the time you make application for your mortgage. Will they have to be paid in cash at the time the loan is made, or can they be spread out over the mortgage loan itself, and if so, for how long a period?

interest rate What will the original interest rate be and to what fluctuations may it be subject? Refer to the escalation clauses noted earlier.

how much down payment is required? The amount of the down payment required, and the amount that you may have available for down payment, may not jibe. If you have more than enough, you're in good shape. If you have less than the required amount, how will you raise the difference? If one lender requires a higher down payment than another, his interest rate may be lower, or his other terms may be more favorable. These must be compared.

term of the mortgage How long will it run? Longer terms mean lower monthly payments, but a much higher interest expense over the long term.

Tables 7-2 through 7-7 (at the end of this chapter) will assist you in figuring the cost involved in mortgages at varying interest rates, terms, and down payments.

types of mortgage loans The most common type of mortgage loan is known as the *conventional mortgage*. A conventional mortgage is a loan agreement arrived at between the borrower and the lender on terms established by the lender. The interest rate is subject to the laws of usury in that state. (The laws of usury dictate the maximum amount of interest that a lender can legally charge on given types of loans.) In a conventional loan situation the lender will have satisfied itself that the borrower is credit worthy and that the value of the property is substantial enough to assure the lender's position. In some cases, lenders may wish a measure of added security for the loan and may request or require that the borrower pay for a form of insurance known as mortgage guarantee insurance. Mortgage guarantee insurance will assure that the lender will receive a stipulated amount in the event the borrower defaults and the property does not bring enough money on foreclosure to cover the entire debt.

In addition to the conventional mortgage, a borrower may qualify for one of two forms of mortgage backed by agencies of the United States government. The Federal Housing Administration will insure certain mortgage loans if both the buyer and the property qualify with governmental requirements. These are known as *FHA loans*. The Veteran's Administration will also guarantee certain loans made to eligible armed services veterans, again providing that all qualifications are met. These are known as *VA loans*. Since the government is involved in protecting the lenders in these types of loans, it also reserves the right to establish maximum interest rates on such loans. Often, lenders will find that the governmentally imposed maximum interest rates don't offer enough profit margin to the lender. Thus, lenders may add additional charges to the cost of the FHA or VA loans to offset the difference between those interest rates and current conventional mortgage rates. Fees may also be added to conventional mortgage rates, as circumstances demand.

The borrower should shop and compare carefully among these various types of loans before making a decision.

applying for a
mortgage

The would-be home buyer might be wise to invest a few hours visiting with mortgage lenders in the area prior to beginning the househunting expedition. The purpose would not necessarily be to make an actual application for a mortgage but to determine the prevailing requirements, interest rates, and terms in the area at that time. Knowing these terms in advance can assist the buyer in knowing what price range to be realistically shopping for. Some lenders may be willing to accept a preliminary application that would be processed once specific facts were known regarding the house.

Once the buyer does find a house that he wishes to buy, and purchase terms have been more or less agreed on, the buyer can then approach specific lending institutions to focus on the actual mortgage terms that would be available. At the time of making formal application—which entails a detailed interview between the mortgage lender and the borrower—the institution should disclose exactly what charges will be made for the services and precisely what the terms of the loan will be, assuming that the loan is consummated at the time anticipated by the parties. Prior to receiving a commitment for a mortgage loan, the borrower should expect that the lender will require an appraisal of the property (generally at the buyer's expense) and that the buyer's credit history will be thoroughly checked by the lender.

If the application is approved, the borrower should obtain a copy of the commitment in writing so that there is no mistake about the terms of the arrangement.

☐ *What if conventional, FHA, or VA financing isn't available?* Perhaps because of the credit history of the borrower, or because of the size of the loan in relation to the value of the property, a home buyer may not be able to obtain mortgage financing. If the buyer is not successful in obtaining a mortgage approval through a commercial bank, a savings and loan association, a mutual savings bank, or a life insurance company that deals in mortgage lending, he might turn to private mortgage brokers in his community. Private mortgage brokers act as intermediaries in finding mortgage loans for property buyers, usually obtaining the funds through private investors. In all likelihood, the interest rates for such loans will be higher than through normal channels, and in addition the mortgage broker will likely be entitled to a fee for his services in obtaining a loan. Before one enters into any commitment with a private mortgage broker, the terms of such an arrangement should be explicitly understood.

☐ *What if a normal mortgage loan isn't enough?* You wish to buy a home that is selling for $40,000. You have $8000 cash available to use as a down payment, but the most anyone will lend you on a mortgage is $25,000. That leaves you $7000 short. How can you close the gap? It may be possible—

though not necessarily advisable—to seek what is known as a "second mortgage." A second mortgage is a loan against the property that is secondary to the main, or first, mortgage. In other words, the holder of the second mortgage stands in line behind the holder of the first mortgage in the event of a default and foreclosure on the property. When a piece of property is sold on foreclosure, the first mortgagee gets first crack at the proceeds of the sale. If the property sells for more than the amount of the first mortgage, what's left will go to the holder of the second mortgage. And so on through third mortgages, fourth mortgages . . .

Obviously, then, the holder of the second mortgage is taking a higher degree or risk and can be expected to charge a higher rate of interest for the money. Further, the second mortgage is usually established for a much shorter period than the first mortgage. Getting back to the above example: you're $7000 shy of what you need to buy the property. You might be able to obtain a seven year mortgage, which might run for seven years. The interest rate and other charges you're likely to pay for obtaining a second mortgage will prove quite expensive. And the high payments necessitated by the relatively short term will drastically increase your monthly outlay.

Very careful arithmetic and a very precise analysis of your budget is necessary before becoming involved in a second mortgage situation as a home buyer. It might be far cheaper and far more prudent in the long run to simply forego the higher priced house and seek something of a more modest nature that you can more easily afford within your existing budget.

What's best: making the biggest possible down payment and having lower monthly payments, or making a smaller down payment and investing what's left? In Table 7-7, a homebuyer has up to $12,000 available to use as a down payment. His budget will allow for monthly payments (interest and principal) of $273.58. He is buying a $40,000 house, and the mortgage will run for 30 years, at a nine percent interest rate.

For purposes of this example, and to help guide you in making your own decisions regarding mortgage financing, the individual plans to invest whatever he doesn't use as down payment; he also plans to invest the difference between his monthly mortgage payment and his budgeted allotment of $273.58. In other words, if he decides to make a down payment of only $8000, he'll have a lump-sum of $4000 left to invest. We'll call that the "lump-sum nest-egg." With an $8000 down payment, monthly payments will total $257.48, or about $16 less than he can take out of his budget. He'll invest that $16 every month, and we'll call that the "monthly nest-egg."

Investment of both the "lump-sum nest-egg" and the "monthly nest-egg" will be in a passbook savings account paying 5½% interest per year, compounding quarterly.

The table shows the effect of the various alternatives over varying periods of time. The column on the far right—"Out-of-pocket difference: total paid out less total of nest-eggs" gives a relative view of the various alternatives. The example is based on the ideal assumption that savings will be regular and without fail. Figures are rounded, and income tax considerations (neither deductibility of interest expense nor taxation on interest earned) are not included.

the closing

Depending on what the parties have agreed to, the closing may take place at the offices of the mortgage lender, at one of the attorney's offices, at the title insurance office, or at the offices where the recording of the documents will take place. The signed deed, in accordance with the purchase contract, will be delivered to the buyer, and the appropriate monies or IOU's delivered to the seller. Also, the appropriate "adjustments" will be made, and payment passed accordingly.

adjustments

The adjustments are a pro-rating of any expenses that will have been incurred on the property by the seller. For example, property taxes on the house total $800 per year, payable in installments on January 1 and July 1. The closing between the buyer and the seller takes place on April 1. The seller will have previously paid a $400 property tax installment on January 1. This covers the first six months of the year. Thus, the buyer will have to reimburse the seller for $200 worth of property taxes, representing the period from April 1 to July 1, during which the buyer will have occupancy of the property.

By the time of the closing, the buyer should have also made arrangements with his insurance agent to have the property insurance in effect in his own name. He should also arrange with the local utility companies—gas, electricity, water—to have the meters changed over to his name effective as of the date of the closing. Even though the new buyer may not take occupancy until sometime after the closing, he will be responsible for these costs from the time of closing onward.

The closing is also the appropriate time for the seller to pay any real estate commissions to the agent who represented him; the lawyers for the parties and the title insurance company will also receive payments due them. With all these payments changing hands at the closing, it's wise for the buyer to determine well in advance how much cash will be required of him so that all payments can be made without embarrassment.

recording Individual state laws govern the recording requirements for the appropriate documents. The recording of the mortgage agreement is the responsibility of the lender, and the recording of the deed is the responsibility of the buyer. Recording these documents in the fashion required by state law puts the world on notice that the lender has a mortgage lien on the property and that the owner has ownership of the property. The buyer's attorney or title insurance company will theoretically have searched the title to the property up to the time of closing. But if the search was concluded days, or even hours, prior to the closing, it is possible for a lien to have snuck in against the property. Although this happens rarely, it can cause tremendous problems. Thus, the ultimate precaution is to have a search conducted at the time of closing to be certain that no liens have attached themselves to the property prior to the actual moment of transfer.

selling your property

All of the elements of the property transaction referred to in the foregoing discussion apply equally to the seller. But the seller has some additional considerations that must be evaluated.

using a real estate agent

Does it pay to use a real estate agent to sell your house, or should you try to sell it on your own and save the commission costs? Real estate commissions on the sale of a house are usually at least 6% of the selling price, and they could exceed that depending on the locale, the nature of the property, and unusual difficulties that the agent might anticipate in selling the property.

If time and money are no object to the seller, he or she might want to try for a limited period of time to sell it personally. But except in rare cases, time and money are of concern. The seller no doubt has made arrangements to move into another dwelling, and wishes to shed the old dwelling before making the move. If he hasn't sold his old home before he takes occupancy of the new dwelling, he'll be making payments on two properties at once, be they apartments or houses. It only takes a few months of these double payments to quickly equalize what the real estate commission might have been.

What can a real estate agent do for the seller? As a professional the agent is equipped to write and place appealing advertisements that will lure prospective buyers. The ads are at the agent's expense. If a seller attempts to dispose of his own home, he'll have to absorb that advertising cost.

Real estate agents are knowledgeable about local market conditions, and can assist you in establishing a realistic price for your property. They're aware of what comparable sales have been in the area, and can quickly determine asking prices that may be too high or too low. If you attempt to establish your own price, you could delay a sale by asking more than market conditions warrant, or you could end up with less than you should have gotten because your price was too low.

The real estate agent has access to local lending institutions and can make it easier for prospective buyers to obtain financing, if that's necessary. The agent can, in effect, put together a "package deal" that would include the sale of the house and the financing. You might have difficulty in duplicating this feat. It can facilitate a sale considerably if the prospective buyer is told that a mortgage loan is available, his or her credit worthiness permitting, at acceptable terms. Without this assistance, the seller going it alone will have to inform the prospective buyer to go out and find his own financing. This can be a discouraging element in your negotiations.

The real estate agent who is a member of a brokerage firm has other affiliated agents who will be seeking prospective buyers. Further, if the firm is associated with the local multiple listing service, the property will be made available to all brokerage firms who do subscribe to that service. In effect, you have an extensive sales force working on your behalf throughout the entire community, as opposed to your trying to do it on your own.

Normally, a real estate agent will require you to sign an exclusive listing agreement that will bind you to him or her for as long as the exclusive runs, with six months being a normal minimum in many communities. If another firm other than the one you're dealing with brings in the ultimate buyer, your own firm will still get a portion of the commission. The listing agreement will set forth your asking price, but there is no assurance whatsoever that the agent will be able to deliver a buyer willing to pay that price. Thus, the asking price included in the listing agreement is not binding on anyone. It's merely a target toward which the agent will be shooting.

It is possible for abuses to occur in this area. An agent, overanxious to get your listing, may lead you to believe that he can deliver a buyer at a much higher price than you might have expected. You could thus be lured into signing a long-term exclusive agreement with an agent whose actual performance may be far less than what you would have wanted. As in acquiring any other kind of professional help, it's important that you determine the reputation and integrity of the real estate firm you're dealing with. The real estate industry has an ethics code designed to protect the public, but, as in any industry, abuses will occur. Before you sign an exclusive listing agreement with any agent or firm, you should attempt to gather personal references from other individuals who have used the services of that individual or firm. You should also check with your local county Board of Realtors to determine if the individual or firm is in good standing, and with the state Board of Licensing that controls real estate brokers and sales agents to determine that their license requirements have been met and maintained.

If an agent delivers a buyer who is willing to offer terms that you are willing to accept, and you enter into an agreement accordingly, then you will be obliged to pay the real estate commission. Under such circumstances, if you as the seller are unwilling or unable to follow through with your part of the deal, you can expect to still be required to pay the commission.

preparing your house for sale

The real estate agent may also be able to assist you in putting your house in the best possible condition to facilitate a sale. For example, it may seem insignificant, but you may have long ceased to notice certain odors in your home, emanating from cooking, pets, pipe smoking, and so on. The agent might rightfully indicate to you that such odors exist and might be detrimental in attempting to sell the house. Some simple adjustments during the period when your house is being shown to prospective buyers can eliminate that problem. Landscaping, brightening the lighting, and adjusting certain traffic patterns might also enhance the salability of the house.

moving expenses

Whether you're buying a house or selling a house, you're going to be moving, and moving involves many important considerations. Whether you decide to hire a moving company or do it yourself will probably depend on the amount of household goods you'll be moving, the distance, and the time of year (a do-it-yourself move during the snowy season may involve more travail than you're willing to put up with).

If you hire a moving company for an interstate move (moving from one state into another), the rates regarding weight and distance are controlled by the Interstate Commerce Commission. Such moves of equal weight and equal distance will cost virtually the same with all moving companies. There may be distinct differences, though, in the overall cost of the move based on the amount of packing and unpacking you wish the moving company to do. These rates may vary from company to company; and you may wish to do some of your own packing and have the moving company do some of it, particularly for glassware and other breakables. Representatives of moving companies can give you *estimates* on the cost of your move, but bear in mind that these are *only estimates* and *not firm bids.* The actual cost won't be determined until the van is loaded and weighed prior to its departure.

tax considerations when you move

If you meet certain requirements of the Internal Revenue Service, a major portion of your moving expenses (for which you are not reimbursed by your employer) may be tax deductible. Because moving expenses can amount to a considerable sum of money, you should keep a careful record of all such expenses and take advantage of whatever the law allows.

You must meet two tests in order for the expenses of your move to be deductible. The first is the distance test. First, measure the distance between your old home and your former place of work. Let's say it's 10 miles. Now measure the distance between your old home and your new place of work. Let's say that's 50 miles. Thus, the distance between your old home and your new job is 40 miles greater than the distance between your old home and your old job. You would then pass the distance test, for the law requires that the difference between these two distances be at least 35 miles. On the other hand, if your old home and your old job were 5 miles apart, and your old home and your new job were 30 miles apart, you would not pass the distance test. The difference between the two distances would be only 25 miles—not enough to meet the 35 mile minimum requirement. Note that the distance test does not refer to the location of your new *residence*, but rather to the location of your new *place of work.*

The second test that you must meet in order to have the eligible moving expenses deductible is the time test. During the 12 month period immediately following the move, you must be employed full time for at least 39 weeks in order to pass the time test. If you're self employed, you must be employed full time for at least 39 weeks during the first 12 months immediately following the move, and you must also be employed full time for at least 78 weeks of the 24 month period immediately following the move.

If you meet both the distance test and the time test, the following expenses of your move may be deductible.

1. Travel expenses, including meals and lodging for yourself and your family while en route from your old residence to your new one.
2. The costs of moving your household goods and personal effects.
3. The costs of househunting trips before you have moved, including transportation and meals and lodging during your househunting trip.
4. The cost of temporary quarters at your new location, if such are needed, for up to 30 days after you've obtained your work.
5. The costs of selling your residence or settling your lease at your old location, and the cost of purchasing a residence or acquiring a new lease at the new location. These costs can include brokers' commissions, attorneys fees, points, and similar expenses incident to the sale or purchase of a home.

These deductible expenses are based on the presumption that you will be working in your new location.

There are limitations to the amount you can deduct. Items 3, 4, and 5 are limited to a total of $3000, of which no more than a total of $1500 may be used for househunting trips (item 3) and the cost of temporary quarters (item 4). Check with an accountant or with the nearest office of the Internal Revenue Service for more specific details on the deductibility of moving expenses.

income taxes on the proceeds of selling your residence

If you sell your property and realize a gain, that gain may be subject to income taxes in the year in which you sell. If you sell your property and suffer a loss, the loss will not be deductible. As with most all tax laws, the specific regulations that apply to this situation can be very complex, and professional assistance would be advisable.

You have to assume that the Internal Revenue Service will be aware of the fact that you have moved, simply by virtue of the new address on your tax return. Your move, of course, may not necessarily mean that you have sold a residence. You may have moved from a rental unit, or you may not have actually sold your house. But if you have sold a house, the pertinent facts of the transaction should be reported on Schedule D of your 1040 form.

Although a sale of a residence at a gain is reportable and taxable, the law does permit certain factors that you can take advantage of; the gain might not be as much as it would appear to be, and the tax may be deferred or postponed for an extended period.

The gain that is taxable is not simply the difference between what you originally paid for the house and what you finally sold it for. For example, if you originally paid $20,000 for the house and you now sell it for $30,000, that would appear to represent a gain of $10,000. Not necessarily so. The difference between what you bought it for and what you sold it for can be decreased by a number of factors. These factors include selling expenses, such as real estate commissions, advertising expenses, legal fees, and loan charges. The original cost of the residence may be adjusted by virtue of certain improvements that you made to the property and fixing up expenses that you incurred in order to get it in shape to sell at the best possible price. In other words, if you had added $1000 worth of eligible improvements to the house, and spent another $500 on fixing up expenses in preparation of selling it, your "adjusted cost basis" on the house would be increased from $20,000 to $21,500. Further, if you incurred selling expenses of, say, $1800 in real estate commissions and $500 in other eligible expenses, your selling price would be reduced from $30,000 to $27,700, which is the "amount realized." The taxable gain would then be the difference between the $27,700 and the $21,500, or $6200.

The tax on any such gain may be deferred if, within 18 months before or 18 months after the sale, you buy and occupy another principal residence, the cost of which equals or exceeds the adjusted sales price (as defined by the IRS) of the old residence. Additional time is allowed if you construct the new residence, or if you are on active duty in the U.S. Armed Forces at the time you sold your house. If, though, the purchase price of your new residence is less than the sale price of the old residence, a portion of the gain, or all of the gain, may be taxable during that year. If you do not purchase a new principal residence, the gain similarly will be taxable during that year.

The tax on the gain can be postponed virtually indefinitely or at least until such time as you sell your residence and do not reinvest the proceeds in another principal residence. Specific rules on this subject pertain to individuals who have reached the age of 65, in which case the gain on a sale of a residence may be totally excluded within IRS limitations.

In order to minimize any gain, and to take fullest advantage of the deferral of the taxes due, careful record keeping of all expenses related to your housing and to the sales transaction is essential.

renting: the lease and its key clauses

Renting a dwelling—be it a house, a mobile home, or an apartment—involves numerous rights and obligations between the landlord and tenant. Those rights and obligations may be spelled out in a full-fledged contract called a lease. Although many tenancies will be based on a handshake or a brief letter between the parties, the fullest protection is not available to you as a tenant without the detailed documentation that the lease will contain. A lease is not of the same financial magnitude as the purchase of a house and the mortgage that corresponds to it, but it can entail many thousands of dollars that you will be paying, and you want to make sure you're getting what you bargained for.

The lease, basically, entitles you to occupy certain premises for a certain period of time at an agreed on cost. Here are some of the key clauses that could well affect the nature and cost of your occupancy.

expenses The lease should set forth exactly who is responsible for what expenses in connection with the property. If the landlord is responsible for all utilities and all real estate taxes, the lease should so state. If the tenant is responsible for individual utilities, will the tenant be separately metered so that the true utility costs can be exactly measured? If the tenant is paying based on a certain percentage of the total building occupancy, and is not separately metered, will the tenant be getting a fair shake, or will he or she be paying more than necessary for actual utility usage? If the tenant is responsible for paying a portion of the property taxes, over and above the landlord's own payments, will that obligation be based on the proportionate rental of the individual unit to the total rental role of the whole building? Or will the tax obligation be based on an arbitrary percentage? These details should be explicit in the written agreement.

repairs
Who will be responsible for *making* which repairs? And perhaps more important, who will be responsible for *paying* for the repairs that are made? The landlord may be responsible for seeing to it that repairs are made, but some repairs may be done at the tenant's expense, while others at the landlord's. Generally, the landlord is responsible for repairing structural defects and for keeping the central heating unit in proper working order. The tenants may be responsible for attending to their own repairs on minor items within the premises, including but not limited to plumbing leaks and defective appliances. If you have examined the premises before you sign a lease, you should be able to determine what possible repair bills you might be facing during your occupancy. If you, or the contractor you hire to assist you in your evaluation, determine that you would be more than normally vulnerable to repair costs, you might want to consider renegotiating the repair clause of your lease with the landlord before you sign.

quiet enjoyment
Quiet enjoyment is a legal term that assures you of the right to privacy and quiet in your occupancy of the premises. If the landlord fails to deliver quiet enjoyment—that is, fails to keep the adjoining neighbors from playing air hockey next to your bedroom wall at four o'clock in the morning—you will have the right to either withhold your rent payment or get assistance in the courts in upholding your rights.

extra fees
Does your monthly rental include all of the features of your occupancy, or will added costs be hidden in the small print on the back page of the lease, such as parking fees, use of recreational facilities, and assessments for improvements in the common areas? All rental costs and fees should be clearly understood prior to the signing of any lease.

renewal options
Will you have a right to renew your lease on the expiration of the original term? Not all leases contain this privilege, and it may be one worth bargaining for. Without a renewal option, the landlord can ask whatever the market would bear when the original lease term expires. If the tenant is not willing to pay

what the landlord is asking, the landlord has the right to have the tenant move out. A renewal option is for the protection of the tenant: he or she has the right to either stay on at the agreed on rental or move out. It's reasonable to expect that the rental rate on a renewal would be higher than on the original term, so that the landlord can be protected against rising costs. Even at a higher rent, though, the renewal option does offer the tenant flexibility and choice, things often worth paying for.

sublease privileges

You may be subleasing *from* another party, or you may wish to sublease *to* another party. If you are subleasing from the original tenant, you will be subject to the terms of his or her lease. Prior to subleasing from another party, you might want to determine if in fact that party has the right to sublease to you, and if the landlord has given consent, if such consent is called for in the original lease. If you sublease from another party, and that party does not have the legal right to sublease to you, the landlord technically could evict you, and perhaps the main tenant as well, for the lease would have been violated.

On the other hand, if you wish to have the right to sublease to other parties while you are the main tenant, you had best make certain that the lease contains this privilege. In the sublease clause, the landlord may or may not reserve the right to approve of any sublessee, generally for reasons of credit worthiness. Unless the landlord consents, the fact that you subleased to another party will not relieve you of your obligation to pay the rent.

A sublease privilege is one that favors the tenant. It gives the tenant the flexibility of being able to move out before the lease has expired, and be able to defray obligations by allowing another party to live in the apartment or house. If you do sublease to another party, you must make certain in advance that the party is credit worthy and reliable. It would pay to obtain a credit history on the party to whom you're subleasing to determine these relative factors.

security deposits

There are three possible types of security deposits that you might be required to pay: deposits to insure the payment of the rent, cleaning deposits, and breakage deposits. The rental deposit is usually designated to cover the last month's rent of the lease. This gives the landlord some protection in the event you move out early. The fact that you do move out early does not necessarily relieve you of your remaining obligations under the lease. Technically, if you move out after 18 months of a 24 month lease, you'll be liable for the remaining 6 months. The landlord will apply the one month's deposit that you have paid toward that six months obligation, and will be able to commence legal proceedings to collect the remaining five months worth of rent from you.

An additional clause that can be to the tenant's benefit would be one stating that the landlord must make a reasonable attempt to rent vacated space, and if he is able to rent the premises during the term of your vacancy, that all or a portion of the rent that he collects from another tenant occupying your premises will apply toward your obligation. For example, you vacate your premises six months early. Your monthly rental is $300. The landlord has received a $300 security deposit from you that he applies to your remaining obligation, which leaves you owing the landlord $1500. The landlord is successful in renting the apartment for $200 a month for the six month period. The $1200 that he thus takes in should apply toward your $1500 obligation, leaving you with a debt of $300.

Cleaning and breakage deposits may or may not be refundable, depending on the agreement between the tenant and the landlord. If the premise does need cleaning, the landlord can be expected to apply the cleaning deposit to that task and the tenant will not receive any of his or her deposit back. If damage or breakage has occurred, the damage deposit will be applied to making the necessary repairs, but the tenant's obligation may not be limited to the amount of the breakage deposit. If the breakage or damage exceeds the amount of the deposit, and the lease stipulates that the damages aren't limited to that amount, the landlord can pursue the tenant for the excess needed to make the appropriate repairs.

For the fullest protection of the tenant, both parties should closely examine all aspects of the premises before the tenant takes occupancy to determine the condition of cleanliness and what damages exist at the time the tenant takes occupancy. For example, there may be a crack in a wall that would normally be covered by a piece of furniture or a wall hanging. If it's there when the tenant takes occupancy, the fact should be noted on the lease document so that no one can claim that you as the tenant caused the damage during the period of your occupancy. The tenant and the landlord may trust each other implicitly, but the tenant has to remember that when he or she moves out there may be a different landlord who will not remember that the crack was there at the time the tenant moved in.

improvements   The tenant of an apartment or a house may wish to make certain improvements on the premises during the term of occupancy. Normally, if improvements are easily removable, such as carpeting, they would remain the property of the tenant. Some improvements, however, may not be quite so portable. For example, a tenant may install built-in bookcases, or a wet bar. Unless the tenant and the landlord have agreed in advance, the nature of improvements of this sort might be such that the landlord could claim them as his property. If any improvements are to be made in the premises, the landlord and tenant should agree before the improvements are made as to who will have the benefit on the termination of the lease.

amending the lease   Even though a lease is a binding legal contract, it can be amended at any time on mutual agreement of the landlord and tenant. (The same holds true in a purchase contract for a house or condominium.) If the parties do agree to any amendments in the contract, and proper consideration (payment) is made between the parties, and the amendment is properly signed by both parties, changes can be accomplished. Any of the above clauses could thus be inserted into a lease agreement even after the agreement has originally been signed and occupancy has been taken. Whether or not to make any amendments on the lease is a matter of bargaining, and if one party is giving up certain rights, he or she will naturally want to receive certain other rights in exchange. Before any rights or obligations are exchanged, legal advice should be sought as to the specific consequences of such actions.

combinations of leasing and buying

There can be situations in which an individual becomes a tenant and then an owner. He or she may have a lease with an option to buy, or one with a first refusal to buy. Arrangements of this sort may be particularly favorable to the occupants who are not certain of their future. For example, a job transfer moves a family to a new city. They're not sure if the job will work out or if they'll want to stay in that new city. Because of their uncertainty, they don't want to commit themselves to purchasing a house, but they do want to live in a nice dwelling. At the end of the year, if they've decided to stay, they don't want to have to trouble themselves with moving again from a rental unit to a house that they may then decide to purchase. They might therefore look to lease a house or condominium for a one year period, with the right, after one year, to buy that house or condominium should they so desire.

a lease with an option to buy

A lease with an option to purchase puts the parties in this status: as tenants they have the right to occupy the premises for the stated time and for the stated rental. At any time during their tenancy, they have the right to notify the owner of their intent to purchase the property at a previously agreed on price. During the period of the tenancy, the owner cannot sell the property to any other party, unless the tenants agree to release their option to buy.

Here's an example. The Greens lease a house at $400 per month with an option to buy the house for $30,000. They may exercise their right to buy at any time during their tenancy, but at least 30 days before the end of the lease. If they wish to exercise their option, they give the owner the proper notice and enter into a sales agreement. If they fail to give the proper notice within the allotted time, their option will expire and they will no longer have the right to purchase at the agreed on price.

By entering into a lease with an option to buy, the owner of the premises is taking his property off the market for at least the term of the lease. He has no assurance that the tenant will in fact buy the property from him, and he may be foregoing an opportunity to lease or sell the property to others at a better rental or purchase price. Thus, the owner of the property can well be expected to charge a premium for the lease, and perhaps for the purchase as well. In other words, although the property might normally rent for $350 per month, he may charge $400 per month. Also, the property might normally have a market value of $27,000, he may put an asking price of $30,000 on it.

Market conditions existing at that time will also have a bearing on the pricing. If there are more houses on the market than there are willing buyers, the owner may be happy to enter into such a lease/purchase arrangement. If, though, there are more buyers than houses available, the reverse could be true and a heavy premium might have to be paid.

Depending on individual circumstances, a lease with an option to buy can be a very desirable arrangement for certain individuals. In exchange for the premium rental or purchase price that may have to be paid, a considerable measure of flexibility can be obtained. The arrangement can also eliminate the need for making a second move, the cost of which may well offset the premium price being paid on the lease or purchase.

a lease with a right of first refusal

A lease with a right of first refusal to purchase is another alternative that should be considered by persons falling into the above circumstances. Under a lease with a right of first refusal to purchase, the tenant does not have an outright guarantee that he can purchase the property at a pre-established price. The tenant and the owner will agree on an ultimate purchase price, but the owner will still be free to offer the property for sale to others during the term of the tenancy, subject however to the right of the tenant to meet or beat any bona fide offer that the owner may acquire. Here's how such an arrangement might work. The tenant and the owner agree on a $400 per month rental, and a $30,000 purchase price after one year. The tenant is not obliged to purchase at all, but may do so at that price if the property is still available at that time. During the period of the tenancy, the landlord has the right to offer the property for sale to anyone at all. Another would-be buyer offers $32,000. The tenant then has the express right to meet or beat that $32,000 offer within a period of, say, 10 days after he's been notified by the landlord of the offer. If the tenant wishes to meet the offer, he can become the owner. If the tenant does not wish to meet the offer, he must give up the property.

In the case of a lease with a first refusal to purchase, the landlord is not taking the property off the market, as he does under a lease with an option to purchase. Thus, the landlord might be less inclined to charge a premium price for either the rental or the purchase. The tenant under such an arrangement, however, does run the risk of not being able to buy the property at the desired price. The trade-off—a possibly lower rent and purchase price versus a possible inability to buy the property—has to be carefully evaluated. Leasing with a right of first refusal can be an attractive alternative to leasing with an option to purchase, and either of these may be more desirable than an outright lease or an outright purchase, unless the family is so certain of its plans that it doesn't need the flexibility offered by these alternatives.

table 7-2 **mortgage reduction schedule**
Percent of Original Balance Remaining on a
Mortgage

Years elapsed	Original Length of Mortgage			
	15 yrs.	20 yrs.	25 yrs.	30 yrs.
1	96.7	98.1	98.9	99.3
2	93.1	96.1	97.7	98.6
3	89.1	93.8	96.3	97.8
4	84.8	91.4	94.9	96.9
5	80.1	88.7	93.3	95.9
6	74.9	85.8	91.5	94.8
7	69.2	82.6	89.6	93.6
8	63.0	79.1	87.5	92.4
9	56.3	75.2	85.2	91.0
10	48.9	71.0	82.7	89.4
11	40.8	66.4	80.0	87.8
12	31.9	61.4	77.0	85.9
13	22.2	55.9	73.7	83.9
14	11.6	49.9	70.2	81.7
15	—	43.3	66.2	79.3
16		36.2	62.0	76.7
17		28.3	57.3	73.8
18		19.7	52.2	70.7
19		10.3	46.6	67.3
20		—	40.4	63.5
21			33.7	59.4
22			26.4	54.9
23			18.4	50.0
24			9.6	44.6
25			—	38.8
26				32.3
27				25.3
28				17.6
29				9.2
30				—

The above table is for mortgages with a nine percent annual interest rate.
Factors will vary slightly for mortgages carrying different interest rates. *Example*:
On a 25 year mortgage with an annual interest rate of nine percent, 80.0 percent of
the original balance will still be due after 11 years of payments have elapsed.
Thus, after making 11 years worth of payments on a $30,000 mortgage, set to run
originally for 25 years, a balance of $24,000 will still be remaining (80% of
$30,000 is $24,000). Similarly, on a 30 year, 9% mortgage, 63.5% of the original
balance will still be due after making payments for 20 years.

table 7-3   **monthly mortgage payment finder**

Annual interest rate (percentage)	Length of mortgage			
	20 yrs.	25 yrs.	30 yrs.	35 yrs.
7.0	7.76	7.07	6.66	6.39
7.25	7.91	7.23	8.83	6.57
7.50	8.06	7.39	7.00	6.75
7.75	8.21	7.56	7.17	6.93
8.0	8.37	7.72	7.34	7.11
8.25	8.52	7.89	7.51	7.29
8.50	8.68	8.06	7.68	7.46
8.75	8.84	8.23	7.87	7.66
9.0	9.00	8.40	8.05	7.84
9.25	9.16	8.57	8.23	8.03
9.50	9.33	8.74	8.41	8.22
9.75	9.49	8.92	8.60	8.41

Note: This table will enable you to determine the approximate monthly mortgage payment (interest and principal) for any mortgage at the above listed interest rates and terms in years. The above factors are calculated for mortgages of $1000. Thus, a mortgage of $1000 at a 9% annual interest rate, running for 25 years, will have a monthly payment of $8.40 (see where the 25 yr. column intersects with the 9% row). To find the monthly payments, then, on a mortgage of $30,000, at 9% annual interest, running for 25 years, you would multiply the 8.40 factor by 30, resulting in a monthly payment of $252. Similarly, what would be the monthly payment for a 30 year mortgage of $25,000 if it carried an annual interest rate of 9.25%? *Answer:* the 30 year column and the 9.25% row intersect at the 8.23 factor. A mortgage of $1000 at those terms would thus have a monthly payment of $8.23, and a $25,000 mortgage would have a monthly payment of 25 times 8.23, or $205.75.

table 7-4   **how interest rates affect your cost—a $30,000 mortgage running for a 30 year term**

Annual interest rate (%)	Monthly payments (interest and principal)	Total amount paid out after			
		5 yrs.	10 yrs.	20 yrs.	30 yrs.
8.	$220.20	$13,212	$26,424	$52,848	$79,272
8.25	225.30	13,518	27,036	54,072	81,108
8.50	230.40	13,824	27,648	55,296	82,944
8.75	236.10	14,166	28,332	56,664	84,996
9.	241.50	14,490	28,980	57,960	86,940
9.25	246.90	14,814	29,628	59,256	88,884
9.50	252.30	15,138	30,276	60,552	90,828
9.75	258.00	15,480	30,960	61,920	92,800

As the table indicates, a difference of one-quarter percent in the annual interest rate—such as between 9.5% and 9.25%—will mean a difference in the monthly payment of $5.40. Over a period of five years the higher interest rate will have required $324 more in total payments than the lower rate mortgage. Over a 20 year period the difference would be $1296.

A difference of one-half percent—as between 9.5% and 9%—will mean a difference in the monthly payment of $10.80; and a difference in total payments over five years of $648, and over 20 years of $2592.

A difference of one full percentage—as between 9.50% and 8.5%—means a difference in the monthly payment of $21.90; and a difference over five years of $1314, and over 20 years of $5226.

Although available rates might not vary by more than a quarter to one-half a percentage point in any given city at any given time, this table indicates the value of shopping for even modest rate difference.

table 7-5 how long should your mortgage run

| Size of mortgage* | No. of years | Monthly payment | Total amount paid after | | | Total interest paid over full term |
			10 yrs.	20 yrs.	Full term	
$20,000	20	$179.95	$21,594	$43,188	$43,188	$23,188
20,000	25	167.84	20,141	40,282	50,352	30,352
20,000	30	160.93	19,312	38,623	57,935	37,935
20,000	35	156.80	18,816	37,632	65,856	45,856
25,000	20	224.94	26,993	53,986	53,986	28,986
25,000	25	209.80	25,176	50,352	62,940	37,940
25,000	30	201.16	24,139	48,278	72,418	47,418
25,000	35	196.00	23,520	47,040	82,320	57,320
30,000	20	269.92	32,390	64,781	64,781	34,781
30,000	25	251.76	30,211	60,422	75,528	45,528
30,000	30	241.39	28,967	57,934	86,900	56,900
30,000	35	235.20	28,224	56,448	98,784	68,784
35,000	20	314.91	37,789	75,578	75,578	40,578
35,000	25	293.72	35,246	70,493	88,116	53,116
35,000	30	281.62	33,794	67,589	101,383	66,383
35,000	35	274.40	32,928	65,856	115,248	88,248

* Figured at a 9% annual interest rate—figures rounded off.

table 7-6 how much of a down payment should you make—based on a total purchase price of $40,000, a term of 30 years, and an annual interest rate of 9%

| Down payment | | Amount of mortgage | Monthly payment | Total amount paid after | | |
% of cost	Dollars			10 yrs.	20 yrs.	30 yrs.
10%	$4,000	$36,000	$289.67	$34,760	$69,521	$104,281
15	6,000	34,000	273.58	32,830	65,659	98,489
20	8,000	32,000	257.48	30,898	61,795	92,693
25	10,000	30,000	214.39	28,967	57,934	86,900
30	12,000	28,000	225.30	27,036	54,072	81,108
35	14,000	26,000	209.21	25,105	50,210	75,316
40	16,000	24,000	193.11	23,173	46,346	65,520

Note: The major difference between larger down payments and smaller ones is that larger down payments require a much smaller monthly payment, and pay out far less in total over the long term.

table 7-7 **size of down payment and savings plans**

Down payment	Lump sum left to invest	Monthly payment	Monthly amount left to invest	After ten years				
				Total paid	Lump-sum nest-egg	Monthly nest-egg	Total, both nest-eggs	Out-of-pocket difference: total paid out less total of nest-eggs
$6,000	$6,000	$273.58	-0-	$32,830	$10,248	-0-	$10,248	$22,582
8,000	4,000	257.48	$16	30,898	6,832	$ 2,560	9,392	21,506
10,000	2,000	241.39	32	28,967	3,416	5,120	8,536	20,431
12,000	-0-	225.30	48	27,036	-0-	7,681	7,681	19,355
				After twenty years				
6,000	6,000	273.58	-0-	56,659	17,506	-0-	17,506	48,153
8,000	4,000	257.48	16	61,795	11,670	6,981	18,651	43,144
10,000	2,000	241.39	32	57,934	5,835	13,962	19,797	38,137
12,000	-0-	225.30	48	54,072	-0-	20,944	20,944	33,120
				After thirty years				
6,000	6,000	273.58	-0-	98,489	29,900	-0-	29,900	68,589
8,000	4,000	257.48	16	92,693	19,932	14,616	34,548	58,145
10,000	2,000	241.39	32	86,900	9,967	29,231	39,198	47,702
12,000	-0-	225.30	48	81,108	-0-	43,847	43,847	37,261

Explanation: If the home buyer made a down payment of $6000, he would still have $6000 left from his total starting available sum of $12,000. He would invest that amount, and after 10 years it would have grown to $10,248 (lump-sum nest-egg). But the $6000 down payment would necessitate using his entire budgeted allotment of $273.58 for monthly payments. Thus he would not have any monthly nest-egg building for him.

If he used his entire $12,000 for down payment, he would have no lump-sum nest-egg building for him, but he would have an excess of $48 each month between his budget allotment of $273.58 and his required monthly payment of $225.30. This amount he would invest as his monthly nest-egg. After 10 years it would have grown to $7681.

After 10 years, the $6000 down payment mortgage would have required total payments of $32,830. The nest-egg would total $10,248. Thus the buyer would be effectively "out-of-pocket" by $22,582. On the other hand, the $12,000 down payment mortgage would have required total payments of $27,036. The nest-egg would total $7681, leaving the buyer effectively "out-of-pocket" by $19,355—an advantage of $3227 over the smaller down payment mortgage.

After 20 years the difference between the two is $15,033, and after 30 years the difference is $37,261.

An Interview between Ralph and Janet Hadley of Westport, Connecticut, and their Attorney, Mr. J. J. Fancher.

FANCHER: What can I do for you today folks?

HADLEY: Well, we bought a piece of land and made a down payment to a contractor to build a house on it. We found out the land is worthless, and the contractor has skipped with our down payment. We'd like to see if you can help us get any of our money back.

FANCHER: Why didn't you contact me before you signed the contracts and paid the money?

HADLEY: We were planning to. But it all happened so fast. We just never had a chance to.

FANCHER: Where is the land?

HADLEY: It's out West. For a long time we've been thinking of moving out there.

FANCHER: Did you see it before you bought it?

HADLEY: We didn't exactly see the land. But we know the area it's in. A few years ago, we were on vacation, and stopped in Las Vegas for a few days. We were approached in our hotel lobby by a pleasant young chap who said he was a public relations consultant and was conducting a public opinion survey on various kinds of investments. He told us if we would participate in his survey he could arrange free tickets for one of the big shows in town. It seemed like a reasonable deal so we went along with him. That afternoon he took us to a meeting room in another hotel. There were ten or fifteen other couples in the room, and the first thing we got was complimentary tickets to the show. They sat us down and the program got under way. The speaker introduced himself as the president of the public relations company and proceeded to discuss various kinds of investments. He told us how risky the stock market was, and how our savings accounts get eaten alive by inflation. Then he started talking about how an investment in land is where the real fortunes are made, and he showed us a short film on a new city that was being built by a firm that his company was representing.

FANCHER: It sounds like you were getting a sales pitch.

HADLEY: Well, it didn't seem like a sales pitch. The new city—they called it Agua Caldo Estates—had the best of all worlds. Skiing two hours away in the winter. The beach two hours away in the summer. And, according to the film, it was a beautiful community that was growing by leaps and bounds.

FANCHER: Let me guess. He told you residential building lots were selling for $4000 the year before, they're selling for $5000 right now, and next year they'll be selling for $6000. Right?

HADLEY: How did you know?

FANCHER: Never mind. How many lots did you buy?

HADLEY: We really didn't plan on buying any. After the film ended, the speaker called for a slight intermission. During the intermission, a fellow who was sitting next to us introduced himself. He said he was a bank executive from Ohio. He told us he had come to this meeting on a lark, just to get the free show tickets, but that he was really impressed with the presentation and thought he'd make an investment. Today, we realize he worked for the promoters. One thing led to another, and shortly after the meeting was over, we found ourselves signing a contract to buy a lot.

FANCHER: I'll bet the sales agent clinched the deal by

telling you, if you never built on the lot, you would be able to sell it off at a handsome profit within a year or two.

HADLEY: Right. By this point we were convinced we had found our dream come true, and we asked the salesperson to have the building company contact us to make arrangements to construct a house. The next day a representative from the building company called on us. He showed us a set of elaborate plans and brochures, and he quoted prices that seemed very reasonable. He could, he said, deliver a completed house on our lot within a year, fully financed at very attractive terms. All he asked was a $2000 down payment to bind the deal. We signed those papers too, and as soon as we got home a week later, we withdrew the money from our savings account and mailed them their checks—$4000 for the lot and $2000 as a down payment on the house. The lot price they quoted us was actually $5000, but they said they could give a $1000 discount if we paid in cash rather than finance it. So we went along.

FANCHER: What happened?

HADLEY: We thought we had found utopia. We just couldn't wait for the months to pass to give up our work and make our move. Two months later we called to check on the progress of our new house. We were told that there had been a slight delay because of a construction workers' strike, but we were reassured that everything would be completed on schedule.

FANCHER: Did that start to give you any doubts?

HADLEY: Not really. Not until another two months passed and we called again to check on the progress. A very rude person told us there had been another delay and they didn't know when construction would be completed. That really bothered us. Two months later I flew out West to get a first hand look at just what was going on. I rented a car at the airport and drove almost fifty miles into the wilderness; when I finally got to our homesite, I was devastated. It was barren wasteland. There was no sign of any kind of community, only some wooden stakes pounded into the ground with street signs painted on them. There was an abandoned trailer with a "Sales Office" sign on it.

Not a soul could be seen for miles. I tried to contact both the public relations firm and the building firm, but both seemed to have disappeared into the night.

FANCHER: So, you're out $6000 plus a round trip plane ticket out West?

HADLEY: Afraid not. About three months after my trip out there, I received a call from a firm in Florida. They said they were representing some foreign investors who were looking for land in the United States. They had learned I owned land out West, and asked if I would be willing to sell it. They thought they might be able to find a buyer who would pay as much as $8000. I almost jumped out of my skin when I heard that. This seemed like a chance to get out from under and make a profit to boot. They said their fee, payable in advance, would be $500. I couldn't send them a check fast enough. Two weeks later, I got a letter from them thanking me for the check and as-

suring me the prospect for finding a buyer looked exceedingly favorable.

FANCHER: And you just sat back and waited for your check to arrive in the mail. Right?

HADLEY: Sure! Another month later, I received another letter telling me they had found a buyer, and that I could expect a contract for my signature in the mail within a few weeks. As soon as I had signed the contract, they would send the check to me. I waited two weeks, and then a few weeks more, but never received the contract. Finally, I tried to reach them on the telephone. The operator told me there was no such listing. Like a fool, I realized if I had only made that telephone call before I sent the check, and not months later, I might have avoided throwing away another $500.

FANCHER: Did you ever ask yourself where this Florida firm found out you owned a piece of property out West? Did you ever stop to think that it might be the very same people from whom you bought the lot originally acting under a different guise, Mr. Hadley?

HADLEY: Do you . . . do you . . . think you can . . . help?

FANCHER: Mr. Hadley, you have been had, partly as a result of your own gullibility, and partly as a result of your own lack of precaution in

seeking help before you sign contracts. If we could find the people who did this to you, and, if they had any money available to make restitution to you, the legal fees alone would probably eat up a substantial portion of anything that you'd get back. It's one of those cases that consumes tremendous amounts of time. This is a confidence game that can hopscotch around the country from one week to the next, assuming different guises, and cleverly hiding any money they have from investors and creditors.

You're lucky in a way. You found out early about your mistake, and you're young enough to recover from it. Many folks get involved in these land deals and don't realize for many years that they've been swindled. Imagine the couple who wants to build a retirement home and buys into one of these phony deals. Then, when the couple move out to their heavenly villa to find it's a chunk of murky swamp or scorpion-infested desert, it's often too late.

HADLEY: Doesn't the government protect people in situations like this?

FANCHER: A little. The offices of the state Attorney Generals in many states keep some surveillance on these promoters, and have had occasion to sue them. Once in a while some of the perpetra-

tors are actually convicted and sent to jail, but I bet that more of them are running loose than will ever see the insides of a jail.

The federal government maintains the Office of Interstate Land Sales registration, which is a division of the Department of Housing and Urban Development. They require builders who are involved in interstate commerce to file certain documents with them, and the builders are also required to provide certain documents to would-be buyers. There are many legitimate developers but the industry as a whole has been badly spotted by the phonies. The federal offices are woefully understaffed, and there's little they can do to help someone who's already been taken.

I'll be happy to pursue the matter for you, but I have to be candid. I really don't think there's much chance of any kind of recovery.

HADLEY: We'll have to think about it, Mr. Fancher. Thank you very much. One question. How do you happen to know so much about these land schemes?

FANCHER: Yours is the sixth case I've had like this in the last eight months. The situations are all virtually identical. Only the names of the guilty have changed, because they know how to do that very quickly.

**review
questions**

1. What are two advantages of an older mortgage compared with a new one?
2. Describe the essential disadvantage of an older mortgage.
3. To determine your housing costs you must estimate utility costs. How would you get the information to do this?
4. What is an easement?
5. When is a title search made as part of the purchase transaction?
6. You have a $42,000 9% 30-year mortgage on a house. What is the approximate balance on the mortgage after 10 years?
7. Harry Schwartz is buying a house for $50,000 with a $40,000 mortgage. The lender wants to charge him 2 points. How much money is this?
8. Explain the purpose of an escrow or reserve account.

**cases
for
study**

1. It is 15 miles from Sarah's old house to her old job. It is 50 miles from her old house to her new job. It is 10 miles from her new house to her new job. Does Sarah have all the requirements for deductible moving expenses? If not, list any other requirements.
2. Explain why lenders use variable rate mortgages. Discuss why a buyer would be willing to accept a variable rate mortgage.
3. Mary Jarvis and her husband have combined take home pay of $1500 per month. They are looking at a house that they can buy for $50,000. They have obtained the following loan quotes:

  90% loan with 2 points + $50 fee, $9\frac{1}{4}$% 30 years
  90% loan with 2 points + $50 fee, $9\frac{1}{4}$% 20 years
  90% loan with 3 points + $50 fee, 9% 30 years
  80% loan with 1 point + $50 fee, 9% 30 years

Select their best financing choice and defend it.
4. Ben Klein and his wife have decided that they do not have enough savings for the down payment on a house. They are now wondering if they should rent a furnished or unfurnished apartment. Discuss the factors involved in the choice.

chapter 8 **life insurance**

coping with risk

Life is full of surprises—risks—that we don't adequately anticipate or prepare for. Some of these risks we accept willingly: driving a car, taking on a new job, investing or betting our money. Others may be strictly a matter of fate: illness, natural disaster, an employer going bankrupt.

When an event occurs for which we have not been adequately prepared, we may suffer disappointment, wasted time, physical harm, and financial loss. The danger inherent in many risks can be avoided or minimized simply by taking some minimal evasive or defensive actions.

There are many events, though, whose occurrence we can neither foresee nor control. They happen in spite of our most precautionary efforts. But we can take steps, prior to their happening, to reduce the loss that we would otherwise suffer, by, in effect, "hiring" others who will be willing, for a fee, to reimburse us for losses that we may suffer.

insurance is protection against risk

This is what insurance is all about. *Example:* on an average given day, 1000 skiers will run a slope and one will end up in

273

the hospital. The cost of hospitalization may be $1000. You never know whether that injured skier will be yourself or one of the 999 others. If it should be you, it will cost you $1000. But if each skier chipped in $1 to cover the cost of that day's accident—whoever it might happen to—you have eliminated your risk at a very insignificant cost. For the price of $1, you may have saved yourself $1000. You may run the slope 1000 times and never be hurt, but actual experience indicates that that's not likely.

If all the skiers aren't willing to chip into a mutual kitty to protect themselves, some enterprising business executive will offer to make the arrangements for them. He will point out the risks that each skier faces, will arrange to collect and hold all of the money in safe-keeping, and will see to it that the proceeds are paid out to the injured parties as the injuries occur. For this service, he is entitled to a fee; thus, instead of charging $1 per skier, he may charge $1.05 or $1.10—whatever he and the skiers agree his services may be worth. In so doing, he is acting as a one-man insurance company.

That, in a nutshell, is how the insurance industry operates. The insurance company will determine the probability of risk in many given situations, such as a house burning down, an automobile crashing, a person dying before their normal life expectancy, and so on. The company will further determine how much money it must collect from each individual to properly protect those individuals should the stated risk occur. That money will be invested prudently, so that the fund can grow, until it comes time to pay benefits to people who have suffered the risks. These calculations are known as the "actuarial" phase of insurance. The money that's taken in from each individual is called a "premium," and the money paid out to individuals who do suffer the stated risks is called "benefits." The portion of each premium dollar set aside to pay future benefits is called the "reserve."

Part of each premium dollar that is received by the insurance company is used to pay the agents for their work in selling the insurance to the public. Part of it is set aside to pay for the buildings that the insurance company occupies, the machines and computers they need, the clerical help, the supplies, the advertising, and the educational material.

When an individual, or a business, enters into an agreement with an insurance company regarding a specific risk, the parties sign a contract that sets forth all the specific rights, duties, and obligations of the parties. This contract is called an "insurance policy." Its specific details are discussed later.

Broadly speaking, there are five kinds of common personal insurance that we must be aware of: life, health, income, property, and liability. Life insurance pays an agreed on amount of money to the named survivors of one who has died. We obtain life insurance to protect the interest of those who depend on us and would be in need should we no longer be able to provide for them. We may also obtain life insurance so that we may pass along a large sum of money to those who survive us.

Health insurance is obtained to reimburse us for the costs of medical care, should the need arise.

Property insurance is obtained to reimburse us for any loss we may suffer as a result of our property (house, car, furnishings, jewelry, and other personal items of value) being lost, damaged, or destroyed by certain stated occurrences.

Income insurance protects us against certain losses of income. For example, disability insurance protects us and provides us with a level of income should we be unable to work due to illness or accident. Social Security provides a measure of income in the event of certain kinds of disability. Unemployment insurance, required by law, provides a level of income if we are laid off from our job.

Liability insurance protects us against the claims of others to whom we may have caused damage or harm. A guest in our dwelling may slip on a banana peel and break a leg; we may hit another person with our automobile. We are responsible for the loss suffered by the victims in such cases, and we have to reimburse them. We obtain insurance to defend us against their claims, and to pay any claims that are valid.

The balance of this chapter discusses the various aspects of life insurance that are important to the average individual or family. In the next chapter, we'll take a close look at the other forms of personal insurance.

the life insurance industry

A brief look at the life insurance industry in the United States will serve to illustrate the scope and importance of insurance in our lives. Statistics from the American Council of Life Insurance indicate that 86% of all adult males and 74% of all adult females are covered by some type of life insurance. The following tables break this down further:

Age	Percentage of Adults Covered by Some Form of Life Insurance
18–24	81%
25–34	79
35–44	85
45–54	87
55–64	80
65 and over	62

Family Income	Percentage of Adults Covered by Some Form of Life Insurance
Under $5,000	63%
$5,000–$7,499	76
$7,500–$9,999	87
$10,000–$14,999	89
$15,000 and over	86

Education of Household Head	Percentage of Adults Covered by Some Form of Life Insurance
High school not completed	74%
High school graduate	83
Some college	84
College graduate or more	81

Americans carry life insurance protection in the total sum of $2.14 trillion. If this total were divided equally among all U. S. families, each family would have $28,100 of protection. Excluding families with no life insurance, the average for *insured* families was about $33,100 as of the start of 1976. The size of the average policy purchased was, at that time, $15,050—a sharp increase from the 1965 average sized policy, which was then $8400.

The following table illustrates how rapidly the average American family has increased its amount of life insurance coverage.

Year	Life Insurance Per Family	Disposal Personal Income per Family
1945	$ 3,200	$ 3,200
1950	$ 4,600	$ 4,000
1955	$ 6,900	$ 5,100
1960	$10,200	$ 6,100
1965	$14,600	$ 7,700
1970	$20,700	$10,100
1975	$28,100	$14,100

It's interesting to note that from 1945 onward, the average amount of life insurance per family has grown from a point where the average insurance and the average disposal income were about equal, to a current point when the average life insurance per family is roughly double the disposable income. In other words, the average family is carrying enough insurance to match two years worth of disposable income. It should come as no surprise, therefore, that the average benefits payable on life insurance to survivors last for about two years, before the insurance proceeds are exhausted.

The total amount of life insurance in force in the United States—$2.14 trillion—is about double what it was in 1967 ($1.08 trillion) and about four times what it was in 1959 ($542 billion) and ten times what it was in 1949 ($213 billion).

There are about 1800 life insurance companies operating in America currently. The vast majority of these are "legal reserve" companies. A legal reserve life insurance company is one operating under state insurance laws, which specify the minimum amount of reserves that the company must maintain on its policies in order to pay expected future benefits to policy holders.

the money: where it comes from and where it goes

In 1975, the total income of all United States life insurance companies was $78 billion. Of this total, $58.6 billion, or 75%, came from premiums paid by policyholders. $16.5 billion or 21% came from earnings on investments—the funds that have been put into reserves by the insurance company. The remaining $3 billion, or 4%, came from other sources.

How are these dollars spent? Benefit payments to policyholders, 51.8¢; additions to policy reserve funds, 25¢; additions to special reserve and surplus funds, 1.5¢; commissions to agents,

6.6¢; home and field office expenses, 9.9¢; taxes, 4.2¢; dividends to stockholders of stock life insurance companies, 1.0¢.

Benefits paid to policyholders take a number of forms. The most common are death payments, where the insured has died, and the proceeds of the policies are paid to the beneficiaries. Other forms of benefits include disability payments; dividends paid to policyholders of certain kinds of policies; surrender values where the insured has, in effect, "cashed in" a policy; and annuity and endowment payments where the insured has received funds due under the terms of the contract. (Annuities and endowment policies are discussed in more detail in the later section describing the workings of various policies.)

life insurance company assets

As indicated above, roughly one-fourth of all the insurance companies' income is put into various reserve funds, where it will be invested, it will grow, and ultimately be used to pay future claims as they fall due. These reserve funds, along with other property and securities the insurance companies may own, comprise their "total assets." Because the companies know they will have future obligations that must be met out of readily available sources, they must invest prudently and conservatively.

Here's how the total assets of United States life insurance companies are invested: corporate bonds, 36.6%; mortgage loans, 30.8%; corporate stocks, 9.7%; government securities, 5.2%; real estate, 3.3%; loans to policyholders, 8.5%; cash, .7%; miscellaneous, 5.2%. Individual companies may have different mixes of their specific investments; these percentages represent the *average* of all United States life insurance companies.

The total assets of all U.S. life insurance companies at the end of 1975 were $289 billion. As noted earlier, the total amount of life insurance in force throughout America is $2.14 trillion. That's the amount the companies will ultimately have to pay to all policyholders as of the date of those statistics. How can the insurance companies meet future obligations of $2.14 trillion when they only have $289 billion in actual assets available? The insurance companies, through their actuarial departments, have very carefully calculated how much each dollar they take in will grow over the anticipated period of time before they must make payments out of that dollar.

The reserve funds grow each year by the addition of investment income, and by the addition of new money generated from premiums that are allocated to the reserve funds. Actual history indicates how long the company will be able to hold the money of each individual insured until it has to pay claims. For example, the average 20-year-old American has a life expectancy of 53 years, and the average 40-year-old American has a life expectancy of 34.5 years. If a 20-year-old and a 40-year-old each buy a $10,000 life insurance policy on the same day, the insurance company knows that it will probably not have to make payments to the survivors of the 20-year-old for 53 years, whereas it will probably have to make payments to the survivors of the 40-year-old in 34.5 years. Because the company will have the use of the 20-year-old's money, to invest and to grow, for almost twenty years longer than it will the 40-year-old's, it can afford to offer the same $10,000 benefits to the 20-year-old at a much lower price, or premium, than it will have to charge the 40-year-old.

In addition to calculating the life expectancy of each insured, the company also calculates the kind of return it can expect on its invested funds over the long period. These calculations, plus the sound management of the companies and the state laws that require minimum reserves, give assurance to policyholders that there will be money on hand to pay the claims as they occur. Failures of life insurance companies are rare, though they do occur. Most life insurance companies that discontinue business are either merged into larger companies, or their policies are picked up by other companies. Instances of beneficiaries failing to collect on life insurance policies that are otherwise valid are extremely remote. The success of the life insurance industry is based on management expertise, which has proven its worth in even the most difficult economic times. Although life insurance policyholders do not have the benefit of governmental protection, as they do in the federal insurance on their savings accounts, the historical record can stand on its own merits.

Nonetheless, the prudent insurance buyer will want to make sure that he or she is dealing with a company whose reputation is established. If a would-be buyer has any questions or doubts about the stability of any given company, he or she can refer to *Best's Insurance Reports* and *Best's Recommended Life Insurance Companies*, which are available at most major municipal libraries. Reference might also be made to the Insurance Department in your state.

the basic elements
of life insurance

kinds of companies: stock and mutual

There are basically two different kinds of life insurance companies: stock companies and mutual companies. Stock companies are owned by stockholders, in much the same fashion as stockholders own other companies such as General Motors, American Telephone and Telegraph, and so on. The stockholders of these companies elect the Board of Directors to run the company. If the company is run profitably, the stockholders of those companies will likely receive dividends on their stock, again much in the same way as stockholders of industrial companies.

Mutual companies, on the other hand, are in effect owned by their policyholders. The policyholders elect the Board of Directors who manage the company. In a mutual company, where the premium income exceeds the expenses (benefits paid and other expenses) by a certain amount, the policyholders/owners will receive back a portion of the excess needed to make expenses. These sums are also referred to as "dividends," but they are technically not the same thing as dividends received on common stock.

"par" and "nonpar" policies

The kinds of policies issued by mutual companies, wherein dividends are paid to policyholders, are referred to as "participating" policies—the policyholders participate in a distribution of excess income over expenses.

Stock companies generally do not pay such dividends to their policyholders. These policies are referred to as "nonparticipating." In some instances, however, stock companies do issue participating policies.

Participating and nonparticipating policies are commonly referred to as "par" and "nonpar."

The difference between stock and mutual companies may be better understood by referring back to the earlier example of the skiers. Where the skiers banded together on their own to chip in $1 for each run, that would be in the nature of a mutual company. Where the skiers declined to do this on their own, and were approached by an outside business executive who would do it for them, more closely resembles the stock company.

Premiums on participating policies will customarily be higher than premiums on nonpar policies, all other things being equal.

But the owner of a par policy has the hope of receiving dividends each year that may be used to offset the cost of the premium. Very possibly the amount of dividends received by a par policyholder could reduce the out-of-pocket cost of his or her insurance to a lower level than what an otherwise equal nonpar policy would cost. For example, an individual shopping for a life insurance policy may find that two policies of equal face value, one par and one nonpar, have annual premiums of $300 and $250. If, over a period of time, the par policy pays a dividend of $60 per year, then the par policy will actually end up being less expensive than the nonpar policy. But insurance companies cannot give any guarantee of what dividends will be paid in any given year. It will depend on their actual experience of premium dollars received and expense and benefit dollars paid out.

how is life insurance acquired

Life insurance is generally acquired in one of three ways: group plans, private plans, and credit plans.

group plans

Group life insurance is designed for large groups of people in similar circumstances. Your employer, for example, may provide a group life insurance plan for all employees who meet the necessary requirements of tenure on the job. Group insurance may also be issued to members of social organizations, professional organizations, and unions. Frequently, group life insurance is issued in relatively small amounts, and the insured individuals may not be required to take physical examinations to prove the state of their health. The group insurance policy will cover all eligible employees, and each participating individual will receive a copy of the master policy, or an outline of it. In some cases, the employer or union may pay the premiums for all of the individuals; in other cases, such as with professional associations, each individual makes his or her own payment.

When an individual ceases to be a member of the group, his insurance may terminate. But in many cases, it's possible for the individual to make arrangements to continue the coverage, provided he makes the necessary premium payments on his own.

Because administration costs on a group policy can be much lower than the administration costs connected with many individual policies, the premium cost to the insured individuals in a group plan is generally lower than what it would be in a private plan.

private plans Private insurance is contracted for directly between the individual and the insurance company. Depending on the issuing company and the amount of insurance involved, a physical examination of the insured may be required.

credit plans When you borrow money, the lender may offer you a program of life insurance that is designed to pay off any balance on the loan should you die before the loan is paid off. This is available in mortgage loans, as well as in small personal installment loans, such as for an automobile, home improvements, and other similar types. The amount of the insurance coverage decreases as the balance on the loan decreases. (This is known as "decreasing term" insurance.) In a long-term mortgage, the insured will generally make payments on the policy each year. In the shorter term installment loans, the insured will generally pay the full premium in one lump sum at the inception of the loan. Frequently, the amount of the insurance premium is added to the amount of the loan so that the insured is not out-of-pocket anything at the outset.

types of life insurance Basic types of life insurance are generally either permanent or temporary. Permanent insurance is designed to run permanently: that is, for the life of the insured individual. This type of insurance is commonly known as ordinary insurance or straight insurance or whole life insurance.

Temporary insurance is designed to run for a specific period of time, such as one year, five years, or ten years. This is known as "term" insurance. At the end of the term specified in the contract, the insurance ceases. However, in renewable term policies the insured has the ability to renew for an additional term; however, it will be at a different premium rate. Term policies may also be convertible to ordinary policies.

A third type of life insurance is the "annuity" wherein the insured is guaranteed a fixed monthly payment, which will begin at a specified time and will last for the agreed on amount of time. Let's take a closer look at these various types of life insurance.

permanent insurance Permanent insurance is a lifetime contract. You agree to pay a fixed level premium and the insurance company agrees to deliver a stated sum of money upon your death, or, in certain cases, at some earlier time. If the money is to become payable at a date prior to death, the insured may elect to receive it in a lump sum at that date, or may elect to have the company pay in periodic installments, which would include an agreed on amount of interest. Or, the insurance company can hold the money (paying interest on it) for as long as the insured lives, and then pay it to the beneficiaries. The rate of interest that an insurance company will pay on monies held for the benefit of the insured or survivors will be specifically set forth in the contract.

In addition to the benefits payable on the death of the insured (or earlier, if called for), the permanent policy will also build up "cash values," also referred to as "nonforfeiture values." These values will permit the insured to terminate the policy and obtain either cash or some other form of insurance, if desired at some later time. These values are discussed in more detail later.

Examples of permanent insurance include:

1. You agree to pay the stated premiums for, say, 20 years. At the end of that period the policy will be "paid up"—the full face value will be payable on death, and you don't have to pay any more premiums. This policy would be referred to as a limited pay plan, or, in this case, "20-pay life": 20 years of payments pays it up in full.

2. You agree to pay the stated premiums for the remainder of your life. Upon death, the full face value will be payable. This policy would be referred to as a "whole life" policy.

3. You agree to make certain premium payments, and the full face value then becomes available to you in cash at a stated age, say 65. If you don't elect to take the cash, you can exercise other options, as noted above, such as installment payments or having the company hold it for you plus interest, for later payment to yourself or to your beneficiaries in the case of your death. Such a policy is of the endowment species, and might be referred to as "endowment at age 65."

The amount of premiums involved for these various policies will differ considerably. For example, in the "20-pay life" policy, the insurance company must accumulate from the insured all the premiums it will need to make the necessary payments on the death of the insured. It only has 20 years in which to do so, even though the life expectancy of the individual may be much longer. Consequently, the insurance company must charge a higher premium for this kind of insurance than it would for whole life, for it has fewer years in which to accumulate the needed funds.

In the endowment policy, the full face value will become payable to the insured when he or she reaches a specific age. The person may live many years after that. In such a case, the insurance company has fewer years in which to accumulate the needed funds in which to pay off the face value, so again it must command a higher premium to meet its own obligations.

term insurance
Term insurance is "pure" insurance. With rare exceptions, term insurance policies do not build up any of the cash or nonforfeiture values found in permanent policies. As each term expires, the insured may, by exercising renewal rights, obtain another policy for an additional term, but at a higher premium rate because the individual is now older and has a shorter life expectancy.

Many term insurance policies contain a right to convert to a permanent insurance policy at stated points. Depending on the company and the amount of insurance, the insured may or may not have to take a physical examination, either upon initiating or renewing the term policy, or on converting it to a permanent policy.

Because term insurance does not have any cash value build-up as a rule, it is the least expensive among all forms regarding initial out-of-pocket premium expenses. But, as term insurance is renewed at ever increasing ages—and thereby at ever increasing rates—the ultimate out-of-pocket expenses can reach, and possibly exceed, those of permanent life.

As indicated earlier, another, and still cheaper, form of term insurance is the decreasing term insurance, which accompanies mortgage loans and installment loans. Such insurance is cheaper because the amount of actual insurance decreases each year as the balance on the loan decreases.

annuities
We've noted that the main emphasis of life insurance is to provide a fixed sum of money to the beneficiaries when the insured party dies. In some cases, however, the insured may retrieve monies paid into the policy while still alive. This occurs in the case of an endowment policy or an ordinary life policy where the insured takes advantage of the cash values that he or

she may borrow against or use to convert the policy to another form, or simply cash in the existing policy.

An annuity is technically not an insurance policy. It is designed basically to provide a source of income to an individual who purchases such a contract. This individual is called the annuitant. Although technically not an insurance policy, it is sold as a major product of insurance companies. And, in some cases, there may be death benefits with annuities. The buyer of an annuity contract pays money to the insurance company either in one lump sum or in periodic payments over a number of months or years. An insurance company agrees to then pay back to the contract holder a sum of money each month for an agreed on amount of time.

That sum of money may be fixed in the contract (a fixed dollar annuity) or may vary (a variable annuity), but there is a guaranteed minimum. With a fixed dollar annuity the funds are invested conservatively—predominantly in government and corporate bonds as well as mortgages—and the company can thus assure the amount of monthly payments to the annuitant.

In the variable annuity, a substantial portion of the money is invested in the stock market. The theory is that the stock market can provide protection against inflation. If the theory works, the annuitant may get more back than he or she might have received under a fixed dollar annuity. The annuitant is guaranteed at least a certain minimum back from the insurance company. Variable annuities rise and decline in popularity as the stock market rises and declines.

Here's a brief description of the common types of payment programs available with annuities.

A straight life annuity. Payments used to buy an annuity are called a "consideration," not premiums as in normal life insurance. In a straight life annuity, once you have made your payments, you will begin to receive the agreed on monthly sum at the agreed on date. Annuities will usually begin payments on retirement. In a straight life annuity, the payments last for as long as you live. If an annuitant dies one month after the payments have commenced, no further payments will be made to any party. If the annuitant lives far beyond the normal life expectancy, he or she will continue to receive the monthly payments from the insurance company, even if they have to pay out much more than they received at the outset from the annuitant. The company, in effect, is taking the risk that the annuitant will live no longer than the life expectancy.

Annuity with installments certain. This type of annuity is set up to provide monthly payments for a fixed period of time—perhaps ten or twenty years. If an annuitant dies before the agreed on time has elapsed, the beneficiary will continue to receive the payments until the term finally elapses.

Refund annuities. If an annuitant dies before receiving back all the money paid in, then the beneficiary will get back the balance still due. It may be in installments or in one lump sum, depending on the agreement between the parties.

Joint and survivor annuity. This can cover two people, such as a husband and wife. When one dies, the other continues to receive the payments until the agreed on fund or the length of time has been exhausted.

Certain tax advantages can be obtained through annuities. While the insurance company is holding your funds, they are investing the money and it will be earning interest and/or dividends. Generally, you do not have to pay income taxes on the earnings while the insurance company is holding the money for you. Once you do begin to receive the annuity payments, the interest that has been earned is taxable. But presumably, you will have retired and you'll be in a lower tax bracket—thus the tax bite will be far less than it would have been if you had had to pay taxes on the income while you were still actively working.

Many pension funds are set up through annuities. If you are making payments to a pension fund, you won't have to pay income taxes on the annuities payments as you receive them with regard to that portion that you yourself have contributed. True, it really amounts to getting your money back without having to pay taxes on it, but it could have been earning tax-free interest for an extended period of time, so the tax advantage is not inconsiderable.

In the chapter on fixed income investments we discuss the Individual Retirement Account and the Keogh plan. Both of these plans can be funded through annuities, in which case the amount that you contribute each year to your program will be tax deductible on your income tax return; in addition, the funds will continue to earn on a tax-free basis until the fund begins to pay out to the annuitant.

Generally speaking, annuities might be considered a fixed

income form of investment offered by insurance companies. The fixed dollar annuity guarantees a fixed income for the agreed on amount of time; and the variable annuity guarantees at least a minimum level of income with the chance of reaping more if market investments are correct. Some individuals may prefer to assure themselves a future source of income via annuities rather than through the stock market, where the level of security is always questionable. But the return offered by annuities may not be as attractive as that available through other forms of fixed income securities, such as bonds and savings plans.

the parties to an insurance policy

There can be as many as five parties involved in an insurance policy contract: the owner of the policy; the person whose life is insured; the beneficiary; the contingent beneficiary; and the company itself. In a great many cases the owner and the insured are one and the same party. In many instances a contingent beneficiary will not be named in the policy. The roles of each of these five parties are important to an overall understanding of life insurance. Let's take a closer look at each of them.

the insured

This is the person whose life is insured by the policy. It is on the death of the insured that the proceeds are paid. The insured may also be the owner of the policy, but it is also possible for the insured and the owner to be different parties.

the owner

The owner is perhaps the most important person referred to in the policy, for it is the owner who has the power to exercise various options within the policy, including naming and changing the beneficiary and making loans against the policy or cashing in the policy.

Consider Harold and Esther Klein. Harold applies for a life insurance policy on himself, and retains ownership in his own name. He names Esther as the beneficiary. In this case, Harold is both the insured and the owner. Or, Harold makes application for the policy with himself as the insured and with Esther as the owner. Or, Harold names himself initially as both insured and as owner, but at some later point decides to transfer ownership to Esther.

Here are other examples where the owner and the insured would not be the same party: Arthur is a valuable employee, so his boss takes out a policy on Arthur's life payable to the company. The premium is also paid by the company. This is to protect the company in the event of Arthur's death—it would alleviate, for example, the cost of training a replacement and the expense of getting along temporarily without Arthur's services. This is generally known as "key man" insurance. The company is the owner of the policy and Arthur is the insured.

Jose needs a loan from his bank. The bank, in conjunction with making a loan, may offer Jose a life insurance policy, with the proceeds payable to the bank in the event of Jose's death. As discussed earlier, this is known as "credit life insurance." In such a case, the bank is the owner of the policy and Jose is the insured. (The bank will also be named as the beneficiary of the policy.)

The owner has important powers regarding a life insurance policy. The owner can assign the policy to a creditor. For example, Ed, instead of buying a new credit life policy, assigns an existing policy to the bank to protect the bank in the event of Ed's death before the loan is paid off. Should Ed die before the loan is paid off, the bank may either receive the proceeds of the policy; or, should Ed default on the loan before his death, the bank would have the right to take whatever cash values exist in the policy. (An assignment is valid only if the insurance company itself has been properly notified and has accepted the assignment.)

The owner, and only the owner, can change the beneficiary of the policy, assuming that that right has been reserved in the original policy.

The owner can transfer ownership from himself to another party, and this might be wise in certain instances of estate planning.

The owner can exercise the nonforfeiture provisions in the policy.

The owner can dictate the manner in which the face amount will be payable to the beneficiary, where a choice exists.

It is only the owner who can make these changes, and they must be done in accord with the insurance company's stipulations in the contract. The insured cannot exercise these powers unless the insured is also the owner. If Harold conveys a life insurance policy on his own life to Esther as the owner—either as a result of an estate planning recommendation, or as a gift, or for any other reason—then it is Esther, and Esther only, who can exercise the various rights granted in the policy. As long as Harold retains ownership, only he can exercise those rights.

the beneficiary

The beneficiary is the one who receives the stated payments to be made on the death of the insured. The choice of the beneficiary is up to the owner of the policy, who, as noted above, may be the same party as the insured. The beneficiary may be one or more persons, a charity, a business concern, or the estate of the insured.

contingent beneficiary

There is always the possibility that the originally named beneficiary will die before the insured. The owner of the policy can name a contingent beneficiary, who will take the place of the original beneficiary if he or she dies before the insured. If no contingent beneficiaries are named, the terms of the policy will probably set forth how the proceeds will then be distributed. As with the original beneficiary, the contingent beneficiary can also be one or more persons, a charity, a business concern, the estate of the insured, or any other recipient the owner wishes to name.

the company

The company is, of course, the insurance company with whom you are entering into the contract. You, as the insurance buyer, will deal with a representative of the company—either an agent connected directly with the company, or an independent agent who may represent a number of various companies. Once you have entered into the contract, you may or may not see that agent again. It all depends on the level of service he wishes to provide, and the prospective sales he may feel he can generate from you and your family. Generally, the agent is the primary representative of the company as far as the insured is concerned, and the party to whom the insured should turn when any question arises. Some companies maintain service offices in communities throughout the nation to handle questions, problems, and complaints. Otherwise, you will turn to the agent directly.

the life insurance contract and its clauses

A life insurance policy is a legally binding contract once it has been properly signed by the necessary parties—the owner and the company. The policy, as a legal contract, sets forth all the rights, duties, and obligations of the parties to the contract. The only way the contract can be amended is by agreement between the parties. If an agreement is reached, it must be set forth in writing and attached to the policy. Changes to a life insurance policy—or any other kind of insurance policy—are called endorsements or riders.

the application   An important part of a policy itself is the application, which is the questionnaire that the applicant for the insurance must fill in to have the policy issued. The application contains pertinent information about the individual applying for insurance, including medical data. If the application contains false or misleading information, and the insurance company issues the policy not knowing this, the policy might later be voided if the insurance company does learn the truth. For example, an individual applying for life insurance may have recently had a severe heart attack but states that he is in perfectly good health. If he can somehow prevent the insurance company from learning of his physical condition and the policy is granted, he has entered into the agreement on false premises, and the policy might be voided if the company learns of the circumstances within the stated time limit.

Insurance companies go to considerable length to assure that they will not be defrauded. Physical examinations will be conducted, and interviews of neighbors may be undertaken to learn an individual's personal habits. All doctors that the applicant has seen in recent years may be questioned by the insurance company to determine the reason for seeing these doctors.

In recent years, an organization known as the Medical Information Bureau has assisted the insurance industry in minimizing fraudulent applications. Currently, in most cases, when one applies for life, health, or disability insurance, he or she will sign a statement giving the insurance company permission to relay all health information to the Medical Information Bureau (MIB) and seek out any information that may exist there relative to the individual's health. The computer banks of the MIB can reveal information on you that you may not have been aware anyone knew about. By reducing fraudulent applications, the insurance industry is able to reduce the claims that it otherwise might have had to pay out and thus can offer a lower premium base to the vast majority of the public dealing on an honest and forthright basis.

Recent life insurance statistics reveal that of all applications made for life insurance in the United States, only 3% are declined. Eighty-five percent of all applications have policies issued at the standard risk levels, and 4% of the applications have policies issued at extra risk levels. (Extra risk policies may be issued in cases where there is an obvious health problem but not one so great that the company will refuse the coverage. They will accept coverage, but usually at a higher premium level or in some cases, particularly in health insurance policies, will exclude certain physical conditions.) Eight percent of all applications are approved by the company but are not accepted by the applicants.

the face amount, or face value

This is the amount of money due the beneficiary on the death of the insured. The face amount is set forth on the policy, and it is what we usually refer to when we talk about the amount of an insurance policy. For example, if we say a "$10,000 life insurance policy," we're talking about the face value of the policy.

It is possible that the beneficiary could receive more or less than the original face value. The beneficiary may receive more than face value if a double indemnity clause was activated in the policy. Or the beneficiary may receive more than the face value if the owner had applied dividends that he or she had received toward the purchase of additional insurance.

The face value might be decreased if the owner has borrowed against the policy and has not paid off the loans against the policy. And, in some policies, the face value may change (usually decreasing) when the insured reaches a stated age.

double indemnity, or accidental death benefit

A double indemnity clause, which is generally available at a slightly additional premium, provides for the payment of double the face amount in the event of accidental death as opposed to natural death.

incontestable clause

Commonly, the insurance company will have a set period of time, usually two years, during which they must take issue with any suspected false or misleading information contained in the application. During that initial two-year period, a company may contest statements made by the applicant, and can void the policy if they find that improper statements were made. But once the two years have elapsed, they can no longer contest any statements.

premium, and mode of payments

The policy contract will spell out how much the premiums are on the policy, and how they can be made. The policyholder may elect to pay premiums annually, semiannually, quarterly, or monthly. The more frequent the mode of payment, the more costly it will be for both the insurance company and the insured. Monthly or quarterly payments might be more convenient to an individual's budget, but the individual should be aware of the probable added cost in paying more frequently than once a year.

lapse, grace period, and reinstatement

The general agreement in a life insurance policy is that the company will pay the face value to the beneficiary as long as the policy remains "in force." The term in force means that the owner of the policy has continued to meet his obligations: he has made his premium payments regularly and without fail. If a policyholder does not meet premium obligations, the policy can lapse. When a policy lapses, it is terminated. There is no more insurance. A lapse should be distinguished from a surrender of a policy. In a surrender, the policyholder will cease his ongoing program of insurance, but will receive something else in exchange: he will have taken out the cash value of the policy, and the policy will thus terminate or will convert the existing program to one of the other nonforfeiture values, such as extended term or paid up life. In a lapse, though, the policy ceases altogether, and the policyholder has nothing to show for it. In 1975, 6.7% of all policies in force either lapsed or were surrendered. Of the total, 20.9% of all policies that were in force for less than two years lapsed or were surrendered; and of policies in force for two years or more, only 4.5% lapsed or were surrendered.

A policy may be surrendered where the policyholder needs the money represented by the cash values; or it may be surrendered because the policyholder's needs for insurance have changed and he or she prefers to cease paying premiums and have one of the other forms of coverage available in the nonforfeiture options.

Unless financial circumstances leave little or no alternative, it can be most imprudent to let a policy lapse. Money paid in up to the date of lapse will be forfeited, and an individual may find that if he or she wishes life insurance at a later time, it will cost more because of increased age; and in some cases, because of the onset of physical conditions, the person may not be able to get the insurance at all. He or she may fall into that small but important 3% of all applications that are turned down by the company.

Lapsing of policies is not in the best interests of insurance companies either. They stay in business because of the continuity of insurance programs, not their termination. The insurance industry has structured the typical life insurance policy so that a lapse does not occur that easily or that automatically.

If a premium is not paid by the stated due date, the policyholder will have a "grace period" of usually 31 days, during which he or she can still make payment and continue the policy in force without any penalty. As the end of the grace period approaches, the policyholder will usually be notified, either in person by the agent or through the mails from the company itself concerning the approaching deadline.

If payment still has not been made by the end of the grace period, many permanent policies have an automatic cash loan provision. If cash values have already begun to build up in the policy, and there is enough to cover the payment of one premium, the company will automatically borrow against those values and use the proceeds to pay the premium and thus continue the policy in force for another period. If there are no cash values in the policy—either it's a term policy with no cash values, or it's an ordinary life policy not yet old enough to have adequate cash values—the policy will then lapse.

Even after a lapse has occurred, the policyholder has a limited time within which to exercise his or her rights to "reinstate" the policy. If a policyholder wishes to reinstate the policy, he or she may have to take a new physical examination, or may simply sign a statement about their health condition. Whichever approach taken will depend on the amount of the face value and the company's general regulations in that regard. If the company is satisfied about the state of the insured's health, and if the person pays all back due premiums and any interest owing thereon, the policy can then be reinstated.

waiver of premium

This protection is available at a slight additional cost to most life insurance policies. It provides that if the insured is totally disabled, the need to make premium payments will be waived. In other words, the insurance can continue in force, without the insured having to make premium payments during the period of disability. It's like a miniature income disability policy built into the life insurance policy itself.

nonforfeiture provisions

These are important values that become available to policyholders under permanent life insurance policies. The amount of the values builds up as you pay your premiums over the years, but the rate of build-up will vary from policy to policy. In shopping for an insurance policy, the prudent individual will carefully compare the rate of growth and relative size of these values. Policy A may have a lower premium than policy B for the same face value. Thus, policy A may seem to be the better value. But policy B may have a higher level of nonforfeiture values, which could be of considerable importance to the policyholder many years later. Thus, what you get for your premium dollar isn't just the face value of the policy. These other values must be considered most carefully.

Here's how nonforfeiture values work. If you cease paying your premiums by choice or otherwise, these nonforfeiture values will allow you to convert your policy into a number of alternative plans.

cashing in

You can cash in the policy. You then receive the amount of cash set forth in the Cash Value table (which is usually the same as the Loan Value.)

borrowing

You can borrow against the policy, usually up to the amount stipulated in the Loan Value table. For policies issued before the mid-1960s, a policyholder usually can borrow at the very attractive rate of 5% per year. In the late 1960s and continuing through the 1970s, insurance companies began to boost the annual interest rate on policy loans to be more in keeping with the general upsurge in interest rates throughout the country. Thus, policies issued in more recent years will carry a higher borrowing rate, but it still might be a very attractive rate compared with what one might have to pay for a simple interest loan at a normal lending institution.

Borrowing against a life insurance policy may be quick and convenient and inexpensive, but it's not always prudent. The act of borrowing is simple: notify the company of your wishes, sign the appropriate papers, and receive a check shortly thereafter. Repayment is up to you: you need not repay the principal at all; but you must pay interest annually. If you do not repay the principal, the face value will be diminished by the amount of the outstanding loan at the time of the insured's death. For example: if the face value on a given policy was $10,000 and the owner borrowed $1000 against it, then died before repaying the loan, the beneficiary would receive only $9000.

Some policyholders have found it wise to borrow against their policies at the available low rates, and use those funds for investment. This can be done either prudently or imprudently. If the purpose for the life insurance program is protection of the family—the most common and reasonable purpose—you can enhance that protection by investing borrowed proceeds in conservative situations, such as bonds and savings accounts. The owner of a seasoned policy could, for example, borrow against the policy and pay a 5% interest rate, then deposit the funds in an insured savings certificate paying 7% or $7\frac{1}{2}$%. Or, he or she might choose well-rated corporate bonds paying upwards of 8% or 9%. The difference between what one has borrowed and what one earns on an investment is additional income.

On the other hand, one might borrow those funds and use them to speculate with. In so doing, one risks losing the funds, thereby impairing the overall degree of protection.

converting to extended term insurance

You can convert your existing program to "extended term insurance." With such insurance, you will still be covered for the same original face value of the policy, but only for *a limited period of time* rather than for the rest of your life, had you continued the policy in force.

converting to paid-up insurance

You can convert to "paid-up insurance." If you cease paying premiums, you can still be covered for a *portion* of the face value for as long as the original policy would have protected you.

automatic premium loan

This provision, as noted earlier, will allow the company to automatically borrow against your loan values in order to make premium payments that you have neglected to make.

nonforfeiture tables Each policy will contain a "Table of Nonforfeiture Values" indicating the precise level of these values at specific points. Table 8-1 is an abbreviated sample of the normally much longer table of nonforfeiture values. Nonforfeiture values are based on the age of the insured at the time the policy is taken out. Values will vary from company to company, and from type of policy to type of policy.

Here's how the tables work. The face amount of the insurance

table 8-1   **nonforfeiture values, sample policy, $10,000 face value**

End of Policy Year	Cash or Loan Value	Paid-up Insurance	Extended Term Insurance
5	$ 590	$1410	14 yrs. 48 days
10	$1340	$2900	20 yrs. 310 days
15	$2100	$4130	22 yrs. 288 days
20	$2890	$5180	22 yrs. 303 days

policy is $10,000 and the age of the insured at the time the policy was taken out was 25. At the end of the tenth policy year, (when the insured is 35), he will have $1340 worth of cash/loan values. That means he can stop making payments, cash in the policy and the insurance will be terminated altogether and he'll have $1340 cash in hand. Or, he can borrow that much against the policy at the interest rate stated in the policy, and otherwise continue the policy in force by continuing to make annual premiums.

If he wishes to convert to paid-up insurance, he will, at the end of the tenth policy year, have the right to convert to a permanent policy with a face value of $2900. That means he no longer need make any premiums, and he's protected for the rest of his life for $2900 in face value. The last column indicates the extended term insurance provisions. At the end of ten years this individual could convert to extended term, in which case he would be covered for the full face amount ($10,000) for twenty years and 310 days. At the end of that time, the coverage would cease altogether.

In order to take advantage of any of the nonforfeiture provisions, the insurance company should be notified of your intention, and you should receive documentation that verifies exactly what steps you're taking. It would be advisable in any case to discuss the ramifications of making such a move with your insurance agent and any other financial advisors before you actually proceed.

dividend options   Earlier in this chapter we noted that some types of life insurance policies—particularly those issued by mutual life insurance companies—pay dividends to policyholders. If you own such a policy, you'll probably have a number of choices as to the manner in which those dividends are paid. You may wish to receive the dividends in cash to do with as you please; you may want to apply the dividends toward the next premium due on the insurance policy; you may let the premium "ride" with the insurance company where it will draw a rate of interest set forth in the insurance policy; or, you may use the dividends to purchase additional life insurance.

In 1975, policy dividends amounted to over $5 billion. Of this total, 32% was used to buy additional life insurance, 28% was left with the companies to earn interest, 21% was used to help pay the premiums, and 19% was taken out in cash.

An annual statement from your insurance company will indicate what dividends are payable to you, and will instruct you as to how you may choose the mode in which the dividends will be applied. If you have any questions, discuss the matter with your agent. As the statistics indicate, many insured individuals find it a wise, simple, and painless way to increase their insurance protection.

settlement options

In addition to the options available under the nonforfeiture provisions and those available under the dividend provisions, policyholders may also have options concerning the manner in which the payment of proceeds will be made. These are called "settlement options." In many cases, the beneficiary of the policy may decide how the monies are to be paid out—either in a lump sum, or spread out over a period of time (in which case interest will be paid on the proceeds that remain in the company's control.)

In some plans, the owner of the policy may determine how the proceeds are to be paid out, and only the owner will be able to amend that plan. For example, a husband may determine that he does not wish his wife to have the entire proceeds in one lump sum. He may then dictate that she is to receive periodic payments; or perhaps he may determine that the wife as beneficiary will receive the interest only, and that a subsequent beneficiary on the death of the wife will receive the full proceeds. Each policy will spell out exactly what options are available and how to go about choosing them and changing them.

who needs life
insurance, and
how much is
needed?

When we're hungry, we go out and buy the food we need. We don't have to wait for someone to tell us that our stomachs need refilling. And we certainly don't wait until a sales agent from the supermarket comes knocking at our door offering us a selection of edibles. We buy what we reasonably need, what we can reasonably afford, and we select those items that will satisfy our taste and nutritional requirements.

Not so with life insurance. The need is not as clear cut. Indeed, contemplating the need for life insurance necessarily reminds us of our own mortality, and it's no surprise that human nature would short circuit such thoughts.

With life insurance, many of us have to be told of the need and indeed we frequently don't take any action to satisfy that need until a representative of the company comes knocking at our door offering a package of insurance programs. He's telling us, in effect, that we need something we don't want to think about. The dilemma may be further compounded by the fact that the agent may talk in terms and concepts we don't fully understand, and may be a person whose presence we don't find pleasant or comfortable—whose best interests are really at heart here?

The perplexity continues; we understand that with other forms of insurance—car, fire, health, theft—we will be reimbursed for an actual out-of-pocket cost. But life insurance is different. It's not such a reimbursement and, unlike the other forms of insurance, it's assured that the stated risk will occur. The vexing problem is: when?

An example: Charlie is 40 years old, with a wife and three children aged 11, 13, and 15. He's in good health, makes about $15,000 a year with good prospects for improvement. His 30-year mortgage is only five years old and still seems gigantic, particularly as college for the kids creeps closer. The mortality tables say that Charlie should live for roughly 35 more years. Eying that prospect, Charlie might say, "Heck, my kids could be grandparents themselves by then. They'll be well into their own careers, and the insurance dollars I might leave them will be so shrunken by inflation that it's hardly worth the cost now to set up a program."

On the other hand, he could also say, "What if I die tomorrow? That's an extremely long shot, but my family would need close to $9,000 a year to live on. If I had $100,000 worth of life insurance, they could get by in pretty much their current life style for perhaps 20 years. Then they'd all be on their own. But can I afford to do this?''

Somewhere between these two extremes—tomorrow and 35 years hence—Charlie must establish the extent of protection to provide for his family.

purposes of life insurance

The main purpose of life insurance is protection. Some may also view life insurance as a form of saving or investing.

The protection aspect of life insurance is unique, exclusive, and obtainable in no other way. Savings and investing are incidental, for an individual has many alternative forms available.

What is so unique about the protection offered by life insurance?

First, it can be created instantly (or, more correctly, in the simple few weeks it takes to process an application). Charlie might buy a winning lottery ticket or do well in the stock market, but the odds are very long against either. Another way to create a $100,000 fund would be for him to put away $100 each month in a savings account, for almost 32 years. But at that rate he'd have only about $7000 five years from now, and only about $16,000 in ten years from now—the years when his family would need the money most. With life insurance, the level of protection is available immediately, as soon as the policy has been issued.

Second, the protection is guaranteed as long as the premiums are paid and the insurance company remains financially healthy.

Third, it's payable in full (less any loans against the policy), cash on the line. Other assets may be available to provide the desired protection, but many would have to be sold in order to convert them into cash. We never know what the economic circumstances might be at that indeterminate future date. If they should be difficult, the sale of other assets might involve sacrifice and loss. With insurance we don't have to take that risk.

life insurance and inflation?

Life insurance is often criticized as being a poor hedge against inflation. Indeed, as the future purchasing power of our dollars continues to shrink—and there's no reason to think this trend will stop, although it may slow down—the protection we're buying today will be worth far less ten, twenty, or thirty years from now. If Charlie buys $100,000 worth of life insurance today, there's no knowing how much that money will purchase at some future point.

Although this thought can be discouraging, there are other factors the would-be insurance buyer should consider. With the phenomenon of inflation, as prices go up, so does personal income. Thus, if it takes Charlie five hours of work each month to make his life insurance premium payment, he should, as his personal income increases, be able to make that payment in the future with fewer hours of work—perhaps four or three or even two. In terms of needed work hours to meet the obligation, Charlie is able to provide the ultimate protection package with increasingly less work.

Also, if Charlie's life insurance policy is participating—that is, it pays dividends—and he applies the dividends to purchase additional insurance, he is able to increase his ultimate protection package without taking any money from his own pocket to do it. This type of program can constitute an effective protection against inflation.

creating an inheritance

One facet of the protection element of life insurance is the creation of an inheritance for one's family. The assumption involved here is that the insured *will* live his or her full life span, and the proceeds will not be needed to provide current living expenses for the survivors. Rather, on the death of the insured, the proceeds will go to the named beneficiaries to do with as they please. Many individuals will carry their insurance program throughout their life for this purpose. Others will amend their program at some future point by taking advantage of one of the nonforfeiture values—cashing in the policy or borrowing against it to use the funds for current needs and desires, or switching to paid up life or extended term life to continue a measure of protection, but at the same time eliminating the requirement of annual premium payments.

The concept of using life insurance to create an inheritance is far less tangible than the more immediate protection aspects. One must decide how much of an inheritance one wishes to pass along, at the expense of current needs and desires. In other words, once the basic protection for the family has been accounted for, how much more life insurance, if any, does one want to create for the benefit of survivors? How much current disposable income should be directed to that end? This is a very personal decision that can't be answered with a simple formula. If children become self-sufficient, an insured may feel the need for a future inheritance via life insurance has been curtailed or even terminated, and may wish personally to take advantage of the cash values and premium dollars. One of the benefits of permanent life insurance is that it does allow the insured to exercise these choices and retain some values of what has been paid into the policy over the years.

who needs protection?

At the center of our circle of protection is our immediate family: spouse and children. Out toward the fringes, depending on personal situations, may be other family members who do, or might, depend on us as a source of financial aid.

For the younger, growing family (children ranging from infancy to high school), we are protecting against the sudden loss of income that would see them through, at least until their maturity. With the older family (children in college or on their own), we are protecting against the loss of security and added comforts that would otherwise be available as the breadwinner reaches peak earning, and childrearing expenses diminish. To a surviving spouse, it might be the peace of mind for later years. To a surviving child, it might be a nest egg to buy a home, achieve a career goal, or start a similar program for his or her own children.

As we evaluate and plan, we must constantly be aware that those within our circle of protection, as well as our ability to provide for their needs, are constantly changing. It's important, therefore, to develop a program that allows maximum flexibility, to best cope with changing circumstances.

One major national insurance company used an advertising slogan that very aptly pinpoints what any would-be insurance buyer must be aware of—"There's nobody else like you." You, and your family, as you are today and as you may be in the future, are indeed unique. Your needs, desires, aspirations, life expectancy and goals are yours alone. An insurance program that might be perfect for Charlie might be improper for you. Only through careful planning—based on your own unique situation—can you develop your own individual program.

how much insurance is needed?

The first task in evaluating how much insurance is needed by any individual is to determine, as noted earlier, who is going to be protected by the insurance program and to what extent? These are your goals, and you must define them most specifically in order to reach dollar figures. For example, do you want to insure that the children will have at least half of their college tuition guaranteed in the event of your premature death? 75%? 100%? Are they on their own after that? Or do you want them to have a nest egg to help get them started in their chosen career? These are individual questions that only you can answer.

Now comes the time for some thoughtful arithmetic. You must determine, as accurately as possible, the following:

1. What might be the possible extent of "final" expenses? These would be expenses arising as a result of death, and they would include the possible uninsured costs of a terminal illness, burial expenses, estate taxes, and a certain sum to help survivors get through the early difficult time of adjustment. In evaluating these matters, one must also take into account the extent of one's health insurance program regarding possible major expenses connected with a costly terminal illness—an item of considerable expense. If you feel you're amply protected against such costs through your health insurance program, you need not necessarily include them as part of your life insurance program.

2. How much existing debt—mortgages, personal loans, and so on—might the survivors have to pay? Obviously, the amount of your indebtedness can fluctuate considerably from year to year. If you don't now own a house, you won't have to worry about a mortgage being paid off. But if you buy a house tomorrow, there will be a sizable debt that will eventually have to be paid. And if you don't want the family to sell the house to eliminate the debt, you might wish to cover such contingencies through life insurance. Careful planning will cover existing debts, with flexibility retained to increase or decrease as future circumstances warrant.

3. How much per year will the survivors need to maintain themselves in whatever style of living you and they feel would be suitable? Looking at this question in terms of the husband/breadwinner, consideration must be given to the possibilities of the wife remarrying, of her going to work, of children going to work, of other potential sources of income materializing or failing to materialize. Elimination of the husband's own cost of living—food, clothing, recreation, and so on—must also be evaluated. It would probably be simplest to base estimates on a continuation of the current life style, with allowance for possible upward or downward adjustments.

4. Beyond the immediate annual cost of living, estimate the extraordinary expenses that survivors will face, and how much of those expenses you want to assure them of being able to meet. Such expenses might include education, weddings, having a stake to go into business on their own, and so on.

5. For how many years would you want them to continue your particular life style on a worry-free basis?

6. What benefits will be provided by Social Security? A visit with your nearest Social Security office can provide this information.

7. Inventory all current assets, paying particular attention to current market value, potential future value, liquidity (how easily and at what cost the assets can be converted into cash), and the earning potential of any assets. Outline a program showing when certain assets could, or should, be converted to cash to meet family needs. Such a program should also show which nonearning assets might be converted to earning ones. (*Example*: should that vacant lot you bought for speculation or as a site for your future summer home be sold and the money put to work as an earning asset?)

8. Evaluate what other realistic sources of income there might be in the future, such as inheritances or scholarships. You can't count on these sources materializing, but you should be aware of the possibility.

9. Evaluate current life insurance programs, including group plans and any others. Determine what the proceeds could earn annually if they were conservatively invested, and determine how long the proceeds would last if the principal were invaded by a certain amount each year. (The savings charts in the chapter on fixed income investments can assist you with this.) Evaluate all your other assets in the same manner. This information might not be easy to compile and you may want the help of an accountant, or perhaps your insurance agent could assist you impartially and objectively. Even though it may be difficult to obtain, this information is essential for an intelligent plan to evolve.

a case history

When you've surveyed your data, the gaps can be measured and the alternatives for filling those gaps can come into focus.

Let's take another look at the case of Charlie, discussed earlier. Charlie is 40, has a wife who currently does not work, and three children, aged 11, 13, and 15.

Charlie takes home about $15,000 a year (after taxes and other deductions from his gross income) and anticipates solid increases in the forthcoming years, for he has now advanced to a managerial capacity and raises (and responsibilities) are increased at a greater rate in his company from this age onwards. Based on recent past history, Charlie reasonably estimates that his salary could be double his current level within about ten years.

He is anxious to have his children attend college, and would like to provide them with some help, if possible, beyond college in either getting started on their careers or helping them to buy a home. Neither he nor the children feel that Charlie owes this to them, and if he's not able to do so, it will be no great loss—but if he can, he'd like to.

Charlie's other assets are as follows: he has $5000 in savings accounts and checking accounts; he has $17,000 in investments—stocks, bonds, and what is owed him in the company's profit-sharing plan. The equity in his home he values at $20,000 currently and he estimates that in five years, with the mortgage paid down and home values rising, the equity will be worth $30,000. Mortgage payments on the house total $200 per month. In addition to the mortgage payment, Charlie has continuing installment loan payments of approximately $100 per month. He currently has a group life insurance policy with a face value of $10,000, and a private policy with a face value of $10,000.

A few weeks ago, a very close friend of Charlie's suffered a severe heart attack. This sent Charlie off to his insurance agent to work out a program that would protect Charlie's family to the extent he deems himself capable of affording.

After taking into account the above factors, Charlie also determined that in the event of his death in the near future his survivors would receive $300 per month from Social Security, but that sum would dwindle as each child reached the age of 18. He considered his health insurance program adequate to cover the bulk of all expenses involved in a terminal illness; and he estimated that $5000 would cover any other final expenses resulting from his death.

Charlie and his agent estimate that in the event of Charlie's death, his family would need close to $900 per month in basic living expenses for the next few years at least, in addition to the

$300 a month to cover the ongoing debts for the home mortgage and other installment loans.

Charlie and his agent then arrived at the following conclusions: his estate will not be subject to any estate taxes, so there's no need to worry about having cash for that purpose. If Charlie were to die tomorrow, the $300 a month from Social Security would be enough to temporarily take care of the $300 debts per month. The $5000 in the checking and savings accounts could be used to pay the estimated final expenses. The proceeds from the $20,000 worth of existing life insurance would be invested conservatively to provide a fund for educating the children. This amount, he estimates, would be adequate to send each of the children through the local state university. If they needed more, they'd either have to seek out scholarships or work to supplement their available income.

But what about the $900 per month that the family will need to live on? To be on the completely safe side, Charlie determines that the $17,000 worth of investments should be converted into a savings account, which could yield 5½% interest per year. By taking out the interest and dipping into the principal, this nest egg could generate a monthly income of $323 for the next five years. At the end of the five years, the nest egg would be completely depleted. Charlie would want the family to remain in the house for at least another five years, until the youngest child was nearing maturity. If his estimates are correct, the equity on the house in five years will be $30,000. That sum, also invested conservatively in a savings account, could then provide a monthly income of $200 per month for 20 years, at the end of which time the total amount would be completely depleted.

But in the interim, he is still almost $600 shy of his goal. The agent points out to Charlie that if he had a life insurance policy of $85,000, that sum, invested in the same conservative type of fixed income security, paying 5½% per year interest, could generate a monthly income of $526 for a period of 25 years. With such a plan, Charlie's family would have a spendable income of $859 per month for the next five years ($323 from the $17,000 investment fund, plus $536 from the invested insurance proceeds). At the end of five years, the investment fund would be depleted, but the home equity fund would come into being to provide an income of $200 per month. Thus, from a period five years hence, there would be a monthly income of $736 available. By that time, Charlie estimates, the older children will be off on their own, his wife most likely would find an apartment to live in, and her monthly expenses would be considerably reduced because of the children's absence. She would then have a monthly income of at least $736 assured to her for the next twenty years, until she was in her middle sixties.

In other words, assuming that his wife neither remarries nor goes to work, an $85,000 life insurance policy in addition to all his other assets will give very close to what Charlie wishes to provide for his family. He has discussed his situation with his own parents and with his in-laws, and has determined that they will be leaving sufficient inheritances to Charlie and Charlie's wife to assure her of adequate comfort and security in her later years.

Charlie decides to buy a whole life policy for $85,000. At his then current age, 40, the annual premiums will be $1700. This is a nonparticipating policy that pays no dividends. Charlie is aware that dividend payments over the years could reduce his costs, but the initial premium on a participating policy would be somewhat higher, and Charlie is content to go with the less costly premium at this time. He realizes that time may prove he made the wrong decision, but he is content with his thinking. He also declined a term insurance policy, which would have been considerably cheaper at the outset. The first five years of a convertible term insurance policy would have cost $510 per year, compared with the $1700 per year with the whole life policy. The second five years of the convertible term policy would have cost $722 per year, and the third five years $1105 per year. By the fourth five-year cycle, however, the annual premium for the term policy would have increased to $1785, and to $2380 by the fifth five-year cycle.

Over a 25 year period, the total term premiums would still be roughly $10,000 less than the whole life premiums for the same period of time, but the whole life program offers Charlie the nonforfeiture options—the flexibility that he's seeking for his later years. Charlie realizes that if he took the term insurance instead of the whole life insurance, he could invest the difference between the term cost and the whole life cost. But he's not confident in his discipline to invest that money regularly and profitably, and he decides to go with the whole life program.

After paying in on the policy for ten years, Charlie will, at age 50, have been out-of-pocket a total of $17,000. But at that time, the cash values in the policy will be $13,000. Charlie can examine his personal circumstances at that time and may decide to cancel the policy and take out his cash values. In so doing, he will have been out a total of $4000 over the ten-year period, while still having the full $85,000 face value protection.

Or Charlie could, at age 50, convert his policy to a paid up status and would have fully paid up life insurance with a face value of $26,435 with no need to make any more premium payments for the rest of his life. He will have paid in $17,000 in premiums, and on his death his beneficiaries will receive $26,435.

Another alternative would be to convert to extended term insurance, which would eliminate the need for further premium payments, and would leave Charlie fully insured for $85,000 for 11 years and 258 days. With the term policy, he would have been out-of-pocket $6160 by age 50 with no residual values.

By age 60, Charlie realizes, his children will be adults on their own in the world, and his need for insurance to protect them will have diminished considerably. By age 60, Charlie will have paid in $34,000 on the whole life policy, and the policy will then have a cash value of $32,980. He can thus get back almost all that he has paid in, and will have had the benefit of $85,000 worth of protection during that 20-year period. Or, he can convert to paid up status, and have a paid up policy for the balance of his life of $52,190. He can also convert to extended term insurance and remain covered for the full $85,000 for 13 years and 118 days.

By age 60, with the term policy, Charlie would have paid in $20,610 with no residual values.

what's right for Charlie?

This is certainly not the only plan that Charlie had available to him, and it may well not be the best. There's ample room for discussion of the various alternatives, ranging from the whole life to the term life and many points in between, such as the limited pay life programs, the endowment programs, and so on. We have simply illustrated the kind of thinking, planning, and estimating that is to be done in arriving at a base on which alternatives can be examined and decisions made. Each individual and family circumstance must be weighed carefully, and the future estimated rationally.

Charlie may have put himself into a minor financial bind by committing such a large portion of his current income to life insurance premiums. But he knew that in a few years it would represent an ever smaller portion of his income, and he'd feel more comfortable with it. Further, he was aware of the flexibility built into the plan. To a large extent, Charlie was investing in peace of mind—an intangible thing of different value to different people. But it is one aspect of the overall insurance program that must be considered. There is no standard rule or even a suggestion on this point, other than that each individual must personally evaluate this factor.

what's the "right" price to pay for life insurance?

Regretfully, shopping for the "best buy" in life insurance makes shopping for the "best buy" in a car seem simple by comparison. There are hundreds of companies from which to choose, and each may offer up to 20 or 30 different plans. Comparing life insurance plans *on the basis of premium cost alone* can be mind-boggling.

A price comparison of just two popular companies illustrates this point. A 40-year-old male is seeking a "stripped down" whole life policy. It's a nonparticipating policy (no dividends), contains no accidental death benefit (double indemnity), and no waiver of premium clause (the premiums are paid automatically in the event of the insured's total disability). The annual premium per $1000 of face coverage is $23.28 in company A and $19.09 in company B. On a policy for $10,000, the annual difference in premiums between the two companies will be more than $42, with company B being cheaper.

Comparing the nonforfeiture values presents a different picture, however. After ten years, company A, on the above policy, will have a cash value of $174 per $1000 of face value, while the cheaper company, B, will have a cash value of only $153 per $1000. Similarly, after ten years, company A's policy will have a paid up value of $330 per $1000 of face value, and company B will have a paid up value of $311 per $1000 worth of face value. The extended term insurance with company A will run for 12 years and 38 days, while the extended term insurance of company B will run for 11 years and 258 days.

When we look at the nonforfeiture values after 20 years, though, the picture again changes. The cash value with company A will be $391 per $1000 worth of face value, and company B will be nearly equal to that, $388. In the paid up department, company A will have $605 worth of paid up insurance per $1000 of face value, and company B slightly exceeds that with $614. Extended term insurance after 20 years will be 12 years and 294 days with company A, and 13 years and 118 days with company B.

If all other factors are equal (which they always aren't), company B would seem to have the slight edge in this comparison. Its overall premium cost is lower, and even though the cash values build up more rapidly for the first ten years in company A, company B's cash values have pretty much caught up with A by the end of 20 years.

There is one very critical factor in comparing the two companies that may not be equal: the service the insured can expect from the agent and the company. The advice and counsel that the insured may receive from the agent for company A may far offset the difference in price between the two policies. We discuss this aspect of service in more detail shortly.

Table 8-2 illustrates the different pricing and value structures for six of the more than twenty plans offered by a single company. The numbers shown in the first five columns indicate the annual premium cost for $1000 worth of face value for a thirty-five year old male. The four columns on the right indicate the cash and paid up value for each plan after 10 years and after 20 years. Although the company is a stock company, it does, like many other stock companies, offer participating policies much the same as issued by mutual companies.

table 8-2 **costs and values in various life insurance policies offered by a single company**

Type of policy	Features of Policy					Future Values			
	Nonpar	Nonpar with Waiver of Premium	Par	Par with Waiver of Premium	Accidental Death Benefit	Cash Value 10 yrs.	Cash Value 20 yrs.	Paid Up 10 yrs.	Paid Up 20 yrs.
Whole Life	$19.46	$20.08	$23.90	$24.62	$1.10	$148	$344	$315	$586
20-Pay Life	30.16	30.59	36.44	36.92	1.35	245	588	520	$1,000 (fully paid)
30-Pay Life	23.85	24.43	29.29	29.97	1.15	181	428	385	729
20-Year Endowment	44.73	45.27	50.69	51.27	1.10	408	1,000 (mature)	542	$1,000 (mature)
30-Year Endowment	28.77	29.44	34.12	34.87	1.20	236	567	399	742
Term: 5-Year Convertible	6.08	6.40	—	—	1.00	0	0	0	0

Note: Figures illustrate annual premium cost per $1000 worth of face value insurance, for a 35-year-old male. Policy values are per $1000 worth of face value.

All the policies indicated, except for the term policy at the bottom of the list, are forms of "permanent" insurance. The term policy is a five-year term, convertible to ordinary life. The premium for a nonparticipating policy of five-year convertible term is $6.08. If a waiver of premium is added, the annual premium is $6.40. The company does not offer participating term policies. If accidental death benefit is desired by the insured, $1 is added to the indicated premium price. The term policy does not have any cash values or paid up values as long as it remains term. If it is converted to whole life, it will begin to accumulate those values after conversion. After the initial five years of the term policy, the premium will increase to a higher level for the second five year term, and will continue to do so throughout the life of the insurance program.

With the permanent plans, the premium remains level throughout the life of the policy, and cash values begin to build up at the inception of the policy, or within a year or two after the policy has begun. Of the five illustrated permanent types of insurance, whole life is the cheapest, followed in ascending order by the limited pay life programs (20 pay life and 30 pay life), then by the endowment programs.

In the limited pay life programs, such as the 20 pay life, the premiums are made for 20 years, at the end of which time the policy is fully paid and the total face value will be payable to the beneficiaries (less any loans outstanding against the policy). However, the cash values will not have reached their highest level at the end of the 20 years. Even though the policy is fully paid, and no more premiums need be paid, the cash values will continue to increase after the 20 years have expired.

In the endowment plans, such as the 20 year endowment plan, both the paid up value and the cash value have reached full maturity at the end of 20 years. In other words, the insured could cash in the policy for full face value, or could remain fully insured for the full face value for the remainder of his or her life without paying any more premiums.

Which is best? As discussed earlier, each individual must determine how much current income he or she wishes to devote to protection and future security, and how much time must pass before how much security is available. In other words, do we scrimp a bit today for the sake of future security and flexibility? Or do we possibly sacrifice future security and flexibility for the sake of more breathing room today? These questions must be resolved, or at least put into focus, before a shopping expedition for a life insurance plan begins.

| | There is no such thing as a typical insurance agent.|

the importance
of the agent

There is no such thing as a typical insurance agent. His training might range from minimal to the rigorous demands of the courses leading to the CLU (Chartered Life Underwriter) designation. His experience might encompass weeks or decades. His income level can range from paltry to six figures. And his personality, sales techniques, and sense of ethics can run the full spectrum of human potential.

There will be many trying to seek you out. If you can find the right agent, you've made a valuable catch. But how do you know what to look for? Before we get into a shopping list, let's take a quick look at some of the dilemmas in the industry.

Dilemma #1: The insurance agent makes his living by selling insurance policies. Proper counselling may be of equal or greater value to you than the policy itself, but the agent doesn't make a penny unless he actually makes a sale. Needless to say, good counselling can produce a good sale, but it might not.

Any agent, therefore, finds himself taking a calculated risk on how much time he'll spend with any given prospect in counselling sessions. This can result in counselling and selling efforts becoming intermingled, to the point where you might not be able to tell them apart. With the agent's help, you should define your protection goals and recognize the gaps between what you have and what you need, and what various alternatives there are that can help you fill those gaps to reach your goals. Those items are the subject of counselling. Once that's in hand, it's time to get into the specifics of various policies.

If the agent is not willing to take the time you need to understand your goals, you might not be getting the service you need. And the agent might not take the time if he's not confident that there will be a sale as a result. This dilemma is perhaps best resolved by open and frank communications at the outset: "Mr. agent, this is what I have to learn from you before I will even consider doing business with you. If you're willing to teach me what I think I have to know, I may well be a customer, but there's no guarantee. If you're willing to proceed on those terms, fine. If not, perhaps it would be best if we didn't waste each other's time."

Dilemma #2: With rare exception, people closer to the top of the economic ladder have better access to more sophisticated insurance counselling than those closer to the bottom of the ladder. This, for better or for worse, is the way of our world.

It might take an agent the same, or more, time to sell a $10,000 policy to a working family as it would to sell a $100,000 policy to an executive. The reward to the agent for his time is obviously drastically different. Further, the agent who is going for the big sale will probably have to be better equipped to handle the more sophisticated problems wealthy prospects will have. People on the lower rungs of the economic ladder also need more sound advice, but it may be more difficult for them to get it.

The more an individual learns about life insurance, the better able he or she will be to take advantage of whatever advice is given, and the better prepared to seek and understand the more sophisticated advice that could be of greater value.

Dilemma #3: Each of us has so many dollars to spend. Some of those dollars will be spent on our current needs, and some will be put away to cover future needs and desires. There are many institutions that would like to take care of our future dollars for us—insurance companies, mutual funds, banks, savings institutions, stockbrokers. They all make their living by putting our future dollars to use until we need them, and the competition is keen to get access to these dollars.

In varying degrees, each of these giant industries has become envious of the success of the others. Some segments of the life insurance industry have reacted, for example, by putting mutual funds in the same attache case as their insurance policies. The funds might be good, so might the policies. Mixing them together too much may not be.

With all these financial industries competing with each other for our future dollars, it's essential that we keep a clear distinction between insuring and investing. Each has its separate set of purposes and goal fulfillment abilities. Insurance offers certainty; some forms of investment offer a measure of certainty, others offer little more than possibility.

Keeping these dilemmas firmly in mind, what then do you look for in an insurance agent?

As in choosing any professional advisor, you must have trust in his ability, confidence in his training, and knowledge of his integrity. You don't usually get these on a hunch or a first impression, though it's not impossible. Personal familiarity, recommendations from others, reputation in the community are indicators. The individual who comes on with a hard sell after his first "how do you do?" may have the same program to offer you as the agent who holds his fire until after the proper rapport has been established. The choice is up to you.

What are the agent's credentials, background, training, and prior experience? These are important factors to determine and evaluate. It is, of course, possible for an eager-to-get-established novice to serve you just as well as an old pro. But the Perennial Job Hopper is liable to leave you with some loose ends hanging.

the CLU   In evaluating an agent's credentials, the question of whether he is a CLU (Chartered Life Underwriter) might arise. A CLU is an insurance agent who has been through a rigorous course of instruction to better equip him to serve his public and make his living. Only a small percentage of all agents are CLUs. The time and educational requirements may scare off many from pursuing the credential. These educational requirements include five separate courses on economics, taxes, estate planning and conservation, corporate law, contract law, pensions and profit-sharing plans, accounting, and the technical aspects of life insurance itself.

Each course requires about 60 hours of classroom work, plus abundant outside homework. On completing the courses, each agent then must pass a four-hour written exam on each of the five subjects.

If all exams are passed, the candidate must then be recommended by his peers, and if so, he then becomes a CLU.

CLUs must subscribe to the following pledge:

In all my relations with clients, I agree to observe the following rule of professional conduct: I shall, in the light of all of the circumstances surrounding my client, which I shall make every conscientious effort to ascertain and understand, give him that service which, had I been in the same circumstances, I would have applied to myself.

A CLU doesn't have any product or secret policies to offer you that any other agent may not have, but he does possess the education that might enable him to better determine your needs and find the right policy to satisfy those needs. (Certainly there are many fine agents who do not have the CLU designation, who can serve your needs most adequately.)

In dealing with a CLU, you are working with an individual who has invested hundreds of hours of his own time to become more of an expert in his own field. That fact alone might cause many insurance shoppers to lean in favor of doing business with a CLU.

Remember that no insurance agent, CLU or not, can make a living unless he sells policies. The amount of time he can give to counselling any client is limited. But the *quality* of counselling is important, perhaps more so than the amount of time given it. And that might well be where the CLU has another edge.

Does an agent seem overanxious to push one specific program? If so, you may not be getting the benefits of the full and clear perspective that you need to choose between possible alternatives.

The company that an agent represents may have a bearing on your thinking. You might feel more comfortable with older, larger, better known companies, though many smaller companies offer excellent choices. Very small, very new companies might be absorbed by bigger firms as time passes, which might entail a measure of inconvenience to you with regard to access to records, service, and so on.

Does the company maintain a well-kept local or regional office where questions can be answered and information and service readily obtained? If you're dealing with an independent agent, who might represent many companies, a look at the housekeeping in his office might be of interest to you regarding the manner in which he handles his overall business and personal affairs.

A major portion of your efforts must be directed to meeting and evaluating a number of prospective agents. The difference between *choosing* an agent and *being chosen by* an agent can be very important. The selection process is up to you, and if you make the most of it, you'll get the most from it. This may seem an undue amount of work simply to buy an insurance policy. But remember that you are not buying a simple product that you'll use today and be done with tomorrow. You're striving to build a structure that will shelter you and your family for many years. If it's built right, it will last, it will perform, and it will have been worth the time and the money involved.

Life Insurance—For Adult Males Only?

In ever increasing numbers, women—single, married, working, or nonworking—are acquiring life insurance. Why? Because of a well-organized sales technique by insurance companies? Or does a real need exist for women to obtain insurance? And if so, how much?

Another sales target of the life insurance industry is the young person—the late teenager or college student who has yet to enter the job market, hasn't formed a family unit, does not have dependents to protect. Does it make sense for an individual to obtain life insurance prior to the age of financial responsibility? Clever sales pitch or real need?

Let's examine both questions more closely.

In terms of general priority, life insurance needs of a working mother rank at the top, followed by the nonworking mother, the working single woman, and the nonworking single woman.

The working mother is making a two-sided contribution to the economic welfare of the family unit. Her income helps to support the family's needs; and her activities in the household, if they had to be replaced, would cost money. The specific functions of life insurance for the working mother, in the event of her premature death, would be as follows: to replace the income she had been generating; to provide funds for housekeeping expenses and for companionship for young children; to defray the possible heavy costs of a terminal illness where health insurance did not fill the gap.

As children grow up and move out, the needs for life insurance obviously diminish, as housekeeping and companionship expenses diminish. Further, when the children have gone off on their own, the need to replace the working mother's income may also diminish, thus cutting down on the need for life insurance on the woman. But the ability to meet uninsured illness costs from life insurance proceeds may still remain.

Except for the matter of replacing lost income, the insurance needs of the nonworking mother regarding child care and housekeeping expenses, as well as terminal illness costs, indicate a valid need for some life insurance. For a mother—whether working or nonworking—a term policy may be more desirable in many cases than an ordinary life policy. Such a program might be geared to continue until the children have moved out and the needs have been minimized accordingly. A greater amount of protection can be obtained for the dollars available through term policies as compared with ordinary life policies.

The working single woman who anticipates raising a family may want to consider a life insurance program so as to create an early foundation of protection when the family unit comes into being. The earlier a program is started, the lower the premiums will be, and the better protection will exist against the possibility of an individual becoming uninsurable.

If a young woman has other individuals who may be dependent on her income—such as elderly parents—a program of life insurance can help protect such dependents in the event of the woman's premature death.

Life insurance needs are least for the young woman who is not working—perhaps a college student, or one supported by parents. However, in anticipation of possible future family involvement or that others may become dependent on her generation of income, a life insurance program can be envisioned at some future point. The closer the reality of family involvement or other's dependency, the more seriously such a person should examine a life insurance program to cover the expected needs.

In a small minority of cases—perhaps less than 5% of the population—life insurance for the woman can fill yet another need. If a woman inherits a substantial sum of money, there well may be estate taxes to pay on her death. Her inheritance may consist of nonliquid assets: property such as the family house, the family business, investments in real estate, and the like. On the widow's death, there may not be enough ready cash to meet the estate tax obligations, and assets might have to be sold, perhaps at a sacrifice, in order to pay those taxes. A life insurance program can provide ready cash to meet that contingency, and can thus avoid the possible need of having to sacrifice other property to pay the tax bill. Generally, unless the widow's inheritance exceeds $150,000 to $200,000, this should not be a problem. But where an inheritance begins to exceed that range, the estate tax bite can be deep. It would be to the advantage of any married couple to examine the potential effect of estate taxes on the death of a surviving widow, and

to plan well in advance as to how the tax obligation will be met. This matter should be reviewed periodically—at least every three to five years—so that the tax planning can remain in line with the inflating value of family assets and the possibility of changing tax laws and other circumstances.

What about the single mother? Her life insurance needs will largely depend on her overall financial circumstances—what outside support can she reliably depend on to meet the needs of her children in the event of her death? Outside support would include alimony and child support payments in the case of a divorcee, inheritances in the case of a widow, and parental assistance in the case of the single parent. Lacking an assured source of outside support, the single mother may find that a life insurance program is the ideal way to fill the gap that could arise regarding the care and education of her children.

Insurance for the young.

When should a young person

commence a life insurance program? At age fifteen, for example, when financial responsibility is minimal and the future is virtually unknown? At age twenty when career goals are beginning to come into focus and the age of financial responsibility is dawning? At age twenty-five, when marriage is likely to have occurred, and when the career path is already started? At age thirty, when a family is likely under way and a career program is well established?

The question can be debated vigorously. "It's a waste of money to start an insurance program until the individual has a clear sense of family obligations and overall financial status!" "The earlier one starts a life insurance program, the bigger and stronger a foundation will be built for the future!"

There is no ultimately correct answer that suits everyone. The matter must be examined in the light of individual circumstances and desires. There are, however, certain factors that must

be considered. On the one side, it may indeed be a financial hardship to begin a life insurance program. The premium dollars could well be put to better use in such other areas as college education, for example. On the other hand, the earlier an individual commences a program, the lower its cost, and, perhaps more important, by commencing a program at an early age, the individual is protecting against the possibility of becoming uninsurable at a later age.

1. What is the term for the mathematical calculations relating to risk and premium?
2. List the five kinds of personal insurance.
3. Explain the difference between stock life insurance companies and mutual life insurance companies.
4. Jim Langton has worked for the Tiny Toy Company for seven years. During that time he acquired two group insurance policies. Jim has invented several new toys and decided to go into business for himself. What should he do about his group insurance?
5. Why might a person decide to buy a policy of endowment at age 65?
6. Jose and Maria bought an annuity contract. Payments are made to both of them or to the survivor after one of them dies. What is this type of annuity called?
7. What is a contingent beneficiary?
8. Describe what a table of nonforfeiture values is and where it is found.

1. George and Barbara Cook are excellent financial managers. They are interested in buying term insurance so that they will have more cash left in the budget to put into a conservative investment program. They are, however, concerned that they might not be able to continue with the investments. Could they go ahead with the term insurance but still have a backup plan?
2. Mike and Elaine Green have been working on their life insurance program. They would like to have enough insurance to provide an additional $800 per month from the invested proceeds. They are planning to invest these proceeds at 8%. Use Table 14-2 in Chapter 14 to determine how much insurance would be required.
3. Phil is now 25 years old. He is considering the purchase of term insurance, but has been comparing it with straight life. The cost of $50,000 for straight life is $650 per year with a level premium. When he reaches age 60, this will have a cash value of $24,000. The cost of the term is as follows: $220 at age 25, $230 at age 30, $260 at age 35, $330 at age 40, $460 at age 45, $680 at age 50, and $1000 at age 55. Compare Phil's two options. Try to point out the personal factors affecting the choice.
4. Mathew and Carla Paine have evaluated their insurance needs and concluded that they would like to reduce that need by improved planning. Discuss the ways in which they could do this.

chapter 9 **other insurance**

insurance when the risk may not occur

There is a very distinct and important difference between life insurance and the other common forms of personal insurance. With life insurance, as long as the policy remains in force, the company must pay the agreed on benefits to the designated beneficiary at a fixed date: the death of the insured. There is no question that the risk being insured against—the death of the insured—will occur. Because of the broad base of statistical information available, the insurance company is able to make a reasonably accurate estimate as to when that date will probably occur. And the insurance company knows precisely how much it must pay on that occurrence.

With the other common forms of personal insurance—health, income, property, and public liability—the risk that is being insured against may not occur. If it does, it might occur tomorrow or ten years from now. When it does occur, the company may have to pay a token amount to the insured, or a moderate or substantial sum. There may be a dispute as to whether or not anything should be paid, depending on the possibility of who

321

was at fault. And there may be disagreement about the amount of damages actually suffered, and thereby reimbursable.

With life insurance, you know for certain that a fixed sum of money will be available to you or your beneficiaries. With the other forms of insurance, the money you pay out may never be seen again. Human nature may lead us to think—perhaps dangerously so—that these kinds of risks will occur to others but never to us. We thus would never be out of pocket as a result of such occurrences, and perhaps we should therefore keep our costs for such insurance to a minimum.

In many respects, the potential losses that can be suffered as a result of risks relating to health, income, property, and public liability can be far more devastating than when a breadwinner dies leaving no life insurance. Vague and unpredictable though these risks may be, it would indeed be imprudent to fail to acquire the appropriate level of protection that can prevent a financial disaster.

The basic mechanics are generally the same for life insurance and the other forms of personal insurance. A contract (policy) is entered into between the insured party and the insurance company. The contract sets forth all of the rights and obligations of the parties, including the stated risks that are insured, as well as precise definitions of all the appropriate terms in the policy that can have a bearing on the rights of the parties. The insurance company holds and invests the premium dollars until claims have to be paid.

But the claim procedures with these other forms of personal insurance can often be much more complicated than with life insurance. When an insured individual dies, the company is notified of the death and makes the payment. But in the other forms of insurance, there may be many questions about the status of the insured or of the injured parties, and the extent of damages suffered may be subject to question.

Presenting a claim for payment with these various types of personal insurance may require filling out numerous and extensive forms. The information you submit on the forms may be subject to further investigation by the insurance company to determine the validity of the claims. Some forms of personal insurance may have a fixed sum that will be paid to a policy holder, such as in a medical insurance policy.

In other situations, the extent of loss may be subject to dispute between the parties. For example, a fire in your home may damage certain items. You claim that they are totally destroyed and must be replaced. The insurance company feels that they are simply in need of cleaning and refurbishing that can be done at a much lower cost than actual replacement. They state that that's the extent of their obligation to you. Unlike the obvious difference between life and death, the problem of pinpointing specific claims and damages in these other forms of personal insurance can be very perplexing to the insured.

Although the vast majority of all claims are clearly defined in insurance contracts, and are paid in accordance with the company's obligations, there is a continuing burden on the insured individual to comply with the requirements for getting satisfaction and for seeing to it that the full measure of the claim is clearly stated and received.

health insurance

The average American family might spend as much in a given year on hot dogs and breakfast cereals as it spends (directly or via fringe benefits) on health insurance. If the hot dogs are too fatty or the cereal is nonnutritive, nobody will suffer any great loss. But if money spent on health insurance—either privately or through an employer—isn't wisely planned and maintained, the results can be catastrophic.

the gap

Currently, out of every $3 spent on private health care and health insurance premiums, only about $1 is returned to the public in the form of health insurance benefits. The other $2 is out of pocket. This is in spite of the fact that close to 90% of the working population is covered by one or more plans of health insurance.

Why should there be such a tremendous gap between what we pay for medical expenses and protective insurance, and what we get back in insurance benefits? Many individuals simply prefer to take their chances that they will not be exposed to risk, rather than spend a lot of money for insurance protection. Others may think they are protected by an existing health insurance program when in fact they are far less protected than they believe. Many people are adequately protected for minor and probable medical expenses, but are unprotected for the major catastrophic expenses. Many insurance policies do not increase their benefits at the same rate that health and medical expenses have been skyrocketing in recent years.

One of the single most frequent causes for financial distress is poor health and the lack of proper protection against medical expenses. Many segments of the population have been so poorly protected that the government has intervened—at enormous expense to taxpayers—to provide forms of basic medical care for those segments. Medicare is designed to take care of a substantial portion of medical expenses for the elderly; Medicaid, as administered by the various states and supported by the federal government, does the same service for those economically distressed. Further, for many years, the federal government has been debating the merits of a form of national health insurance to protect the population at large.

Whether or not the government sees fit to close the medical expense gaps for those who don't do this on their own, the prudent individual and family will see that their welfare is protected by designing and maintaining a sensible health insurance plan.

reasons for the gap

The following case histories illustrate some typical situations wherein people learn the hard way about the coverage gap in their health insurance programs.

arthur's case history

Arthur considered himself in the peak of health, and never paid much attention to the sick-pay policies of his employer. It wasn't until a co-worker suffered an injury and was laid up for four months that he realized how vulnerable he was. Through his co-worker he learned that the employer would provide full pay for the first two weeks of any disability, then half pay for another month and a half, then nothing. After two months of disability, the co-worker had ceased to receive any income, and the total cost of his disability and recuperation put his family into a critical financial bind.

Arthur was thus a ripe prospect for an advertisement that offered "$200 a week extra cash when you're hospitalized. . . . and $100 a week when you are recuperating at home!" Those were the two inch high letters that caught his eye. He skimmed over the small print in the advertisement, for it seemed too complicated. He bought the policy, and, even though he had ten days in which to return it if he wasn't satisfied, the small print in the policy also seemed too complicated. He retained the policy, assured that he was protected come what may.

A freak accident landed him in the hospital with a broken hip a few months later. Arthur was hospitalized for three weeks, and sent in his claim for $600, and received a check shortly thereafter. This was in addition to the sick-pay benefits he was receiving from his employer.

But he was in for a long siege of convalescence and rehabilitation, and wasn't able to return to work for ten weeks after he left the hospital. Three weeks after leaving the hospital he submitted another claim for the $100 per week that was due him, and again he got a check immediately.

Now the sick-pay benefits from his employment were near an end, but Arthur was not aware that his insurance policy benefits were also at an end. After another month, Arthur filed a claim for his $100 per week, but this time the insurance company notified him that he was entitled to no more benefits.

The small print that he had skimmed over and had not understood explained that the recuperative benefits were payable for no longer than the time he spent in the hospital. Three weeks in the hospital would entitle him to three weeks of at-home benefits. But no more. He had thought that the benefits would be payable for as long as any recuperation lasted, but the policy said otherwise. The remaining weeks of recuperation, with no source of income at all, made a serious dent in Arthur's savings account.

brian's case history

Brian was a bright business executive who was keenly aware of his family's need for protection against medical expenses. Ten years earlier, he had carefully shopped around for and had obtained a comprehensive medical insurance program. He filed the policy away, satisfied that he had insulated himself from any problem in the medical expense field, particularly major catastrophes. And he was fortunate, for ten years elapsed with no major health care obligations. He dutifully paid his premiums, but, being a busy man, never took the time to review the coverage offerred by the policy, even though he was aware that medical costs were steadily rising.

Then his wife developed some strange intestinal pains, and the siege began—tests, X rays, specialists, surgery, hospitals, drugs, post-operative care, nurses, consultations, more drugs, more X rays, more tests, more nurses. But Brian never had a worry about getting it all paid for.

Finally, the doctor pronounced his wife cured, and Brian started to add up the bills. His ten-year-old policy had provided $25 a day toward the hospital room. That had seemed ample ten years ago, but today the cost was in excess of $100 a day. The surgical schedule in the policy allowed $100 for the needed operation, but the surgeon's bill now was $500. And so it went throughout all of the specific items Brian had to pay.

The insurance company paid fully and promptly, but the total payments that Brian received were only a fraction of the total bills. Brian realized too late what a costly error he had made by not periodically reviewing and updating his policy. For the sake of a few minutes every few years, he could have saved many thousands of dollars that were now gone forever.

cora's case history

Cora was widowed a few years ago, and though she was left with adequate income, she had no protection against medical expenses. Cora was not yet old enough to be eligible for Medicare, but she was old enough to believe what her friends told her about the cost and difficulty of obtaining health insurance at her age. She inquired of a few agents and found, indeed, that what her friends said was true. It was a costly proposition to acquire adequate protection, and she feared dipping into her limited sources of income to obtain that protection.

Like Arthur, she was ripe for the lure of an advertisement offering a medical insurance plan that "required no medical exam . . . absolutely no age limit." Cora mailed in the coupon attached to the ad, and a few days later was visited by an aggressive sales agent who, after scaring her with tales of what might happen to her, sold her a medical and hospital expense plan that, he said, would give her all the protection she might need.

Time passed, and an old kidney ailment came back to haunt Cora. She had all but forgotten about the condition, since she thought it had been cured many years ago.

She submitted her claim to the insurance company, and was shocked to learn that they would not pay her anything. She was told that pre-existing conditions weren't covered in the policy. Any condition that developed after she had acquired the insurance policy would be covered but none that had existed previously, which reoccurred, would be covered. Cora had been totally unaware of this clause. As a gesture of good will, the insurance company offered to return all the premiums she had paid in. But that was a small token compared to the medical expenses she had incurred. Her assets drained by the uninsured illness, Cora had to turn to public welfare.

big print/small print

The big print giveth and the small print taketh away. As the case histories illustrate, a clear understanding of precisely what the insurance contract states is essential if an individual is to have protection. And this requires reading the small print, and understanding it. If the small print is too garbled by legal mumbo-jumbo, seek the assistance of the insurance agent, your family doctor, and any friends or associates who may be helpful. Sadly, many documents—particularly insurance policies—that we must understand to protect our financial situations are not worded in the language of the common person, but in the language of the lawyer. To an extent this is necessary, for the wording must clearly define the legal obligations and rights of the parties. Some companies have attempted to present the contractual matters in a more easily understandable format, but not enough are doing so. Even when they are, the client does not always take the time to read beyond the big print to see what the small print says and means.

The big print says: "We will pay you up to $5000 if you are hospitalized because of illness or accident." But the small print says: "Payments shall not exceed $500 in any given year."

The big print says: "No more worries about surgical expense! We will pay you up to $10,000 on your surgical bills." The small print says, in effect, that the $10,000 is the outside maximum payable over the entire life of the contract. Any single claims are subject to a precise schedule of benefits, which may provide payments well below the actual costs. Also, coverage may be for the surgeon's bill only, and may not cover such things as anesthetic, operating room fees, assistant surgeon, surgical nurse, and recuperative costs.

The big print says: "This policy is guaranteed renewable!" The small print says: "Guaranteed renewable to age 65 only, and annual renewals will be made at premium rates at the time of renewal."

the contracts

Before we delve into the specifics of different kinds of medical costs and the forms of insurance you can obtain, it is necessary to have an overall understanding of the workings of the contracts themselves.

The following precautions are necessary.

□ Compare a number of plans in detail. Lay out a chart, perhaps, itemizing each point of coverage for each kind of insurance protection: how much and for how long are you covered? What exceptions or exclusions or limitations are there? What will the premium costs be? Only by doing this can you really get an accurate comparison of what the policies will offer you.

☐ Examine the policy carefully before you buy it. If an agent won't provide you with a copy of the policy he is selling, you can find other agents who will. Without a copy of the policy, you are buying big print, but getting small print.

☐ Examine the policy after you buy it. Conditions may have been imposed on the contract as a result of information contained in your application. This can be especially true with contracts heavily promoted in advertising.

☐ Before you buy any policy, determine what actual current costs are in your area for various forms of medical care. This can be done with a few phone calls—to your local medical society, your doctor, and a local hospital. If the policy benefits aren't in line with actual costs, you'll find yourself footing the balance of the bill on your own.

☐ Review policies periodically, be they group, Blue Cross/Blue Shield, individual. Old policies can be out of touch with current costs and may need updating or supplementing. Many policies contain riders that permit you to increase your limits from time to time. You may want to take advantage of these rights.

☐ Remember that it is the policy itself, and not what the sales agent says, that spells out the obligations of the insurance company. If, later on, the company refuses to pay a claim, you'll get nowhere if you tell them, "But the agent said . . ."

☐ Be well aware that the policy that seems the cheapest isn't always the best.

☐ Don't be fooled by some of the wording and language that may appear in mail order or promotional insurance advertisements. Many private companies will attempt to lure buyers by using slogans, replicas, and names that sound like government-sponsored programs. Examples may include such wording as, "Medi-Care," "Veterans Insurance Division," "Armed Forces Policy," and so on. Envelopes may be created to resemble official U.S. government envelopes. Plans offered by these companies may be legitimate, but the sales approach may be less than ethical and you might end up paying for far more than what you are actually getting. If you have any questions, check out the reputation of the insurance company. One source of such information is *Best's* directory, a rating service that will probably be available at your local library. Your local agent may also have a copy, and you may need help in deciphering the language in *Best's*. Other information sources include your state Insurance Department, your local Better Business Bureau, the National Council of Better Business Bureaus, and the Bureau of Deceptive Practices of the Federal Trade Commission (Washington, D.C.).

understanding health care costs and risks

The first step in building a sound program of protection is to determine precisely what your existing health insurance coverage consists of. If you are protected under a group plan at work, the personnel office at your place of employment should be able to offer you the counselling needed to help you understand the precise limits of your coverage.

If you are privately insured, you may have to depend on your agent for help in understanding the details. If a policy—be it group or private—has not been updated within the last year or two, or if it does not contain automatic escalation clauses that increase the benefits in line with increasing costs, it will likely be necessary to amend your policy, or find supplemental policies, that will bring your level of coverage up to a par with current actual costs.

In addition to determining what existing coverage you now have, you'll also want to evaluate what this coverage is costing you, and how much more you can afford for added protection.

Health care costs and the risks you'll be facing can be broken down into three ranges.

necessary minor expenses

In the first range are the necessary minor expenses: periodic check ups for all family members, the inevitable smattering of doctor bills for injuries and common illnesses, prescriptions, first aid, and the like. Do you need insurance to cover these relatively minor predictable costs? Are you just swapping dollars with the insurance company—dollars that might better be spent protecting you against the major, unpredictable, possibly crippling costs? No two individuals are alike. Some may prefer to budget these costs in their normal expense program. Others may want the security of insurance even though, over the long pull, it's possible that they may be spending as much or more on premiums than they may get back in benefits. In any event, it's worth looking at your current program to determine whether or not you are covered for expenses that you'd rather take your chances on, and save the administration costs that go to the insurance company.

heavier costs

The second range of health care costs involve the heavier, less predictable situations that entail hospitalization, extensive doctor bills, and surgery. These situations, in turn, can lead to loss of income due to the length of disability. In addition to out-of-pocket medical expenses and lost income, the convalescent expenses connected with such medical situations can be considerable.

the heaviest expenses

Major diseases and injuries can entail expenses that swiftly mount into the many thousands of dollars. The initial expense is often followed by protracted periods of disability in which no work can be done and no income received. In addition to conditions that threaten life itself, many impose limitations on one's ability to work and otherwise function normally in society. It is this area of health care problems—often referred to as "catastrophic"—that has been the primary focus of recent government attention looking to establish some form of federal protection for the public against such costs.

Slightly more than half of the American population has adequate or good protection against catastrophic medical costs. The balance is unprotected or has less than adequate protection.

Although it's logical to assume that a major disability to the family breadwinner would be most damaging (largely due to loss of income), a similar fate befalling any individual can be nearly as severe.

The difficulty in predicting potential costs increases from the first level of health care (the necessary minor expenses) up to this highest level. Fortunately, the health insurance industry in America has devised a variety of programs that can be tailored to fit our available budgets and help us achieve the necessary circle of protection that we're seeking.

basic hospital, surgical, and physician insurance

These three forms of insurance protection cover three different areas of medical costs. Frequently, they are lumped together in one type of basic policy, such as in group programs and Blue Cross/Blue Shield programs. If an individual has more than one plan—such as a group plan at work plus a private plan—care must be taken to determine that coverage does not overlap, or, in other words, that you are protected for the same expense twice. Some policies will not pay you benefits if you have in fact received benefits from another policy. Further, duplication of coverage means that you're paying more in premiums than you need to.

hospital insurance | Hospital insurance is designed to reimburse you for hospital expenses: room and board, nursing, minor supplies, and perhaps X rays, tests, and medications. The major item—room and board—will generally be limited to a maximum amount per day, for a maximum number of days. The other items may also be limited to specific dollar amounts. In evaluating the adequacy of hospital insurance, you must take into account the following:

☐ What are the actual going rates at hospitals in your area, particularly the one you'd use if the need arose? What are the costs for a private room, a semi-private room, and a ward? What about emergency room costs? Intensive care unit costs? To what extent would the proposed insurance plan cover these costs?

☐ Do your local hospitals anticipate raising their rates and, if so, to what levels? It can almost be automatically assumed that hospital expenses will increase in the future. If you want complete coverage, does your plan contain provisions that allow you to increase the benefits for hospital care expenses? Would it make sense to pay an added premium to obtain higher limitations than are currently needed if such limitations can in fact be obtained?

☐ Is the hospital you'd use covered under the proposed insurance plan? Some hospitals may be excluded from certain kinds of insurance policies, and you must determine this in advance.

☐ Must you be an "in-patient" in order to be covered? That is, do you actually have to be registered in the hospital as a patient? Is there coverage for emergency room treatment and for out-patient visits?

☐ For how many days of hospital stay are you fully covered?

☐ Are you covered for any cause that may put you in the hospital, or are there exclusions? For example, mental disorders may not be covered, even if you are hospitalized.

☐ Are there extra benefits for intensive care? These costs can be considerable, and not all policies will protect an individual against intensive-care confinement. If the policy offers optional intensive care coverage, what is the cost, and what are the limitations?

☐ Must you be in the hospital for a minimum number of days in order to be covered, or are you covered from the very first day? This type of clause is generally referred to as a "waiting period." Bear in mind that the average hospital stay is only about eight days. If there is a waiting period that leaves you unprotected for the first six or seven days, you'll recover very little for an eight day stay, and you'll actually be out of pocket for the days during the waiting period.

☐ What limitations are there for such miscellaneous expenses as X rays, radiation treatments, lab tests, nurses, anesthesia, oxygen, traction gear, plasma, ambulance costs, drugs, and medications? How does the protection offered by the policy actually compare with current going costs for these items?

☐ What benefits are payable, if any, for nursing care? Benefits may only cover a certain number of hours per day of nursing care, or they may offer twenty-four hour coverage. There also might be limitations on the hourly amount payable for nursing care regardless of the number of hours, and other limitations regarding the type of nurse that you'll be reimbursed for.

surgical insurance

Surgical insurance pays for surgeon's fees and related expenses such as anesthesia, operating room fees, and assistant surgeons. Surgical policies may also provide some coverage for post-operative care and follow-up surgery if needed. Surgical benefits are usually tied to a specific schedule, and related expenses are often expressed as a percentage of the fee allowable to the surgeon. For example, a surgeon may be allowed as much as $400 for a specific type of surgery. The policy may further state that an assistant surgeon will be paid up to, say, 15% of the surgeon's fee, which would mean that $60 would be payable toward the fees of the assistant surgeon.

In analyzing the surgery insurance aspect of your protection program, you must consider the following:

☐ What are the current going rates for various surgical services in your area? For comparison purposes, ask your family doctor or your local medical society for approximate surgical fees for some of the most frequent surgical procedures such as: stitching of lacerations; setting a fracture; setting a dislocation; tonsilectomy; appendectomy; hysterectomy; and childbirth. How do the surgical benefits of the insurance policy compare with actual current costs?

☐ A surgical procedure may require more than one incision. Or you may have two more operations through the same incision. Determine what the extent of coverage would be in such cases. Further, if an incision has to be reopened for further surgery related to the original cause, would this be partially or totally covered in your policy?

☐ How much is allowed for the cost of assistant surgeon, anesthetist, surgical nurses, and operating room fees, and do the benefits payable compare with the current going costs in your area?

☐ In order for surgery to be covered in your policy, must the surgery be done in the hospital in order for you to recover benefits? Some minor surgery may be done in a doctor's office, and this may or may not qualify for coverage under the policy. Further, a great deal of surgery is now being performed in ambulatory care facilities. These are not hospitals, but they are equipped with virtually all surgical facilities and are designed so that the patient spends a minimum amount of time in them. It's a fairly new phenomenon, and you must determine whether any older policy, or a new policy, will provide coverage for surgery conducted in such situations.

☐ In many policies, the surgical schedule may be connected with the room rate schedule for the hospital portion of the policy. In other words, you would be entitled to a higher schedule of surgical fees if you select a higher schedule of room rate protection. Do you have the right to increase the surgical benefits at any time in the future? If so, to what limits?

physician insurance Generally, physician insurance, or basic medical insurance, is designed to pay doctor bills for hospital visits, office visits, and house calls. There may be a dollar limit per visit, and there may be a limit to the number of visits that will be paid for. All plans differ. In determining the breadth of coverage offered by your physician insurance, you must determine the following:

☐ What are the actual going rates for doctor's visits in your area, including office visits, house calls, hospital calls, "overtime" visits (such as nights, weekends, and holidays), telephone consultations. Consider the costs involved, not just with your regular doctor, but with specialists as well, such as pediatrician; ear, nose, throat; internist; eye; skin; obstetrics and gynecology; and surgeons (for nonsurgical consultations).

☐ How much will your plan pay for each type of visit with each type of doctor, and how many visits will be paid for per family per illness or accident, and per year? There may be limitations in all these respects. Two seemingly identical policies may pay the same amount per doctor visit, but one may be much more strictly limited in the number of visits that will be covered during a given period of time.

☐ Will you receive benefits for diagnostic as well as for treatment calls?

☐ Are there any limitations concerning the type of doctors that you'll be covered for? For example, will you be covered for visits with chiropractors, osteopaths, podiatrists?

☐ What about dental coverage? In recent years, dental protection has increased considerably, particularly in group policies. Although a group policy is something that's made available to you, and your only choice is to accept or reject it, many people will want supplementary insurance beyond what their group policy offers, for both dental and regular medical purposes. Thus, it's important to understand what even a group policy will provide regarding these professional services.

major medical insurance

A major medical policy—or "major med" as it's frequently called—is designed to protect you against the major, unexpected, and catastrophic medical expenses that seem to be so commonplace. The basic philosophy behind major med insurance is that you, the insured, will pick up some of the minor costs on your own (either out of pocket or through the basic hospital/physician/surgery protection), and the major med coverage will then assume all or a substantial portion of the heavier costs. The initial costs that you yourself absorb are referred to as the "deductible." For example, a major med policy may have a $500 deductible per family per year. This would mean that the major med coverage would not come into effect until after the family had absorbed $500 worth of eligible expenses during that year. In such a case, if one individual used up the deductible, then all of the other family members would be eligible for the major med protection. But if each of the four members of the family spent $125 during the course of the year, the major med coverage would not become effective for any of them.

Another form of deductible might be, for example, $100 per person per year. In such a case, any member of the family would become eligible for the major medical coverage once he or she had incurred $100 worth of eligible expenses during the year. But the other members of the family would not become eligible until *each of them* had accumulated his or her own expenses up to the deductible amount.

Once the deductible has been met, the typical major med policy will pick up 80% of all additional costs, and the insured will have to absorb the other 20%. (Some major med policies may split this on a 90/10 basis, and a few might even pick up 100% of all costs over and above the deductible).

Most major med policies will also have schedules for room rates and for surgical benefits similar to those contained in the basic policies. The company's obligation to pay, say, 80% over and above the deductible may be limited by these specific room rates and surgical benefit schedules. If a major med policy has a $50 a day limit on hospital rooms, that's all it will pay, even though the policy otherwise states that it will pay 80% of your costs over and above the deductible. Where specifically excluded, the hospital room and surgical benefits will not fall into that 80% payment obligation of the insurance company. Many policyholders overlook this very important clause, and are distressed to learn that the major medical plan has not paid all that they thought it would.

There will also be a maximum ceiling—a top limit of total expenses that the policy will pay. If, for example, the maximum is $25,000, then that's all the company will pay, and the insured will have to absorb any costs exceeding that.

Here's an example of how a typical major medical policy might work. The policy calls for an annual deductible of $500, with the company then paying 80% of all qualifying expenses above the $500 deductible, up to a total of $25,000.

The insured party, Mr. Ramez, has a 60 day hospital siege resulting from a severe heart condition. His total expenses are $16,000, including hospital room and board, X rays, private nurse, cardiologist fees, physician's fees, lab tests, and so on. Mr. Ramez has to pay the first $500 worth of expenses, and the insurance company pays 80% of the next $15,500, or $12,400, subject to room rate and surgical rate limits. Mr. Ramez has to pay the remaining 20%, or $3100. The total out-of-pocket costs for Mr. Ramez are $3600—the initial $500 deductible and the remaining 20% of the excess over the deductible, which was $3100.

Mr. Ramez has now eaten into the maximum benefits payable under the policy, reducing his available protection by $12,400, from $25,000, the original limit, to $12,600.

If Mr. Ramez had a basic protection package—surgical/hospital/physician—in addition to the major medical plan, that would have reimbursed him for a portion of the $3600 he was out of pocket. But the limitations in the basic plan might not have protected him adequately for the major portion of the total expenses.

Depending on the type of policy, the costs, and the family's financial circumstances, it might be advisable for some families to forego the basic coverage and use those premium dollars toward building a sound major medical insurance program.

Some homework is essential in buying a good major med policy. From company to company, and even within the same company, the coverage can vary widely. Here are some of the factors to consider and compare when shopping for a major med plan:

☐ How much is the deductible? Does the deductible apply per family, or per person? What expenses can be applied toward the deductible and what expenses cannot?

☐ Does the deductible run for the full year regardless of the claims that may be made against the policy? Or does a new deductible start after each claim is paid? The latter situation might provide far less coverage, particularly if one person has more than one claim in a given year.

☐ How much above the deductible will the company pay—70%, 80%, 90%, 100%? This can make a considerable difference in both the level of protection you're receiving and in the premium you'll pay for the coverage.

☐ What is the maximum amount that the company will pay, and is it per person, per family, per claim, per year? If the maximum is used up, does it terminate the policy altogether? In some policies the maximum can be replenished over a period of time, thus allowing continued coverage.

☐ How much expense can you afford without major medical insurance? Determine the maximum limits on your basic insurance plan, and talk with your doctor to get an idea of the possible costs involved in major situations, such as heart disease, cancer, lung disease, and the effects of major fractures or other disabling accidents. How well prepared are you, between your existing assets and your existing basic insurance, to stand the cost of any such major medical catastrophe?

☐ How long does the "benefit period" run? The benefit period is the amount of time that benefits will be payable once the deductible has been covered. For example, a major med policy may state that the benefit period will run for one year. That means that if you incur medical expenses, the policy will pay benefits owing to you for up to one year. At the end of the one-year period, you must accumulate a new deductible before a new benefit period will begin to run again.

general health insurance provisions

There are a number of provisions that can appear in any of the foregoing insurance policies that can affect your rights. They should be given careful attention when choosing a policy. The more important of these provisions are:

Maternity benefits. What is covered and what is not? How much of a waiting period is there before maternity benefits will be payable? Maternity benefits may be optional, and obviously if you anticipate the birth of children, you'd want to take advantage of the insurance protection. If you've had coverage for maternity benefits in an ongoing policy, as you have reached a point of not having any more children, you should look into deleting that area of coverage from your policy because it can be costly. How will complications arising from pregnancy be treated—under obstetrical surgery benefits, under maternity benefits, or regular sickness benefits?

Dependents. To what extent are dependents, particularly children, covered? If children are born to you or adopted by you after your plan has begun, will they be covered and to what extent? If you have children now who may be incapacitated—mentally or physically—will they be covered by the plan, and with what limitations and up to what age? Until what age are children generally covered under your policies? Once they have passed that age, will they be permitted to continue coverage either on their own or under your wing, by the payment of an additional premium?

Waiver of premium. As in life insurance policies, if you become totally disabled, a waiver of premium clause will protect you: there will be no need to make premium payments during the period of such disability. Do your health insurance plans carry such a provision, and if so, at what cost?

Termination. This can be particularly important in group health insurance situations. If you leave the job, presumably your protection under the group plan would cease. Will the insurance company allow you to maintain your protection individually once you have left, and if so at what cost? The extent of coverage offered by group plans can differ widely. If you have comprehensive coverage under an existing group plan, and you are anticipating changing jobs, will your new employer offer you comparable coverage? If not, you'll probably want to supplement the group coverage with a private plan. The costs of doing this should be anticipated before a job change occurs, since the cost can be considerable and may offset what seems to be a higher earning level at a new job.

Pre-existing conditions. As Cora's case history illustrated, many policies will not provide coverage for conditions that have already been known to exist. Some policies will permit coverage of these pre-existing conditions after the passage of time, sometimes one year, but more likely two years. If you do have any known pre-existing conditions that are even remotely likely to reoccur, this clause can be very critical to your overall protection package.

Excluded or rated risks. Many policies will not provide coverage for certain stated risks, such as injuries occurring during acts of war or riots. Other policies may exclude coverage from more likely risks, such as the onset of mental illness and the costs connected thereto. Still other plans might offer full protection, but at a higher premium cost if the individual may be deemed to be risk-prone, either as a result of a pre-existing condition or as a result of occupation. These specifications should be clearly understood before entering into a policy agreement.

Renewability and cancellability. If a policy is guaranteed noncancellable and renewable, you have the right to renew it on its expiration. If a policy is cancellable by the company, or you do not have a right to renew, the insurance company could terminate your insurance at the end of the policy term, or could renew at a higher rate than you had been paying. In a guaranteed renewable policy, though, the rate can only be increased if the entire class of insured have had their rates increased. The company cannot single just you out for an increase. Generally, policies that are noncancellable and guaranteed renewable will cost more than those that can be cancelled or be denied renewal. You're paying more money for the assurance of continued protection, and the expense may well be worth as much as any other facet of your health insurance policy.

Grace period, lapse, and reinstatement. If you don't pay your premium on the due date, what grace period is there during which you can still pay the premium and continue coverage? Is there a penalty? If the policy does lapse, what rights, if any, are there to have the policy reinstated? If a policy has lapsed, the insurance company may examine your recent medical history as a stipulation for permitting reinstatement. If they determine that you have suffered certain conditions, they may only allow reinstatement if those conditions, or recurrence of them, are excluded from coverage. Consequently, it can be most imprudent to allow a health insurance program to lapse, particularly if such a condition has occurred during the time you've been covered.

other forms of health insurance protection

In addition to the basic forms of medical insurance, there are other modes of protection that may be available. One—the health maintenance organization (HMO)—can offer a fairly comprehensive package. Others, such as Workers Compensation, offer only a limited level of coverage.

health maintenance organizations (HMO's)

HMO's are a form of prepaid medical care facility. Instead of paying premiums to an insurance company and then being reimbursed later, if and when medical expenses occur, with the HMO you pay in advance a fixed amount each month, for which you are entitled to a broad range of medical services. Generally, you use the doctors and facilities provided by the HMO, rather than choosing your own. Preventive medicine is at the heart of the philosophy behind HMO's—regular check-ups for all family members are provided as a part of the overall fee you pay. It is hoped that major expenses can be avoided if early diagnosis and treatment of various diseases can be accomplished. HMO's have their own schedules of how much treatment is provided for what types of need; additional fees may be payable to the HMO for treatment and care beyond the normal maintenance programs. HMO's are a fairly new phenomenon. A handful have existed throughout the country for a number of decades, but it wasn't until the mid 1970s, when the federal government encouraged their development with substantial grants, that they began to occur in any number. They are still relatively few in number, and the financial stability of some has not yet been proven. Some HMO's are backed by major insurance companies, and it would seem reasonable that their financial stability offers a greater level of assurance to subscribers.

workers compensation

If you are injured at work, or if you contract an illness related to your work, you will likely be protected by state Workers Compensation laws. These laws provide a fixed schedule of benefits for medical care, and certain disability income benefits, as well as rehabilitation expense reimbursements. Each individual should consult the personnel office where he or she works to determine the extent of coverage provided by Workers Compensation.

Medicare

Medicare is a health insurance program administered by the Social Security Administration designed to protect citizens 65 and over. The costs of, and the benefits provided by, Medicare are amended from time to time, and anyone currently eligible for Medicare, or soon to become eligible, should check with the local Social Security office to determine what current costs and benefits are.

There are two aspects of Medicare: hospital insurance (the basic plan), and medical insurance (supplementary plan). These are referred to as "Part A" and "Part B."

Persons eligible for Medicare must pay an initial deductible amount with Part A, and a monthly premium in order to be protected by the medical insurance coverage, Part B. Part A, after the deductible has been paid, covers the bulk of the cost of hospital services and extended care facilities, including rooms, meals, nursing, and certain drugs and supplies. Part B is designed to defray the cost of doctors' services, as well as related medical expenses for such things as X rays, various equipments, laboratory fees, and so on. Medicare will cover a major percentage of these various expenses, but the insured may be responsible for a certain percentage as well. Part A, the hospitalization insurance, is also limited to a specific number of days.

Many older citizens have had the mistaken belief that Medicare is the ultimate protection for them against health care expenses in their later years. Although Medicare does cover a substantial portion of normal medical expense needs, many people have found themselves still heavily burdened by expenses not covered by the program. A number of supplemental programs are available through major insurance companies, and any existing or prospective Medicare recipients should explore the advisability of obtaining some supplemental protection.

Do not mistake comprehensive supplemental health care programs for the often heavily promoted hospital supplemental programs, which offer "tax free cash while you're in the hospital." Those programs only offer cash payments during periods of hospitalization, usually on a per day basis. The lure of "$1200 a month cash while you're in the hospital" may seem attractive, but it's far less so when you realize that you're only being paid $40 per day, and that if there's a waiting period of, say, six days, and you end up in the hospital for eight days, you'll only end up with $80 in benefits, a far cry from $1200. These hospital supplemental plans can fill a very minor portion of the gap, but they should not be relied on as being any form of full-fledged comprehensive protection.

medical coverage in homeowner's and automobile insurance

These other forms of personal insurance may contain medical payment plans that will reimburse you for certain medical expenses where guests are injured in your home, or anyone is injured in your automobile. The amount of such protection may be minimal or extensive, depending on the premium you're willing to pay in your homeowner's or auto insurance policies. Although they provide only a limited health protection plan, they can fill small gaps, and should not be overlooked as part of your overall package.

the agent

As with life insurance, the agent who handles your health insurance program can be a most valuable ally. He or she can assist you in determining the coverage gaps that you face, and can present a variety of ways by which these gaps can be covered within the budget you have available. If you're covered only by a group plan, it would be advisable for you to meet with a representative of the company carrying that plan and seek assistance in judging the extent of protection offered and ascertaining the gaps that remain.

The same general suggestions regarding a life insurance agent hold true with health insurance and the other forms of personal insurance. The agent willing to take the time to study your needs, who can communicate clearly and simply, and who is staffed to provide the measure of service you expect for the dollars you're paying is a most important professional within your overall financial structure. Professional help can be well worth seeking out.

income insurance

How long could you get by without any income? One week? One month? Six months? A year? What other sources could you call on for funds to live on? Your savings account? Your investments? The equity in your home? Friends or relatives or institutions who might loan you money?

Income can be lost in one of four ways: quitting your job, being fired, being laid off, or being laid up due to physical disabilities. With the possible exception of quitting your job, all of these occurrences are totally unpredictable.

Loss of work due to physical disability can mean more than simply lost income. With the disability may come added expenses of rehabilitation, recuperation, medicine and drugs, nursing, and other miscellaneous medical costs. Further, there can be intangible costs: the psychological depression that the laid-up breadwinner may suffer, the extra demands imposed on other members of the family, the natural worry over what prospects the future holds.

existing programs

There are a number of existing programs that give a moderate degree of protection against lost income. But for many people these programs won't be enough, and they will want to examine the opportunities offered by private disability income insurance policies. Before we delve into the specifics of that kind of personal insurance, let's briefly examine some of the other ongoing programs that may already be protecting your income.

sick pay plans

The sick pay plan at your place of employment should be examined to determine the level of protection it may offer. Some employers have a set policy on how much sick pay they will provide for ill or injured employees. Others, particularly in smaller concerns, may "play it by ear" when an employee is unable to work due to physical disability. It would be sheer folly not to take the time to learn what your employer's program is regarding sick pay, for this is the core of your basic income protection plan. A private plan, should you acquire one, must be tailored around and built on the foundation of your employer's sick pay program.

workers compensation

Workers Compensation offers a measure of disability income to workers who are injured on the job, or who contract an illness that is job-related. But, needless to say, you could be physically disabled from causes not related to your work, in which case Workers Compensation would be of no help to you. Through your personnel office, determine what Workers Compensation benefits for disability income would be, because this, along with the sick pay plan, is an important consideration in structuring any private plan for your ultimate protection.

social security

If you become totally disabled—that is, "unable to engage in any substantial gainful activity," according to the Social Security laws—you may be eligible for monthly benefits under the Social Security system.

If the disability occurred before you reached the age of 24, you must have one and one-half years of work in the three years prior to the disability to be eligible for the disability benefits. If the disability occurred between the ages of 24 and 31, you must have worked half the time between when you turned 21 and your date of disability. If you're over 31, you must have worked at least ten years, five of which had to be during the ten years prior to the date of the disability.

In order for the coverage to commence, the disability must be construed as expected to last at least 12 months or to continue for an indefinite period. Benefits will begin after six months have elapsed from the date of disability. The benefits will be equal to what you would get if you were retired. You can obtain more specific details from your local Social Security offices.

unemployment insurance

Unemployment insurance offers a measure of income if you are laid off from work. Your state Unemployment Office can assist you in learning what benefits are payable and for how long. You will be expected to seek out other work if you are receiving unemployment benefits, and you may waive your rights to the benefits if you do not comply with the state regulations.

waiver of premium clauses

Waiver of premium provisions in your life insurance and health insurance policies can protect you, at least to the extent of those obligations. If you are disabled and unable to work, the premiums for those policies would be automatically paid for you. This is only a minimal level of protection, but it would at least assure that those important payments were being met, so that you do not further jeopardize your overall financial situation.

credit health insurance

This is similar to credit life insurance, which is obtained in conjunction with a loan to pay off the loan in the event of the borrower's death. With credit health insurance, if you are disabled and unable to work, the loan payments will be made for you during the period of disability. The same protection may be available with your home mortgage. The cost of such insurance, and the benefits payable, will vary from lender to lender. If you believe this is valuable protection, you should determine the costs and the benefits available from various sources at the time you are negotiating the loans.

evaluating your needs for disability income insurance

In order to determine how much, if any, disability income insurance you may need, you must evaluate the foregoing sources of protection as well as the other personal sources of income that may be available. These latter sources would include the ability of other family members to work and generate income; the size of your personal savings and investments and how much you'd be willing to dip into them and for how long; other assets that may be converted into cash such as the equity in your house, the cash values in your life insurance, plus vested rights in profit-sharing and pension funds that you may be able to get access to; part time or temporary work that you yourself could do that could help reduce the strain; and loans or gifts from family, friends, associates.

Some of these sources you may dip into without hesitation. Others you might not want to attempt to utilize until and unless all else failed. This is an individual matter that you must examine and resolve yourself. But once you have made a reasonable determination of outside sources of supplementary income, you can begin to examine closely the benefits available from private disability income policies.

private disability income policies and how they work

Like life insurance and health insurance, disability income insurance is available in a vast variety of sizes and shapes. You may obtain an individual policy directly through a company, or you may obtain a policy on a group basis, such as through a professional association, a union, or a trade group.

Depending on your age, your occupation, and your income, you may be required to take a physical examination for a policy to be approved. The cost of the disability income policy can also vary depending on your age, income, and occupation.

the waiting period

One of the most important factors in shaping a disability income policy is the waiting period—the amount of time that you have to be disabled before the insurance will begin to pay benefits. It's possible to obtain a policy that will begin payment of benefits on the very first day of disability due to accident. Or, you might obtain a policy with a waiting period of fifteen, thirty, sixty, ninety days, or even longer. Waiting periods may differ for accidental disability, and disability caused by illness (usually a seven day minimum wait). Obviously, the shorter the waiting period, the higher the premium, for the company will become obliged to pay you all that much sooner. This is why it's so important to know what your sick-pay plan is at work. If your sick-pay plan will cover you fully or substantially for, say thirty days, there's not much point in beginning the disability plan until after thirty days of disability have elapsed. You can do so, of course, but you'll be paying a substantially higher premium, and you may not recover in disability benefits what the actual premium will cost you. Once your sick pay benefits have been exhausted, you might want to look to your ready sources of other income before you begin the disability plan. If you feel that the sick pay plan will last thirty days, and that readily available other sources can provide for another thirty days worth of income, it might make sense to have the disability plan begin after sixty days from the date of the disabling incident.

total disability and
partial disability

Disability income policies agree to pay you a flat fixed monthly amount in the event that you are totally disabled. Should you be partially disabled, the company will pay you a portion, usually half, of the full total disability benefit. The definition of total disability can be very important. If, in order to receive total disability benefits you must be totally unable to perform *any kind* of work, it may be more difficult to obtain such benefits. Many people who become disabled are unable to perform their normal job, but still may be able to perform other jobs on a limited basis.

If the definition of total disability states that you are not able to perform *your own specific tasks*, you might be more readily able to obtain total disability benefits. In this case it would not matter that you could perform other duties. The important distinction is whether or not you can perform your own normal duties in order to be considered totally disabled.

You should also determine if the policy requires you to be either bedridden, home-bound, or under the care of a physician in order to maintain continuing benefits, whether total or partial. As with all insurance, the more liberal the benefits, the higher the premiums. You're probably getting more protection, thus you're paying extra dollars for the desired security.

how much protection?

Once the disability payments begin, how long will they continue? One year? Five years? Ten years? Lifetime? Policies may differ widely in this respect, as will the cost of the policy. There may also be maximum limitations on how much the policy will pay you over a lifetime. Many income disability policies will cease paying benefits or will curtail the benefits once you have reached age 65, even though you may still be working. Naturally, when you do cease work, it can be expected that the disability income policy will also cease, since it's designed to protect you against lost income.

Benefits that you receive from a disability income policy are not subject to income taxes. Thus, it's not necessary for you to try to obtain a monthly benefit that's equal to your actual income.

Some disability income policies will offer extra benefits in the event of loss of a limb or limbs, and loss of eyesight. Some will also offer death benefits.

All things considered, a sound program of disability income protection is similar to a sound program of medical expense protection. You may determine that you'd be better off dollar-wise taking your own chances on short-term minor disabilities, and using the available premium dollars to amply protect yourself against the major long-term crippling disabilities. And, as with other forms of personal insurance, the right agent will help you evaluate your needs and illustrate the alternatives you have for protecting yourself against the probable risks.

property and liability insurance

Technically, property and liability insurance are two distinctly different kinds of insurance. But because we generally find these different forms lumped together in the same packages—homeowners or tenants insurance and automobile insurance—we will consider them within the same section.

Property insurance reimburses us if our property is damaged, destroyed, or lost. Our property includes our homes, furnishings, appliances, personal items, and automobiles, boats, and other vehicles.

Liability insurance protects us in the event we cause harm to other people, or to the property belonging to others. Public liability insurance can supply two forms of protection for the policyholders. It will provide legal defense for us against claims that we may have inflicted damage or harm to others. And it will pay those claims for which we are found to be legally responsible.

With property insurance, the amount of coverage we need is generally related to the value of the property in question. The insurance will reimburse us in the amount needed to replace or repair lost or damaged property, based on its replacement value. Some kinds of property tend to increase in replacement costs—such as a house and articles of jewelry. Other types of property tend to decrease—such as furnishings and an automobile. These changes in value are known as appreciation and depreciation. In spite of the fluctuations in replacement cost, it should be relatively easy to determine what those costs would be from year to year.

With public liability insurance, the amount that we may become liable to pay is completely unpredictable. Your child may hit a baseball through a neighbor's window, causing property damage, and the amount of damages will be relatively slight. On the other hand, a member of your family could be involved in a serious automobile accident in which other people are severely injured or killed. The amount of claims in such a case could easily be in the hundreds of thousands of dollars. If our public liability insurance doesn't adequately protect us against such large claims, we will have to make up the difference out of pocket.

homeowners insurance

Homeowners insurance, next to auto insurance, is the most common form of personal insurance for property. For the house owner, the condominium owner, the mobile home owner, the various forms of homeowners policies provide protection against damage to the structure and damage to furnishings and personal items. For those who rent, there is a special policy called the tenants policy, which provides protection against loss or damage to furnishings and personal items.

The cost of your homeowners or tenants insurance will depend on a number of factors: the company you deal with, the risk ratings of your property, and the amount of protection you seek.

the company you deal with

As with all other forms of insurance, property insurance is competitive. Rates for similar coverage can differ from company to company. The cheapest protection is not necessarily the best.

You must try to gauge the extent of service you'll get from the company, their response to claims, and the possibility of increased premiums when claims have been submitted.

the risk ratings of the property

Each property insured will be rated by the insurance companies according to relative risk factors. These factors can include location of the building and proximity to fire departments and fire hydrants; construction of the building (for example, brick as opposed to wood frame); proximity to other buildings; and fire and crime statistics in the neighborhood in which the building is located. Check with your agent to determine what precautions you might take to keep your property insurance premiums as low as possible. Such precautions might include the installation of fire extinguishers and fire retardant materials, the cleanliness of attics and basements (piles of combustible rubbish or souvenirs do not please insurance raters), security devices such as smoke detectors and burglar alarms, as well as the locking mechanisms used throughout the premises.

the amount of coverage you desire

If you have a mortgage on your house, the lender will require that you carry at least enough fire insurance to protect his interest in the event the building is destroyed. That may be all the fire insurance you care to have—you'll take your chances, come what may. On the other hand, you may insure your property against virtually any hazard conceivable with the possible exceptions of earthquake, land slides, and tidal waves. (Floods may not be insurable in certain areas; but check with your local agent regarding the federal flood insurance program that may provide protection for you against that hazard.) The amount and extent of coverage can affect your insurance costs considerably for obvious reasons. Prudent individuals will carry enough insurance to see to it that their routine is not materially disrupted by most foreseeable hazards. Likely, they will be willing to take certain chances that some hazards won't occur, or if they do, they can get by without reimbursement for particular losses.

the types of policies and coverage

Homeowners insurance comes in three primary forms: the basic form, or "Homeowners 1"; the broad form, or "Homeowners 2" (the tenants form is similar to the Homeowners 2 and is known as the Homeowners 4); and the comprehensive form known as "Homeowners 5." A special form, "Homeowners 3," combines the broad form (HO2) coverage on personal property with the comprehensive form (HO5) coverage on the dwelling itself.

the basic form (HO1)

With HO1 your premise is protected against the most common risks. These risks include:

Fire

Lightning

Windstorm

Hail

Explosions

Riots

Aircraft

Vehicles

Smoke damage

Vandalism and malicious mischief

Theft (except for certain exempt items, among which are credit cards)

Breakage of glass in the building

Loss suffered to personal property where you remove it from endangered premises (e.g., the building next door to you is on fire and you flee into the night clutching some private possessions that are later lost or damaged—they are covered under your basic form policy.)

the broad form (HO2)

The broad form (HO2) and the tenants form (HO4) provide protection against additional risks at a nominal extra cost. These additional risks include:

Falling objects

Collapse of the building

Damage to the building due to the weight of ice or snow

Certain damage caused by escape of steam and water from a boiler, radiator, or similar device

Certain accidents involving electrical equipment, such as an overloaded circuit that blows out an appliance

the comprehensive form (HO5)

The comprehensive form is sometimes referred to as an "all risk" policy. But the comprehensive form will generally exclude certain risks from coverage that may include earthquake, tidal wave, sewer backups and seepage, landslides, floods, war, and nuclear radiation. See each specific policy to determine what exceptions do exist on the comprehensive form. Even though flood may be excluded from coverage, the federal government has acted to make flood insurance more easily available to homeowners in flood prone areas. Your agent can give you details on this coverage, and its cost. The added cost of the comprehensive protection may not be worth it to many home-owners, but each must examine his own circumstance to determine what kind of protection is best for the dollars available.

protecting other property

The basic insurance applies to loss or damage occurring to the building itself. In addition, the typical homeowners policy also provides extended coverage for other forms of property. For example, such auxiliary buildings as garages and storage sheds will customarily be covered for 10% of the full value on the main building. In other words, if the main building is covered for $30,000, the auxiliary buildings will be covered for a total of $3000. Your personal property within the home will be covered for 50% of the coverage on the house itself. Personal property that you take with you while away from home, with the possible exception of jewelry and securities, will be protected for 10% of the primary value. In the comprehensive and special plans, the protection for personal property away from home may be as much as 100% of primary value on the house itself.

If your home or apartment suffers damage, and you are required to live elsewhere while the damage is repaired, the typical homeowners and tenants policies will provide you with additional living expenses—usually 10% on the basic HO1 policy and 20% on the broad and comprehensive policies—with the percentages calculated on the total primary value. In addition, your trees, plants, and shrubs will be covered for up to 5% of the primary value in the event they are damaged.

public liability

Homeowners policies will also contain public liability protection. Commonly, the homeowners policy will have up to $25,000 liability protection per occurrence, $500 in medical expenses payable to others, and $250 in property damages. For example: a guest in your house slips on a banana peel that you have negligently left lying in the hallway. The guest is unable to walk and an ambulance is summoned. X rays reveal that he has fractured his hip, and has also broken his wrist watch in the fall. The homeowners policy will provide up to $500 in medical expenses, which would probably have been required in such a case. They will reimburse the injured party for up to $250 in property damages, which would likely cover the expense of replacing the watch. The injured party then learns that he will be unable to work for a number of months, and makes a claim against your homeowners policy. The public liability provision would pay him up to $25,000 in damages—loss of income—as a result of the accident, assuming that all facts proved that you were legally liable.

The limits on these items of public liability can be increased considerably by paying an added premium. Vastly higher limits for public liability can be obtained at a fairly modest increase in premium, and the prudent homeowner might do well to consider obtaining a much higher level of protection than the basic policy offers.

valuables

Valuable personal property, such as jewelry, paintings, sculptures, china, silver, cameras, projectors, expensive collections of stamps, coins, medallions, golf clubs, furs, and securities may be specifically covered for any loss whether at home or away from home. In order to do this, you must obtain a separate "personal property floater" that will increase your premiums noticeably. Because the cost of this protection is high, you should seek the assistance of your agent in determining exactly what personal property is covered under what circumstances, and where you may wish additional protection.

the deductible

The amount of your premium will vary in relation to the deductible that you choose. The deductible is the amount you pay out of pocket for any losses before the insurance company becomes responsible. Some policies have a no-deductible clause, which means that the insurance company is responsible for the first dollar onward. A $50 deductible means that in any given occurrence, you must absorb the first $50 worth of expense before the insurance company becomes responsible. Deductibles may be obtained for as much as $250 or $500. In choosing the higher deductibles you are exposing yourself to more potential risk in return for a lower premium. The premium will not be lowered as much as the risk will be enlarged. For example, the difference in premium cost between a $50 deductible and a $250 deductible may be only $20 or $30 but you're exposing yourself to $200 more potential risk. However, the premium expense is an actual out of pocket cost that you can save, whereas the added risk is only a possible expense that you may never incur. If you prefer to take your chances with the larger risks, then the higher deductible would be more economical for you.

the co-insurance clause

This can be extremely important. The co-insurance clause states generally that if you wish to receive full replacement value for any damage to the premises, you must insure the premises for at least 80% of its replacement cost. For example, a house has a current replacement cost (not counting the land and foundation) of $40,000. That means that at current going prices, it would cost $40,000 to duplicate the house, in its depreciated condition, on the existing foundation. (The land and the foundation are not included in figuring costs for insurance coverage because theoretically they can not be destroyed.) But the owner has insured the building for only $28,000, which is $4000 shy of the 80% level of $32,000. The owner has a fire in the house that results in an actual loss of $16,000. But because he has not insured up to the 80% co-insurance level, the company will only pay him $14,000 instead of the full $16,000. Why? Because the owner's coverage was only seven-eighths what it should have been under the co-insurance clause ($28,000 is seven-eighths of $32,000). Thus, the owner will receive only seven-eighths of the actual damages ($14,000 is seven-eighths of $16,000). If the owner had insured the property for the full 80% co-insurance value, or $32,000, he would have recovered the full $16,000 on the loss. The difference in premium between the full 80% value and the lesser value would have been so relatively small that the owner could be accused of being woefully imprudent for not obtaining the balance of the 80% coverage.

The prudent homeowner or tenant will make a careful inventory of all furnishings, appliances, and personal property and evaluate current market or replacement costs of those items in order to determine if he or she is adequately covered by a basic homeowners policy. The owner or renter will also be aware of the effects of inflation in most areas of the country; the value of housing is steadily increasing and, in order to maintain the proper level of insurance protection, continual upward adjustments must be made. Many policies offer clauses that automatically increase the amount of coverage in line with inflation, for as the replacement value of the house increases, so must the amount of coverage if the owner is to be adequately protected.

If a homeowner or tenant acquires new property, such as personal items, or disposes of old items that have been insured the owner must see to it that the insurance company is properly notified so that the new acquisitions can be properly covered, and the old dispositions properly deleted. When the insurance company is notified, they will issue an endorsement amending the policy, and that endorsement should be checked for accuracy and then attached to the policy itself.

automobile insurance

An adequate package of automobile insurance can protect us against the hazards inherent in owning and using an automobile: damage to the machine itself, and damage that it may bring to others for which we might be responsible. Each state has imposed a requirement that motorists must maintain a minimum level of financial responsibility in the event that they are involved in an automobile accident. Most commonly, this minimum responsibility is met by obtaining an automobile insurance policy, which includes the all-important public liability protection.

The typical automobile insurance policy packages up to seven different types of insurance all together. These types of coverage are:

- *Public liability for bodily injury.* This is the single most important financial aspect of your automotive insurance policy, and possibly of your entire personal insurance program. Should your car injure or kill other people, this aspect of coverage will defend you against claims, and will pay any claims for which you're found to be legally responsible. Coverage is generally broken down into two phases: one for injury to a single individual involved in an accident and a second phase for all individuals involved. The limits of coverage are usually expressed as follows: $10,000/$20,000. This coverage limit would protect you for up to $10,000 worth of claim from any single individual, and for up to $20,000 for all parties injured in the accident. The amount of protection you choose is up to you. You may have to comply with a minimum required by your state, which may be as low as $10,000/$20,000 (more commonly expressed as 10/20). Of, if you are prudent and aware of the potential circumstances, you may choose much higher limits, perhaps as high as $100,000/$300,000, or even higher if it's available. The difference in cost between the minimal coverage and the more extensive coverage is only a few dollars per month—an investment that many would have a hard time turning down.

- *Public liability for property damage.* If your automobile causes damage to the property of others, this aspect of coverage will defend you against claims and will pay claims for which you are found to be legally responsible. The limit of coverage is usually expressed as a number following the limits for bodily injury liability. For example, overall public liability limits of 25/50/10 would mean that your property damage liability limits are $10,000 (following the bodily injury limits of $25,000 and $50,000). In this case, if you caused injury to the property of others, you would be protected for up to $10,000 of such damage.

  Property damage liability covers damage to the property of *others*—not to your own property. It can include damage to the automobiles of others when involved in an accident, or damage caused to buildings if a driver hits a building. Property damage coverage will usually not be less than $5000 and a ceiling of $25,000 should be adequate in most situations. It's difficult to conceive of an auto accident causing much more physical damage to property than that, although it is possible if you crash into a new Rolls-Royce or careen through the lobby of a modern retail building.

  Your public liability protection for bodily injury and property damage will cover you in your own car or if you're driving someone else's car, and covers other persons who drive your car with your permission. It also provides legal defense for claims made against you.

- *Medical payments.* If you, or members of your household, or guests who are driving in your car, are injured while driving (or even if struck while walking), the medical payments provision will reimburse all reasonable actual medical expenses arising out of the accident up to the limits of the policy. Generally, these payments will be made regardless of who was at fault. The minimum may be as low as $500, but much greater coverage than that can be obtained at a reasonable added annual cost. As with the public liability portions of the coverage, the prudent motorist would do well to consider taking much higher than minimal limits on the medical payments provisions, for the added extra cost is small indeed compared with the immediate protection obtained

- *Uninsured motorists.* Regretfully, not everyone who drives an automobile is insured, or is adequately insured. You might be caused serious harm by a motorist with little or no insurance protection. You could be out of pocket tens of thousands of dollars in medical expenses and lost income, and the party at fault may have little or no money with which to reimburse you for the damage he or she has caused. (Generally, property damage is not covered) Although the courts may find the person legally responsible for making payments to you, he or she may not be financially responsible and you may never be able to recover. Uninsured motorist protection is designed to take care of this problem, providing you with reimbursement for your losses through your own insurance company.

  Unfortunately, we don't have a choice as to who might cause us harm in an automobile. It could be a perfectly adequately insured individual, or it could be the uninsured individual, or a hit and run driver whom we will never see again. This form of protection is quite inexpensive and the motorist is assuming an unnecessary risk by not having it.

- *Comprehensive insurance.* This is a broad form of protection for loss caused other than by collision. It includes damage to your car due to fire, loss due to theft, glass breakage, riots, windstorm, hail, and other types of miscellaneous damage. Limited protection on contents is also available. Deductibles are common in such policies. If the deductible is, for example, $50, then the motorist will have to absorb the first $50 worth of any such loss, and the insurance company will pay for damages over the deductible amount. You should check your policy to determine if you are protected against theft if you leave your car unattended and/or unlocked. Some policies will not protect the motorist under these circumstances.

- *Collision insurance.* This coverage protects you against damage done to your own car, should you be in a collision with another car, or an object such as a telephone pole or a building. Collision insurance also usually carries a deductible amount. If car A and car B collide, and the accident was the fault of the driver of car A, his property liability insurance will pay for the damage to the owner of car B, and car A's owner's collision insurance will pay for the damage to car A. Compared with the other forms of automobile insurance, collision protection tends to be fairly expensive. If you're driving a car more than five or six years old, the cost of the collision protection might be so high as to discourage you from obtaining that protection in view of the limited recovery you can expect on an older car. Weigh the cost and the protection accordingly.

• Some auto policies also offer protection against towing costs and road breakdowns. These forms of protection are also available through automobile clubs. It's generally a fairly modest sum, and the protection can come in handy.

how much will it cost?

The cost of automobile insurance can vary considerably depending on the age, safety record, owner, occupation and purposes for which the car is used. It's common knowledge that younger drivers have to pay a higher rate for their automotive insurance, primarily because those drivers have a generally bad statistical record when it comes to accidents and claims. Some companies will offer discounts for drivers with safe records, for younger persons who have taken certain driver education courses. Other discounts may be available where more than one car is insured, and where compact cars are involved. In shopping around for the best automobile insurance protection package, all available discounts should be inquired about from each agent.

The amount of the various deductibles can also have a bearing on the total premium cost. As with deductibles in other forms of personal insurance, you are assuming a higher risk, in exchange for paying a lower premium. The premium saved is an actual savings, whereas the higher risk may never occur.

a word about "no-fault" auto insurance

If you've ever witnessed the typical fender-bender, you've seen both drivers leap out of their cars and commence bleeping at each other in a furious rage. Even though both drivers may be totally insured, and neither may end up out of pocket as a result of the accident, it's a matter of pride, if nothing else, that each establish blamelessness. Each will want the other's insurance company to pay for the damages, and each may be concerned that if his insurance company has to pay, premiums may be increased as a result of the accident. This, in fact, may be true in certain cases.

Where extensive injuries or damages are involved, the question of who is at fault can become critical to the rights of all the parties. If the solution is not clear cut, and if the damages are extensive enough, each party may find itself involved in a lawsuit to determine who is at fault. The question of fault will ultimately determine which insurance company has to pay for what damages. In addition to actual physical damages to property or to a person, injured parties might also claim that they had endured "pain and suffering," knowing that the courts may award damages to parties who have so suffered in many cases. It may be difficult to understand why a dollar value can be placed on physical pain and mental anguish, but the concept has been embedded in our legal system for close to two centuries.

For many years, the hassles over who was responsible for automobile accidents, and who suffered how much damage, either physical or mental, had created extraordinary congestion in our courts and added extravagant costs to the settlement of claims. It was not unusual for a lawsuit involving an automobile accident to take three or four years to be heard by the courts in some states, and the addition of medical costs, legal expenses, and related fees boosted the asking price on many claims to levels that tested the imagination.

The result was that injured parties might have to wait years before they received their settlement. In the meantime, insurance companies that were having to pay out very high settlements had to pass the cost along to their insureds, which meant ever-increasing automobile insurance premiums for the general public.

All parties involved in these lawsuits agreed that something had to be done to correct the situation. The best available solution, at least to date, has been the advent of what's known as "no-fault" auto insurance. Many states have adopted such plans, and there has been talk in Washington for a number of years regarding a federally mandated no-fault form of automobile insurance for the entire nation.

Under the typical no-fault legislation, insured parties are paid for certain losses and medical expenses (including lost income) regardless of who is at fault in the accident. These expenses are limited by state law.

Although many states have reported good experience with no-fault, the public at large has still not noticed any improvement in the cost of its automobile insurance. There are a number of reasons for this. One is that the costs of repairing automobiles, along with the costs of repairing people's bodies, has continued to skyrocket in spite of the existence of no-fault legislation. Because premiums have to be kept in line with the payments that the insurance company anticipates it will have to make to claimants, the cost of premiums has accordingly continued its climb.

Another possible reason for the lack of overall success with the no-fault program has been the so-called "threshold" concept. If an innocent party is injured by another, the sums he or she may be paid under a no-fault plan may not nearly fully compensate for the actual damages suffered. The no-fault concept can eliminate bickering between the parties on relatively minor amounts of money, yet it would be contrary to our legal rights to prevent an innocent party from seeking full compensation for actual damages incurred. The threshold concept suggests that if your actual immediate medical expenses are nominal, then the ultimate losses you might suffer from being out of work, or pain and suffering, would likely be minimal or nonexistent. If your actual medical expenses are high, it's more likely that you will truly have suffered related losses.

Although the law differs from state to state, the threshold concept generally allows for further lawsuits if the actual medical expenses have exceeded a certain level or threshold. Let's say that the threshold is $2500. If your immediate medical expenses do not exceed that amount, you may not be allowed to pursue further claims. If your actual expenses do exceed it, you may be able to proceed with your other claims. Critics of the system have suggested that doctors and patients will conspire together to create a medical expense history high enough to satisfy the minimum threshold, thus allowing the injured party to pursue a higher suit.

Items from a Reporter's Notebook

I was curious about the kind of protection and service one might get in a health insurance policy when dealing directly with a company or one of its agents, compared to dealing through the mail order route. I talked to several agents directly, and all were willing to give me sample specimens of the policies, and they all sat with me for varying amounts of time to explain the kind of coverage I'd be getting for my premium dollar. Some were a bit brusque, while others were more than happy to take all the time I requested to learn what I felt I needed to know. Naturally, all of them hoped I would buy a policy from them, and their level of disappointment ranged from none to moderate. Apparently, they're well accustomed to having to spend their time without reaping a sale.

On the promotional approach, I sent in six mail order coupons with the required amount of money to obtain the policy, ranging from 25¢ to $1 for "the first month's premium." These were the results.

INQUIRY #1.

Eight weeks elapsed after sending in the coupon, and no reply received. Had I really been in need of the insurance, or had I suffered any malady that could give rise to a claim, I would have been totally out of luck.

INQUIRY #2.

I never received a policy from the company, but I did receive bills urging me to pay the premium before my "valuable coverage" (whatever that may have been) lapsed and left me in danger.

INQUIRY #3.

I received a policy by return mail, and the bills started flowing in. It was a disability income policy, and I compared it in detail with other plans received directly from the agents. Dollar for dollar there was no comparison. The agents' plans offered far broader coverage for about the same cost.

INQUIRY #4.

An agent called on me without an appointment. He was personable and tried to be helpful, but would not talk about any of the limitations of his policies unless I asked him directly. He seemed surprised that I knew to ask such pertinent questions, and in some cases, he wasn't sure of the answers.

He had no literature to leave with me, and said that there was absolutely no way for me to see a sample policy unless I signed up with him. Then, he said, I would have ten days to cancel if I wanted to. His main concern was to sign me up on the spot. Can't blame him for trying.

INQUIRY #5.

The agent called without an appointment. The interview was very similar to the one above. He did leave some vague literature, but no sample policy. "It simply can't be done," he repeated. My expressed wish to study and compare the policy terms at my own leisure fell on deaf ears.

INQUIRY #6.

Another agent called on me without an appointment, but I was busy at the time. Three weeks later he telephoned to set up an appointment. Over the phone I requested a copy of the policy so that I could prepare myself for the appointment. "Can't be done," he commented, just as the others had done.

From the limited descriptions given me by numbers 4, 5, and 6, it appeared that the protection they were offering was far less comprehensive than that available through the direct agents' plans.

My curiousity was also aroused regarding celebrity endorsements of various products, particularly certain kinds of health insurance plans. Somehow, Madison Avenue has gotten us to believe that Joe Namath really knows a good pair of panty hose when he puts them on, or that Danny Thomas is an expert when it comes to making coffee. What strange quirk of human nature leads us to believe that the appearance of a celebrity makes a product any better or different from one without a celebrity advertising it?

With these thoughts in mind I was intrigued with the marketing of certain supplemental hospital insurance policies that appeared in the Sunday supplement of my local newspaper.

Art Linkletter and Roy Rogers were locked in combat pitching "$40-a-day-when-you're-in-the-hospital" plans. In the ads, both admitted that they have a financial stake in the deal, and nowhere is there any mention that these entertainers have any kind of expertise in knowing a good insurance plan from any other plan. The ads appeared within two weeks of each other, first Art's then

Roy's. Hundreds of thousands of people, if not millions, were exposed to these ads. No doubt the effect of seeing two well-known personalities pushing similar products could lead people to believe that not only is the product valid, but also that their competition with each other is sure to produce price advantages to the public.

But are they competing?

Art's company is the National Home Life Assurance Company. Roy's is the National Independent Insurance Company. But in each pamphlet there are identical pictures of the same office building. The caption un-

der the picture in Roy's booklet reads, "Administrative headquarters for National Liberty Corporation, parent of National Independent Insurance Company." The caption in Art's booklet reads, "World headquarters for National Liberty Corporation, parent of National Home."

Opposite the picture of the building is a photo, in each booklet, of a happy-looking couple, smiling as if they'd just received a claim check. Same couple. Same photo, except that Roy's is enlarged a little bit more than Art's.

Except for some minor differences in coverage and cost, the policies as described are virtually identical. And the value of the coverage? Well, as Roy puts it, "Don't be caught short of cash! Many group insurance plans like the one you probably have at work do not pay all the bills." Or, better yet, as Art claims, "Don't be caught short of cash. Many group insurance plans like the one you probably have at work do not pay all the bills!" Catch the subtle difference? Art didn't put an exclamation mark after the word "cash."

Most of the language in the two "competing" brochures is identical. So what's going on here? If Art doesn't get ya, Roy will—is that the ploy? Or is this nothing more innocent than what General Motors does, by selling competing cars with different brand names? Intriguing, isn't it?

If you have a valid need for such supplemental hospital insurance, you may want to do business with Art or Roy. Or, you may prefer the less glamorous, but more accessible, local agent of any number of major national insurance companies that offer a wide variety of plans to suit your specific needs.

But whatever you buy, and from whomever, buy the steak, not the sizzle.

1. What should you do if you are trying to buy health insurance and you cannot understand the contract?
2. What rating service rates the financial strength of insurance companies?
3. Which health care loss would be most damaging to a family?
4. Describe the losses covered by hospital insurance.
5. Mary Ann Volk has company paid health insurance. Why is it important for her to know the extent of her group coverage?
6. What is a pre-existing condition?
7. How can an insurance company drop a customer if his or her policy is noncancellable?
8. List four ways of losing income.

cases for study

1. Bob and Luann's apartment was robbed while they both were working. After the loss they found that their insurance agent was very cooperative but they had a problem in knowing what was taken and its worth. Bob and Luann tried to remember what they had, but it was difficult. What would you suggest to avoid this problem?
2. Joyce and Ron have no-fault auto insurance in a state that has a $200 threshold. It seems as though the claims always seem to go over $200, so the no-fault has little advantage. Comment on this problem.
3. In reading this chapter, you should have noticed many problems with the fine print on health insurance policies. To quite an extent this is due to a lack of standardization. Discuss how much of the difficulty is eased by having group coverage.
4. Barbara and Kirk are self-employed. They are attempting to set up a program of health insurance, but the cost seems more than they can afford. List, *in order of importance*, the types of coverage you think they should carry.

chapter 10 **saving & investing: an overview**

today dollars and tomorrow dollars

One of the most essential parts of anyone's financial program involves putting away dollars that you don't need today so that they can be available to you in the future. Some of the many different ways we can go about accumulating tomorrow dollars will involve a relatively high degree of risk, others, a relatively low degree. Some ways might offer a relatively comfortable measure of protection against inflation while others may grant little or none. Some ways may seem simple, others complicated; some require luck, others prudence.

The challenge is to find the right program that will enable you to accumulate the needed amount of future dollars safely, comfortably, and in such a manner that the accumulation program does not interfere with your ability to pursue your current needs and desires.

The relative importance of your own personal future needs and desires will be a major factor in shaping what accumulation techniques you choose. In the opening of this book we discussed the importance of establishing future goals, and each individual was urged to set specific targets subject to the inevitable changes that will occur as we mature, and as our needs and objectives change. Now let's examine the specific vehicles you can utilize to help reach your specific destinations.

automatic accumulating

In shaping our long-range accumulation program we must remember that some tomorrow dollars are being created automatically as a result of other transactions we may be making. For example, a home owner makes monthly payments on a mortgage. A portion of those payments is applied toward interest on the debt, and a portion is applied to reducing the debt. Eventually, when the house is sold or refinanced, that portion of the payments that had been applied to the debt may be recaptured in cash. This recaptured money is commonly referred to as "equity." It's a form of automatic accumulating.

Another form of automatic accumulating can occur with life insurance. Here a breadwinner is putting away today dollars to be used by the survivors after his or her death. In ordinary life insurance policies, the policy will also build certain values that allow the policy owner to either cash in the policy at a later date or borrow against it or convert the values into other forms of insurance. The insured is building these future values as an automatic part of paying the life insurance premium.

Deductions from our paycheck represent another form of accumulation of future dollars. Social Security taxes are automatically deducted from everyone's paycheck and in many cases pension and profit-sharing plan contributions are also deducted. Thus, we are joining with our employers and our government to create a pool of future dollars. We may have little or no control over how these tomorrow dollars are being put to use, but we do have some reasonable assurances as to how much will be available to us at the pre-established time when we're entitled to retrieve them.

active accumulating

Active accumulating of future dollars can take two broad forms. First, we can loan or entrust our dollars to another person or institution or firm with the understanding that they will pay us a prearranged sum for the use of our money and will return the principal sum. This type of accumulating is referred to as "fixed income investing," and a savings account is perhaps the most familiar form of accumulating dollars within this category.

A savings account is, in effect, a loan to a financial institution, accompanied by an agreement stating that the institution will pay us "rental" for the use of our money—interest.

We may also make "loans" to governments and corporations. A U.S. savings bond (series E bond) is an example of one of the many kinds of loans that we can make to the federal government. Loans made to cities and states are referred to as municipal bonds. Loans made to corporations are referred to as corporate bonds.

These forms of accumulating future dollars normally carry a high degree of assurance that we will get all of our money back plus the agreed upon interest at the agreed upon time. When we entrust our money, we receive a binding legal contract from the debtor that promises to pay us what we are due, regardless of whether or not the debtor operates efficiently or profitably. If the debtor should fail, the interest and principal due us might be in jeopardy. Although there have been remote instances of corporations and municipalities defaulting on their debts, defaults by the federal government have never happened, nor have insured amounts in federally insured banks and savings institutions ever lost money as a result of the failure of the institution.

When we loan or entrust our money to others in these forms, we're minimizing both the risk of loss and the chance of gain, and in return we're getting a fairly assured program that will take us to our appointed destination on time.

The other broad form of active accumulating of future dollars is to buy something that we hope will generate income, and also possibly increase in value while we own it. As owners, either in part or in whole, we have a stake in another entity—an equity. This broad form of accumulating future dollars can also be referred to as investing.

We buy a portion of ownership in a company, hoping that the company will be profitable and that it will distribute a portion of its profits to its owners. We also hope that the company will prosper and that the value of our ownership interest will increase, allowing us to sell it at a profit in the future.

We may invest in real estate, hoping to operate that property so that it shows a profit and further hoping that the property will increase in value and allow us to reap a profit when we sell. Similarly, we may invest in our own business interest where, in addition to earnings and profits, we may also be able to pay ourselves a living. When we invest our money in a piece of ownership of another entity, there may be many outside forces that can shape the destiny of our future dollars.

The distinction between lending or entrusting our money to reliable debtors on one hand and buying something with our dollars is critical. When we lend, we have a binding legal contract that assures us of getting back our principal. When we buy with our dollars, we are owners and we have to take our chances in the marketplace and with the forces beyond our control that we can get back our money at any time we wish.

This distinction should always be remembered in establishing any kind of accumulation program.

The following are additional factors to bear in mind when establishing our long-range tomorrow dollars program. They include the risk/reward rule, liquidity, yield, pledge value, hedge value, and income tax implications.

the risk/reward rule

This rule is simple and has virtually no known exceptions. It's this: The bigger the possible reward, the higher the risk. The more conservative individual may look at this axiom a bit differently: The safer my money, the less return I'll have to be satisfied with. And yet a third, and perhaps more elemental viewpoint: In planning a program of savings and investments (commonly known as a portfolio), much depends on whether you'd rather eat well or sleep well.

liquidity

Liquidity refers to how quickly and conveniently you can retrieve your money and at what cost, if any. Often a price may have to be paid for liquidity.

For example, in a regular savings account, you can get all of your money plus accrued interest immediately, simply by making the request in the proper fashion to the institution. But with a savings certificate—where you have placed your money with the institution for an agreed upon minimum amount of time— you might have to forfeit a portion of the interest that you might otherwise have earned if you want to get your money out right away. But generally the certificate will pay you a higher rate of interest than the regular passbook savings account.

In other words, the passbook savings account is more liquid than the savings certificate, but at a price. The passbook account offers a lower rate of return in exchange for the ability to get your cash out that much more readily.

The need for liquidity varies from portfolio to portfolio. If you're putting the money away for the long term, and are confident that you won't need it for an extended period of time, you can afford to give up liquidity in favor of higher return. On the other hand, if you think you'll need the money sooner, you may feel better foregoing the higher return for the chance of being able to get at your money in a hurry. The amount of liquidity that you need, or are willing to forego, depends on the nature and timing of your own individual goals.

yield

Generally, yield refers to how much money your savings or investments will earn for you. For example, if a savings account is paying 5% interest per year and you put $100 into the account, you will receive $5 during the first year that your $100 is in the account. Your yield may be expressed as "5%" or as "$5 per $100 per year." The term "yield" is often used interchangeably with "return" and "return on investment."

In making any form of investment, you should determine not only what yield you can expect immediately, but whether or not that yield will continue, for how long, and what degree of fluctuation it might be subject to.

If you put your money into long-term corporate or government or municipal bonds, you are assured of a constant yield for the amount of time you own the bonds, assuming that the debtor continues to pay the interest promised. The actual face value of the bond may fluctuate up and down during the time that you own it, and you may sell the bond for more or less than what you originally paid for it. But the actual income you receive for the term of your ownership will remain constant. If you buy a government bond for $1000 that promises to pay 5% per year, you will receive $50 for each year that you own the bond, regardless of whether the face value of the bond increases or decreases, which it might.

Passbook savings accounts might be somewhat subject to minor fluctuations in yield over the years. At various times in recent years, at various localities throughout the country, passbook savings rates have fluctuated up and down by one-quarter of one percent to one-half of one percent.

If you buy a share of ownership in a company—stock—and that company distributes a portion of its profits to its owners—dividends—your yield, or return, is expressed as the amount of dividend dollars you receive. If you pay $100 for a stock and during the first year of your ownership the company pays you $5 in dividends, your yield can be expressed as 5% or $5 per $100 per year.

Many companies have long histories of dividend payment records, and many also increase their dividends from time to time. Even more companies have erratic dividend payment histories, while some companies pay none at all. If a company runs into hard times, a dividend payment record may suddenly halt. On the other hand, if a company suddenly has a surge in business, it may start to pay dividends unexpectedly. Investing in the stock market, then, offers a broad range of yield possibilities.

An investment in real estate also offers a wide range of yield potential. If you own a property and it's leased for a long term to respectable tenants, and those tenants are responsible for paying escalating costs such as property taxes and utilities, your yield (total income less total expenses) could remain quite constant for long periods of time. On the other hand, if you have less reliable tenants, and you as the owner are required to pay those escalating operating costs, your yield could be far less constant and far less satisfactory.

Following the risk/reward rule, you'll find that the more respectable tenants will bargain for and receive a lower rental rate than the less reliable tenants. Although your rental income may therefore be higher from the less respectable tenants, the chances of it ceasing or being eroded by vacancies and added costs are that much greater.

gain and loss

It's important to keep a clear distinction between yield and gain or loss. For example, you buy stock for $100 and during the first year of ownership it pays a dividend of $5. But at the end of the year you sell the stock for $120. You have realized a gain of $20 on your investment, plus a dividend of $5, for a total overall increase in your fund of $25. Would this be considered a yield of 25%? Technically no. It is indeed an overall gain of 25%, but it comes from two different sources: the dividend yield of 5% and the increase in value of 20%. Similarly, if you sold the stock at year end for $80, you still would have had a dividend yield of 5%, but you would have suffered a loss of $20 or 20% of your original investment.

Generally, in embarking on an investment program, the expected yield is a relatively known quantity—at least with savings accounts, bonds, and stocks with good dividend payment history. The aspect of possible gain or loss, particularly with stocks, is a relatively unknown factor, if not totally unknown. In building toward a specific future goal, a relatively predictable yield can be a far more useful aspect than the relatively unknown gain or loss. The prudent investor should structure his or her program accordingly.

pledge value

The need may arise to get at the money you have invested, but you don't want to actually cash in the investment for one reason or another. Can you then borrow against the investment, and how readily, and on what terms? These questions refer to the "pledge value" of a given type of investment. Savings accounts—both passbook and certificate—have the highest level of pledge value among the common types of investments. Most depositors can usually borrow virtually all of the money in their savings account at favorable rates, without any delay. This can be an excellent device for obtaining short-term funds in a hurry, and is often preferable to actually invading the savings account or cashing in the certificate.

Because stocks are prone to fluctuation in value, they have a somewhat lower pledge value than savings accounts. The amount you can borrow against any given stockholdings will depend on the quality of the stock itself. You can borrow either from your broker—on a "margin" account—or from your banker. In either case of course you have to surrender the certificate as collateral for the loan.

Good quality real estate has a high pledge value, but because of the nature of the documentation required in borrowing against real estate, the process can be costly and time consuming. This, in effect, detracts from real estate's otherwise good pledge value.

hedge value

Particularly since the inflationary epidemic of the early and mid 1970s, investors have become ever more concerned over the ability of their investments to withstand the ravages of inflation. This aspect of investing could be referred to as the "hedge value" of an investment. Historically, it had been claimed that the stock market always provided a good hedge against inflation; in theory, as costs rise, so do profits for companies, and so thus do their stock prices. However, the severe stock market plunge in 1974 to 1975 during a period of rampant inflation tended to convince some observers that perhaps the stock market no longer offers that same protection against inflation. Others maintain that over the long term, as measured in decades, the market still provides good protection against inflation. But with thousands of stocks from which to choose, the average investor may find selecting the right one for inflation protection more of a challenge than he or she is prepared for.

Savings accounts have long been accused of having no protection against inflation, for the principal amount invested doesn't grow, except for periodic additions of interest to the account. Although it's true that the principal does not increase on its own, there is some protection against inflation because interest rates paid on savings plans will tend to rise in line with rising costs. By the same token, interest rates paid on savings plans may also decrease slightly in the face of slackening inflation.

Real estate has long been considered a good hedge against inflation, but again this depends on the nature of the property and the community in which it's located.

In short, there is no form of investment with a guaranteed hedge against inflation. But there is one important caution to note regarding the dangers of inflation, because it can affect your portfolio. In 1974 to 1975, when inflation was hitting its "double digit" levels—prices were tending to rise on various common goods at a rate of more than 10% per year—savings accounts were commonly paying 5% to 6% per year, and it was obvious that the increase in the cost of common goods was growing at a greater rate than an individual's nest egg was. Consequently, many savers figured their savings accounts were a "losing proposition."

They thus fell prey to the wily advances of salespeople who were touting other forms of investment, many of which had much higher degrees of risk than the existing savings plans. Tempted by a purported better protection against inflation, thousands of small investors shifted their funds from the security of their savings accounts into these other forms of investment. They did not adequately take into account the risks involved, and stories were legion of people losing substantial portions of their life savings as a result of the switch.

Historically, the level of personal income has increased at a faster rate than the cost of living, thus enabling individuals to save an ever increasing portion of their total dollars. The Social Security Administration has estimated that this trend will continue for at least the next fifty years. From time to time, there will be slight aberrations; the 1974–1975 period was one. There is no assurance as to when, if ever, further deviations from the traditional pattern will occur. It's impossible to anticipate them, but when a deviation does occur, it can be more dangerous to switch from the tried, true, and secure than to remain with it for what one hopes is a short distortion of the long-term trend.

tax implications

There has been so much tax legislation in recent years—affecting both large and small investors—that neither can afford to ignore the implications taxes have on their investment portfolios. Today, even the most modest investment portfolio can take advantage of tax-deferred investments, tax-sheltered investments, tax-exempt investments—in addition, of course, to the plain old garden variety of taxable investments.

taxable investments

Taxable investments are those in which the return to the investor is fully taxed.

Savings accounts are the most visible example of taxable investments. Every dollar you earn through your savings account is subject to federal income tax. So is interest received on corporate bonds. Stocks are also considered fully taxable, but there are some minor tax advantages in investing in the stock market. Up to $100 worth of dividends received each year by an investor can be excluded from income in calculating income tax (up to $200 for married couples filing a joint return). In other words, at least that much of your dividend income is tax free. Further, if you sell a stock at a profit after having held it for the appropriate amount of time, it's considered a long-term gain and that profit is subject to taxation at a lower rate than ordinary income rates. Although such income is taxable, it's not *fully* taxable in the sense of being taxed at ordinary income rates.

tax-sheltered investments

The most common form of tax-sheltered investments is real estate. Because buildings physically depreciate in value, tax laws allow real estate investors to deduct "depreciation" from their income. This depreciation factor does not represent an actual loss in value on the building, but rather a paper loss. Indeed, a building may be increasing in value, even while depreciation is being taken on it. Because of the depreciation factor, the income realized on the investment may not be subject to taxation, in whole or in part. However, if the building is ultimately sold, the investor may have to pay a tax on a larger profit than if the depreciation were not taken. In other words, a portion of the investor's income is being sheltered from taxation for an indefinite period. This aspect of investing is discussed in more detail in Chapter 13.

Prior to 1961, it was difficult, if not impossible, for the small investor to muster enough capital to invest in real estate and take advantage of this form of shelter. But in 1961, Congress gave birth to the "Real Estate Investment Trusts," or REITs, which were a form of mutual funds in which small investors' monies could be pooled to obtain real estate and the tax shelters that went along with them.

tax-deferred investments

In a tax-deferred investment, you do not have to pay taxes on the income now, but will later. The best example of this is the Individual Retirement Account, which allows workers not covered by a pension plan at their place of work to put away money each year for their ultimate pension. The amount they contribute to the plan each year is a form of tax deduction, thus reducing their immediate tax obligation to the government. Further, the earnings on these funds are not taxed. However, when the entire fund is withdrawn, which normally can not be before age 59½ without penalty, the taxes on the funds must then be paid. The presumption is that when a fund is withdrawn on retirement, the individual investor will be in a much lower tax bracket than at the time the contributions were made. Thus, there can be a considerable tax break. Further, all of the money contributed into the fund has been allowed to work without being subject to taxation, which can again make a substantial difference in an overall nest egg over the long term.

tax-exempt investments

When local governments, such as cities and states, borrow money, the interest they pay on their IOUs is not subject to federal taxation in the hands of the investors. The income the investor receives is thus "tax exempt." (In most cases, however, it will be subject to state and local taxation.) Tax-exempt municipal bonds, as they're called, have long been the preserve of investors in the highest income brackets. The minimum amount that can normally be purchased is often far beyond reach of the small investor, running to as high as $50,000 or $100,000. In order to buy smaller amounts, a steep extra commission must be paid, thus offsetting the benefits of the tax-exempt status. Prior to the Tax Reform Law of 1976, there were a few mutual funds specializing in this type of investment, but for reasons explained later they were not attractive to the small investor. Then, with the passage of the 1976 Reform Law, the doors were opened wide to mutual funds to offer tax-exempt securities to investors large and small. Beginning in the fall of 1976, by early 1977 they had sold several hundred million dollars worth of securities. Experts in the industry estimate that the ultimate pool of funds obtained by these mutual funds will approach $10 billion. Now the small investor can take advantage of the tax-exempt fields that previously were outside his domain.

investigation

"Investigate before you invest" is one of the essential maxims to remember when putting your money to work. An equally important statement all too frequently overlooked is "investigate before you un-invest." Homework is a necessity before you place your funds in any kind of situation, and there's no form of investment for which homework can't and shouldn't be done. But the homework doesn't stop once you've made the investment. You should develop an ongoing, disciplined program to keep you aware of all the alternatives that could improve your situation. This does not mean that you have to keep your nose buried in the *Wall Street Journal* every day, nor that you should jump from one investment to another as the mood strikes you.

Varying forms of investment dictate varying levels of ongoing homework. If you determine that a portfolio of fixed income investments, such as savings and bonds, is best suited to your needs and goals, many months or even years might elapse before an opportunity comes along that can better your situation within your fixed framework. A periodic check with your banker or stockbroker can reveal emerging trends and can alert you to new opportunities you may want to explore. For example, the investor prefering the safety and security of a passbook savings account could have taken advantage of numerous opportunities during the 1970s to considerably improve yield without materially affecting safety. Many highly regarded corporations issued bonds, and even the federal government was offering IOUs with yields considerably higher than what had generally been available in passbook savings accounts. Many savers did not take advantage of these trends because they were either unaware of their existence or did not understand their meaning. This lack of knowledge may have proved costly in terms of the lower yields that were accepted instead of the higher rewards.

Knowing when to get out of a situation is as important as knowing when to get in. "But," many say, "I don't want to become a slave to my investment. I don't want to have to worry about it. I just want to be able to put it away and have it grow and deliver what I'm seeking without the worry or the constant checking."

All well and good—but beware that such a course may result in a diminished nest egg compared to what it might have been. The decision is up to each individual; you don't have to become a fanatic. But you're planting a tree and you want it to bear the most and the best possible fruit. This involves care, nurturing, and an awareness of all steps you can take to improve your crop. In short, your ability to prosper will depend largely on your willingness to work. And your need to work will be minimized by your initial efforts in understanding how the various forms of investments function and what they can and cannot do for you.

sources of investable funds

All sources of investable funds must be accurately evaluated. You have little or no control over the inactive investment activities that you're now engaged in, such as building the equity in your home, your life insurance policies, your pension or profit sharing programs, or your Social Security. But these funds can become actively investable at some future time, and you must, in line with your goals, determine how much will be available and when. These sources may not materialize for many years, but it's senseless to play guessing games about their amounts. Reasonable estimates, periodically revised, will be needed to help assure that you reach your goals. Check periodically with your employer and with your local Social Security Office to determine what you can reasonably expect from those respective sources.

discretionary income

The major source for active investment funds is your discretionary income—the difference between what you take home in earnings and what you currently spend for all your present needs. "But," says the majority, "I'm just living hand to mouth as it is. By the time everything is deducted from my paycheck and I keep up with rising costs and allow some modest improvements in my lifestyle, there's barely a penny left to put away."

Or, as it's also said: "There's too much month left at the end of the money." True enough, and in many cases there's little you can do about it. However, a close examination of your current living style, in comparison with your *desired future* living style, is in order. Investable funds can be provided by creating disposable income. And disposable income can be created by cutting down on current expenditures, or by increasing current income. Simply translated, this means additional work and/or belt-tightening. Whether you wish to do either depends on how closely your *existing* investment program meets your targeted goals. If your current program is adequate, there may be no need to either increase your income or tighten your belt. If, though, the development of your nest egg will not be adequate to meet your targeted goals, you may have to consider one of these two steps to expand your discretionary income. The alternative, of course, is to cut down on future goals. But that, perhaps, is the most dangerous course of all.

Consider that the most critical goal for most individuals and families is to have enough income to live in the desired style when work ceases and retirement begins. If, when that time rolls around, you don't have what you had hoped you might have, *you don't get to do it over.* You're locked in. Again, it's up to each individual: how much, if anything, are you willing to sacrifice in your current lifestyle in order to assure a future lifestyle? When you can approximate an answer to that question, you'll be more readily able to determine what adjustments you want to make in your current discretionary income.

inheritances and gifts

Other sources of investable funds can include inheritances and gifts. This is a touchy area that must be handled delicately, but nevertheless must be faced. A great many people will receive inheritances from parents and other family members, and the amount may be token or may be considerable. It may occur soon, and it may not occur for many, many years. The amount ultimately received can have an important bearing on your own overall plans. If you know or can determine what can reasonably be expected in the way of an inheritance, you may want to adjust your existing investment program or your current lifestyle accordingly.

what we'll explore

We'll now examine the most common types of investments available: what they are, how they work, and their respective features regarding yield, liquidity, safety, hedge value, pledge value, taxation, and investigation.

There are no specific rights or wrongs in structuring an investment portfolio. Each must be tailored to the needs, both present and future, of a particular individual or family. And it must be structured with the thought that those needs can and probably will change over the years. Thus, although the discussions are presented from a relatively conservative viewpoint, there's ample room for disagreement.

The Recorded Conversations of Howard Ackerman—Investor

January 20:

MR. ACKERMAN, this is J. Fairly Nicely calling from Amalgamated Universal Investments in St. Louis. You recently responded to our ad offering guaranteed 12% investment opportunities.

ACKERMAN: Ah, yes. You've caught me at a very busy time.

NICELY: Well, if you just have a few minutes, I can explain the whole matter to you.

ACKERMAN: Well, all right. Please be quick. I have people waiting.

NICELY: Fine sir. Have you ever heard of the *Beauty Burger* chain of family restaurants? I'm sure there are some in your community.

ACKERMAN: A food franchise operation? Forget it! I've heard too many horror stories about people getting ripped off in those deals. I want no part of it.

NICELY: No, no, you don't understand. I agree that some people get taken. It's scandalous. Of course, *Beauty Burger* is a well-established chain with an excellent track record. But I know you're not interested in running a burger house. I know you're doing quite well with your business there in Dallas.

ACKERMAN: Well, then, if it isn't a hamburger house, what is it?

NICELY: We've obtained the exclusive *Beauty Burger* rights for New York state and New England. We build the buildings and then sell them to the franchise operators. We make our profit on the sale of the building, the equipment, the supplies. We also get a portion of the franchise fee. The rest of the fee and a percentage of the operating profits go to *Beauty Burger, Inc.* Some of the franchise operators are able to pay all cash for the property. But many can't. We don't want to kill a good deal because the buyer doesn't have all the cash needed, so in some cases, where the buyer's credit is absolutely perfect, we're willing to take his mortgage for a ten-year term. We do that as a convenience to the buyers. But we really don't want to sit around and wait ten years for the payments to come in. We need the cash in order to develop additional properties. So we sell those mortgages to other investors. We can offer a most attractive return, with guarantees of course.

ACKERMAN: What kind of returns? What kind of guarantees?

NICELY: Let me give you an example of a case I have right here in front of me. Perhaps you'd be interested in this one. We have a Dr. Martin Singer in Rutland, Vermont, who has signed the papers to open a *Beauty Burger.* Actually, he's doing it for his son, to put him in business. The property costs $100,000, and Dr. Singer is giving us $70,000 in cash, and his IOU for $30,000. The mortgage will run for ten years with a 10% interest rate. We've checked Dr. Singer out thoroughly. His credit is Triple A, and he has an excellent reputation in the community. We'd be willing to offer that mortgage to an investor for $25,000. In other words, you put up $25,000 and over the next ten years you get back $30,000 plus interest calculated at 10% on the original $30,000 amount. It all works out to better than a 12% return on your capital.

ACKERMAN: What about the guarantees?

NICELY: Well, you have Dr. Singer's personal guarantee on the mortgage for starters. He is A-1. He pays his debts like clockwork. We have a title insurance policy on the property with a value of $150,000—50% more than the actual cost. Indirectly, you have the guarantee of the *Beauty Burger* company. They have over 500 units around the country, and not one has ever failed. If one does fail, I'm certain that the company would go in and operate the franchise successfully enough to make all payments on any debts. But most important, you have the guarantee of Universal Amalgamated. We give you a written guarantee that if the debtor, Dr. Singer, should ever default in his payments, we will substitute a mortgage of equal amount in its place. This assures you continuity of payments.

ACKERMAN: Why don't you just take it to a local bank in Rutland and sell it to them?

NICELY: As a matter of fact, we do sell most of these deals to the local bank. But on occasion—and I'm sure you can understand this—the debtor doesn't want to have local lines of credit taken up by an obligation of this size. Dr. Singer requested that we not sell it to the local bank, and we're merely complying with his wishes.

ACKERMAN: Look, I need time to investigate the deal.

NICELY: We have a problem. We only have a limited number of these deals available. Business is booming. Buyers get a substantial discount if they pay cash, so we don't have these financing opportunities coming along every day. We only have four or five available, and it's my guess that there may not be any more for as long as six months. During that six months you could be making 12% on your money instead of 6%. And I'm not even sure that we'll have any six months from now. This is an opportunity . . . Hold on just a minute would you please. . . . Yes . . . OK . . . Yes, I'll tell him. . . . Mr. Ackerman, are you still there?

ACKERMAN: Yes.

NICELY: Our executive vice-president informed me that three mortgages have just been sold to another investor. The only one we have left is this Dr. Singer in Vermont. I'm not sure we'll have this by the time I go home tonight. Let me make a suggestion. If you want this deal, tell me you'll put your check in the mail for $1,000 tonight. We'll send all of the papers right out to you, and you can mail us the remaining $24,000 within three days after you get the papers. If you decide you don't want it, let me know and we'll send you back $1,000 less $100 for our time and costs involved up to that point. Is that fair enough? You're risking at most $100 to get a firm commitment on a deal that will pay you 12% guaranteed for the next ten years. *How far wrong can you go?*

ACKERMAN: Well . . . I'm still not sure. After all, $100 bills don't come that easily . . .

NICELY: Mr. Ackerman, you're an intelligent business executive and I can't blame you for being hesitant. Normally, I wouldn't do this, but you seem so interested in the project that I'm going to make a special concession. If you decide that you don't want the deal after you've examined all the papers, I'll *personally* make sure that you get your $100 back. I'm not supposed to do this, and if I'm caught, I could be in trouble, and I could end up being out the $100 myself. But if you'll give me your commitment right now, then that's my promise to you and I assure you that you won't regret it. . . .

May 20

NICELY: Hello, Mr. Ackerman, this is J. Fairly Nicely of Amalgamated Universal. How's everything going with your investment?

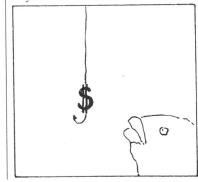

ACKERMAN: You know I have to apologize for having been so skeptical when you first called. To tell you the truth, I'm thrilled. Dr. Singer pays like clockwork. I appreciate your putting me onto this. As a matter of fact, I told some of my friends about it, and they'd like to get involved too. If you have any more deals like this, I'm sure I can put you in touch with some investors.

NICELY: Thanks! Right now we don't have any opportunities, and I don't think we're going to since we've about wrapped up our operation in New York and New England. I'll let you know if something does come up, but in the meantime you let me hear from you if you have any questions or problems with your Dr. Singer. Remember we stand behind it 100%. . . .

August 20

ACKERMAN: Tom, this is Howard Ackerman calling. . . . Listen, Tom, I'd like you to do a little favor for me if you could. You don't live very far from Rutland, Vermont . . . what is it, a few hours drive? Here's my problem. I have a mortgage on some property in Rutland and everything had been going along beautifully until two months ago when the payments stopped coming in. I've tried to reach the fellow who makes the payments, but he's not listed in the directory. Could you take a run over there and check it out. I've got a lot invested. I'm not too worried. It's guaranteed by the brokerage firm that placed the deal, but the guy I dealt with is on vacation for the month and no one knows how to reach him.

September 20

ACKERMAN: Hello, operator, I'd like the new number of Universal Amalgamated Investments in St. Louis. I just called, and a recording said their old number was no longer in service.

OPERATOR: I'm sorry, sir, there is no new listing.

December 20

ACKERMAN: I'd like to make a person-to-person call to the head of the Consumer Protection Division (CPD) of the Vermont Attorney General's Office in Montpelier, Vermont.

CPD: Can I help you?

ACKERMAN: I hope so. I think I've been the victim of a swindle. Earlier this year I invested in a mortgage on property that was supposed to hold a *Beauty Burger* restaurant in Rutland. The mortgage was signed by a Dr. Martin Singer. Everything went fine for the first few months—the payments came in promptly. But then the payments stopped, and I started doing some investigation. The firm that sold me the deal seems to have disappeared, and there never was a Dr. Martin Singer or a *Beauty Burger* restaurant in Rutland.

CPD: You found out that the credit report was forged and the title insurance policy was phony. Am I right?

ACKERMAN: Yes, I'm afraid so.

CPD: You really really believed you couldn't go wrong. Right?

ACKERMAN: Yes.

CPD: I'll bet he sent you all the necessary papers but you didn't investigate them.

ACKERMAN: Yes, you're right. Is there anything that can be done about it? Do I have any hope of ever finding them or getting my money back?

CPD: I rather doubt it. We've already had a dozen cases like yours, and we've run into a brick wall. Some of the victims were residents of our own state, who could have investigated the location just by getting in their cars and driving a short distance. We're supposed to protect consumers, but we can't protect them against their own greed and laziness. Schemes like this are in operation all around the country. No one knows how many hundreds of millions of dollars they take in. I'll take down the particulars of your case and give it to one of our investigators, but I'm afraid for now all I can tell you is to be more careful next time. Have a happy holiday.

1. Gradually paying off the principal on a mortgage, building up cash value on a life insurance policy, and payroll deductions for a pension are examples of what?
2. What types of accumulating could be labeled "fixed income investing"? What types of accumulating come to mind when you buy something you *think* will increase in value?
3. Explain the risk/reward rule.
4. What is the difference between the yield on common stock and the gain?
5. Give two examples of taxable investments and two examples of tax-sheltered investments.
6. Explain the difference between the terms tax exempt and tax deferred.
7. What do we call the difference between take home pay and what we currently spend for all our present needs?
8. Given the situation presented in Issues and Incidents, which policies would you suggest for dealing with investment solicitors?

**cases
for
study**

1. Complete the following chart, rating the investments as good, average, or poor:

	Passbook Savings	Common Stock	Real Estate
Liquidity	————	————	————
Yield	————	————	————
Pledge Value	————	————	————
Hedge Value	————	————	————

2. Don and Marie Johansen have the following goals:
   1. Down payment on a house they want to buy in three years
   2. College for their children, ages 2 and 5

   Which of the savings and investments methods discussed in this chapter seem most appropriate for each goal?
3. Many individuals find that having investments taken from their pay is the easiest way of saving. Examine the possibilities of payroll deduction available to you or your family. Some companies will send your pay directly to a bank, savings and loan association, or credit union, and many companies have plans for automatically transfering amounts to other financial institutions.
4. After studying investments, most students agree that it would be a good idea to invest. Not all are able to find the money in their budgets. There are two choices: you either spend less, or you earn more. Try to think of some ways of increasing your income by about $50 per month.

chapter 11 **investing: fixed income**

what is "fixed income"?

When you live in an apartment, you agree to pay a fixed amount of rent for the privilege of using the landlord's property. When you borrow, you agree to pay a form of "rent" for the privilege of using someone else's money. This rent is called interest. As with apartment rentals, loan agreements generally state that the borrower will pay a fixed amount of "rent," or interest, during the period of time that he or she has the use of the money.

Fixed income investments are those in which you, in effect, lend your money to an institution, and they agree to pay you a fixed amount of interest for the period they are holding your money. The income you receive is fixed by the agreement between you and the institution; thus, the term: "fixed income investments."

The most common form of fixed income investment is the passbook savings account. Other forms include savings certificates, government bonds, corporate bonds, and municipal bonds. We'll take a detailed look at each, but first let's examine an important element of fixed income investments—how interest works.

When you loan your money to an institution (or a corporation or governmental agency), you receive an agreement in which the institution promises to return your money to you, either on your demand or at stated date, and also agrees to pay a fixed amount of interest. If the interest rate is, for example, 5% per year, that means they will give you $5 in interest each year for every $100 you have loaned them.

In some instances, they may simply send you a check for the interest at the agreed on time. That's the case with bonds— corporate, governmental, and municipal.

In other cases, you may have a choice: you can receive the interest in a cash payment; or you can have the interest added to the original amount. If you choose this latter course, the interest that you have earned will, like the original amount, begin to earn interest itself. This is what is known as "compounding" and this choice is customarily available with savings accounts, both passbook and certificate variety.

savings accounts— passbook and certificate

A passbook savings account is an "open-end" agreement between the customer and the financial institution. The customer is free to put in as much money as desired at any given time, and can take out as much as he or she wishes at any given time. While the money is in the account it will earn interest in accordance with the agreement set forth between the institution and the customer. (In some institutions there may be a limit on the number of withdrawals a customer can make during a given period. If that number is exceeded, the institution might impose a service charge for the excess number of withdrawals.)

According to the typical passbook savings agreement, the institution generally reserves the right to modify the rate of interest it is paying on the accounts. Notice must be given to customers if an interest rate is to be changed, but the manner of giving notification can vary from institution to institution. A customer may be notified in the mail that interest rates will be changed. Another customer might not know of a rate change because that institution's rules only required the change to be posted in the institution lobby and the customer had not seen such notification. Therefore, it's important for passbook savings customers to periodically determine the rate of interest being paid on their accounts.

A savings certificate (or certificate of deposit, or CD as they're often called) is a fixed contract for a specific amount of money, for a specific length of time, and for a set interest rate. For example, an institution might offer a CD that guarantees to pay 6% per annum on amounts of at least $1000 that remain in the institution for a period of three years. In some cases, the customer might be able to make additional deposits to that certificate; but generally cannot make withdrawals from the account without suffering some penalty on the interest rate.

Financial institutions offer a wide range of CDs, from as short as ninety days in length to as long as ten years. Generally, the longer the term of the certificate, the higher the interest rate.

Commonly, certificates will automatically renew at the currently prevailing interest rate unless the customer notifies the institution that he or she does not want to renew. For example, you have a two-year certificate paying 6% per year. When the two years have expired, the regulations state that the certificate will automatically renew for another two-year period at the then current rate of interest. Assume that the interest rate at that time has dropped to 5½%. It's unlikely that you will have been directly notified of this new interest rate, although some institutions do send out individual notices when such changes occur. If you have neglected to notify the institution that you do not wish to have the certificate renewed, it will automatically be renewed, and at a lesser rate than you might otherwise have been able to find at another institution.

the power of
compound interest

Passbook savings accounts and certificates of deposit have one important feature in common: the opportunity to have interest compound.

Here's an illustration of how the effect of compound interest can benefit the saver. You have a savings passbook account of $1000 that receives interest at 5% per year compounded annually, or once each year. During the first year your account will earn $50. You have a choice of withdrawing that $50 or "letting it ride" in the account. If you choose to have the amount remain in your account, you start off the second year with $1050. During the second year, then, your account will earn $52.50— 5% of the balance at the start of the year, which was $1050.

Most savings accounts and certificates compound more frequently than once a year. Quarterly compounding is common, and many institutions even compound on a daily basis. The more frequent the compounding, the more rapidly your funds will grow—the money goes to work for you that much sooner in the more frequently compounded account.

Let's compare the above annual compounding with a quarterly compounding situation. In an account of $1000 paying 5% per year compounding quarterly, the account will be credited with $12.50 in interest at the end of the first quarter. At the start of the second quarter your account has $1012.50 at work for you. With more money at work for you, your earnings during the second quarter will be greater than during the first. During the second quarter, you'll earn $12.66 that will be added to your account giving you a total of $1025.16 to go to work for you at the start of the third quarter.

During the third quarter, your fund will earn $12.81, giving you a total fund at that start of the fourth quarter of $1037.97. That will earn $12.97 during the fourth quarter, and you thus finish off the year with $1050.94 in your account, or 94¢ more than you would have earned in the account that compounded only once a year.

Following the same arithmetic through to the end of the second year, the quarterly compounding account would have $1104.49 in it compared with $1102.50 in the once-per-year compounding account. As each year passes, the amount in the more frequently compounding account will grow at a more rapid pace than the less frequently compounding account.

(Although savings accounts and savings certificates give you the choice between taking the interest out or letting it remain in the account to compound, corporate and government and municipal bonds do not offer such a choice. They simply pay you the interest—usually twice a year—and you can do with it as you please. However, there are mutual funds that specialize in bonds, and by utilizing those mutual funds, you can achieve the same effect as from compounding. The payments that are due you can be reinvested in additional shares of the mutual funds—thus, in effect, letting your money ride in the mutual fund.)

yield Determining the true yield on a savings account or a certificate requires more than just examining the interest rate being paid. You must examine the frequency of compounding and crediting of interest to the account. Some institutions may pay interest on a deposit from the day the funds are deposited to the day they are withdrawn. For example, if you made a deposit in such an institution on January 15 and withdrew the total balance of December 15, you would earn interest for the full eleven months your money was in the account.

However, some institutions use different methods to calculate the interest. One method states that interest payments begin at the start of each quarter, and interest will not be paid on an account unless the funds remain in the institution for at least a full quarter. Looking at the transactions in the above example, you would earn nothing during the first full quarter, January 1 through March 31, for you did not have funds in the account at the start of the first quarter, and you will have to wait until the beginning of the next quarter for interest to be credited to your account. Likewise, you'd earn nothing during the last quarter for you would have withdrawn your funds prior to the completion of the quarter. In other words, in such a case, though your money was in the bank for a full eleven months, you might only earn interest for six months. As you can see, two institutions can pay the same rate of interest, but by using different means of crediting the interest to your account they can create a considerable difference in the actual yield you earn.

Another method of calculating interest uses the low balance in any quarter as the amount on which interest is computed. For example, you start the first quarter of the year with $1000 in your account. On January 15, you withdraw $600 to pay certain bills until your income tax refund comes in. The refund comes in on February 15, and you put the money back into your account. During that first quarter of the year you will be credited for interest on only $400, even though you had $1000 in the account for the majority of the time. In a day-of-deposit to day-of-withdrawal account, the interest would be calculated on the balance in your account each given day of the quarter, and you wouldn't suffer as you do in the low balance type of calculation.

As noted earlier, the frequency of compounding can also have an effect on the yield you'll receive.

Because deposits to and withdrawals from savings certificates of deposit are rare, the yield question is barely affected. Your yield will be the stated interest rate, but again, the frequency of compounding must be taken into account. Certificates of deposit also have a penalty stipulation that you must be aware of: if you withdraw funds prior to the maturity of the certificate, you will lose much of the interest that otherwise might have been paid to you. An investor in a savings certificate should determine what this penalty is in advance and should arrange a financial program to avoid the need of making premature withdrawals.

liquidity   Savings accounts are as liquid an investment as one can make short of storing the money in a cookie jar. Subject to possible sacrifice of some interest as noted previously, you can withdraw your entire fund without question, at any time, simply by submitting your passbook and the appropriate withdrawal slip. Liquidity is high for certificates, but in cashing one in before maturity you may end up having no more interest than you would have in a passbook account, and in some cases perhaps less.

safety   Savings accounts and certificates insured by the federal government have the highest degree of safety. The Federal Deposit Insurance Corporation (FDIC) offers insurance of up to $40,000 per account for all accounts—checking and savings—in commercial banks and in mutual savings banks. Similar coverage is offered in savings and loan associations by the Federal Savings and Loan Insurance Corporation (FSLIC). Federally insured credit unions are covered under the National Credit Union Administration Program (NCUA). Practically all savings accounts throughout the nation are thus insured. In rare instances, state-chartered institutions and thrift companies may not offer the federal insurance and although many of these institutions may be sound and well managed, occasional abuses do occur when the depositors' funds are lost by a failure of the institution. Institutions insured by the federal government must post prominent notices of that fact in their place of business and in their advertising.

Although relatively few families have more than $40,000 in savings, it is possible to insure more than $40,000 by dividing the total into a number of accounts. For example, separately insured accounts for up to $40,000 each can be established in the name of the father alone, in the name of the mother alone, in the name of the father and mother jointly, in the name of the father and daughter jointly, and so on.

hedge value   Savings accounts and certificates offer modest protection against ever-increasing prices. If you put $1000 in today and withdraw it in ten years, you'll have only your $1000 plus the interest it has earned. But as prices of common products tend to increase over the years, so do interest rates. Thus, that deposit you make today at, say, 5%, might be earning 7% ten years hence when you withdraw. This is an unknown factor and can't be relied on, but historically the trend has held fairly true.

pledge value   Savings accounts and certificates have a high degree of pledge value. You can normally borrow up to 100% of the total amount at favorable rates simply by presenting your passbook or certificate to a loan officer and signing the simple documents. Naturally, you'll pay more in interest on your loan than you'll earn on the account, but on occasion it may make sense to borrow against your account rather than withdrawing from the account. If, for example, you need a certain amount of money for a short period of time, until other expected funds come in, and if the account is one that does not pay from day-of-deposit to day-of-withdrawal, it may be cheaper for you to borrow against the account and pay the interest on the loan rather than withdrawing the funds and losing interest for an extended period of time. If you face this situation, consult your banker, who can help you work out the specific figures.

tax implications   Generally, the interest that you earn on a savings account or on a certificate is fully taxable by both federal and state taxing authorities. Thus, there is no tax advantage or shelter to the standard savings account or certificate. However, in recent years, the advent of the Individual Retirement Account (IRA) has cast a new light on the picture. If you qualify for an IRA plan (See p. 415) or for its equivalent for the self-employed, the Keogh plan (see p. 415), it is possible to have the interest earned on your savings account or certificate tax deferred for an extended period.

investigation   The availability of federal insurance on most types of savings accounts eliminates the need to check the stability of a federally insured financial institution. Yes, there have been bank failures throughout the United States over the years, but accounts insured within the limits of the federal agencies have never suffered a loss. It would be extremely difficult to gather any valid information concerning the financial stability of a federally insured institution simply because improper information, or correct information in the wrong hands, could cause unnecessary damage to an otherwise healthy institution and subsequent loss to many members of the community. Thus, information about the condition of banking institutions is maintained under fairly close secrecy by the examining authorities and bank officials. Additional investigation would examine the other services available at the institution, its hours, distance from home or work, and, of course, the yields offered.

Careful shoppers might want to investigate the opportunities available at institutions in other localities. Interest rates will vary, and if you don't feel the need to visit your money regularly, you might have better opportunities available elsewhere. Most public libraries receive newspapers from major cities around the country, and a scanning of a number of those papers might reveal higher interest rate opportunities. Transactions can be handled safely and efficiently through the mail.

bonds   Just as you often borrow money—to buy a car, to fix up your home, to pay your bills, or to refinance existing older debts—businesses and governments likewise borrow money for similar needs. They may borrow for a long term, upwards of forty years, or for a short term, a few years or even a few months. When they borrow for a long term, the IOU that they issue is referred to as a bond. Short-term IOUs may be referred to as bills, notes, and, in the case of corporate short-term IOUs, "commercial paper."

There are three major categories of bonds—federal government, local government, and corporate. And there are three kinds of ways that an investor can get involved in bonds: directly, semidirectly, and indirectly.

You can buy various bonds *directly* through a stockbroker, and in some cases through the investment department of major banks. You can invest in them *semidirectly* through mutual funds that specialize in various bonds. The mutual funds pool the investments of many individuals and spread them out over a wide assortment of different issues. This is something that the ordinary investor can't do individually.

And, although you may not be aware of it, you *already* have *indirect* investments in the bond market. If you have a bank account, an insurance policy, or pension fund, it's very likely that some of your money is already invested in the bond market—and that in itself is a good reason for you to become familiar with the workings of bonds.

Of every dollar you leave on deposit with your local bank, they invest roughly 25¢ to 30¢ in government IOUs, predominantly those of the United States Government, plus states and cities. Roughly 60¢ out of each dollar is loaned to individuals and businesses for their various needs, and the balance of the bank's assets are in cash, their banking premises, furniture, fixtures, and so on.

When you pay your life insurance premium, the life insurance company puts the money aside for the day that it will have to pay off on the policy. How does it invest? Taking a broad national average of all life insurance companies, out of every dollar's worth of assets over 40% is invested in government bonds and corporate bonds. About 32% is invested in real estate mortgages, about 11% in stocks, about 3% in owned real estate, about 7.5% in policy loans, and the balance in miscellaneous.

Individual investors may learn a valuable lesson regarding why successful institutions such as banks and insurance companies invest so heavily in the bond market, and relatively so negligibly in stocks—they have fixed obligations that must be fulfilled and must take positive steps to fulfill them. Insurance companies must have funds available at anticipated future dates to pay off policies when claims are made. Banks must have funds available at all times to meet whatever withdrawal demands their customers may have. If they were any less certain of meeting these fixed requirements, you, as the customer or the insured, might be in jeopardy.

Similarly, you as an investor have certain fixed goals in mind. There's something to be learned from the policies of banks and insurance companies as to how they fulfill their fixed obligations and meet their goals.

categories of bonds— federal government

The federal government is the biggest borrower of them all. Federal IOUs range from the common series E savings bond for as low as $18.75 to the multimillion dollar obligations issued frequently by the U.S. Treasury. The federal government even borrows from itself. For example, the Social Security Administration invests its own funds in U.S. Treasury IOUs. Federal government obligations are further broken down into three subcategories: U.S. Treasury borrowings, Federal agency borrowings, and savings bonds.

U.S. treasury

The U.S. Treasury borrows frequently on a short-term, medium-term, and long-term basis. Short-term obligations are called treasury bills, and their maturities range from three months to one year. Medium-term obligations are called treasury notes, with maturities ranging from one year to seven years. Long-term issues are called treasury bonds, with maturities ranging from five years to thirty years. Any of these treasury debts can be obtained at a nominal commision through a stockbroker or the investment department of a bank; or directly from the Federal Reserve Bank at no commission.

federal agency securities

A number of federal government agencies are frequent borrowers of large sums of money. The money they borrow is generally pumped back into the economy to subsidize such things as mortgage loans for home buyers and farm loans for the agricul-

tural industry. Investments are available in a wide range of
maturities. Short-term obligations, usually for a year or less, are
commonly called "notes." Medium-term obligations, which may
run from one to five years, are commonly referred to as
"debentures." Long-term obligations that run from five to twenty-
five years are referred to as "bonds." Some of the more popu-
larly traded federal agency obligations are the Federal National
Mortgage Association, the Federal Home Loan Bank, Banks for
Cooperatives, Federal Land Banks, Federal Intermediate Credit
Banks.

The prices and current yields (before commissions) of treasury
obligations and agency obligations are quoted daily in the *Wall
Street Journal* under the heading "Government, agency, and
miscellaneous securities." They're also quoted in some major
daily newspapers.

savings bonds   Series E bonds are the most commonly known and popular form
of bond issued by the federal government. Lesser known are
series H bonds. E bonds and H bonds offer a return of 6% and
their maturities are five years and ten years respectively.

When you buy an E bond, you pay less than the face value for
it. For example, you pay $18.75 for a bond that, at the end of five
years, will be redeemable for $25. The difference between what
you pay and what you ultimately receive is the interest that the
bond will have earned. Other denominations of E bonds, and
their purchase price are as follows:

PURCHASE PRICE	REDEMPTION PRICE
$ 37.50	$ 50.00
56.25	75.00
75.00	100.00
150.00	200.00
375.00	500.00
750.00	1,000.00
7,500	10,000.00

The annual limit of E bonds that a single individual can buy is
$10,000. However, if two or more parties are co-owners of bonds,
the maximum annual purchase limit can be extended to $20,000,
apportioned between the two co-owners.

When E bonds are bought for individuals, they may be
registered in single ownership, co-ownership, or beneficiary
form. If a bond is bought in the name of a public or private
organization, it can only be registered in single ownership form.

E bonds can not be redeemed during the first two months after issue date. But after that time, they can be redeemed at most financial institutions. Banks have schedules issued by the government indicating the redemption value of all E bonds. You can check with them to determine the current value of any E bond that you may hold.

E bonds cannot be sold or transferred to another party, and they cannot be used as collateral or security for a loan. This is also true of H bonds.

H bonds are issued in denominations of $500, $1000, $5000, and $10,000. With H bonds you receive interest checks twice each year from the government starting six months after the issue date. The registration provisions and the annual limit on purchases of H bonds are the same as for E bonds. Your local bank can make arrangements for you for the purchase of either H or E bonds. H bonds can be redeemed after six months from the issue date.

yield The yield offered by government issues tends to be in the same range as that available on passbook savings accounts and certificates of deposit. With Treasury and agency obligations, the yield is fixed throughout the life of the IOU. E and H bonds have a somewhat different status. During the early years of those bonds, the interest rate is lower, and it rises as the years pass. For example, with E bonds the interest yield during the first year is 4½%, and it gradually increases over the five years so that your total average for the full five years is 6%. Thus, if you redeem an E bond during the third year, your average annual yield would be in the 5 to 5½% range. You can only get the full 6% if you hold until the five year maturity time. Once an E bond has reached its maturity, the government commonly extends the continuation of interest payments for at least a ten year period. In other words, all E bonds currently outstanding are still earning interest.

Interest on H bonds is figured as follows: the yield is 5% during the first year, 5.8% during the next four years, and 6% during the second five years. This gives you an average rate of return of 6% over the ten year period. But if you redeem at the end of the first year, you will have earned only 5% during that year. If you redeem at the end of the second year, you will have earned roughly 5.4% during that two year period, and so on.

liquidity There is an active market on most government and agency issues, which would allow you to cash in your holdings prior to maturity if you so wished. Commissions on such transactions are generally less than commissions on stock transactions. As noted earlier, there are some slight restrictions on the liquidity of E and H bonds: you can't redeem them during the first two and six months respectively of the issue dates.

safety Government issues are considered to be in the highest safety category. To the ultimate skeptic, it's safe to presume that before the government falls, everything else will have long since fallen.

hedge value An investor in long-term government issues has virtually no protection against inflation. The rate of income is fixed, and the fluctuations in the value of the bond are relatively minor. Traders in shorter-term government IOUs can realize better protection against inflation, for as their issues mature, they can move into new issues whose interest rate would reflect prevailing trends throughout the country. If interest rates have moved up, the short-term trader can thus take advantage of higher new rates at the time of reinvesting.

pledge value E bonds and H bonds cannot be pledged as security for a loan; they thus have no pledge value. Other government agency bonds can be pledged as security, usually at a very high percentage of their value. Because of the high safety of such bonds, the pledge value would be greater than for corporate bonds of equal size and maturity.

tax implications U.S. Government IOUs, agency IOUs, and Series E and H bonds are fully subject to federal income taxation, but not to state and local income taxation.

E and H bonds offer some tax advantages that many small investors are not aware of and could well take advantage of. In normal bank savings accounts, the interest you earn each year is subject to taxes during the year you earn it. If you have $1000 in your savings account and it earns $50 during the year, you have to pay income taxes on the $50 you have earned. But with E bonds you have a choice: you can either pay income taxes on the amount of interest earned during that year, or you can delay payment of income taxes until you actually redeem the bond. This aspect of E bonds is especially attractive to those nearing retirement. If you wait until after retirement when your income and tax bracket are lower before you cash in your E bonds, you thus pay the income taxes at a lower tax bracket level.

Example. A family has accumulated E bonds with a face value of $5000. The bonds originally cost $3750, and there thus will be taxable interest earned of $1250. The family has a taxable income of $15,000 and they file a joint return. If they cash in their E bonds during that year, there will be a tax of approximately $312.50 to pay on the interest earned over the years. But, say, the breadwinner retires and his taxable income drops to $5000 per year. If he cashes in the bonds then, the tax on the income will be only about $200. Further, the available credit for the elderly may reduce that tax by even more.

The tax payable on interest earned on E bonds can be delayed even further by switching from E bonds to H bonds. As noted earlier, H bonds pay interest twice each year, and the interest you receive each year on the H bonds is then subject to federal income taxes. For example, you have a $1000 E bond that originally cost $750. At the time you cash it in, you'll be obliged to pay federal income taxes on the $250 worth of interest that has accumulated. Your ultimate amount of cash in hand will thus be reduced accordingly. But you may wish to get your interest out and have it available to spend. If so, you can convert your E bond to an H bond. In effect, you'll now own a $1000 H bond. In six months you'll get a check for roughly $21 in interest. Six months later you'll get a check for about $29 in interest. Each six months for the next four years you'll get $29 and each six months for the five years thereafter you'll get $32.56. Each year you pay the taxes on the interest you've actually received. Thus in the first year you will have received $50 and that's the amount you pay your federal income taxes on. In other words, instead of paying your income taxes on one lump sum, which would occur if you cashed in your E bonds, by converting to H bonds you spread the tax bite out over as much as a ten-year period. This can be advantageous to any investor, particularly to those nearing retirement. The minimum amount of E bonds that you can convert into H bonds at any time is $500.

A reverse situation holds true where minors are concerned. Where bonds are being accumulated in a minor's name, it might be more desirable to report the interest earned each year for income tax purposes. Because the minor is your dependent and entitled to a personal exemption on his or her tax return, it's very likely that the minor won't pay any income taxes, or little if any, during these years when the interest is accumulating on the bonds. If the minor waits to cash in the E bonds until he or she is earning income and paying taxes accordingly, the tax bite on the interest earned from E bonds will be in accordance with the earning bracket the individual is in.

investigation

Government bonds are of the highest quality. But an investor should compare the returns available on government bonds with those available in other forms of fixed income investments to determine what the best current available yield would be at the time of making the investment. In early 1977, for example, E bonds were offering a 6% return, compared with passbook savings returns in the 4½% to 5% range. That's a favorable comparison. But certificates of deposit at federally insured institutions were offering 6% to more than 7% returns, for periods ranging from two to 10 years. Although the differences may be slight, the tax advantages mentioned earlier regarding E bonds and H bonds might tilt the scale slightly in favor of those instruments for certain investors.

municipal bonds and notes

States, cities, towns, water districts, school districts, sewer districts, highway authorities, and a variety of other local entities have periodic needs to borrow funds. To enable these local entities to borrow easily in the open market, the interest that these bonds pay has been deemed exempt from federal income tax obligations. This, of course, benefits the local residents of the particular jurisdiction. It makes the cost of building and maintaining schools, roads, sewers, whatever, cheaper than if the holders of the municipal bonds had to pay income taxes on the interest they earned. If the bonds were not tax exempt, they would have to be issued at a higher interest rate, thus costing higher interest expenses that would be passed along to taxpayers.

There are two major types of municipal bonds: general obligation bonds and revenue bonds. The general obligation bonds are backed by the taxing authority of the locality. The revenue bonds are backed by the revenues produced by the entity, such as toll roads on a highway authority bond, or water usage fees on a water revenue bond.

tax implications

The most notable aspect of municipal bonds is that the interest they pay is exempt from federal income taxes. (Municipal bonds, however, are not exempt from state or local income taxes—except if you live in the jurisdiction issuing the bond; the interest received may then be exempt.)

Here's an example of how the tax-exempt factor works. A couple filing a joint tax return has a taxable income of $16,000 per year. This puts them in the 28% federal income tax bracket. They invest $1000 in a 6% municipal bond. They receive $60 per year in interest from the bond, and it's all theirs to keep (except for any state or local income taxes). If that couple had a fully taxable bond also paying 6%, they'd receive $60 in interest, but they'd have to pay $16.80 (28%) of the $60 back to the government in federal income taxes. This would cut their true yield to 4.32%. They would end up keeping $43.20 after taxes, which is 4.32% of $1000.

What kind of taxable bonds would they have to buy to allow them to keep the same $60 that they can get on the 6% tax-exempt municipal bonds? If they had bought a fully taxable bond with an 8.33% yield, they would earn $83.33 on their $1000 investment during the year. In the 28% tax bracket, they'd pay $23.43 back in federal income taxes, leaving them a net return of $60, the same as they get on the 6% tax-exempt bond. In other words, in their particular tax bracket you'd have to find a taxable bond paying 8.33% to equal what they'd be getting on the 6% tax-exempt bond.

The higher one's income tax bracket, the more attractive tax-exempt yields become. If in the 36% bracket, you would have to find a taxable bond paying 9.37% to equal, after taxes, what you'd get on a 6% tax-exempt bond. In the 42% tax bracket, you'd have to find a taxable bond paying 10.34% to equal your net return on a 6% municipal bond. Table 11-1 shows a comparison of tax exempt yields with taxable yields.

safety   The financial crisis that surfaced in New York City in 1975 cast a dark shadow over the municipal bond market. When it became apparent that the nation's largest city was dangerously close to the brink of bankruptcy, many began to take a much closer and harder look at the financial condition of other cities and states throughout the country, and indeed it was found that the problem was not an isolated phenomenon.

A joint study conducted by the University of Michigan and the Price Waterhouse accounting firm reported in late 1976 that a very large percentage of major American cities were not adequately reporting their future pension and lease obligations. Cities are legally obliged to pay pension benefits to their current workers, and to pay rental on space they occupy over a long

table 11-1 **comparison of yields: tax-exempt versus taxable securities**

Taxable Income		Tax Bracket	Tax-exempt yield					
			4%	5%	5½%	6%	6½%	7%
Joint Return	Single Return		Equivalent taxable yield					
$16–20,000		28%	5.56%	6.94%	7.64%	8.33%	9.03%	9.72%
	$14–16,000	31%	5.80	7.25	7.97	8.70	9.42	10.14
$20–24,000		32%	5.88	7.34	8.07	8.82	9.56	10.29
	$16–18,000	34%	6.06	7.58	8.34	9.09	9.85	10.61
$24–28,000	$18–20,000	36%	6.25	7.81	8.59	9.38	10.16	10.94
	$20–22,000	38%	6.45	8.07	8.87	9.68	10.48	11.29
$28–32,000		39%	6.56	8.20	9.02	9.84	10.66	11.48
	$22–26,000	40%	6.67	8.33	9.17	10.00	10.83	11.67
$32–36,000		42%	6.90	8.64	9.51	10.34	11.21	12.07
$36–40,000	$26–32,000	45%	7.27	9.09	10.00	10.91	11.82	12.73
$40–44,000		48%	7.69	9.61	10.57	11.54	12.50	13.46
$44–52,000	$32–38,000	50%	8.00	10.00	11.00	12.00	13.00	14.00

period of time. But their current operating budgets—income and outgo—did not properly take into account these long-term obligations.

Let's compare it with a common family situation. A family may have a realistic grasp on its current budget—how much is coming in and how much will have to be spent. But the family also has two teenage children who anticipate entering college within the next three to five years. The family must, if it's to be realistic and prudent, determine where the money will come from to meet those expenses, unless a fund is already saved up. If the family is not currently setting aside a fixed amount to cover those future expenses, they'll have to borrow the funds when the tuition bills come due. And when the bills do arrive, the family's specific financial situation will suddenly and dramatically alter. Similarly with cities: if they do not realistically and prudently project those future expenses, and make *current* arrangements to meet those expenses, then the cities' taxpayers might find themselves looking at an unanticipated and costly burden within a few short years. If the taxpayers rebel against having to pay those expenses, a city's ability to pay its debts becomes jeopardized.

Another aspect of municipal borrowing can be compared with the family situation. If a family's credit history is questionable or seems unsafe to a lender, that family will have a more difficult time borrowing money, and will likely have to pay a higher interest rate when it does borrow. Where credit worthiness is questionable, the lender is obviously taking a higher risk in making such a loan. So also with cities: as their credit worthiness becomes more questionable, due to a high debt level in relationship to taxable income, the city faces a higher borrowing cost each time it seeks to borrow. And, obviously, as interest costs go up, the burden on the taxpayers of that city increases proportionately. Thus, the problem compounds itself—the greater the need to borrow, the more expensive the borrowing can become. And the more expensive the borrowing becomes, the closer the flash point at which the taxpayers will rebel.

rating the bonds

To aid investors, municipal bonds are rated by two major rating services: Moody's and Standard and Poor's. These rating services examine the financial status of cities and corporations; the ratings compare the relative qualities of the various issues.

The formats of both rating systems are similar. One, Standard and Poor's, will serve as an adequate example of both:

AAA-Prime: these are obligations of the highest quality. They have the strongest capacity for timely payment of debt service.

General Obligation bonds: In a period of economic stress the issuers will suffer the smallest declines in income and will be least susceptible to autonomous decline. Debt burden is moderate. A strong revenue structure appears more than adequate to meet future expenditure requirements. Quality of management appears superior.

Revenue bonds: Debt service coverage has been and is expected to remain substantial. Stability of the pledged revenues is also exceptionally strong because of the competitive position of the municipal enterprise or the nature of the revenues. Basic security provisions (including rate covenant, earnings test for issuance of additional bonds, debt service reverse requirements) are rigorous. There is evidence of superior management.

AA-High grade: The investment characteristics of general obligation and revenue bonds in this group are only slightly less marked than those of the prime quality issues. Bonds rated AA have the second strongest capacity for payment of debt service.

A-Good grade: Principal and interest payments on bonds in this category are regarded as safe. This rating describes the third strongest capacity for payment of debt service. It differs from the two higher obligations in the following ways.

> *General Obligation bonds*—There is some weakness, either in the local economic base, in debt burden, in the balance between revenues and expenditures, or in quality of management. Under certain adverse circumstances *any weakness* might impair the ability of the issuer to meet debt obligations at some future date.

> *Revenue bonds*—debt service coverage is good, but not exceptional. Stability of the pledged revenues could show some variations because of increased competition or economic influences on revenues. Basic security provisions, while satisfactory, are less stringent. Management appears adequate.

BBB-medium grade: This is the lowest investment grade security rating.

> *General Obligation bonds*—under certain adverse conditions several of the above factors could contribute to a lesser capacity for payment of debt service. The difference between A and BBB ratings is that the latter shows *more than one fundamental weakness*, or *one very substantial fundamental weakness*, whereas the former shows only one deficiency among the factors considered.

> *Revenue bonds*—debt coverage is only fair. Stability of the pledged revenues could show substantial variations, with the revenue flow possibly being subject to erosion. Basic security provisions are no more than adequate. Management performance could be stronger.

BB-Speculative grade: Bonds in this group have some investment characteristics, but they no longer predominate. For the most part, this rating indicates a speculative, noninvestment grade obligation.

B-low grade: Investment characteristics are virtually nonexistent and default could be imminent.

D-Defaults: Payment of interest and/or principal is in arrears.

Not all municipal bonds are rated by the rating companies. But generally when nonrated bonds are issued, they are examined by the issuing brokerage firms and the interest rate they pay will usually be in line with issues of comparable quality rated by the rating services.

underwriting: how the bonds are sold

When a city wishes to borrow money, it usually approaches an underwriter, which acts as a wholesaler might. The underwriter will be a major brokerage firm, or a group of firms acting as underwriter partners. Depending on current market conditions and the quality of the issue, the underwriter will determine the interest rate the offering will probably bring, and will then offer the bonds to specific investors.

The same procedure exists regarding the sale of corporate bonds. There has been, however, one major difference between the underwriting of municipal bonds and that of corporate bonds. Traditionally, cities have had to divulge only a relatively minimal amount of information to the underwriters, whereas corporations have to disclose their books in extreme detail. Perhaps the experience with New York City and other cities will amend this practice, requiring cities to more fully disclose all of their current and future financial situations. Though the image of municipal bonds has been somewhat tarnished, municipal bonds are still regarded as being relatively high on the safety ladder among the various kinds of investments.

yield   The yield on a municipal bond, as with other fixed income investments, is based on the original promise to pay a fixed rate of interest for the life of the bond. If a bond is issued with a 6% interest rate, an investor will receive $60 per year for each $1000 worth of face value. Municipal bonds do fluctuate somewhat in their value over the years. This can be due to fluctuating interest rates, changing market conditions, and changes in the circumstances of the issuing municipality. The effect of these fluctuations is discussed in more detail under the yield section of corporate bonds.

liquidity   There are thousands of various municipal bond issues available on the market at all times, but the trading activity in them tends to be much lighter than with corporate or government bonds. Thus, an investor wishing to sell municipal bond holdings may have to wait until a willing buyer comes along. It may be a matter of minutes, hours, or days. The seller may have to settle for a lesser price in order to find a willing buyer.

pledge value   Holders of municipal bonds should be able to borrow against their holdings without much difficulty. The percentage of the total value that they can borrow, and the interest rate they'll have to pay will depend on the quality of the issue itself. The higher the quality, the higher percentage of face value they'll be able to borrow, and at a respectively lower interest rate than the lower rated issues.

hedge value   Municipal bonds offer a rather indirect protection against inflation. Although the bond itself pays a fixed rate of income for as long as one holds it, the tax-exempt factor can be translated into some protection against inflation for the investor whose income is on the rise, either as a result of inflation or because of his or her own energies, or a combination of the two. As income passes from one tax bracket level into a higher level, the tax-exempt income increases in its relative value to the investor. For example, an individual owns $1000 worth of municipal bonds, has a taxable income of $15,000 per year, and files a joint return. He's in the 25% tax bracket, which means that he'd have to find a taxable bond with a yield of 8% to equal what he now receives on his 6% tax-exempt bond.

If his income jumps above $16,000 (and up to $20,000), he moves into the 28% tax bracket. In that tax bracket, his 6% tax-exempt bond is equivalent to an 8.33% taxable bond. The next highest bracket, 32% (taxable income between $20,000 and $24,000) means that the 6% tax-exempt bond is equivalent to an 8.82% taxable bond.

In other words, as income increases, the taxable equivalent of the tax-exempt bond also increases. The tax-exempt investment, which has not changed with inflation, is providing a return comparable to what he could get with increasingly higher returns available in the taxable market.

investigation   Prior to 1977 an investor seeking to put money into municipal bonds would have found very little opportunity to do so. In most cases, the minimum denomination that could be bought would be beyond the ability of most small investors. Or, in the alternative, a minimum purchase of, say, $1000 could have entailed a commission cost so high as to offset the tax-exempt advantages of the bond. In short, municipal bonds had been the almost exclusive preserve of the large and sophisticated investors, such as pension funds, major institutions, and the relatively wealthy.

A small number of investment companies had set up mutual funds that would allow smaller investors to pool all of their dollars into a larger fund that would, in turn, invest in municipal bonds. But prevailing tax laws prior to 1977 put certain technical restrictions on these mutual funds to make them unappealing to the average small investor.

the new MUNIfunds.   The 1976 Tax Reform Law, however, eliminated those restrictions; MUNIfunds will provide the first relatively simple opportunity for millions of small investors to take advantage of the tax-exempt type investment previously out of their reach.

In addition to providing tax-exempt income to investors, MUNIfunds also allow earnings to compound. Before MUNIfunds, an investor could buy a specific bond, but had no means of reinvesting the interest received back into the bond. In short, the compounding effect was not available as it is in savings accounts where interest is automatically reinvested and put back to work. Further, the owner of a municipal bond could not add small additional amounts periodically to the investment. He or she bought a bond, or bonds, and that was it. The investor could also not withdraw anything from the investment other than periodic interest payments. Either the bond was cashed in totally, or the investor waited until it matured, or borrowed against it if necessary.

MUNIfunds offer great flexibility. The owner of MUNIfund shares can have earnings automatically reinvested in additional fractional shares of the fund; can add minimal amounts to the original investment at any time; and can withdraw monthly or quarterly sums from the investment, in many cases at no service charge. Specific regulations on these various techniques may differ from one MUNIfund to another.

the prospectus: a shopping guide.

An investigation into buying MUNIfunds may prove time consuming, but it's essential. A great many investors make their investment decisions based on a talk with the salesagent and a quick reading of the advertising material. But the prudent investor will take the time to study the prospectus issued by the fund and to compare a number of such prospectuses to determine the explicit terms and conditions of the investment and how it will be handled. The following is a "shopping list" of factors that should be examined in various prospectuses for any investor considering putting money into MUNIfunds.

☐ *Loading charge.* Some MUNIfunds will charge a sales commission that can range to as much as 4½% of the amount invested. In other words, on an investment of $1000, $45 will be taken off the top as the selling commission. Thus, the investor only has $955 invested. Other MUNIfunds will not impose a sales charge, and thus allow the total investment to go to work. The amount of any loading charge can significantly affect the yield the investor can expect.

☐ *Maintenance.* Most of the MUNIfunds will impose an annual or monthly maintenance or management fee, whether or not they also charge a loading fee. The management or maintenance fee will customarily be a percentage (usually less than 1%) of the total assets in the fund. In addition, some funds may also take a fee based on the earnings of the fund during the year. These fees may be deducted from the total fund assets, or directly from each individual account. Either way, they are an added cost and can affect your yield. The loading charges and the annual fees are legal: it's the cost to the investor of having professionals manage your money for you.

☐ *Distribution of assets.* How will the fund invest the money it receives from each individual? A sampling of various MUNIfund prospectuses will disclose that there are differences in the proposed distribution of investors' dollars. Some funds, for example, may state their objective as being "at least 80% or 90% in AAA, AA, or A rated municipal bonds." Others may include BBB bonds within their projections. The mix of higher quality investments will result in a slightly lower yield, but a higher degree of safety and less likelihood of fluctuation.

Further, all of the MUNIfunds reserve the right to make temporary investments that *may include certain taxable issues* of varying quality. They also reserve the right to make "defensive" investments in the face of a declining market. These defensive investments *may also include certain taxable issues.* Thus, it's likely that not all of the income received on a MUNIfund will be totally tax exempt. If a fund does make temporary or defensive investments in taxable issues, that portion of income represented by those temporary or defensive investments could be taxable.

Other taxable income might be generated by a MUNIfund if it sells a specific issue at a gain. Municipal bonds are tax exempt only to the extent of the *interest* they pay to the investors. If an investor, or a mutual fund, sells a particular bond at a profit, that *profit* is subject to federal income taxation.

☐ *Extra privileges.* Many MUNIfunds are part of a family of other mutual funds. The owner of shares in a MUNIfund may therefore have the privilege of exchanging all or a portion of his or her MUNIfund shares for shares in another fund managed by the same investment advisory group. A switch might take place, for example, from a MUNIfund holding into a common stock fund holding or vice versa at the investor's desire. There may be a slight charge in order to make such an exchange. Reinvestment privileges—whereby your earnings can be automatically reinvested in additional shares of the fund—are commonplace, usually at no charge. Withdrawal privileges—taking out a fixed amount each month or each quarter—are also available, with some minimal restrictions as to the amount that can be withdrawn.

☐ *Minimum investments required.* Many MUNIfunds require a minimum initial investment of $1000, but some are available for as low as $100. After the initial investment, the investors may make additional investments in smaller amounts. Some funds allow "any amount" as a subsequent investment while others may have a minimum of $100.

☐ *Size of fund and management expertise.* The MUNIfund concept is in its infancy, and it may take many years before specific MUNIfunds prove the kind of performance that investors are looking for. Municipal bond trading is a sophisticated area. Many new MUNIfunds may not have the management skills needed to trade effectively and competitively in this sophisticated field. Those with the more experienced and skilled investment advisers may be in a better position to help achieve the fund's objectives. It's also possible that the size of a fund—the total assets—can have a bearing on the fund's success in meeting its objectives. Municipal bonds tend to be traded in very large blocks, and funds with a greater reservoir of assets might be better able to take advantage of a particularly attractive offering than smaller funds.

An investor should also examine that portion of the prospectus refering to the permissible turnover of a given fund. The turnover rate controls how much trading in and out of bonds a fund can do in a given year. The higher turnover permissible, the greater the temptation may be for a fund manager to buy and sell more frequently than prudence might otherwise dictate.

MUNIfunds are advertised in daily newspapers (usually on the financial pages) and in a variety of financial periodicals, such as the *Wall Street Journal*, *Forbes*, *Barron's*, and *Business Week*. They can also be obtained through stockbrokers.

private dealers   There are a number of private municipal bond dealers throughout the country. They actually own and sell bonds at whatever profit margin they can generate and don't deal on a commission basis as normal brokers do. They will have bought the bonds themselves to hold in their own account for the subsequent resale to investors. Typically, they will add a markup to the current prevailing market price, thus adding to the total cost. These brokers often deal in unrated bonds that may have a limited marketability. Investors may thus pay a higher price for bonds of a given caliber than they otherwise could obtain through normal stock exchange brokers who deal more extensively in rated bonds, which are more heavily traded and thus more marketable.

corporate bonds   The third major category of bonds is corporate bonds. Under the overall heading of corporate bonds are included the IOUs issued by railroads, public utilities (such as local electric and gas companies), and industrial firms (manufacturers, service companies such as airlines, retailing firms, etc.). Broadly speaking, there are two classifications of corporate bonds: straight and convertible. The straight bond is a simple long-term IOU of the issuing company, wherein a fixed interest rate is agreed to be paid to the investor. The convertible bond carries with it the right for the holder to convert the bond into shares of that same company's common stock. Convertible bonds, or convertible debentures as they're sometimes called, are discussed in more detail in the section on investing in stocks.

sinking fund and   When corporations borrow money, they typically do something
call privileges   most individuals and families should be well advised to do. They set up what is called a "sinking fund" out of which they will eventually pay off the bond. They put aside so much money each year toward the eventual redemption of that bond and

actually use those monies to pay off the investors, either at maturity, or in advance of maturity if market conditions so dictate. For example, a company has issued a bond paying 7% interest per year. After the passage of a number of years, the interest rates prevalent throughout the economy have dropped to 6%. The company sees an opportunity to refinance the existing IOUs and drop their interest rate from 7% to 6%, thus cutting their interest expense considerably. In order to take advantage of this possible occurrence, many bonds have written into them a "call privilege," which means that the company has the right to call in the existing bonds and pay off the holders at an agreed on price.

A would-be investor in corporate bonds should determine what call privilege or protection exists. Because a bond is usually a relatively long-term investment, it would be to the investor's advantage to know that the company can't call the bond for at least five to ten years.

Corporate bonds can usually be bought in denominations of $1000, and the commission payable to a stockbroker is generally much less than when buying stock. Further, when you buy a bond at its initial offering (and this applies to government and municipal bonds as well as corporate bonds), there's usually no commission to pay. Likewise, if you hold a bond until maturity, and it's redeemed directly by the issuer, there'll be no commission to pay.

how to read
bond quotations

Many major daily newspapers carry bond quotations, as does the *Wall Street Journal*. *Barron's*, a financial newspaper issued weekly, also contains a full listing of traded corporate bonds. In bond price quotations, a bond selling for $950 would be quoted as 95. A bond selling for $985 would be quoted as 98½, and so on.

An example: in 1950 the XYZ Company borrowed some money from public investors and issued their bonds as IOUs. These bonds contained a promise to pay 4% interest per year for 40 years to everyone who bought the bonds, issued in $1000 denominations. The bonds would thus mature in the year 1990, at which time the XYZ Company would pay all holders of the bonds $1000 for each $1000 bond. Over the years, investors traded the bonds back and forth among each other. Due to market conditions that bond today sells for $950. The quote in the newspaper would look like this, on a day when there was no fluctuation in its price:

XYZ Company 4s 90 95 95 95

This bond would be referred to as the XYZ Company 4s of 90. The 4s refers to the original interest rate that the company agreed to pay, or 4%; the 90 refers to the year of maturity of 1990; the three 95 figures refer to the high, low, and closing prices for the day. (Remember we said that the price didn't fluctuate on this particular day.)

how bond yields are figured Bonds have three different yields, and the difference must be clearly understood. (This can be equally true for government and municipal bonds.) The following description does not take into account brokerage commissions or income taxes payable on bond interest received.

Referring back to the earlier example of the XYZ 4s of 90. The 4% interest that the company originally agreed to pay is known as the *coupon rate*. In other words, the company guarantees that it will pay $40 each year (usually in semiannual install-ments) to each holder of each $1000 bond. The bond may fluctuate in price up and down, but the holder will continue to get $40 per year for each $1000 bond held, regardless of the price of the bond.

We noted that the bond was quoted at $950 on a given day. If an investor purchased a $1000 bond for $950, and received $40 per year in interest from the company, the actual *current yield* is 4.2% ($40 of $950, which is your actual investment). If, on the other hand, you had paid $1050 for the bond, your *current yeild* would be roughly 3.7% ($40 is 3.7% of $1050, which is your actual investment.)

The third concept of yield is called the *yield to maturity*, and it's a bit more difficult to understand. Say that you buy a $1000 face value bond for $950, and you buy it exactly one year before its maturity date. Assume that it's paying the same 4% per year as the bond quoted above. When the bond matures one year after your purchase date, you get back the full face amount, or $1000. That's $50 more than you paid for it, and that $50 is considered a capital gain. Also, you're going to get the $40 in interest during the year you hold the bond. Altogether you will receive $90 in one year for your $950 investment, or a *yield to maturity* of just over 9.4%. You've invested $950, and one year later you've received back $90, which is a 9.4% return for the year.

If, though, you purchased the bond five years before maturity date, that $50 gain would be prorated over the remaining five years. Thus you would be getting the $40 each year in interest plus an eventual extra $50 on redemption, which is equal to an extra $10 on average each year, assuming that you hold the bond until maturity. Your annual average yield to maturity would then be approximately $50 each year, or about 5.2% of your initial $950 investment.

how bonds
fluctuate in
value

The above illustration discusses a bond whose original price has fluctuated in value. Why do bond prices fluctuate? At the time XYZ Company originally borrowed the money back in 1950, the prevailing interest rates for companies of XYZ's caliber seeking loans of that particular size for that particular duration was 4% per year. A company of higher credit standing than XYZ might have been able to borrow at a somewhat lower interest rate. And a company with a lesser credit worthiness might have had to pay a higher one. But for XYZ, at that time, 4% was the going rate.

The general rule in the bond market is that bond *prices* tend to move in the *opposite* direction of *interest rates.*.

Let's say that by 1960 the prevailing interest rates for companies of XYZ's size and quality had increased to 5%. In other words, if XYZ wanted to borrow in 1960, they'd have to pay 5% for their money instead of the 4% they had contracted for ten years previously. If you had originally bought a $1000 XYZ bond in 1950, what would that bond be worth in 1960 when the prevailing interest rate had increased from 4% to 5%?

If you wanted to sell it, you'd have to take less than the $1000 you had paid. Why? Because another investor could go into the new bond market and buy a new issue at 5%, getting $50 on a $1000 investment. Why then should he pay you $1000 and only get $40 for his investment? For this reason, your $1000 bond might now only be worth $880 to $900. If you wanted to sell it in 1960, you'd have to take a loss of $100 to $120. That's because a buyer in 1960 would be seeking 5% on his investment and, in order to achieve a 5% return on your older bond, would only be willing to pay you the lesser amount for it.

By 1970, prevailing interest rates for a company of XYZ's size and quality have jumped to 7%. That means that if XYZ were borrowing in 1970, they would have to pay 7% interest on their money for a long-term loan. This would mean that your $1000 bond bought in 1950 might only be worth about $750. If an investor paid you $750 for your $1000 bond in 1970, he'd receive $40 in interest per year, plus an average of $12.50 per year once the bond matured in 1990—assuming it was held until 1990. At that time he'll get his full $1000 from XYZ company. (He'll receive $250 more than he paid for the bond on maturity, which is an average of $12.50 per year.) Thus, he'd be getting roughly $52.50 per year, on average, and that would equal 7% on his $750 investment.

The value of your bond has thus slipped from $1000 in 1950 to $750 in 1970.

As the general rule indicates, the price of the bond has declined as the interest rates have gone up. But at some point—depending on the length of time remaining until maturity and the prevailing interest rates—the general rule begins to change. As the bond nears maturity, the price may start to move back up again, even though interest rates are continuing to rise. The primary reason for this is that the maturity date is acting like a magnet regarding the price of the bond, pulling it upwards toward face value. With redemption date in sight, an investor can more easily foresee the day when he'll get the full face value of the bond directly from the company when the bond is paid off.

Thus, while the general rule is that bond prices move in the opposite direction of interest rates, the rule may change as maturity of the bond gets closer, when the price of the bond tends to move toward its face value.

We've looked at an example of how a bond price declines in the face of rising interest rates until some indeterminate time, when, nearing maturity, the redemption date begins to draw the price of the bond back up to face value. The same situation holds true if interest rates decline: bond prices then tend to rise for the same reason, and they may well rise above face value. Again, there will be an indeterminate point at which the redemption date will begin to draw the price of the bond back down to face value. For example, say that a bond had been selling at a premium—more than face value—or $1050. As maturity nears, the holder of the bond knows that the company will pay off only $1000 for the bond and will see the price begin to slide from the $1050 toward the $1000 to be paid off at maturity.

Another factor that can affect the bond price is the change in the quality of the issuing company. If the company falls on hard times financially, investors may become pessimistic about the company's ability to meet its debts and the interest due thereon. This can have a negative effect on the value of the company's bonds. Naturally, in such cases, the stock of the company will have also been affected, most likely in a more drastic fashion than the bond. Similarly, an improvement in the financial status of the issuer can have an upward effect on the value of the bond.

Although the yield on a bond can be accurately calculated as of the time it's purchased, an investor must, for reasons noted above, be well aware that the total *value* of an investment can fluctuate over a long period of time. Bond prices will tend to fluctuate more slowly and gradually than will stock prices, but this can mean that an investor might get caught in a downtrend for a longer period and suffer a loss if the need arises to sell the bond. The closer a bond is to maturity at the time it's purchased, the less that risk. If a bond is purchased at a price *above* face value, the investor must be aware that as maturity approaches, the value of the bond will *drop* to meet the ultimate redemption price. This obvious effect on the ultimate yield must be taken into account at the time of purchase.

safety Like municipal bonds, corporate bonds are also rated as to quality by both Moody's and Standard and Poor's rating services. The Standard and Poor's ratings are as follows.

AAA. Bonds rated AAA are highest grade obligations. They possess the ultimate degree of protection as to principal and interest. They move with interest rates (as noted above), and hence provide the maximum safety on all accounts.

AA. Bonds rated AA also qualify as high grade obligations, and in the majority of instances differ from AAA issues only in small degree. Here, too, prices move with the long-term money market.

A. Bonds rated A are regarded as upper medium grade. They have considerable investment strength, but are not entirely free from adverse effects of changes in economic and trade conditions. Interest and principal are regarded as safe. They predominantly reflect money rates in their market behavior, but also economic conditions to some extent.

BBB. The BBB, or medium grade category, is borderline between definitely sound obligations and those where the speculative element begins to predominate. These bonds have adequate asset coverage and normally are protected by satisfactory earnings. Their susceptibility to changing conditions, particularly to depressions, necessitates constant watching. Marketwise, the bonds are more responsive to business and trade conditions than to interest rates. *This group is the lowest that qualifies for commercial bank investment* (author's emphasis).

BB. Bonds given a BB rating are regarded as lower medium grade. They have only minor investment characteristics. In the case of utilities, interest is earned consistently, but by narrow margins. In the case of other types of obligors, charges are earned on average by a fair margin, but in poor periods deficit operations are possible.

B. Bonds rated as low as B are speculative. Payment of interest cannot be assured under difficult economic conditions.

CCC-CC. Bonds rated CCC and CC are outright speculations, with the lower rating denoting the more speculative. Interest is paid, but continuation is questionable in periods of poor trade operations. In the case of CC ratings, the bonds may be on an income basis and the payment may be small.

C. A rating of C is reserved for income bonds on which no interest is being paid.

DDD-D. All bonds rated DDD, DD, and D are in default, with a rating indicating the relative salvage value.

liquidity

An active bond trading market is maintained by the New York Stock Exchange, and quotations on traded bonds are contained daily in the *Wall Street Journal* as well as major local daily newspapers. Weekly quotes are found in *Barron's.* Generally, bond trading is not as liquid as stock trading, and a holder of bonds, particularly of a small amount or of a seldom traded company, may not be able to get the desired price immediately. A few days wait may be necessary, or a lower price may have to be accepted, or both.

hedge value

If a bond is bought at or near face value, there is little protection against inflation. If prices move upwards—interest rates being among those prices—the bond will likely decrease in value as noted above. Thus, the hedge value might be considered negative. If a bond is bought below face value, and maturity is within sight, the bond will move upwards as maturity approaches, thus offering a measure of protection against prices, which might be rising during the same period.

pledge value
The amount that one can borrow against bonds, and the interest rate paid on such a loan, depends on the quality of the bond, determined by the rating services. Generally, well-rated bonds should provide ample opportunity for pledging, at reasonably favorable interest rates.

tax implications
Interest earned on corporate bonds is taxable. There is no shelter or protection with this kind of income. However, if a bond is purchased at less than face value, and is redeemed at face value, the difference between purchase price and the redemption is considered a capital gain. If the bond has been held for the requisite long-term capital gain holding period (more fully described in the discussion on stocks), then the capital gain income may be taxed at a lower rate than ordinary income. This is a fairly modest tax advantage, but something worth considering.

investigation
The proper sources from which to buy bonds are established stock brokerage firms and the investment department of banks. (Banks commonly invest in high grade corporate bonds, and on occasion are willing to sell portions of their holding to individual investors. Although the selection from a bank investment department may be limited, the fees and commissions payable may be less than what an investor might have to pay through a stock brokerage firm.)

corporate bond mutual funds and money market mutual funds.

Faced with thousands of corporate issues from which to choose, an investor may prefer to investigate the opportunities offered by corporate bond mutual funds and by so-called "money market mutual funds." These are mutual funds that pool small investors' money to invest in a variety of fixed income securities: government bonds both long and short term, long- and short-term corporate bonds, as well as bank certificates of deposit and other forms of IOUs. Money market funds became popular in the mid-1970s when interest rates throughout the land had boosted the yields on many of these money market instruments to unprecedentedly high levels. As with tax-exempt mutual funds, careful study is necessary for investing in the corporate bond or money market mutual funds. One must observe the objectives of the fund, how it will distribute the assets, what the various commissions and fees are, what reinvestment and withdrawal privileges are, and how the fund has performed in accordance with its stated objectives. As the previous discussion has indicated, the quality of corporate IOUs can vary considerably, and a corporate bond or money market mutual fund that concentrates on the higher quality issues will offer a lower return, with a commensurately lower risk. Conversely, such funds may emphasize the more risky levels of corporate issues, thus offering a higher return with an equally higher risk. Also, as with tax-exempt mutual funds, the salesagents and the advertising materials may not tell you all you need to know. A careful reading and comparison of various prospectuses are necessary if a prudent decision is to be made in line with your own personal investment objectives.

yields on bonds and other money market securities

Table 11-2 illustrates the typical yields for a variety of fixed income securities over the recent years.

table 11-2   **comparative bond yields***

| | U.S. Government bonds | | | | | Municipal bonds | | Corporate bonds | | | | |
| | | | | | | | | By rating | | By group | | |
	3 Mo. bills	6 Mo. bills	12 Mo. bills	3–5 year notes	Long-term bond	Highest rating	Medium rating	Highest	Medium	Industrial	Railroad	Utility
1970	6.39	6.51	6.49	7.37	6.59	6.12	6.75	8.04	9.11	8.26	8.77	8.68
1971	4.33	4.52	4.67	5.77	5.74	5.22	5.89	7.39	8.56	7.57	8.38	8.13
1972	4.07	4.49	4.77	5.85	5.63	5.04	5.60	7.21	8.16	7.35	7.99	7.74
1973	7.03	7.20	7.01	6.92	6.30	4.99	5.49	7.44	8.24	7.60	8.12	7.83
1974	7.84	7.95	7.71	7.81	6.99	5.89	6.53	8.57	9.50	8.78	8.98	9.27
1975	5.80	6.11	6.30	7.55	6.98	6.42	7.62	8.83	10.39	9.25	9.39	9.88
1976	5.06	5.30	5.48	6.80	6.69	5.40	7.34	8.37	9.22	8.63	8.60	8.86

* Figures given are percent per year.
Source: Federal Reserve.

tax-deferred fixed income investing: ira and keogh

Virtually every worker has a portion of his or her earnings put away for future Social Security benefits. And roughly half of the American work force (about 40 million workers) participates in pension programs to which their employers make annual contributions.

In pension plans that meet Internal Revenue Service standards, the contributions made by the employer on behalf of the employee are not considered taxable income to the employee in the years in which the contributions are made. When the pension funds are finally paid out, on or before retirement, the employee will have to pay a tax on those funds. But being retired, and thus in a lower income bracket, the tax will be at a much lower rate. In short, this amounts to a very attractive tax advantage to employees covered by these plans: even though they don't have the use of the money until retirement time, they are relieved of paying taxes on the employer's contributions during their working years. (Pension plans that do meet the tax law standards are referred to as "qualified plans." For simplicity, all references to pension plans will mean qualified plans.)

This concept of tax-deferred income for covered employees is fine. But what about the millions of self-employed individuals and the tens of millions who do not have a pension plan at their place of work?

In 1960, Congress passed a law, referred to as the Keogh Act, or HR 10, which extended some similar benefits to self-employed individuals. But it wasn't until 1974, with the passage of the Employee Retirement Income Security Act (ERISA) that similar benefits were extended to employed individuals who did not have a pension plan.

That law created the Individual Retirement Account (IRA) that permits noncovered employees to establish a form of do-it-yourself pension program with attractive tax advantages.

Because Keogh and IRA funds are frequently placed in fixed income forms of investments, it is appropriate to discuss them in detail at this point.

how they work

The mechanics of the Keogh plan and IRA plan are similar. In an IRA plan a participant can contribute up to 15% of earned income, or $1500 per year, whichever is less. A Keogh plan participant can contribute up to 15% of earned income, or $7500, whichever is less. The amount of the annual contribution is tax deductible to the participant. (Technically, it's listed as an "adjustment" in the income tax return, but the effect is the same as if it were a deduction.) The deduction is available even though the individual does not otherwise itemize deductions. Further, the earnings on the fund are not taxed while the fund is accumulating.

Except in cases of death or disability, the fund cannot be withdrawn before age 59½, and must be withdrawn by age 70½. In the case of an early withdrawal, a penalty must be paid.

Here are some examples of how the programs would work.

☐ An individual eligible for an IRA plan earns $12,000. The maximum that he or she can contribute to an IRA plan is $1500 in a given year. The contribution is limited to 15% of earned income, or $1500, whichever is less, and since 15% of the individual's earned income equals $1800, he's limited by the $1500 ceiling.

☐ A self-employed individual eligible for a Keogh plan earns $30,000. The maximum that he can contribute to the plan in that year would be $4500, which is 15% of his income, and the lesser of that figure and the $7500 ceiling.

☐ An IRA plan participant has a taxable income of $15,000, and files a joint return. Based on the tax tables, she would thus pay an income tax (before any applicable credits) of $3004. If, though, she makes a contribution to an IRA plan of $1000, her taxable income is reduced to $14,000, and her taxes are thus $2754. The $1000 deduction of the IRA contribution has reduced her federal income tax obligation by $250. That's $250 cash-in-hand that the individual can spend or invest.

☐ A Keogh plan participant has a taxable income of $30,000, which, on a joint return, would indicate a tax due of $7880. If he makes a $1000 contribution to his Keogh plan, his taxable income is reduced to $29,000, and his tax is accordingly reduced by $390, to $7490.

☐ An IRA plan participant contributes $1000 into a savings plan paying 6% interest per year. If her taxable income is in the $15,000 range, and she filed a joint return, that $1000 in a *fully taxable* savings plan would mean that $15 of the $60 earned during the year would be returned to the government in the form of income taxes. But under the IRA plan, the fund pays no taxes, and the entire $60 is able to remain in the fund and allowed to go back to work for her.

These examples should amply illustrate the abundant advantages in the IRA and Keogh plans, particularly over the long term in a retirement-oriented investment program. For the taxpayer in the 25% tax bracket, an annual contribution of $1000 over a 20-year period will result in a fund of $20,000 plus all accrued and compounded interest, which will have been tax free. That same annual contribution, placed in a normally taxable situation would, after twenty years, result in a total fund of $15,000 (after federal income taxes have been paid) and a much smaller added accumulation of interest, because the interest earned each year will have also been taxed.

exceptions

Under the IRA regulations, if both spouses are eligible for such a plan, they may each make contributions up to the previous stated limits, thus allowing a total maximum between the two spouses of $3000 per year. Further, if one spouse is eligible for an IRA plan and the other spouse does not work, the working spouse may exceed the otherwise stated limit of $1500 by an additional $250, for a total maximum allowable contribution of $1750, or 15% of earned income, whichever is less. This element of the law, commonly known as the "housewife's pension," was added to the IRA regulations by the 1976 Tax Reform Law.

Another feature of the 1976 Tax Reform Law modified the Keogh program concerning individuals who have part time self-employed earnings. This aspect of the law is frequently referred to as the "moonlighter's pension." If your adjusted gross income is $15,000 or less, you can put as much as $750, or 100% of your self-employed income, whichever is less, into such a plan. In other words, if you earned $800 moonlighting, you can put $750 into the plan. If you earned $600, you can put it all in. If your adjusted gross income is more than $15,000, you can put up to 25% of your moonlighting income into such a plan, but not in excess of $750.

who is eligible?   In order to be eligible for an IRA plan, you must not be an active participant in an otherwise qualified pension, profit-sharing, or stock bonus plan. However, a self-employed individual may be eligible for either a Keogh plan or an IRA plan, if he or she also is not otherwise covered by a qualified pension, profit-sharing, or stock bonus plan.

The self-employed individual may prefer a Keogh plan because it allows a much higher annual contribution limit (if one can afford to take advantage of that higher limit). However, a participant in a Keogh plan must include permanent employees who have served for three years or more. In other words, he must make contributions on their behalf out of his own income sources. Although those employee contributions are tax deductible to him, the cost of making the contributions nevertheless may be more than he cares to bear. In such a case, he may then prefer the IRA plan, which does not require employee contributions, but will then have to accept the lower annual contribution ceiling.

setting up a plan

Both IRA and Keogh plans can be set up relatively simply at local banks and savings institutions. The Keogh plan will likely require a bit more paper work than the IRA. You can't invest your IRA or Keogh money any way you see fit. In order to qualify for the tax benefits, the investment program must meet the tax law standards, generally: a form of savings account, annuity, or special U.S. retirement bonds—all fixed income investments, and in some instances mutual funds.

making your contributions

The amount of your contribution is limited to a percentage of your earned income. Earned income refers to income generated by your work, and does *not* count income received from investments, from other pensions, or from profits on the sale of property. For example: an individual earns $8000 from work and another $2000 from investments. The maximum he or she can contribute to an IRA account in that year would be $1200, which is 15% of the $8000 worth of earned income. The other $2000 does not qualify.

As long as you have the necessary income, you can make contributions to an IRA plan from other sources. For example, you may already have a savings account of the normal variety with, say, a balance of $4,500 in it. With an earned income of, say, $10,000 per year, you're eligible to put up to $1500 into an IRA account. You can withdraw $1500 each year from your existing savings account (or any other sources of funds) and shift that money into a tax-deferred IRA program. In so doing over the course of three years, you can have shifted your nest egg from a taxable status to a tax-deferred status, and have taken the deductions for the annual contributions in the meantime. Only cash contributions count toward an IRA plan. In the chapter on Retirement Planning, we'll take a closer look at some of the means of taking money out of these plans, and their tax implications.

Bleak Future Awaits Empty-Handed Investors

Phoenix, Arizona

Just before Christmas 1975, more than 20,000 investors in a Phoenix-based thrift association were shocked to learn that their nest eggs were in dire jeopardy: the institution had been thrown into receivership on order from the Securities and Exchange Commission in Washington, amid charges of fraud and mismanagement on the part of the thrift association.

After a year of effort by trustees and attorneys to unscramble the situation, Christmas 1976 came and went and investors didn't receive a penny back. The prospect of recovery remains dim for the victims, many of whom had their entire life savings invested with the institution.

Observers close to the scene estimate that investors may ultimately hope to receive between 15¢ and 25¢ for each dollar invested, but years of additional court action may expire before that occurs. The total amount involved is between $50 and $60 million.

The saga of Lincoln Thrift is an object lesson in how greed,

gullibility, and lack of investigation can lead otherwise innocent investors into chaos.

Lincoln Thrift was organized in Arizona under existing thrift association laws in the late 1960s. By the time of its demise in late 1975, it had grown to forty branches throughout the state, and had dozens of subsidiaries operating in Arizona and adjoining Western states.

Unlike banks and savings and loan associations, which are regulated by the State Banking Department and regularly audited by federal authorities, the thrift associations in Arizona were under the jurisdiction of the Corporation Commissioner's Office. That office was not equipped to do any kind of detailed surveillance or auditing of the thrift associations it licensed.

Although Lincoln may have been adhering to the regulations regarding thrift associations, to outward appearances it seemed to be a bank or savings and loan association: it offered "thrift accounts" and "investment certificates" that closely resembled passbook savings accounts and

savings certificates from regular banks and savings and loan associations. The catch—and the appeal—was that Lincoln offered these accounts at 1% to 2% higher interest rates than the other local financial institutions.

Its advertising and promotion also resembled that of other financial institutions: gifts and premiums were offered for new accounts; movie stars lent their names and apparent credibility to the campaigns; and "insurance" was even offered on the accounts. The catch here was that the company offering the account insurance was a subsidiary of Lincoln itself. Federal insurance available at banks, savings and loan associations, and credit unions is under the control of the federal government and is backed by the Treasury.

A brochure describing the account insurance may have been simultaneously accurate and misleading. The amount and type of insurance (up to $40,000 per account) seemed identical with the protection provided by the federal agencies for covered institutions. Lincoln's insuring company was known as Omaha Surety Corporation of America, a name that might conjure up images of an affiliation with the well-known and respectable

420

Mutual of Omaha Insurance Company.

Pertinent questions and answers in the brochure were as follows:

Q: Is Omaha Surety Corporation of America related in any way to the government?

A: No. Omaha Surety Corporation of America is a stock company, operating pursuant to a certificate of authority granted to it by the Department of Insurance for the State of Arizona.

Q: Where is Omaha Surety Corporation of America chartered?

A: Omaha Surety Corporation of America is chartered by the State of Arizona, by and through the Arizona Corporation Commission.

Q: Is Omaha Surety Corporation of America's policy of accountholders insurance approved by the Arizona Insurance Department?

A: Yes.

Q: Who regulates and audits Omaha Surety Corporation of America?

A: The Arizona Insurance Department.

The impression given is that the State of Arizona, its Corporation Commission, and its Insurance Department were keeping close watch on all matters relating to the thrift accounts. In fact, they were not, nor was it their job to do so. But, taken as a whole, it's easy to see how the uninformed public might easily have been led to believe that the insurance had the State of Arizona standing firmly behind it.

Many would-be investors may have been so swayed by the language on the front of the brochure that they didn't take the time or expend the energy to read the ominous paragraph that was printed on the back of the brochure:

"*Caveat*: All materials herein contained are general in nature, and by summary only. The precise extent and content of the applicable coverages available are set forth with particularity in the Account Holders Master Surety Bond and Agreement of Indemnity (Form #OSC-101). Anything herein contained which is and/or may be construed to be inconsistent and/or at a variance with the content of the aforementioned policy shall be deemed to be superseded in toto by the said policy. As to any questions of a technical nature which either involved the contents of the said policy, its coverages, or any matter relating thereto, which might involve the reader's reliance herein, the reader is respectfully referred to the reader's own attorney and/or business advisor, prior to undertaking any steps of any type with relation to the materials herein contained.

Anyone who did take the time to read that statement would likely need an attorney to interpret it. What it said, in effect, was: "Warning—if you really want to know exactly what the insurance does and does not cover, you'll have to read the policy itself. If you have any other questions regarding the policy or your accounts, you should check with your own attorney and/or business advisor before you get involved with us."

Such a warning, if clearly understood, should have been enough to scare away any but the most adventurous investors. But the warning was ignored by enough imprudent investors to result in a flow of $50 million into the coffers of Lincoln Thrift.

What went wrong? Would-be investors who inquired as to how their money would be put to use by the firm were told that a major portion of the assets would be loaned to doctors and dentists to finance their equipment purchases. This would have appeared to have been a relatively conservative investment program on the part of Lincoln: doctors and dentists are reputed to be wealthy and of good credit standing, and loans to them secured by their equipment should assure Lincoln's

ability to pay its promised rate of interest to the investors.

However, when the trustees had completed their accounting of Lincoln's assets, a very substantial portion was found to have been invested in the likes of racing yachts, airplanes, automobiles, fast food franchise real estate, and marginal shopping centers. One of their major investments was a shopping center in Phoenix whose principal tenant was W. T. Grant Company. The original investment may have been well intended, but its worth was severely decreased when W. T. Grant entered its own bankruptcy in 1976.

The trustees' reports indicated that imprudent investments on the part of Lincoln's management were resulting in a severe loss to the company, thus distinctly endangering the investments of all the individual account holders. Investigations by the state Attorney General's office and the Securities Exchange Commission in Washington apparently revealed enough abuse of trust to warrant the imposition of receivership.

"But we thought it was a bank" was the most common complaint of the stung investors. "It looked like a bank, it acted like a bank, it was insured like a bank—so we thought. We believed the state of Arizona was behind it, and that they would protect the depositors." And therein—in the word "depositors"—lies the ultimate rub. For these people who placed their money in the hands of the Lincoln Thrift management were not *depositors* at all. They thought they were, but they were *investors*. What Lincoln was, in effect, saying to the public was: "You give us your money and we'll invest it for you. If at any time you're not happy with what we've done with your money, just stop in and we'll gladly refund the unused portion thereof."

It may be years, if ever, before the responsible parties are brought to whatever justice the law dictates. And it may be years before the empty-handed investors see any of their money again. In the meantime, the 20,000 losers will have gained an expensive lesson in investing: because of a bit of greed, a bit of gullibility, and a failure to investigate, their money has evaporated. Perhaps at least their children, their grandchildren, their great-grandchildren and their great-great-grandchildren will have been amply instructed in how not to make the same mistake.

**review
questions**

1. Rather than send Sonia a check for interest, the financial institution using her money keeps it and adds it to the amount they owe her. What is this procedure called?
2. Sonia likes having her interest reinvested by the financial institution, but she now wants to invest in corporate bonds. Her broker tells her that corporations mail out interest checks twice a year. How can her interest on corporate bonds be reinvested?
3. How do life insurance companies invest most of their money?
4. How good are E and H bonds for collateral?
5. When and where can E and H bonds be purchased and redeemed?
6. What is the most notable feature of municipal bonds?
7. What are the two companies that publish ratings of corporate and municipal bonds?
8. Give the price in dollars and cents of the following bond quotations:

    a. 97 b. $97\frac{1}{4}$ c. $97\frac{1}{8}$ d. $102\frac{1}{2}$

**cases
for
study**

1. After the New York city bond problems, investors have been concerned about financial data behind municipal bonds. Because cities are not covered by the federal law requiring the use of a prospectus, how are they being pressured to disclose this data?
2. Calculate the approximate current yield on the following bonds:

    $4\frac{1}{2}$% bond selling at 90
    6% bond selling at 90
    7% bond selling at 105

3. Generally, bond prices go down as interest rates go up. When will a bond price rise with a declining interest rate?
4. Which taxpayers are eligible for either IRA or Keogh plans? Explain why some taxpayers would choose to use IRA and others Keogh.

chapter 12 **investing: the stock market**

stock ownership as a form of investing

In the previous chapter on fixed income investing we explored the possibilities of creating future wealth by "loaning" your money to another entity, receiving in turn a promise to pay a fee (interest) for the use of your money, plus the promise to return it at an agreed on time. These promises are legally binding obligations of the debtor or institution.

Stock ownership as a form of investment is quite different. With stock ownership, the investor has become a part owner of a business enterprise and has no promise (legal or otherwise) that he will receive any fee for the use of his money, or that anyone will be obliged to pay him any or all of his money back at any future time. He is dependent on the profitability of the business venture to generate a return on his investment and to create the possibility of a gain should he wish to later sell the investment.

425

What's the difference between lending your money to a business (investing in a corporate bond) and buying a portion of ownership in the business (buying stock)? Businesses often need money to develop new products, expand their facilities, buy new equipment, modernize, and for other job-creating activities. Some of the money needed may come from the profits that the business generates, but this isn't always enough. In order to acquire large sums of money relatively quickly, a business will either borrow from investors (issue corporate bonds) or will sell a portion of itself to investors (issue stock). The former route is frequently referred to as the debt market, the latter as the equity market.

Regarding its debt, the company has a legal obligation to pay interest to the investors, and to return the principal sum at the agreed on time. With equity, or stock, the company has no such legal obligation. If profits are in fact generated, the company may distribute a portion of the profits to the stockholders. The company is under no obligation to buy the stock back from a stockholder. If a stockholder wants to sell the stock, he or she hopes to find a buyer willing to pay an attractive price.

The important priority to note in comparing debt with stock ownership is that debt service (interest) must be paid before profits are tallied. Profits are the dollars left over after the business has paid all of its obligations, among which may be the payments due on its debts.

The same holds true when a business is terminated, either voluntarily or otherwise. In such a procedure, commonly called a liquidation, everything that the company owns is converted into cash. Out of that pool of cash, all of the company's debts are paid, including any bonds that may be outstanding. What's left over is split up between the stockholders. In other words, creditors have priority over stockholders in liquidation as well as in the day-to-day operation of a business.

The profitability of any kind of business venture depends on a great many factors, including the management of the business, nature of the competition, overall ups and downs in the nation's economy as well as for a particular category of industry, and the totally unpredictable quirks and whims of the investing public. It's this last element—the whims and quirks of the investing public—that makes the stock market a series of unending dilemmas. In the stock market, you are not just necessarily betting on how profitably the company can perform; you are also betting on how other people think the company might perform.

Virtually every transaction in the stock market, every purchase and every sale of every share is essentially a disagreement. The sellers want to get out because they don't think the stock offers them satisfactory income or potential any longer. The buyers want to get in because they feel the stock does offer satisfactory income or profit potential. In other words, the two parties disagree about the potential of the stock.

The stock market offers a vast spectrum of possibilities. The challenge is to find that small cluster of possibilities that can help achieve your stated objectives. But note the word *possibilities*. In the fixed income investment area, we're dealing with the realm of *probabilities*—in the stock market it's *possibilities*.

In your own personal life, you have a spectrum of future needs and desires: some probable and some possible. It's *probable* that you're going to retire some day and need adequate money to live on. It's *possible* that some day you might be in a position to enjoy a trip around the world. Goals that are probable, or fixed, or certain, need appropriate techniques if they are to be achieved. Those techniques tend to fall into the fixed income investment spectrum. You can't afford to take chances that you will or will not achieve those fixed and necessary goals. You have to be certain that they will be reached, or at least as certain as you can be.

Other goals that are less certain may be appropriately sought after by the less *certain* investment techniques, principally the stock market, *but not until after you have established a disciplined program that you feel confident will put you on the path of achieving your fixed goals*.

In other words, get a reasonable program under way that will take you to your fixed destinations. If you still have funds available to invest after you've put enough away toward those top priorities, you might want to consider the more speculative techniques to help you achieve lesser priority goals—goals that if not achieved, will not cause you to really suffer.

For a more vivid comparison of the difference between fixed income investing and "ownership" investing, let's look at the following scales, which represent the likelihood of achieving stated objectives.

1. Relatively total certainty
2. Fairly certain
3. Highly probable
4. Probable

5. Highly possible

6. Possible

7. Relatively uncertain

8. No degree of certainty

The objective: to put away X dollars today and know that you will have Y dollars at some future date.

The better quality ranges of the fixed income types of investment will fall into the top half of the eight categories, from one to four. The better quality range of stocks will range in the middle, from three to six. Although many high quality stocks have a very strong assurance of continuity of dividends, they are, nonetheless, subject to the fluctuations in value that can have an important bearing on your overall nest egg. Consider, for example, what many think to be the bellwether of all stocks: American Telephone and Telegraph. Its dividends have been increasing over the years, but the stock was selling for about $70 per share in the mid 1960s and below $40 in the mid 1970s.

The majority of investments in the stock market would fall in the four to seven range and a considerable number would be in the six to eight range. A small number of lower rated fixed income securities might fall into the bottom half of the scale, but the risk in such securities is much more self-evident because of the ongoing ratings of the securities.

For the balance of this chapter, we'll examine in greater detail some of the inner workings of the stock market. In no way at all should any of the discussion be construed as recommendations to buy, sell, or hold any types of securities; it is to help you determine whether or not the stock market offers the opportunities that will help you meet your goals, to understand how the mechanism works, and to motivate you to do further independent research to find those specific areas that will provide you with the returns you're seeking.

cautions   As you read and discuss the material on the stock market, bear in mind the following cautions.

1. Aided by sophisticated computers, millions of workhours are spent every day studying every movement, jiggle, and quiver of the stock market. Yet no one can predict with any degree of certainty what direction the market as a whole, or any individual stock, is liable to take even a minute or two from now.

2. There have probably been more statistics compiled about the stock market, and more books written about it, than perhaps any other phenomenon on earth. Yet it continues to be one of the most confusing, mystifying, and frustrating subjects we deal with.

3. The stock market touches our day to day life in more ways than we can imagine, yet we are powerless to control it even in the slightest way. Even though you may have never had anything to do directly with the market, and don't intend to ever have anything to do with it, it can still affect you. If the company that employs you is traded on the stock market, swings in the value of the stock can affect the future profitability of the company and possibly the future of your job. If your employer or boss is a stock market trader, his or her success or failure in the market on a day to day basis can have an effect on his or her personality and attitude which in turn can affect yours. If your pension fund or profit-sharing fund has money invested in the stock market, the investment expertise of those who manage those funds can have a profound bearing on your future.

4. There is no person, no book, no system, no computer, that can *assure* you of making money in the stock market. The stock market can play an important function as an integral part of establishing your future security. But unless one approaches it with the proper frame of mind, the proper expertise, and the proper degree of skepticism, its traps and pitfalls can destroy the very best intentions.

how a business operates

A brief look at how a corporation functions will assist you in understanding the workings of the stock market.

A corporation is a legal entity in its own right. Each separate state has it own specific laws governing how a corporation may be created and how it can be run. Like a person, a corporation can own, buy, or sell property; it can be taxed; it can sue and be sued; and it can conduct business.

A corporation is owned by its stockholders. Operating within the framework of applicable laws, the stockholders determine what they wish their corporation to do. But, particularly with corporations that have a great many stockholders, it is cumbersome for the stockholders to meet and consult over every item of corporate business. Thus, the stockholders elect a group of representatives who will act on their behalf in setting basic

policy and direction for the corporation. This group of representatives is referred to as the *directors*.

In turn, the directors will choose a group of individuals to
carry out the day-to-day and month-to-month operations of the
business. These people are called the *officers* of the corporation.
The chief officer of a corporation is commonly called the President. (Many large corporations also have other titles of high
magnitude that may be equal to or greater in power than the
president, such as Chief Executive Officer.) Under the President,
and answering directly to him or her, will be an array of Vice
Presidents, each with their own area of tasks, obligations, and
responsibilities. Seniority and experience may dictate that there
be a hierarchy of Vice Presidents: Executive Vice Presidents,
Senior Vice Presidents, Vice Presidents, and Assistant Vice
Presidents. Other officers of the corporation will commonly
include the Treasurer, the Secretary, and the Comptroller, and
each of these may have an additional hierarchy of assistants.

The stockholders generally meet once each year, at which
time they are informed of the progress and future potential of the
corporation. It's at the annual meeting that the stockholders—the
ownership—select the managers of the corporation for the forthcoming year—the directors, who in turn select the officers. If an
individual stockholder is unable to attend this annual meeting,
he or she will receive a "proxy," a voting authorization on which
one can indicate the selection of directors, and one's choice on a
number of issues on which stockholders have been asked to
express an opinion or a vote.

Commonly, the Board of Directors will recommend to the
stockholders a slate of nominees for the board for the forthcoming year. If ownership has been pleased with the job that
management has done, the board's recommendations will usually be followed. If ownership has not been pleased with
management's performance, a struggle might ensue. One or
more directors may be voted out, and one or more proposed
policies may be rejected by the stockholders. It is the rule rather
than the exception in most large corporations that the stockholders will comply with the recommendations of the Board of
Directors. Stockholders assume that management knows best,
even though there may have been some setbacks during the
year, or they may simply not care to express any contrary views
when completing their proxy vote. In recent years, though, the
annual meetings of many major corporations have been enliv-
ened by sharp discussions between ownership and manage-

ment regarding corporate responsibility in the fields of discrimination, pollution, and political practices. As a result, many corporations have adopted policies in keeping with stockholder wishes to amend their stance or create a new stance in line with these highly visible public issues.

how the stock markets operate

An individual's share of ownership in a corporation is represented by the stock certificate, which stipulates how many shares the individual owns. The value of each share, and thus of one's overall sum total of shares, is determined by a number of factors: profitability of the company, future potential for the company, amount of dividends the company is paying, and, broadly, what the public at large thinks it's worth. If a stockholder wishes to sell his stock, he must find a buyer who's willing to pay the asking price. If an investor wishes to buy stock, he must find a willing seller. In small local corporations, word of mouth may be all that's needed to find the respective buyer or seller, if one is to be found. But with large corporations, particularly those with hundreds of thousands or millions of shares outstanding, this would be impractical. If a would-be investor in stocks did not feel confident that he could sell his shares quickly and efficiently, he would likely be discouraged from making the investment in the first place.

Thus, throughout the nation and the world, exchanges long ago came into being to provide a ready market place for both buyers and sellers. The most familiar is the New York Stock Exchange, located in lower Manhatten, in an area commonly referred to as Wall Street. Other major exchanges include the American Stock Exchange, the Toronto Stock Exchange, the Montreal Stock Exchange, the Pacific Stock Exchange, the Boston Stock Exchange, the Philadelphia Stock Exchange, and the Mid-West Stock Exchange.

The stock exchanges are basically a form of auction in which buyers and sellers try to achieve the best buying or selling price. An investor who wishes to buy or sell stock places an order with a local stockbroker who works for a firm who owns a "seat" on an exchange. The order is relayed from the local broker's office to the firm's facilities on the floor of the exchange. In some cases, the brokerage firm may fill the order itself. In other cases, the order may be referred to a "specialist" on the floor of the exchange. Each individual stock traded on any given exchange is represented by a specialist whose job it is to match certain buy and sell orders and to keep an orderly marketplace for the stock he represents. In order to do so, he may be required to actually buy or sell stocks from his own account.

When the order is filled, word is relayed back to the local brokerage firm, who informs the customer of the results. Written confirmation of the transaction follows shortly thereafter.

Before a stock can be publicly traded (including on an exchange), it must comply with certain governmental regulations. If a stock is to be sold only to the residents of the specific state in which the company is located, the company must comply with local state regulations. If it is to be traded broadly, beyond state boundaries and across the nation, it must comply with requirements of the federal agency that oversees such matters, the Securities and Exchange Commission (SEC).

The federal regulations require a company to disclose a variety of facts relating to its operation including the identity and experience of its management, its debts, its legal affairs, its overall financial status, and the potential risks that an investor might face in investing in the company. All of this information— usually spelled out at great length in cumbersome legal jargon—is contained in a document called the prospectus.

A prospectus is required when a company initially sells its stock, or when it issues subsequent securities, including stocks or bonds. Once the initial prospectus has been issued, a company need not issue subsequent ones unless it does offer additional securities at a later date. Thus, while the prospectus is an important tool for the investor, if it is substantially out of date (as most are), its value can be diminished. Yet it still might serve as important background material, and should not be ignored.

Corporations do issue annual reports for the stockholders and for the SEC that contain more up-to-date information than the prospectus. A would-be investor should examine the annual reports, and it would be wise to compare these reports with the original prospectus, if for no other reason than to determine how well the company has met its originally stated objectives.

One critical aspect of the prospectus must be emphasized: Investors often believe that because a company has filed a prospectus with the SEC, that the strength of the federal government stands behind that stock, and that in effect Washington has somehow bestowed its blessings on the company and its stock. Nothing could be further from the truth. On the front cover of each prospectus is this often overlooked statement:

These securities have not been approved or disapproved by the Securities and Exchange Commission, nor has the Commission passed on the accuracy or adequacy of this prospectus. Any representation to the contrary is a criminal offense.

That statement means exactly what it says: The government does not in any way stand behind any of the statements made in the prospectus. The government does not say whether the information in the prospectus is accurate or adequate, but corporations found to have included inaccurate or inadequate or improper statements in their prospectus are subject to criminal prosecution. Further, anyone who tells you that the government has approved the issue or any of the specific details can also be subject to criminal prosecution. Thus, if a company lies in its prospectus in order to raise more money through the sale of stock, and stockholders are subsequently damaged as a result of the deception, it is possible that criminal and civil prosecution could result in an order requiring the corporation to reimburse the deceived stockholders. But if there's no money available to make such reimbursement, all is for naught.

investors insurance

The government does offer one measure of protection to investors, through the Security Investors Protection Corporation (SIPC).

When scores of banks folded as a result of the Great Depression in 1929–1935, the government acted to create an insurance program that would prevent a recurrence of such a disaster. The Federal Deposit Insurance Corporation came into being to insure bank depositors against the institution's failure. But until 1970, there was no comparable protection for investors who entrusted their funds to stock brokerage firms. A severe stock market collapse in 1969–1970 caused a number of brokerage firms to fail. Many more, on the brink of imminent failure, were absorbed by larger and healthier firms. As a result of the near panic that ensued, the government, in conjunction with the securities industry, took steps to create the SIPC, which would insure investors' accounts for the value of any securities or fund held by their brokerage firms in the event of a failure of such a firm. Most major firms currently provide this protection to their customers, but some smaller firms may not. (*Note:* The insurance does *not* protect against the value of any stock going down.)

keeping the records

The shares of most major corporations are traded by the hundreds or thousands every business day. It's not uncommon for over 20 million shares of stock to change hands in a single day on the New York Stock Exchange alone. This total volume is made up of many thousands of individual transactions, representing handfuls or major blocks of shares. Smaller corporations whose shares are seldom traded may hire clerical help to administer the necessary bookwork involved in periodically amending the list of stockholders. But most major corporations hire "transfer agents" to take care of this burdensome task. Transfer agents are usually affiliated with major banks.

When you buy or sell shares of a stock, the transfer agent will be notified accordingly, and your name will be either placed on or removed from the list of stockholders of that corporation. As dividends become payable, the transfer agent will see to it that the dividend is transmitted to you, or to your account with the stockbroker.

When you do buy stock, you have the choice of obtaining the certificate registered in your own name (or in the name of whatever parties you choose as owners, such as husband and wife jointly); or you may prefer to have the broker retain custody of the stock. In that case, the stock would be listed "in street name"—technically it is in the broker's name and possession, but he is holding it for your account. Some investors may prefer to obtain the certificate in their own hands, aware of the fact that they should make proper safekeeping arrangements for it. Other investors prefer the convenience of having it remain in the broker's custody. In such cases the investor will receive a monthly statement from the broker indicating the status of the account and which securities are being held in his or her name.

Each buy and sell transaction will be followed up by a written confirmation that indicates the date of the transaction, the price for which the security was bought or sold, the amount of the broker's commission and any appropriate taxes, and the net amount due to the broker or to the investor from the broker. These confirmation slips should be retained by the investor, for they will contain information helpful in determining future gains or losses on the stock. The confirmation slips also indicate the "settlement date," which is the day by which the payment must be made and the stock delivered.

executing an order

Once you have opened an account with a broker by signing the necessary papers, you can execute orders: that is, instruct your broker to buy or sell on your behalf. (If the individual broker with whom you regularly deal is not available at the time you wish to place an order, you can always place an order through another representative of the firm.) You can place an order to buy or sell either "at the market" or at a specific price (sometimes called a "limit order").

If you place an order to buy or sell at the market, the broker will transmit your order to the floor of the stock exchange and you will buy or sell the securities at the then going price. It may be slightly more or slightly less than you had planned on, depending on the supply and demand of the stock at that particular time. If your order is at a specific price, the order will be executed *if* a buyer or seller is available at that particular price. If not, the order will not be executed. You can also place orders with your broker that will remain open indefinitely, or until cancelled by you, or until a specific time has elapsed (the end of a day, a week, a month). Such open-ended orders are not advisable, however, unless you maintain a most stringent supervision over all of your stock market affairs. If you place an open-ended order, then change your mind and neglect to cancel it, you may find that you have bought or sold stock that you wished you hadn't.

Many prudent investors will have a philosophy of selling automatically if the stock drops to a certain level or rises to a certain level, thus assuring their profits or cutting their losses. This can be done via a "stop order," which you can leave with your broker at any time. Such stop orders may be particularly advisable if you will be travelling and out of reach of the broker and the information needed to make decisions.

If you've ever visited a brokerage firm office, you're well aware that a very large percentage of the orders are handled by telephone. It's important, therefore, to make certain that the broker has followed your instructions explicitly, particularly concerning the number of shares you're selling and the price at which you wish to sell them. Although errors may be rare, an order to buy 100 shares that is transmitted as an order for 1000 can be catastrophic, particularly if the stock goes down shortly thereafter.

who invests in the stock market and what are they looking for?

The vast diversity of stock market investors can be broken down in two broad categories: by size and by type.

investors by size

Within the size categories there are individuals and institutions—or, put another way, small investors and large investors. Individual investors (as well as groups of them such as in investment clubs) and small organizations generally trade in small blocks of stock. Blocks of 100 shares are referred to as round lots; blocks of less than 100 shares are referred to as odd lots, and such transactions may carry a slightly higher brokerage commission—called the "odd lot differential"—than round lot trades.

The large investors, such as pension and profit-sharing funds, mutual funds, trust funds, large corporations, insurance companies, and the like, often trade in very large blocks—many thousands of shares at a time. Large block trades can disrupt the normal flow of supply and demand of shares, and can thus cause considerable fluctuations in the price of a given stock at any given time that such an order to buy or sell is placed.

The existence, side by side, of the small investor and the large investor has been referred to as the "two tier market." From the end of World War II until the late 1960s, the securities industry had vigorously wooed the small investor all across the nation. Small investors responded by the millions and became part owners of American business. They were particularly welcomed in the stock market, not only because of the commissions they generated for the brokerage firms, but also because the large mass of small investors tended to exert a stabilizing influence on the market movement as a whole.

But the stock market debacles of 1969–1970 and 1974–1975 chased a large portion of small investors away from the stock market, leaving an inordinately heavy portion of the trading to be done by the large investors. The result is a much more volatile market: day-to-day fluctuations in prices tend to be much broader than they had been during the 1950s and 1960s, thus casting an even more uncertain aspect on the fate of anyone's investment.

investors by type

The following are brief descriptions of eight broad categories of investors. They may represent individuals or institutions. They are all together in the market at the same time, all expressing a constant flow of opinions that may be in total accord or total discord with their colleagues. Generally there is enough disagreement to keep most prices on a relatively even keel most of the time. Let's take a closer look at the cast of characters.

the novice   The novice isn't really sure what he's doing. His obvious motivation is to "make money," but he's not really certain as to how, or
if, he will. If he has done any studying at all, it's probably been
only superficial; most likely he has involved himself in the
market because of the suggestion of someone else, and he's
probably followed the suggestion at its face value. He may
fancy himself as an investor, but his real status is more akin to
that of a blind bettor.

the insider   There are three types: the way-insider, the fringe-insider, and
the pretend-insider. The way-insider is a person on intimate
terms with the day-to-day operation of the corporation—an
officer, an employee, a director, or a major stockholder. He will
be privy to information not yet available to the public that, when
released to the public, can have a good or bad effect on the
stock of the company. He may know, for example, that a
potentially profitable deal is about to be completed; or that a
sharp loss is about to be announced; or that an important new
product is about to be introduced; or that an unsuccessful old
product is about to be withdrawn from the market. Based on his
inside information he may buy shares of the company's stock,
anticipating that the impending announcement will cause a
price rise. Or, he may sell in the anticipation that the news will
cause a drop. If his information is accurate and the announcement has the effect he anticipates, he could reap a substantial
profit, or avoid a sharp loss by selling out his existing holdings.

The fringe-insider may have indirect or delayed access to the
intimate information available to the way-insider. He may, for
example, be the stockbroker for the way-insider, or a close
friend, associate, or relative. He may be a supplier to or a buyer
from the company. He may be a professional advisor (lawyer,
accountant) of a way-insider. He will likely obtain the valuable
inside information sometime after the way-insider has obtained
it. Perhaps he will learn of the important facts in time to act on
his own behalf, perhaps not. He doesn't really known for sure
what will happen, but if he does receive what he believes to be
valid insider information, he's very likely to act on it.

The pretend-insider is another step or two, or more, removed
from the fringe-insider. He is in the "friend of a friend" category.
By the time he gets the information, the upswing or downswing
may have long since occurred. But he won't necessarily be
aware of that. Having just obtained what he believes to be a

valid company secret, he's still likely to act on it, even though it's long after the fact. The pretend-insider is a victim of that common children's party game: the first person whispers a phrase into the ear of the second, who then must repeat what he or she heard to the third person, and so on. By the time it reaches the last person, the original statement is usually drastically changed.

Trading on inside information is illegal. It's not supposed to happen, but it does, and the Securities and Exchange Commission admits that enforcement of their insider information rules is extremely difficult. Even though certain insiders are required to report their buy and sell transactions, it is still very difficult to discover and prove wrongdoing in this area of stock market trading. Illegal though it may be, and successful or unsuccessful though it may be, it does exert a distinct effect on specific stocks and to a lesser extent on the market as a whole.

the hunch player
He will probably be an active trader, and possibly a seasoned veteran of the stock market. He may be convinced that all the study in the world is for nought, because the quirks and whims of fellow investors are imponderable and they have more of an effect on the value of any given stock than the actual true value of the company itself. He'll listen to tipsters avidly, if not actually actively seeking them out. Much of his trading will be based on what can best be described as hunches: a gut reaction, a voice in the night, an omen. If he's canny to the ways of the market and has observed in enough detail the minute ebbs and flows of prices over the years, he might be fortunate enough to generate a trading profit during periods when the market is moving upwards; and he may be astute enough to stay away from the market when it's in a general downtrend. His investment objectives tend to be without any long range plan or pattern: he just wants to make what he can when he can.

the theory trader
Though often mistaken for the hunch player, the theory trader bases his transactions on one or more specific theories that may be directly tied to something as tangible as governmental statistics, or as intangible as trends in international currency fluctuations. Though they may be small in number, the theory traders can be very influential when their theories prove correct; however, they also have a way of disappearing temporarily when their theories have proven incorrect. Many theory traders will often be found reading stock market advisory newsletters,

generally the well-spring of their information and decisions. Because they paid a steep price for these advisory letters, they assume the information has to be correct, otherwise it wouldn't be so expensive.

sentimentalists This well-intentioned group of investors may place their money in stocks of companies that they work for, or that are located in their home town. Sentimentality or loyalty will be their primary reason for investing. Emotionally, it's like rooting for the home town team to win; but rationally this can amount to nothing more than total speculation.

technical analysts The technical analyst (sometimes called "chartist") is a serious student of the stock market. Essentially, technical analysts closely follow, and chart, specific short-, medium-, and long-term trends in individual stocks, in groups of stocks, and in the market movement as a whole. Technical analysts, as a group, have come up with a dazzling array of indicators that supposedly give signals to buy and sell. There are market peaks and market troughs; there are bellwether stocks that purportedly lead the way in one direction or another; high ratios and low ratios; moving averages; overbought and oversold indexes; and charts that plot every conceivable squiggle a given stock may be subject to. (More detailed information on these various techniques can be obtained through the dozens of books available on the subject, and through brokers.)

But in spite of all the information available, the problem is that the meticulously plotted signals of the analysts are often invalidated by the actions of other traders who pay no attention to these signals. Further, the analysts don't necessarily agree with themselves as to which signal means what, and they may often come up with conflicting signals.

the fundamentalist The fundamentalist is the serious investor who has done his homework, and who is willing to continue to do the necessary homework. He has learned how to analyze the financial statements of the companies he is interested in investing in, and he has learned how to seek out the basic sound fundamental value of each company. He's not a trader: he'll be willing to wait perhaps as much as two years or more for the fundamental value of the company to prove itself in terms of price appreciation and dividend payments. He realizes that his market decisions are subject to the actions of all the other types of investors, but he feels confident that his prudent and rational analysis of the facts at hand will survive the whims and flutters caused by other types of investors.

The fundamentalist knows that there's no such thing as a sure thing in the stock market, but is willing to take the time necessary to find the best things available. He'll analyze profit and loss statements, dividend payment records, the amount the company has earned on its invested capital, profit margins, the ratio of the company's assets to its liabilities and debts, and what the trends are in the company's overall performance over recent years. He'll have studied the industry as a whole to determine if it is healthy or failing, and whether or not it appears to have a chance to grow at a more rapid rate than the economy as a whole. He'll shun advice from tipsters. He won't play hunches, he won't let sentimentality get the best of him. And he won't subscribe to any theories that are not rooted in accurate financial analysis of the companies he's considering investing in.

the prudent investor
The prudent investor is the fundamentalist-plus. Plus what? Perhaps plus a bit of technical analyst, for many of the analytical devices can be helpful in the fundamentalist approach. Perhaps also plus a tiny bit of the hunch player, for even the most prudent investor will occasionally need the intestinal fortitude that is second nature to the hunch player to survive unexpected turns for the worst. Further, the prudent investor will have most of the following attributes.

☐ He will have a firm, crystal clear understanding of his current financial situation, and of his overall investment objectives. He will convey this understanding to his stockbroker, and will make a joint commitment with the broker to stick with the stated objectives. If the prudent investor wants the benefit of the broker's expertise, he must give the broker proper instructions. Without that basic understanding between investor and broker, both may be groping in the dark. Periodically, with the broker's aid, the prudent investor will review his objectives, and will determine whether or not they are still reasonable in view of the unpredictable nature of the stock market. Can they still be obtained, and if so, at what potential risk? Or should the objectives be revised, particularly in light of changing financial circumstances?

☐ The prudent investor will clearly define his own role. Is he an investor or is he a trader? The investor, broadly speaking, is putting his money to work and he's willing to let it do the job over the needed span of time. The trader is working his money and he must have the know-how to cope with weekly, daily, and hourly fluctuations and trends. A prudent investor can be a little bit of both, but to do so he must keep his more prudent investment funds and his more speculative trading funds strictly segregated. When the two start to mingle, objectives can get derailed swiftly.

☐ The prudent investor will do his homework. Investment decisions are ultimately the investor's, not the broker's. There are thousands of securities, no two alike, and no human being can keep track of the fine points of more than a few dozen at a time. A broker can give you the research tools and his own opinion, but the investor must reach his own conclusions. And sound conclusions require work.

☐ The prudent investor will avoid the natural quirk of human nature that leads one to want to recover losses as quickly as they may have occurred. This can lead an investor out of one speculative situation into another. When an unexpected loss occurs, it is time for research and cool thinking, not guessing games and gut reaction. Desire to recoup quickly can deter a prudent investor from basic objectives. It can turn one from an investor into a speculator, a role that might not be suitable.

☐ The prudent investor who finds himself holding a stock at a loss will ask himself: would it be consistent with his investment objectives to purchase that same stock today at its current price? If so, that may be a sign to continue holding the stock. If not, what other security would be more consistent with the stated investment objectives?

☐ The prudent investor will look back to learn from his past mistakes. Why did he buy or sell too soon or too late? Did he listen to a tip? Did he play a hunch? Did he panic? The ability to recognize one's own mistakes and benefit from them is a rare quality, one worth cultivating by the prudent investor if he doesn't already possess it.

☐ When a prudent investor invests in a stock, he will determine, at that time, when he will be likely to sell. He will set limits for himself, and will stick to them, barring unforeseen conditions that may dictate otherwise. He will have determined how much of a loss he's willing to take in order to acquire a certain gain. He'll be well acquainted with, and willing to abide by, that old maxim of the investment community: Take your profits when you can, and cut your losses when you can.

☐ The prudent investor will look at his gain objectives in the aggregate: considering both dividend income and appreciation in value. If his objectives for his investment portfolio are to grow by, say, 10% per year, such a goal might be far more attainable if he looked for a situation that will yield 5% in dividend income and the other 5% in growth.

☐ The prudent investor will be well aware of the value of a good night's sleep. Or, for that matter, of a good day's work. Distractions and frustrations caused by involvement in the stock market can detract one from one's own personal productivity and one's pleasures. Whatever gains an investor may be chasing, may not, under keen analysis, be worth it in terms of lost time and lost efficiency in other endeavors. In other words, if your involvement with your investment portfolio begins to interfere with your personal life, whatever gains you may achieve may not, in the long run, have been worth it.

☐ The prudent investor will not waste his time or his money chasing after systems that purport to "beat the market." There are none. And there aren't any books, brokers, newsletters, analysts, chartists, economists, or tipsters who know anything more about where the market is headed than you do. If there were, we'd have heard about them long before now.

basic stock market information

price quotations

The daily trading activity of all of the major stock exchanges is contained in fairly complete detail in the *Wall Street Journal* each day. A number of stocks will be traded on more than one exchange, and their listings will be contained generally in the larger exchange on which they're traded.

Many local daily newspapers also carry extensive listings, though many are abbreviated from the full listings used in the *Wall Street Journal*.

Here's what a sample New York Stock Exchange listing in the *Wall Street Journal* looks like.

—1976–77—		Stocks	Div.	P-E Ratio	Sales 100s	High	Low	Close	Net Chg.
High	Low								
36⅜	31⅜	ACF Ind	1.80	8	53	35¾	35¼	35¾+	½
4⅝	1⅞	AJ Ind		8	250	4½	4⅜	4½+	⅛
24⅜	17⅞	AMF	1.24	11	1617	23	22¾	23 +	¼
17⅜	12¾	APL Cp	1	5	39	14⅛	14	14	
60⅝	44⅝	ARASv	1.20	12	14	48	47¾	48 −	¼
33	12⅝	ASALtd	.80	. .	295	20¼	19¾	20⅛+	¼
11¾	7¼	ATOInc	.40	6	54	10½	10¼	10⅜	
55⅛	37¾	AbbtLab	1	14	416	44¼	42½	42⅞−	1⅛
13	8⅛	AcmeClv	.50	20	85	13¼	12⅞	13⅛+	⅛
4½	2⅝	AdmDg	.04	6	21	3¼	3⅛	3¼+	⅛
13¼	9⅞	AdmEx	1.15e	. .	46	12	11¾	11⅞−	⅛
5¾	3¾	AdmMill		8	5	4⅝	4½	4½	
14⅜	7¾	Addrssg	.10e	19	194	13⅝	13⅜	13½	
36¼	22½	AetnaLf	1.20	9	681	32	31⅜	31⅝−	⅜
53½	36¼	AetnaLf	pf 2	. .	5	49½	47½	47½−	2½
11¾	4⅜	Aguirre		13	10	11	10⅞	10⅞−	⅜
17	9⅝	Ahmans	.22	6	30	15⅞	15⅝	15⅝−	⅛
6⅞	2½	Aileen		68	27	3⅜	3¼	3⅜	
39¾	29⅝	AirProd	.20b	14	x246	31⅝	31⅛	31⅜+	½
15⅛	11	AirbnFrt	.60	12	40	14⅜	13¾	14 −	⅜
34⅜	17¼	Airco	1.15	7	59	32⅛	31¾	31⅞−	⅛
25¾	13⅜	Akzona	1.20	38	110	16⅞	16⅝	16⅞	
16⅞	13⅛	AlaGas	1.28	8	7	16⅝	16⅜	16⅝+	⅛
116	104½	AlaPw	pf 11	. .	z40	115	115	115 +	1½
104¾	89	AlaP	pf 9.44	. .	z210	104½	103	104½+	2½
19¾	11⅛	Alaskin	.60e	7	119	19¼	18¾	19¼+	⅜
21¾	14¾	Albanyin	.72	8	9	18¾	18¾	18¾+	¼
8⅝	5⅞	AlbertoC	.36	15	65	7⅛	6⅞	6⅞−	⅜
23⅞	17⅜	Albertsn	.72	10	12	22½	22¼	22½+	¼
30⅝	19⅛	AlcanAlu	.40	55	914	25⅛	24¾	24⅞+	⅛
21¼	14¾	AlcoStd	.80a	7	103	21¼	20⅝	21⅛+	¼
28	18⅜	AlconLb	.28	15	94	19¾	19	19¾+	¼
9¼	5½	Alexdrs	.36e	7	39	7	6⅞	6⅞−	⅛
13¾	7	AllegCp	.90e	16	42	13½	13¼	13⅜	

Let's examine the details more closely. The eighth listing is "AbbtLab," which stands for Abbott Laboratories, a major manufacturer of various health care products. Though Abbott Laboratories is traded on a number of exchanges, its listing is contained in the New York Stock Exchange listing. Its ticker symbol—a three letter abbreviation that all major exchange stocks carry for ease in relaying information—is ABT.

1976–1977 High/low. This listing indicates that during 1976 and into 1977, up to the date of this listing (January 26, 1977), Abbott Laboratories sold at a high of 55⅛ and a low of 37¾ per share, *before commissions*. Fractions, such as one-eighth and three-quarters, are used as an abbreviation to represent cents. One-eighth equals 12½¢, one-quarter equals 25¢, three-eighths equals 37½¢, one-half equals 50¢, five-eighths equals 62½¢, three-quarters equals 75¢, and seven-eighths equals 87½¢. Thus, the high trading price for Abbott Laboratories during the 1976–77 period was $55.125, and the low price was $37.75. Once a year is well under way—usually by February—the high/low quotation will reflect only the trading during that year. If an investor wants to learn what the high/low was for the previous year, he would have to dig back into previous listings or check with his broker.

Dividend (DIV). The dividend column indicates the rate of dividend paid, based on the most recent quarterly or semiannual dividend. It is not necessarily an indication of the dividend that will be paid in the future. Abbott Laboratories paid a dividend in the prior year of 1, which means $1 per share. An investor would have to dig more deeply to determine the likelihood of any company continuing its indicated rate of dividend for the foreseeable future. The *Wall Street Journal* listings do contain some explanatory notes that may bear on the regularity of dividend payments. You'll note, for example, that AdmEx shows a dividend of 1.15e and that Addressograph shows a dividend of .10e. A bit further down, you'll see that Air Products shows a dividend of .20b. The small e, according to the explanatory note, indicates that the dividend was "declared or paid in the preceeding twelve months," which could indicate that while that was the actual payment history, there may be reason to believe that it is not the normal regular expected dividend. the small b, according to the explanatory note, indicates that this was the "annual rate plus a stock dividend."

The full explanatory notes, as contained in the *Wall Street Journal*, are as follows.

Sales figures are unofficial.

Unless otherwise noted, rates of dividends in the foregoing table are annual disbursements based on the last quarterly or semi-annual declaration. Special or extra dividends or payments not designated as regular are identified in the following footnotes.

a—Also extra or extras. b—Annual rate plus stock dividend. c—Liquidating dividend. e—Declared or paid in preceding 12 months. i—Declared or paid after stock dividend or split up. j—Paid this year, dividend omitted, deferred or no action taken at last dividend meeting. k—Declared or paid this year, an accumulative issue with dividends in arrears. n—New issue. r—Declared or paid in preceding 12 months plus stock dividend. t—Paid in stock in preceding 12 months, estimated cash value on ex-dividend or ex-distribution date.

x—Ex-dividend or ex-rights. y—Ex-dividend and sales in full. z—Sales in full.

cld—Called. wd—When distributed. wi—When issued. ww—With warrants. xw—Without warrants. xdis—Exdistribution.

vj—In bankruptcy or receivership or being reorganized under the Bankruptcy Act, or securities assumed by such companies.

Year's high and low range does not include changes in latest day's trading.

Where a split or stock dividend amounting to 25 per cent or more has been paid the year's high-low range and dividend are shown for the new stock only.

Price earnings ratio (P-E Ratio). The price-earnings ratio is arrived at by simple arithmetic, but determining its meaning is a bit more mystic. The specific figure, which is 14 in the case of Abbott Laboratories, is the result of dividing the *price* per share of the stock by the *earnings* per share of the stock. If a company earned $1 million during a year, and it had 1 million shares of stock outstanding, its earnings per share would be $1. If that same stock were selling for $10 per share, its price-earnings ratio would be 10 to 1 ($10 market price to $1 worth of earnings), or simply 10.

The earnings referred to in the P-E ratio quotes are the actual latest available earnings or the best estimated earnings of the company for a one year period. The prudent investor will determine whether or not the P-E ratio reflects actual past earnings or estimated future earnings. If the ratio reflects actual earnings, it's a picture of reality. If it reflects future estimated earnings, one must gauge the accuracy of the estimate in order to determine the validity of the ratio itself.

For example, say that a stock is selling for $48 per share, and that its actual earnings for the past year were $3 per share. This would give it a P-E ratio of 16. Estimates of earnings for the forthcoming year are $4 per share. This would give the stock a P-E ratio of 12.

What does the P-E ratio mean? As with other stock market "indicators," it is, at best, a broad and general yardstick, essentially indicating the relative conservatism or speculation involved in a given stock. The lower the P-E ratio, the more conservative the investment, and the higher the P-E ratio, the more speculative. But note: this is only a broad general yardstick, and does not necessarily mean that a stock with a low P-E ratio will perform better or worse than one with a high P-E ratio. In the lower P-E brackets, investors are looking more closely at the true investment value of the stock: the actual earnings of the company.

Regarding some stocks, an investor may feel that their actual or currently projected earnings do not truly reflect the ultimate potential of the stock, or the ultimate potential of what other investors may be willing to pay for the stock. Based on this kind of optimism, they may be willing to pay far more for one stock than another, and as the price goes up, so does the P-E ratio. Thus, in the higher P-E brackets, investors are speculating not so much on what the company itself may truly earn, but on what other investors might be willing to bid for the stock.

Sales 100's. This indicates the amount of activity in the trading of the stock for the prior day. Abbott Laboratories shows 416 under this column, which means that a total of 41,600 shares were traded during the prior day. Market analysts will keep an eye on the sales volume of specific stocks, looking for the unusual. If a stock normally has a trading volume within a fairly close range from day to day, and suddenly there seems to be a great surge or a tapering off of activity, this could signal that something out of the ordinary might be happening with the value of the stock. Unfortunately, there's no way to know for sure what that happening might be, or whether it will have a plus or minus effect on the stock. If the stock seems to be moving upwards on heavy volume, it would indicate a high degree of buying interest—investors willing to take the plunge. On the other hand, if the stock moves downward in high volume trading, it would indicate a desire of investors to unload. The only problem is that you never know until it's too late whether you're getting on or off the rollercoaster at the right point.

High/low/close. These columns indicate the high, low, and closing prices per share for the previous day's trading. During the previous day, for example, Abbott Laboratories traded at a high of 44¼ ($44.25) and a low of 42½ ($42.50). It closed out the day at 42⅞ ($42.875). During that day a trader might have bought or sold at prices anywhere within that range.

Net change. Abbott Laboratories closed down 1⅛ ($1.125) from the close of the previous day. In other words, the value of the stock dropped by $1.125 per share from where it had been at its last trade on the prior trading day.

other published listings

More detailed information on specific stocks can be found in *Barron's*, a weekly newspaper, and in the stock guides published monthly and quarterly by Standard and Poor's and Moody's. *Barron's* is commonly available at newsstands, and the stock guides are available at brokerage firms and at most public libraries. The added information consists of historical high and low trading, dividend history and dividend payment dates, the financial status of the company, and a history of its earnings per share. The prudent investor will not rely simply on the daily newspaper quotation, but will make extensive use of these more detailed published statistics.

brokers quotations

Aided by computers, brokers at local brokerage firms are equipped with video terminals that can display up-to-the-second price fluctuations as well as detailed information on any given quoted stock. In addition, the "ticker tape," now computerized, flashes on a large screen each transaction for each stock that's sold on the respective exchanges.

stock market averages

"How's the market doing?"

"Up two."

Or, you may hear a news broadcaster report, "Market was down nine points today in heavy trading. Analysts attribute the decline to investors' concern over the impending automobile workers' strike."

the dow jones industrial average

What do these cryptic sayings mean? The statements "up two" and "down nine" refer to the daily fluctuations in the Dow Jones Industrial Averages, or DJIA. This is the oldest and most commonly referred to measurement of stock market prices. But it does not reflect the movements of all stocks; rather, it refers only to the movement of 30 major industrial stocks. The Dow Jones company, which publishes the *Wall Street Journal*, *Barron's*, and many other financial publications, has historically used these thirty major corporations to reflect the "essence" of the market as a whole. The average is arrived at by tallying the prices of the 30 stocks within the averages, and dividing the total by a divisor that takes into account previous stock splits and stock dividends. The divisor is changed from time to time as any of the companies within the group of thirty declares stock splits or stock dividends. Although other companies have devised more broad-based averages over the years, the DJIA has remained the favorite indicator of most investors.

Even though there are thousands of stocks traded in any given day, the 30 companies represented by the DJIA represent a major segment of American industry. These are the thirty stocks used in the DJIA.

Allied Chemical	Exxon	Owens-Illinois
Aluminum Co	General Electric	Proctor & Gamble
American Brands	General Foods	Sears Roebuck
American Can	General Motors	Standard Oil of Calif
American Telephone & Telegraph	Goodyear	Texaco
	Inco	Union Carbide
Bethlehem Steel	International Harvester	United Technologies
Chrysler	International Paper	US Steel
Du Pont	Johns-Manville	Westinghouse Electric
Eastman Kodak	Minnesota M&M	Woolworth
Esmark Inc		

Although on any given day hundreds of specific stocks may bound off in directions opposite to the DJIA, the market as a whole does tend to follow it because of the importance of its companies to the overall national economy. For example, Chrysler, Bethlehem Steel, General Motors, Goodyear, and U.S. Steel are among the 30 DJIA stocks. The advent of a possible automobile strike could mean curtailed profits for all of these companies. If the automotive industry falls on bad times, it's not just these major firms that will feel it—hundreds of smaller firms, whose stock may also be listed on the exchanges, may also suffer as a result. Firms that supply products and services to the steel, tire, and automobile makers will likely feel the result of a downturn in business. On the other hand, good times for the majors can reflect in optimistic projections for the minors as well, and the stocks could move accordingly.

Much of the movement of the DJIA is rooted in psychology: the fears and hopes of investors, and not so much in the realities of the company's profitability. Companies tally their earnings on a quarterly basis, thus reality might suggest that the true value of these companies would only fluctuate on a quarterly basis as their earnings are announced. That's not the case though. The averages fluctuate on a moment-to-moment basis, reflecting what investors think might be happening, as opposed to what is really happening. The magnetic power of the DJIA can thus affect stocks that really might not have any relationship to the thirty listed companies, pulling them down when they should be going up and vice versa.

In addition to the Dow Jones Industrial Average, there are two other Dow Jones averages: 20 transportation stocks for the transportation averages, and 15 utility stocks for the utility averages. These, respectively, reflect movements within those respective areas: transportation companies and utility companies.

standard and poor's stock price index

The Standard and Poor's Corporation maintains an index of 500 major corporations, of which 425 are industrials, 20 are railroads, and 50 are utilities. All of these stocks are listed on the New York Stock Exchange. Although the Standard and Poor's index represents a much broader spectrum of listed securities, it has not achieved the popularity of the DJIA. Moody's, the other company that lists ratings and statistical data on securities, also maintains an index of 125 industrial corporations listed on the New York Stock Exchange.

new york stock exchange common stock index

This index is maintained by the New York Stock Exchange itself and covers all of the common stocks listed on that exchange.

dividends

A dividend is that portion of a company's profit paid out to its owners, or stockholders. Dividends are commonly paid in cash, but in some instances a corporation may issue additional shares of stock as a form of dividend. This is known as a stock dividend, and the recipient of a stock dividend is free to sell these shares for cash, or retain the investment.

The value of a dividend is usually referred to as the "yield." The yield is the percentage return you're getting on your money, and it's figured very simply by dividing the stock's annual dividend by its price. If a stock is selling at $50 per share and it pays an annual dividend of $2 per share, its *apparent* yield is 4% (2 divided by 50 equals .04). We use the word *apparent* because the yield does not take into account the commission that you'll have to pay when you buy the stock or when you sell it. The commissions must be deducted from your return to come up with a more accurate yield figure.

Further, if you do not hold the stock for at least a full annual cycle, you won't receive the apparent yield. For example, say, the above stock paid its dividend quarterly on the first day of January, April, July, and October. It would pay 50¢ for each share four times a year, for a total of $2. If you bought the stock on January 2 and sold it during the subsequent December, you'd have received only three of the four dividend payments, or $1.50, even though you had held the stock for almost twelve full months. You would not have received the first dividend, payable on January 1, because you were not a "stockholder of record" on the date called for. In such a case, your yield would be only 3%, before the payment of both commissions.

Dividend payments are announced, or "declared," by the Board of Directors of the company at its regular meetings. Here's how it works: At their February meeting the Board of Directors of XYZ Company declares that they will pay a dividend on April 1 to stockholders "of record" as of March 5. If you are recorded on the books of the corporation as being a stockholder as of March 5, you'll be entitled to receive the April 1 dividend even though you sell your stock between March 5 and April 1. The reason for the time lag is to give the company enough time to get an accurate list of all its stockholders, in anticipation of the payment date, so that checks can be prepared and other necessary book work done.

ex-dividend date   What if, following the above example, you instructed your broker to buy XYZ stock on March 2. Would you be entitled to the dividend? Probably not. It usually takes four or five days from the time of an order until you are officially registered on the books of a corporation as an owner of the stock. Thus, the stock exchanges, in listing dividends payable on stocks, generally note that a stock is "ex-dividend" about four or five days prior to the *record* date. When a stock is quoted "ex-dividend," it means that if you buy the stock at that time you won't get the next dividend that has been declared by the company. Following along with the above example, XYZ might be quoted as "ex-dividend" on

March 1—five days before the record date. Anybody who buys the stock from March 1 onwards will not receive the dividend payable in April.

The prudent investor, particularly one bargaining for a known return on invested capital, will pay close attention to the history of dividend payments of any company that he's thinking of investing in. These records can be found in the Moody's and Standard and Poor's guides, or directly from the broker. Some companies have long histories of regular dividends, many of which increase periodically as earnings increase. Some companies pay no dividends, and other companies pay erratically. Companies that pay little or no or erratic dividends tend to fall more into the speculative category of investment. The steady dividend payers are more conservative.

Unlike the movement of a stock's price, which is subject to countless and often indefinable pressures, the dividend payment rate is generally well rooted in the company's earnings, and in its willingness to spread those earnings out among its stockholders. Earnings that are not distributed to stockholders are retained within the company (and are referred to as "retained earnings") for investment within the company itself. Those retained earnings may be used as a cushion against troublesome economic times, or to create new facilities that in turn can create new jobs and new products, which in turn can create additional earnings for stockholders.

commissions

Brokerage commissions are the fees received by brokerage firms for handling your transactions when you buy and sell stock. Prior to 1976, commission structures were quite uniform among all various major brokers. Pressure from the government to break up what was considered a form of price fixing resulted in a wider spectrum of commission charges, depending on such matters as the size of the transaction, the price of the stock, and the total volume of business a given investor does with the brokerage firm during the year. Further, since that time, a number of "discount" brokers have emerged on the scene, offering strictly the execution of orders, and not offering, as major firms do, the full range of research services, custodial services, and the like. The discount firms give the investor an opportunity to transact at lower commission structures. But many investors may feel more comfortable with the size and backup facilities of major firms.

Abuses exist in all industries, and the securities industry is no exception. Though rare, an abuse called "churning" does occur. Churning exists where a broker convinces an investor to continually buy and sell securities, with the net result being large commissions generated for the broker, to the possible detriment of the investor's account. Prudent investors will have committed themselves in all likelihood to ride with their investments for a protracted period of time, and likely will not succumb to the intrigues of churning, which demands frequent in and out trading.

long and short

When an investor buys stock, hoping for an increase in value as well as receipt of dividends, he or she is "buying long." This is the most common type of transaction, constituting the vast majority of all trades on the exchanges.

But what if an investor thinks a stock may go down in value? There is a technique called "selling short" that enables an investor to seek a profit because a stock declines in value.

Selling short is a sophisticated and risky transaction. Here's how it works. Let's say you think that XYZ, which is now selling at $10 per share, is due to slump in price. You want to "sell it short," or bet that it will decline.

In effect, you borrow 100 shares from your broker and you sell them on the open market at the $10 price. You now have $1000 cash in hand (before commissions) and you owe your broker 100 shares of XYZ.

If the stock then dipped to, say, $6 per share, you in effect buy 100 shares at the going market price, for $600, and return the 100 shares to your broker. You took in $1000, then paid out $600 so you're $400 ahead as a result—again, before commissions.

The broker will have obtained the "borrowed" stock usually from his firm's supply of customers' stock that they are holding. You, as the short seller, must have cash or unmargined stock in your account before you can initiate a short sale. This is to assure the broker that you have available funds to repay the stock you've borrowed from him, and those funds are effectively tied up during the life of the transaction.

The element of risk involved in short selling can be indeed frightening. On a regular, or long, transaction, your ultimate loss is limited. If you bought XYZ long at $10 per share, and XYZ goes bankrupt, you can only lose the $10 per share. That's it. It can't go any lower than zero.

But if you sell a stock short at $10 per share, and it goes up instead of down, your loss can run on indefinitely. Say you bought 100 shares short at $10, and then the stock runs up to $50 per share. If you wanted to get out then, you'd have to shell out $5000 to buy enough to pay back your broker the shares you owe him, for a net loss of $4000. If you decide to wait, hoping for a drop, and it goes up another $10 to $60 per share, your loss is even greater. Such run-ups may be rare, but the risk is there.

One further problem with selling short: If you're holding stock in a long position, you receive any dividends the stock pays. But if you're in a short position, you are obliged to pay the dividends to the broker since you technically owe him the stock itself. This can add to your losses or cut into your hoped for gains.

Prudent investors would not find themselves comfortable with short selling.

capital gains and losses

Property that is held for investment purposes, such as stocks and bonds, is considered as a "capital asset" under the Federal Income Tax laws. As such, it may be subject to special tax treatment when you realize a gain from the sale of such assets.

If you have owned such property, as stocks, for a long enough period of time, and you then sell it at a gain, that is considered a "long-term capital gain." For tax years beginning after December 31, 1977, the long-term holding period is one year. In other words, if you own a stock for at least one year before you sell it and you then have a gain on the sale, that gain is taxed at a lesser rate than your normal income tax rate would be. If you do not hold it for at least one year's time, it is considered a short-term situation. If a transaction does qualify for a long-term capital gains treatment, the tax on such a gain does not exceed 50% of the tax on ordinary income.

Prior to 1977, the long-term holding period had been six months. The Tax Reform Law of 1976 boosted the minimum holding period to nine months for 1977, and to twelve months commencing, as indicated, for the taxable year 1978 and onward. The net effect of this new longer holding period will theoretically reduce rapid turnover in stock holdings. In order to take advantage of the lower tax rate, the investor must hold the stock for a longer period of time. There was a great deal of argument over the extension of the holding period. The securities industry felt that it would detract from trading in the market; others felt that it would exert a more prudent influence on investors, and thus be more beneficial to more investors in the long run.

buying on margin

Buying on margin is a means of buying stock on credit. The rate of margin varies from time to time, depending on overall economic conditions throughout the nation and the condition of the stock market. The Federal Reserve Board sets the margin rate. If the margin rate is 40%, you can buy stock by putting up only 40% of the total purchase price. The remaining 60% you borrow from the broker using the stock as collateral for the loan. Say that XYZ is selling at $30 per share, and you wish to buy 100 shares. The margin rate at that time is 40%. You can thus buy $3000 worth of XYZ by putting up $1200 in cash and borrowing the remaining $1800 from the broker. Let's say further that at that time the interest rate that you'll pay your broker on the margin account is 10%, which means that during the course of the year you'll owe him $180 in interest on the $1800 margin loan.

If XYZ goes to $35 per share at the end of one year and you sell, you have realized a profit of $500, less the $180 in interest, for a net (before commissions) of $320. But you've only invested $1200 of your own cash at the outset, so your return of $320 is equivalent to a yield of 26.7% for the year, not counting commissions or dividends. If you had invested the full $3000 and realized a $500 gain, your rate of return would have been 16.7% before commissions. This is what's known as "leverage." The gain on a sale and the rate of return on the dividends are magnified by the fact that you have less of your own money at work for you.

However, margin buying can be very dangerous, particularly if the stock declines in value. If you had purchased XYZ normally—that is, unmargined—for $3000 and it had dipped to $25 per share, you'd have a loss of $500. But if you bought it on the margin account, your loss would be increased by the amount of interest you would have to pay on the loan. In the above example, your total loss would come to $680.

Another potential danger in buying on margin is the possibility of a "margin call." If the margin rate is 40%, as in the above example, you can buy stock by putting up 40% of the amount required. The broker loans you the other 60%. On the $3000 transaction, the broker will originally lend you the $1800 and you put up the other $1200. But in a margin arrangement, the amount of your loan with the broker may not exceed the margin level—in this case 60% of the value of the stock. If the stock should drop to $20 per share, or a total value of $2000, the maximum amount of loan that the broker would be willing to extend to you would therefore be $1200. Since your original loan from the broker was for $1800, he will, in such an event, call you to inform you that you have to reduce your loan from $1800 to $1200. In other words, you have to come up with fresh cash to keep your account solvent with the broker. This is what's known as a margin call, and if an investor isn't prepared to have the necessary cash in the event of a drop in the price of the stock, he ought not get involved in that kind of trading. In all, trading on margin can be a highly speculative form of investing.

stock splits and stock dividends

Occasionally a company will issue a stock dividend to its stockholders. This may be instead of or in addition to a cash dividend. For example, if a company declares a 10% stock dividend, it will give all of its stockholders one share of additional stock for each ten shares already owned. A 100% stock dividend means that stockholders will get one new share for every one already owned. In effect, this doubles the amount of shares of stock outstanding. Frequently, companies will continue to pay the same amount of dividend in dollars after a stock dividend. This has the effect of increasing the return to the investor because he has more shares of stock earning dividends for him.

A company will "split" its stock when it wishes to get more shares of stock out into the marketplace, and also perhaps to bring the price of the stock down into a more attractive range. For example, a two for one stock split means that you will end up owning two shares of stock for every one that you had owned originally. Thus, a two for one split is the same as a 100% stock dividend. Generally, though, when a stock is split, its price will be split accordingly as will its dividend. If a stock was selling for $50 per share and was paying a $2 per year dividend, it will, after a two for one split, probably sell for $25 per share, and the dividend will be $1 per share. Thus, on paper, your actual net worth as an owner of that stock will not necessarily have changed as a result of the split.

However, rumors of a stock split, followed by the actual split itself, will often tend to boost the value of a particular stock, for a split is generally taken as a sign of optimism. Often, however, there will be rumors of a split and the split does not occur. In such cases the value of the stock might spurt up on the word of the rumor, and then drop sharply back down when the split does not actually take place.

preferred stocks

Preferred stocks are often thought of as a mix of bonds and common stocks. Preferred stock is a separate class of stock from common stock, which has been the type under discussion until this point. If a company has bonds outstanding, the bondholders have to be paid before any dividends can be paid to any common stockholders. If a company also has preferred stock outstanding, the holders of the preferred stock also are entitled to preference over the common stockholders. This is the derivation of the name "preferred." In other words, if a corporation has bonds *and* preferred stock *and* common stock outstanding, the bond holders are first paid the interest due them, then the preferred stockholders are paid their dividends, then the common stockholders receive their dividends.

Preferred stock generally pays a higher rate of return on dividends than does common stock, and the preferred stock is less subject to fluctuation than the common stock.

Most preferred stocks are "cumulative." This means that unpaid dividends will accumulate and the preferred shareholders must be paid in full on all back unpaid dividends before common stockholders can be paid any of their dividends. For example, a company has preferred stock outstanding, on which it has set a fixed dividend rate of $3 per share. The dividend rate on its common stock has been $2 per share. The company runs into hard times and for three years pays no dividends. In the fourth year it realizes a healthy profit. Before common stockholders can receive any dividends, the preferred shareholders must be paid $9 for each of their shares for the back accumulated dividends that had not been paid.

Some preferred shares will have a "call price." This means that the company can redeem the preferred shares at a stated price. If the preferred should reach $28 per share and the call price is $25 per share, the owner will suffer a loss if the company does call, or redeem, the stock. If the call price is above the actual selling price, the owner is in no danger of losing, as long as the call price does remain above the selling price. An investor in preferred stock should always check to determine what call privileges do exist regarding the stock.

In stock listings, preferreds are indicated by a "PF" following the name of the company.

convertibles: bonds and preferred stocks

Convertibles are another hybrid form within the overall framework of the stock market. A convertible bond may be converted into shares of the company's common stock at an agreed on price. Similarly, convertible preferred stock may be converted into common stock at an agreed on price. Convertibles can offer an attractive mode for fixed-income investing with an opportunity to convert into a common stock if the common stock appears to be taking a promising move upwards. But because part of the price one pays for buying a convertible is at least indirectly related to the value of the underlying common stock, a plunge in the common stock can adversely affect the value of the convertible bond or preferred stock, perhaps to a greater degree than a nonconvertible bond might suffer. Convertibles are a sophisticated area of investing that require further study on the part of any interested student. Ample literature should be available from most stockbrokers.

warrants

On occasion, when a company is issuing a bond or preferred stock, it may offer "warrants" to purchasers of the bonds or preferred shares as an extra inducement to get them to invest. The warrant will entitle them to purchase shares of common stock at a fixed price for a set period of time. In other words, if the common stock is selling at $20 per share at the time the bonds or preferred shares are issued, the warrant might entitle the holder to acquire a share of common stock at $25. The issuing company will fix the life of the warrant, which may be a few months or a number of years.

Warrants are totally speculative. The owner of a warrant does not have any ownership in the corporation unless or until he or she exercises the warrant—that is, trades it in for the share of stock to which one is entitled. The owner of a warrant receives no dividends, and has no voting rights in the company.

Here's an example of how a warrant might work. If the warrant gives the holder the right to purchase a share of common stock at $25 per share, the warrant theoretically has no value whatsoever until the common stock is selling for over $25 per share. If the common stock rises to $27 per share, the warrant might then become worth $2 per share, or slightly more if the market is generally optimistic about the future of the common stock. In other words, one could buy a warrant for $2 per share, which would give him or her the right to buy the common stock at $25 per share. If such an investor felt that the stock, now selling at $27 per share, might go to $30 per share, the $2 investment in a warrant could indeed bear fruit if the stock did go to $30 per share, for the value of the warrant would rise accordingly. The investor would reap a $3 profit over and above the $2 investment. A warrant, in other words, enables an investor to partake in the comparable price rise potential of the common stock without investing all of the money needed for the common stock purchase. As in the above case, it would take $2500 to purchase 100 shares of the common stock outright, the warrant might be purchased for $1 or $2, depending on the price of the common stock.

The ultimate danger with warrants is that they expire at a fixed point. Once they expire, they are worthless. If the warrant never rises to the exercise price, or above the price at which you purchased, then your investment is totally and completely eliminated. Your loss is complete. Warrants represent a speculative level of trading, and the prudent investor would not normally be attracted to such modes.

rating the stocks

Like bonds, stocks are ranked and rated by both Standard and Poor's and Moody's. The explanation of the stock rankings by Standard and Poor's is not only informational, but also serves as a guide to the prudent investor in the quest to determine the relative values of investments within the broad selection available in the stock market. The Standard and Poor's explanation follows in its entirety (with emphasis by author) and deserves a careful reading and rereading.

Earnings and Dividend Rankings for Stocks. The relative "quality" of common stocks can not be measured, as is the quality of bonds, in terms of the degree of protection for principal and interest. Nevertheless, the investment process obviously involves the assessment of numerous factors—such as product and industry position, the multi-faceted aspects of managerial capability, corporate financial policy, and resources—that makes some common stocks more highly esteemed than others.

Earnings and dividend performance is the end result of the interplay of these factors, and thus over the long run the record of this performance has a considerable bearing on relative quality. **Growth and stability of earnings and dividends are therefore the key elements of Standard and Poor's common stock rankings,** which are designed to capsulize the nature of this record in a single symbol. The rankings, however, do not pretend to reflect all other factors, tangible and intangible, that also bear on stock quality.

The point of departure in arriving at these rankings is a computerized scoring system based on per share earnings and dividend records of the most recent ten years—a period long enough to measure significant time segments of secular growth, to capture indications of basic change in trend as they develop, and to encompass the full peak to peak range of the cycle. Basic scores are computed for earnings and dividends, then adjusted as indicated by a set of predetermined modifiers for growth, stability within long term trend, and cyclicality. Adjusted scores for earnings and dividends are then combined to yield the final score.

Further, the ranking system makes allowance for the fact that, in general, corporate size imparts certain recognized advantages from an investment standpoint. Conversely, minimum size limits (in terms of corporate sales volume) are set for the three highest rankings, but the system provides for making exceptions where the score reflects an outstanding earnings-dividend record.

The final score for each stock is measured against a scoring matrix determined by analysis of the scores of a large and representative sample of stocks. The range of scores in the array of this sample has been aligned with the following ladder of rankings:

A+	Highest
A	High
A−	Good
B+	Median
B	Speculative
B−	Highly Speculative
C	Marginal
D	In Reorganization

Standard and Poor's present policy is not to rank stocks of most finance oriented companies such as banks, insurance companies, etc., and stocks of foreign companies; these carry the three dot (...) designation. NR signifies no ranking because of insufficient data.

The positions as determined above may be modified in some instances by special considerations such as natural disasters, massive strikes, and nonrecurring accounting adjusments. And in the oil industry, for example, "cash flow" is taken into account to avoid distortions that might be caused by differences in accounting practices.

Because of the special impact of regulation on earnings and dividends of public utilities, special parameters have been devised for this group, and such factors as capital structure, operating rates, growth potential of service area, regulatory environment, and rate of return are considered.

These scorings are not to be confused with bond quality ratings which are arrived at by a necessarily altogether different approach. Additionally, they must not be used as market recommendations; a high score stock may at times be so over priced as to justify its sale, while a low score stock may be attractively priced for purchase. **Rankings based upon earnings and dividend records are no substitute for analysis. Nor are they quality ratings in the complete sense of the term. They can take into account potential effects of management changes, internal company policies not yet fully reflected in the earnings and dividend record, public relations standing, recent competitive shifts, and a host of other factors that may be relevant to investment status and decision.**

Preferred Stock Ratings. Quality ratings on preferred stocks are expressed by symbols like those used in rating bonds. They are independent of Standard and Poor's bond ratings, however, in the sense that they are not necessarily graduated downward from the ratings accorded the issuing company's debt. They represent **a considered judgment of the relative security of dividends but are not indicative of the protection of principal from market fluctuations.** These ratings are as follows:

AAA   Prime
AA   High Grade
A   Sound
BBB   Medium Grade
BB   Lower Grade
B   Speculative
C   Non-paying

dividend reinvestment plans

When companies pay their quarterly dividends, stockholders get checks directly from the company or from their broker. Many a well-intended investment program is often led astray by these relatively small checks that come in at quarterly intervals. There's often a temptation to spend rather than reinvest these sums, unlike in a savings account or a savings certificate where the interest is automatically credited to the account and goes to work automatically for the investor. That, as discussed in the section on fixed income investments, is the nature of compounding interest.

It is possible, in a sense, to obtain the same kind of compounding in the stock market. Many companies offer "dividend reinvestment plans" whereby the dividends, instead of being paid directly to the stockholder, are automatically invested in additional shares of the stock itself. If an investor does have faith in the stock over the long pull, and wishes to acquire additional shares at virtually no out-of-pocket cost and no effort, the dividend reinvestment plan is an ideal way to proceed. Of course, there's no way of knowing what the ultimate results of dividend reinvestment will be. If the stock increases in value, then the dividends as reinvested will continually increase in value. If the stock should decline in value, or if the dividends should be reduced, the dividend reinvestment plan may not prove to have been as fruitful as investing the money in a passbook savings account might have been. However, a dividend plan is worth considering by the prudent investor. Details on which companies offer these plans can be obtained from stockbrokers.

price and value: what can affect the worth of a stock?

The distinction between price and value is as important in the stock market as in any other form of commerce. A patch of barren land in the middle of the desert may sell at a very low price, say, $10 an acre, because it seems to have no value. But if there is oil underneath that patch of land, the value can be astronomically high, even though the price was very low.

On the other hand, that same barren patch may have absolutely no value—no oil or anything else hidden beneath it. But a fast talking pitchman can sell the land to a gullible investor, leading him to believe it is a future oil well, a future retirement villa, a potential gold mine, or whatever. In this case, the price may be astronomically high in comparison with the value.

In all of our normal acquisition of the goods we buy, we attempt to make sure that we're getting good value for the money we pay; that value and price are compatible.

In the stock market, we have to maintain the same vigil, for very easily the price and value of a stock can take off in opposite directions. We might speculate on a stock with little intrinsic value, but because of a speculative fever the price of the stock may jump and reap a bonanza. Or, we may invest in a stock with sturdy and dependable values only to find that a reverse form of speculation has condemned the stock to a severe plunge, and our money with it.

There are many factors that can have a direct effect on the *value* of a given stock; and there are many that can have a direct effect on the *price*, although those factors technically have no bearing on the underlying value.

The underlying value of a stock is related to the profitability of the company in selling its product and services to its customers. The essential factors involved are the expertise of management; the cost of its raw materials (which can be affected by weather conditions, labor costs, strikes, and delivery problems); the efficiency in producing its finished product from the raw materials (which can likewise be affected by the foregoing elements of labor, weather, and gremlins); and by the efficiency with which it delivers the finished product to the market, at a price and in a package the public is willing to accept.

Further, with a great many of our major companies now involved in international commerce, international factors must also be considered. These can include fluctuations in currencies between various nations, international politics, trade and tariff regulations, and the same unpredictability regarding weather and labor strife that we have in America, but compounded by the distance and difficulty in communicating between the various parties.

Following are some of the important elements that, although they do not affect the underlying value of the company, can have a distinct bearing on the *price* of the stock.

☐ When a new issue of a stock is being offered to the public, the level of persuasion exerted by the salesagents for the brokerage firms can have a bearing on the price of that issue for some time to come. If the market is receptive to a new issue, the price of the new issue may gravitate upwards and remain there for an extended period. If the market is cold to the agent's persuasions, or if the persuasions themselves are cold, the new issue may sink and remain depressed for an extended period of time.

☐ The general health and outlook of the national economy can give a boost to the market as a whole, and sometimes to specific stocks, or can have a depressing effect if the news is bad.

☐ Financial analysts periodically examine major listed companies to determine the true valuation of the company. But, financial analysts being human, they may see things worse or better than they really are. And management, also being human, might be tempted to exert subtle influences on the report of the financial analysts. The reports by the financial analysts are often reacted to vigorously by the investing public. Optimistic reports can have a positive effect on a stock, and pessimistic ones can have a depressing effect. The reports of financial analysts are far from infallible. In determining, or attempting to determine, the true underlying value of a company, they can, by even minor errors or misstatements, have a sharp effect on the actual price of the stock.

☐ A large investor, such as an institution, might be persuaded to make a substantial investment in a company. This could come about purely innocently; or it could come about because a high official in the company is a close friend or associate of a high official with the investing institution. A major investment could be a sign of optimism for other investors; on the other hand, if a major investor pulls out of a large situation, for whatever reason, this could be construed as a sign of pessimism. There's no way to know what might have persuaded a large investor to get involved or disengaged from a specific situation, but the large block of stock that changes hands is sure to affect the price, at least for a short term.

☐ One of the great imponderables is competition. The threat of formidable competition can have a depressant effect on the stock of a given company; the fading of competition can have a bouyant effect. The presence, or the absence, of competition may not truly affect the ultimate profitability of the company itself. But the public believes that *can* be the case; it can be, but is not necessarily so.

☐ The rumor mill is always a potentially troublesome source of information (or misinformation) that can affect the price of a stock. Wall Street is a tight little community, and word can get around very fast. In all likelihood, the day-to-day ebb and flow of rumors is perhaps one of the most prevalent forces in shaping the direction of the market.

stock option trading

Trading in stock options is a fairly new and fairly sophisticated form of investing, which can range from high speculative to staunchly conservative. Let's examine how trading in stock options works.

Stock in the XYZ company is currently trading at $41 per share. You have that gut feeling that it will rise to $45 per share in the months ahead, and you want to take a flyer on it. The normal way of making such an investment would be to buy the stock (we'll use round lots of 100 shares for example purposes) at $41, or $4100 for 100 shares. You then hope to sell out at $45 per share, or $4500 total, thus realizing a profit of $400 before commissions. Obviously, if XYZ goes to $50 per share, and you're still holding on, your profit before commissions will be $900, and so on.

On the other hand, should XYZ drop to $30 per share, you're sitting on a loss of $1100 should you decide to sell out then. Whatever the price fluctuations may be, you as an owner of the stock can hold on to it for as long as you care to, taking in the dividends as they are paid.

There's another way that you can speculate on a hoped for price rise in a stock. Rather than buy the stock itself, you can obtain the *right to buy the stock*, or an option. An option gives you the right to buy shares of a stock at an agreed on price for a specified amount of time.

buying options

For example, based on today's prices, you can obtain the right (an option) to buy 100 shares of XYZ at $45 per share for, say, the next sixty days. The price you pay for this privilege is called the "premium," and today's price indicates that the premium to buy an option on 100 shares of XYZ at $45 per share will cost you $2 per share, or a total premium of $200 for a round lot of 100 shares. The $45 per share—the price at which you can purchase—is called the "strike price." The option will last for a specified amount of time. When that time has expired, at the "expiration date," the right to buy the stock terminates. In other words, the option expires. (Remember: all prices referred to are before brokerage commissions.)

With XYZ now selling at $41 per share, you put out $200 for the right to buy it at $45 per share within the specified time limit. Now let's say that XYZ goes to $50 a share within a few months. The option that you bought gives you the right to buy at $45. You want to exercise your option so you inform your broker accordingly. In effect, you buy the 100 shares at $45 each and immediately turn around and sell them at the now going price of $50 each. Your profit is $500, less the $200 premium you paid to buy the option, or $300. That's on an investment of just $200. If you had bought the stock itself, you have had to put up $4100 to reap a profit of $900 when XYZ went to $50 per share. By dealing in the options, you put up only $200 and reaped a profit of $300. Your risk was vastly smaller, and your percentage reward was vastly higher.

Further, if you had bought the stock outright and it had plunged to $30 per share, or even lower, you would be sitting on a very substantial potential loss should you sell. But with the options, the most you can lose is the $200 premium that you paid. Thus, your risk of loss is far less.

Actually, the typical exercise of an option does not necessarily involve buying the stock and selling it at the higher price as indicated above. The commissions involved in such a transaction would be extremely expensive. The actual transaction involves just simply selling the option itself. It would have originally cost $200 and as the stock itself moved up, so would the price of the option to a level of about $500. That's how the $300 profit would be realized.

Although all of the foregoing may sound extremely attractive, it is nevertheless extremely risky. Why? Because unlike holding the stock itself, which you can do for as long as you care to, the option *will expire* on a certain date, after which it is *worthless*. In other words, it's a wasting asset. If the stock fails to rise to a price level that can generate a profit for you, you will lose all of your investment whether you wish to or not. If you own the stock and it takes a dip, you can wait it out as long as you like. Maybe it will recover, maybe it won't. But with the option, it does expire, terminate, cease to be.

Buying options is certainly not recommended for the cautious or conservative investor. But it's necessary to understand the buying of options in order to appreciate the other side of the coin, selling options (or "writing" options as it's called in the trade.)

selling, or writing, options

An option transaction, like a stock transaction, requires two parties: the buyer and the seller, or writer. Every time a speculator buys an option, as in the above case, a more conservative investor is selling an option. *Selling options can be a sound and secure way for owners of stocks to substantially increase their return, without increasing their risk.* Bear in mind that this statement refers to those people who already own those certain stocks whose options are traded. What about buying stocks so that you can sell options against them? This involves a greater degree of speculation, for you may choose a stock not basically compatible with your long-term objectives. But if you already own stock, and options are traded on that stock, the options trading market does offer opportunities that you might not now be taking advantage of.

Let's look at the position of a couple selling an option. They have owned XYZ stock for many years and had originally bought it at $35 per share. Through their local stock broker, they place an order to sell an option for 100 shares of XYZ at $45 per share. The premium is $200 and the expiration is sixty days hence. This is the match for the "buy" transaction described earlier.

The owners of XYZ *receive* the $200 premium, cash in hand (before commission). If the stock does rise above the $45 per share level, and the option is exercised, they will have to give up the stock at the $45 per share price. But they will have made a profit of $10 per share over what they had paid for it, plus the $200 premium for the option.

If the option is not exercised, they keep both the stock and the premium, and can sell another option all over again after the original one has expired. Let's say that XYZ stock pays an annual dividend of $1.50 per share, and that the option that's just been sold is not exercised, and the owners drop out of option trading for the rest of the year. In addition to their dividends of $150, they will have earned an extra $200. In effect, they will have more than doubled their return on the stock by this one transaction. If they write additional options during the year, they can improve their situation even more.

What are the risks? The major risk is not different regardless of whether or not they are writing options—will the basic stock rise or fall in value? As long as they own it, they're subject to that risk.

The only other risk is that they are limiting their profit potential. Although they had sold the XYZ option at $45, they were obliged to sell the stock at that price during the life of the option. If, say, XYZ had suddenly zoomed to $60 per share, the owners would not have been able to sell out and reap that larger profit. They would have had to sell the stock at $45, assuming that the option would have been exercised.

In other words, the option seller must be prepared to limit

profit potential in order to receive a known and assured gain. That's a risk that should be more than acceptable to most prudent investors.

Not all stocks are traded on the options exchanges. Most of the stocks that make up the Dow Jones Industrial Averages are traded, plus a number of other popular issues. The options tables are carried daily in the *Wall Street Journal* and many major daily newspapers.

options quotations

Let's take a look at a typical quotation to see how it works:

	Jan.		April		July		N.Y.
	Vol.	Last	Vol.	Last	Vol.	Last	Close
XYZ 35	17	7	13	8	11	9	41
XYZ 40	22	3½	18	4½	17	5	41
XYZ 45	18	2	16	3	12	4	41

Here's what the listing means, assuming that we're now in late November. Look at the line that begins "XYZ 45." Under the January column you'll see a "Vol." or volume of 18 and a "last" of 2. This means that in yesterday's trading session the closing, or last, price for this particular option was $2 per share, or $200 per contract (100 shares in a contract). During that day, there was a trading volume of 18 contracts representing 1800 shares of XYZ. That particular option would expire next January. Options generally expire on the third Friday of each stated month, but there may be exceptions from time to time. Check with your broker concerning the specific expiration date of any given option.

This particular option would be referred to as "the January XYZ 45's."

Similarly, along the same XYZ 45 line, we see that the price for an option expiring next April closed at 3, or $300 for a 100 share contract. This option would be referred to as "the April XYZ 45's." The XYZ 45 expiring in July closed at 4 or $400 per 100 share contract. And the last column indicates that the closing price of the stock itself on the New York Stock Exchange the previous day was $41 per share.

As you can see, the owner of 100 shares of XYZ has many different choices as to which option he or she could sell. For example, the July 35's closed at 9. This means that the aforementioned owner, whose average cost for XYZ was $35, could sell the July 35's and realize a premium (cash in hand) of $900 for the 100 share lot. If the stock drops below the $35 level and the option is not exercised, they keep both the $900 and the stock. If the option is exercised, they must give it up at the $35 per share price.

Or, they could sell the January 45's for the $200 premium. In this case, although their premium is much less than with the July 35's, there is a much smaller chance that they'll have to give up the stock. It is now selling at $41 per share, and will have to rise above the $45 per share level by the January expiration date before a buy-out is likely to occur. If a buy-out does occur, though, at the $45 price, their gain will be $1200: $1000 on the basic increase in the value over their $35 per share cost plus the $200 on the option premium.

In reality, if a *buyer* pays $200 for the January 45's, he probably won't exercise his option unless the stock rises above $47 per share. He won't reap a profit until it passes that point, for in addition to the $45 stock price, he must cover the $2 per share option price, or a total of $47 per share. In other words, if the stock rises to $48 per share, and the option then presumably rises to $3, he will be able to reap a $100 profit. A buyer, though, *may* exercise his option if the price is between the $45 and the $47 range. If he doesn't exercise his option, he loses the whole $200. If he does exercise the option, he may be able to reduce the $200 loss to a lower level.

The above transactions illustrate the spectrum of choices open to the seller of options. They range from the big premium and the higher chance of having to give up the stock to a lower premium and a lower risk.

What if the owners want to minimize the chance of their having to give up their stock? They can just concentrate on the 45's. But which 45's should they sell? The Januarys for $200, the Aprils for $300, or the Julys for $400?

which option to sell?

Is the July deal the best, earning them twice the premium that the January will bring? Not necessarily. Again, assuming that we're in late November, the January deal will give them a $200 premium, which averages out to about $100 per month (late November to late January). The April deal will return $300, or an average of $60 per month over a five month period. And the July deal will return $400 or an average of $50 per month over an eight month span. (In addition to the premiums, which are received in a lump sum at the original transaction, the owners will continue to receive the dividends on their stock.)

If they sell the January option, they may have to make another transaction in January. If their stock has been taken away, they will have to reinvest their money. If their option was not exercised, they still own the stock and they can either sell another option for some future date, or they can just sit it out and not make any transaction.

Much of the decision as to which option to sell will be based on how active an investor may want to become in this kind of trading. As the above example illustrates, selling the January option means having to possibly make another transaction in two months. Selling the further out July option means that an investor can sit tight for eight months. The beginner might do better to go for the longer deal originally, so as to have more time to study and get the feel of the market before it's time to make a new decision.

"rolling over" options

What if you sold an option and the expiration date is nearing and chances look good that you'll be bought out and have to give up your stock? Perhaps you'll welcome being bought out so you can put your money into something else. This will mean paying a commission on the stock sale, and another commission if you buy more stock. Of, you may prefer to hold on to XYZ and avoid those commission costs. What can be done?

Here's another chart, date in mid-January, with the expiration date just a few days ahead (volume is not included).

	Jan. Last	April Last	July Last	N.Y. Close
XYZ 45	1	2	3	$46

This means that the stock of XYZ closed yesterday at $46 per share. You had sold someone else the right to buy your 100 shares at $45 per share, and that right will expire in a few days. It looks as though there's a good chance that that right may be exercised.

You may now want to "roll over" your position. To do so, you would *buy* a contract for the January 45's for $100, thus wiping out your obligation to give up your stock. Then you can turn around and sell another option for the July 45's for $300, thus netting another $200 in the process, again before commissions. In effect, it has cost you $100 to wipe out your obligation to give up your stock, and you have taken in another $300 by selling the July option for a net profit of $200. In so doing, the owners have now protected their position until July, and have gained another premium in the process as well as the continuing dividends.

The brokerage commission on a 100 share option contract will be much lower than the commission on a 100 share purchase or sale of the stock itself. Thus it can be more desirable to be trading in the options rather than in the stock. Bear in mind that if you do sell an option, and the option is exercised and you do have to give up the stock, you must pay a commission on that sale of the stock. Thus, the value of "rolling over" has to be examined in view of the necessary commissions that you'll pay if you give up the stock.

the options exchanges

If an investor owns stock whose options are traded, and that investor is committed to the stock for the long pull, it can make very good sense to consider selling options on them. For further homework on this subject, you should obtain and read the following: "Understanding Options" and "Option Writing Strategies," both available at no charge from your stockbroker or from the Chicago Board Options Exchange, LaSalle at Jackson, Chicago, Illinois 60604. You should also read the prospectus of the Options Clearing Corporation, available at no charge through the same sources.

mutual funds in the stock market

Stock market mutual funds pool the dollars of many small investors and place them in a broad portfolio of various stocks. There are hundreds of different stock mutual funds offering a wide variety of choices to the investor. There are "performance" funds, whose objective is to create as rapid a growth pattern as possible. These funds tend to be more speculative, taking chances on stocks that fund management sees as having a quick short-term potential rise. There are growth funds that are more geared to long-term steady growth, with a lesser emphasis on dividend income. There are income funds whose primary objective is to generate maximum current dividend income. And there are growth/income funds that attempt to achieve a balance between growth and income factors.

The primary task of the investor seeking mutual funds as a vehicle is to determine whether the fund's objectives are in line with his or her own: short-term growth, long-term growth, income, or a combination. These objectives are spelled out in the fund prospectus, which must be read prior to making any investment decision.

Once a group of appropriate funds is selected, the investor must then review all of the pertinent factors that can shape one's investment future: costs involved in buying into the fund, annual charges for management or maintenance, the history of the fund in meeting its stated objectives.

Sales costs (loading fees) vary considerably with stock mutual funds, from as much as 8½% of the investment to as little as zero (no load). Similarly, annual or monthly maintenance and management fees vary considerably. In many cases, the load funds (those without a sales charge) may charge a lesser annual fee than do the no-load funds, and proponents of the load funds claim that this difference over the long pull offsets the initial commission factor. Debate has ranged long and furious over which is better—load funds or no-load funds. Proponents of each side can find specific groups of funds over specific periods of time in which their viewpoint prevailed. There is no simple answer. Like the stock market itself, there's an element of speculation even in choosing one type of fund over another.

Mutual funds are quoted daily in the *Wall Street Journal* as well as in many local daily newspapers, weekly in *Barron's*, and annually in the "Mutual Fund Almanac," and *Forbes* magazine. *Forbes* devotes an entire issue (usually in August) to the mutual fund industry. It rates the funds based on their performance in general up and down markets, giving a perceptive analysis as to how various funds have performed during periods of boom and adversity. The *Forbes* analysis is perhaps the best available for the would-be mutual fund investor.

The daily listings of mutual funds quote the "net asset value" (NAV), the offering price, and the net asset value change. The net asset value of a mutual fund is the actual value per share. It's arrived at by dividing the total assets of the fund by the total number of shares outstanding. If a fund has $10 million in total assets, and 1 million shares outstanding, the net asset value per share will be $10.

The offering price is the price that an investor would have to pay for shares in a particular fund. If the fund is a no-load fund, "N.L." will be indicated in the offering price. If the fund is a load fund, the offering price will be higher than the net asset value price, with the difference being the commission charges. For example, a fund may show a net asset value (NAV) of $12.68, and an offering price of $13.86. The investor pays $13.86 for each share, currently carrying an actual market value of $12.68. The difference of $1.18 represents the loading charge. $1.18 is 8½% of $13.86. In other words, this fund carries a loading charge of 8½%.

Another fund shows a net asset value of $7.70 and an offering price of $8.28. The 58¢ difference is the loading charge, which is equal to 7% of the dollars invested. A no-load fund will sell at the same price per share as the net asset value.

Mutual funds have had a spotty history. They reached the peak of their popularity in the mid and late 1960s, during years when the stock market was generally moving upwards. A number of "performance" funds performed spectacularly during those years, some of them doubling, tripling, and quadrupling investors' money within very short periods. This caught the public attention and many other more conservatively oriented funds began to try to match these performance records in order to attract investor dollars. Investors who had thought they were embarking on relatively conservative courses found their fund management deviating from initial objectives. Those were the years of the "performance cult," and the performance funds became known as "go-go funds." Investors poured their money by the billions into these funds, persuaded by convincing sales pitches that made it seem the funds would go up forever, that there was no end in sight. But there was an end, and it came rather suddenly in 1969–1970 when the stock market went into a severe tumble and with it most of the mutual funds. Many investors had just gotten in at the tail end, and they were the hardest hit, watching their investments dwindle rapidly as the market plunge continued.

The problem was compounded when large numbers of investors began to cash in their shares rather than suffer further losses. When an investor sells shares of stock owned individually, he or she sells to another willing buyer. But when a mutual fund shareholder wants to cash in shares, the mutual fund is obliged to buy them back directly from the investor. Thus, the mutual fund must have cash on hand to redeem shares. If they don't have adequate reserves, they may have to sell off some of their existing stockholdings in order to generate the cash. The surge of redemptions, or cash-ins, following the market decline in 1969–1970 made it necessary for a great many funds to sell off stockholdings at severe losses. As the assets of the fund thus dwindled due to redemptions by investors, the funds were unable to generate new investments when the market began to move upwards again in 1971–1972. Throughout the mutual fund industry as a whole, monthly redemptions (cash-ins) begain to exceed new sales with regularity. For a period of twenty consecutive months, from early 1975 until late 1976, the mutual fund industry had an excess of redemptions over sales every month.

Perhaps the biggest disappointment in the mutual fund industry arose as a result of a feeling by investors that they were paying a fee to have their money professionally managed, whether that fee was in the initial commission charge or in the annual maintenance charges. If an investor buys stocks individually and loses, he can only blame himself and perhaps his broker. But when an investor is led to believe that professional management firms are handling his nest egg, and for a not inconsiderable fee, he casts the blame directly on the fund management during adverse times. And disappointment and word of mouth are quick to spread.

The concept of the mutual fund is a valid one, and there are ample numbers of sound management firms that can handle the public's money effectively. Mistakes have been made by both the public and the mutual fund managers, and more mistakes will happen in the future. But if all parties have learned from their previous errors, the mutual fund as a constructive means of achieving objectives can still be a valuable investment alternative for many individuals and families. Careful study must be done, and each investor must be wary of being "sold" whatever the salesagent is pitching.

choosing your broker: a guide through the investment jungle

All of the above dilemmas are difficult enough for the advanced investor to cope with, let alone the novice. The choice of the right broker can be an invaluable aid in helping to evaluate the various factors an investor is faced with. There is no assurance that the broker will know the truth or falsity of any given rumor, or will be able to evaluate the long-term implications of a new competitor entering the market or an old one leaving it. And a broker can't spend as much time on your account as you might want him to, for he does have other customers. But the good broker, wisely chosen, can direct you to sources of information that can assist you in making a proper decision, and can steer you away from detracting sources.

Choose your broker carefully, remembering at all times that you must make the ultimate decisions based on his recommendations and advice. A good broker can be a valuable ally in helping you meet your objectives, but only if you and the broker take the time to clearly state those objectives, and only if he then adheres in assisting you in meeting them.

Remember that a broker, with rare exception, earns his living by executing trades. He gets a commission on each trade, whether you're winning or losing. In other words, if he's going to eat, you've got to trade. If you invest a given sum of money in a given stock and instruct the broker to stash it away and forget about it for five or ten years and then tell him that's all the market investing you plan on doing, it's no wonder he wouldn't regard you as his favorite customer. Granted, he'll make his commission on your initial investment, and if he's still around when you cash in, he'll make another commission on the sale. But meanwhile your money is sitting idle as far as he's concerned, and he knows he's not going to make anything from you.

Naturally, any broker wants his customers to do well because this enhances his own professional image in the community, and each satisfied customer is like a walking, talking billboard. Many brokers can string along a losing customer for a period of time, blaming the continuing losses on market conditions, international news, and a variety of other factors beyond his control. True or not? It depends. There are indeed many factors beyond the control of any brokerage firm; but there are also many that could work to the broker's advantage yet are overlooked.

The broker may not be keeping close enough tabs on all of his customers' various accounts, and may neglect to advise you to buy or sell at the best possible time. He may be too prone to listening to unfounded rumors and passing them along to his customers. He may not be making adequate use of research materials available in his firm and through other sources. He may be spending too much time hustling and too little time learning. And because there have been all too many lean periods for the brokerage industry in recent years, he may be so worried about where his next meal is coming from that he neglects the application of his own expertise to his customers' needs.

Consider these criteria in choosing your broker: how closely his investment philosophy parallels yours; his reputation for integrity and hard work that you can learn from other customers who have used his services; the amount and continuity of his schooling, scholarship, and research; his willingness to spend time with you in learning or helping you to set your own goals, and the amount of time he will subsequently spend in seeking out the best means of achieving these goals; and finally, faith—something that can't be described, shopped for, or catalogued. It's just got to be there and you'll know it when it is or isn't.

Hope for the Best . . . But Prepare for the Worst

The employer has to learn how to get along with inflated wages that he must pay his workers. Consumers have to learn to get along with inflated prices passed along to them by the business executives who have to pay the higher wages to the workers who are the consumers. It's a vicious cycle that seems to know no end.

What goes up must come down

The investor, too, has a vicious cycle that he or she must learn to cope with. It's known as "inflated expectations," or, more simply, "what goes up, must come down."

Inflated expectations has to do with wearing rose-colored glasses, with believing what one wants to believe, with magnifying the good points and ignoring the bad ones. Nowhere is the inflated expectations syndrome more common and more dangerous than in the stock market. The witches' cauldron of hot tips bubbles incessantly and the bubbles magically seem to become crystal balls foretelling stupendous success. Or at least so we let ourselves think. How easily we believe that fortune lies ahead because our favorite company has just been awarded a major government contract, or has made a new discovery, or is about to unveil a new invention, or has just hired a golden genius away from the competition. And so on.

Ecstasy to nightmare

We don't stop to examine whether or not this new factor, if in fact true, can mean greater profits. Stories of ecstasy turned nightmare may be rare, but they are worth considering. One occurred not long ago in Australia where in 1969 a mining firm named Poseidon, Ltd. was muddling along digging things out of the ground, minding its own business, and its stock was selling for $1 per share. Then the Poseidon people came across a major discovery of nickel in the remote reaches of the western part of the continent. When word of the discovery got out, Poseidon's stock started to climb. Not climb, skyrocket. By early 1970, it had moved from $1 per share to $350 per share!

476

Inflated expectations abounded.

Then came a slight problem: getting the nickel out of the ground *profitably*. The next few years proved to be a horror story of ghastly proportions for Poseidon, Ltd. and its eager investors.

Even though the price of nickel (and thus Poseidon's potential profits) had more than doubled from $1.05 per pound in 1969 to $2.40 per pound in the mid 1970's; and even though the Australian government subsidized the effort with a $24.7 million loan; and even though they brought in the nation's largest nickel mining firm as an expert partner; Poseidon could not get the nickel out of the ground profitably.

In late 1976, with the stock back down under $1 per share, Poseidon gave up the ghost and announced that it would go into receivership.

A history of plunges

Similar stories are in evidence in the American stock market. The January 15, 1977, issue of *Forbes* recounts dozens of American companies plunging from the heights to the depths, as seen through the experiences of major shareholders.

A random sampling of those instances can illustrate the point.

Perhaps the biggest loser ever was H. Ross Perot, chairman of the Board of Electronic Data Systems, a stock traded on the New York Stock Exchange. In 1970 the stock was selling at $162 per share, and Perot owned close to 7½ million shares. His paper worth was then $1.2 billion. When the stock plunged to $16.50 per share, Perot's worth dropped to 10% of its former value, to $122.5 million. You may shed no tears for a man who still has paper worth that much money, but for anyone to lose over $1 billion in the stock market in half a decade a kindly "tsk-tsk" is at least in order.

Meanwhile, on the American Stock Exchange, the Chairman of the Board of Originala, Inc. owned 61,000 shares, selling at a high of $37 per share. The drop to $1.25 per share reduced the value of his paper from $2.25 million to $80,000.

And on the Over-the-Counter Market, the Chairman of Lion Country Safari, a chain of wild life preserves and amusement parks, watched his holdings of $6.2 million plummet to $60,000 as the stock fell from $24.50 to 25¢ a share.

And the President and Chairman of the Board of Leisure Group, who together owned roughly a quarter of a million shares of that company, saw their worth drop from $8.5 million to $30,000, as the stock hit a low of 12.5¢ per share.

More popular major stocks tell similar stories. Over the last two decades, Polaroid Corporation has ranged from a high of $149.50 per share to a low of $10.25 per share; Avon Products ranged from a high of $140 per share to a low of $8.50 per share; Lockheed Aircraft, one of the nation's major defense suppliers, ranged from $73.87 to $2.75 per share; and such former major national industries as PennCentral, W. T. Grant, and Franklin National Bank went off the board altogether and into bankruptcy proceedings. Even the giant of them all, American Telephone and Telegraph, ranged from a high of $75 per share to a low of $39.62.

Many investors were fortunate enough to get in on the way up in these various stocks, and got out before the downturn occured. They no doubt have fond memories and perhaps fat bank accounts. But for every investor who *sold* at the peak, there was an investor *buying*, obviously anticipating still further rises.

All were bedazzled by inflated expectations. It's dangerous and often sad. Watch for it playing at a brokerage office near you.

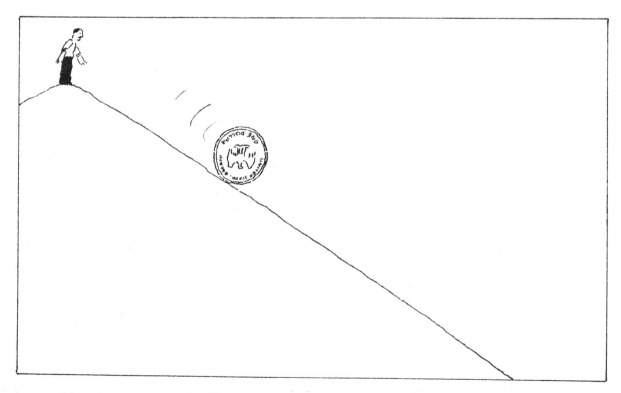

1. Who is the member of the stock exchange who matches orders to buy and sell stock and maintains an orderly market for the stock he or she represents?
2. What federal agency is responsible for supervising the trading in securities?
3. Name the document that discloses information about a corporation preparing to offer securities for sale.
4. What is the term for an order to sell common stock at a specific price?
5. Who are the large investors that trade in lots of thousands of shares?
6. What is an investor who has access to information about a company that has not been released to the public called?
7. What stock market investor is sometimes called a "chartist"?
8. What are some of the sources of information about mutual funds?

1. Karen and Scott Alvarez have decided to enter the stock market. In selecting stocks, they are going to use the fundamentalist approach. What are some of the factors they will be analyzing when selecting their stocks?
2. The securities industry has the Security Investors Protection Corporation. Discuss what losses would be covered by this insurance and what losses are not.
3. Jack and Sue Carlucci have made some nice progress in their financial affairs. They have their budget under control, and are starting an investment program in common stock. Their broker has suggested options. They have heard that this is risky, but their broker says it can be conservative. How can options be conservative?
4. Your friend Steve Hoffman has been investing in mutual funds. He has asked you about sales charges. Since he doesn't have any other information with him, show him how to find out what his sales charges are from the quotations in the newspaper. His three mutual funds are Dreyfus, Keystone S4, and Afuture.

chapter 13 **investing: other alternatives**

In addition to the basic fixed income techniques of savings accounts and bonds and the more speculative opportunities afforded in the stock market, there are other forms of investment that combine certain features of both fixed income and speculation, and have some unique features of their own. The various modes of investing in real estate are perhaps the most common forms of these mixed breeds, and they are discussed in detail in this chapter.

real estate

Real estate offers many attractive investment opportunities—but not without drawbacks, minor and major. Unlike fixed income investments, where large financial institutions are acting as custodians of your money, or the stock market, where large industrial corporations are working on your behalf, the field of real estate is much more personal. You, as the investor, will deal with other individuals, and will have to cope with their quirks, needs, demands, and their own financial ups and downs. Real estate can be very satisfying, offering ample opportunities for both income and growth. But because it is essentially a personal involvement, you must be prepared in advance for the gives and the takes that inevitably arise when dealing with tenants, maintenance and repair workers, building managers, mortgage loan officers, and the like.

There are four basic categories of real-estate related investment: income properties, vacant land, buying and selling houses and other properties, and investing in mortgages. For the small investor who wants to avoid the personal problems and still have a stake in a real estate investment, there is a form of mutual fund for real estate, commonly known as the Real Estate Investment Trust (REIT), discussed later in the chapter.

income-producing property

You purchase or construct a building and lease it to the best tenants you can find. They pay you an agreed on rental, and out of the rental income you pay the expenses on the building. What's left represents the return on your investment. In addition, you may be able to sell the building at some future point and realize a profit. Further, some of the income you receive is sheltered from federal income taxes because of a phenomenon known as the "depreciation deduction."

The following example illustrates most of the common facets of a real estate investment, including various forms of incomes, expenses, return on investment, and depreciation elements.

An investor buys a property consisting of two stores on the ground floor and four apartments on the upper floors, plus a parking lot for twenty cars. The total price for the property is $100,000, which is exactly the amount that the local assessor has appraised the property for at fair market value. The assessor further breaks down the property into land and building components valuing the land at $10,000 and the building at $90,000. The investor's sources of income on the property are as follows.

☐ The two stores each pay a monthly rental of $500 plus their own electricity and a share of the real estate tax. In addition, each store has agreed to pay an extra rental to the owner of 2% of their gross receipts in excess of $50,000 per year—this is known as a "percentage clause." (For example, if one of the stores does a gross volume during the year of $60,000, it will pay an annual additional $200 in added rental.) For the time being, the stores have not yet reached that $50,000-a-year-gross-income figure so their combined payment in monthly rental to the owner is $1000.

☐ Two of the apartments are unfurnished and they each rent for $200 per month. The tenants pay their own electricity and the owner provides the heat, as he does for the rest of the building.

☐ Two of the apartments are furnished and those bring a monthly rental of $250 each. The owner had previously owned the furniture in those apartments and allocates a total cost to the furniture of $2000.

☐ A space on one of the exterior walls is rented to an outdoor sign company that pays a monthly rental of $100.

☐ Ten of the parking spaces in the lot are reserved for tenants in the building. The other ten are rented at $10 per space per month for a total monthly rental of $100.

The owner's expenses are as follows. When he bought the building, he paid $36,000 in cash and obtained a mortgage of $64,000, which was set to run for 30 years and carried an annual interest rate of 9%. His total monthly payments are $515 or $6180 annually. During the first year of ownership, roughly $5700 of that total will go toward interest, with the balance of $480 applied to principal.

☐ Property taxes on the building total $5000 per year. However, the owner has a "tax stop" in all of his leases requiring the tenants to pay a stipulated share of any property taxes in excess of $4800 per year. In other words, the owner's total obligation for property taxes is $400 per month, or $4800 per year.

☐ Heating costs average $147 per month.

☐ Maintenance costs, including snow removal and minor repairs, average $100 per month.

☐ Repairs and replacements average $200 per month.

☐ Total costs for insurance are $200 per month.

☐ Because the owner is busy at his own job and doesn't want to be bothered with the day-to-day details of maintaining and operating the building, he has hired a management firm to whom he pays 6% of the monthly rental, or $138.

Here's how his income and expenses look in statement form.

Income

Two stores	@ $500 per month =	$1000
Two apartments (unfurnished)	@ $200 per month =	$ 400
Two apartments (furnished)	@ $250 per month =	$ 500
Outdoor sign	$100 per month =	$ 100
Ten parking spaces	@ $ 10 per month =	$ 100
Total Income		$2100

Expenses

Mortgage payment, including interest	$ 515
Taxes	$ 400
Utilities	$ 147
Maintenance	$ 100
Reserve and replacements	$ 200
Insurance	$ 200
Management fee	$ 138
Total Expenses	$1700

The owner, therefore, has a cash flow of $400 per month, or $4800 per year. Because he invested $36,000 in cash to purchase the building, his cash flow of $4800 represents a "cash flow return" of 13.3% on his invested capital.

Remember, though, that a portion of the owner's mortgage payment is applied to reducing his debt—$480 during the first year. Investors in real estate occasionally look at their rate of return as being the cash flow plus the debt reduction on the mortgage. If this owner figures in that manner, he would consider his true return to be the $4800 cash flow plus the $480 applied toward the reduction of his debt, or a total of $5280. This would represent a return of 14.7% per year on his invested capital of $36,000. However, because the equity portion is not "cash in hand" until the owner sells or refinances the building, this may not be a preferable way to represent the actual yield on the property.

For the complete story, we have to look at the effect of the real estate investment on the owner's tax return—that's where the depreciation deduction comes into play.

the depreciation deduction

Before the owner put money into the property, he had a taxable income of $20,000 per year. Filing a joint return with his wife, that meant a total federal income tax obligation of $4380.

Because the $480 worth of the mortgage payments that are applied toward principal do not technically count as deductible expenses for tax purposes, the owner reports net income on the building of $5280—the actual cash income of $4800, plus the amount of principal payment that is considered as an added investment.

If the investor had earned $5280 on a normally taxable investment, that amount, when added to the $20,000 base of taxable income, would boost total taxable income to $25,280, on which he would owe a total tax of $6121. In other words, actual cash flow of $4800 from the building investment would be reduced by the extra $1741 he'd have to pay in federal income taxes. Roughly 36% of the income received on the building would thus be taken by federal income taxes. His true cash flow, therefore, after federal income taxes, would be reduced to $3059, which would give him an ultimate true yield on his invested capital of about 8.5%. This would be further reduced by state or local income taxes where applicable.

However, federal tax laws now come to the aid of the real estate investor. These laws recognize that physical property, including buildings, machines, furniture, and so on, will depreciate in value over the years. In theory, the American economy will be aided if property owners are encouraged to replace the property as it supposedly wears out. For this reason, as well as to encourage new real estate construction, owners of real estate can deduct from their income taxes a certain measure of the property's value each year.

The Internal Revenue Service has determined that the particular type of building owned by this investor has a life use of 30 years. The investor's cost for the building was $90,000, based on the breakdown used by the local assessor's office. The land, which cost $10,000, is not deductible. From among the various methods available the investor decides to utilize what is known as the "straight line depreciation" method that enables him to divide the remaining life use of the building (30 years) into the total cost of the building ($90,000), giving an annual depreciation factor of $3000. Each year that he owns the building, he can take a tax deduction on his own income tax return of $3000 for depreciation on the building. This is not an actual out-of-pocket expense, but a mere paper entry permitted by the tax laws. In fact, the building may well be increasing in value. Nonetheless, the law makes these allowances and the investor is quick to take advantage of them.

In addition to the depreciation on the building, the investor is also permitted to depreciate the furniture. He had established a fair value on the furniture of $2000, and for the purposes of this example, the Internal Revenue Service has determined that the furniture has a remaining life use of five years. Thus, the investor can take an additional $400 in depreciation each year on the furniture.

His total annual depreciation for the building and the furniture is, then, $3400.

From his taxable income of $25,280 we deduct the depreciation items of $3400 and arrive at a new taxable income of $21,880. The federal income tax on that amount of taxable income would be $4982.

The net effect is this: the investor has taken in $4800 in cash, and has applied another $480 on a debt, which he ultimately hopes to recapture. The income taxes payable to the federal government have increased as a result of this income from $4380 to $4982. In other words, the owner has paid only $602 more in taxes than he previously had with his base taxable income of $20,000.

The true effect of the depreciation deduction is that the owner's actual cash flow of $4800 has created a net tax liability of $602. Reducing the $4800 by the $602 in taxes, the investor realizes a true cash flow of $4198, which amounts to an 11.67% return on the invested $36,000. This compares with the 8.5% return he would have received if all of that investment income was taxable, as opposed to being tax sheltered via the depreciation deduction. Table 13-1 outlines this transaction.

The above calculations represent only the first year of the investor's ownership. As each year goes by, the interest portion of his mortgage will get smaller and the principal portion will become larger, thus slightly altering the true yield on his actual investment. Further, the investor has not taken into account the possibility of vacancy factors in making his investment. The foregoing figures are based on 100% occupancy, which is a hoped for situation, but not always an actuality. Obviously, if the owner suffers some vacancies, income will go down but expenses may not go down proportionately. Further, the investor has to face the possibility that in later years the operating

table 13-1 **comparison of nonsheltered and sheltered (real estate) income tax implications**

Base taxable income (tax = $4,380)	$20,000
Nonsheltered extra income (fully taxable)	5,280
Total taxable income	25,280
Tax = $6,121 (extra tax due as a result of added	
nonsheltered income of $5,280 is $1,741)	
Base taxable income (tax = $4,380)	$20,000
Sheltered extra income $5,280	
3,400	
1,880	
Reportable extra taxable income	1,880
Total taxable income	21,880
Tax = $4,982 (extra tax due as a result of added sheltered	
income of $5,280 is $602)	

expenses on the building will increase, and he may not be able to increase rents to keep up with the increase in operating costs.

These factors add a measure of uncertainty to this or any other kind of real estate investment. But an astute landlord, coupled with a talented management firm, can anticipate many of the turns of events and plan to cope with them accordingly.

later effects of the depreciation deduction

The investor purchased the above property for $100,000 and owned it for ten years, taking an annual depreciation deduction of $3000. Let's say that he sold it after ten years for $150,000. During his ten years of ownership, the total depreciation deductions would be $30,000 (excluding furniture for the moment).

According to the tax laws, the investor's "cost basis" is reduced by the amount of depreciation he has taken during his ownership of the building. Therefore, on his sale, the difference between his "cost basis" ($100,000 cost less $30,000 depreciation or $70,000) and the selling price of $150,000 would be $80,000. That $80,000 is the taxable amount. Thus, while depreciation gives the real estate owner some benefits during the years of ownership, it can theoretically catch up with him on a subsequent sale. However, the depreciation benefits during ownership generally offset this other factor considerably. The sale at a profit would be taxed at capital gains rates if the property was held for the required time (one year, for taxable years beginning in 1978). Thus, he would pay an income tax at half the normal ordinary rates on the subsequent sale. Had he not taken the depreciation, he'd have to pay his taxes at the higher rate on each year's worth of income.

Further, the investor might not sell the building until after he has retired, and the profit could therefore be taxed at a much lower rate assuming that his taxable income had dropped accordingly. Or, the investor might not sell the building at all. He may make a gift of the building to his children, or he may pass it to them in his will. Ultimately, if they then sell the building, they'll have to pay the capital gains tax, but it's possible for a building to pass down through a few generations before it's ultimately sold and the tax is paid.

There's also the possibility that the building may actually decrease in value. Although this could cause a loss to the investor, it might also eliminate the problem of paying a tax on any gain. In the meantime, the owner still has the benefit of the annual depreciation deduction.

factors that can affect income-property investments

The possible variety of income-producing investments in real estate is infinite. Risks can range from exceptionally high to exceptionally low, depending on the many factors that can affect ownership, use, and resale potential of any given property.

the quality and type of tenants

In residential property, for example, consider the problems involved in an apartment complex that rents primarily to "the swinging single" crowd, particularly if it's in the vicinity of a university. An owner can expect a relatively high rate of turnover, and with each turnover comes the chance of a vacancy and the possible need to repaint and refurbish each apartment as it's vacated. On the other hand, an apartment complex catering to married couples or older persons might experience a relatively low rate of turnover, thus minimizing the chance for vacancies and the need for refurbishment. Applying the reward/risk rule, which relates as much to real estate as it does to any other form of investment, the properties with the higher chance of turnover and higher refurbishing costs should carry a proportionately higher rent than the more stable properties.

In commercial properties there is a broad spectrum of possible tenants that could occupy any given space, limited only by the landlord's willingness to accept certain types of tenants, and zoning ordinances that might control the usage permitted in certain locales. Consider, for example, the possible uses that can occur in a small neighborhood shopping center—a popular type of moderate real estate investment for small to medium-sized investors. A given space might be occupied by a business or professional firm, such as an insurance agency. It will have relatively little public traffic, and will need no special plumbing, electrical, or drainage installations. The same property might be occupied by a coffee shop or a tavern, which could have a high level of public traffic that can contribute to the more rapid deterioration of the premises; in addition, such installations need specialized plumbing, plus electrical and drainage connections that might not be suitable to other tenants who would want to occupy the space after the coffee shop or tavern moved out. Further, these uses could generate smoke and possible fire hazards that could increase the insurance rates on the building and of the adjoining tenants.

Two similar businesses, one new and one established, can have very different meanings to the landlord. The established business will have a seasoned clientele, and theoretically a more dependable credit history that the landlord should study in making rental decisions. Even though the owner of the new business may have good credit, he or she may be undercapitalized and unable to cover obligations during the usually difficult first two to three years of business. Thus, the landlord might face a vacancy far in advance of expectations. And, as in residential projects, commercial vacancies mean not only a temporary loss of rent, but the likely need to refurbish to make premises attractive to new would-be tenants.

The credit worthiness of a prospective tenant is not to be overlooked. When entering into a legitimate business venture, such as a lease, the landlord can and should check with the local credit bureau to determine the tenant's credit worthiness. A sloppy credit history might indicate a number of possible actions the landlord should consider: He might want to decline renting to that particular tenant altogether; he might feel the credit problems justify asking a higher rent; he might seek a co-signer to insure payment of the rent; he might request a substantial rental deposit, as well as a breakage and cleaning deposit, from the tenant to help assure that the rent will be paid or, if it isn't, that the landlord will at least be partly compensated for a period of vacancy that he might have to endure before he can rerent the premises.

A tenant who is tardy with rent can cause more than one problem. In addition to the headache and aggravation that the landlord must undergo in collecting overdue rent, the landlord might have to dip into his own funds to meet *his* monthly payments as they fall due. If the landlord has to borrow money to meet his own obligations on the building while awaiting past due rents, the interest cost for such borrowed funds can substantially eat into his return on the property itself.

the nature and
the quality of
the building

The potential risks and rewards for the landlord are directly related to the quality, location, and nature of the building itself. As in buying a house (Chapter 7), the would-be investor in income-producing real estate must pay explicit attention to all the various mechanical and structural details of the building. If not familiar with building construction, it would behoove the investor to hire a construction specialist to provide a detailed inspection and report on the building. A building with hidden defects can cause serious and costly problems for the unsuspecting landlord; one in good physical condition will keep risk at a minimum and cut down problems of maintenance, repairs, and replacements. Many investors in real estate are content to take the word of the seller or the real estate agent representing the seller concerning condition of the building. The more prudent investors will determine on their own, with professional assistants, that the building does meet the standards they are seeking.

Location is important to the would-be investor; one must determine whether or not traffic patterns or changes in adjoining neighborhoods can have an effect on the investment. An attractive gas station, motel, shopping center, or restaurant on a heavily trafficked thoroughfare might seem most appealing. But if a new highway diverts all the traffic away from the street, the result can be disastrous. A neighborhood shopping center might seem to offer attractive possibilities; but when a bigger and better shopping center is constructed a few blocks away the unaware investor may regret the day he signed his down-payment check.

There are several sources that the prudent investor can check to determine the continuity of the status of the proposed location. The local zoning map discloses what uses are permitted in which areas of the city. If adverse uses exist in close proximity, or could possibly exist, the investor should be forewarned. A visit with the local and state agencies that control traffic and highway patterns might reveal whether any changes in these patterns or street routings are anticipated. A check with local real estate firms might reveal new developments pending within the trading area of the subject property that could have either a good or bad effect on the investment.

The nature of the building must also be considered. Many buildings are limited by their size, shape, and type of construction in the uses to which they can be put. Food franchise buildings often fall into this category; they might prove very unadaptable to other uses should the original tenant move out. On the other hand, some buildings are easily converted to suit many different purposes. The more limited the use of a given building, the more difficult it may be to find tenants and maintain the level of investment return sought.

the tax base

The tax base is the aggregate of buildings (and their taxpayers) in a given community that provide the local real property tax payments that flow into the city coffers. Many cities have been having severe problems with their tax base in recent years; some are older with shrinking populations; others are in financial distress.

Before entering into any real estate investment, the prudent investor will visit with the local tax assessor to determine the recent history of property taxation in the community and the projected future. In order to properly evaluate the cash flow on a given investment situation, the investor must bear in mind the likely cost of property taxes over a relatively long term—or at least as long as he or she plans to own the building. An investor may be able to blunt rising taxes by requiring tenants to agree to a tax stop clause in their lease. But not all tenants will agree to such clauses, and in that case, the landlord will have to absorb the higher taxes and should be prepared in advance to do so.

utility costs

Before the energy crisis of the 1970s, little thought was given by real estate investors to the cost of electricity and fuel for heating. Those costs rarely changed from year to year and in cases where the landlord was responsible for electricity and heat the effect was relatively minimal. However, since the crisis, utility costs have been leaping upwards rapidly. Although it's difficult for anyone to predict what level the costs might ultimately reach, the prudent real estate investor must be ready for whatever comes.

A landlord obliged to provide utilities for tenants would thus do well to consider negotiating a "utility stop" clause in any new leases and lease renewals. This clause would provide that the landlord pay for utilities up to an agreed on amount; any usage of electricity or fuel over and above that amount is absorbed by the tenant. This not only offers some protection against rising utility costs, but also serves as a caution to the tenant not to be wasteful.

management of the property In the previous example of how a real estate deal works, the investor hired a management firm to take care of the day-do-day operation of the building. Management, in the overall sense, includes the leasing of premises when they become vacant, collection of rentals, supervision of repairs and maintenance as needed, maintaining good public relations with the tenants, and generally advising the owner about the needs of the property and the steps the owner can take to improve the investment.

A skilled property manager can be a very valuable ally for the real estate investor. In addition to day-to-day operations, a manager is in close touch with the general real estate market within the community, and might be able to spot potential tenants or buyers. A manager's experience helps detect the need for preventive maintenance that can avoid serious repair or replacement costs. And—perhaps most valuable—the manager absorbs the headaches inherent in real estate ownership: dealing with tenants, with repair and service personnel, with tax assessors and lawyers and accountants, and so on. In short, the property manager removes the personal problems from this type of investment and leaves the owner with a much more simple and clearcut situation.

One of the most serious mistakes made by real estate investors, particularly novices, is attempting to tackle management alone, without any outside professional assistance. Unlike those investments where your money is at work for you and there's not much you can do to change what's happening, real estate requires direct involvement. The efficiency of that involvement can make a bad deal good, or its lack can make a good deal turn bad.

A building owner must keep tenants happy, but not too

happy. A happy tenant will be more inclined to pay rent and other obligations promptly, as well as to renew a lease on favorable terms to the landlord. The tenant who is unhappy, perhaps because the landlord has reluctantly or improperly fulfilled his obligations, can make matters difficult during the term of his or her lease and is more likely to be looking for other quarters when renewal time rolls around. The tenant who is coddled and spoiled by an overindulgent landlord can find it easy to take advantage of the landlord, requesting more than may be legally due, and costing the landlord both time and money. A tenant may request the landlord to fix a leaky toilet when the lease clearly states that this is the tenant's obligation. But the tenant has not read the lease and is not aware of this. The landlord can do a number of things in response to such a request: he can tell the tenant to take care of the matter himself, in such a way that the tenant might be irritated at the manner in which he has been treated. Or the landlord could be cordial and proper about the matter, causing no rift and no dissatisfaction. Or, out of the goodness of his heart or from fear that the tenant might do further damage to the toilet, the landlord will fix it himself. The ultimate reaction of the tenant might depend on the mood the landlord happened to be in at the moment the tenant called. A property manager is geared to handle such matters in routine fashion, keeping in mind the welfare of all parties. There's less risk of irritation or of overindulging a tenant, when a professional intervenes.

In assuming the task of managing one's own property, the investor also must have a reasonably workable knowledge of how a building and all of its mechanical components function. When mechanical equipment fails or needs to be replaced, or when other work has to be done on a building, a good deal of comparison shopping, pricing, and evaluating may be in order. This can be very time-consuming, and a wrong decision may prove costly.

In addition to repair and replacement of the building and its components, the owner will be subjected to a continuing barrage of sales persons who offer a variety of products and services.

An owner will have to take the time to listen to the various sales people offering these products. Discerning the best buy for the money and the purpose is a task requiring experience and a sharp head for figures. A two year supply of fluorescent lightbulbs may be offered at a discount, and indeed might be an attractive purchase. But how will this affect the owner's cash flow if the bulbs have to be paid for in advance; what will it cost to store them until they're needed; are there better deals elsewhere? If the owner doesn't have the head or temperament for such matters, professional management would be recommended.

financing   The mechanics of financing income property are generally the same as financing one's own home. The investor (unless paying all cash) gives a down payment to the seller of the property and either assumes an existing mortgage or obtains a mortgage loan from outside sources.

But there the similarity fades, for the real estate investor must arrange financing geared to his or her investment objectives: obtaining a satisfactory return on invested capital. If the mortgage payments are so high that, when combined with the other expenses of operating the property, there is no cash flow available to the investor, one is involved in a totally speculative situation—hoping that someday the property will be sold at a substantial profit. Yet some investors may prefer to pay off any mortgage debt as rapidly as possible so that when the debt is finally eliminated, the cash flow on the property will be all that much greater.

But the prudent investor will seek a good return on invested capital (the cash down payment), and to that end will attempt to structure the mortgage so that there is adequate cash flow to meet objectives. Clauses in a mortgage that allow the lender to increase the interest, and thus the total monthly payment, can have an obvious effect on the investor's cash flow, and such clauses should be closely scrutinized. If there are interest rate escalation clauses, the owner will have to be prepared to adjust rents accordingly if he or she wants to maintain a constant rate of cash flow.

The real estate investor may also need large sums of money at indeterminate future dates in order to accomplish major renovations and repairs. If possible, the investor will negotiate with the mortgage lender to obtain such funds by adding them on to the existing mortgage, hopefully at favorable terms.

When a lender is considering a mortgage loan application on income property, he or she will examine not only the owner's credit worthiness, but the caliber of tenants that currently occupy the building. The owner's ability to make payments on the mortgage is, of course, directly related to the ability of the tenants to make their regular rental payments. The better the tenants, the more favorable terms the borrower should be able to negotiate with the lender. Better quality tenants will, as noted earlier, be able to bargain for a lower rental from the landlord. The landlord can make up this difference by seeking the most favorable terms on his mortgage payments.

the lease At the heart of any real estate investment is the lease: the agreement between the investor/owner and the tenant/user. Whether the property is commercial, residential, or a combination, the specific terms of the lease can have an important bearing on the investor's overall success. Residential leases tend to be shorter and simpler, usually running for a period of not more than one or two years. Commercial leases can be more complex, and because the property might be usable in many different ways by different tenants, a variety of clauses should be carefully considered by the investor. In either case, residential or commercial, the prudent investor will see to it that an attorney prepares a lease best suited to the investor's interests.

The following are some of the more important terms that should be evaluated, particularly in commercial leases.

length of the lease

How long should a lease run? One year? Five years? Ten years? If the tenant and landlord agree, negotiations should be relatively simple. If they disagree, someone will likely have to compromise. Is there any ideal length of time for a lease? Not really. As noted above, residential leases usually only run for one or two years, sometimes slightly longer. But for commercial leases it's quite a different story. The tenant will want to know that he or she has the right to use the property at a fixed rental rate for as long as the property is profitable. If it ceases to be profitable, for whatever reason, the tenant will probably want to depart. On the other hand, if the landlord feels the space could be rented out more profitably after the passage of time, he may wish to replace the tenant or increase the tenant's rental.

A preferred situation for a tenant would be to have a medium-term lease—say, three to five years—with options to renew at agreed on rentals. This offers the tenant both flexibility and fixed overhead. But this might not be to the landlord's advantage. By giving a tenant the privilege to renew, he is effectively taking the property off the market for the length of the original term and possibly the period of renewal.

Customarily, where renewal clauses exist, the tenant is obliged to give notice of intention to renew two or three months prior to the expiration of the lease. Technically, the landlord does not know until notice is given whether or not the space will be available after the expiration of the lease. The landlord can certainly make inquiry, but tenants are legally not obliged to express their intentions to renew or depart until the time stated in the lease agreement. Where there are no renewal privileges, the landlord knows exactly when he can expect the premises to be vacated, and can begin seeking new tenants with an assurance of when they can take occupancy. Or the landlord can renegotiate the lease with the existing tenant and hope that conditions will permit an equal or better rental on the renewal term.

The landlord should bear in mind that because a tenant has a right of renewal at an agreed on rental this does *not* guarantee that the tenant will pay that rental. Renewal date may roll around and the tenant may want to continue in the space, but at a reduced rental. This can put the landlord in a predicament, for he now has a relatively short period of time in which to try to find a better tenant for the premises. Working out such problems often comes down to nothing more than plain old hard-nosed bargaining, the outcome of which will generally depend on the condition of the local real estate market at that time. If there's a surplus of tenants looking for space, the landlord is in a better position and vice versa. There's no way of knowing what these conditions will be like years in advance, so the parties just have to be prepared to cope with the situation as it arises.

An alternative position—part way between a renewal option and no renewal option—is a lease with a *right of first refusal to renew.* Here's how such a clause might operate: the tenant is paying, say, $300 per month for a two year period. At the end of the two years, the tenant has a right of first refusal to renew the lease at $400 per month. During the initial two years, the landlord still has the right to offer the property to other potential tenants, but before he can lease it, he must allow the initial tenant to meet or beat any bona fide rental offered by another would-be tenant. The offer must be acted on within a specified period.

With six months to go before the end of the initial two years, the landlord finds a new tenant who is willing to pay $450 a month for the space. Before the landlord can make a deal with this tenant, he must first offer it back to his original tenant, who has, say, ten days in which to meet or beat the $450 offer. If the tenant wishes to equal the offer, the space is his for a renewal term. If not, the new tenant will take over the space at the expiration of the original term. If the landlord does not come up with any other bona fide offers, the original tenant can renew for the originally agreed on $400 per month.

This device offers a measure of protection to both parties. The landlord can still offer his property for rent to the highest bidder, subject to the tenant's rights, and the tenant has the ability to remain on the premises at a rental that should be in line with current market conditions, as they change.

Another important factor to consider concerning the length of a lease is that mortgage financing can depend on the term of the lease. A long-term lease—ten or more years—with a well-qualified tenant will be more attractive to a mortgage lender than a short-term one. The lender is obviously better protected on the longer term lease, assuming that the credit worthiness of the tenant meets the lender's standards otherwise. Thus, a landlord might have to offer a longer term than he otherwise might in order to satisfy the requirements of the mortgage lender and get the best financing terms available. All of these elements must be weighed and balanced before decisions are made, and before leases are signed.

the rental rate   In most cases, market conditions will determine the probable amount of rental a given tenant will pay. In commercial rentals, the rent is often expressed in terms of "per square foot per year." A space of 1000 square feet rents for $500 per month, or $6000 per year. The rental is thus quoted as $6 per square foot per year. In the jargon of real estate agents, it might be referred to as "$6 a foot."

Commercial rentals are also referred to as "gross" or "net." In a gross lease, the landlord is responsible for virtually all operating costs on the property, including real estate taxes, utilities, maintenance, cleaning, and generally servicing the premises. In a net lease, the tenant is responsible for most of these expenses. There is no precise definition of a gross lease or net lease, for circumstances and practices may differ from area to area, and one slight amendment to a lease can tend to change the definition of gross or net. But the jargon of the trade does refer to what's commonly called a "net-net-net" lease, which customarily requires the tenant to pay for absolutely everything, except for the owner's own mortgage payments.

In a gross lease situation, the landlord will receive a considerably higher monthly payment from the tenant. But out of that payment he has to meet all of his related expenses and obligations on the building. The landlord who wants a minimum of involvement in the operation of the building will prefer the most net lease he can get, preferably the net-net-net lease. Some tenants may prefer a net-net-net lease because they can more directly control the operating expenses on the building, and end up paying less money for their occupancy costs. Whether gross or net, someone does have to take care of the operation of the property, be it landlord or tenant, which will take time—an ultimate cost to somebody. A landlord with a net-net-net lease is less likely to need a property management firm than one with a gross lease.

Rental payments may be fixed for the term of the lease, or they may escalate upwards in line with rising prices, or simply by agreement between the parties. In addition to the basic flat rent, commercial leases often have percentage clauses, as illustrated in the earlier example of the combination commercial/ residential property. The existence and terms of a percentage rental clause are a matter of negotiation between the parties. If a landlord feels a particular business will prosper in his location, he may be willing to settle for a slightly lower base rent and a good percentage deal so that he can have his share in the prosperity of the business. If he has anticipated correctly, he may be far better off than he might have been with a flat rental. If he anticipates wrongly, he could be very sorry. A percentage lease with a new business can be highly speculative; one with an existing business might be more conservative, for the landlord can, and should, determine the volume of business the tenant has done in the past years. This should give a good indication of what he might be able to expect on a percentage lease. A percentage lease allows the landlord the right to look at the books and records of the tenant so that the correct amount of the percentage can be determined. The percentage clause would have to spell out this right explicitly.

use of the property   The lease stipulates the purposes for which the premises can be used by the tenant, or by any subtenants, if there is a right of sublease. If, for example, a tenant rents a store property for a retail shoe business, the landlord does not want the tenant, or a subtenant, to later change the premises to a tavern.

In addition, particularly in a multiple occupancy situation

such as a shopping center, the tenant may request a "noncom-petition" clause. This would prevent the landlord from allowing other spaces in the center to be rented to competitors. The landlord will have to evaluate such a request in light of current market conditions, his eagerness to rent the space, and the rent that the tenant is willing to pay.

repairs and restoration The lease should stipulate who is responsible for each and every kind of repair. Customarily, the tenants are responsible for making minor interior repairs, and the landlord is responsible for structural repairs and matters affecting mechanical equip-ment, such as the heating plant and the air conditioning unit. Of course, the parties can agree to any combination of who does what and who pays for what. A prudent landlord might prefer that the tenant pay for certain repairs, but that the landlord will see to the actual work. By so doing, the landlord can choose the firms to do the repair work, and might get a better level of satisfaction than by having the tenant make the choice.

A restoration clause is again subject to negotiation between the parties. This clause would require the tenant to restore the premise to its original condition at the time he or she first took occupancy. If tenants have made renovations within the prem-ises, they will have to see to it, at their own expense, that the property is brought back to its original condition unless the landlord later agrees otherwise. If a restoration clause is agreed on between the parties, it would be necessary for them to include a careful description of the premises at the time of the start of occupancy (including colored photographs as an added precaution) to assure that the amount of restoration needed is also agreed on.

default What if the tenant doesn't live up to the agreement? He or she may damage the property and not repair it. Or the tenant may leave in the middle of a lease and try to escape making further payments. The lease should clearly state that the tenant remains responsible for any default. But including such a clause within a lease does not necessarily mean that the tenant will automati-cally make good on a default. The landlord must still pursue his rights, through the courts if necessary, to gain satisfaction.

As a measure of protection against default, the prudent real estate investor will insist upon a rental deposit and breakage and damage deposit from a tenant. The rental deposit, usually designated as the last month's rent on the lease, assures that the landlord will at least have some cash in hand should the tenant skip. The breakage and damages deposit will protect the landlord to some extent in the event that the tenant neglects to make such repairs. But it should be clearly understood that the amount of the rental deposit and the breakage and damage deposit are not the limit of the tenant's obligation. He or she will still be obliged to make whatever payments are due over and above the amount of the deposits.

"compounding" your income in real estate investments

In fixed income investments your earned interest can be automatically reinvested in your account and go to work for you. This is known as compounding interest. The same ends can be accomplished in the stock market, either through a dividend reinvestment plan or a mutual fund that pumps your earnings back into additional shares of the fund. But can you "compound" your earnings in a real estate investment? In a sense, yes, at least to a certain extent. Prudent real estate investors realize that a portion of their income should be reinvested back into the property, by way of refurbishing and modernization. The net effect of this *should* be to generate higher income from tenants of the property.

It's not as simple or as automatic as the compounded interest on your savings account and it requires some expertise to know which dollars can generate additional rentals. The investor may prefer to take all income out and invest it in some other fashion, if in fact he or she is not spending it. But the investor should examine the possibilities of reinvesting the money back into the property before making an ultimate decision.

For example, a tenant might agree to an increase of $20 per month if the landlord repaints the premises. The paint job might cost $1000, but the landlord will be getting an additional $240 per year for the balance of the lease. That's a 24% return on the investment, which shouldn't be tossed off lightly. Other modes of refurbishing might be more or less profitable to the landlord, and much will depend on negotiations between landlord and tenant. The prudent investor will be continually on the alert for ways to increase income by plowing profits back into the property.

investing with partners in income property

Because so many real estate investments require a fairly substantial down payment, an individual might wish to seek partners on a particular venture. A $30,000 down payment on a building might be more than a single investor can stand, but if the individual has $10,000 available and can find two other partners with the same amount, he or she can become a one-third owner of a property.

Although partnership arrangements can make real estate investments more available to the smaller investor, there are obvious problems. All of the individuals involved must be firmly committed to the same long-term objectives. For example, investment partners must determine how much of the income will be pumped back into the property for refurbishing and modernization. They must agree on how much vacant space should be rented as vacancies occur. They must determine who will be responsible for managerial duties, bookkeeping, tenant relationships, and other personal matters. They must agree on how and by whom major repairs and replacements should be done.

If one partner wants to sell out, will he or she be required to first offer the share to the other partners, and, if so, on what terms? What kind of "vote" will it take to determine if the property should be sold? If the property should be refinanced?

The natural human tendancy is to not worry about such matters until they arise. This can be foolhardy, for nothing can stand between friends or business associates more distinctly than a disagreement over money. All possible items of dispute, particularly those noted above, should be reduced to a binding contract among the parties at the inception of the deal. A contract can't eliminate the disputes, but it can minimize them.

investing in vacant land

Investing in vacant, or raw, land can be one of the most extreme forms of speculation. We do hear of "killings" made in land by investors; and we hear statements, such as the one Will Rogers made, "You ought to buy land, cuz they ain't gonna print no more of it." But success in raw land investment, for the most part, remains the province of the skilled professional who has the expertise, the capital, and the selling skills needed to turn a profit most of the time. *Note* "most of the time." Even the skilled professional will have setbacks.

Other forms of investment pay a form of income to the investor—interest on fixed income investments, dividends on stocks, rentals on income properties. But raw land requires the investor to be constantly *paying out* money: real estate taxes, public liability insurance, and money for necessary signs and security. Further, the investor in raw land has put his or her capital beyond reach until the land is actually sold. It's extremely difficult to borrow against raw land, and if one does, then the interest expense has to be added to the other expenses.

An investment in raw land will usually take one of two forms. It may be land that you hope to use some day for your own purposes, such as for building a summer home, a retirement home, or a principal residence. Or, an investment in raw land may be for the purpose of a hoped for profit on a subsequent resale.

land for personal use

Buying land for future personal use can make sense as an investment if a number of criteria are met. If you are certain that you want to eventually build a particular type of home at a specific location; and if you are certain that the price you pay for the land today will be less than what you'll have to pay for it at some future point (considering the ongoing cost of owning the land as noted above); and if you are certain that the specific piece of land, or anything comparable to it, will not be available at the future date you plan on building, then it might be wise to put your money in the land today. If, in fact, your anticipations prove to have been correct—that at some future time you still do wish to build a home, the price of the lot has increased tremendously, and you wouldn't have been able to purchase anything comparable—then you may score a successful investment. But, if your building plans change, or if the land does not go up in price as you had thought it would, or if many other comparable lots are still available to you at a lesser price, then your investment may have been in vain.

"known" land

There's a much better chance for success in such an investment if you're dealing with known land—that is, land that exists in a community with which you're familiar, and on which you can get professional estimates from real estate professionals concerning probable future value. Known land also implies that you are certain of the availability of utilities, sewers, roadways, schools, shopping, and other necessary facilities.

"unknown" land

Uncounted millions of dollars are lost every year by people who sign contracts and checks to buy parcels of unknown land—generally, land in distant places that is being sold as part of a development program for the creation of a "new city," or a resort, or a retirement village. Although there are legitimate developments in all parts of the country, the abuses, intentional or otherwise, that have arisen have been all too frequent.

Anyone considering investing in raw land for future personal use, particularly if it's unknown land, must observe the following cautions.

see the land

It's necessary to actually view the land, and walk it from corner to corner, before you sign any documents. The majority of people who have been bilked on such deals haven't done this. Fancy brochures and high pressure sales pitches lead them to believe that they may be getting an idyllic lot in an ongoing development, when in fact they may be buying a barren patch of wasteland.

hire an attorney before you sign anything

The attorney should help you determine if the land you actually saw is the land you'll actually be buying. He or she will also scrutinize the other documents involved and will help you ascertain exactly what you can expect for the money you're paying. If you sign documents before you have had legal counsel, it may be too late for the attorney to help you. If you're planning on spending many thousands of dollars for a piece of land that you hope to use in the future, it's only prudent to make sure that you're actually getting what you're paying for, and an attorney is the proper party to give you that assurance.

read the property report

If a developer is selling land on an inter-state basis—to buyers in many states—federal law requires the provision to prospective buyers of a Property Report. The Property Report must contain certain information prescribed by the Interstate Land Sales Act, a federal law. If a developer fails to provide the Property Report within the prescribed time limits, the buyer might be entitled to revoke the contract and obtain a refund. However, many gullible buyers have signed receipts stating that they have received the Property Report within the prescribed time, when in fact they may not have.

Further, buyers have often been misled into believing that because the Property Report is required for federal law, the federal government has in effect made some form of approval of the property. Nothing could be further from the truth.

The following bold message is required by law to appear on

the Property Report:

This report is not a recommendation or endorsement of the offering herein by the Office of Interstate Land Sales Registration, nor has that office made an inspection of the property, nor passed upon the accuracy or adequacy of this report, or any promotional or advertising materials used by the seller.

That statement is crystal clear: the U.S. Government does *not* recommend, endorse, approve, or advocate the land being offered. It has *not* examined the property. It has *not* passed on the accuracy or adequacy of the Property Report or the promotional or advertising materials. Yet in spite of this, many gullible buyers continue to believe that the U.S. Government has, in some fashion, expressed its approval, and that therefore the investment is "safe."

The only protection that the government does offer is that if the developer has filed false or misleading information in the Property Report, he can be subject to penalties. Prior to the passage of the Interstate Land Sales Act, would-be investors had no such protection. Developers were not required to produce a Property Report, and whatever statements they made about the land were not subject to any scrutiny by the government.

A Property Report may contain information not contained in the sales pitch. In fact, it may contradict some information. One large land developer (large enough to have its stock traded on the American Stock Exchange) produced a slick movie as a selling tool for one of its developments. The following items were actually contained in the Property Report, but they were not presented in either the movie or the sales pitch that followed the movie. The reasons these items were not included in the sales pitch should be obvious.

1. "There are no recreational facilities currently available . . . other than green belt areas."
2. "At the present time, there is no garbage or trash collection service available."
3. "At present time there are no roads completed within the subdivision."
4. "Over and above the purchase price there will be an estimated fee of $500 for each lot when the water and sewer lines are installed and are available for use. Water will be

by private well at the expense of the purchaser . . . estimated completion cost to the purchaser is from $700 to $850."

5. "There are no bonds or escrows to insure completion of any of the facilities mentioned above."

6. "The nearest elementary school is almost ten miles away. The nearest medical facilities are over forty miles away. A small general store is three miles away, but the nearest major shopping center facilities are over forty miles away."

7. "As of the date of this report, there were only five mobile homes occupied on the development."

Those were the facts, as presented by the developer in the Property Report. Ample promises were made that all of the facilities would be completed, but the actual terms of the purchase contract raised even further doubts.

the contract

The ultimate investment is made when the contract is signed, and the clauses of that contract specifically spell out the investor's or buyer's rights and obligations, as well as those of the developer. The contract for the aforementioned property contained a number of troublesome clauses, outlined as follows.

1. The seller agrees to complete the streets and other improvements before the end of the year in which the payments are scheduled to be completed. Since the payments are scheduled to run for ten years, that means, in utter simplicity, that the seller is not obliged to install these improvements for up to ten years. Repeat, ten years. Even if the buyer pays up in advance.

2. The buyer does not get his deed until he has completed all of his payments, plus payments for water and sewer taps, which will be many hundreds of dollars extra.

3. If the buyer fails to make any payment within the specified time, the seller may terminate the contract, keep all of the money that the buyer has paid in, and resell the lot as if it were the seller's own.

4. If the seller defaults, they agree to refund all payments made to the buyer. However, the Property Report states that all of the buyer's payments go directly to the seller, and are not placed in any kind of escrow account. Thus, if the seller has spent the money that the buyer has paid, there may be no source out of which refunds can be paid.

5. The contract gives the buyer the right to transfer his paid-in equity to any other available lot of equal or greater value. This may be attractive on the surface, but beware of the arithmetic. The contract is talking about the buyer's *equity*, not total payments. In the early years of such a deal, the bulk of the buyer's payments is applied toward interest, and the actual equity is very low. And if, during those years, the price of the lots are boosted (justifiably or not), a transfer of existing equity is no privilege at all. The buyer may have gained virtually nothing.

6. By signing the contract, the buyer is acknowledging that he has received and examined the Property Report, whether or not he has actually done so. A buyer could thus be waiving certain rights regarding cancellation and refund.

In 1973, the Office of Interstate Land Sales Registration (a division of the Department of Housing and Urban Development) conducted extensive hearings in seventeen major cities throughout the nation. The purpose of the hearings was to determine the nature and extent of land sales abuses, so that the Office of Interstate Land Sales Registration could take appropriate steps to correct or prevent the abuses. At one such hearing, which went on for a marathon twelve hours, scores of property buyers stood in front of the Washington panel to air their gripes. Before they made their complaints, they were asked three simple questions by the chairman of the commission.

1. *Did you see the property before you signed the contract?* The virtually unanimous answer was "No."

2. *Did you read the Property Report before you signed the contract?* Again, the "nays" were virtually unanimous.

3. *Did you read the contract before you signed it?* And again, the answer was "no."

The chairman of the commission shook his head and expressed his dismay. "How can we protect the public, if the public doesn't take the obvious steps to protect itself?"

investing in land
seeking a future
profit
Here, too, we must consider the difference between known land and unknown land. All of the above cautions regarding unknown land bought for future personal use apply equally, if not moreso, to land purchased on the hope of a future profit on

resale. Indeed, many of the lots sold for personal use are sold with the following inducement: "Even if you never do decide to build on the lot, you can always sell it for a profit." This obvious appeal to everyone's greed has been eminently successful. Personal case histories abound of people who have bought such lots, vaguely anticipating that they might build a home on them some day, but with the principal motivation of "turning a quick profit" when enough years had passed. Their disappointment was immeasurable when they later learned they couldn't sell their land, or even give it away.

Regarding known land—land located within a community with which you're familiar and within which you can get expert appraisals and advice—there are additional cautions to follow if a successful investment program is to be realized.

appraisal

Success in a raw land investment depends on two critical decisions: the price you pay for the land, and the price you get when you sell. Before an investment is made, the prudent investor will obtain an appraisal on the land at its current market value, and at least a reasoned estimate as to its potential future worth.

The seller's asking *price* may or may not bear a resemblance to the current market *value*. Current market value is determined by the sale of comparable property, which can be put to comparable uses in comparable neighborhoods. A real estate agent or a professional appraiser can assist you in determining these facts. The professional can also advise you about the elements that may or may not contribute to the increase in value of the property, such as improving traffic patterns, increasing population trends, the stability of the tax base, the scarceness of such land for designated uses, and the attractiveness of the terms with which you can buy and later sell.

Many forms of speculative investment, particularly raw land, are subject to the operation of what's known as "Greater Fool Theory." The Greater Fool Theory states that if someone buys a piece of property at a given price, then at some later date, a greater fool than the original investor will come along and buy it from him or her at an even higher price. In times of a rising stock market and a rosy economy, the Greater Fool Theory has been known to operate with extremely high efficiency. But in times of stability or decline, the Greater Fool Theory is totally unreliable. The problem is that one never knows what times are ahead when one makes a major investment. The willingness to pay for, and make proper use of, available professional assistance in establishing an investment in land can negate the Greater Fool Theory.

the tests

If you buy a piece of raw land with the hope to sell it to someone at a profit, you have to consider the likelihood that that ultimate buyer will want to erect a building on the property. If he is a prudent buyer, he will want to be certain that the land is adequate for the use he intends. The buyer may thus require that certain tests be conducted on the land, and may expect you, as the owner/investor, to bear their costs. On the other hand, you as the owner/investor, anticipating the possibility of such necessary tests, may want to do them on your own well in advance. The availability of the appropriate test results might enhance your ability to sell the land. But the costs of the tests have to be taken into account.

The soil test determines the bearing capacity of the soil. In other words, how much of a building load can the soil withstand? The soil may be compact enough, and of the right composition, to support a small, one story cinder block or brick building, without needing any expensive footing or foundations. On the other hand, the soil may not be proper to support a multi-story building, without getting into expensive substructures.

The percolation tests determine the drainage capacity of the land—how much rainfall and moisture the land can absorb without turning into a swamp or a sea of mud. The condition of the ground in this respect can obviously have a bearing on the use of the land and the cost of constructing a building on the land.

the surveys

Although not technically tests, the boundary survey and the topographical survey will assure a would-be buyer/builder of the true boundaries of the property, and of the precise slopes that may exist on the property. If there is, for example, too much slope to the property, a prospective builder might be faced with expensive land moving costs, and those costs could be reflected in a price that a buyer is willing to pay for the property.

The prudent investor in raw land might deem it wise to have these tests made, even before making his purchase, so as to determine the ultimate usability of the property and/or the cost of making it most usable to most prospective buyers.

the dollars and cents

If a parcel of raw land doubles in price within the short space of five years, an investor might break even. Here's the arithmetic. Say that an investor pays $10,000 in cash for a piece of vacant land. He is foregoing a return on his money of, conservatively, $600 per year. That's how much he could have earned by simply investing the money in a savings certificate insured by the federal government. In addition, he may have the following typical expenses: property taxes, $500; insurance (mainly for public liability, to avoid lawsuits if anyone is hurt while crossing the property), $200; signs, advertising, and security, $200. (These figures are just rough estimates, but within the bounds of probability.) His total annual expenses (including lost interest) are thus $1500, or a total over five years of $7500.

Assume that five years later he is able to sell the property for $20,000. If he has used a real estate agent to find a buyer—which is likely—his commission to the real estate agent will be 10% of the selling price, or $2000. In addition, he'll probably have expenses related to the sale, particularly legal fees and recording costs that can easily total $500. His total expenses then are $10,000—$1500 per year for five years, or $7500, plus the $2500 at the time of sale. His selling price of $20,000 thus results in a net of $10,000. Over a five year span, the property has doubled in value and the investor has broken even.

This example may be pessimistic; but it's intended to provide a would-be investor the kind of "what if" arithmetic one faces before making a decision. The time to evaluate this very clear risk is before making any commitments to invest in raw land. Once the commitment is made, you can't get out of it as you could selling a share of stock or cashing in a savings certificate. You're stuck with it until a buyer comes along, and if that buyer isn't willing to meet your price, you may have to take whatever is offered. And the longer you hold on, the more it costs.

investing in buildings as a buyer/seller

Probably somewhat more speculative than higher quality income property investing, and probably less speculative than raw land investing is the purchase of existing homes for subsequent resale. It's a tricky business requiring expertise, hard work, and patience. But many small investors have found handsome profits in such endeavors, so that they have become semi-businesses, rather than just investment modes.

Many opportunities exist involving homes that need refurbishing, and these might prove particularly attractive to the investor with repair talents. Such talents will allow you to make reasonably accurate estimates of what renovations might be needed, how much they'll cost, and how much they can boost the potential selling price. A few hundred dollars wisely spent on paint or panelling or flooring, for example, could increase the potential selling price by a thousand dollars or more.

The overall procedure involves seeking out houses that have good underlying basic value, but can be bought for less than normal market conditions, perhaps because the owners have had financial difficulties and are anxious to get out.

The success of any venture will depend on the investor's ability to buy right and to finance right.

buying right

Buying right requires the careful evaluation of the neighborhood as well as of the physical structure itself. A run-down house in an area of better homes could command a handsome price if it's spruced up to be on a par with its surroundings. Another run-down house might offer little or no profit potential regardless of how much you do, because the general neighborhood isn't that desirable. Remember that your buyers are looking for location as well as a house itself, and the selling price is affected accordingly.

There are three major sources where an investor might find attractive situations. First, you can scout around privately for people who are hard pressed to sell, either because of time or money pressures. The more pressure on them, the better the deal you might strike. Word of mouth, or simply driving around looking for "for sale" signs are ways of discovering such opportunities. Advertising is another way. The seller may place a classified ad with a tipoff that indicates a good buy; or you, as the investor, can advertise under the "homes wanted" or similar classifications in the want ad pages.

A second source would be real estate agents in your area. Make it known to a number of them that you're in the market for such houses, and ask them to contact you if they spot any. Often, agents might be reluctant to take a listing on run-down houses from the seller, but if they know they have a possible buyer, they could put you on to a number of opportunities.

A third source would be banks and savings and loan institutions who have taken back properties on foreclosures, and who don't relish owning a lot of unused residential property. This possibility deserves particularly careful attention because you might well find a source of automatic financing when you sell.

financing right

If you've bought right, and if you've refurbished correctly, your chances of finding a willing buyer who will pay you the sought after profit will be greatly enhanced if you can offer the property fully financed. This means that a credit worthy buyer can step right into a mortgage situation for which you have made prior arrangements. In order to make such arrangements it will be necessary to develop a relationship with a mortgage lender, or lenders, in your community who will be willing to cooperate with you in such transactions. As part of the negotiations involved in setting up such a relationship, you may have to guarantee all or part of any given loan that is arranged on behalf of your buyer. Although this can improve your potential profitability in the sale of the house, it does put you on the hook for an extended period, and you should be particularly careful that the buyer pays an adequate down payment, and that his credit history justifies your assuming that possible risk. As noted earlier, many mortgage lenders in the community may have an inventory of used homes that they'd be willing to sell at attractive prices to investors willing to fix them up and offer them for resale. In such cases, they might be willing to cooperate in advance in making commitments for long-term financing to credit worthy buyers.

the profit margin

Perhaps the biggest challenge in this kind of investment is building enough of a profit margin into the deal to cover your initial expenses, as well as your continuing expenses, and yet not price the property out of the market. The investor must be well aware that once renovations are completed and the property is on the market, time can start working against him or her. Every month that goes by in which the house remains unsold means added costs—interest, taxes, insurance, advertising, and so on. As these costs mount, the investor, for lack of a buyer, might drop the price. As the expenses rise and the asking price drops, the investor might succumb to a feeling of panic. That's the worst danger. The difference between what you will pay out for the purchase, the renovations, and the continuing expenses and what you'll take in at the time of sale must be most carefully estimated.

Here, for example, is how such a deal might be structured, and what theoretically could become of it.

An investor/handyman finds a house for sale in a neighborhood with homes that generally sell in a range from $25,000 to $30,000. This one has been neglected and the owners are anxious to sell and move out. The investor/handyman makes an offer of $20,000, which the owners accept. He is to pay $5,000 in cash, and assume the balance on the existing mortgage of $15,000. He feels confident that if he puts in $2000 worth of carefully planned renovations, the house can be brought up to a par with the other homes in the neighborhood, and can be sold for $28,000. He makes arrangements with a local bank, pending approval of an ultimate buyer, for a mortgage of $23,000 running for thirty years and carrying a 9% interest rate.

The investor is therefore working on a potential profit margin of $6000, assuming he can sell the house immediately once the renovations have been completed. Here's the arithmetic: He will have taken in $28,000 ($5000 in cash down payment from the ultimate buyer and $23,000 from the bank on the mortgage loan). He will have paid out $22,000 (his $5000 down payment to the seller, $15,000 to pay off the old mortgage, and $2000 for the renovations).

If he does not sell the house immediately, his monthly expenses will be as follows: $185 on the mortgage, $65 for utilities and maintenance (for the house must be properly heated and cared for when it's not occupied to keep it in tip-top salable condition), $50 in real estate taxes and property insurance, and $100 per month in advertising expenses, which is what the investor estimates he'll have to spend to attract buyers. His total monthly outlay, therefore, comes to $400, which is what he'll have to spend each month until he finds a buyer.

Further, the investor is aware that a buyer might be brought to him by a real estate agent. In such a case, he would have to pay a commission equal to 6% of the selling price, for that's the going commission rate in his community at that time. In addition, he estimates that he'll have to spend an additional $500 in legal and related costs pertaining to the closing of the deal.

Here are three scenarios of what might happen to the investor/handyman.

1. He sells the house for the $28,000 asking price one month after he has completed the renovations. During that one month, his expenses have been $400. His apparent profit, then, is $5600. From that he deducts his selling costs of $500, giving him a profit of $5100. If he has sold through a real estate agent, the commission will be $1740, leaving him with a final net profit of $3360 (before payment of income taxes), a most attractive return on his investment.

2. Three months elapse with no buyer in sight. Concerned that his asking price may be too high, the investor drops the price to $27,000. He then finds a buyer. Reducing the price of $27,000 by the $1200 in accumulated monthly expenses, he shows a profit of $3800. Reducing this by the selling costs of $500 he stands to gain a total of $3300. But if he has had to pay a real estate commission (6% of $27,000 or $1620), he'll end up with a net profit of $1680. That's still a handsome return on his investment over a three month period.

3. Six months elapse with no buyers in sight. Particularly concerned now, the investor drops his asking price to $26,000, and a buyer is readily found. His monthly expenses have now totalled $2400, which leaves him with an apparent profit of $1600. (He took in $26,000, and paid $22,000 for the original purchase and renovations, plus an additional $2400 for monthly expenses). His $1600 apparent profit is reduced by the $500 selling costs, to $1100. If he has had to pay a real estate commission (6% of $26,000, or $1560), the payment of his real estate commission will leave him showing a net loss on the whole project of $460.

The ultimate catch is readily apparent: As time passes without a buyer, there's a natural inclination to drop the price. The combination of a lessened price and the added monthly costs can quickly erase the profit potential in such deals. A well-structured deal offers the opportunity for substantial profit if a buyer is found in the early months. But as time goes by, profitability rapidly erodes. This risk must be well considered by anyone investing in homes for resale purposes.

investing in mortgages

Technically, mortgages are not really real estate investments, but many people think of them as such. It falls more aptly into the fixed income category: you're actually buying someone else's IOU with a piece of real estate as security for the IOU. But because you could end up owning the real estate if the borrower defaults on the mortgage payments, it can, and perhaps should, be considered within the overall category of a real estate investment.

The prudent investor must scrutinize the value of the property itself as much as he must scrutinize the credit worthiness of the borrower. In effect, he or she must exercise the same precautions that a bank would in making an original mortgage loan: appraising the property, determining the credit status of the borrower, and seeing to it that there is adequate protection regarding title and property insurance. The assistance of an attorney is necessary for preparing all the required documents, and the cost of the legal service must be taken into account. It's not unusual in private mortgage investing for the costs of legal matters and related documentation to be passed along to the borrower. In addition, the private mortgage lender might be able to impose extra fees or "points" in much the same way that institutional lenders do.

Prior to becoming an investor in mortgages, it would be valuable to meet existing mortgage brokers in your community and determine what the current going prices and interest rates are. You might even, as a would-be investor in mortgages, prefer to deal through such brokers before you embark on your own. The mortgage brokers will, in effect, place your money for you in mortgage situations, and will take a fee for their service. Most communities have a number of private mortgage brokers who are always looking for funds that they can invest, content to take a service fee for their efforts. You can find them listed in the Yellow Pages of your telephone directory, and in the classified section of your newspaper, usually under the heading "Money to Loan."

A mortgage investment can take one of three forms.

"taking back" a mortgage

If you sell property that you own, and you agree to accept the buyer's IOU in full or partial payment thereof, this is commonly known as "taking back" a mortgage. The buyer of the property becomes obligated to you to make the monthly payments called for in the mortgage agreement. In recent years the common going rate for institutional mortgages has been in the 9% range. This has been generally much better than the typical yield an investor can get in savings accounts and certificates. However, many well-rated corporate bonds do offer yields comparable to going mortgage rates. Many people who sell their homes or business properties don't have immediate use for the full proceeds, and might prefer to let the money stay in the property as a form of investment.

initiating a new mortgage

This is very much like the above situation, except that instead of taking back a mortgage on a property that you own, you are making a new mortgage loan to an individual who is buying a different property. The interest rate, costs, and added fees that you as an investor can generate out of the deal are subject to negotiation between the parties. Some important cautions are in order, though, if the deal is to be structured to your best advantage.

First, you must determine why the individual is not able to obtain conventional financing through a normal lending institution. If it's because his or her credit status is weak, you might be asking for trouble. In such cases, you might be able to command a higher interest rate (subject to state usury laws) because you are taking on a higher than normal risk. Or, the property buyer may simply not have enough down payment to meet the requirements of the institution, even though the credit status is perfectly acceptable. This is a lesser risk, but one that you should evaluate nonetheless.

Or, an individual may find that you are offering better terms than the local institutions offer. For example, the current going rate at banks might be 9% and you might be willing to take back or grant a new mortgage at an 8½% interest rate. The bank might not be satisfied with that lower return, but you might be perfectly pleased with it.

Another caution must be noted regarding the term of the mortgage. Mortgages commonly can run for 20 to 30 years, and a large institution can absorb that long-term debt easily into its overall loan portfolio, for it has a substantial amount of short-term loans outstanding to balance off the long-term one with regard to cash flow. But you as an individual don't have that advantage, and a 20 to 30 year term might be far longer than you care to have your money tied up. To offset that problem, it is possible to structure the mortgage so that payments are based on a long-term payout, but you reserve the right to have the full balance come due at some much shorter point, perhaps five to ten years hence. This matter, too, is subject to negotiation between the parties. The borrower may not like the prospect of having to refinance at the end of five years, but may be willing to go along if there is no other choice or if, all things considered, it's still a better deal than can be gotten elsewhere.

Your documents should be structured so that the borrower (the property owner) cannot sell the property to another party without your express permission. For obvious reasons you would not want him to sell the property to a person whose credit status is unacceptable. You might permit him to do so on the condition that he remain liable for the debt in case the other party to whom he sold defaulted. A subsequent buyer of the house whose credit history is unacceptable may damage the premises in some way, or decrease its value, so as to jeopardize your investment.

In establishing the interest rate on a new mortgage or a "taken back" mortgage, you might also want to consider what many institutional lenders are doing: putting in clauses that permit them to alter the interest rate, when and if interest rates in general throughout the country change. This matter was discussed in more detail in Chapter 7, where it was described from the borrower's viewpoint. As a potential investor in mortgages, consider the same factors, but from the lender's viewpoint.

buying mortgages at "discount"

There's an active market in most communities in this type of investment. Here's how it works.

Fifteen years ago Miss Klein sold her house to Mr. Smith. As part of the payment, Miss Klein "took back" Mr. Smith's mortgage for $20,000. The mortgage was to run for 30 years, and it carried an interest rate of 6%, which was the going rate at that time. Mr. Smith has been making payments on the mortgage for fifteen years, and Miss Klein has been satisfied with the situation. But now Miss Klein feels she would like to get her cash out of the deal. She has asked Mr. Smith to pay off the remaining balance, but Mr. Smith doesn't have the cash on hand. Could Mr. Smith refinance the mortgage? Yes, he could, but he'd have to do so at the current going interest rate which now is 9%. Legally, Mr. Smith does not have to go through a refinancing. He's protected with the original interest rate of 6%.

How then can Miss Klein get some cash out of the deal? She can sell her mortgage to another investor, but probably for less than it's worth at its face. A mortgage investor in today's market would probably not be interested in buying the Smith mortgage, which now has a balance remaining on it of $14,200. Why not? Because the investor would only be getting a 6% return when out in the open market today he could easily obtain a 9% return. But a mortgage investor might be willing to buy the Smith mortgage at a discount, if it meant he or she could obtain a 9% return.

Over the next 15 years, Miss Klein will be receiving $14,200 in principal from the mortgage, plus interest based on a 6% figure. If she can sell the IOU to another investor for $11,800, that new investor will be getting a return of approximately 9% on the invested $11,800 over the next 15 years, with payments continuing at $120 per month. Mr. Smith will continue to make his payments as agreed, but the new investor, having bought the mortgage at a $2400 discount, will get the higher return. The higher return results from the 6% interest due on the mortgage itself, plus the additional $2400 ultimately received from Mr. Smith. The new investor has purchased the existing seasoned mortgage for $2400 less than its current face value, which is the same as a 17% discount.

Miss Klein has not gotten all of her money out, but has gotten a substantial amount of it. She may consider that it's well worth selling at a discount to have $11,800 cash in hand today compared with $14,200 spread over a 15 year period.

The amount of the discount on a transaction of this sort is subject to negotiation between the parties. The individual wishing to sell the mortgage will obviously want to do so at as small a discount as possible, whereas the investor will want a discount as large as possible. The investor will have to determine the credit worthiness of the property owner who's making the mortgage payments and will also have to carefully ascertain what defects might exist in the property itself and the result that these might have on the investment.

For example, if a seller of a mortgage offers a discount that seems "too good to be true," the investor might well be suspicious that there is a problem lurking somewheres. The borrower (the property owner) may be in severe financial straits, or the property may be in dilapidated condition. Further, the mortgage documents themselves should be examined closely to determine whether or not the owner has the right to sell the property with or without the permission of the new mortgage holder, whether or not there are any rights to call the full balance due, even if there is no default, and whether there are any rights to increase the interest rate on the mortgage. As with the other two types of mortgage investing, the service of an attorney is just as necessary in buying mortgages at a discount; and comparable attention must be paid to the credit worthiness of the debtor and the physical condition of the property.

return of principal

There's one catch in investing in mortgages investors are not always aware of. Each monthly check that you receive contains some interest and some of your own principal that you're getting back. In the previous example, Miss Klein was receiving $120 per month from Mr. Smith, at a time when the balance due on the mortgage was $14,200. This amount of $120 per month, or $1440 per year, actually equals about 10% of $14,200. Yet, as we noted, this was a 6% mortgage. The reason for the apparent discrepancy is that part of that $120 monthly payment represents interest, and the balance represents a return of principal. (See the section on mortgage financing to refresh your recollection on how this aspect of mortgages works.)

Thus, each month as you receive the payments, you have less and less of your original investment working for you, and unless you take steps each month to reinvest your principal, your ultimate investment won't generate as much money as you had thought it might.

Let's look at some examples, using a $10,000 lump sum for ease in figuring. This amount invested in a savings account paying 5% interest will grow to roughly $17,700 in 10 years. All of your principal is working for you all of the time, and the interest that it earns goes to work for you immediately, automatically, and without any expense or bother on your part.

Put that same $10,000 into a mortgage paying 7% and running for ten years. The monthly payments, rounded off, will be $116, or a total of $13,933 over ten full years. You're getting back your original $10,000 plus $3933 in interest over the ten years. If you do not reinvest each monthly payment as it comes in, that's all you end up with—$13,933. It's a far cry from what the savings account would earn.

Of course, if you don't reinvest each monthly payment as it comes in, you have that much more cash in hand to spend. But that may detract from your long-range objectives.

The basic problem is that it's difficult to find an investment vehicle where you can put the small monthly mortgage payments at a yield equal to what the basic mortgage itself is paying. Your original principal has gone to work for you, at, say, 9%. But as you receive each small piece of principal each month, you may not be able to put it back to work for more than say 5 or 6%. You are thus diluting the overall long-term yield. Lending institutions can avoid this problem because they are constantly reloaning all of the money as it comes in at the higher mortgage rates. But as an individual you can't do this that easily.

If you're dealing through a mortgage broker, he can pool all of his various investors' payments as they come in and put them back to work in new mortgages. This advantage may offset the fee that you have to pay for keeping your money at work for you at the highest possible yield. But, if you do deal with a broker, it's essential that you find a party whose investment and payment record is completely unsullied—one who will virtually guarantee your payments regardless of whether a loan goes bad. His or her reputation should be checked most strenuously before you get involved.

"mutual funds" for real estate investments

There are two ways that a small investor can pool his or her money with that of other small investors to get involved in real estate and take advantage of the depreciation laws discussed earlier.

syndication

The first of these is syndication. Usually, a promoter, or syndicator, will embark on a single major project such as an apartment complex or a shopping center. Shares will be parceled out in denominations of $5000, $10,000, and so on to small investors who wish to become involved in the project. The promoter will likely take a fee for efforts in organizing the syndicate, and may also share in the profits of the project. These syndicates are usually structured so that the promoters reserve to themselves all control over the management of the funds and the property, and the investors have no say in the matter.

real estate investment trusts (REITS)

These are specialized forms of investment programs set up under the federal tax laws to allow small investors access to the real estate investment market. An REIT is like a mutual fund. It will acquire a variety of properties, mortgage investments, and the like, and as long as it adheres to the Internal Revenue Service regulations, it can pass its profits, income, and depreciation deductions along to each investor. The REITs tend to be much larger and broader based than syndicates, which usually restricts their deals to one or a few individual properties. REITs are available in shares of stock, comparable to buying stock in a company itself.

problems with syndicates and REITs

Regretfully, during the money/energy/inflation crunch of the early and mid 1970s, many real estate syndicates and REITs ran into considerable difficulty. Some of them embarked on highly speculative ventures and ended up absorbing severe losses. Further, since REITs are sold in much the same manner as shares of stock, the value of the REITs are reflected not only by the income and profitability of the real estate that they own, but they're also subject to some extent to the whims of the stock market. Thus, in highly fluctuating stock market periods, the REITs lose much of their element of certainty for prudent investors.

By 1977 many of the nation's largest REITs had progressed all the way to receivership, and those that survived the hard times were struggling to gain back their prestige and profitability.

investing in small businesses

existing businesses

Many people will come across opportunities to invest in small local existing businesses, becoming involved either as a "silent partner," as an "active partner," or may actually buy a business outright and become sole proprietor. An existing business may be seeking fresh capital for expansion, renovation, or for the purchase of machinery or other equipment. The owner may prefer to seek private financing rather than bank financing so as to cut down on the interest cost. The owner might prefer to offer a share of the profits to an investor rather than be obliged to pay interest on a loan. Or, an owner may wish to sell all or a part of his interest for a variety of reasons. He may be anticipating retirement; he may be ill; he may just wish to move on to something else; or he might be trying to get out from under a bad situation.

In any of the above instances, a would-be investor in a going business must do extensive and detailed investigation, and will need the assistance of a lawyer and an accountant. Here is a checklist of matters that the prudent investor must examine with the aid of those professional assistants.

how will funds be used?

If the business is seeking funds for expansion, renovation, or new equipment, how will the funds specifically be put to use? What are the prospects of the new capital being able to generate added profits? Often, small businesses will overexpand, anticipating substantial additional business when little or none actually results. Or the cost of the expansion will be too great to permit increased profits. There's a high level of risk in such investments, and the would-be investor should turn to outside sources for help. The Small Business Administration office in your community can direct you to sources of information on specific types of businesses, how they function, and how profitable they might be. Such background information would be advisable for the prudent investor in any kind of business investment situation.

why is a business being sold?

If all or a part of a business is being sold, you must determine the reasons for the sale. Is it a genuine case of retirement, illness, dissatisfaction with an associate, or lack of a successor? Or is there some problem that might not be visible on the surface? With the aid of your accountant, you should examine at least three years of the business's operating statements, as well as three years of its federal and state income tax returns. You should attempt to trace the flow of income and expenses to determine whether you can spot any trends that could indicate danger ahead.

You should obtain a credit report on the business and on the principal owners to determine if they have been meeting their obligations. These obligations would include the payment to suppliers, lease payments, utilities, and taxes. If you spot any pattern of delinquency in meeting obligations, you might be looking at a danger sign. The pattern might indicate, for example, that the owner has been subsidizing the business out of his own pocket, and these subsidies might not show up in the business's operating statement. The owner may have considered such transactions to be private loans to himself, and may not have entered them in his books. Although you as a buyer would not necessarily have to repay those loans, you would find, in short order, that the business was not capable of maintaining itself without further subsidy from you.

Other reasons for selling a business might include threat of future competition. The owner may be aware of plans for a major shopping center near the retail outlet, and might want to sell out while the selling is good rather than risk being wiped out by the competition. Local realtors in the area might be familiar with such pending plans, and they could aid you in making your long-term projections concerning the future profitability of the business. In addition to competition, there are other developments that might affect your investment, such as changes in highway routings, nearby construction projects whose noise and dirt could be troublesome for an extended period of time, zoning changes that could permit uses of land and buildings near your premises that would be incompatible with your business.

If you're considering investing in a business that relies on a particular product for its success (such as a brand name item that the business may have a territorial exclusive on), determine whether or not that particular product will continue to be available to you, and if at a relatively predictable price.

Determine whether or not there are any claims or law suits pending against the business, such as tax liens, claims for refunds, law suits arising out of unpaid obligations, or damages suffered by individuals where there is no insurance to cover the cost.

Find out whether the business has maintained a good record with the local Better Business Bureau and any other consumer protection agencies in the community. You don't want to discover after the fact that a business has a bad public image, which can seriously detract from your investment. Determine whether the business has met all of its federal, state, and local government obligations including proper payment of federal and state withholding taxes, unemployment insurance taxes, workman's compensation insurance premiums, and all necessary filings regarding its business status with all appropriate agencies.

"good will"

If you will be replacing the existing owner in the day-to-day operation of the business, either totally or partially, you'll want to determine how much of the business's success (or lack thereof) may be due to the owner's presence. Does he, for example, have a large loyal following that may disappear when he is no longer there on a day-to-day basis? Such a situation could jeopardize your investment. On the other hand, you might be able to determine that the existing owner has a bad public image, and that by replacing him or her the business can actually improve, thus enhancing your investment.

the lease

Your attorney should review the lease on the premises to determine how well protected you are. How long does the lease run and what kind of renewal options do you have? What provisions are there for increases in the basic rent or in the cost of utilities, property taxes, and maintenance? To what extent will you be responsible for repairs? Will there be any percentage clauses requiring you to pay a portion of your gross business volume to the landlord as additional rent? If a landlord owns additional space, for example, in a shopping center, do you have any rights to expand into such space should you so desire, and if so, at what cost? Further, are you protected against the landlord allowing undue competition to rent space near you in the same center?

how much to pay for a going business

There are many elements to conjure with when determining how much of an investment is justifiable in an existing business situation. There is the hope for expanded profits as the business enlarges and improves in its efficiency. There is a hope for a profit on a later resale. There is the matter of a salary that one might gain from becoming active in the business situation.

But the ultimate question is: What kind of return will you get on your invested capital? The potential increased profits and the potential profit on a later sale are speculative, and the prudent investor will not be satisfied with mere hopes and promises. The question of a salary is not truly an investment concern. If you do earn a salary from becoming involved in the business, theoretically you'll be giving up some other form of earning to take over the tasks of running the business. Or, if you're moonlighting while retaining your existing work, you'll have increased your income as a result of your involvement. But you can always moonlight without making a substantial investment in an existing business situation.

Thus, the question of return on investment becomes all-important, and this can be arrived at, with the help of your accountant, by examining the books closely to determine how much money is left after all expenses, including the business's own taxes and any salary paid to you have been paid.

Depending on economic times, America's major corporations have an average return on invested capital per year ranging between 10 and 15%. If a local business investment doesn't generate at least 10%, you might do better to look elsewhere for a source of investing your funds. If the business promises a return of greater than 15%, there may be undue risks attached to the investment.

the legal documents   With the aid of your lawyer, you will enter into a contractual agreement with the seller or borrower. The contract will spell out all of the rights and obligations of the parties particularly regarding the ongoing management of the business. The contract will stipulate how any profits are to be split, and how any losses are to be made up. The contract should also give you protection if you later determine that the seller or borrower made misrepresentations to you about the business.

If, by becoming involved in the business, you are becoming liable for any of the business's debts, you should make arrangements with the creditors so that the extent of your obligation is clearly understood. You should also see to it that you are properly protected as an individual regarding the business's lease on its premises; and on all insurance policies relating to the operation of the business, including fire and public liability insurance. If the business provides group health, life, or other insurance, and if it provides a pension or profit-sharing plan, you should also see to it that all documents are in order to protect you to the extent that you and your associate have agreed on. These things will not take care of themselves. Many documents may have to be amended to assure that you are getting what you have bargained for, and what you're entitled to.

investing in a   Starting up a business from scratch, either on your own or
new business   through such means as a franchise arrangement, does not fall into the investment category at all. It's pure speculation. There can be no assurance whatsoever of your getting any kind of return on the money you put into such a situation. You could reap a bonanza, and you could go broke in short order.

Yet, many will regard such situations as a form of investment. Indeed, during the late 1960s and early 1970s, thousands of Americans invested millions of dollars in franchises and distributorships, and a very high percentage of them are still bemoaning the loss of a life's savings as a result of imprudent or impulsive reactions to high pressure sales pitches.

It's one thing to dive into an *existing* business where there is some record of the business's success available for your examination, and established clientele, patients, customers, what have you. But to start from scratch, where you have nothing on which to base even estimates, can be extremely hazardous.

Some major national franchises, on the order of MacDonald's, Kentucky Fried Chicken, and the like, have indeed produced many successful investor/restauranteur/operators. But for each MacDonald's there were dozens of "Beauty Burgers" that proved to be a disaster for one and all. Of course, each new franchise operation that comes along envisions itself as the next MacDonald's, and they sell as such to the would-be investors. This is where dreams are turned into nightmares. Proceed, if you must, with complete awareness of the risks that you face, and remember that the salesperson is trying to sell you something on which he or she will make a profit. There's no assurance that you too will make a profit, or ever see your money again.

If you're starting up your own business from scratch, be well aware that, on average, it takes from two to three years before a typical new business venture begins seeing a profit. This is not a casual warning, but a fact of life. Many businesses will fail because they were not adequately capitalized at the outset. The owner may have gotten an overdose of glamor, and failed to see the realities of running a business.

In any kind of new business venture, the efforts of your legal, insurance, and accounting advisors are essential before you proceed with any expenditure of funds. And bear in mind this simple but important caution: if you're prepared to risk it all on a new business venture, you have to be prepared to lose it all.

investing in commodities

The only reason for including commodities in this section on investments is to emphasize the fact that, contrary to what many think, commodities *are not* a form of investment. Like raw land and new business ventures, the commodity market represents a form of pure speculation. It's one of the most volatile, unpredictable, and high pressure gambling devices yet devised. Next to a commodity exchange, a Las Vegas casino might seem tame by comparison.

In the commodity market, in brief, you are betting on the future price of a variety of crops, metals, and international currencies. In the middle of March, for example, you can place a bet on what wheat or corn might be selling for next September; what hogs and cattle will be worth in December; what the future price of sugar or orange juice or cocoa might be a few or many months hence. You can, in effect, buy a contract for the future delivery of 5000 bushels of wheat on the Chicago Board of

Trade (which also deals in corn, soybeans, soybean oil, oats, silver, and plywood).

Or, you can buy a contract for the future delivery of 40,000 pounds of cattle, which is traded on the Chicago Mercantile Exchange (which also trades in hogs, pork bellies, fresh eggs, russet potatoes). The New York Coffee and Sugar Exchange will sell you a contract for the future delivery of 112,000 pounds of sugar or 37,500 pounds of coffee, and the New York Cocoa Exchange will sell you contracts for 30,000 pounds of cocoa.

The International Monetary Market (an adjunct of the Chicago Mercantile Exchange) deals in foreign currencies, trading contracts for Mexican pesos, Swiss francs, British pounds, Canadian dollars, German deutschemarks, and Japanese yen, as well as U.S. Treasury Bills. If you think you know what any of those commodities might be worth a month, six months, or a year from now, the commodity exchanges offer plenty of action where you can place your bets.

The chances of any bet succeeding are based not only on how the other bettors are betting, but on such other totally unpredictable factors as weather conditions, crop blights, the law of supply and demand, governmental and international politics, major shifts in the world's economy, minor shifts in the economy of any given nation, and even consumer boycotts.

In 1974, for example, American homemakers, shocked at the sharply rising cost of beef, boycotted that product. They simply cut back on their buying. Cattle breeders, with millions of tons of ready-for-market cattle on their hands, found the demand for their product sharply dropping, and with it the price. As the market price of beef dropped, speculators in beef futures (those who had bet on the future price of beef) were taking a beating. Other speculators may have profited mightily when sugar prices skyrocketed in 1975, when coffee prices skyrocketed in 1976 as a result of frozen crops in Brazil, and when orange juice prices skyrocketed in 1977 as a result of unexpected freezes in the Florida citrus groves. But for every profit, there is probably a corresponding loss.

Any student interested in learning more about speculating in the commodity markets can obtain abundant material through a stockbroker or through the respective Exchanges. Before making any speculations, it would also be advisable to attempt to gain admission to and spend an hour or so on the trading floor of any of these Exchanges. That experience might be enough to convince anyone of the nature of the commodity market as a form of extreme speculation.

Reminiscences of a Real Estate Investor

"My dad and I considered ourselves professional real estate investors. We'd both been involved in it extensively, on a near full-time basis, he for over fifteen years, and I for close to five. Further, we were both attorneys and well versed in the ways of finance, in addition to having excellent connections with lending institutions throughout our part of the country. Thus, we were as well equipped as anyone could be to find good deals and make the most profit from them.

"It's a strange quirk of human nature, but nobody likes to think he's capable of making mistakes, particularly not someone who calls himself a professional—and that goes in any field. Well, we made some mistakes. Fortunately, our successes far outweighed the mistakes, but when we made them, they were something to behold.

"We had concentrated our real estate investment activities in a number of smallish cities in upstate New York where we had purchased small parcels on the fringe of downtown areas, demolished the existing buildings and erected small office buildings for a major national life insurance company. Other investors in those communities wondered how we, as outsiders, could have found the opportunities and capitalized on them. It's the old saying: You can't see the forest for the trees. They were so close to their own situation that they couldn't envision the opportunities available.

"But that same inability of seeing the forest for the trees is what caused us our problem.

"As natives of upstate New York, we lacked the perspective to see many of these communities for what they really were becoming; their industrial heydays, built on the surge of immigrant labor at the turn of the century, had passed. For the most part, these communities were shrinking in size, in affluence, in opportunity and in investment potential. Our mode of real estate investing—as of most professionals—depends on a generally continuing upward trend in property values.

"We had failed to recognize that the bloom was off the rose; that the traditional pattern of upward moving prices had for the most part ended in most of these communities.

"Then Geneva, New York, happened.

"A banker friend from New York City called us one day to see if we were interested in a proposition that he had. His bank had made a substantial mortgage loan on a large property in downtown Geneva. The major tenant in the building had been the W. T. Grant company, but they had moved out to a new suburban shopping center location. (This was in the early 1960s, long before W. T. Grant had taken its own demise in 1976.) At about the same time, the owner of the building had died, and the building was the only thing of value in his entire estate. With no major tenant, there was no money left to make the mortgage payments. So the building had gone into foreclosure, and the bank had now taken it over and was trying to sell it.

"We were told that the building was old and in need of renovation, but that it occupied a prime site in downtown Geneva, next door to a major department store. We had made similar investments in the past in other cities—buying old buildings, sprucing them up, and turning them over at a profit shortly thereafter, or finding a suitable tenant that could enable us to generate considerable returns on our investment.

"Based on our previous experience, we realistically estimated that a building of this size and location, even without a tenant, would be worth $100,000. The bank's asking price: $100,000. It seemed like a "how-far-wrong-can-we-go" deal. That is, until we drove to Geneva and took a look at the building. It was a shambles. To bring it into any decent kind of rentable condition would have cost at least $30,000 to $50,000. We politely declined the offer and returned home.

"We all but forgot about the Geneva building until a few months later when our friend from the New York City bank called us back again. Even though the building was empty, it was still obliged to pay the very high real estate taxes that downtown commercial properties are subject to. And winter was coming on, which meant that the building would have to be at least minimally heated in order to keep the plumbing—what there was of it—from cracking. The payment of property taxes, the ongoing need for insurance and security, plus the advent of more expenses through the winter months, had reduced the bank to be willing to take 'any offer.' A shudder went through my spine when I heard my dad agree on the telephone to pay $20,000 for the building. I had to admit that the land alone was worth at least $50,000, and we reasoned that at that low price we could certainly do *something* with the building to generate a profit. That was the beginning of our great mistake.

"In the ensuing winter months, I drove the 200-mile round trip to Geneva at least fifteen times seeking tenants for the property. Because our purchase price was so low, we were able to offer the space at far below what comparable space was renting for in the downtown Geneva area. But there were no takers at any price.

"We approached the owners of the department store next door to our building. We offered them a deal 'they couldn't refuse.' But they refused. The only salvation through that long winter was that we were able to convince the city assessor to reduce the assessment on the building and therefore reduce our tax obligation.

"As spring approached, we became convinced that it was futile to try to rent the building. Our attempts to sell it at even a slight profit had met with no response whatsoever. We thus resolved that as soon as the weather turned, we would demolish the building. We would then have an extremely desirable empty lot in the center of downtown Geneva, which would be easily rentable as a parking lot.

"But it's neither easy nor cheap to demolish a four-story brick building covering roughly 12,000 square feet of land. The demolition bill totalled more than what we had paid for the building in the first place. But at least we had our parking lot.

"It wasn't until after the building had been demolished that we got a good look at the wall adjoining the department store. The two buildings had been butted together, and when our building was removed, the remaining wall was a crazy quilt of splotchy colors from all of the various rooms in the upper floor apartments that had been in our building. The department store owners, rather than welcoming the opportunity to rent an ideal parking lot right next to them, instead threatened us with a law suit if we didn't do something to remove the eyesore that was left after the demolition: the crazy quilt wall, which now, in effect, was their outer wall. Another few thousand dollars down the seemingly bottomless pit.

"Now, though, with our property tax burden lightened considerably by the removal of the building, we looked forward to an attractive lease of the parking lot. The 200-mile round trip journeys began again.

"Would the city rent the parking lot as a municipal lot? No, the city budget was in a bind and they couldn't make any such commitments. Would an association of other retailers in the downtown area rent it, with the hopes of attracting their lost customers back from the suburban shopping center? No, they didn't think it was really big enough to do the job. Our only recourse then was to operate the parking lot ourselves. We hired a local citizen and paid him a decent salary to operate the lot, but it never gen-

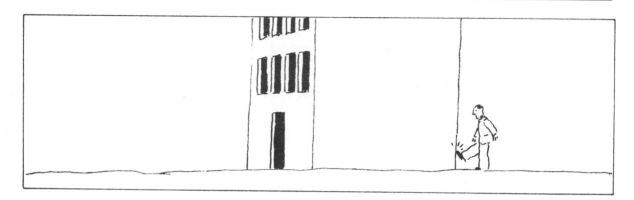

erated enough income to pay the overhead. And now another winter was nearing.

"In a classic gesture of throwing good money after bad, we finally decided that our only salvation was to build a modern retail structure on the property, which could be divided up into as many as three or four stores.

"The onset of winter prevented us from getting our construction under way, and building didn't commence until the following spring. Supervision of the construction required another dozen or so 200-mile round trips, but in spite of the close scrutiny we couldn't complete the shell until shortly before Christmas, too late to attract tenants who wanted to take advantage of the Christmas shopping season. So the shell sat empty through the winter, awaiting the advent of still the next spring.

"The light at the end of the tunnel! A regional retail firm of good repute expressed an interest in taking half of the building. We were ecstatic. The half of the building that they wanted, and were willing to pay a reasonable rental for, meant that the remaining half of the building would be very unattractive to other tenants. But good quality tenants were few and far between in downtown Geneva, New York that spring, and we went along with the deal.

"It was almost a full year later before we were able to cajole another business into taking over the remaining space, and they did so at a rental so low that we had to swallow hard when we signed the leases.

"The whole ordeal—from the day we purchased the property until there was enough cash coming in to stem our losses— took almost five years, and that was over ten years ago. In the meantime, tenants have come and gone, but no return on our investment is in sight. Our best hope is to sell the building for what we have in it, and even if we do that, we'll still have a considerable loss over the years.

"We were professionals. I guess we still are. But now we're better professionals, because we're able to realize and admit our own mistakes. Even with our expertise we missed some critical warning signs along the way: the effect of the suburban shopping center; the general downward trend in business in small cities like these; and the financial condition of the local business executives whom we looked to as would-be buyers or tenants of the property.

"Perhaps our greatest mistake was at the very beginning in thinking we were getting a deal so good that we could never go wrong with it. Our judgment got clouded by what I guess you'd call pure greed. And that's a danger for any investor, whether in real estate or anything else. It all seemed too good to be true. And it was.

"If you're interested in investing in real estate, let me know if you ever get up around Geneva, New York. Have I got a deal for you!"

**review
questions**

1. What is the income tax advantage of taking depreciation on the physical property portion of a real estate investment, since this deduction will increase the tax due when you sell?
2. Compare the property lease with option to renew with the lease with right of first refusal. Which is most advantageous to the investor/owner?
3. What does the government guarantee in a Property Report required for interstate property sales?
4. Where may a prospective investor in real estate obtain an appraisal of business property?
5. What principal concern, other than the buyer's credit rating, does the lender consider in evaluating a mortgage loan application on income property?
6. Did the governmental hearings conducted in 1973 reveal whether purchasers of unknown land saw the property purchased?
7. What are soil tests and percolation tests designed to determine?
8. How long does it take a typical new business to show a profit?

**cases
for
study**

1. Explain the manner in which tax stops and utility stops limit the liability of a lessor, or landlord, in terms of expenditures for taxes and utilities. Explain why utility stops tend to reduce utility bills.
2. Kenneth and Odessa Washington have purchased a commercial building as an investment. What are the advantages and disadvantages of engaging a property manager rather than managing it themselves?
3. Fletcher and Laura Knebel have $200,000 to invest. They want to put in real estate. What are the main factors that they should consider in deciding whether to invest in vacant land or in a commercial building?
4. What are the factors that make investing in commodities speculation rather than investment? What are some of the factors typically responsible for fluctuations in the prices of agricultural commodities?

chapter 14 **financial planning for later years**

reaching financial maturity

There comes a time—it's different for everyone—when we reach a plateau that might be referred to as "financial maturity." This time, particularly for families, generally coincides with those years when children have grown up and moved out on their own. It may be in the early to late forties, perhaps even later. It's a period when we find ourselves looking at our personal and financial affairs from a new perspective. Many of our needs have changed, and many previously long-term, vague goals now begin to achieve sharper focus.

As we reach financial maturity our needs and attitudes toward a great many important financial matters are in a state of change. These matters include housing, investing, insurance, use of leisure time, and the ultimate direction of our working career. Many of the financial decisions we make in our twenties and thirties can have a profound bearing on our ability to fulfill later goals during the mature years. Thus, thinking about and making plans for the years of financial maturity should begin at the earliest possible time.

The most dangerous course is to totally ignore the future. We live in an age of instant gratification, constantly urged and teased into buying things for the here and now. If we succumb

533

to such urges excessively, we can end up ruining tomorrow for the sake of today. Tomorrow *will* come and we must be ready for it.

Let's take a close look at some of the major elements of financial planning for the later years, so that alternate choices can be properly envisioned and anticipated. We can only conjure with possibilities and probabilities; specific solutions will be strictly up to each individual and family.

housing

"This is the old homestead. This is where we raised our family. This is where we feel comfortable. It's almost all paid for, why should we move?"

Or, "Without the children, we don't need this house to rattle around in any longer. Do we sell or do we stay, and what are the ramifications of either choice? If we sell, do we find another place in our present community or do we move to a new community? Do we find another house? A condominium? Apartment?"

Our housing requirements are often drastically altered with the onset of financial maturity, and our personal feelings may easily stand between us and many thousands of dollars that could help provide added security and comfort in the years beyond.

The dilemma is simple enough: retaining the old "family homestead" with its comforts and its memories, or exchanging it for another dwelling that may be more practical and economical.

Most home-owning families in their forties and fifties will have a substantial equity in their homes. In addition to what they have paid in on their mortgage debt, the value of the property itself will probably have increased considerably. But as long as that equity is tied up in the house, it's not working for you—except to provide a roof over your head. You may be perfectly content with that roof and not wish for any other pleasures the equity may be able to buy for you. However, by selling or refinancing the house, you could avail yourself of the means to provide personal satisfactions previously unavailable because your money was tied up in the property. In addition to equity dollars, sufficient thought must be given to the costs involved in maintaining a home.

Further, one of the main financial advantages in home ownership—the deductibility of mortgage interest and real estate taxes—may be of far less value to you in the later years, particularly on retirement, than they had been in the earlier years. All these considerations must be carefully evaluated.

Let's examine the case of the Johnson family to see what alternatives faced them. The basic thinking in this example can be used to determine the specific dollar advantages in most any other situation.

The Johnson's bought a house fifteen years ago for $30,000. They paid 20% down, and took out a thirty year mortgage for $24,000 at 6% interest. Their monthly payments on the mortgage for principal and interest were $145. Today, with fifteen years to go on the mortgage, they still owe roughly $16,000.

Their house is now worth $46,000 on the open market. Thus, if they were to sell it and pay off their existing mortgage, they would have a $30,000 cash-in-hand nest egg to do with as they please.

In addition to their current mortgage expenses of $145, they have real estate taxes of $75 per month, property insurance costs of $20 per month, utility costs averaging $60 per month, and maintenance expenses averaging $50 per month. Their total outlay for shelter is, therefore, $350 per month.

The Johnsons are about to enter retirement, which will drop them into a drastically lower tax bracket. The advantage of being able to deduct mortgage interest costs and real estate taxes on the property will be of far less value to them, not only because of their lower income tax bracket, but also because the standard deduction has increased manyfold since they originally bought the house, and the amount of interest they're paying on their mortgage is far less than it was in the earlier years of the mortgage. (Where families are still working and in higher income tax brackets, those matters should be taken into account on an individual basis.)

what are the johnsons' alternatives?

staying as is:

Let's assume that the Johnsons are willing to spend $350 per month for their basic shelter for the foreseeable future. They could remain in their current house, and at the end of fifteen more years the mortgage would be paid off and their monthly expenses, assuming no inflation, would have dropped to about $200 per month (for the property taxes, insurance, utilities, and maintenance). At that time they could either continue living in the house at the lower monthly cost, or they could then sell it and free their equity to put to other uses. But that's fifteen years from now, and who knows what the future holds?

selling and becoming renters:

If they sold the house now, they could rent either an apartment or another house. By wiping out all the obligations of home ownership, they'd have $350 per month to put toward apartment rental. They'd also have $30,000 in cash, free and clear, to spend as they saw fit. If they couldn't find a rental situation for $350 per month that pleased them, they could invest the $30,000 and use some of the income from that fund toward their rental.

If, for example, they invested the $30,000 in a savings account yielding 5.5% interest, that would generate $130 per month in interest income, (before income taxes, which in their situation might be minimal). That, added to their initial $350, would allow them to spend $480 in rent per month. Assuming that they could find a satisfactory rental situation at that price, they'd have their shelter *and* a $30,000 cash nest egg.

Or, if they invested the $30,000 in a savings certificate yielding 7.5% interest, the income would be about $188 per month, which they could either use for shelter or spend. It would seem reasonable in most communities that a family spending $350 per month for housing could find a satisfactory rental situation for $500 per month. If, in fact, the Johnsons invested their equity at the 7.5% level, they could have a $500 apartment plus an extra $38 per month in spending money. This would be their situation indefinitely. If the rental inched up on the apartment, there's a fair assumption that the available yields on the $30,000 investment fund would also inch up proportionately, thus allowing them to maintain a fairly level standard of housing over the long term.

buying another dwelling:

Another alternative would be to *buy* another dwelling—house, town house, or condominium—with the proceeds of the sale. Let's say that the Johnsons find a new but smaller dwelling with a $43,000 price tag. They put $20,000 of their total $30,000 nest egg toward a down payment on the new house, and sign up for a $23,000 mortgage for twenty years at 9%. Their new monthly mortgage payments would be $210 and it's reasonable to expect that the taxes, insurance, utilities, and maintenance would be lower in their new dwelling than in their older dwelling because it's a more modest house.

Assume that those monthly expenses are $60 for taxes, $15 for insurance, $40 for utilities, $25 for maintenance. This brings the grand monthly total outlay to $350—the same amount they had been paying before. But now they have a $10,000 nest egg left over from the sale of their previous house. If they put that to work in a 7.5% savings certificate, they'll have an extra $62.50 per month cash to spend or to put back into their nest egg. If they prefer to let the money ride, in ten years the $10,000 nest egg will have more than doubled to over $20,000.

Another alternative is to buy a still more modest dwelling, say in the $33,000 price range. They could use $10,000 of the $30,000 proceeds as down payment, and take out the same mortgage as in the above case—$23,000 for twenty years at 9%. The monthly mortgage payments would be the same as above—$210 per month—but let's say that the more modest dwelling required $50 less in total expenses than the $43,000 house. They would then have $50 per month more spending money, plus a $20,000 nest egg, which, if invested at 7.5%, would give them a yield of an additional $125 per month.

All things considered, this move to a more modest dwelling would put an extra $175 per month cash in their hands, if they chose to spend all the income received from their investment. Or, if they chose to let the income compound in the nest egg, they'd have an extra $50 per month cash, plus a nest egg that would build over the next ten years to an excess of $40,000.

what about refinancing?

What if the Johnsons decided to stay put? Would it make sense for them to refinance their existing mortgage even though the current interest rates on mortgages are considerably higher than the rate on their old mortgage?

Assuming it was feasible, if they were to refinance their existing $16,000 balance for a new period of twenty years at 9% interest per year, their monthly payments would drop only by about $10 per month. This might not be worth the time or the cost involved in obtaining the refinancing. But if they wait another five years, the balance remaining on their existing mortgage will have dropped to about $13,000. If they refinanced at that time for a new twenty-five year term (also at the 9% interest rate), their monthly payments would drop to about $110 per month, or a $35 per month saving over what they are currently paying. Another alternative would be to refinance the existing mortgage for a higher amount—say, $30,000. This would give them a $14,000 cash-in-hand nest egg, but would necessitate accordingly higher payments. The value in taking these steps will depend on the amount of equity in the house, the prevailing interest rates both with the mortgage itself and what can be earned on investments, as well as the overall financial status of the family. Each family should determine for itself, with the help of a banker, when, if at all, it would pay to refinance an existing mortgage.

investing

Our investment attitudes and tactics will likely undergo a considerable change as we reach the plateau of financial maturity. Until now, we've been concerned with generating capital to meet the heavy expenses of housing, educating the children, and other family needs. Now, with those needs substantially accomplished, we turn to the philosophy of preservation of capital. While we were younger, we could afford to make mistakes and still recoup. Now we may be at an age when the spectre of a financial loss via investments is more fearsome: we may neither have the time nor the ability to recoup.

The advantages of fixed income investing, as opposed to more speculative forms, become clearer. Although many individuals are just reaching their peak earning years at this stage, the feasibility of taking risks is diminishing. We simply have less time to recover from a poor risk. And, anticipating some future time when work may cease, we begin to realize the importance of preserving our capital so that there will be adequate funds available. This does not imply that all attempts to generate capital in more speculative modes should be abandoned altogether. But the risk factor must be examined more closely, and should be considered with much more respect than it may have been a decade or two earlier.

A portfolio of fixed income investments to preserve capital can take many shapes. Perhaps the line of least resistance is to take whatever lump sum you may have accumulated and put it into a long-term high yielding bond or savings certificate and forget about it for as many years as it has to run. This minimizes the need to have your nose buried in the *Wall Street Journal*, keeping tabs on your capital and constantly looking for better opportunities. If you're locked into a given situation, you may regret it later if better opportunities do present themselves. On the other hand, nothing better may come along in the foreseeable future, and you'll be very content to ride it out with your locked in situation.

But the prudent investor in the mature years must be aware of the value of liquidity and flexibility. To obtain liquidity and flexibility in the fixed income portfolio, one must consider the advantages of building a portfolio based on *staggered maturities*.

What are staggered maturities? Instead of investing a whole lump sum for one long period, the investor would break up the lump sum into perhaps three or four or five nearly equal segments and invest them for different lengths. For example, you have a $10,000 lump sum that you want to put into fixed income securities. Consider breaking it into four equal parts of $2500 each, and investing each of the four segments for a different maturity: one segment for two years, one for three years, one for four years, and one segment for five years. Within each time span, you can take advantage of the highest yielding security available. Then as each segment matures, starting in two years, you can redirect that money into whatever is best at that time, considering safety and yield.

With a portfolio like this, after two years you'd have one-quarter of your total nest egg roll over every year. In some years you might have to take a lesser yield than you had previously been earning on that segment because of a drop in overall interest rates. In other years you might be able to obtain a better return. With a program of staggered maturities (not exceeding a five or six year maximum) you're going to have a higher degree of control and liquidity with your nest egg that could bring you a greater sense of satisfaction and financial return.

Overall, as noted in the chapter on fixed income investing, the fixed income portfolio allows you to predict with a reasonable degree of certainty how much money you will have available at any given future point. By sticking to fixed income investments with shorter maturities, you can avoid the problem of being caught in a long-term downtrend of prices on such fixed income securities as bonds. If you need to tap your nest egg, you will have minimized any worry that the value will have shrunk because of fluctuations in those securities.

insurance

Financial maturity brings accompanying changes in our insurance program. We may have had a life insurance program designed to protect our family in the event of the premature death of the breadwinner. Now the family is on its own and we may have far better uses for those premium dollars. And, because age renders us more susceptible to the risks of injury and illness, we must be increasingly concerned with our ability to cope with such circumstances both psychologically and financially.

Life insurance programs begun when one is in the twenties and thirties can have a most important effect on financial status in the fifties and sixties. If a young person is willing to sacrifice a bit of current pleasures for the sake of greater security and comforts in the future, he or she can create a life insurance program that will serve well in the later years. In the chapter on life insurance, we examined some of the deliberations and alternatives facing the younger person in making a choice of various kinds of life insurance programs. Let's now look at the effect of one particular choice decades later.

When Joe was thirty, he embarked on a straight life insurance program by buying a policy with a face value of $50,000. His annual premium for this life insurance protection was $653. From the very first day the policy was issued, Joe and his family had the peace of mind in knowing that $50,000 would be payable to his family in the event of Joe's death. Joe has lived a full and healthy life, and today, twenty years later, he is pleased to observe the nonforfeiture values in his life insurance program.

In the past twenty years, Joe paid premiums totalling $13,060. Now, at age 50, the policy has cash surrender value of $14,850. Joe can cash in the policy and receive back *more* than what he has paid in. If he invests the $14,850 at 7% per year, he will have a return of $1040 per year, leaving his $14,850 nest egg intact. The net results: For the past twenty years he has guaranteed his family a substantial lump sum of money—$50,000—in the event of his premature death. Now, instead of being out-of-pocket $653 each year, he can have an *added income* of $1040 per year, plus a nest egg of $14,850.

Joe may also elect to borrow that $14,850 and otherwise continue the policy.

Joe's other alternatives are to convert the policy to a paidup or an extended term status. If he chooses the paid-up method, he can cease paying the annual $653 premium and will have a life insurance policy with a face value of $28,550, paid up for the rest of his life. He doesn't have to pay any more premiums and, on his death, his survivors will receive that stated sum. If he converts to extended term insurance, he will be able to stop paying premiums, and be insured for the full $50,000 face value for a period of 19 years, 103 days—until he's almost 70.

What if Joe decides to continue paying on the policy and keeping it in force for another fifteen years, until he's 65 years old? By that time he will have paid in a total of $22,855. During the entire 35 years, from the first day onward, his family has had the protection of the $50,000 face value payable in the event of his death. Now, at age 65, the cash value in the policy is $20,550, almost $5000 more than what he has paid in premiums. If he cashes in the policy and invests that sum of money at 7% per year, he will have an annual income from that fund alone of $1930, and will no longer have to pay the $653 premium.

He might convert to paid up life insurance, in which case he could cease making payments and be covered for the balance of his life for $39,950. Or, more likely, he might prefer to convert to extended term insurance, in which case he would be covered for the full $50,000 for 14 years, 160 days, almost until age 80.

Joe might have taken out a term insurance policy at the outset, which could have cost him far fewer dollars and could have left him more leeway for investing other available dollars. Such a program could have provided Joe with greater benefits over the long pull, but quite possibly the benefits would not have been as extensive. In any event, he never would have been able to know for certain what the ultimate benefits would be, unless he had invested the other available dollars in a prudent form of fixed income situation with a predictable twenty or thirty-five year picture.

The important thing is that the 30-year-old Joe did in fact create the program that the 50-year-old Joe or the 65-year-old Joe can now either continue or convert to suit current needs. The young man created a liquid and flexible package that the older man can benefit from.

Health insurance is also important. Many individuals reach retirement age and find that leaving their job means the cessation of a group insurance plan that had given them the protection they've needed throughout their working years. Now they might become totally dependent on Medicare, and on costly supplemental programs to it. The person who had taken out a good supplemental or Major Med program in the younger years can leave a legacy for the older one: a well-rounded program that can continue beyond the cessation of work and provide abundant protection to the older family during years when they might be most susceptible to the crippling costs of medical care.

activities and idleness

Our personal activities and leisure pleasures may undergo substantial alteration when we reach financial maturity. Much of our free time in the younger years may have been devoted to family affairs or community activities. We may also find that our contemporaries are shifting from old patterns into new ones, and there's an obvious and natural need to pursue various interests jointly with friends.

One very serious problem for retired individuals arises from neglecting to develop outside interests that would provide a measure of satisfaction and constructiveness in later years. In spite of all the money some may have accumulated, children and grandchildren, and the lovely bungalow in the sparkling retirement village, the loneliness and the boredom and the helplessness that can attack are overpowering.

The critical time when a person may begin developing such outside interests could well be at the onset of financial maturity. Many of the diversions of the earlier years will have ceased of their own accord; now, in the mid-forties or later, there still can be ample time to explore, to test, to sample new ideas and new activities.

to work or retire?

As financial maturity begins, so starts our thinking about how long we wish to continue working. This might be the most drastic forthcoming change of all. If you're in a work situation where retirement is mandatory at a given age, will you want to seek some other form of work, either part- or full-time, when retirement occurs? Or will financial circumstances dictate that you'll *have* to seek other work to maintain yourself in a given style?

If you intend to continue working, either voluntarily or out of necessity, what kind of employment might be available relative to your skills, desires, experience, and your needs? If mandatory retirement is not in your future, when will you voluntarily want to begin to taper off and how quickly? Will you want to take some new direction in your career, albeit at a later age? Will you want to try that certain something that "you'd always wished you could do"?

If even the vague possibility of wanting to continue work beyond the normal retirement age is on your horizon, the earlier you can start shaping those thoughts into something tangible the better. If you anticipate a work activity that will take some investment on your part, the earlier you can start setting aside the necessary funds the better you'll be able to accomplish your desires. If no investment will be needed, you'll have all that much more time to establish extra reserve funds to see you through should the business venture not work out.

some particular thoughts for the older single person

The single person reaching financial maturity has some considerations slightly different from those of the married person. (By single we're referring generally to someone who does not have a family dependent on him or her, and does not plan to do so in the future.) The single individual might easily justify spending more of his or her disposable income on personal pleasures than the married person. But the single person must be every bit as aware as the married person of the impending future, and, unchecked by a constant companion, should avoid developing spendthrift habits that could be regretted later on.

Regarding insurance, the single person probably has fewer concerns and fewer budgetary obligations. A single who does not have a family dependent on him or her has obviously less need for life insurance, and can reallocate those dollars elsewhere. To the extent that a single wants to leave an inheritance to anyone, life insurance does provide a good vehicle for that purpose, as it does for a married person. But if insurance is simply for the welfare of surviving dependents, the single may choose to do without such protection.

Many singles may have life insurance policies acquired many years ago. If the original need for the insurance has diminished, the single might do well to examine the conversion privileges in the policies, as noted earlier in the case of Joe.

In health and disability insurance the single has some other matters to be concerned about. Being alone, only one person's health has to be insured. And that can represent a savings on premiums compared to what the couple and the family will pay. But if disability strikes, the single can be at a disadvantage— long-term convalescence can be a costly and time-consuming proposition. With a couple, the well spouse can assume many of the obligations and duties that the single might have to pay someone to do. Housekeeping, shopping, nursing care, and the like must be considered, and the costs can run high. It's essential for the single to maintain a comprehensive insurance program that will protect an individual in the event of long-term disability.

A single facing a long-term disability may be involved in some problems that need a lawyer's attention. If you are unable to act on your own behalf, for whatever reason, someone trusted should be allowed to step into your shoes and take care of important matters for you. These matters could be as simple as writing or endorsing checks, or as complex as selling a home. The Power of Attorney can be a valuable tool for the single, particularly in the event of an extended disability.

A Power of Attorney need not be given just to a lawyer; it can be granted to anyone you choose. But a lawyer should definitely draw up the documents. A Power can be limited to specifically stated acts or can be general in scope. A general Power of Attorney is very broad and should be entered into only in the most compelling circumstances. Your lawyer can give you more details.

financial arrangements for the later years

How much will you have to live on when your active working career tapers off and/or ceases altogether?

Before we take a closer look at some of the specific details involved in planning your retirement budget, we must discuss one very frequent comment: "Whatever we have to live on, it won't be enough because inflation will eat away at it."

We occasionally hear horror stories of elderly people forced to turn to public welfare or to pet food in order to survive during their later years. Such stories may be true and sad indeed, but they represent only an extremely small fraction of all those who have entered their later years, the vast majority of whom are able to live comfortably and contentedly within their fixed income situation. The prudent individual who has planned properly and saved scrupulously should not have these fears.

the spectre of inflation

Inflation can be a spectre, particularly if the ability to work has diminished or disappeared. But it can be coped with. Much of the fear about inflation devouring people's fixed incomes arose in the recession of 1974–1975 when the rate of inflation exceeded the rise in personal income. Or at least so it seemed. By 1976 and 1977, the trend had been reversed, and we were back into the historical pattern of personal income continuing to exceed the rate of inflation. Of course, there's no assurance about what the future might hold, although the Social Security Administration has estimated that for the next fifty years (just as with the past 50 years) that historical pattern will hold true.

The fear of inflation can be almost as dangerous as inflation itself. During the 1974–1975 recession, many people became convinced—often by high pressure salespeople—that their investments were being erroded by inflation. Their reaction was to abandon the safety and security of their current high quality fixed income investments to take a "too good to be true" plunge in supposed inflation-beating opportunities. In all too many cases, these opportunities turned sour and people ended up losing far more than they would have if they had stayed with their original programs.

Upon reaching the later years, many individuals automatically and without deliberation curtail their living expenses and thus blunt the effects of inflation. Moving to smaller quarters, moderating clothing needs, having only one car can sharply reduce financial needs. Many families will have paid off the mortgage on their home, and many will terminate or convert existing life insurance programs. These steps can create additional spendable dollars previously applied toward these purposes.

Beyond what a family or an individual does unconsciously to meet its diminished needs, they might also take some conscious steps to cut back so that their disposable income can still provide satisfaction. A review of any budget can reveal minor excesses that can be reduced or curtailed without materially affecting life style.

The effects of inflation can also be blunted on the income side. Social Security payments are scheduled to increase in line with consumer price index fluctuations, and many pensions have escalation clauses also tied to rising prices. Also, as costs move upwards, so inevitably do yields available on secure fixed income investments. If inflation starts to nibble away at a nest egg, the proper shifts into higher yielding investments can offset the inflationary bite.

shaping the budget

There are two primary sources of sustenance that must be considered in detail: income and principal. Income is money received from all sources such as Social Security, pensions, investments, and work. Principal is accumulated money working for you that may be dipped into for living purposes as the need arises. Until an individual or family determines how much it wants to spend, it can't adequately determine how much, if any, principal will meet their needs. The obvious and prudent tendency is to attempt to live off income, and keep principal in reserve until needed. A careful review of your savings and investment program is necessary. How much principal do you have? How well is it protected? Can you count on the projected income from principal? If not, how can you restructure your investment program to offer better protection?

the income sources

The farther you are from a termination of work, the more difficult it will be to get specific figures on the sources of income that will be available. But at least ten or fifteen years before you anticipate retirement, you should begin to obtain some estimates as to what might be expected. As the date approaches, you should check with regularity—at least every second year, tapering down to every year—in order to focus more clearly on the ultimate income figures. One very sad mistake is to conjure up in one's own mind what these income sources might be—those who guess too high can be grievously disappointed. The proper way to go about this is to check with the specific sources and get their most reasonable conclusions as to the true amount of dollars that will become available.

social security

Laws passed in 1972 dictate that Social Security payments be increased periodically as the Consumer Price Index increases. Because there is absolutely no way of knowing what those fluctuations might be in the future, there is no way of predicting what your ultimate Social Security check might be. But a visit with your Social Security office can be helpful in instructing you about probable trends. The closer you get to actual retirement, the more closely the Social Security Administration can estimate your income.

pensions, profit-sharing plans

Visit with your employer's pension or profit-sharing plan administrator to determine as closely as possible what money you may have coming from those sources. What options do you have with those funds? Will you be paid a fixed monthly amount, and, if so, for how long? Will you be able to obtain a lump sum payment; what will it be and when can you get it? Will payments continue beyond the death of the working spouse and be available to the surviving spouse, and, if so, for how long? The Pension Reform Law, passed in 1974, makes many provisions for the benefit of pensioners-to-be. The appropriate details of that law are discussed later in this chapter.

income from investments

As retirement nears and the ability to earn income from work diminishes, you'll seek more assurance that a fixed amount will be available to meet your needs. The trend toward fixed income investments becomes more pronounced under these circumstances and the more you solidify such a program, the more clearly you'll be able to see the kind of return that you can expect once you have retired. The greater your need to know what your investment income sources will be, the more motivated you will become to create a portfolio that clearly defines the sources.

income from working

This is a very unpredictable item. The prudent and conservative person will probably estimate a lower level of income than may actually be realized. You may simply reach a point when you just don't care to work as much or as hard and income level will diminish accordingly. As with other sources of income, the closer you get to the actual day, the more carefully you'll be able to peg a prospective figure. But for how long will this income continue? This is even more difficult to estimate. You might plan to work for one year, or three or five years, and find that after awhile you have changed your mind. Perhaps this is voluntary, or it may be dictated by physical circumstances. And you may find, as many do, that the strange quirk in the Social Security laws inhibits working—in many cases, you can have nearly as much income by not working as you do by working. This may be counterproductive to an individual who feels the desire to continue being of service to society, but it must be taken into account.

income taxes, social security, and net spendable income

The arithmetic of the federal income tax laws and Social Security laws has to be examined by any people nearing retirement age. They hold some interesting surprises that should be examined in view of individual circumstances.

For example, Bernie and Flora are both 64 years old. They both work and have no personal exemptions other than themselves. In the last year of their careers (they both will retire next year on turning 65), they had an Adjusted Gross Income of $20,000. Using the tax laws applicable to 1976 income, Bernie and Flora are entitled to two personal exemptions of $750 each, for a total of $1500. They take the standard deduction of $2800. The exemptions and the deductions are subtracted from the Adjusted Gross Income, giving them a taxable income of $15,-700. Their tax on that amount is $3191, which leaves them with a net spendable income after taxes of $12,509. (For ease in comparing situations, we won't consider available credits against the taxes in this illustration.)

The following year, on retirement, their income picture looks like this: they have $3000 actual earned income from part-time work. This is the amount they can earn without curtailing their

Social Security benefits. In addition, they have $3000 income from a pension plan, all of which is taxable income since the employer contributed the full amount to the plan. They thus have an Adjusted Gross Income of $6000. But now, being 65, they're entitled to double the personal exemptions for a total of $3000. The minimum standard deduction is $2100, and subtracting the exemptions and deductions from their income they end up with a taxable income of $900, which results in a federal income tax of $128.

In addition, they receive a total of $600 per month from Social Security, for an annual total of $7200. Their total income is thus $6000 (earned and from the pension) and $7200 from Social Security for a grand total of $13,200. The Social Security income is not subject to taxes. Subtracting their federal income tax bill of $128 from their total available income of $13,200, they end up with a net spendable income after all tax considerations of $13,072.

They are making more money after retirement than they were while they were still working.

We never know what income tax laws will be beyond the current year, so it's difficult to do this kind of arithmetic until one gets quite close to actual retirement. But the basic formula should be applied as soon as it becomes appropriate.

losing your social security benefits

Once you've become eligible for Social Security benefits and you start receiving them, they can be curtailed or lost completely if you return to work. The amount that you'll lose depends on the amount you earn at work. Income received from investments is not considered earnings for purposes of reduction of Social Security benefits. Earnings refer to actual wages and salaries.

Here's how it works. *As of 1977*, you could earn as much as $3000 in a given year without losing any Social Security benefits. If your annual earnings go above $3000, you lose $1 in benefits for every $2 in earnings above $3000. In other words, if you earn $6000 in a year, and you would have otherwise been entitled to $4800 in Social Security benefits, you will lose $1500 worth of your Social Security benefits. Why? Because your $6000 earnings exceeded the $3000 ceiling by $3000. You lose $1 in benefits for every $2 earnings over the ceiling. The amount, $1500, which is one-half of $3000, is the loss you'll suffer. The net result is that your Social Security benefits will total $3300 instead of $4800 for that year.

There is an exception to this rule: If in any given month your earnings do not exceed $250, you can still get your full Social Security benefits *for that month*, even if your *annual* total exceeds the $3000 ceiling. In other words, if you earn $6000 in a given year after you've started receiving Social Security benefits, but your earnings are broken down to ten months at $600 each and two months at zero each, you will still get your full Social Security benefits for the two months in which you had no earnings. (The same would be true if your earnings were under $250 during any other months.) This is so despite the fact that your total annual earnings are $6000.

But if your earnings are spread out equally, at $500 per month for twelve months, you'll lose the benefits as indicated earlier for each and every month. Thus, if you do plan to continue working past age 65 (or 62 if you choose to start your benefits at that time), you should attempt to structure your work and payment arrangements so that there will be a legitimate number of months in which your earnings are below the $250 level to provide yourself with maximum benefits available and to minimize the penalty for working.

Once you have reached age 72, your earnings do not affect your Social Security benefits.

If you decide to return to work after age 65 and are willing to forego your Social Security benefits, you may do so. You then will receive a slightly higher check when you do decide to cease work and take your benefits. However, the added credit amounts to only 1% per year between the ages of 65 and 72, which is really quite slight and may not even be worth considering.

Let's look at an individual who wishes to continue working after he has started receiving his Social Security benefits. We'll assume that his earnings are equally divided over the full twelve months of the year, that the Social Security benefits he'd be entitled to are $4800 per year, that he's married, and that his spouse is also over 65, thus entitling them to the $3000 worth of exemptions on their income tax return as opposed to the $1500 they received prior to age 65.

We'll assume that the couple takes the standard deduction on its income tax return instead of itemizing deductions. And further, we will not consider any outside investment income or retirement tax credits that the couple might be entitled to. We'll look just at a relatively pure situation of earned income, Social Security benefits, and the net number of dollars available after paying federal income taxes, Social Security taxes, and the reduction, if any, of Social Security benefits. For illustration purposes we'll use 6% for the Social Security tax rate.

The couple earns $6000 in a year after both have turned 65. The earnings are at the rate of $500 per month. Based on the assumed exemptions and deductions noted above, the couple will have an income tax obligation of $159 for the year. Based on a 6% factor for Social Security contributions, they will pay into the Social Security fund $360 during the year. Subtracting these two tax items from their income, the couple will have a $5481 net from earnings.

The couple is entitled to Social Security benefits of $4800. However, their $6000 earnings exceed the annual ceiling of $3000 by $3000. As we previously noted, the Social Security benefits will thus be reduced by $1500, leaving the net available from Social Security of $3300. We add the net available after income taxes of $5481 to the net from Social Security of $3300 and we see that the couple has a total *disposable* income, after all tax considerations, of $8781.

Now let's compare this with a couple earning $9000 during the year after Social Security benefits have started. The federal income tax on earnings (using the same assumptions as above) will be $644, and total Social Security taxes will be $540, giving a net from earnings after taxes of $7816. Because this couple has earned $6000 over the allowable Social Security ceiling, their Social Security benefits will be reduced by $3000 in accordance with the formula. This will give them a net income from Social Security of $1800. Adding that to the net income from earnings of $7816, the couple ends up with a total *disposable* sum of $9616.

The shocking conclusion is that the couple earning $6000 ends up with $8781 spendable money, while the couple earning $9000 ends up with $9616 spendable money. The couple that earned $3000 more ends up with only $835 more cash in their pockets! Was it worth the effort to earn that much more money, only to be left with so little difference after the tax factors have been considered?

This phenomenon may be altered by the time many who read this book reach the age when retirement must be considered. But it is the law now, and anyone currently nearing retirement age, or at retirement, must consider this rather drastic government action on one's desire to work and remain productive.

the principal sources

The principal sources of future spendable dollars may be easier to estimate than income sources, particularly if an investment portfolio is in fixed income situations. The potential principal sources are the following.

equity in your home

As noted earlier in this chapter, many people will sell their existing home or refinance an existing mortgage to get access to the dollars they've been paying in over the years on their mortgage. This equity can represent a substantial portion of anyone's ultimate future nest egg, and should be estimated as carefully as possible, and as far in advance as feasible.

life insurance values

Individuals with conversion values in their life insurance policies should determine precisely what those values currently are and what they will be in future years, assuming premium payments are continued until a conversion is made. Personal circumstances will dictate whether to continue the protection of the life insurance in full, convert it to one of the other forms of life insurance, or retrieve the cash that's available.

pension and profit-sharing funds

If lump sum distributions are available instead of monthly payments, these should be counted in your overall sources of principal.

business interests

If you have an interest in a business situation, either wholly or partially, how might that be converted into investable funds, and at what time? How can you best sell out your business or professional interest and on what terms?

Anyone in these circumstances must recognize when a business or professional practice is at peak potential and reach a decision as to how much energy should be devoted to the business compared to other pursuits. A common problem arises when a business executive begins to feel a diminution in energies regarding operation of the business. As energies diminish, so can profitability, and, in turn, the opportunity to reap the best possible price on a sale of the business. The sad end result can be that the business falls far short of being able to provide for the needs of the owner at the time of retirement because the ability to sell it has been so negatively affected.

Prudent planning may dictate that when the business executive or professional recognizes the peak potential in his or her occupation the individual should immediately begin to consider the feasibility of a gradual phase-out. This generally would involve selling the business to a younger successor, or turning over the reins to a family member.

existing investment portfolio

This would include all money you now have invested. Some of it currently may not be offering any return—you are hoping for a gain in value to realize your ultimate rewards. As retirement approaches, you may deem it advisable to convert these nonearning assets into earning situations where you can specifically gauge how much will be available to you at future points.

potential inheritances

Realistically, try to estimate inheritances from family members in the foreseeable future. Will the funds be in cash, securities, property, or in some other form? Will they be earning assets or nonearning assets, and what would be involved in converting them into situations best suited to your personal needs? For example, you might inherit a parcel of income-producing real estate. Although this could generate an attractive measure of income, you might not want to continue ownership of the building. It might be a great distance away from where you live or you simply may not have the desire or expertise to deal with income-producing real estate. What are the prospects of selling the building, and what sacrifice, if any, would be made in your income picture if you convert the property into cash or other securities? These considerations apply to any inherited assets, except perhaps cash.

how much and for how long?

Most of us face the ultimate dilemma in the later years: to have enough money available to live within a desired framework for an *indeterminate* time, and possess the security of having sufficient funds to take care of virtually any contingency. Life expectancy and health factors are unknown quantities, but the amount of money available should be a known quantity. If, after work has ceased, you can live comfortably on income alone, your later years should be relatively worry free. The dilemma is compounded in those many situations where principal has to be invaded, minimally or substantially, to provide for necessities and contingencies.

In many cases, it's necessary for a life style to be trimmed in order to conserve enough principal to guarantee future comforts and necessities. Temptations to dip into principal should be examined carefully. When the principal is reduced, so is your earning power.

the 1974 pension reform law: how it affects the rights of workers and retirees

In September 1974, Congress passed the Employee Retirement Security Act of 1974, more commonly known as the Pension Reform Law or ERISA. The purpose of the law was to correct abuses that occurred in the administration of pension funds that resulted in pensioners being deprived of monies that otherwise have been due them. About 350,000 existing pension plans had to be revised to conform with the requirements of this new law.

The administration of the law is under the jurisdiction of two governmental agencies: the Internal Revenue Service and the Department of Labor. Both agencies will be producing regulations and guidelines, and the courts undoubtedly will be interpreting the regulations and guidelines for years to come, so specific elements of the law are bound to be modified. The following discussion is intended to acquaint you with the overall concepts. Anyone accumulating pension benefits subject to ERISA should determine from their employer exactly what their benefits will be, and what their rights are under the law as it becomes amended.

the abuses

The law was created to deal with certain abuses and shortcomings in pension practices throughout the nation. These abuses may not have affected more than a very small percentage of the population, but they caused headlines and created considerable fear when they did occur. The Department of Labor revealed in a study that in 1972 a total of 1227 pension plans were terminated when the companies sponsoring them went out of business. These terminations left almost 20,000 would-be pensioners without $50 million in benefits to which they would have been otherwise entitled. One particularly severe example occurred in 1963 when a major automobile plant suddenly closed its doors. Reportedly, more than 4000 workers then under 60 could collect no more than 15% of what they would have been entitled to had the closing not occurred.

Aside from a company's actually going out of business, other abuses occurred in ongoing companies where the persons responsible for investing pension funds erred and severe losses were incurred, leaving the pension fund accounts too depleted to pay promised benefits.

And there were numerous individual cases where workers were deprived of benefits. Case history: A 64-year-old man had spent his career as a janitor for a large manufacturing firm in Georgia. Just two months shy of his retirement, his employer asked him to "do the company a favor" and retire two months earlier than scheduled. He was a loyal employee and consented without ever realizing what the consequences might be.

Shortly after his retirement began, he started receiving his pension checks and was shocked that they were one-third of what he had been anticipating! On inquiring, he was told his early retirement curtailed his pension benefits and that what he was getting was all he could expect. In effect, he had been conned into the "early retirement" by an employer who realized that legally he could deprive the worker of substantial benefits. If the worker had been able to establish how he had been inveigled into his actions, he might have persuaded the state labor department and the federal labor department to intervene on his behalf.

In a sense, the law itself might be considered somewhat of an abuse. The highly publicized wrongs represent only a small fraction of the vast number of pension plans that provide satisfactory benefits, without any hitches, to the workers who have earned those benefits. But the law seemingly is designed to protect against the few potential abuses at the expense of reputable plans. Indeed, during 1975, immediately following passage of the law, almost 5000 existing pension plans were terminated by employers because they feared the cost of the paperwork required to comply with the new law.

what the law says

The law is aimed at those pension funds that are "qualified" under the Internal Revenue Service regulations. Qualified pension funds, generally, are those maintained in such a way so as to allow the employer tax deductions for the cost of contributions, and allow the employee receiving the benefits to not have to report those contributions as income until the money in the fund is later withdrawn. About 40 million Americans are thus covered by the blanket protection of the law regarding pensions.

The Pension Reform Law does *not* require any company to start a pension plan. But if a company does begin one, it must meet the requirements of the law. Further, the law does *not* stipulate how much money an employer should pay in pension benefits for employees, nor how much, if any, an employee should contribute. But the law does establish that once promises are made regarding pension contributions, those promises must be kept.

If your employer does not have a pension or profit-sharing plan, you should still be aware of the benefits available under the law. You may change jobs and go to a company that does have a pension plan, or people close to you may be affected by the law and your awareness of its benefits can be helpful to them.

The Pension Reform Law attempts to correct abuses in these main areas: vesting, funding, folding, reporting, and managing. In addition, the law establishes the do-it-yourself program known as the Individual Retirement Account or IRA.

vesting   Vesting refers to that point when your benefits are "locked up," or guaranteed as a result of the time you've spent on the job. Say you've worked for a company for twenty years and you leave, either to change jobs or to retire. When you try to collect your pension, you're told you hadn't been on the job long enough to receive a full pension. You had not worked long enough to have rights "vested" in your behalf.

The Pension Reform Law is designed to eliminate this problem of when it is that you are entitled to how much money. It requires an employer to establish one of three fixed formulas for vesting your rights. To better understand what this means, let's follow the three basic steps involved in obtaining pension benefits from a company.

First you must become eligible to participate in the plan. Before the Pension Reform Law, an employer could have required, for example, that an employee serve at least 20 years before becoming eligible to participate in a plan. If the employee left before the 20 years had elapsed, he or she might be entitled to no pension benefits because of being ineligible for participation in the plan.

The law now states that any employee who is at least 25 years old with at least one year on the payroll must be taken into the pension plan if the company has a plan.

Once you become eligible, the company supposedly credits a certain sum to your pension or profit-sharing account each year. This is the second step in obtaining pension benefits from a company. That amount should be allocated to your account each year until you either leave the company or retire.

The third step in receiving the benefits is vesting, or locking up of whatever accrued benefits have been set aside in your name.

Before the passage of the Pension Reform Law, an employer could determine when employees would become vested. He might contribute money to their account once they had been eligible, but if they did not stay at the job for the full vesting period, they could forfeit everything that had been paid into their account. For example, as noted earlier, if the vesting requirements were twenty years, and you left the job after nineteen years and six months, you could forfeit everything that you might otherwise have been entitled to.

But under the Pension Reform Law, an employer can not arbitrarily determine when employees will become vested. The employer cannot delay the guarantee of pension benefits until a late age. Thus, the employee who resigns or wants to retire early cannot be denied benefits. His accumulated funds cannot be spread among the other employees or returned to the employer.

The employer must choose one of three vesting plans and stand by it. This requirement is retroactive from January 1, 1976. Vesting programs for all who have worked since that date must fall into line with the new requirements.

The three vesting choices are the following.

1. At least 25% of all your accrued credits must be vested in your account after five years of service; then at least 5% per year must be vested for the next ten years; then 10% per year must be vested after that until you're fully vested, which will be by the fifteenth year.

For example, let's say your employer is contributing $500 per year to your pension fund account, once you have become eligible to participate in the plan. Under this first choice, at least 25% of all your accrued credits must be vested after the first five years in the plan. During those first five years, the employer will have contributed $2500 to your account. The law states that 25% of this amount, or $625, must be irrevocably yours by the end of five years. *Nothing* need be vested until the *end of the fifth year*, but the 25% *must then become vested by the end of the fifth year*. During the sixth year, the employer contributes another $500, bringing your total account to $3000. By the end of the sixth year, under this choice, 30% of the total, or $900, must be vested, and so on until the end of the tenth year when 50% of the then accumulated $5000 will be vested irrevocably in your name. After the tenth year, the amount vested each year goes up to

10% per year. That means that during the eleventh year 60% of your fund will be vested. The fund after the eleventh year will total $5500, of which $3300 will be vested. By the end of the fifteenth year, when the fund totals $7500, 100% will be vested in your name. That's the amount you'd eventually be entitled to. If you continued with the company beyond that time, the money would remain in your account, earning interest or dividends through the pension fund investment portfolio and, it is hoped, would increase by that investment return as well as by additional contributions that the employer has been making to your account.

Note that where employees themselves make contributions to their own accounts, those funds are always available to them on their termination.

2. The second choice is that the employer need not vest anything for the first ten years, but the employee must become 100% vested after ten years of service. In other words, if you work for nine years and then leave the job, you will lose all your accumulated rights to your pension. But if you work eleven years and then quit, you will still be entitled to those benefits accrued during those eleven years and can begin receiving them when you finally do reach retirement age, or sooner, if the plan calls for an earlier payout.

3. The third choice is called the "rule of 45." You become 50% vested when the sum of your age and your years of service total 45. You become additionally vested by 10% each year after that until you become 100% vested.

For example, at age 38 you have been working for a company for seven years. The sum of your age and the sum of your years of service totals 45, so you become 50% vested at that time. If, say, the employer had paid in $3000 toward your pension account by that time, being 50% vested would mean that $1500 was irrevocably locked away in your name, to become available to you at the proper time. Over each of the next five years, you become additionally vested by 10% so you would end up being 100% vested at age 43. (One exception to the rule of 45 is that you must, in any event, have at least five years of service. Thus, if you join a company at age 44, you don't fall under the rule of 45, when, after one year of service, you reach the 45 total. After five years of service, when you're 49, you would become 50% vested.)

These vesting choices do not mean that you're entitled to a full pension once you've achieved full vesting. You may have to wait until you actually retire before any of the funds are available. In certain cases, an employer may be willing to pass on the vested funds to an employee in the event of an earlier termination. This must be determined directly with each employer in any specific individual case.

Note also that these vesting requirements refer to the employer's contribution to the pension fund. If you are making your own contribution, either directly or through payroll deduction, you are fully and immediately vested regarding those contributions.

Can vested rights ever be lost? Not generally, but under the law a plan could stipulate that vested rights resulting from an employer's contribution could be forfeited if an employee died, and if the pension plan was not *joint with survivor benefits*. In other words, if a pension plan provides benefits only to the worker, and on the worker's death his or her survivors do not receive any of the still unpaid benefits, then, in such a plan, vested rights could possibly be lost prior to retirement if the employee dies prior to retirement.

Vested rights can also be lost or diminished if the whole pension plan is in jeopardy because of severe business hardships. Under such circumstances, the Secretary of Labor must grant approval, and if so, a pension plan can be amended to reduce vested benefits.

What if an employer contributes only very small benefits in your younger years and very high benefits in your later years, thus in effect locking you into the company? This practice, called "backloading," is minimized by the Pension Reform Law. The law requires that contributions must be spread fairly evenly throughout the years in accordance with complicated requirements.

Another important aspect of the vesting provisions regards joint and survivor benefits, briefly referred to earlier. Prior to the Pension Reform Law, an employer did not have to provide for survivor benefits in his pension plan. Now, however, if a pension plan provides for benefits to be paid to the retiree over the *remainder of his or her life*, it must provide for joint and survivor benefits. In order for these benefits to be paid, the employee must have been married for at least one year at the time retirement benefits began. The survivor benefits are to be at least one-half of those payable to the employee while he or she was alive.

What if an employee doesn't want a survivor to obtain these benefits? The individual can then sign a statement that will reject the survivor benefits. This means that one's own benefits will likely be larger. These regulations may vary where early retirement is involved. This could be an important consideration for many families—if, for example, the spouse is protected upon the death of the retiree by adequate life insurance or other proceeds, the retiree may prefer to relinquish the survivor benefits in order to get the higher payments while still living.

An employer's plan must state which vesting alternative is being used. The employer must keep records of every employee's service and vesting. Each employee is entitled to a yearly statement from an employer concerning vesting and accrued benefit status. As a result of these vesting provisions, workers may be entitled to a larger guaranteed sum of money than before the Pension Reform Law. You must consult your employer to determine exactly what your benefits are under this important aspect of the Pension Reform Law.

funding   Funding refers to putting enough money into the pension fund to meet the future promises to pay the benefits.

Say that XYZ company has ten employees in its pension plan. By reasonable estimates, each of the ten employees will receive pension benefits of $50,000 over his or her lifetime after retirement. Let's assume that all ten employees retire on the same day and that they all request a single lump sum distribution of their benefits. On this mass retirement day, therefore, the XYZ pension fund should theoretically have at least $500,000 in it.

But what if the XYZ pension fund only has $200,000 in it? Why might this be so? Perhaps through some bookkeeping shenanigans or some imprudent investment, or perhaps due to a simple shortfall in the amount it was contributing, the company has missed the mark considerably. What then happens to the ten employees? They split up the $200,000 into lumps of $20,000 each and sit there in amazement wondering what happened to them.

The Pension Reform Law attempts to correct this possible abuse. It imposes very stringent requirements on all pension funds to put away the amount that they, according to reasonable expectations, will need to meet the targeted promises.

folding   Despite the rigid requirements of the Pension Reform Law, a company may still violate that law and not properly fund enough money to meet its obligations. You may not discover this until the time for your retirement at which point, of course, it's too late.

Similarly, a company might have the finest pension plan in the world, and may meet all of the requirements of the law. But just before you're ready to retire, it goes bankrupt. It simply fails. Down the drain with it could go all of the pension fund money.

Or, a company for whom you've worked could fold after you've already started receiving your pension benefits, thus putting those benefits in jeopardy.

The Pension Reform Law has created an insurance program that will guarantee retirees at least a *portion* of their benefits if their company folds. The law established the Pension Benefit Guarantee Corporation (PBGC) to administer this program.

This insurance program is intended to provide for benefits that are *vested*. If you become entitled to your benefits under the PBGC, the *most* you can receive is $750 a month. The actual amount you will receive depends on your highest paid five consecutive years while working for the company. The $750 limit is subject to change depending on future changes in the cost of living index.

What can cause the termination of a pension plan? An employer can voluntarily terminate his pension plan, but if he does, he can become liable to the PBGC and have to repay a substantial amount of the benefits that the PBGC has paid out to covered employees.

Or the PBGC can start termination proceedings on its own if it feels the plan has failed to meet minimum funding standards or has failed to pay the benefits it has promised when due. It can also start termination proceedings if it otherwise determines that the plan and its beneficiaries are in jeopardy.

In effect, the PBGC is like a safety net under the overall pension programs throughout America. But don't rely on it to the exclusion of any other safety nets that you might provide on your own through individual initiative and planning.

Also, do not be misled by the $750 per month figure publicized in connection with PBGC. That's the *maximum* a worker can receive; in fact, the amount any worker might receive could be *much less* than $750. Although the odds of termination of a pension plan are small (about one in forty according to a Treasury Department estimate), a worker could be in for a rude awakening by believing that he will always receive at least $750 through PBGC when he might actually only receive a small fraction of that depending on his vested benefits.

reporting The law has created these benefits and protections for the individual worker, but how is the average individual supposed to learn about them and keep up to date with them?

The law has seen to that too. Every eligible participant in a plan must be given a description of the plan plus a periodic summary of the plan "written in a manner calculated to be understood by the average plan participant." This summary must explain in detail the participant's rights and obligations under the plan. Additionally, the company must maintain open access to the latest annual report on the plan, and related documents must be available for examination by participating employees.

The written explanation shouldn't be treated lightly. You should study the booklet when you get it and ask questions if you don't understand. Sound financial planning requires that you know the exact status of your pension rights at all times.

managing Let's say the person who manages your company's pension fund investment portfolio takes an ill-advised fling in the stock market and suffers severe losses. How will the losses be replaced to pay out pension benefits when they fall due? The new law proposes stringent guidelines for the management of pension funds. It sets forth fiduciary duties, the punishment for their breach, prohibited transactions, and steps to avoid conflicts of interest between the respective parties. In short, it can be expected that the investment philosophy of pension funds will become much more conservative to comply with this requirement of the Pension Reform Law.

the individual retirement account The Individual Retirement Account was outlined in detail in the chapter on fixed income investing. We now discuss some of the particular matters concerning taking your money out of an IRA plan. (The same discussion holds generally for a Keogh plan for those self-employed individuals who participate in it.)

When you do withdraw your IRA fund, the amount is then subject to income taxes. However, since you are presumably withdrawing the money after retirement, you will be in a much lower earning bracket, and the taxes you then pay on the fund will be much lower than what you would have paid had you received such monies during your working years.

Under the law, you cannot withdraw your IRA fund until after age 59½. If you do withdraw before then, you will pay a penalty on the amount withdrawn, plus taxes on the amount withdrawn. (There are exceptions in certain cases of disability or death.) The penalty was originally set at 10% of the amount withdrawn. Although this may seem harsh, it's probably not much greater than the interest you'd have to pay on a bank loan if you had to borrow the needed dollars.

The money must be withdrawn no later than the close of the tax year during which you reach age 70½. When you do withdraw the money, presumably between the ages of 59½ and 70½, you can either take it out in a lump sum or withdraw it over the span of years. Tax laws do permit you to spread the tax treatment out over as much as five years if you do withdraw in one lump sum. This can further lessen the tax bite, and should be seriously considered by anyone withdrawing money from an IRA plan.

the IRA roll-over

You've been working for an employer for a considerable amount of time, and you have a substantial fund vested in your pension account. You are leaving the job now, either to retire or to take another job.

Prior to the Pension Reform Law, if you received the funds due you at that time, you'd have to pay income taxes on at least that portion of the fund that represented what the employer had contributed. If you had not wanted to make use of that money at that time, you'd still have to pay the taxes.

Now, under the Pension Reform Law, an individual can use an IRA plan to hold the monies received on termination of a job and delay the payment of taxes until a later ultimate withdrawal.

Further, an IRA plan can be used to transport accumulated pension benefits from one company to another if both the old employer and the new employer are willing.

The procedure is referred to as a "roll-over." Here's how it works. You leave a job and you receive in a lump sum the pension benefits to which you are entitled. Any portion of that fund that exists because of contributions you made will be taxable at the time you receive the lump sum. But the portion the employer contributed can be spared from income taxes by depositing the total sum into an IRA account within sixty days. You can then leave the money in the IRA account indefinitely, until you are ready to withdraw the money. Or, if you obtain new employment where a qualified pension program is available, you can, if the new employer is willing, deposit your IRA funds from the previous job into the new plan.

If you do roll-over money from a former pension plan into an IRA plan, you must maintain a separate IRA account for that money. You can't put your previous pension distribution into any other investment plan in which you are a participant if you want to retain the IRA benefits. The basic regulations of the regular IRA plan apply to the roll-over IRA plan.

If you are leaving one job, whether you intend to go back to work or not, and you had substantial pension benefits payable to you that you may not be needing for a number of years, the IRA roll-over provides very attractive shelter from taxation for an extended period of time.

one final caution

The Pension Reform Law takes a lot of the guesswork out of how much a worker can expect to have on retirement. The provisions of the law can serve as an excellent planning guide for the 40 million American workers covered by pension plans. But a pension, unless it's most generous, should not be relied on solely as a means of support during retirement years. Regardless of what your pension rights might be, you still have to properly evaluate all other sources of income and structure your program in line with your needs. The pension may fall far short of fulfilling your needs, yet many people have made the mistake of assuming that it, plus Social Security, will be all they need. It's a mistake from which there may be no ability to recover.

Further, for the other 40 million individuals not currently covered by pensions, arrangements must be made to provide for necessary living funds when they do cease work. The IRA plan is a most attractive mode, along with other fixed income programs, plus the addition—where prudent—of more speculative techniques. The law can only help answer questions; it can't solve basic problems. For that, you must look primarily to yourself, and to your own ability to do the necessary homework and planning.

Reporter's Notebook: Excerpts from a Survey of Recent Retirees

"One year before retirement we made up a fairly liberal budget and lived with it for that one year. Kind of like a trial run. Then we knew we could really make it go. Advice for would-be retirees? Frank talks. Communicate and be prepared. The first year of togetherness can be difficult."

* * *

"Think young and resolve to be independent as long as you're able. Neither your children nor any organization owes you anything. If you think you've reached the age where now someone will take care of you, you're sadly mistaken.. If you haven't long ago accepted the fact that only you are responsible for your future, then you're in for a rude awakening. Your family will keep in close touch, especially your children, but be prepared if they don't. They have their own lives to live and probably have their own problems. You'll be hurt and feel neglected, but don't throw their neglect up to them for it will only alienate them. Let them see that you're happy.

* * *

"On retirement, we moved from the New York City area to a retirement community in a warm climate. We wanted to get away from the large city and the cold climate. Why did we choose a retirement community? We felt that as we grew even older, we would need the protection and slower pace of such an area. We'd have done it sooner if we had it to do over again. I'd advise others to consider the same. Young people are not interested in senior citizens, and it's easier to live with a group of one's peers. General advice? Retire while you are still young enough to adapt to new surroundings. A sense of humor helps too."

* * *

"I retired from my dental practice ten years ago, at age 62. We had no children, and quite honestly I never became involved in any hobbies or activities. Now I'm paying the price. We moved to a retirement community two years ago, but I think it was a mistake. We're going to move back to our former home where we had more friends. There are too many old people here. Even though I'm in my

seventies, this place is only old people. The worst part of retiring is too much time on your hands. Retirees should have hobbies or sports interests consistent with their health. The worst habit is getting bored and turning to the bottle."

* * *

"I retired at age 66 from my own drycleaning business about two years ago. Looking back, though, I wish I had done it earlier, perhaps at age 62.

What applied to me may not fit others, but at age 50 I began to think about retirement and realized that I would need things to do. So I cultivated hobbies—many of them. I've long been an amateur color photographer, but to that I added the collecting of rocks, old bottles, sea shells, and so on. As a result, everywhere I go I'm looking for something. I deliberately built up associations with others who like the same things, so I always find someone to go with. I cultivated these hobbies so assiduously before retirement that I found it hard to wait until I could spend all the time I wanted on them.

I believe, therefore, that I looked *forward* to doing these things and haven't looked *backward* at not having to go to work. Having observed many

564

other retirees in the last fifteen years, I think 95% of them would have been better off to have adopted my theory."

*   *   *

"Before considering moving to a new location, a couple should investigate the area and the situation, taking all possibilities into consideration. They should talk it over with their family, clergymen, banker, lawyer, and doctor—and anyone else who can offer an intelligent opinion. They should be willing to accept these opinions with an open mind. If they do move, it can be a big emotional upset that may require care and kindly consideration to overcome. Should they decide to stay in the same neighborhood, they must be prepared to adjust to changes that are inevitable—old friends dying or moving away, changes in the community, and so on. It can be just as difficult a situation if they later decide to return to their old neighborhood where things have not stood still.

The best advice is for the couple to get as mentally close as they were when they were married, and to remember that they can not enjoy leisure without doing some work, nor can they enjoy pleasure without having some pain."

*   *   *

"It's been ten years since I left my executive position. I'm now 79 and living quite comfortably in a happy retirement. To other executives on the verge of retirement, I offer these words: Be prepared to accept the change as a form of partial exile from former habits as well as emancipation from previous compulsory activities. Don't expect to be missed for long by former business associates and do not visit them unless invited. You should be realistic and accept the loss of clout gratefully."

*   *   *

"I'm 64 years old and formerly an attorney with a major national corporation. Two years ago I was forced to take early retirement, and it hit me like a bolt out of the blue. It happened to me as well as to 800 other employees in my company, and it's going to happen to many other people in the months and years ahead.

In spite of the fact that my pension was generous and my financial sacrifice not great, and in spite of the fact that early retirement had not been directed solely at me, and that from my position in the company I knew and understood the sound judgment behind the early retirement program, *I still resented being forced to take early retirement.*

Only now, three years later, is my resentment beginning to abate. I would wish for anyone reaching retirement age that he or she be able to adjust to the change and avoid the underlying resentment that plagued me. No matter how carefully you may prepare yourself, you still can feel cast aside, no longer needed. In my case I had adjusted my thinking to retirement at 65 and was at short notice chopped off at 62."

*   *   *

"My career with the Social Security Administration put me in daily contact with retiring persons from 1936 until 1967, and I personally observed the problems of old age, retirement, survivorship, disability, and medical care programs.

The indisputable lesson for pre-retirement financial planning is that the earlier start, the better. Specifically, these points should be noted: (1) analyze in writing your entire financial picture with a balance sheet of all assets and net worth. Go into particular detail on present income and expenses, and prospective future income and expenses. That is the basis you need to proceed sensibly. (2) Be as debt free as you can within the projected lifestyle that you wish to enjoy. Interest on borrowings is a heavy drain. (3) Be careful not to let too large a portion of your total assets get frozen into your housing.

General advice? Relax. Don't expect retirement to be served

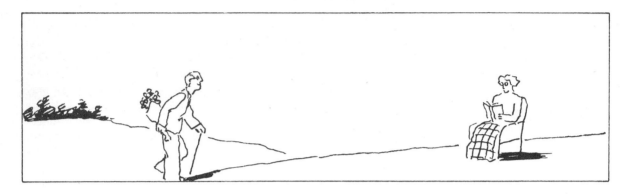

up to you on a silver platter. Be satisfied with the small joys, and, if bored, blame yourself. Philosophize constructively.''

*   *   *

"When I was thirty years old, my employer told me that my pension plan would provide $511 per month at age 65. That, plus my Social Security, seemed enough to meet all my needs and allow my wife and I to have a leisurely and comfortable life at retirement. I left it at that and didn't make any other plans. We spent what we earned and lived well.

Then came the blow. I was made to retire at age 62 at a $405 per month pension benefit. And times have changed. Not only am I getting more than $100 less than I expected, but the money I am getting doesn't go very far at all. If I had my life to live over again, I'd have anticipated this possibility and would have salted away some of my earnings in an investment program. I'd certainly recommend that to any other would-

be retirees. It's absolutely essential that you constantly update your retirement plans. History tells us that we have to put away far more for the future than we think we do. It can be a sad mistake to rely on a fixed pension program or Social Security alone. Nobody is going to take care of you later on better than you can take care of yourself.

Another burden, though I really hate to use that word, is having to care for elderly family members. My wife's mother is 84 and quite ill. Aside from the expense, which we can stand, the psychological burden on my wife weighs very heavily. Obviously, there's no easy solution to that kind of problem. It can happen to anyone and we have to learn to live with it. But we can prepare for it if we plan far enough in advance.''

*   *   *

"I'm a spinster, and I made a decent living, now I'm living decently in retirement. Some general advice for would-be re-

tirees? Here are a few thoughts I've found helpful:

☐ Make as many necessary purchases as you can a year or so before your retirement, while your earning power is still good and you can afford it better.

☐ Diversify your activities as well as your funds.

☐ Don't waste your anger on someone you like.

☐ Retire to, not from.

☐ Try to keep your "want" list within reasonable bounds. Don't be an advertiser's dream.

☐ Use the easy payment plan— pay cash.

☐ Try to enjoy the present moment just as much as you anticipate the future or relish the past.

☐ Keep your sense of humor.

☐ When you make an important decision, stop mulling it over and go forward with confidence.

☐ Always leave room for an orchid in your budget.''

1. Why are income tax deductions such as those allowed for taxes and interest of less value to most retired persons than to those still working?
2. If a life insurance policy is converted to a paid-up status, is the amount paid at death the same as or less than the original face amount?
3. What does a Power of Attorney authorize another to do for the person granting it?
4. How is the increase paid under Social Security due to inflation determined?
5. If a person drawing Social Security benefits earns $4800 during a year at the rate of $400 per month, how much will this reduce the Social Security benefit per year?
6. Who is responsible for the administration of the Pension Reform Law?
7. What are the two significant aspects of a qualified pension plan?
8. What aspect of the Pension Reform Law protects a worker who has been with a company for many years, but is then fired before retirement?

1. How could a person with substantial equity in a home put that equity to use without selling the home?
2. What are the advantages of a staggered maturity for bonds or savings certificates, compared to a single long-term investment?
3. Read over the case of the Johnson family. Select one of their alternatives and discuss why you would make that choice if you were the Johnsons.
4. One critical problem of retirement is finding activities to provide mental and physical exercise. Pretend that you are now ready to retire. Discuss what you feel would be best for maintaining your physical and mental health.

chapter 15 **estate planning**

this chapter should not be at the end of the book

Books and courses on the subject of personal money management traditionally place a discussion of estate planning at the tail end. Why? Probably because estate planning deals with something ultimately occurring at the end of life, therefore it seems appropriate to include the material at the end of the book, or course.

Wrong! The subject of estate planning can be as important early in life as later on, and the prudent individual should begin to become aware of its implications in the twenties or thirties. Estate planning is most definitely not something to be left until the later years.

By placing this chapter at the end of the book, the author is simply bowing to tradition, but does so with the strong admonition that material contained herein should be considered with as much personal concern and acted on with as much practical expedience as earlier chapters on investing, insurance, and the like.

there is a whole new set of rules

In late 1976, Congress enacted the 1976 Tax Reform Law. That law has been referred to in many other chapters because it affects income taxes, investments, and other aspects of financial planning. One of the most profound areas of change brought about by the 1976 Tax Reform Law was in the field of estate planning, particularly regarding federal and estate gift taxes. These laws underwent a major overhaul—the first time in more than forty years that Congress had brought about revisions of the existing law to conform with modern circumstances. The essentials of the new law are included in this discussion.

It should be noted, however, that laws are subject to revision and constant interpretation by courts and taxing authorities. Any discussion of the changes wrought by the 1976 Tax Reform Law should take into account subsequent changes and interpretations.

there is only one proper way to accomplish correct estate planning

Each of the fifty states has its own separate body of laws regarding how property passes from a deceased person to survivors. In our highly mobile society, individuals move from state to state, and may own property in states different from the one in which they live. Thus, it's possible to be affected by the estate laws of more than one state.

In addition, federal laws on estate and gift taxation can have a bearing on the estate of any individual, regardless of which state he or she resides in.

There are a number of ways in which property can be passed from one generation to another: by will, by trust, by virtue of joint ownership, by gift, and by intestacy (when there is no will).

Each of these different modes of passing property is subject to its own laws as to how instructions are prepared and carried out.

Because of this jumble of laws, documents, and customs, *there is really only one proper way in which a desired estate plan can be carried out: with the aid of a capable attorney.* Any attempts—repeat, *any* attempts—at do-it-yourself estate planning can be fraught with danger. Last wishes may not be carried out as expressed; taxes may have to be paid when they could have been avoided; survivors could be left in a variety of predicaments when all could have been avoided.

Citizens of the United States have a very precious right: to pass a substantial portion of their acquired wealth to the survivors of their choice. These rights are protected by our courts. But in order to achieve their fullest protection, the wishes of any individual must be expressed in full and complete accordance with the law.

A lawyer—particularly one specializing in estate matters—is the qualified party for tending to the problems of estate planning. This chapter is intended to acquaint you with the rudiments of estate planning. *It is not by any means a guide to preparing one's own estate plan.* But with the understanding that can be obtained by reading this material, and the supplementary material and class discussions accompanying it, you will have the basic knowledge to discuss personal matters intelligently with professional counsellors.

a minor device to aid in your reading

One of the most commonly used devices in estate planning is the "last will and testament," commonly called a "will." To minimize the confusion between a "will" and the other uses of the word ("I will follow my lawyer's advice"), "will," as used in this chapter is spelled as follows: WILL.

what is an estate?

While a person is living, his or her "estate" is all that the person owns, less all of that person's debts. On the death of the person, the estate becomes a legal entity in its own right. When John Doe ceases to exist, the "estate of John Doe" comes into existence. This estate becomes the legal machinery that pays the estate taxes, distributes the property and money, and carries out all other legal wishes of the decedent.

If the decedent has executed the proper legal documents, most commonly a WILL, the activities of the estate will be carried out by the Executor, a person or an institution named by the decedent to carry out these functions. If the person has died without a WILL, the state in which he or she resided at the time of death will name an administrator who will be responsible for carrying out the laws of intestacy of that state as they apply to the individual's estate.

what is estate planning?

Estate planning, simply stated, is the development of a program that will insure that any individual's last wishes are carried out regarding the estate.

We have two primary choices of distributing our estate. *The first choice* is to take steps on our own to insure that our wishes are *clearly stated*, that they will be *carried out*, and that they will receive the *full protection of the courts*.

There are many devices to establish the desired program. The most common is the preparation of a WILL. Other devices include life insurance, gifts, trusts, and simply spending it all, leaving nothing behind.

The second choice is to do nothing, in which case the laws of the state of residency at the time of death will determine the distribution of any estate.

In order to make a sensible choice between the two alternatives, we really have to understand the effects of each choice. If we exercise the first choice, and see that it's done properly, we can determine who will get what, and who will attend to the fulfillment of our wishes. On the other hand, if we choose not to take steps on our own, we owe it to ourselves and our families to know what the state laws are regarding distribution of an estate where there has been no other legal distribution set forth by the individual.

Each state has its own laws concerning this, known as "laws of intestacy." All state laws are somewhat similar, yet different. Each person must determine what the state laws of intestacy are, and how they might affect you.

the rights involved in estate planning

Rooted deeply in our legal tradition, and its English origins, are the rights of an individual to determine what will happen to his or her accumulated wealth upon the person's death. Our freedom is not total in this respect, but it is precious enough to take the fullest possible advantage of. Over the years, certain limitations have been placed on the overall freedom to distribute our accumulated wealth as we wish. For example, it was long ago determined that the federal government and some state governments would have a right to a certain share of our wealth. When the estate itself, as a legal entity, is required to pay taxes, these taxes are known as "estate taxes." The federal government levies estate taxes—though the 1976 Tax Reform Law has eliminated the federal estate taxation from all but a very small percentage of estates. Further, many states levy estate taxes.

In some states, those who *inherit* may become liable to pay taxes to the state. These are known as "inheritance taxes."

Our wishes may be limited because they are contrary to public policy. For example, a court may not carry out the wishes of a deceased person who leaves money to an individual on the condition that the individual marry or divorce a certain person, or change religions, or do, or refrain from doing, other things that society at large would deem improper or immoral.

Another form of limitation exists regarding surviving spouses. Laws differ from state to state in this respect, but, generally speaking, a surviving spouse has a right to at least a certain minimum portion of the deceased spouse's estate. If, for example, the laws of a specific state proclaim that a surviving spouse is entitled to at least one-third of the deceased spouse's estate, and the deceased spouse has expressed in his WILL that his widow will receive only 25% of the estate, the surviving widow has a "right of election against the WILL." In effect, she can disclaim that portion of the WILL that gives her only 25%, and, if everything else is in proper legal fashion, the spouse will then be entitled to the minimum allowed by the state, or one-third.

The overriding limitation on our freedom to distribute our wealth as we wish is that we must do so in accordance with the law. If we want the full protection of the courts, we have to play the game by the established rules.

The most obvious purpose of an estate plan is to determine who will get the money and property of the deceased. But there are other important purposes. In addition to distributing property, the legal documents of the estate plan can establish who will be responsible for carrying out the wishes of the deceased. If the individual has not named a party to do so, the courts will appoint an executor.

The proper use of an estate plan can minimize taxes; it can name guardians of orphaned children or other individuals previously under the guardianship of the deceased; and it can set forth specific instructions, such as funeral and burial procedures.

The deceased individual will of course never know the difference once dead, but he or she can live with a greater degree of peace of mind knowing that their wishes will be carried out because of a proper estate plan.

the terminology of estate planning

Among the various techniques of estate planning, any one or a combination thereof might offer the proper solution to an individual. In order to build the most efficient program for your estate, it is necessary to examine the alternatives that can be obtained through the use of different techniques. To better understand these techniques and how they are used, it's essential that you learn the terminology used in estate planning.

testator (female—testatrix)

This is a person who makes out a WILL. When you ask your attorney to prepare your WILL for you, you are regarded as the testator or testatrix.

decedent

A decedent is a person who has died. The testator eventually becomes the decedent.

beneficiary

A beneficiary is one who receives an inheritance in the estate of a decedent. For example, your WILL may say, "I leave my summer cottage to my sister, Melba." Melba is thus a beneficiary of a portion of your estate, namely your summer cottage. But what if Melba should die before you? In your WILL, or in other estate documents, you can name a contingent beneficiary. A contingent beneficiary is one who takes the place of a named beneficiary who has already died. For example, "My summer cottage shall go to my sister, Melba, and if she dies before I do, it shall go to my other sister, Lucy." In this case, Melba is your beneficiary and Lucy becomes your contingent beneficiary in the event that Melba dies before you do. Had you not named a contingent beneficiary, the summer cottage may have passed through Melba's estate, to whomever she may have named to receive whatever she might have owned.

bequest (legacy)

A bequest is the specific property or money given to a beneficiary. In the above example, the bequest consists of the summer cottage.

a life estate

A life estate is a form of bequest with some strings attached. To create a life estate, the WILL might read: "My summer cottage shall go to my sister Melba for as long as she lives, and on her death it shall go to the Boy Scouts of America, local chapter 123." In other words, Melba has the use of the cottage for her life, but she has no right to pass it on to anyone else on her death; at that time it will go to the local Boy Scout chapter. You have given her a life estate in the summer cottage, and you have further directed who shall get in after her death.

executor (female— executrix)

This is a person, or an institution, that one names in a WILL to handle the affairs of the estate. Generally, the executor will be granted broad powers to allow him or it to carry out the directions of the WILL. For example, the executor commonly will be given the power to buy and sell properties and securities, and to do whatever else may be needed to carry out the wishes of the deceased as closely as possible. The executor may be entitled to receive a fee for his duties, but it is possible to arrange for an executor to serve without a fee. This will all depend on personal circumstances. The testator may request or require that the executor post a bond. This is a form of insurance that would protect the estate from financial harm at the hands of the executor.

The duties of the executor can be considerable. In addition to following the specific wishes of the decedent, he may also have responsibilities of a more personal nature to the family members involved. In all likelihood, the executor will need the assistance of a lawyer and an accountant in fulfilling all the needs of the estate, which can include the payment of estate taxes and income taxes when the estate has earned income on investments or properties prior to the disbursement of the funds to the ultimate beneficiaries. If an executor is incapable of, or unwilling to, fulfill his duties, the court will generally appoint a successor executor.

administrator (female—administratrix)

If an individual dies without a WILL, the court will appoint a person or an institution to handle the affairs of the estate. This person is called the administrator or administratrix. Duties are similar to those of an executor, and the question of fees and bonds will probably be determined by the court.

probate

Probate is a court proceeding in which the validity of a WILL is established. The term probate comes from a Latin word meaning "to prove" or "to examine and find good." If the WILL is properly drawn and executed and no one challenges its terms, the court will direct that the terms of the WILL be carried out. If a challenge arises that can't be settled by the parties, the WILL is thus "contested" and additional court proceedings might be needed.

As with other matters relating to the distribution of an estate, the laws of probate can differ from state to state. Generally, the attorney for the estate, acting in conjunction with the executor, will request that the appropriate court commence the probate proceedings. All potential heirs will have been notified and will be given the opportunity to accept or challenge the WILL as written. A would-be heir who wishes to challenge an otherwise valid WILL will have to do so at his or her own expense, which can be considerable.

A challenge to a WILL, or a contest, can be a most bitter and costly struggle. Even the most carefully planned and painstakingly drawn estate plan cannot guarantee that an outside party will not challenge it. But the chances of an outside party succeeding in such a challenge will be drastically reduced by virtue of the professional expertise that has gone into creating the plan.

Some brief examples of how a WILL contest can arise: A father dies and leaves a large sum of money to his children who loved him dearly during his later years. But one wayward son who ran off to sea years ago in disgrace comes charging in after the funeral. He claims that "the Old Man was off his rocker," and that his WILL, which cut out the wayward son, was consequently not valid. He therefore stakes his claim and the battle begins.

Or, to reverse the situation, the WILL surprisingly leaves everything to the wayward son. His loving children storm back, claiming that the wayward son snuck into the father's room as he lay on his deathbed and twisted his arm to make him sign this WILL. They ask that the court judge the WILL invalid because it was signed under duress. And the battle begins.

Probate procedures are constructed so that frivolous claims or challenges will be quickly dismissed. In order for a challenge to be successful, the challenging party must have fairly clear and convincing proof that all or part of a WILL was invalid, or that the WILL being probated was not in fact the last WILL of the decedent.

the will

The first necessary step in the creation of an estate plan is a visit with your attorney. During this initial meeting, you should disclose all of your assets, liabilities, and objectives. The attorney will then be able to determine what estate planning documents might be best suited to your needs. As noted, a WILL is the most common form of device utilized in the formation of an estate plan. A simple WILL, which is adequate for most individuals, can be prepared quickly and inexpensively.

what goes into a will—the basic clauses

In a sense, a WILL is a form of contract: it is a legally binding document that sets forth certain rights and responsibilities of the parties, and cannot be changed without the consent of at least the person who drew up the WILL. If the testator has had his WILL prepared in full compliance with the laws of his state, then, on his death, the executor has the responsibility for carrying out the stated wishes in the WILL, and the courts of the state are responsible for seeing to it that the rights of the survivors are given the full protection of the law.

The major clauses of a WILL that set forth primary responsibilities and rights are as follows.

the introductory clause

This generally is the opening clause of a WILL and it should clearly and unmistakably state that "this is my last WILL and testament," or, "my WILL is as follows." It is essential that this clause establish that you are creating the WILL and that the document is in fact your WILL. If both you and the document are not clearly identified as to who and what they are, it's conceivable that another party might claim that this is not your actual WILL. For example, an individual might intend to create a WILL by writing a personal letter to his spouse, his children, or his attorney. He does not clearly identify the letter as being his purported WILL. In the letter he disinherits one of his children. After his death, the letter is introduced as being his actual WILL. The disinherited child, who would stand to gain considerably if there were no WILL (and the property passed through the laws of intestacy, which would assure each child of a certain percentage of the estate) attacks the letter claiming that it is not in fact the true WILL of the deceased. The court will probably uphold the disinherited child, thus invalidating the purported WILL, and requiring that the property pass through intestacy.

revocation of prior wills

If an individual is creating a WILL, and has previously made another WILL, he should, assuming these are his wishes, clearly revoke the entire prior WILL by stating so clearly in the new WILL. If he does not do this, it's possible that the prior WILL, or at least portions thereof, might be included in the probate with his new WILL. If there are two WILLs, the latter one will generally control, except to the extent that the specific provision of the two WILLs are consistent with each other. But even this can cause unnecessary complications, which can be avoided by a clear revocation of the former WILL.

For example, a testator prepares a WILL in which he leaves a bequest of $10,000 to each of his grandchildren. At the time he drew the WILL he had two grandchildren. Many years later, he draws another WILL, but does not clearly revoke the earlier WILL. The new WILL contains the same clause giving $10,000 to each of his grandchildren. But now he has eight grandchildren, which means a total bequest to them all of $80,000. This is now a very substantial portion of his total estate. The question may well arise as to whether or not only the original two grandchildren were entitled to the $10,000 bequest or whether all eight are entitled to it. If all eight are entitled to it, other heirs might receive much less. The actual wording of the old WILL and the new WILL, perhaps with the assistance of the court in interpreting the clauses, will ultimately determine who gets what. But the example illustrates how confusion and disagreement can result where there are two WILLs that may convey the same intentions, but each with a substantially different effect on the overall estate.

debts and final expenses

Before your survivors can receive their share of your estate, the remaining debts, funeral expenses, and taxes must be paid. Commonly, a testator will include a clause in his WILL instructing the executor to make all these appropriate payments. But even if there is no such clause, the executor will still be required to make them.

Each individual state law sets forth the *priority* of who gets what and in what order. If your state laws require that a "widow's allowance" be paid, that generally is the item of first priority. This is not the widow's ultimate share of the estate, but is usually a minimum allowance to enable her to get by for at least a short time. After the widow's allowance, the priorities generally run as follows: funeral expenses; expenses of a final illness; estate and other taxes due to the United States; state taxes; taxes of other political subdivisions within the state, such as cities and counties; then other debts owed by the decedent.

Creditors of the estate must generally file a claim against the estate if they wish to be paid. The executor may determine, or the testator may have instructed the executor accordingly, that certain claims are not valid. A testator can not invalidate legitimate claims against his estate by simply stating in the WILL that those claims are not valid. However, if claims are in fact invalid, or even questionable, the executor's powers might result in eliminating such claims or minimizing them, particularly if the creditor does not wish to press the matter with the executor and the courts.

If, after all debts, taxes, funeral costs, and final illness expenses are paid, there is enough left in the estate to make payments to the survivors, such payments are then made in accordance with the "legacy clauses." If, however, these debts and expenses consume all that there is in the estate, then the survivors may receive nothing. In such a case, the estate is considered to be insolvent.

legacy, or bequest, clauses

These clauses determine which of your survivors gets how much. Broadly speaking, there are four ways in which property can pass on death to the survivors: through joint ownership with right of survivorship; through a specific bequest; through a general bequest; and through the residuary.

If property is owned in joint names—such as a home, or a savings account—the property will pass to the survivor of the two joint owners on death, assuming that the ownership had been structured in that form. The WILL need not necessarily specify such matters, but it would be probably advantageous to make note of these items in the WILL to avoid possible misunderstanding.

A specific bequest, or legacy, will refer to a particular item or security. For example, a testator may bequeath to a child, "my stamp collection which is located in safe deposit box 1234 at the Fifth National Bank." The collection will pass to the survivor on the death of the testator, assuming that the testator still owns it at the time of death. If he no longer owns it, then obviously it cannot pass, and the gift will dissolve. The heir will receive nothing in its place unless the testator has specifically instructed the substitution of other items of value, or money, should he no longer own the collection. Further, if the subject of a specific bequest is not free and clear—it has been pledged, for example, as collateral for a loan—the heir will receive that property subject to the debt against it, and will be responsible for paying off the debt unless the testator has instructed that he is to receive it free and clear. For example, the stamp collection may have been pledged as collateral for a loan. The collection is worth $10,000 and the balance on the loan is $2000. If the testator has not stated that the heir is to receive it free and clear, the heir can be responsible for paying the $2000 owed. If, though, the testator has instructed that the heir should receive it free and clear, the $2000 debt will be paid out of other estate resources.

General legacies are those payable out of the general assets of the estate. Commonly, general legacies will be in the form of cash, such as "I bequeath to my housekeeper, Marsha Margolis, the sum of $3000."

Occasionally, there will be a form of legacy that is a cross between a specific and a general legacy. It's referred to as a "demonstrative legacy." For example, the testator instructs that his two nephews, Tom and Dick, each receive $3000 from the proceeds of the sale of his stamp collection, which is to be sold to the highest bidder at auction after his death. This may be construed as a demonstrative legacy. If the auction of the stamp collection only brings $5000, Tom and Dick might still be entitled to receive their full $3000 by dipping into the general assets of the estate for the remaining $500 apiece.

After all property has passed through either joint ownership, specific legacies, or general legacies, everything that's left is called the "residual." Commonly, this will represent the bulk of many estates. A typical residual clause might read as follows: "All the rest, remainder, and residual of my estate I hereby bequeath to my wife and children, to be divided equally among them." There may be further detailed instructions concerning the manner and timing of such distributions, including the possibility of trusts that would parcel out the payments over a specific period of time.

In planning a WILL program, it's essential that the testator and attorney discuss all these various provisions for distribution in detail. Further, as individual circumstances change over the years, these clauses should be reviewed to determine that the bequests are still what the testator wishes; and if the subjects of specific bequests are no longer owned by the testator, provisions should be made as desired for the proper substitution.

(Another minor definition should be noted: personal property generally passes through a WILL as a "bequest." When real estate is transferred, the transaction is commonly referred to as a "devise." For example, I bequeath to my son my diamond ring; and I devise to my daughter my summer cottage at the lake.)

Other elements of who gets what—and who doesn't—may include clauses of disinheritance; clauses that set forth a preference among various heirs; gifts to charitable causes; and clauses that release individuals from debts owed to the decedent.

survivorship clauses
Though rare, it can happen that a husband and wife will be killed in a common disaster, such as an automobile accident or an airplane crash. Each of their WILLs should have been created with this possibility in mind, particularly if there are minor children. The couple will want to determine who will be the guardians of the children in the event of such a disaster. If estate taxes are of concern to the couple, a survivorship clause should also set forth the sequence of the deaths (who is to have been presumed to have died first) in such a way as to minimize the effect of estate taxes.

appointment clauses
In this clause, the testator will appoint the person or institution who will be the executor of the estate. Where personal circumstances dictate, a testator may also want to name an attorney for the estate to act in conjunction with the executor.

If other individuals—such as minor children or elderly parents—are dependent on the testator, the testator should also name the guardian for such individuals. This guardian will have the duties and responsibilities, and fee if any, that are specified in this appointment clause.

It's common for one spouse to name the other spouse as executor (or executrix). The testator wants to know that someone who is deeply concerned with the welfare of the survivors will be in charge of carrying out the duties of the executor. It should be noted, however, that the duties of the executor can be rigorous and demanding; the more complicated the estate, the more exacting the duties. A surviving spouse may not be equipped to handle many of the duties; thus, many prudent individuals will name an institution, such as a trust department of a bank, as a co-executor. The institution is fully staffed and capable of carrying out the specific legal and accounting responsibilities of the executorship, and in cases of substantial estates should prove to be well worth their fees. The testator, in naming such a co-executor, has the added peace of mind of knowing that the burden on the surviving spouse will be minimized, yet the personal concern will remain, while adding to it the expertise of the financial institution.

the execution   The final clauses of a WILL are very important. They are called the "testimonium clause" and the "attestation clause." The testimonium clause contains language in which the testator expresses that he or she is signing this document as his or her true last WILL and testament, as of the specific date on which the document is being executed. The attestation clause contains language in which the witnesses to the WILL agree that they have witnessed the signing of the WILL in each other's presence and in the presence of the testator on the specific date.

The combination of these two clauses should serve as ample proof that the document is in fact the last WILL and testament of the testator, and that the document has been properly signed, and that the witnesses can verify all of this.

The execution of a WILL is a ritual that should follow the letter of the law. Each state's law determines how many witnesses should attest to the signing of the WILL by the testator. It is generally imprudent for any individual who may receive a share of the estate—either as a family member or as a recipient of a specific or general bequest—to act as a witness at the signing of the WILL.

In addition to the signing and witnessing at the end of the WILL, the attorney may have the testator and each witness sign or initial each separate page of the WILL. This may help serve as added proof that the WILL that is finally presented for probate is the true and complete total WILL of the testator.

Until the WILL is finally signed and witnessed, it is not in fact valid. Any attempt to shortcut the execution procedure might open the doors to anyone with thoughts of contesting the WILL if this person can prove that the WILL was not properly signed or witnessed by the appropriate parties.

changing a will

A WILL can be legally changed in one of two ways: it can be totally revoked by a brand new WILL, in which case the brand new WILL should expressly state that the former WILL is totally revoked. Or, minor changes can be affected by means of a "codicil."

A WILL can *not* be legally amended by crossing out or adding words, by removing or adding pages, or by making erasures. A codicil should be drawn by an attorney and should be executed and witnessed in the same fashion as the original WILL itself. The codicil should then be attached to the WILL. If a WILL is amended in any way other than the creation of a new WILL or the creation of a properly executed codicil, it's all that much easier for anyone who wishes to contest the WILL to be successful. Further, a court might not admit to probate a WILL that has been changed by hand. Such improper changes could conceivably invalidate the entire WILL, and could render the estate subject to the laws of intestacy. In short, a testator should not destroy all that he or she has created in the estate plan by making changes unless they are made in the proper legally prescribed fashion.

Once a WILL has been drawn and executed, it's common for the attorney to keep the original in a safe or a fireproof file. You should keep a copy or two for your own reference, and if you've named a bank or other institution as executor or co-executor, they should also receive a copy for their files.

when should a will be altered?

A prudent individual should review his or her WILL and overall estate plan at least every three years. Depending on the extent of change in the individual's circumstances, revisions may or may not be called for. These are the common circumstances that might dictate the need to amend a WILL or any other portion of an estate plan:

☐ If the individual has moved to a different state, the WILL should be reviewed. Remember that the law of WILLs and estate distribution are state laws and there can be slight or significant differences from one state to another. A change in state residence could therefore have a slight or significant impact on an estate plan. You won't know until you've had your plan reviewed by an attorney in your new state of residence.

☐ Changes in family circumstances might dictate the need to alter a WILL. Children may have grown up and moved out on their own. If one child has become particularly affluent and another has suffered economically, you might want to make provision to assist the less fortunate child. You may wish to add or delete charitable contributions, to amend your funeral and burial instructions, to add or delete specific bequests that you have made to individuals, and there may be a myriad of other possibilities. The testator himself must see to it that changes are covered in the proper legal fashion.

☐ If there have been substantial changes in your assets and liabilities, a review of your WILL might indicate that changes are in order. If you have acquired substantially greater wealth since the original drawing of the WILL, this may dictate different modes of distribution to your heirs. If your estate has been diminished by financial reversals, appropriate changes might also be in order.

☐ If heirs named in your WILL have died before you, you might want to review the effect that would have on the distribution of your estate.

☐ If an executor or guardian named in the WILL has died or has become incapable of acting in the desired capacity, or if you simply no longer wish to have that person representing your interests, an amendment to your WILL would be in order.

☐ If tax laws change regarding estates, a review of your WILL would most certainly be in order. The changes wrought by the 1976 Tax Reform Law can have a sweeping effect on millions of estate plans already in existence. Virtually all estate plans and WILLs prepared prior to the effective date of the Tax Reform Law—January 1, 1977—should be at least reviewed by an attorney, and changes should be made where called for.

It's impossible to know when further changes may come about in the laws, but there are always court decisions that cast slightly new and different interpretations on existing laws. Any of these decisions could conceivably have an effect on your own estate distribution, and your attorney should be aware of such possible effects and advise you accordingly to make the appropriate changes.

uncommon wills

Occasionally a court will receive for probate a WILL that has been prepared by the testator in his own handwriting. It may or may not have the appropriate number of witnesses. A WILL that's prepared in the handwriting of the testator is called a "holographic WILL." Some states permit the probate of holographic WILLs under certain circumstances, but such WILLs are definitely not substitutes for WILLs prepared under proper legal guidelines. The courts recognize that individuals may be in dire circumstances and are unable to acquire the proper legal counsel to prepare a totally valid WILL. Thus, allowances are made for the occasional probate of a holographic WILL.

In more extreme cases, a WILL may be spoken by the dying individual to another party or parties. Such a WILL, oral or spoken, is referred to as a "noncupative WILL." It's allowed only by some states, and then only under strictly defined conditions.

Neither a holographic WILL nor a noncupative WILL should be relied on as a substitute for a properly prepared WILL. A court may find such a WILL invalid and could throw the entire estate into a situation of intestacy. Where at all possible, proper legal assistance should be sought in creating a WILL. A store-bought WILL, with the blanks filled in, or a WILL prepared under the instructions of a "do-it-yourself" guidebook could prove to be totally futile and foolish. This is one of the most glaring forms of false economy—saving the legal fees involved in creating an estate plan could result in a far more costly and aggravating situation when a do-it-yourself WILL is either invalidated or contested with great bitterness by survivors or subjects the estate to unnecessary taxation.

other devices for passing one's accumulated wealth

trusts

In addition to the common WILL, there are other means whereby one may pass wealth to heirs and other generations. A trust is a "strings attached" way of passing money or property to another party.

For example, you have the sum of $10,000 that you would like eventually to pass to your son who is now 25 years old. But you're concerned that he might run through that money imprudently. You thus decide that until he reaches the age of 40, he should only be entitled to the income that the $10,000 would generate through investments.

When he reaches 40, he can have the entire amount. In order to accomplish this, you create a trust.

To be sure that your wishes are carried out without further concern on your part, you make an arrangement, for example, with your bank to administer the trust. The bank then becomes the "trustee." You deposit the $10,000 with the bank, which then agrees to invest it prudently and pay out the income to your son until he reaches the age of 40, at which time he will be paid the full principal amount.

That's an oversimplified view of the creation and function of a trust, but it's intended to make the point that passing money by trust is not an outright transfer. There are, as noted, strings attached. The trust agreement itself can stipulate just how much the beneficiary (your son) will get at what time and under what circumstances.

In the foregoing case, both parties involved in the trust are still living. This would be called an *inter vivos* trust, or a trust between the living.

Or, a trust can be established in one's WILL to take effect upon death. Instead of property passing outright to the beneficiary of the WILL, it may go in trust. For example, you might leave $10,000 in your WILL in trust for your son until he reaches the age of 40, with the full amount payable to him on that date. Where a trust is established in one's WILL to take effect on death, it's referred to as a "testamentary trust."

A trust can be revocable or irrevocable. A revocable trust is one that can be revoked or cancelled. An irrevocable trust may not be cancelled; it is permanent.

Under certain circumstances, trust arrangements may be desirable in place of a WILL, or may be used in conjunction with a WILL. There is no fixed rule—it all depends on individual circumstances.

The law of trusts is complicated. A great deal can be accomplished with trusts, both in the control of property and in the minimization of estate taxes. An attempt at a do-it-yourself trust might be even more foolhardy than a do-it-yourself WILL because of the added complexities of the trust laws.

The trustee is the person or firm who has the duty of carrying out the directions of the trust. The trust document, which is a form of contract, spells out the trustee's powers and responsibilities. Many people prefer to use a financial institution as a trustee instead of an individual. Bank trust departments are operated by professionals, and there is an assurance of permanence. Such permanence has obvious advantages if a trust is designed to continue for many years. As with naming executors in a WILL, an individual might prefer to name both a corporate trustee (such as a bank) and a person close to the family as co-trustees.

gifts

Making gifts of money or property is another form of estate planning. Gifts have long been popular with more wealthy individuals as a means of cutting down on their potential estate tax liability. By giving them away prior to death, money or property may escape taxation, wholly or partly. The overall desirability or feasibility of making gifts a portion of an estate plan should be discussed in detail with professional advisors.

insurance

For a great many families, life insurance is the predominant way of passing wealth from one generation to the next. Indeed, in families of lesser means, a life insurance program may be the only form of estate planning necessary. But it would be imprudent to rely on the existence of life insurance policies as a substitute for sound estate planning. Even the most modest estates should attempt a review with the proper professionals to determine what will occur on the death of each individual. Insurance can pass money from one generation to another, but it may not assure that the parties who need the money most, or who are most entitled to it, will get what the testator wishes. For example, an individual may have little estate other than life insurance policies and if his children are named as beneficiaries, his widow may not receive what she needs for her own survival. If the children aren't willing or able to help her, she could be in dire straits. On the other hand, the widow could be the sole beneficiary of the life insurance policies, and the children could thus be deprived of funds that the individual wished them to have. These matters should be discussed with a life insurance agent, in conjunction with an attorney and accountant.

joint names

Putting property in joint names, such as husband and wife, often seems a simple and attractive way to insure that the surviving spouse will receive everything in the event of the other spouse's death. This may be true in many cases, but it can subject the total value of the estate to estate taxes that could have been avoided, and may prevent the money from ultimately going where you had wished it to go. For families of more modest means, a joint names program might suffice in many cases. It's not safe to make any assumptions about the ultimate distribution of an estate wherein everything is owned jointly—the advice of a competent attorney is still essential.

spending it all

For many, spending it all may be the ultimate form of estate planning. If you can make arrangements, such as through gifts or trusts, for your survivors to be taken care of according to your wishes, you might then proceed to spend everything available and pass on without leaving any problems over probate, estate taxes, or squabbles among heirs. For example, it might be feasible in certain situations to establish a trust for the children, with the individual testator receiving all income from the trust, and the principal going to the children upon the testator's death. If you're fortunate enough to have ample assets that, if invested, could generate enough income for you to live comfortably on, you might have a program that will allow you to "spend it all" without any need for a further estate plan.

what should your estate plan accomplish?

Four main objectives should be kept in mind when creating and amending any estate plan.

1. To establish the proper liquidity and distribution of assets.
2. To establish a program of sound management of assets.
3. To provide for the assured continuation of a family's life style in the event of death, or disability, or retirement.
4. To minimize taxation. Three aspects of taxation must be taken into account: the federal gift and estate taxes that would come out of the overall estate assets; the taxes that the heirs may ultimately have to pay on inherited property; and, perhaps of slightly lesser concern, the income taxes that the estate may have to pay, where it has had earnings before the ultimate distribution of the assets to the heirs.

Let's now take a closer look at each objective.

establishing proper liquidity and a proper distribution of assets

Mike was a good planner up to a point. He prepared his WILL some years ago leaving one-half to his wife and the other half to be divided equally between his three children. Mike worked hard and provided well for his family. He had a one-half interest in a successful plumbing supply firm; owned a twelve-unit apartment house that he had bought as an investment, which was providing a satisfactory return; owned a number of promising parcels of vacant land in the suburbs of his community; and had a stock portfolio that had performed fairly well, but at the time of his death was considerably depressed below what Mike had paid for it.

Mike also had a portfolio of life insurance, and his children were named as the beneficiaries of all the policies.

Mike reviewed his WILL periodically, and was particularly pleased when the passage of the 1976 Tax Reform Law removed any concern about possible estate taxes. Although his estate was considerable, it was not large enough to cause any worry about estate taxes. His lawyer had helped him revise his WILL to conform with the requirements of the new law.

But Mike had failed to take other matters into account. Although Mike's estate represented ample wealth, the wealth was not liquid. That is, upon his death there was not enough ready cash available to take care of the needs of his survivors, or to accomplish other transactions that could have helped assure their welfare. Had his estate been subject to estate taxes, there wouldn't have been enough cash on hand to pay the taxes. The only liquid asset of any consequence was his life insurance payable to his children. If they hadn't been willing to provide for their mother's needs, certain assets would have to be sold—perhaps at sacrifice—to take care of those needs.

Mike's oversight regarding liquidity and distribution of assets caused problems he would have dearly regretted. Without Mike at the helm of the business, its value dropped sharply. Mike had been the "outside man" and had developed a strong personal relationship with the clientele. His partner was the "inside man" and had neither the know-how nor the temperament for dealing with customers. Further, the partner did not have the cash or the desire to buy out Mike's share. Mike's heirs were left with a difficult choice: either try to revive a suddenly floundering business or sell it for far less than it could have been worth or might yet be worth if new blood were injected into it.

Regarding the business, Mike and his partner could have better protected their families by entering into a program of "key man" life insurance. This program would have insured each man for an agreed on sum of money, and, in the event of the death of either, the insurance proceeds would have been payable to the business. This could have provided a substantial sum of cash if the parties agreed to liquidate the business; or it could have given the remaining partner an ample sum to help tide the business through its difficult times without one of its partners; or it could have supplied the capital for the surviving partner to buy out Mike's interest, thus giving Mike's heirs ample cash. Mike could have accomplished all this by amending his existing life insurance plan to name the business as the beneficiary rather than his children.

With regard to the apartment house, the land, and the stocks, Mike's heirs were divided over what should be done with them: sell them, borrow against them, hold them for a better price? There were ample assets for distribution, but dividing them was difficult.

As Mike's case illustrates, liquidity is an essential part of building a sound and prudent estate plan. Liquidity, more simply stated, is the ability to put cash on the table as quickly as possible and with as little expense as possible. The more liquid one's assets, the easier it will be for everybody to get whatever it is that they are supposed to have. It's not necessary—and may indeed be unwise, depending on personal circumstances—for all assets in an estate to be maximally liquid. As the chapter on fixed income investments pointed out, liquidity comes at a price: more liquid investments might return a lower yield, and many estates in their growth process may necessarily be locked into nonliquid assets, such as interests in a business (as in Mike's case).

Each individual's circumstances will dictate the proper balance in the estate between liquid and nonliquid assets. The mode of distribution of the assets will, to a large extent, depend on the liquidity of the assets. A major factor to be determined is the amount of ready cash survivors will need to live on until other less liquid assets can be properly converted into more liquid assets or into cash. When a family depends on a breadwinner for support, the need for liquidity is higher. As children grow up and become more financially independent, the need for liquidity may diminish.

In many families, life insurance is used as the device to provide the needed liquidity on the death of the breadwinner. As he grows older and the need for liquidity diminishes, the breadwinner can perhaps put his life insurance premium dollars to other uses, or can convert a program of ordinary life insurance into one of the nonforfeiture items available. (See the chapter on life insurance for more details.)

The program of distribution of assets can also include instructions by the testator as to what should be done with certain assets that are to be distributed. Mike might have exerted more effort to direct what should have been done with the various assets upon his death, and thus have saved his family considerable aggravation. For example, he might have instructed them to sell certain assets at the time of his death, regardless of their own personal feelings. They may have disagreed with him, but the matter would have been accomplished and the cash would have become available.

The plan for the distribution of assets must be revised from time to time as both the nature of the assets and the circumstances of the family change. Mike's situation illustrates some of the common problems that can arise in establishing a sound plan for the distribution of liquid assets, but individual circumstances may produce dozens of other similar problems that need comparable attention, anticipation, and execution.

establishing a program of sound management for estate assets

The bulk of Ned's estate consisted of life insurance and stocks. By the time Ned reached his mid-forties, he had accumulated a large enough estate to provide for his family in a most comfortable style, including education for the children and total peace of mind for his wife, in the event he should die suddenly, which he unfortunately did.

Ned's plan had been carefully prepared, but he had made one major miscalculation. When left on her own, Ned's wife proved to be a very poor manager of money. Between her grief at having become a widow at such a young age and her lack of familiarity with the specifics of investments, Ned's estate was wiped out within a few short years.

Ned had at one time thought that because there was a sizeable sum involved, he should arrange to have it flow through some form of managed program whereby the money would be allocated to the family as needed. But because of his faith in his wife and because of the cost involved in a managed program, he didn't do so.

Proper management of assets in an estate is a factor all too often overlooked, as is the distributional plan discussed in the case of Mike. Tales are legion of widows and children who have squandered money, been bilked, or were ill-advised.

The prudent individual planning an estate program must be aware of the need for sound management of assets for as long as the survivors will have use or need of those assets. Management can be accomplished in a number of ways. Assets can flow through a trust arrangement whereby income is paid to the survivors, and they can further have a right to tap the principal as and if the need arises for specific purposes. Insurance policies can be arranged so that the money is paid out over an extended period rather than in one lump sum. Similar extended withdrawal plans can be set up with annuities, mutual funds, pension and profit-sharing plans. Whether a management program is set up formally, as through a life insurance company or a trust, or whether it's established by common consent among the parties, there is still no substitute for a basic knowledge on the part of family members about the nature of the assets of the estate, an awareness of the pitfalls that can jeopardize those assets, and a cool collected head to keep things on an even keel, particularly during the difficult early months and years following the death of the breadwinner. In short, education and knowledge are essential for a sound management plan.

As with all other elements of estate planning, the matter of management must be reviewed from time to time and amended as needed.

assurance of continued life style

Oliver worked out a fine estate plan, taking into account all the foregoing questions of distribution and management of assets. But his mistake came in viewing the estate plan as something that commenced at the time of death. His primary concern—the concern of many—was to provide ample funds so that his family could continue to live in their accustomed manner upon his death.

But he erred in failing to provide for that same life style while he was still living. When Oliver first fell ill, his business associates continued to pay him a full salary for a number of months even though he was contributing nothing to the business. All his medical expenses were paid by a very comprehensive health insurance program. But after several months, his associates came to him and said they'd have to reduce salary since the business was hurting by his continued sick pay benefits and the loss of his energies.

Oliver could understand this and consented to it, feeling that he would soon be on the road to full recovery and back at full earnings. But it didn't work out that way. A few months later his associates told him sadly that they would have to cut his salary down to a minimum level, and a few months after that it was terminated completely. Even though his medical expenses continued to be paid, there was no income, and Oliver had to start dipping into his reserves.

His illness lingered, and when he died three years later, the bulk of his estate had been used up. His heirs received virtually nothing. Oliver's case illustrates a most tangible problem that has very intangible solutions: an otherwise adequate estate demolished by unforeseen risks. In Oliver's specific case, a solid program of disability insurance could have provided ample protection and allowed him to leave his estate much more intact. That's an insurable risk, as is most any medical situation. But other occurrences are less insurable. A portfolio of investments can suddenly turn sour—stocks, real estate, business interests. The need to support elderly or disabled family members can drain one's assets suddenly and sharply.

Prudent individuals will insure against all foreseeable risks, within reason, and without becoming "insurance poor." And they will further structure their portfolio of investments and business relationships to at least minimize the chaos that could result from unforeseen sources.

Perhaps most important is to communicate with family members about the size and extent of the estate, and what they can expect from it. They should be prepared for the contingencies they will face, realizing that the more knowledgeable they are, the better they will be able to cope on their own.

minimization of taxation

One of the paramount objectives of estate planning is to devise a program that will enable an individual to pass as much of his or her accumulated wealth to survivors as possible. But federal and state tax laws can take a bite out of what we have created and it's only natural to want to reduce that bite as much as possible.

Prior to the passage of the 1976 Tax Reform Law, only about 7% of all estates were subject to taxation. That's a relatively small percentage of the entire American population. Under the new law, the percentage of estates taxed will be even smaller—it's estimated that only about 2% will be depleted by federal estate taxes. A discussion of the implications of the federal estate tax would seem to be unwarranted in this book because the tax will only affect a very small percentage of the population, that being the most affluent segment.

Not so. A general understanding of the overall concept of estate taxation is an important element in one's general knowledge of family finance and money management. There are other provisions in the Tax Reform Law of 1976, moreover, that can have a very broad effect on a large segment of the population. In short, while many estates will escape taxation, many *heirs* will find themselves facing tax obligations that previously would not have confronted them.

Here's a brief illustration. Under the law as it existed *before* the 1976 changes, Uncle Willy bought $5000 worth of XYZ Company stock in 1970. When Uncle Willy died in 1975, the stock was worth $15,000, and you were the recipient of that stock under the terms of Uncle Willy's WILL. You immediately sold the stock for $15,000. For purposes of taxing Uncle Willy's estate, the stock would have been included in the estate at its value at the time of Uncle Willy's death, or $15,000. You, as the recipient of the stock, own it at that same value—$15,000, the value at the time of death. If you sold it for $15,000, you did not realize a gain; your selling price was the same as the value at which you received it. Because you had no gain, you as the recipient are not required to pay any tax.

Under the law as it now exists as a result of the 1976 tax changes: if Uncle Willy acquired $5000 worth of XYZ stock in 1977 and at the time of his death in 1982 it was worth $15,000, you as the recipient of that stock would have a valuation on it of $5000—the original cost to Uncle Willy. If, after receiving the stock, you sold it for $15,000, you would have realized a gain of $10,000 and that would be subject to income taxes on your own individual return. It would still be included in Uncle Willy's estate at the $15,000 value, where it may or may not be subject to estate taxes, depending on the size of the estate.

The critical change, therefore, is that heirs receive property valued at the cost of acquisition by the original owner, and no longer valued as of the time of the owner's death. The net result is that in many cases heirs are subject to taxes that they previously had not been subject to.

Thus, while one major aspect of the law will relieve many estates from the burden of estate taxation, it will subject many heirs to taxation that had previously not existed.

how the estate and gift tax laws work

There are two primary ways in which an individual can pass property on to others. He or she can make gifts of the property while alive, and can distribute the property through the estate, by WILL or by trust agreements. Both types of transactions are subject to possible taxation. When property is given away, there is the possibility of a gift tax. When property passes through an estate, it is subject to a possible estate tax. With regard to the gift tax, the individual who makes the gift, not the one who receives it, is responsible for paying any tax that may be due. With regard to the estate tax, it is the estate of the deceased individual that will be responsible for paying the tax, not the individual who receives it. (Generally, we're now referring to the estate and gift taxes at the federal level. Various states may levy estate taxes, and some also levy inheritance taxes that the heirs are required to pay. But because those laws differ so much from state to state, space does not permit comprehensive coverage of each. Every reader should learn his or her own state laws.)

In addition to estate and gift taxes, a death can also create certain income tax situations. For example, Uncle Willy dies on January 1. The assets in his estate total $100,000. His estate will be exempt from estate taxes. But it takes a full year until all the assets are finally distributed to the heirs. During this time the $100,000 is invested in a savings certificate that earns 6% or $6000. During that year, therefore, the estate of Uncle Willy has had income, on which it must pay income taxes, just as if it were an individual.

The other aspect of income taxes arising out of a death occurs when an heir receives property that is then sold at a gain. That gain is to be included in the heir's income for that year, and income taxes must be paid on it.

As noted, there are two primary kinds of federal taxation that can be imposed when one conveys property to another: gift taxes and estate taxes. In essence, the 1976 Tax Reform Law effectively combines the federal estate and federal gift tax concepts into one—a tax on taxable transfers of property, whether made during life or at the time of death.

estate taxes

Let's first examine how the tax applies to transfers of property made at the time of death—the estate tax.

The federal estate tax is calculated as follows: everything that an individual owns is totalled up (including some assets that may have been in joint names and pass directly to the surviving spouse). This total is known as the *gross estate*. Certain items are then subtracted from the gross estate. Those items include funeral expenses, the costs of administering the estate, certain debts of the deceased, charitable bequests. After deducting those expense items from the gross estate, we arrive at the *adjusted gross estate*.

The adjusted gross estate can be further reduced by one very important deduction, known as the *marital deduction*. The marital deduction consists of a portion of the estate that is left, in proper legal fashion, to one's surviving spouse. The marital deduction can be as much as $250,000 or 50% of the adjusted gross estate, whichever is larger. *Note:* the transfer must actually be made to the surviving spouse in proper legal fashion in order to allow the marital deduction. It's not available automatically. The marital deduction is subtracted from the adjusted gross estate, and the result is the *taxable estate*.

The taxable estate represents the amount of *taxable transfers* made by the individual. Table 15-1 is used to calculate the tax.

table 15-1 **estate and gift tax rates***

Taxable Transfers	Tax Due (Before Credit)
(via gift or estate, after all proper expenses, deductions, marital deduction)	
Under $10,000	18% of Taxable Transfers
$10,000 to $20,000	$1,800 plus 20% of excess over $10,000
$20,000 to $40,000	$3,800 plus 22% of excess over $20,000
$40,000 to $60,000	$8,200 plus 24% of excess over $40,000
$60,000 to $80,000	$13,000 plus 26% of excess over $60,000
$80,000 to $100,000	$18,200 plus 28% of excess over $80,000
$100,000 to $150,000	$23,800 plus 30% of excess over $100,000
$150,000 to $250,000	$38,800 plus 32% of excess over $150,000
$250,000 to $500,000	$70,800 plus 34% of excess over $250,000
$500,000 to $750,000	$155,800 plus 37% of excess over $500,000
$750,000 to $1,000,000	$248,300 plus 39% of excess over $750,000
Over $1,000,000	The rates continue to escalate upwards until the highest level is reached; after $5,000,000 taxable transfers the tax (before credit) is $2,550,800 plus 70% of any excess over $5,000,000.

* Unified Federal Estate and Gift Tax Rates as a result of passage of the 1976 Tax Reform Law. *Note:* The credit referred to in the text applies directly against the tax due.

table 15-2
credit available against federal estate and gift taxes.

Year	Credit	Eliminates tax on cumulative taxable transfers not exceeding:
1978	$34,000	$134,000
1979	38,000	147,333
1980	42,500	161,563
1981	47,000	175,625

The tax due is then reduced by a *credit* that the federal law allows. During the first year of the new law, 1977, the credit totalled $30,000. That credit will increase each year until 1981, when it reaches a total of $47,000. Table 15-2 illustrates the amount of the credit available each year under the 1976 Tax Reform Law.

Here are some simplified examples of how the estate tax would be calculated. Able, Baker, and Charlie all have *gross estates* of $400,000, and they all have deductible expenses totalling $20,000. Thus, they would all have an *adjusted gross estate* of $380,000.

Able decides to leave only 25% of his adjusted gross estate, or $95,000, to his wife. The balance he leaves to his children. His marital deduction of $95,000 thus reduces his adjusted gross estate, leaving Able's estate with a taxable transfer of $285,000. Looking at Table 15-1, we see that the tax on a taxable transfer of $285,000 would be $82,700. (Look at the line where the taxable transfer is $250,000 to $500,000. The tax due before the credit is $70,800 plus 34% of the excess over $250,000. The excess in this case is $35,000, and 34% of that, $11,900, is added to the $70,800 to arrive at the total tax of $82,700.)

Able died in 1981 when the credit was $47,000 (Table 15-2). The $47,000 credit is subtracted from the tax of $82,700 leaving an actual tax due of $35,700. Table 15-3 illustrates Able's case more graphically.

table 15-3   Able's estate tax calculations

$400,000	Gross estate
−20,000	Deductible expenses
380,000	Adjusted gross estate
−95,000	Marital deduction
285,000	Taxable transfer

Tax, from Table 15-1, is   70,800 + 34% of 35,000

or   11,900

Tax =   82,700

−47,000   Credit (Table 15-2)

35,700   Tax due

Baker, who also died in 1981, decided to leave one-half of her adjusted gross estate, or $190,000, to her surviving spouse. Her taxable transfer thus totalled $190,000, which would result in a tax of $51,600. Subtracting from that amount the $47,000 credit, Baker ended up with an actual tax due of $4600. Table 15-4 illustrates Baker's case.

Charlie, who suffered a similar fate in 1981, had left the full allowable $250,000 to his wife, which qualified for the marital deduction. Charlie thus had a taxable transfer at death of $130,000, which resulted in a tax of $32,800. But the credit of $47,000 exceeded the tax; thus, Charlie's estate actually has no federal estate taxes to pay. Table 15-5 illustrates Charlie's case.

The role of the marital deduction in minimizing possible federal estate taxes is quite obvious from this example: Able, who made a relatively small bequest to his wife, was exposed to a relatively high estate tax. Charlie, who made the maximum bequest to his wife, escaped estate taxes altogether.

But long-range estate planning must take into account both spouses, not just the first one to die. Let's look a little further into the future and see what kind of estate tax liability the spouses of these three individuals will be exposed to. We'll assume that the gross estate of each consisted of exactly what they had received from their spouses—$95,000 for Mrs. Able, $190,000 for Mr. Baker, and $250,000 for Mrs. Charlie. We'll also assume that

table 15-4   **Baker's estate tax calculations**

$400,000	Gross estate
−20,000	Deductible expenses
380,000	Adjusted gross estate
190,000	Marital deduction
190,000	Taxable transfer

Tax, from Table 15-1, is	38,800	+ 32% of 40,000
or	12,800	
Tax =	51,600	
	−47,000	Credit (Table 15-2)
	4,600	Tax due

table 15-5 **Charlie's estate tax calculations**

$400,000	Gross estate
−20,000	Deductible expenses
380,000	Adjusted gross estate
250,000	Marital deduction
130,000	Taxable transfer

Tax, from Table 15-1, is   23,800 + 30% of 30,000
                      or   9,000

Tax =   32,800
       −47,000   credit (Table 15-2)

        −0−   Tax due

they each had ample funds available on which to live comfortably, that they all died in 1983 (the $47,000 credit will remain the same from 1981 onwards unless Congress decides otherwise), and that they all had $10,000 worth of deductible expenses.

None of these three people remarried after their spouse's death, so that none of them would be allowed to take advantage of a marital deduction. Thus, their taxable transfers would be the gross estate less the allowable deductible expenses. In Mrs. Able's case, she would have a taxable transfer of $85,000 (the gross estate of $95,000 less the deductions of $10,000), which would result in no tax payable. Mr. Baker would have taxable transfers of $180,000 that, according to the tax tables, would result in a tax on his estate of $1400.

Mrs. Charlie would have taxable transfers of $240,000, which according to the table, would result in taxes of $20,600.

Summing up: the Ables paid total federal estate taxes of $35,700—$35,700 on his estate and nothing on hers. The Bakers paid a total of $6000—$4600 on her estate and $1400 on his. The Charlies paid a total of $20,600—nothing on his estate, and $20,600 on her estate.

Thus, even though it would have appeared that Charlie did the best planning regarding his own estate, escaping estate taxes altogether, the couple actually ended up paying considerably more than did the Bakers, who in the long run, were the best off of all with regard to federal estate tax liability.

taxation on gifts

Every individual is permitted to make gifts to others up to a certain limit before any federal gift tax liability will be incurred. There are three main areas limiting the amount of gifts that can be made before taxation is imposed.

1. Every individual can make gifts of up to $3000 per year to as many individuals as desired. Let's say that Reed had five children. Every year he could make $3000 gifts to each of the children, totalling $15,000. He could do this every year, as long as he cared to, without ever becoming involved in a gift tax liability. If a spouse joins in the making of the gift, the amount that can be made to each individual each year is $6000 before any gift tax liability will be imposed. In other words, if Reed and Mrs. Reed joined in making gifts to their children, they could give up to $6000 per year to each of their five children, for a total annual gift of $30,000, without worrying about federal gift taxation.

   An estate that might otherwise be subject to taxation can be reduced considerably by making gifts of this nature over a period of years. Naturally, one does not want to make gifts imprudently, and the counsel of your estate planning attorney would be advisable before embarking on any program of gifts, whether to minors or others.

2. On gifts made from one spouse to another, the first $100,000 is not included as a taxable gift. However, such a gift can reduce the marital deduction available at the time of death. Looking back at Charlie's case, for example, if he had given his wife a gift of $100,000 prior to his death, the allowable marital deduction available to him in his estate tax calculations would have been reduced to $150,000. Gifts to one spouse from another in excess of $100,000 can be subject to gift taxation.

3. The credit available against estate taxation is similarly available against potential gift taxation. See Table 15-2. Using the 1981 figure in that table, the $47,000 credit eliminates tax on transfers—either by gift while living or by estate on death—equivalent to $175,625. That's over and above the annual gifts of $3000 per donee (which may be made as indicated in paragraph one above.) In other words, an individual can, in 1981, give away $175,625 (over and above other nontaxable gifts), in which case he or she will have used up the total

credit and will have none available in the estate tax calculations. Or, on the other hand, the individual may make no gifts at all, and have the full credit available.

To summarize the impact of the unified estate and gift tax laws that came into being as a result of the 1976 Tax Reform Law: Every individual is allowed to pass property to others free of any federal estate or gift taxes of at least the following amounts: $134,000 in 1978; $147,333 in 1979; $161,563 in 1980; and $175,625 in 1981 and onwards unless Congress amends the law. Individuals may be able to give additional amounts to others tax free by making use of the annual $3000 per donee gift provision and by making use of marital deduction provisions. Transfers made in excess of the stated amounts will be subject to taxation based on the rates contained in Table 15-1. If an individual makes no gifts of any kind, takes no marital deductions, and has no deductible estate expenses of any kind, he or she can have an estate of $175,625 in 1981 and will not be subject to any federal taxation as a result. By making use of the gift provisions and the marital deduction provisions, an estate of many hundred thousand dollars can possibly escape taxation.

the heirs may feel the bite

The changes wrought by the 1976 Tax Reform Law will relieve all but an estimated 2% of American estates from taxation. But while the estates may be freed from taxation, other changes in the law may impose severe taxes on heirs.

Earlier in this chapter we discussed how, under the law prior to the 1976 changes, an individual who received property through an estate would own that property at a value equal to the owner's value as of the date of death. If the property had originally cost $5000, but was worth $50,000 at the owner's death, the basis of value for the heirs would be the value at the time of the original owner's death, or $50,000. If the heir then sold the property for $50,000, he or she would have realized no gain and would not be liable to pay any income tax as a result of that transaction. The new law states that the heir now takes the property with a value equal to the original owner's cost. Following the above example, an heir would, on selling the property at $50,000, have a taxable gain of $45,000, on which income taxes must be paid. This would be so whether or not a property in question was subject to estate taxes in the estate of the individual who bequeathed the property.

There are some important exceptions to this general law. For securities (such as stocks and bonds) acquired prior to December 31, 1976, the basis will be the value as of December 31, 1976. For example, Uncle Willy acquired $5000 worth of XYZ stock in 1970. On December 31, 1976 that stock was worth $15,000. On Uncle Willy's death in 1980, the stock had a market value of $20,000. The cost basis to the heir receiving that stock will thus be $15,000—the value as of December 31, 1976. If the heir then sells the stock for the then market value of $20,000, he or she has a taxable gain of $5000.

For property acquired after December 31, 1976, the original owner's cost will be the ultimate heir's basis. If Uncle Willy acquired the stock for $5000 on January 2, 1977, and it was worth $20,000 on his death in 1980, the heir will then have a cost basis of $5000 and a gain of $15,000 if he sells at the $20,000 market price.

For property other than marketable securities acquired before December 31, 1976, the new law sets forth a complex formula for determining the value as of the date of death. If, for example, an individual had acquired real estate in 1970 that had appreciated in value by the time of his death in 1980, the law would pro-rate the increase in value from the time of original acquisition until December 31, 1976, and thereby establish the heir's value as of the December 31, 1976, date.

Small estates are excluded from this "stepped up" basis. The value of property in an estate may set at a minimum of $60,000, and $10,000 worth of household and personal effects may also be excluded from the new basis rules. For example, an individual's total gross estate at the time of her death consisted of her house and nothing more. The house had originally cost $30,000, but because of inflation it had a market value at the time of the owner's death of $60,000. The estate would be small enough so that no estate taxes would be payable.

However, the difference between the owner's cost and the fair market value at the time of death is $30,000. If her heir sold the house, there would be a taxable gain of $30,000. But the new law permits the basis to be stepped up to at least $60,000, therefore there would be no gain. The estate would still be exempt from taxes and the heir would not have to pay any taxes on the sale of the property because the basis of $60,000 and the market value of $60,000 are the same. Thus there would be no profit on the sale.

This $60,000 minimum basis can not exceed the fair market

value of a property. For example, if, as in the above example, the house had originally cost $30,000 and at the time of the individual's death it was worth $40,000, the $40,000 basis would be used—not $60,000. The heir would thus own it with a cost basis of $40,000. If he sold it five years later for $65,000, his profit would be $25,000, not $5000, which it would have been had he been able to use a $60,000 basis as a basis.

estate planning under the new law

Because the 1976 Tax Reform Law exempts all but a very small segment of the population from possible estate taxes, this is no reason to think that estate planning can be ignored. This chapter has pointed out many of the other important elements of estate planning, including the arrangements for proper liquidity and distribution of assets, management of the assets, and the need for assurance of a continued comfortable life style for one's survivors. The new law does nothing to assist one in making those provisions. The need for sound and prudent planning is every bit as important today as it was before the changes in the law.

The 1976 Tax Reform Law is still relatively new. Tax laws are always subject to interpretation and amendment, and there's no way of knowing what modifications may occur in the law within the next few years. A prudent individual who has established an estate plan will find it necessary to keep abreast of modifications within the law as they might affect his or her estate and the financial welfare of survivors.

Unless and until modifications occur, an individual should be aware of the implications in the new law that require heirs to pay income taxes on inherited property when sold at a profit. This could create a larger diminution in the overall accumulated wealth than under the previous law. The effect of this potential tax can be made even more burdensome as the value of various properties increases with inflation. But the individual who is alert to the overall workings of estate taxation, and who makes an effort to keep up to date with changes in the law and in the customs of estate planning, will be better equipped to take advantage of any tax reduction devices that come along in the future. These devices could save even the modest estate thousands of dollars. It's worth a bit of continuing education to be aware of how those savings can be obtained.

Interview with a Lawyer who has Done Extensive Work in Financial Counseling and Estate Planning

Q. "What percentage of families actually go through a proper estate planning program?"

A. "Very few. I don't know whether any statistics are kept, but I would say it's probably under 5%. Some larger percentage than that may have had wills prepared at one time, either on a do-it-yourself form that they've bought at a stationery store or through an attorney. But I doubt that more than 5% have actually created a plan that is kept up to date periodically and amended when necessary."

Q. "Why do you suppose so few families have availed themselves of estate planning? Is it a matter of cost?"

A. "No, I don't think it's cost. For the average family, the cost would not be great at all. A one or two hour interview plus the time to draw a simple will would be all that's entailed. Anybody can check with the Bar Association in their own community to get at least a rough average of what the going rates are with most attorneys in the community. And a simple phone call to any lawyer will disclose what the rates would be for a sim-ple estate plan. Unless a lawyer becomes involved in a very large estate, I don't really think a full estate planning program is particularly lucrative to a lawyer. Maybe that's part of the reason why many lawyers don't actively encourage clients to do a full-fledged estate planning program. There's a modest amount of income in preparing the original estate plan and keeping it up to date, and perhaps more down the line if he should act as the attorney for the estate as well. Then, too, a lot of lawyers simply aren't familiar with the basics of estate planning because they specialize in other areas, particularly if they are involved in a small firm. Larger firms have specialists in a variety of fields, and they could probably be more able to assist a client's estate planning needs."

Q. "Then what are the reasons why most people don't get involved in estate planning?"

A. "I think superstition has a lot to do with it. Strange as it may seem, a lot of people feel that once they've prepared a will, they're going to walk out of the office and lightning will strike them on the street. I know it sounds silly, but I and many other lawyers have seen that reaction all too often. Many times we'll convince a client of the value of estate planning and they'll have us go ahead and create the will or other documents that may be necessary. Then when it comes time for them to come back to the office to sign the documents, they find dozens of convenient excuses to cancel the appointment. Again, it's probably a matter of superstition. And believe me, it can be expensive superstition. I've seen many cases where proper estate planning could have saved many thousands or tens of thousands of dollars for an individual who has passed away. And when I've spoken to their families after the death, they're shocked to learn how much estate taxes have to be paid and how poorly distributed the assets are. When they ask why nothing had been done to prevent these chaotic situations, I explain that the deceased simply never got around to signing the will that had been prepared for them. You can't

604

force them to sign, you know.''

Q. ''Any other reasons?''

A. ''Well, a lot of people think that estate planning is only to avoid taxes, and under the new tax law, it's a fact that most estates don't have to worry about estate taxes. People simply aren't familiar enough with the other objectives of estate planning. Frankly, I'm afraid that I have to say that the legal profession in general has done a relatively poor job in acquainting the public with the advantages of estate planning. Much of this has to do with that tired old ethic about lawyers not advertising. I don't think it ever will come to a point where lawyers put ads in the paper offering special sales on estate planning— this week only—but I certainly do feel the Bar Associations in each community and state can do more to educate the public concerning their legal rights and obligations. A lot of lawyers and Bar Associations might argue with me but I'm only speaking from my viewpoint as I've seen it over the years.''

Q. ''Where could this education be most effective?''

A. ''I'd like to see some programs developed in the public school systems, at the higher grade levels. Community colleges and four year colleges are also an appropriate place for people to start learning

the rudiments of estate planning. That, of course, brings up another aspect of the problem. People generally think that estate planning is something that's done in the later years. For the most part, that's when a large segment of the population that does estate planning finally gets around to it. But the younger the better, because estate planning is something that grows with you and that you grow up with. If kids in school just learned what estate planning was all about, even if they never actually did anything, they would have a greater sense of awareness of the needs and advantages of estate planning as they matured.''

Q. ''Is it just the breadwinner who needs an estate plan, or should both spouses become involved?''

A. ''Without a doubt, both spouses should become involved. For the most part, the man is still the breadwinner, but in ever increasing numbers women are contributing to the overall family income and accumulation of wealth. Further, the wife—and statistics indicate that every average American wife will probably be a widow for close to four years—should be aware of the implications of estate taxation and distribution of assets on her death. And aside from the specific tax aspects of estate planning, this is one of the most important areas in which families have to communicate openly and frankly about what they want to do with their accumulated wealth, however large or small. For example, families simply have to determine how much, if anything, they want to leave to their children, and how much they want to spend on their own pleasures when they can.''

Q. ''That may be the biggest dilemma of all: how does a family determine what to leave their children and how much they want to spend on their own?''

A. ''The person who discovers the answer to that question can sell the formula for a billion dollars. The problem is, there is no formula, no pat answer. It's something that each family has to hammer out on their own. Some families will struggle mightily to create such a large nest egg for their children that the children will never have any financial worries. This may be laudable and worthy, and yet it can be a detriment to the children. It all depends on the parents and children. No two examples are identical. Everything returns to the primary rule of communications.

I think that if children are brought up with a sense of values regarding self-sufficiency they'll be more prone to strive in that direction regardless of what kind of nest egg may be awaiting them in the future. If children aren't made aware of the values of self-sufficiency, no amount of money will be able to resolve the frustrations they may be in for. That's just one man's opinion, of course.''

Q. ''Do you ever advise parents as to how much they should strive to set aside for their children?''

A. ''Not really. You might easily say that all you can really give children as they're growing up is love, devotion, a sense of ethics, and an awareness of their self-worth. That, and a good education, and they're off on their own to do as they please anyway. And again, many families have struggled through economic hardship and they want to do as much as they can for their children so that they won't have to make the same struggle. That's all well and good too.''

Q. ''In a sense, then, are you telling me that part of estate planning is the communications between members of the family simply with respect to growing up, maturing, becoming adults, and making one's own pathway through life?''

A. ''Yes I am. Most distinctly.

Estate planning has its legal aspects, its tax aspects, its accounting aspects, its insurance aspects. But when you boil it all down, estate planning is *life* planning. Estate planning is putting the numbers and details on what you are doing with your life, your career, your whole process of maturing and raising a family. Your estate is more than simply your financial worth. In a sense, it's also your spiritual worth, your philosophy, your direction, your desire for achievement. It may not be within the lawyer's province to try to direct a family along those lines. But I feel I'm doing my job most adequately if I can at least encourage families to think that the estate plan is more than dollars. It's attitudes. Feelings. Goals. If families never did embark on a formal estate plan, I can't help feeling that they'd be better off and more in touch with themselves if they at least thought about the whole program rather than ignoring it or feeling that it's only something that 'rich people' have to do.

''Perhaps one of the most unfortunate aspects of estate planning is the name itself— estate planning. Perhaps if we had learned to call it life planning, instead of something that seems to refer to death planning, we'd all be able to take better advantage of it.''

1. How can property be passed from one generation to the next?
2. Jane Ikuno died without a will. The state named a person to carry out the laws with regard to Jane's property. What is the legal term for this person?
3. Explain the difference between an estate tax and an inheritance tax.
4. Byron Michaels left his home to his son for as long as the son lives. When his son dies, the home will go to the university where Byron received his degree. What is such a bequest called?
5. When should you change your will?
6. Which trust is set up to become effective upon death?
7. Describe liquidity and explain why it is important in your estate plan.
8. Kirk bought some common stock in 1977 for $4000. He died in 1978 leaving the stock to Susan. At that time the stock was worth $6000. Susan sold it in 1979 for $7500. What was the amount of her gain?

1. Tony and Ann are planning to see a lawyer about drawing up a will. What information should they prepare before their appointment?
2. Jack and Susan were discussing their married son who wants to buy a house. Susan was interested in helping him with the down payment, but she would also like to avoid gift or estate taxes. She consulted their financial advisor, who said, "Since it is this close to the end of the year, you could give your son and daughter-in-law $24,000 without any gift tax and without using any credit against your estate tax." How is this possible?
3. Jack and Susan were telling their friends, Mike and Elaine, about their planned gifts. Elaine said, "Well, what's the catch? There has to be something wrong with the deal." Explain the negative factors to consider before making gifts.
4. Joan Ritter has two sons. She would like to leave all her estate to them, but she is concerned about the possibility of their spending it all quickly and unwisely. This would not have been a problem if the boys had studied personal finance in college; however, what would you suggest for Joan's will?

index

about the author   Robert Rosefsky received his B.S. degree from Yale University and his Juris Doctor degree from Syracuse University. For several years, he was a practicing attorney and served as a vice-president and director of a commercial bank. He thus became aware of the public's lack of information and degree of misinformation on subjects relating to their financial well-being and turned to writing and education as a full-time activity.

As a writer, Robert Rosefsky has accepted many challenges. He has written five books on the subject of personal finance. In recognition of his contributions, he has been granted the John Hancock Award for Excellence in Financial Journalism and has been elected by his fellow financial writers to the Board of Governors of the Society of American Business and Economic Writers.

As an international lecturer and educator, Robert Rosefsky has been honored many times. Most recently he has served as program consultant and lecturer for a personal finance television series produced and distributed by the Consortium for Community College Television.